LOCAL EXPLORER

BRISTOL & BATH

www.philips-maps.co.uk

Published by Philip's a division of
Octopus Publishing Group Ltd
www.octopusbooks.co.uk
Carmelite House,
50 Victoria Embankment,
London EC4Y 0DZ
An Hachette UK Company
www.hachette.co.uk

First edition 2022
BABDA

ISBN 978-1-84907-602-9

© Philip's 2022

This product includes
mapping data licensed from
Ordnance Survey® with the
Map data permission of the Controller of
Her Majesty's Stationery Office.
© Crown copyright 2022. All rights reserved.
Licence number 100011710.

*All streets named in the source Ordnance
Survey dataset at the time of going to press
are included in this Philip's Street Atlas.

Photographic acknowledgements:
Alamy Stock Photo: /robertharding front cover;
/John Boothroyd III top left; /PA Images III top
right. Dreamstime.com: /Alexey Fedorenko
II top; /Andrew Emptage II left; /Chris Dorney
III bottom.

Printed in China

CONTENTS

II Best places to visit

IV Key to map pages

VI Route planning

VIII Key to map symbols

1 Street maps at 3½ inches to 1 mile

141 Street maps of Bristol and Bath city centres at 7 inches to 1 mile

144 Index of towns, villages, streets, hospitals, industrial estates, railway stations, schools, shopping centres, universities and places of interest

Best places to visit

◄ The Roman Baths and Bath Abbey

▲ Bristol's Floating Harbour and SS Great Britain

Bath Beautiful city, a UNESCO World Heritage Site since 1987, renowned for its elegant Georgian architecture and its Roman history. The city was founded by the Romans on the site of hot mineral springs and named Aquae Sulis, soon becoming one of the great religious spas of the ancient world. Its Roman history is told in the well-preserved **Roman Baths**. The site contains the remains of the temple built to honour Sulis Minerva, the goddess of wisdom; the Sacred Spring, source of the hot spring waters; and the Great Bath complex itself, where the Roman public could bathe in the healing waters. Important artefacts are on display in the attached museum, including a gilt-bronze head of Minerva. The hot spring waters can be enjoyed in the thermal baths at the privately owned Thermae Bath Spa.

Bath Abbey church was built in the early 16th century on the site of a ruined Norman cathedral, which had itself replaced an 8th-century monastery. It was substantially restored in the 19th century by the English Gothic revival architect Sir George Gilbert Scott. The fan vaulted ceiling is impressive, as are the numerous memorial stones on the wall and the floor. Other highlights include the ladders of carved stone angels on the West Front, and the stained glass. Visitors can climb the **Abbey Tower** on a tour and see the vaulted ceiling and bells from a different angle. There are impressive views over the city.

There are well-preserved Georgian buildings throughout the city centre. The Georgian **Assembly Rooms** – a Ball Room, Tea Room, Octagon and Card Room – were completed in 1771 and were the most elegant public rooms of fashionable society life in 18th-century Bath. Now owned by the National Trust, they house the **Fashion Museum** on the lower ground floor, with its world-class collection of historic and contemporary dress. There are family activities and a dressing-up area. The **Jane Austen Centre** housed in a Georgian building on the street where she lived, gives a flavour of Austen's life in Regency Bath. The museum is an interactive experience, with guides in period costume and a variety of hands-on activities, including dressing up and tasting food from the era. The **Herschel Museum of Astronomy** is in a restored Georgian townhouse, home to siblings William and Caroline Herschel. The museum relates their achievements in music and astronomy, not least William's discovery of the planet Uranus in 1781,

using a seven-foot reflecting telescope of his own making in the back garden here.

Great Pulteney Street is the widest and one of the grandest streets in Bath. It leads from the famous Palladian-style Pulteney Bridge, designed by Robert Adam in the 1770s, to the Holbourne Museum (see page III). It was commissioned in the late 18th century in order to expand the boundaries of the city and is lined with imposingly elegant townhouses. **No. 1 Royal Crescent** museum occupies one of the grand terraced houses in the Grade 1-listed Royal Crescent, widely considered to be one of the UK's finest examples of Georgian architecture. The museum's many rooms are decorated and furnished as they would have been in the period from 1776 to 1796, soon after the crescent was built, and they provide an insight into the lives of fashionable residents and their servants at that time. There are interactive activities and events. **Royal Victoria Park** is a large park overlooked by the Royal Crescent. It has facilities for all, ranging from a children's play area, crazy golf and a bowling green, to a botanical garden with interesting shrub roses and trees, and a replica Roman Temple. There is a bandstand with frequent outdoor concerts. The **Victoria Art Gallery** near Pulteney Bridge, houses an interesting collection of paintings, sculpture and decorative arts. There are frequently changing exhibitions, often of contemporary art, and a permanent collection which includes works from the 15th century to the present day. Artists who lived in the area, such as Thomas Gainsborough and Walter Sickert, are well represented.

🖥 www.visitbath.co.uk **141**

Bristol Historically significant city which can trace its roots to Iron Age hill forts at the confluence of the rivers Frome and Avon, and which owes its wealth to its position near the Severn Estuary. It was the starting point for voyages to the New World, including that of John Cabot, who in 1497 sailed across the Atlantic to become the first European to land on mainland America. Bristol prospered in the 17th and 18th centuries, processing sugar and tobacco from the American colonies, and in the 18th century it played a major role in the transatlantic slave trade. Many of its historic buildings were destroyed by German air raids during World War II. Bristol's port is now at Avonmouth and the city centre docks have been transformed to become the home of many of its heritage and cultural attractions.

Dominating the waterfront is the historic ocean liner the **SS Great Britain** in the dry dock where she was built in the 1830s. Visitors can explore the ship, inside and out, and learn about Isambard Kingdom Brunel in the attached museum. There are hands-on activities for all. Also on the harbourside, in a former warehouse, is the **Arnolfini**. Its art galleries, performance space and programme of lectures and readings focus on contemporary arts of all kinds. Nearby is **M Shed**, housed in an old dockside transit shed, which relates the history of Bristol, its involvement in international commerce and the slave trade, its experience in World War II, and the lives of ordinary people. Outside are restored cranes, tugboats and trains, from the area's time as a working dock. There are hands-on activities, as well as trips on the trains and boats. **We the Curious**, more of an experience than a museum, is all about interacting with science, through hands-on exhibits, workshops and shows. It has a planetarium.

Castle Park, on the harbourside, occupies the site of what was Bristol's main shopping district before its destruction during the Blitz in World War II. **St Peter's Church**, heavily damaged, stands in the park and acts as a memorial to the lives lost during the bombardment. Further memorials commemorate other victims of the war. There is a physic garden and the partially excavated remains of Bristol Castle. Away from the harbour, Bristol's medieval **cathedral**, founded as an abbey in 1140, is one of the world's most important 'hall' churches, with nave, choir and aisles all built to the same height, resulting in a strikingly light and spacious east end. Also notable are the Lady Chapel and the Romanesque Chapter House with its magnificent stone carvings, and the garden.

Queen Square is an attractive park in Bristol city centre, originally laid out in 1700 and named after Queen Anne.

After riots in 1831 destroyed many of the buildings, the area was largely rebuilt, and is now full of imposing Georgian houses and cobbled streets. The park underwent a substantial restoration in the last decade of the 20th century, after a long period of decline, and now hosts outdoor theatre and events. Life in an affluent 18th-century home – both above and below stairs – can be explored in the **Georgian House Museum**, a four-storey townhouse restored and decorated as it would have been when it was built in 1790 for a wealthy slave owner and sugar merchant. The **Red Lodge Museum** relates its history from its roots as an 'overflow' house for the Tudor Great Hall (now the Bristol Beacon concert venue). There are Tudor rooms, complete with original oak panelling and stone carvings, extensive Georgian additions, a recreated Elizabethan knot garden, and exhibits from its time as a Victorian girls' reform school.

The **Royal West of England Academy** is housed in an imposing building in the city centre, widely considered to have the best exhibition spaces in the country. It exhibits world-class contemporary and historic art, and has an annual open exhibition. Its Drawing School hosts regular workshops and courses. There are frequent children's activities. The broad-ranging collections at the **Bristol Museum and Art Gallery** encompass art, archaeology, geology and natural history, all housed in a large Edwardian building. There are well-preserved dinosaur skeletons and fossils, ancient Egyptian and Assyrian artefacts, and an important collection of both European paintings and Eastern glass and ceramics. There are hands-on activities and children's trails. The city is also famous for its **street art** – the world famous graffiti artist Banksy was born here, and his work can still be seen around the city.

🖥 www.visitbristol.co.uk **142–143**

Outdoors

Cadbury Camp Remains of an Iron Age hill fort with fine views across Somerset and towards the Bristol Channel. It was constructed in the 6th century BC and remained occupied until the 1st century; it is also believed to have been used in Roman times. Wildflowers and butterflies flourish on the limestone grassland, and there are walking trails. *Tickenham* 💻 www.nationaltrust.org.uk **59 A5**

University of Bristol Botanic Garden Gardens with a vast number of different plant species both outside and in glasshouses divided into climatic zones. Among the collections are medicinal plants, rare local flora, and displays telling the story of plant evolution from prehistoric times. Highlights of the glasshouses are the Giant Amazon Water Lily, Chinese sacred lotus, and plants of the cloud forest. *Bristol* 💻 www.botanic-garden.bristol.ac.uk **48 F4**

Chew Valley Lake Reservoir that supplies much of Bristol's drinking water. It is popular with birdwatchers for the large variety of wildfowl, some rare, that visit the lake. There is an accessible walking route around the lake, picnic areas, playground and refreshments. Fishing and sailing can be arranged. *Chew Stoke* 💻 www.bristolwater.co.uk/chewvalleylake **113 A7**

Dolebury Warren Nature reserve on the site of an Iron Age hill fort, overlooking the Mendips and North Somerset. Unusual wildflowers and rare butterflies flourish on the mainly limestone grassland that covers the summit and slopes of the hill. The double ramparts of the fort can be made out, as well as a medieval rabbit warren. There are walking trails, although access is not easy. *Churchill* 💻 www.avonwildlifetrust.org.uk **109 A3**

Gordano Valley National Nature Reserve Valley that runs between two limestone ridges, comprising 126 hectares of woodland, grassland and fen. The wet meadows and ditches of the valley are home to rare wildflowers and insects, water shrews and otters. Walks on the northern and southern ridges of the reserve provide fine views and the opportunity to spot other rare species. *Walton-in-Gordano* 💻 www.woodlandtrust.org.uk **58 E8**

Leigh Woods Nature Reserve Beautiful woodland on the plateau overlooking the Avon Gorge, with fine views of Bristol and the Clifton Suspension Bridge. It has been designated a Site of Special Scientific Interest for its abundance of rare plants and animal species. The ancient trees and – in autumn – wide variety of fungi can be enjoyed on the walking routes. There is a specific mountain-biking trail and a permanent orienteering course. *Abbots Leigh* 💻 www.nationaltrust.org.uk **62 D8**

Prior Park Landscape Garden Georgian landscaped gardens on a steep slope descending from Prior Park house, designed in the 18th century with input from 'Capability' Brown and the poet Alexander Pope. A beautiful Palladian bridge crosses one of the many lakes, which were created by a series of dams. There are paths and children's nature activities, and it offers easy access to the longer circular walking route above Bath known as the Bath Skyline. *Bath* 💻 www.nationaltrust.org.uk **102 C3**

Sydney Gardens Former Georgian Pleasure Gardens, now a public park behind the Holbourne Museum (previously Sydney Hotel). The gardens opened in 1795 and – for a fee – visitors, who included Jane Austen, could enjoy all kinds of entertainments, among them dancing, concerts and fireworks. Visitors today appreciate the wide lawns, peaceful woodland and parkland, pretty buildings and bridges, as well as walks beside the Kennet and Avon Canal. There are frequent events in the summer. *Bath* 💻 www.bathnes.gov.uk **102 B7**

Buildings

Clevedon Court Medieval manor house, dating from the 14th century, with an 18th-century terraced garden. The house has been altered over the years, but it retains a medieval core, notably the Great Hall and chapel. The Elton family, who

▼ *Tyntesfield*

acquired Clevedon Court in 1709, created the terraced garden, which rises up steeply behind the house. The family's collections of glass and Eltonware pottery are on display. *Clevedon* 💻 www.nationaltrust.org.uk **58 A4**

Clifton Observatory Observatory, built in 1828 on the site of a ruined 18th-century windmill, with dramatic views over the Avon Gorge and the Clifton Suspension Bridge. The observatory tower houses a museum, with a rare Victorian camera obscura, and a café. A tunnel leads down from the observatory to the Giant's Cave, a natural limestone cave with a viewing platform in the face of the gorge. *Clifton* 💻 www.cliftonobservatory.com **62 F7**

Dyrham Park Baroque manor house surrounded by ancient parkland and formal gardens. The house was built for William Blathwayt in the 17th century, and is filled with the fine art and Delftware he gathered on his travels as a diplomat and colonial administrator. There are walks and children's trails in the grounds, fabulous views from the sloping parkland, and year-round colour in the formal gardens. *Dyrham* 💻 www.nationaltrust.org.uk **54 E4**

Tyntesfield Originally a smaller Georgian home, it was remodelled in the 1860s, with the addition of elaborate turrets, gables and carvings. Visitors can see the lavishly decorated interior, complete with Gothic-style chapel, and some original carpets, wallpaper, furniture and paintings. The formal gardens include a Rose Garden and Kitchen Garden. There are walking trails within the large estate and woodland, children's activities and play areas. *Wraxall* 💻 www.nationaltrust.org.uk **60 F4**

Museums & galleries

See also Bristol and Bath

Aerospace Bristol Aerospace museum on the former Filton Airfield, with numerous aeroplanes, helicopters, missiles and other aviation-related exhibits on display. Its centrepiece is

▲ *Concorde at Aerospace Bristol*

Concorde Alpha Foxtrot, which visitors can board, alongside information about supersonic flight and the jet's history. There are conservation projects in a World War II hangar and interactive activities for all. *Patchway* 💻 www.aerospacebristol.org **35 F6**

American Museum and Gardens Museum dedicated to American decorative arts and culture, housed in a Georgian manor house. Founded by two antiques collectors – one British and one American – the museum has important collections of quilts and textiles, folk art and maps. The Period Rooms were created using original materials from demolished historic American houses. The gardens reflect traditional English and American landscape design. Highlights include a replica of George Washington's Garden at Mount Vernon and an arboretum with American trees. There are changing exhibitions and frequent events. *Claverton* 💻 www.americanmuseum.org **3 A5**

Blaise Museum Museum of social history housed in an 18th-century manor house surrounded by parkland. The museum's collection includes toys from the 1800s onwards and domestic items, such as kitchen and washing equipment. Within the grounds are a dairy dating from 1805, kitchen gardens and an orangery. Other points of interest include the folly-like Blaise Castle, which was built in 1766 as a summer house for a previous manor on the estate. *Bristol* 💻 www.bristolmuseums.org.uk **34 E2**

Holbourne Museum Museum and art gallery named after Sir William Holbourne, whose extensive collection of fine and decorative arts was bequeathed to the city in 1882 and forms the core of the present-day collection. Decorative arts on display include porcelain, silver, maiolica and bronze sculptures; the fine art collection includes portrait miniatures and works by Gainsborough, Stubbs and Turner. The museum is housed in what was the Sydney Hotel, and backs on to the Sydney Pleasure Gardens. *Bath* 💻 www.holburne.org **102 B7**

Family attractions

Ashton Court Estate
850-acre estate comprising parkland, woodland and a deer enclosure, surrounding Ashton Court Mansion. As well as walking trails, there are orienteering and mountain biking courses, and the park lies on the National Cycle Network. Activities include golf of varying kinds, and a miniature railway. *Bristol* 💻 www.bristol.gov.uk/museums-parks-sports-culture/ashton-court-estate **62 C4**

Avon Valley Railway
Victorian train station and railway, opened in 1869 and closed in the 1960s. Locomotives and carriages have been restored, as has the Victorian railway station, and steam trains now run on a three-mile section of track. Engines and rolling stock are stored in the original goods shed. There are trips on both diesel and steam trains, and there is a small museum on site. *Bitton* 💻 www.avonvalleyrailway.org **66 B1**

Noah's Ark Zoo Farm
Farm park and zoo, with both traditional and exotic animal species, many of them endangered. The animals on site range from rabbits to rhinos, via African elephants, spectacled bears, giraffes and snakes, as well as cows, chickens, and many more. There are frequent keeper talks and birds of prey flying displays. Children's activities include a wildlife maze, indoor and outdoor play areas. *Wraxall* 💻 www.noahsarkzoofarm.co.uk **60 B6**

Wild Place Project
Large zoo park and outdoor attraction, focused on the protection of threatened habitats. Visitors can spot brown bears, wolves, lynxes and wolverines from raised walkways through a large area of ancient woodland that has been enclosed to form Bear Wood. Other highlights include open grassland, with giraffes, zebras and eland, and a lemur walkthrough. There are play areas, woodland walks and an outdoor climbing experience for all ages. This will also be the location of the new Bristol Zoo which is due to open in 2024. *M5 junction 17* 💻 www.wildplace.org.uk **35 B8**

▼ *The Royal Crescent, Bath*

IV

Key to map pages

| 75 | Map pages at 3½ inches to 1 mile |
| 237 | Map pages at 7 inches to 1 mile |

Abertillery Abersychan

Usk

Cwmbran

Chepstow

Caerleon

A48

M4 Caldicot

Newport

Northwick **12**

Severn Beach Pilning
21 **22**

Rumney

32 **33** Hallen **34**

Avonmouth Henbury

Cardiff

Portishead Shirehampton Sea Mills
44 **45** **46** **47** **48**
Redcliff Bay Pill
Clapton In Gordano Portbury

Penarth

Leigh Woods

57 **58** **59** Wraxall **60** Failand **61** Long **62**
Clevedon Tickenham Ashton
Nailsea

Kenn West Town Backwell
71 **72** **73** **74** **75** **76** **77** Dundry **78**
Claverham Brockley Barrow Gurney
Kingston Seymour

Wick St Lawrence Yatton Cleeve Bristol Felton Winford
87 **88** **89** West Hewish **90** **91** International **94** **95**
Kewstoke Congresbury **92** **93**
Weston-super-Mare Wrington Redhill

Chew
Butcombe Stoke
104 **105** **106** **107** **108** **109** Blagdon **110** **111** **112**
Uphill Hutton Locking Banwell Sandford Burrington Ubley

Bleadon Shipham Ubley Sideling
Brean **121** **122** **123** **124** **125** **126** **127** **128** **129**
Loxton Compton Bishop Charterhouse East Harptree
Lympsham Axbridge

Cheddar

Burnham-on-Sea

Wedmore Wells

Highbridge

Scale
| 0 | 5 | 10 km |
| 0 1 2 3 4 | 5 miles |

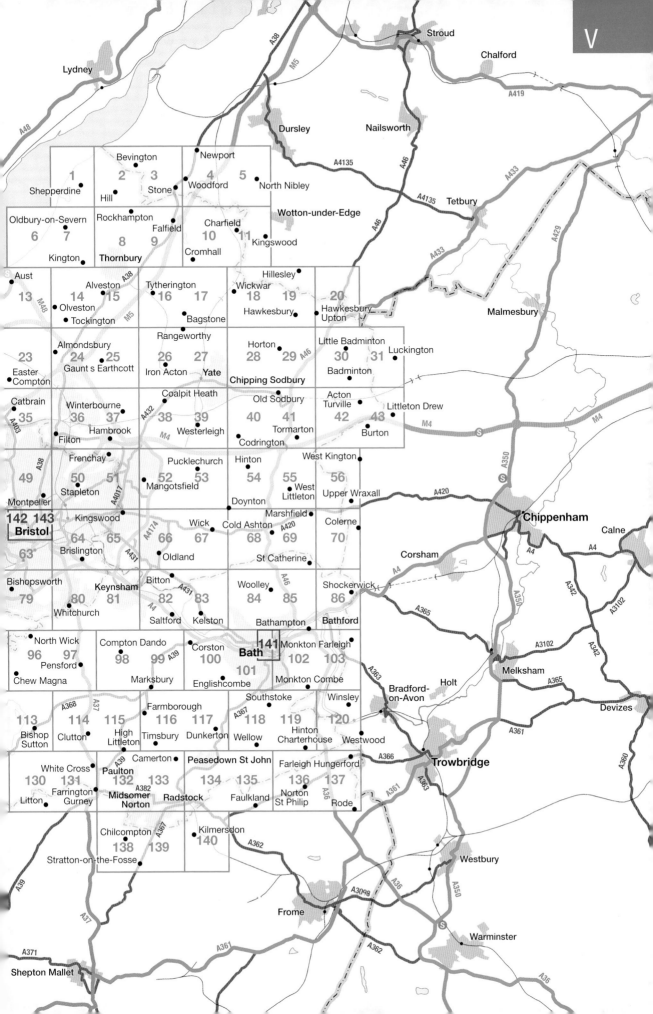

Scale

0   5   10 km

0   1   2   3   4   5   6 miles

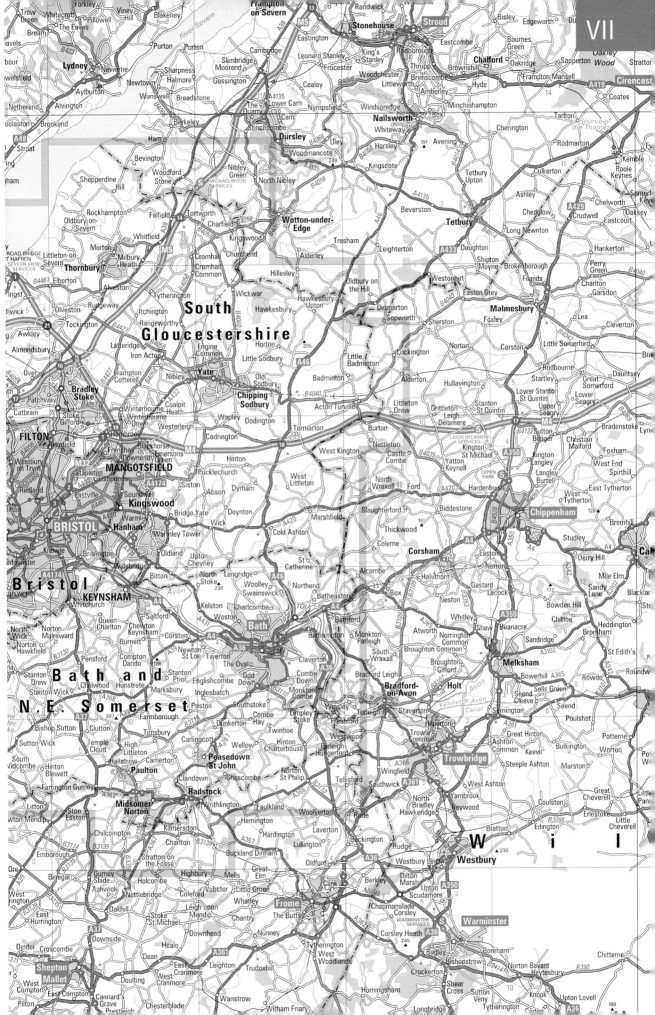

Key to map symbols

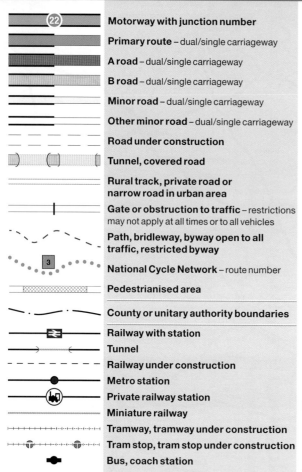

	Motorway with junction number
	Primary route – dual/single carriageway
	A road – dual/single carriageway
	B road – dual/single carriageway
	Minor road – dual/single carriageway
	Other minor road – dual/single carriageway
	Road under construction
	Tunnel, covered road
	Rural track, private road or narrow road in urban area
	Gate or obstruction to traffic – restrictions may not apply at all times or to all vehicles
	Path, bridleway, byway open to all traffic, restricted byway
	National Cycle Network – route number
	Pedestrianised area
	County or unitary authority boundaries
	Railway with station
	Tunnel
	Railway under construction
	Metro station
	Private railway station
	Miniature railway
	Tramway, tramway under construction
	Tram stop, tram stop under construction
	Bus, coach station

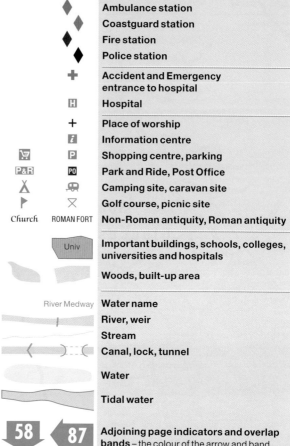

	Ambulance station
	Coastguard station
	Fire station
	Police station
	Accident and Emergency entrance to hospital
H	Hospital
+	Place of worship
i	Information centre
P	Shopping centre, parking
P&R PO	Park and Ride, Post Office
	Camping site, caravan site
	Golf course, picnic site
Church ROMAN FORT	Non-Roman antiquity, Roman antiquity
Univ	Important buildings, schools, colleges, universities and hospitals
	Woods, built-up area
River Medway	Water name
	River, weir
	Stream
	Canal, lock, tunnel
	Water
	Tidal water

Adjoining page indicators and overlap bands – the colour of the arrow and band indicates the scale of the adjoining or overlapping page (see scales below)

The dark grey border on the inside edge of some pages indicates that the mapping does not continue onto the adjacent page

The small numbers around the edges of the maps identify the 1-kilometre National Grid lines

Abbreviations

Acad	Academy	Meml	Memorial
Allot Gdns	Allotments	Mon	Monument
Cemy	Cemetery	Mus	Museum
C Ctr	Civic centre	Obsy	Observatory
CH	Club house	Pal	Royal palace
Coll	College	PH	Public house
Crem	Crematorium	Recn Gd	Recreation ground
Ent	Enterprise		
Ex H	Exhibition hall	Resr	Reservoir
Ind Est	Industrial Estate	Ret Pk	Retail park
IRB Sta	Inshore rescue boat station	Sch	School
		Sh Ctr	Shopping centre
Inst	Institute	TH	Town hall / house
Ct	Law court	Trad Est	Trading estate
L Ctr	Leisure centre	Univ	University
LC	Level crossing	W Twr	Water tower
Liby	Library	Wks	Works
Mkt	Market	YH	Youth hostel

Enlarged maps only

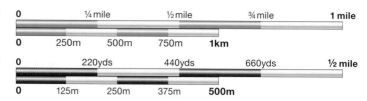

	Railway or bus station building
	Place of interest
	Parkland

The map scale on the pages numbered in blue is 3½ inches to 1 mile
5.52 cm to 1 km • 1:18 103

0	¼ mile	½ mile	¾ mile	1 mile

0	250m	500m	750m	1km

The map scale on the pages numbered in red is 7 inches to 1 mile
11.04 cm to 1 km • 1:9051

0	220yds	440yds	660yds	½ mile

0	125m	250m	375m	500m

Gloucestershire STREET ATLAS

A   B   C   D   E   F

8

7

97

6

White House

Chapel House

Manor Farm

The Laurels

5

Severn Way

+

96

PH

Shepperdine Farm

North Ham Corner

Shepperdine Farm

4

River Severn

Shepperdine

Brickhouse Farm

Shepperdine Withybed

3

95

SHEPPERDINE RD

Harestreet La

Jobscreen Farm

2

Oldbury Power Station (decommissioned)

Lowgoods Farm

Knight's Farm

Mast

41

HILL LA

1

STONEYARD LA

94

60   A   B   61   C   D   62   E   F

Gloucestershire STREET ATLAS

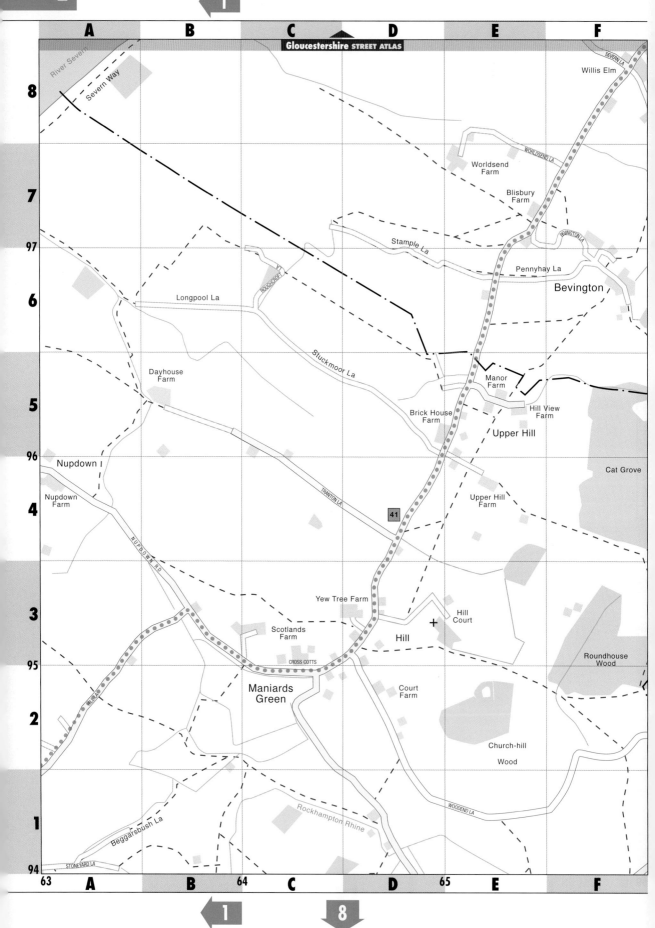

Gloucestershire STREET ATLAS

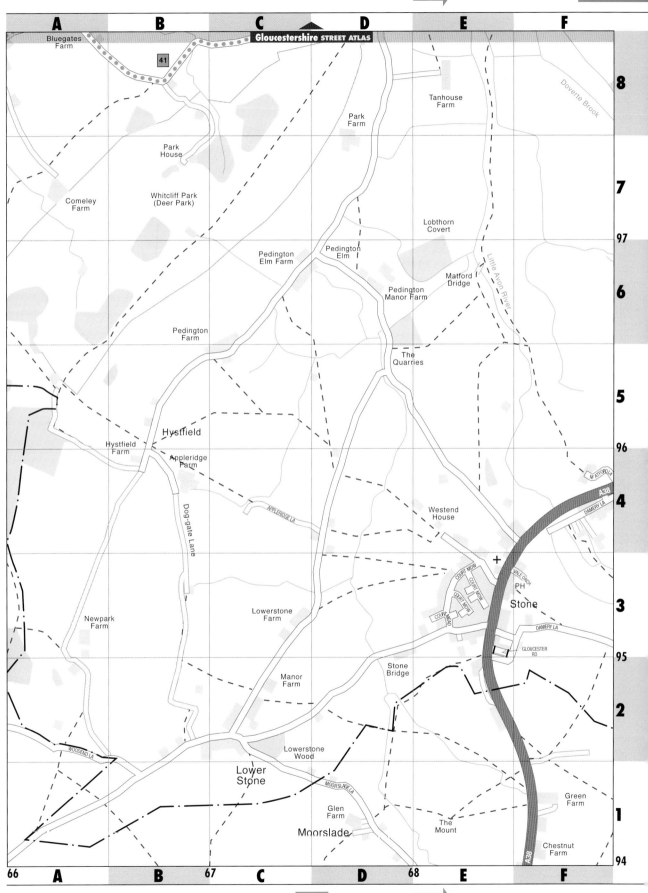

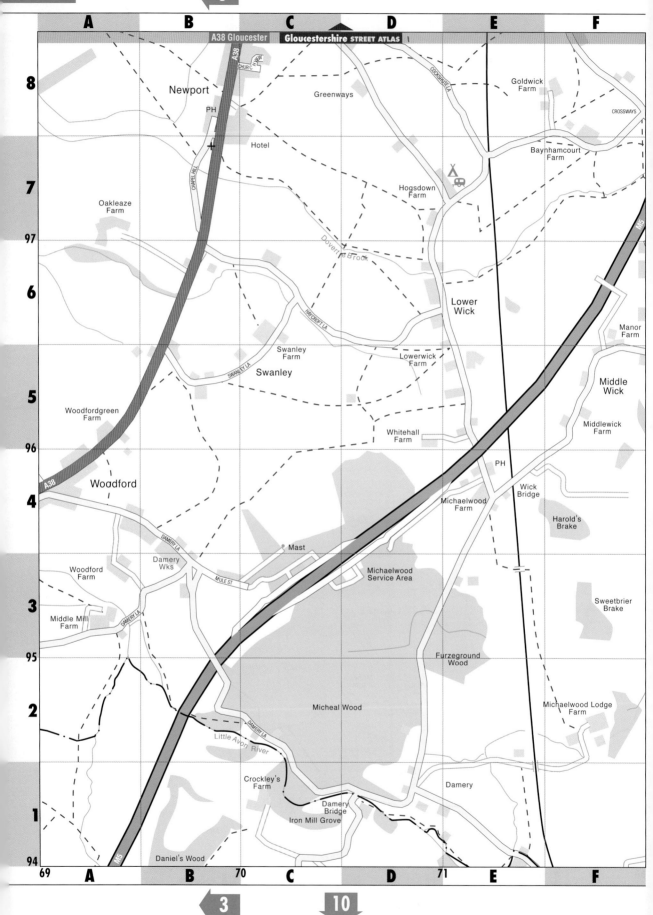

A   B   C   D   E   F

A38 Gloucester   **Gloucestershire STREET ATLAS**

8

Newport

PH

Greenways

Goldwick Farm

CROSSWAYS

CHURCH VW

Hotel

Baynhamcourt Farm

7

Oakleaze Farm

Hogsdown Farm

97

Dovert'e Brook

Lower Wick

6

Manor Farm

Swanley Farm

Lowerwick Farm

Middle Wick

Swanley

Middlewick Farm

5

Woodfordgreen Farm

Whitehall Farm

96

PH

A38

Woodford

Wick Bridge

Harold's Brake

4

DAMERY LA

Michaelwood Farm

Damery Wks

Mast

Michaelwood Service Area

Sweetbrier Brake

Woodford Farm

MULE ST

3

Middle Mill Farm

DAMERY LA

95

Furzeground Wood

2

Micheal Wood

Michaelwood Lodge Farm

DAMERY LA

Little Avon River

Crockley's Farm

Damery

1

Damery Bridge

Iron Mill Grove

94

Daniel's Wood

M5

69   A   B   70   C   D   71   E   F

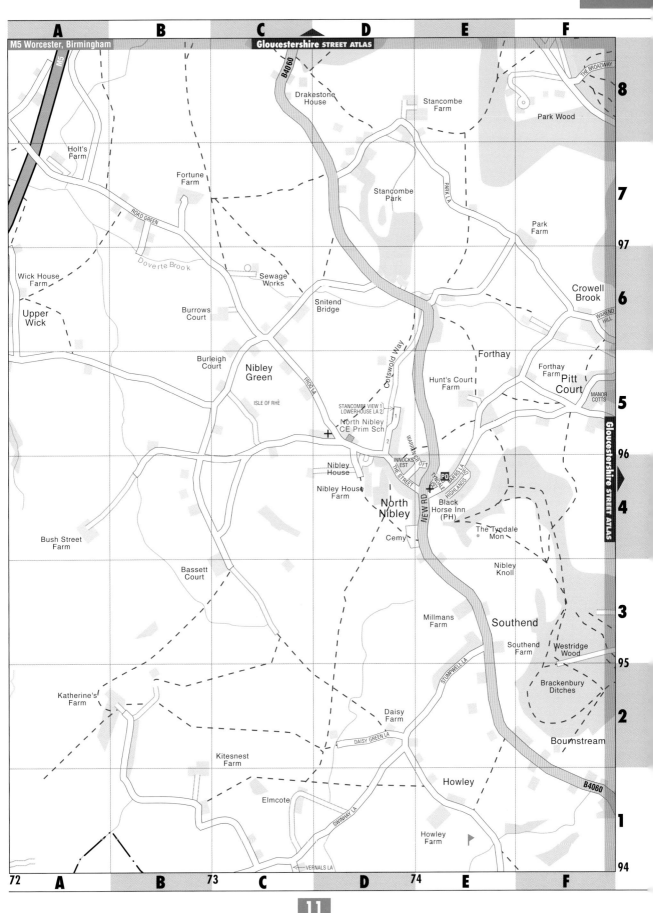

A B C D E F

M5 Worcester, Birmingham

8

7

97

6

Gloucestershire STREET ATLAS

5

96

4

3

95

2

1

94

Drakestone House

Stancombe Farm

Park Wood

THE BROADWAY

Holt's Farm

Fortune Farm

Stancombe Park

PARK LA

Park Farm

ROAD GREEN

Doverte Brook

Wick House Farm

Sewage Works

Snitend Bridge

Crowell Brook

WAREND HILL

Upper Wick

Burrows Court

Cotswold Way

Forthay

Forthay Farm

Pitt Court

MANOR COTTS

Burleigh Court

Nibley Green

ISLE OF RHÉ

FROG LA

STANCOMBE VIEW 1
LOWERHOUSE LA 2

North Nibley CE Prim Sch

Hunt's Court Farm

Bush Street Farm

Nibley House

Nibley House Farm

WARREN CROFT

INNOCKS NEST

TYNDALE HIGHLANDS

BEARS LA

The Street

PO

North Nibley

NEW RD

Black Horse Inn (PH)

The Tyndale Mon

Cemy

Nibley Knoll

Bassett Court

Millmans Farm

Southend

Southend Farm

Westridge Wood

Katherine's Farm

STUMPWELL LA

Brackenbury Ditches

Daisy Farm

DAISY GREEN LA

Bournstream

Kitesnest Farm

Howley

B4060

Elmcote

SWINHAY LA

Howley Farm

VERNALS LA

72 A B 73 C D 74 E F

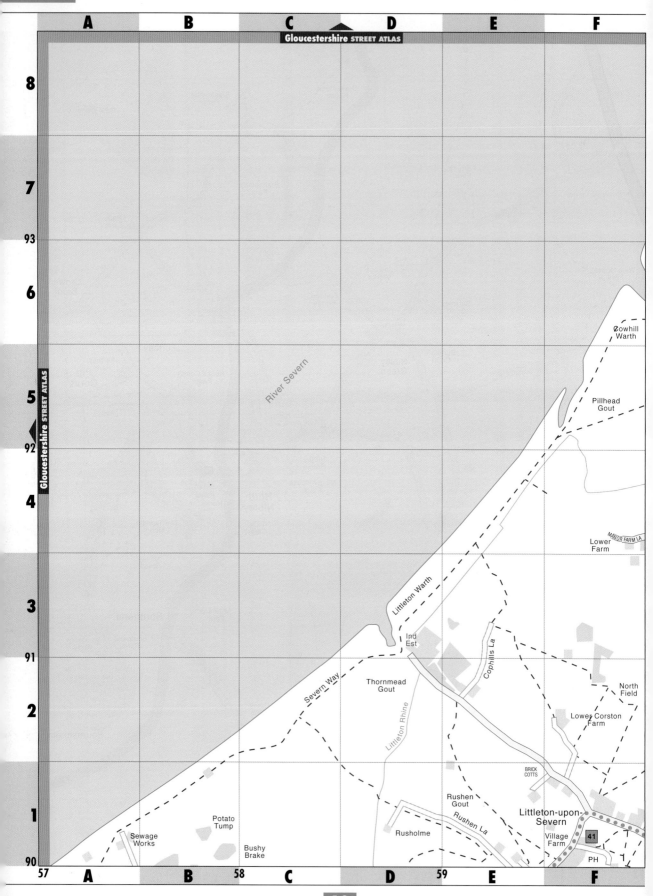

River Severn

Cowhill Warth

Pillhead Gout

MANOR FARM LA

Lower Farm

Littleton Warth

Ind Est

Cophills La

North Field

Severn Way

Thornmead Gout

Littleton Rhine

Lower Corston Farm

BRICK COTTS

Rushen Gout

Rushen La

Rusholme

Littleton-upon-Severn

Village Farm

41

PH

Sewage Works

Potato Tump

Bushy Brake

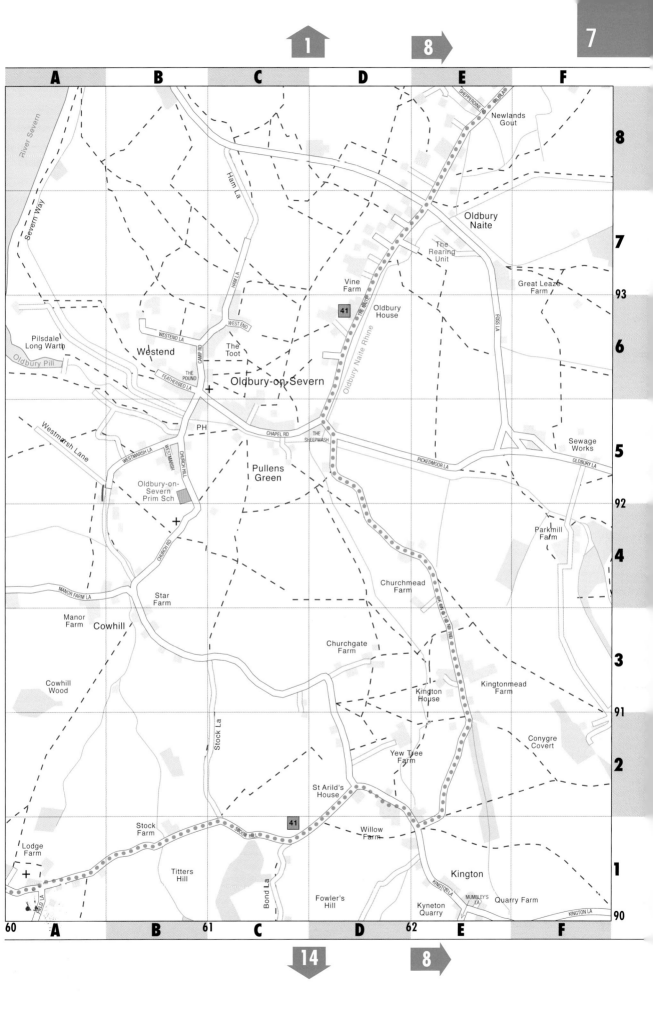

	A	B	C	D	E	F

8

Northfield Lane

Northfields

Rockhampton Rhine

The Old Rectory

Sundayshill La

7

Lodge Farm

CHURCH VIEW

Rockhampton

Court Farm

The Hollies

Pennywell Farm

Gully La

93

Henridge Hill

The Firs

Rockhampton Rhine

6

Luce's Farm

Yew Tree Farm

Newton

Groves Tully

5

Pound Mill Farm

Maypole Farm

Longman's Grove

Pound Mill Bsns Ctr

HORSE LA

CATSBRAIN LA

Oak Farm

Duckhole

92

Spring Farm

OLDBURY LA

MORTON ST

Lower Morton

4

Morton House

1 SWALLOWTAIL CL
2 SPECKLED WOOD RD
3 MEADOW BROWN CL
4 PURPLE EMPEROR RD
5 MARBLED WHITE CL

Manor Farm

Upper Morton

WILD FLOWER RD

Park Farm

GLOUCESTER RD

Mile End Farm

Yewtree Farm

B4061

3

Morton

The Knapp

Knapp Farm

91

Manorbrook Prim Sch

THORNBURY

The Castle Sch

Shelling Sch

2

Thornbury Castle

St-Mary's CE Prim Sch

Crossways House

Crossways

Christ the King RC Prim Sch

New Siblands Sch

WHITEWALL LA

1

Cemy

The Castle Sch Sixth Form Ctr

Thornbury

PO

Crossways Jun & Inf Schs

Crossways Rd

HACKET LA

MUNDY LA

B4061 HIGH ST

90

| 63 | A | 64 | B | C | D | 65 | E | F |

B1
1 QUAKER CT
2 ST JOHN ST
3 PULLINS GN
4 CRISPIN LA
5 SAW MILL LA
6 ST MARYS WAY
7 SILVER ST
8 ST MARY ST
9 ROCKLEASE
10 GROVESEND RD
11 BUCKINGHAM PAR
12 GLOUCESTER TERR

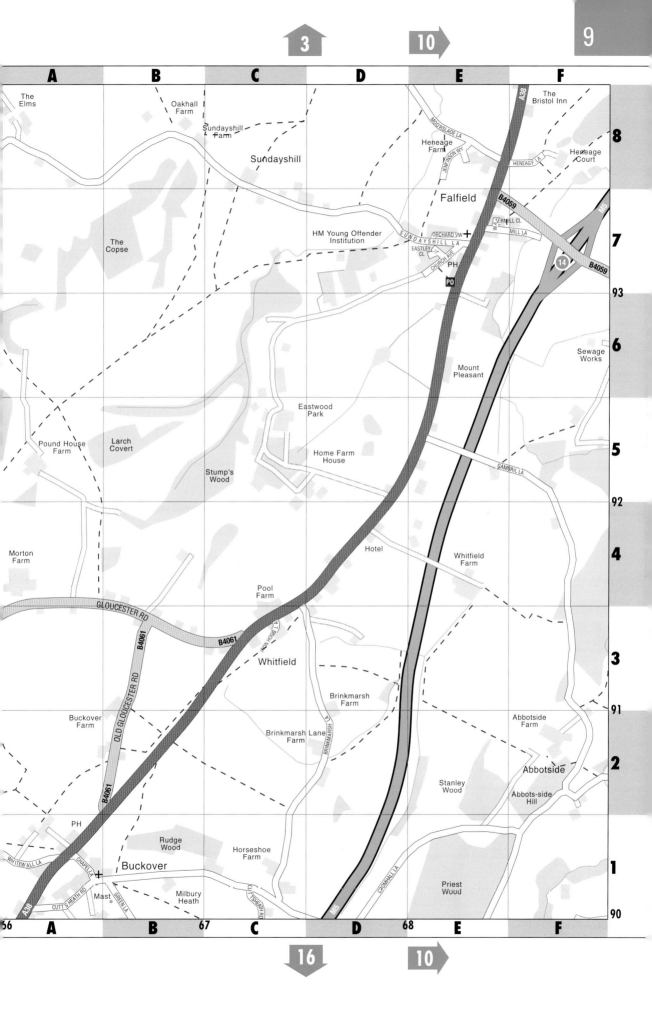

	A	B	C	D	E	F

8

M5

Daniel's Wood

Old Court Farm

Avening Green

Huntingford

Huntingford Farm

Little Tortworth Copse

Little Avon River

Hotel

Brook Farm

Howcroft Cottages

Tortworth

Old Court

7

B4059

Chestnut

Tortworth Prim Sch

93

Old Lodge Farm

Kennel Plantation

Tortworth Copse

Underwood Farm

6

Gall Pond

Arboretum

Lodge

Elmtree Farm

Tortworth Court

Tortworth Green

Poolfield Farm

Charfield Prim Sch

5

HM Prison

Charfield Hill

WOTTON RD

B4058

MANOR LA

PO

92

The Lake

Tortworth Park

Leyhill

Tafarn-bach

B4059

The Old Rectory

4

Harris's Wood

PARK RD

WOODLAND RD

MEADOW RD

Woodend Farm

Hammerley Down

B4059

Poundhouse Farm

Bloody Acre

CHURCHEND LA

3

Parkend

Royal Oak (PH)

Brand Wood

Manor Farm

Churchend

Wick's Hill

KNAPP LA

Bibstone

Church Farm

DEER LA

91

Sodam Mill

FARLEIGH LA

2

THE BURTONS

TOWNWELL

PO

Townwell

Talbotsend Farm

HAWLEY'S LA

DUDLE CL

CHURCH LA

LONGCROSS

BRISTOL RD

St Andrew's CE Prim Sch

Cromhall

Court Farm

RECTORY LA

Talbot's End

FOXHOLE LA

1

B4058

B4059

90

69	A	B	70	C	D	71	E	F

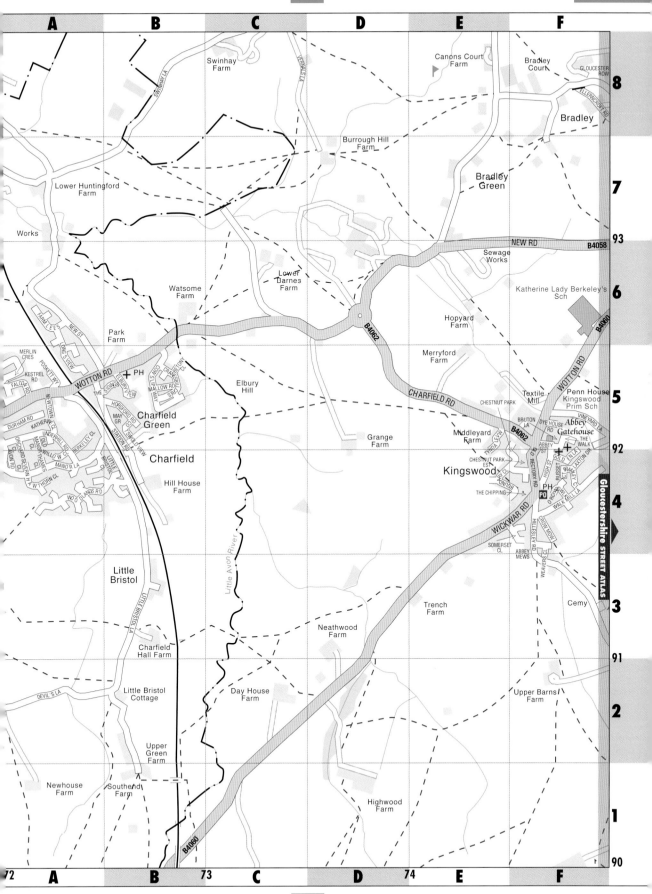

M48 Chepstow, Newport

8

Severn Road Bridge

Footpath/Cycle Way

M48

Mast •

Toll

Severn Way

7

Aust Cliff

PASSAGE RD

89

New House Farm

Old Passage

Old Passage House

A403

6

Aust Warth

River Severn

MILLHILL LA

Foss Ditch

5

Cake Pill

Cake Pill Gout

Asnum Copse

88

4

Lords Rhine

Severn Way

Bilsham Rhine

Northwick Pig Farm

Bilsham Farm

3

87

CASTLE LA

AUST RD

Laural Farm

Church Farm

Northwick

41

2

SEVERN RD

B4055

Mill Farm

Manor Farm

B4055

NORTHWICK RD

Holm Rhine

DANGER AREA

Red Lodge

Rifle Range

North Worthy Farm

A403

M4

1

Severn Lodge Farm

New Passage

NEW PASSAGE RD

BLANDS ROW

B4064

B4055

86

54   55   56

Herefordshire & Monmouthshire STREET ATLAS

Severn Way

• Mast

Motel

Severn View
Service Area

THE VILLAGE

ORCHA RD DR
THE ROW
SANDY LA
A403
BRUNEL W SMR
Severn Way

PASSAGE
RD

Aust

PH

Tenhouse
Farm

COMMON LA

Villa
Farm

A403

MANOR
FARM

B4461

Cote
Farm

Cote
Lodge

Littleton Rhine

Lynch
Farm

41

Littleton-upon-Severn

Home
Farm

Rock House
Farm

MARSH A CRE LA

Village
Farm

Redhill Farm
Bsns Pk

Redhill
Farm

REDHILL LA   B4461

Red
Hill

Hephills Rhine

Priestpool

Priest
Pool

HELM W LON RB

Priestpool
Farm

Box Bush
Farm

New
Leaze

JAUNT RD

Old Splott Rhine

Ingst Manor
Farm

41

Valley
Farm

Manor
Farm

Ingst
Farm

Ingst

INGST RD

M48

Willow
Gout

DR SMA NR LA

Ingst Rhine

Olveston
Common

THE COMMON

LEY LA

CH URCH   Church
HILL   Farm

DENISS

Olveston Court
(remains of)

Catherine
Hill

CATHERINE HILL

Port
Farm

Holm
Farm

MEAD LA

Mead
Farm

Olveston Mill Rhine

HOLM LA

Greenditch
Farm

GREENDITCH ST

M48

NIXLEY LA

M48

M48 M4

21

Walning
Farm

REDHAM LA

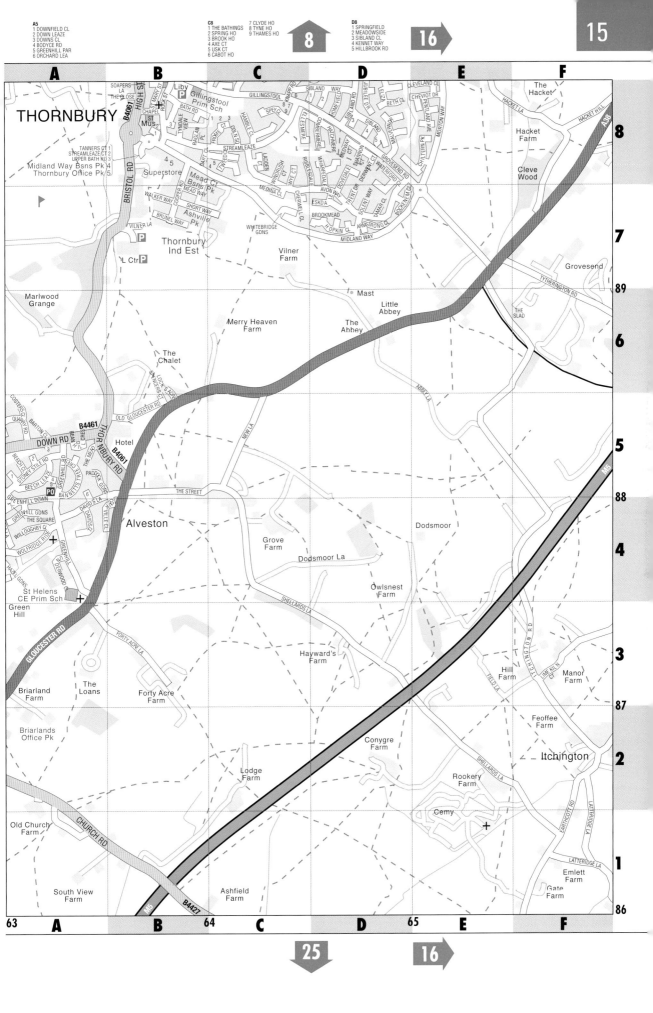

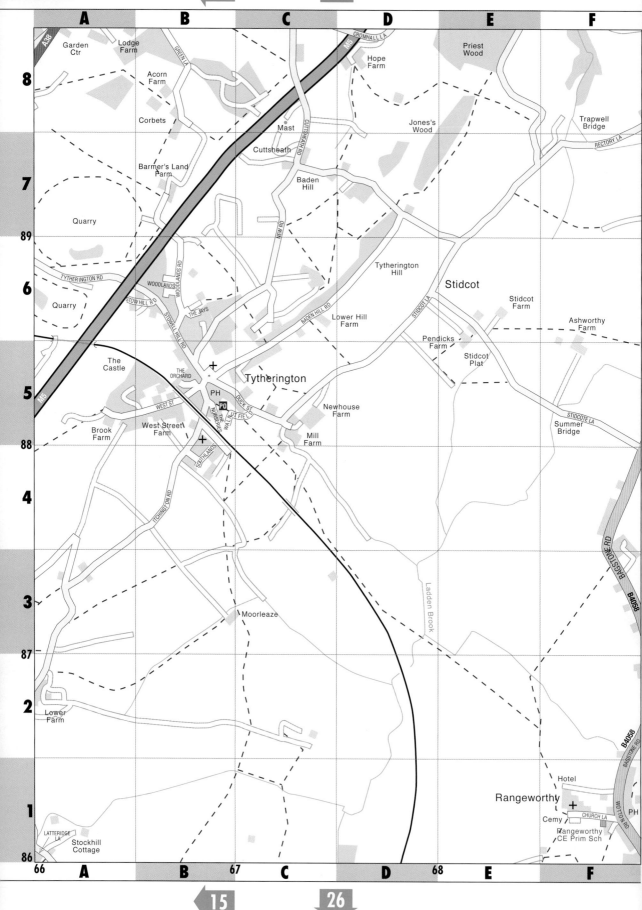

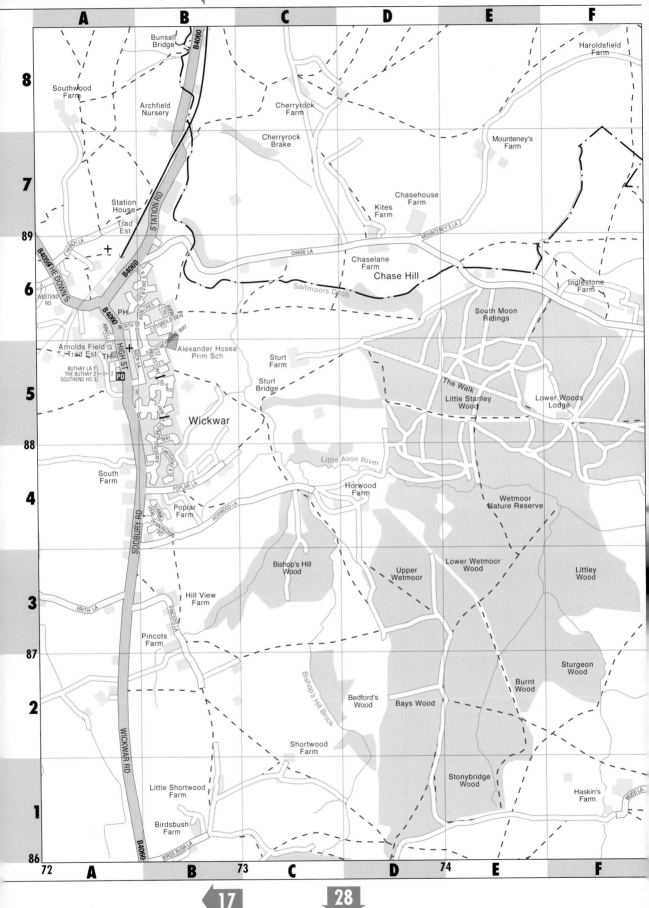

A B C D E F

8

Southwood Farm

Bunsall Bridge

B4060

Archfield Nursery

Cherryrock Farm

Cherryrock Brake

Haroldsfield Farm

Mounteney's Farm

7

Station House

STATION RD

Trad Est

Kites Farm

Chasehouse Farm

89

CHURCH LA

+

Chase La

MOUNTENEY'S LA

6

THE DOWN'S

WESTEND RD

B4059

B4060

PH

Chaselane Farm

Chase Hill

Saltmoors Ditch

Inglestone Farm

South Moon Ridings

NORTH ST

TOR PIKE GT

AVON CRES

CO

AVON CRES

SMOLD VIEW

NEWMINE WAY

Arnolds Field Trad Est

TH

HIGH ST

BACK LA

INGLESTONE RD

Alexander Hosea Prim Sch

Sturt Farm

The Walk

Little Stanley Wood

Lower Woods Lodge

BUTHAY LA 1
THE BUTHAY 2
SOUTHEND HO 3

PO

2

3

ARKELLS CT

Sturt Bridge

5

Wickwar

Little Avon River

88

AMBERLEY CT

GARDEN

CARTERS CL

WAY

South Farm

POPLAR LA

Horwood Farm

Wetmoor Nature Reserve

Littley Wood

4

SUMMER VIEW

PENNINGTON RD

Poplar Farm

HORMOOD LA

Bishop's Hill Wood

Upper Wetmoor

Lower Wetmoor Wood

SODBURY RD

Hill View Farm

FRITH LA

PINCOTS LA

3

Pincots Farm

Bishop's Hill Brook

87

Sturgeon Wood

Burnt Wood

2

WICKWAR RD

Bedford's Wood

Bays Wood

Shortwood Farm

Stonybridge Wood

Haskin's Farm

WOOD LA

Little Shortwood Farm

1

B4060

Birdsbush Farm

BIRDS BUSH LA

86

72 A B 73 C D 74 E F

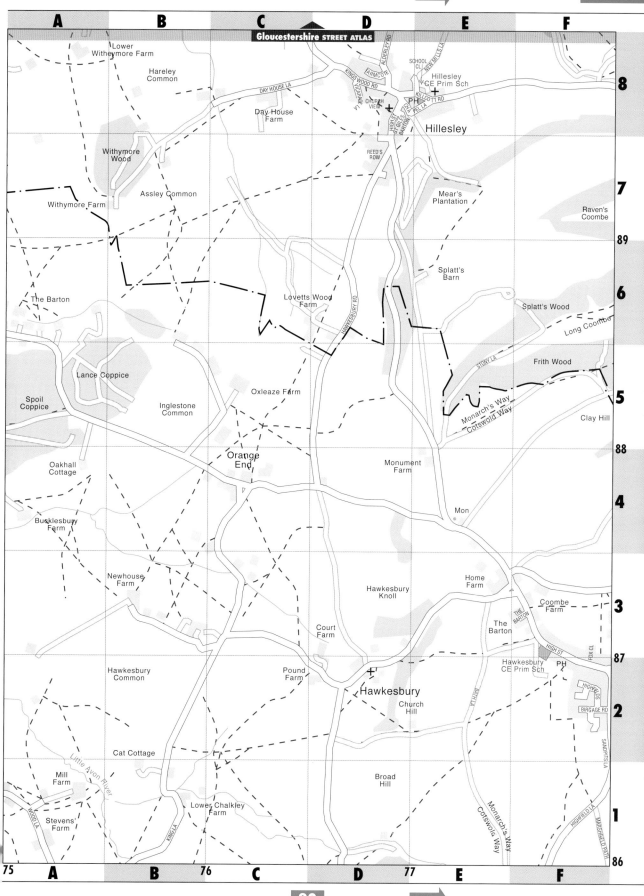

Gloucestershire STREET ATLAS

Lower Witheymore Farm
Hareley Common
Day House Farm
FARMCOTE
KINGS WOOD RD
DAY HOUSE LA
VICARAGE LA
ALDERLEY RD
NEW MILLS LA
SCHOOL CL
Hillesley CE Prim Sch
CHURCH VIEW
HIGH ST
ST GILES
BARTON
PEL LA
KILLCOTT RD
PH
Hillesley

Withymore Wood
Withymore Farm
Assley Common
REED'S ROW
Mear's Plantation
Raven's Coombe

The Barton
Lovetts Wood Farm
HAWKESBURY RD
Splatt's Barn
Splatt's Wood
Long Coombe
STONY LA
Frith Wood

Lance Coppice
Spoil Coppice
Inglestone Common
Oxleaze Farm
Monarch's Way
Cotswold Way
Clay Hill

Oakhall Cottage
Orange End
Monument Farm
Mon

Bucklesbury Farm

Newhouse Farm
Hawkesbury Knoll
Home Farm
Coombe Farm
THE BARTON
The Barton
HIGH ST
FOX CL

Court Farm
Hawkesbury CE Prim Sch
PH
HIGHFIELDS
BIRGAGE RD

Hawkesbury Common
Pound Farm
Hawkesbury
Church Hill
BATH LA
SANDPITS LA

Little Avon River
Cat Cottage
Mill Farm
Broad Hill
Monarch's Way
Cotswold Way
HIGHFIELD LA
MARSHFIELD PATH

Stevens' Farm
WOOD LA
KING LA
Lower Chalkley Farm

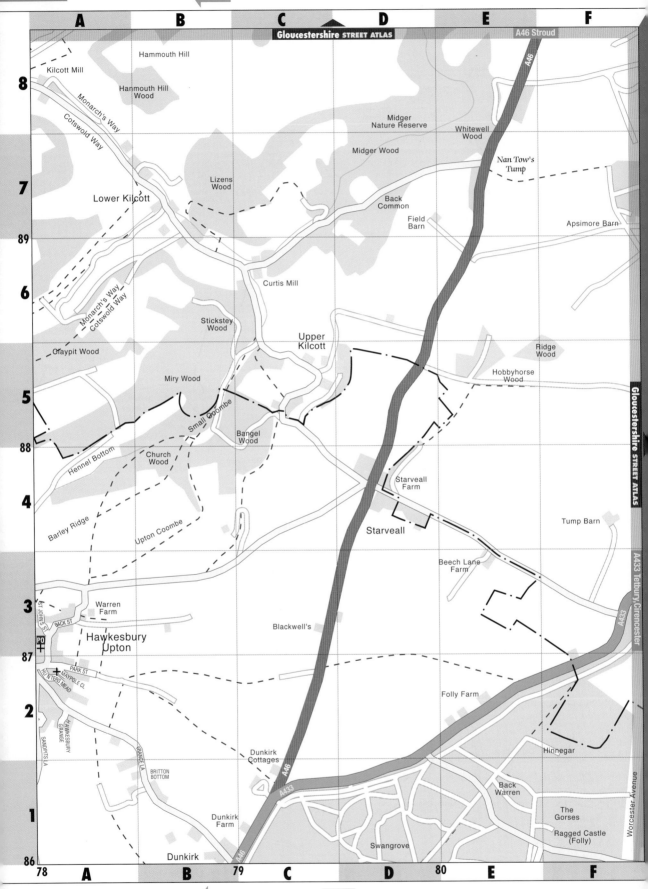

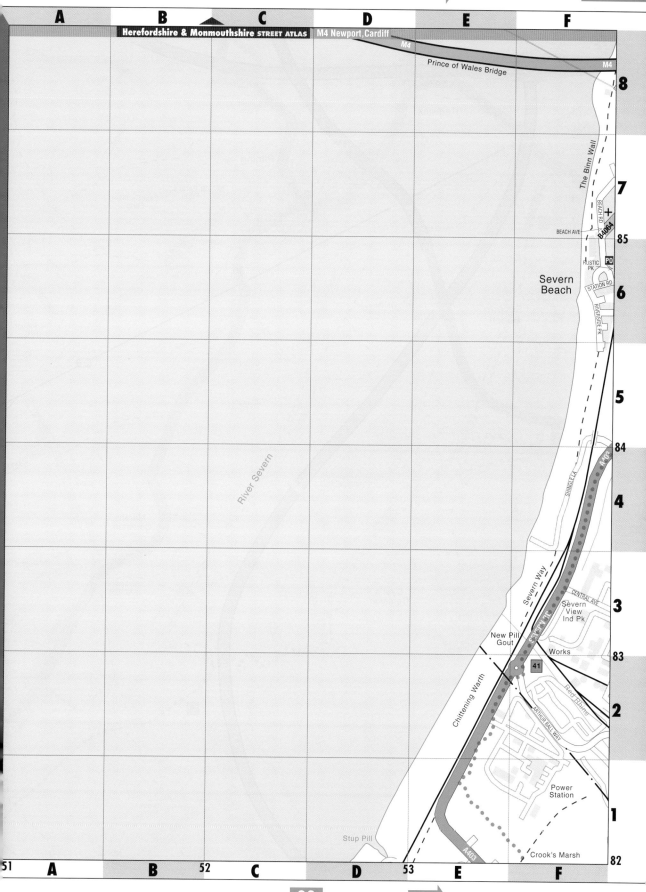

Herefordshire & Monmouthshire STREET ATLAS | M4 Newport, Cardiff

M4

Prince of Wales Bridge

M4

8

The Binn Wall

7

BEACH RD

B4064

BEACH AVE

85

RUSTIC PK

PO

Severn Beach

STATION RD

6

RIVERSIDE PK

River Severn

5

84

A403

SHINGLE LA

4

Severn Way

CENTRAL AVE

Severn View Ind Pk

3

New Pill Gout

SEVERN WAY

Works

83

Chittening Warth

41

Red Rhine

2

ARTHUR BALL WAY

Power Station

1

A403

Stup Pill

Crook's Marsh

82

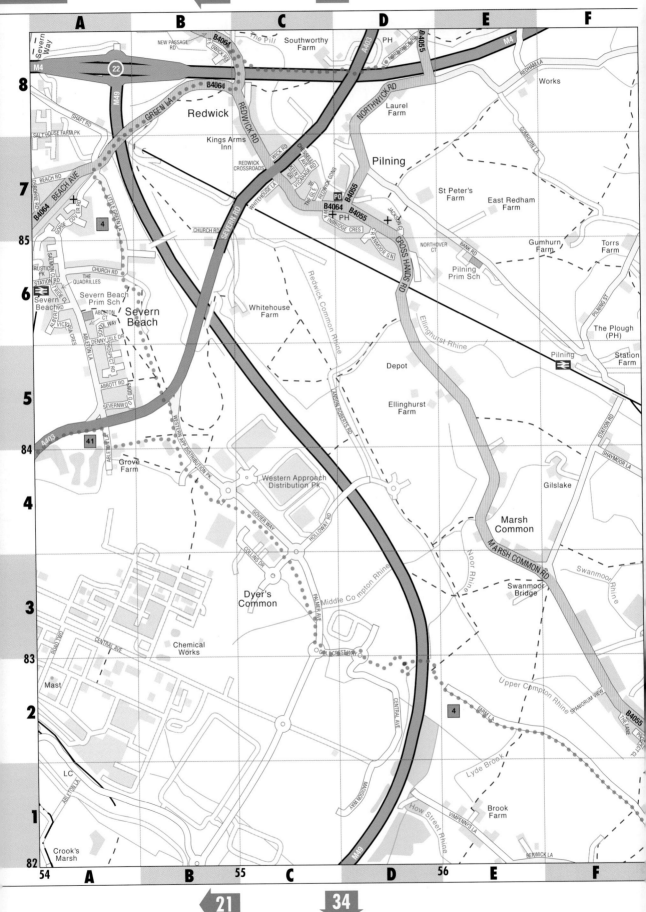

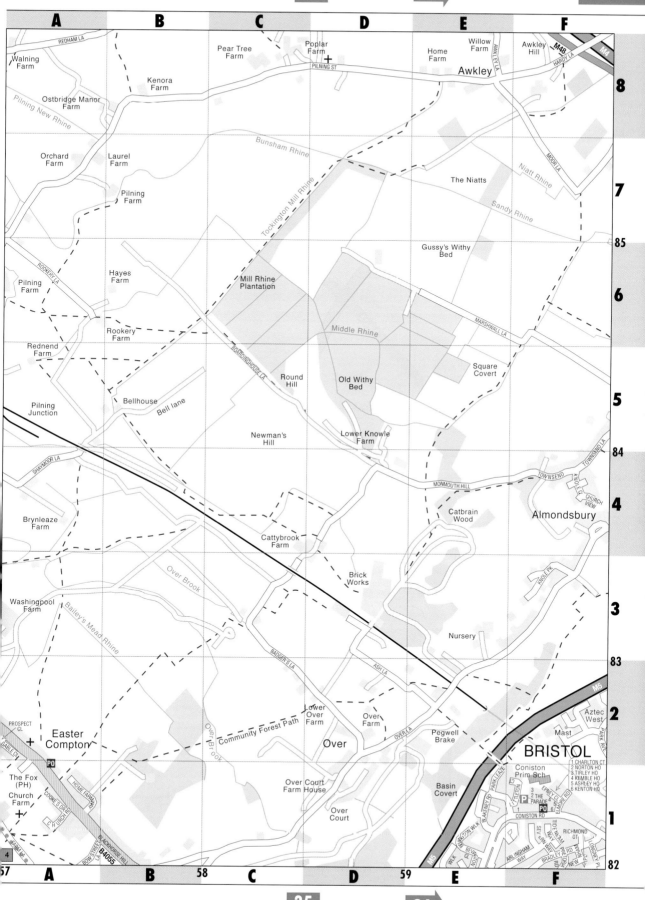

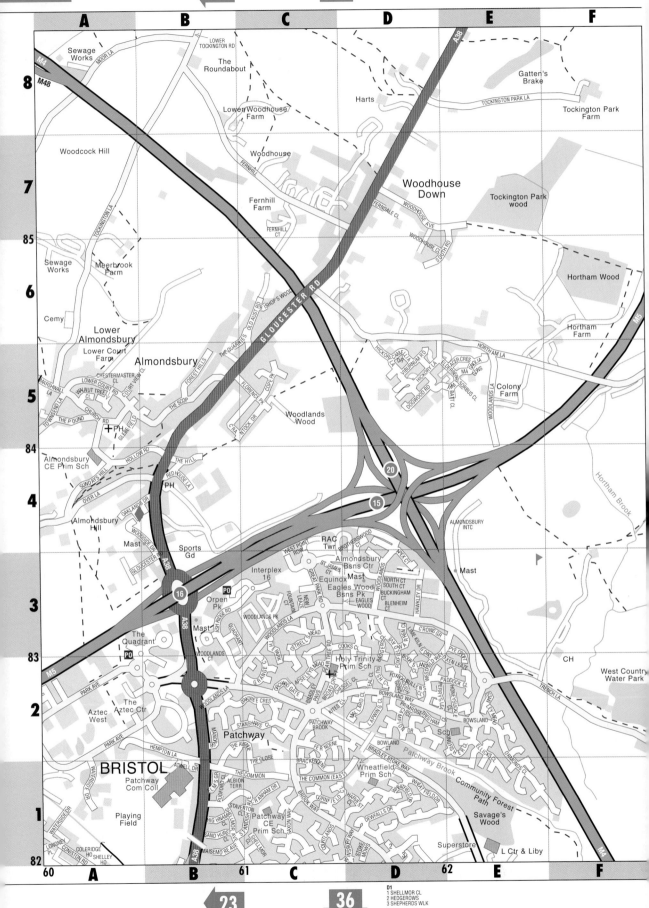

D1
1 SHELLMOR CL
2 HEDGEROWS
3 SHEPHERDS WLK

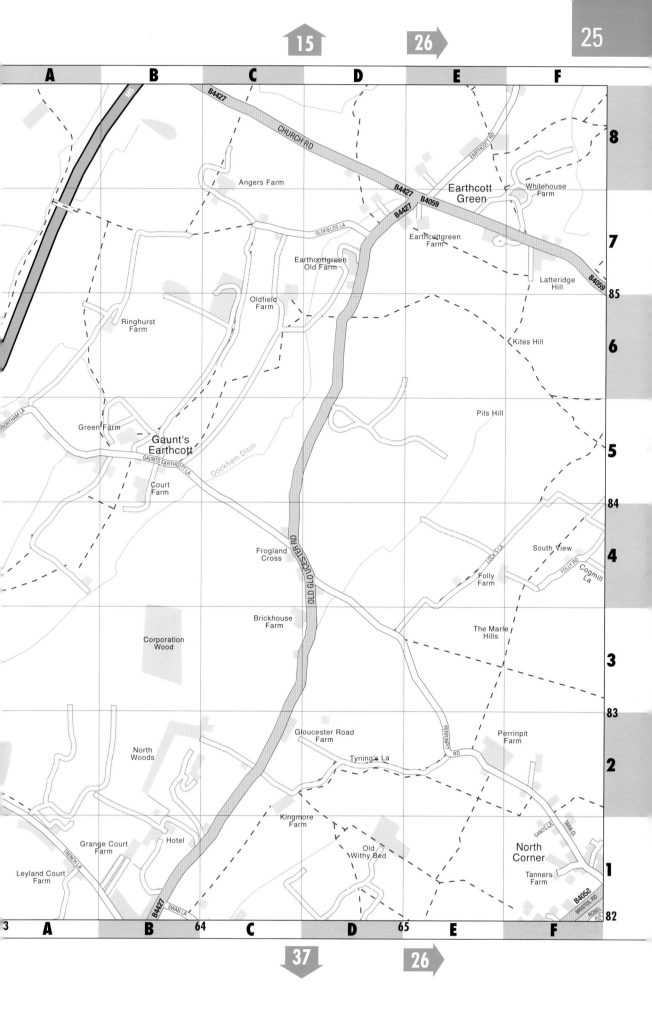

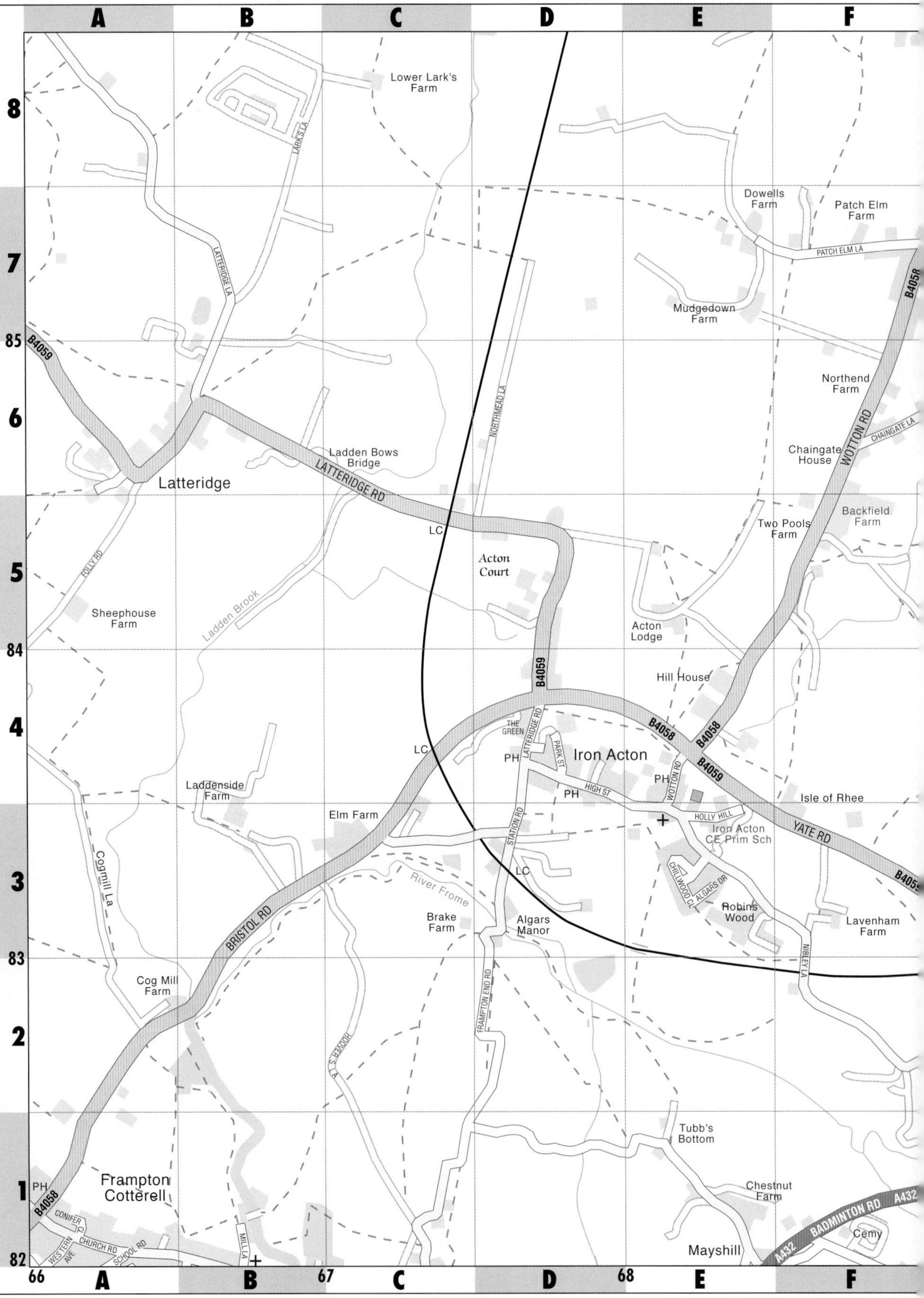

A **B** **C** **D** **E** **F**

8

7

85

6

5

84

4

3

83

2

1

82

Lower Lark's Farm

Dowells Farm

Patch Elm Farm

PATCH ELM LA

B4058

Mudgedown Farm

Northend Farm

LATTERIDGE LA

LARKS LA

B4059

Latteridge

Ladden Bows Bridge

LATTERIDGE RD

NORTHEND LA

LC

Chaingate House

CHAINGATE LA

WOTTON RD

Two Pools Farm

Backfield Farm

FOLLY RD

Sheephouse Farm

Ladden Brook

Acton Court

Acton Lodge

Hill House

B4059

B4058

B4058

B4059

LC

THE GREEN

LATTERIDGE RD

PARK ST

Iron Acton

Isle of Rhee

YATE RD

PH

PH

HIGH ST

PH

WOTTON RD

HOLLY HILL

Iron Acton CE Prim Sch

B4059

Laddenside Farm

Elm Farm

STATION RD

LC

River Frome

Brake Farm

Algars Manor

CHILWOOD CL

ALGARS DR

Robins Wood

Lavenham Farm

Cogmill La

BRISTOL RD

FRAMPTON END RD

NIBLEY LA

Cog Mill Farm

ROVER'S

Tubb's Bottom

Chestnut Farm

BADMINTON RD

A432

A432

Cemy

PH

B4058

Frampton Cotterell

CONIFER AVE

CHURCH RD

WESTERN AVE

SCHOOL RD

MILL LA

Mayshill

66 **A** **B** 67 **C** **D** 68 **E** **F**

A   B   C   D   E   F

8

7

85

6

5

84

4

3

83

2

1

82

Oxwick Farm
OXWICK FARM LA
B4060
Lady's Wood
Horwood Riding Farm
BURY HILL LA
The Chase
Springfield Farm
VINNEY LA
Bury Hill
Lattimore Farm
Little Wood
Brinsham Wood
Brinsham Farm
Brinsham Bridge
BRIN SHAM LA
Hares Farm
MAPLERIDGE LA
Ashlea Farm
Horton Bushes
GRAVEL HILL RD
Quarry
Quarry
Home Farm
Rockwood
ROCKWOOD HO
B4060
PEG HILL
SOUTHFIELD WAY
LOVE LA
LIME CROFT
BARNHILL CL
CARMARTHEN CL
Sodbury Common
Totteroak
HORTON RD
Totteroak Farm
Star Vale Farm
Little Sodbury End
Winchcombe Farm
Greystone Ct
Stub Riding
Mead Riding
CH
The Windmill
Lodge
Monarch's Way
Great House Farm
WICKWAR RD
YATE
GREENWAYS RD
WILTSHIRE AVE
DORSET WAY
ELMHIRST GDNS
NUT AVE
MELROSE AVE
JUBILEE GDNS
BROADWAY
FIRGROVE CRES
RIDGEWAY
HIGHWAY
STATION RD
RENN E
B4060
BOWLING HILL
Works
Bowling Hill Bsns Pk
Mill
LIMESTONE LA
WEAVERS WAY
DROVERS WAY
QUARRY BARN
SODBURY VALE
MELROSE CL
Cemy
BARNHILL RD
STONE HOUSE MEWS
THE PARADE
ROUNCEVAL ST
HIGH ST
B4060
TH
BROAD
HORSESHOE LA
HOUNDS
COLLIERS CL
LEMAN CL
Liby
Prim Sch
STREAMSIDE
ASTORIA RD
WISTARIA RD
CHESTNUT CT
HIGHFIELD RD
VIRGINIA RD
MEADOW
CHERRY
GRASSINGTON DR
COTSWOLD
ARNOLD CT
HOUNDS CL
ABBEYFIELD HO
B4060
HORSE ST
MEAD CL
Chipping Edge Est
BEAUFORT MEWS
TRINITY LA
ST MARYS
COND
CAROLINE CL
COUZENS CL
ROSS CL
HATTERS LA
HORTON RD
BROOKFIELD CL
CH
MANOR WAY
ST JOHNS WAY
FAIRWAY CL
TRI
YATRE CL
G RACE RD
BRANDASH RD
ROGERS
BATTEN CT
TT Trad Est
T
WALSHE AVE
WHITEFIELDS
GORLANDS RD
RIDINGS
HARTLEY CL
CESSON CL
PO
River Frome
Harwoodgate Farm
Park's Farm
PORTWAY LA
COMMONMEAD LA

CHIPPING SODBURY

A B C D E F

8

7

85

6

5

84

4

3

83

2

1

82

Petty France Farm

THE STABLE YD

Hotel

Petty France

Bodkin Wood

Bodkin Hazel Wood

BODKIN HAZEL LA

STROUD RD

A46

A46

Seven Mile Plantation

American Barn

Peaked Down Clump

Landing Strip

SWANGROVE LA

Swangrove House

Worcester Avenue

Worcester Clump

Shepherd's Lodge

Withy Bed

Little Badminton Farm

Little Badminton

CHURCH LA

WELL LA

Badminton Park

Mount Pond

Deer Park

The Mount

Park Pond

Slait Lodge

Badminton House

SHOP LA

KENNEL DR

Castle Barn

The Tyning

HIGH ST

HAYES LA

SCHOOL LA

THE TIMES

CENTRE WALK AVE

Badminton

Bath Lodge

Bath Verge

ROACH'S LA

LIME AVE

LIME AVE

Vicarage Plantation

OLD DOWN RD

STATION RD

Badminton Farm

Cape Farm

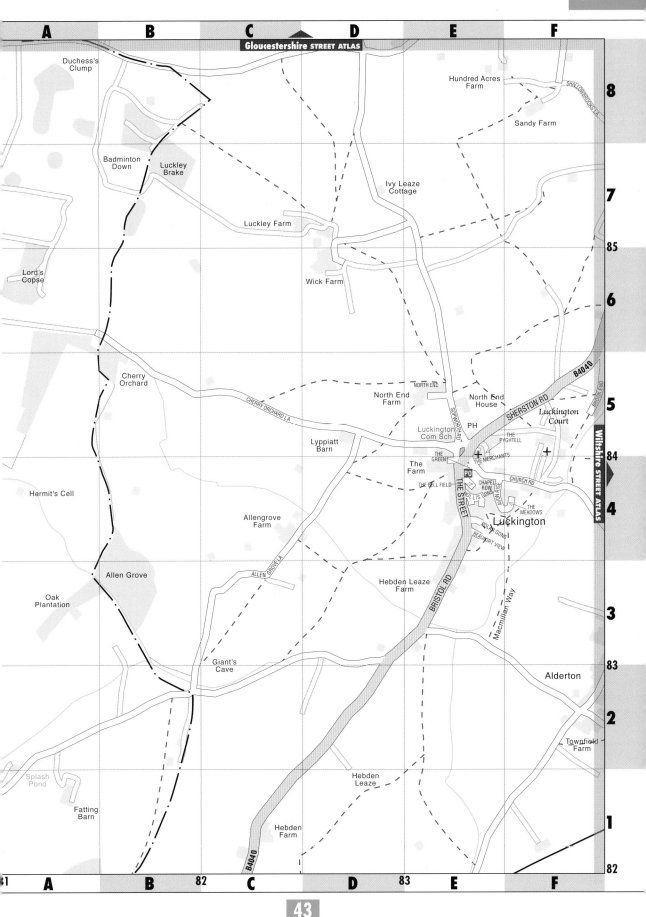

A B C D E F

8

7

85

6

Wiltshire STREET ATLAS

5

84

4

3

83

2

1

82

Duchess's
Clump

Badminton
Down

Luckley
Brake

Luckley Farm

Lord's
Copse

Cherry
Orchard

CHERRY ORCHARD LA

Hermit's Cell

Allengrove
Farm

Allen Grove

ALLEN GROVE LA

Oak
Plantation

Giant's
Cave

Splash
Pond

Fatting
Barn

B4040

Hebden
Farm

Hebden
Leaze

Hebden Leaze
Farm

BRISTOL RD

Ivy Leaze
Cottage

Hundred Acres
Farm

Sandy Farm

SHALLOWBROOKS LA

Wick Farm

North End
Farm

NORTH END

North End
House

SOPWORTH RD

Luckington
Com Sch

PH

SHERSTON RD

B4040

BROOK END

Luckington
Court

THE PYGHTELL

THE MERCHANTS

THE GREEN

THE FARM

THE BELL FIELD

PO

HOLLIS GDNS

CHAPEL
ROW

AVON RISE

CHURCH RD

THE
MEADOWS

BOLDS GDNS

THE STREET

Luckington

BEAUFORT VIEW

Macmillan Way

Alderton

Townfield
Farm

Lyppiatt
Barn

A B C D E F

81 82 82 83 83 82

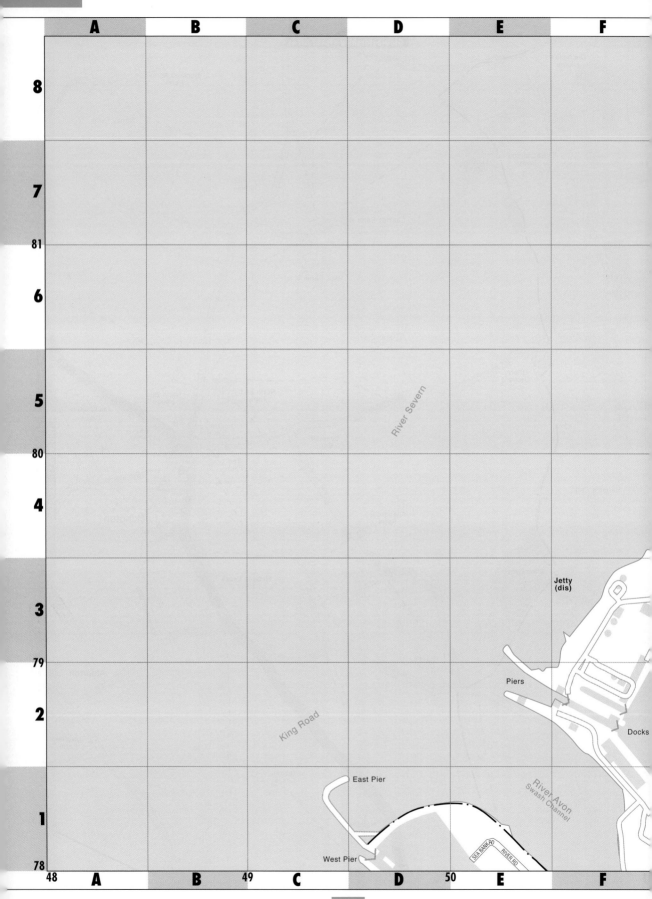

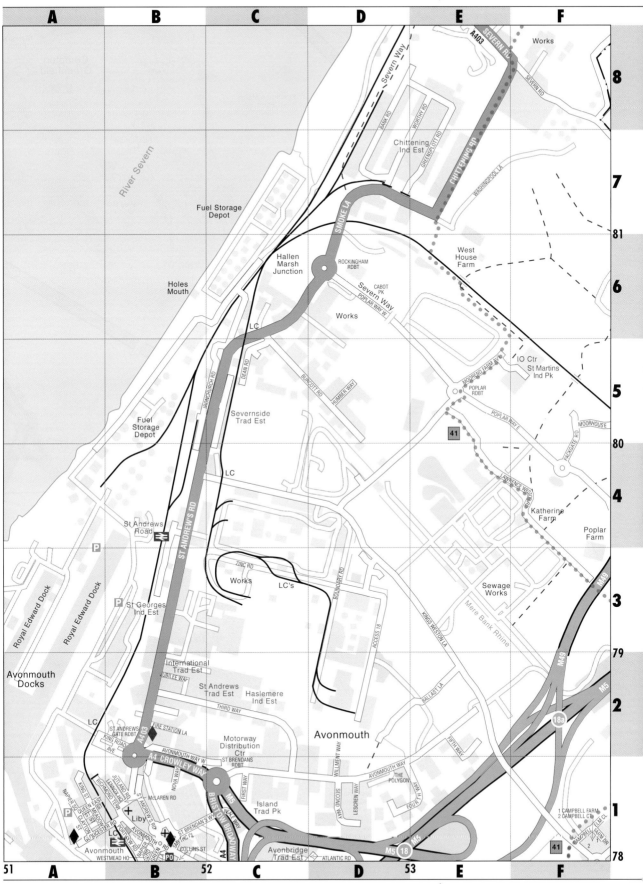

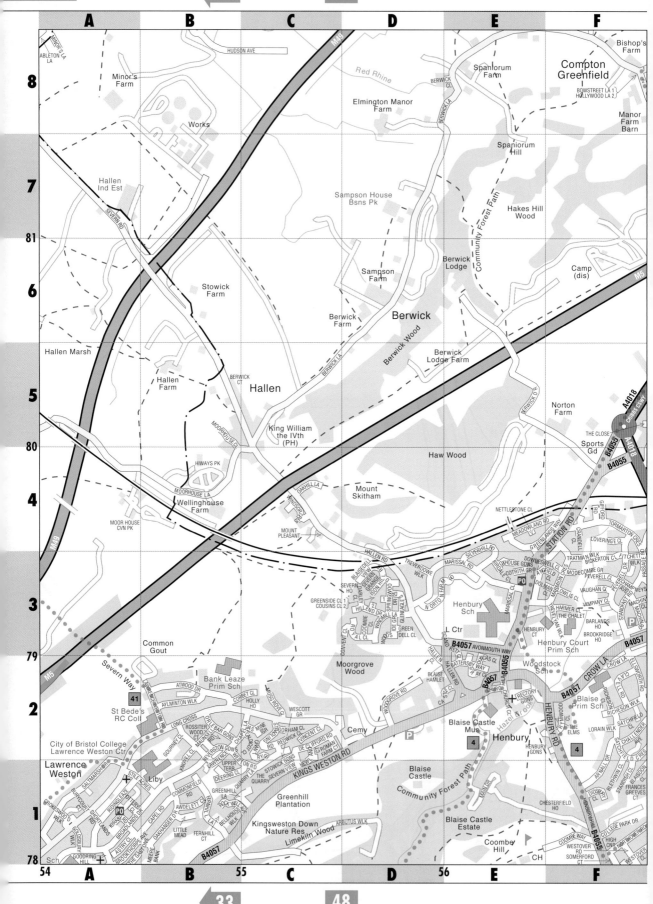

F7
1 CHARLES ENGLAND HO
2 WEST FIELD
3 GREEN SANDS RD
4 SOLDIERS RD
5 BROAD LEAZE
6 HOLLOW MEAD
7 HADWELLS RD
8 HIGH LEAZE RD
9 CROSS FIELD

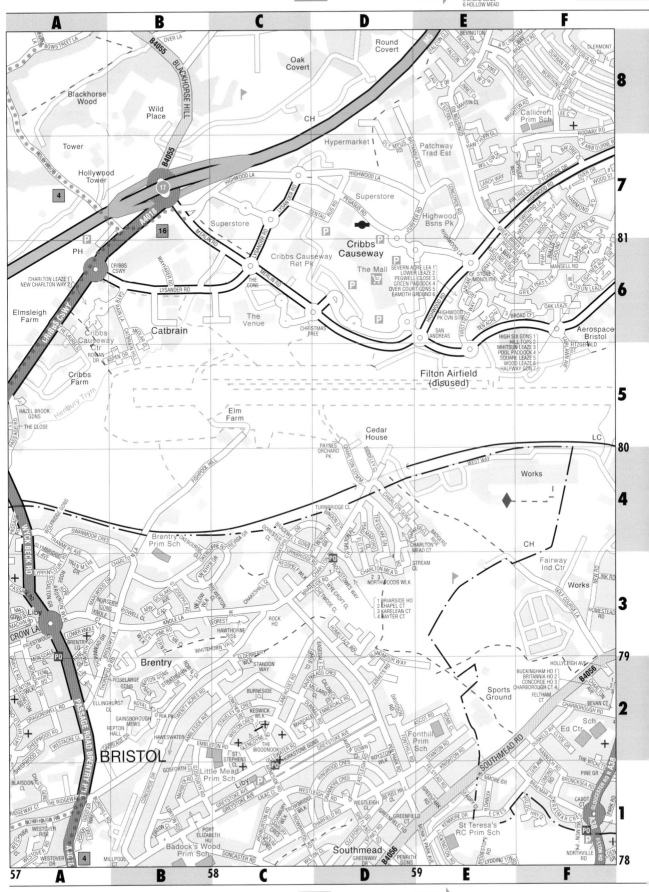

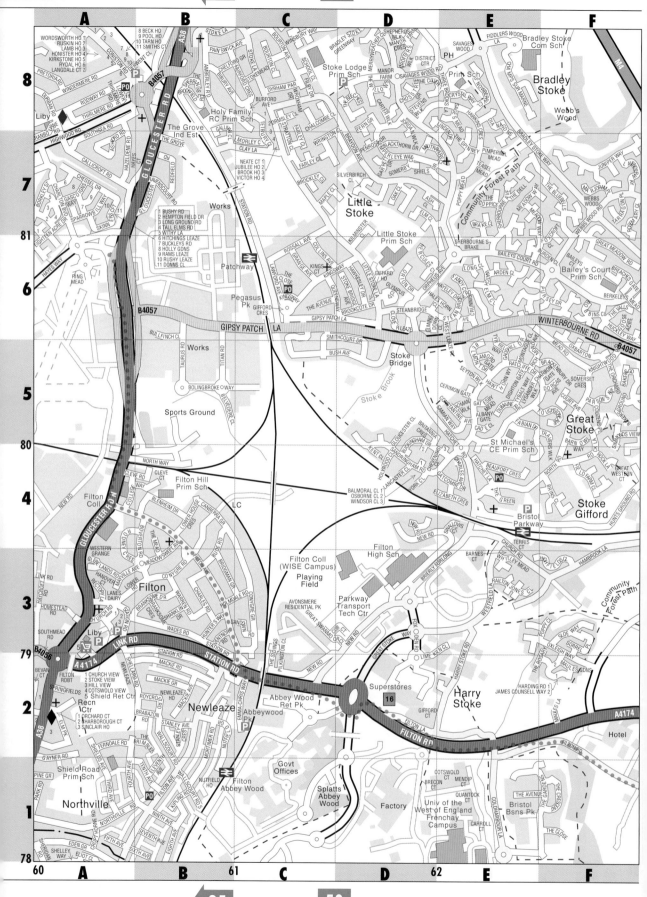

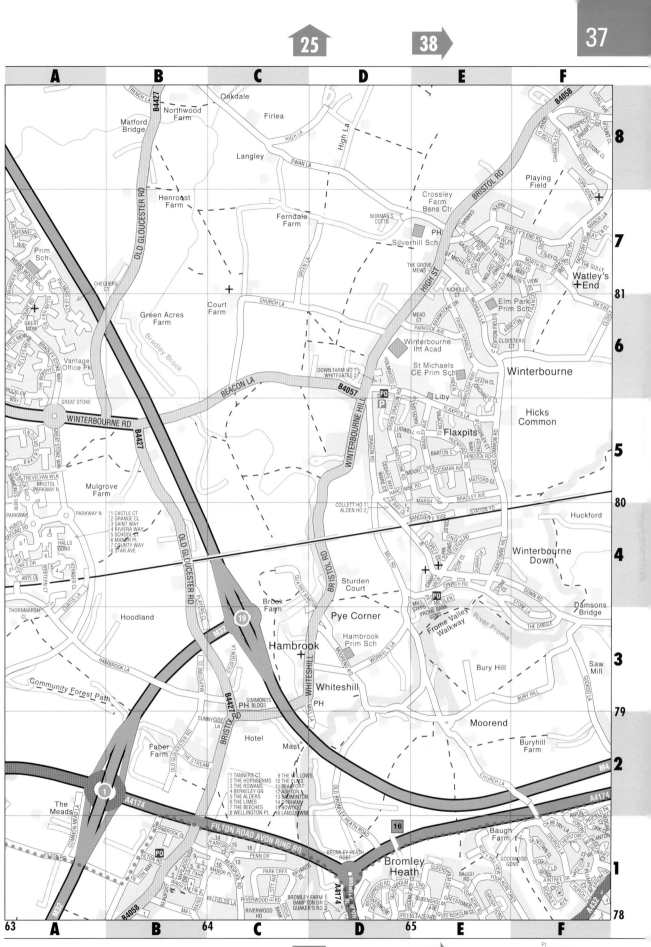

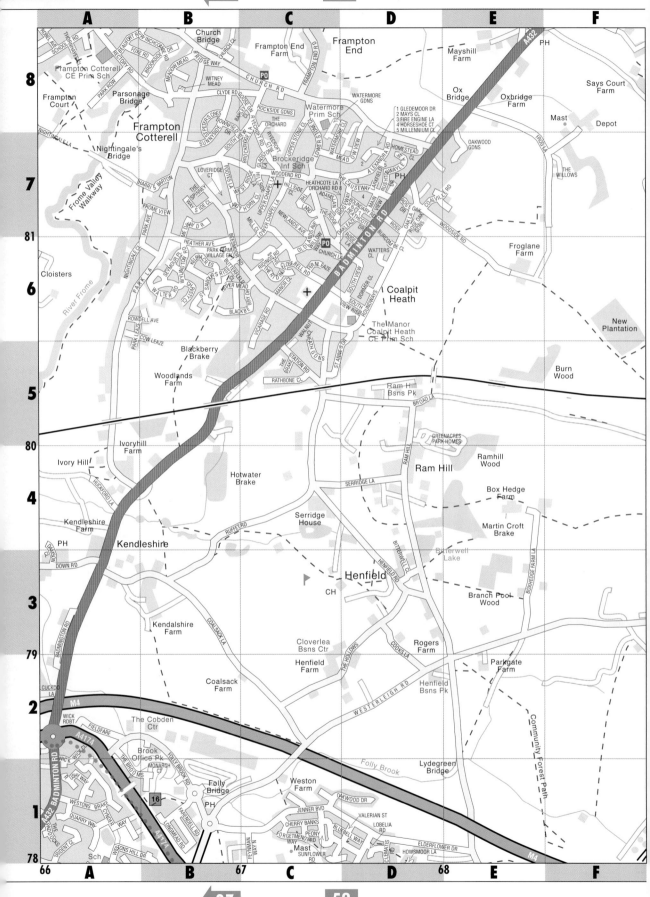

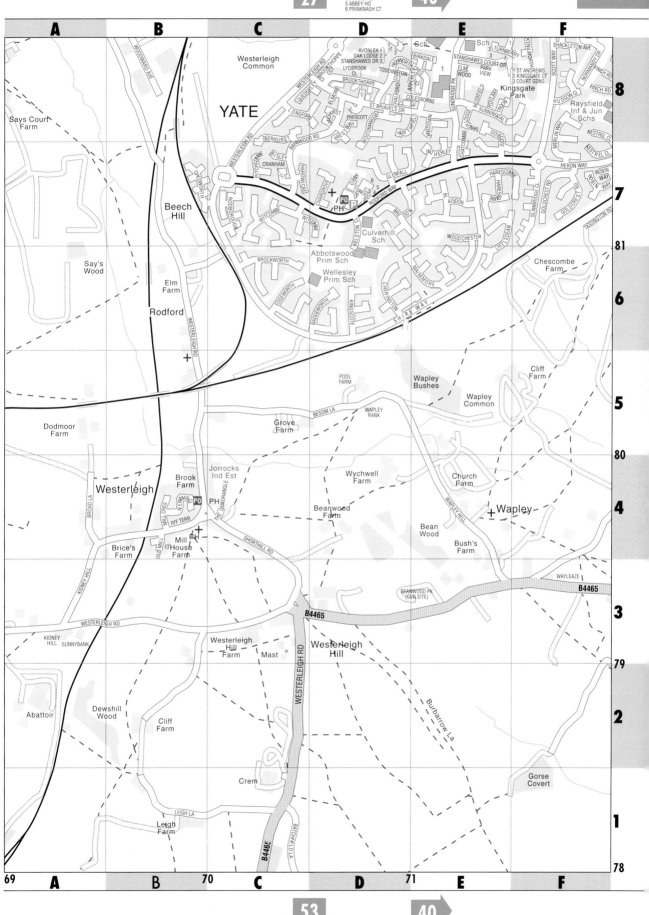

27

D7
1 MINSTER CT
2 FOUNTAIN CT
3 MONKS HO
4 FRIARS HO
5 ABBEY HO
6 PRINKNASH CT

40

E8
1 The Ridings' Federation
Yate Int Acad

39

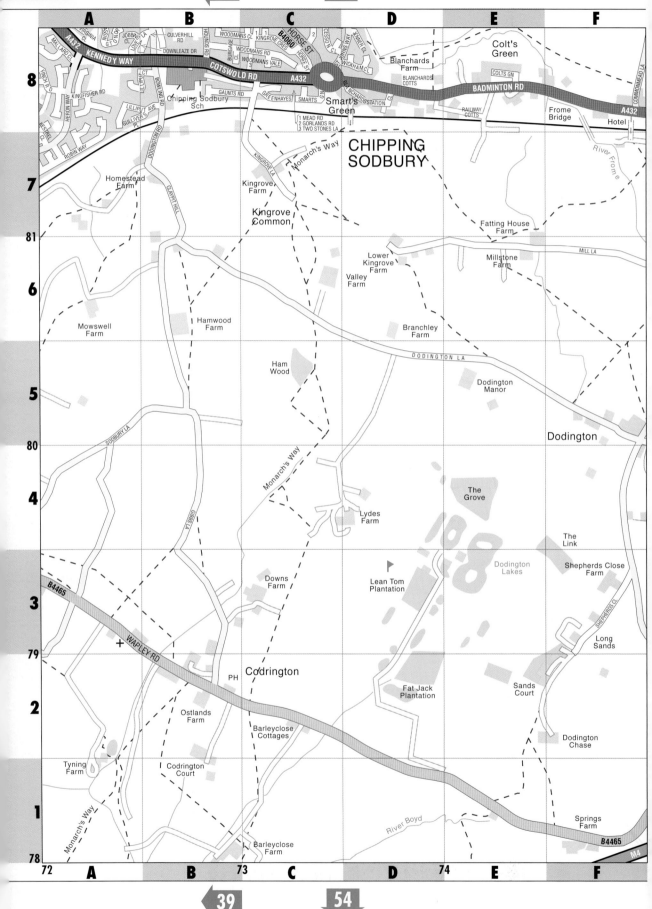

A **B** **C** **D** **E** **F**

A432

Virginia Cl

MALLARD CL

FINCH RD

NISS GT

LDR LA

JOBBINS CL

CULVERHILL RD

DOWNLEAZE DR

HOUNDS RD

BURGAGE

WOODMANS CL

WOODMANS RD

WOODMANS VALE

KINGROVE CRES

HORSE ST

B4060

CESSORS

JOHNS WAY

JOINER CL

WICKHAM CL

KENNEDY WAY

COTSWOLD RD

A432

Blanchards Farm

Colt's Green

COLTS GN

HERON WAY

KINGFISHER RD

ROBIN WAY

KESTREL

LILLIPUT AVE

GULLIVER'S PL

LCT

LHAPLEY PL

BOWLING RD

DODINGTON RD

Chipping Sodbury Sch

GAUNTS RD

GREENHAYES

GREENHAYES

SMARTS

BR. RICHARDS STATION

BLANCHARDS COTTS

RAILWAY COTTS

BADMINTON RD

Frome Bridge

Hotel

A432

8

Smart's Green

1 MEAD RD
2 GORLANDS RD
3 TWO STONES LA

CHIPPING SODBURY

River Frome

KINGROVE LA

Monarch's Way

7

Homestead Farm

Kingrove Farm

CLAPIT HILL

Kingrove Common

Lower Kingrove Farm

Valley Farm

Fatting House Farm

Millstone Farm

MILL LA

81

6

Mowswell Farm

Hamwood Farm

Ham Wood

Branchley Farm

DODINGTON LA

Dodington Manor

5

SODBURY LA

Monarch's Way

The Grove

Dodington

80

GIBBS LA

Lydes Farm

The Link

Dodington Lakes

Shepherds Close Farm

4

B4465

Downs Farm

Lean Tom Plantation

SHEPHERDS CL

Long Sands

3

WAPLEY RD

PH

Codrington

Fat Jack Plantation

Sands Court

Dodington Chase

79

2

Ostlands Farm

Barleyclose Cottages

1

Tyning Farm

Codrington Court

Monarch's Way

Barleyclose Farm

River Boyd

Springs Farm

B4465

M4

78

72 **A** **B** **73** **C** **D** **74** **E** **F**

A | B | C | D | E | F

COMMONMEAD LA

Haye's Farm

Old Sodbury CE Prim Sch

COTSWOLD LA

THE GREEN

Old Sodbury

PO

PH

Overndale Sch

CHAPEL LA

MILL LA

CHURCH LA

HILL LA

BADMINTON RD

CATCHPOT LA

Coomb's End

Hammerdown Clump

Frenchpiece Wood

Dodington House

Dodington Park

Cotswold Way

Vineyard Clump

Bailey Clump

River Frome

Black Brake

Old Farm

Southfield Clump

Watt's Barn

Dodington Wood

DODINGTON ASH

B4465

Hawkes Tyning Clump

TORMARTON INTC

18

A46

Long Plantation

BATH RD

A432

A46

Plough Farm

Tyning La

Sodbury Tunnel

Hotel

WESTMORLAND TERR

B4040

B4040

Windylands

The Clovers

Bennett's Gorse

Lyegrove Wood

Lyegrove House

Lyegrove Farm

Sheepcot Barn

CHURCH RD

Tormarton

OLD HUNDRED LA

PH

Old Hundred

PH

HIGH ST

CAVENDISH CL

NORLEY LA

LAPDOWN LA

MARSHFIELD RD

M4

8

7

81

6

5

80

4

3

79

2

1

78

5

76

77

78

A B C D E F

8

Lyegrove Wood

Egg Clump

Withy Moor

LIME AVE

OLD DOWN RD

STATION RD

7

Sodbury Tunnel

B4040

81

SODBURY RD

Limes Farm

B4040

Newhouse Farm

Acton Turville

B4039

THE STREET

6

PH

BURTON RD B4039

OAKES LA

TORMARTON RD

Vicarage Cottage

5

Warren Barn

80

Fagot Pile

M4

4

Pike Cottage

ACTON TURVILLE RD

Old Warren

Wall Leaze Wood

Brotton Hill Wood

Parks Farm

3

Warren Gorse

79

2

Westfield Farm

M4

Phyldornick

Little Westfield

1

Fox Covert

78

78 A 79 B C 80 D E F

A B C D E F

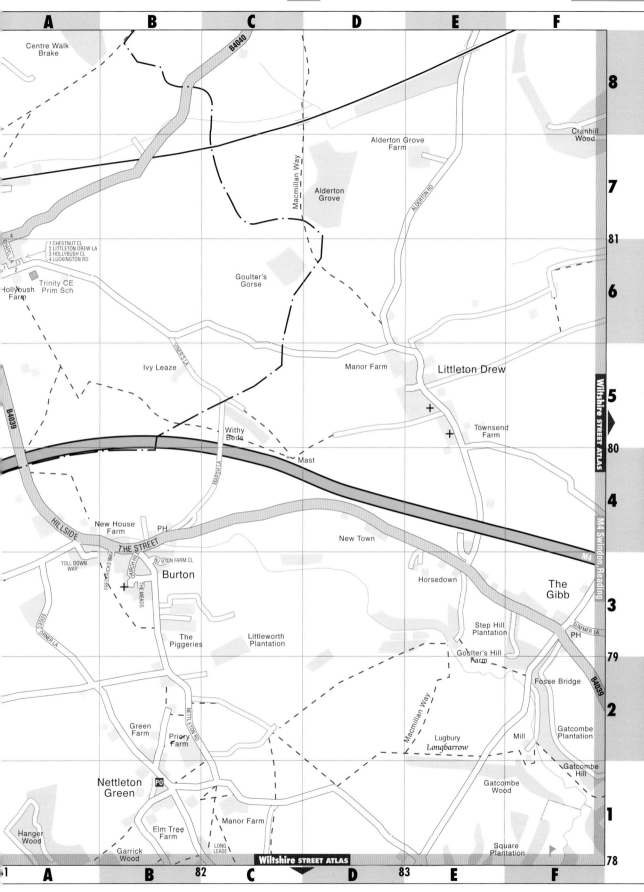

A   B   C   D   E   F

8

Centre Walk Brake

Cranhill Wood

7

Alderton Grove Farm

Macmillan Way

ALDERTON RD

81

Alderton Grove

4

CHAPEL LA

1 CHESTNUT CL
2 LITTLETON DREW LA
3 HOLLYBUSH CL
4 LUCKINGTON RD

3

2

6

Hollybush Farm

Trinity CE Prim Sch

Goulter's Gorse

VINER'S LA

Ivy Leaze

Manor Farm

Littleton Drew

5

B4039

Withy Beds

MARSH LA

+

+

Townsend Farm

80

Mast

4

HILLSIDE

New House Farm

PH

New Town

M4

The Gibb

3

M4 Swindon, Reading

Toll Down Way

FREDERICK'S WAY

THE STREET

CHURCH HILL

BURTON FARM CL

Burton

Horsedown

Step Hill Plantation

SUMMER LA

PH

79

THE MEADS

The Piggeries

Littleworth Plantation

Goulter's Hill Farm

Fosse Bridge

B4039

2

EDGEC ORNER LA

Green Farm

NETTLETON RD

Priory Farm

Macmillan Way

Lugbury Longbarrow

Mill

Gatcombe Plantation

Gatcombe Hill

Nettleton Green

PO

Gatcombe Wood

1

Hanger Wood

Elm Tree Farm

Manor Farm

LONG LEASE

Square Plantation

78

Garrick Wood

1

A   B   82   C   D   83   E   F

Wiltshire STREET ATLAS

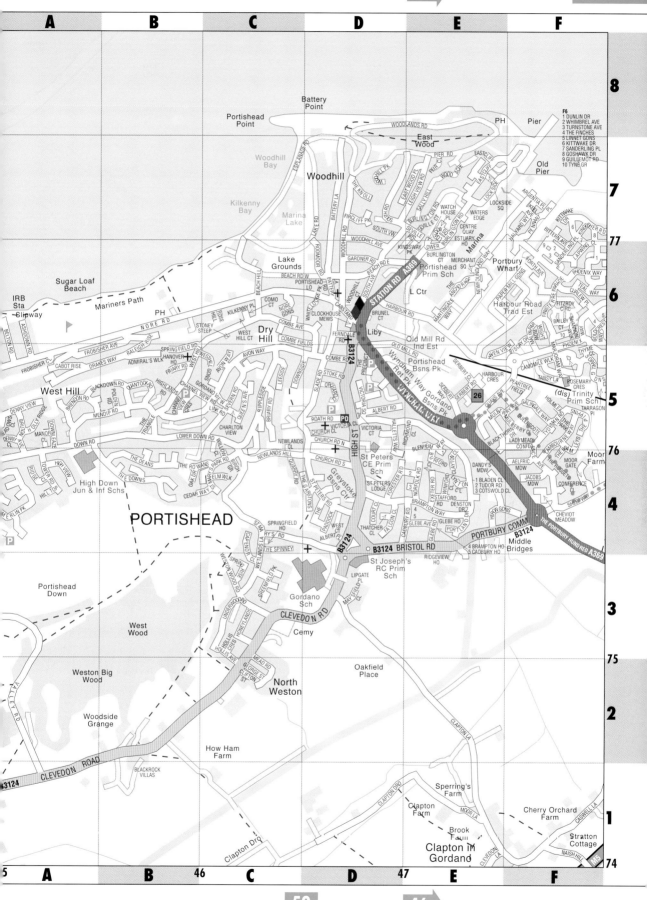

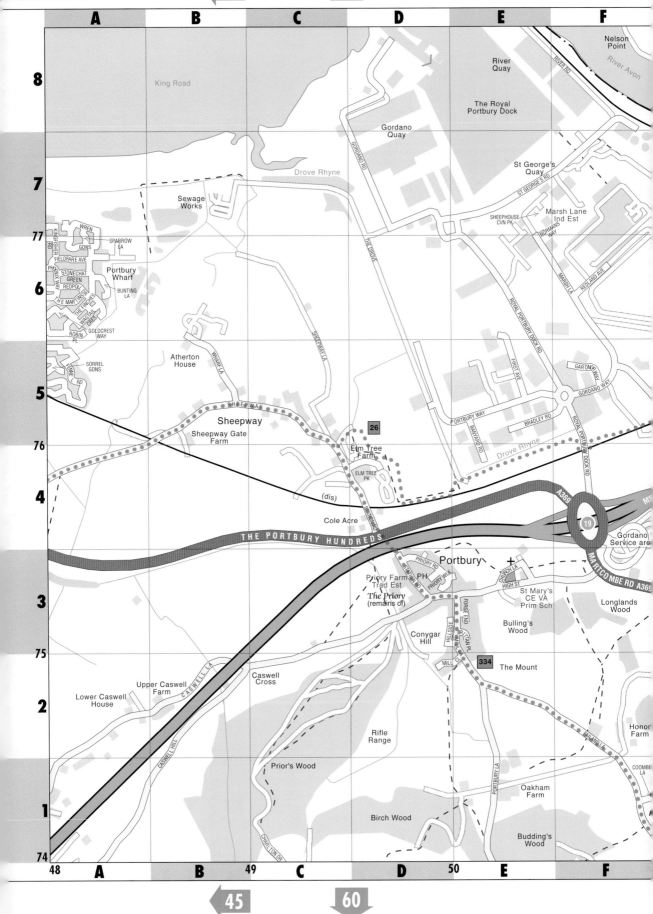

King Road

Drove Rhyne

Sewage
Works

Nelson
Point

River
Quay

The Royal
Portbury Dock

Gordano
Quay

GORDANO RD

RIVER RD

River Avon

St George's
Quay

ST GEORGE'S RD

SHEEPHOUSE
CVN PK

Marsh Lane
Ind Est

NORMANS WAY

WREN
GDNS

SPARROW LA

KINGFISHER RD

FIELDFARE AVE

PH

STONECHAT
GREEN

PHEASANT WAY

REDPOL

THE FINCHES

WAGTAIL
CRES

THE MARTINS

GOLDCREST
WAY

ROBIN
PL

SORREL
GDNS

FENEL RD

Portbury
Wharf

BUNTING
LA

THE DROVE

SHEEPWAY LA

WHARF LA

Atherton
House

ROYAL PORTBURY DOCK RD

FIRST AVE

MARSH LA

REDLAND AVE

GARONOR WAY

GORDANO WAY

Sheepway

SHEEPWAY

Sheepway Gate
Farm

26

Elm Tree
Farm

ELM TREE
PK

PORTBURY WAY

BANYARD RD

BRADLEY RD

Drove Rhyne

ROYAL PORTBURY DOCK RD

A369

19

M

Gordano Service are

(dis)

Cole Acre

SWITHIN RD

THE PORTBURY HUNDREDS

Portbury

PRIORY RD

PRIORY WLK

PH

CHURCH LA

+

High St

St Mary's
CE VA
Prim Sch

Longlands
Wood

Priory Farm
Trad Est

The Priory
(remains of)

Conygar
Hill

FORGE END

MILL ST

BRITTAN PL

Bulling's
Wood

MILL CL

334

The Mount

MARTCOMBE RD A369

75

Upper Caswell
Farm

CASWELL LA

Caswell
Cross

Lower Caswell
House

CASWELL HILL

Rifle
Range

PORTBURY LA

FAIR VW LA

Oakham
Farm

Honor
Farm

COOMBE
LA

Prior's Wood

Birch Wood

Budding's
Wood

CHARLTON DR

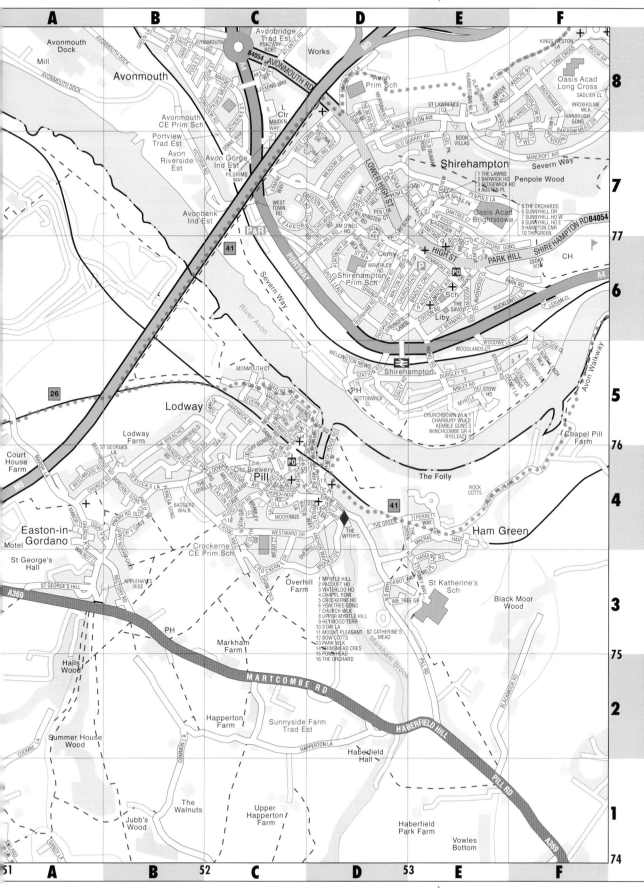

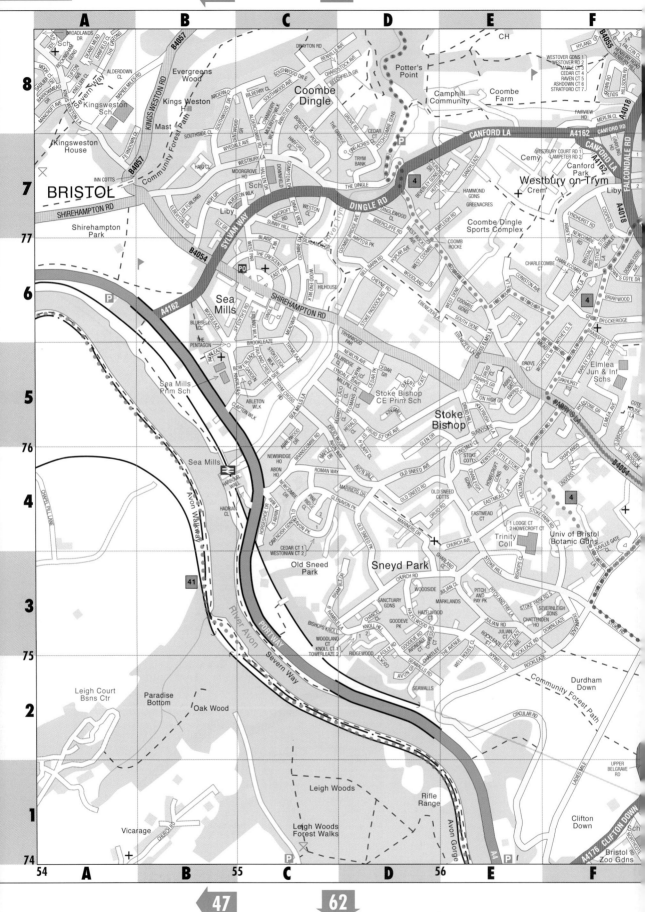

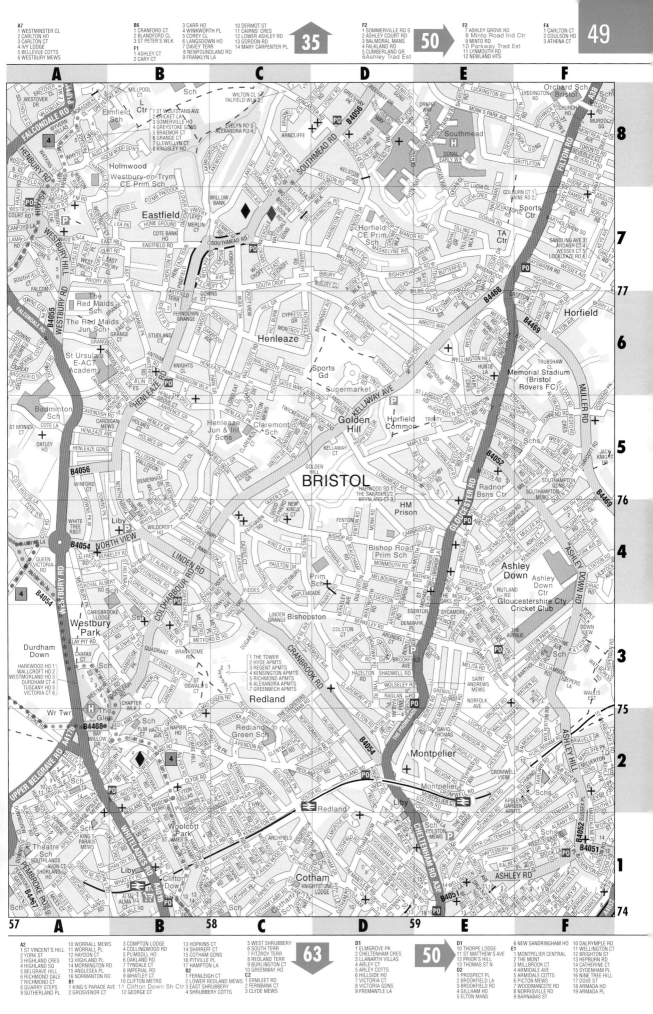

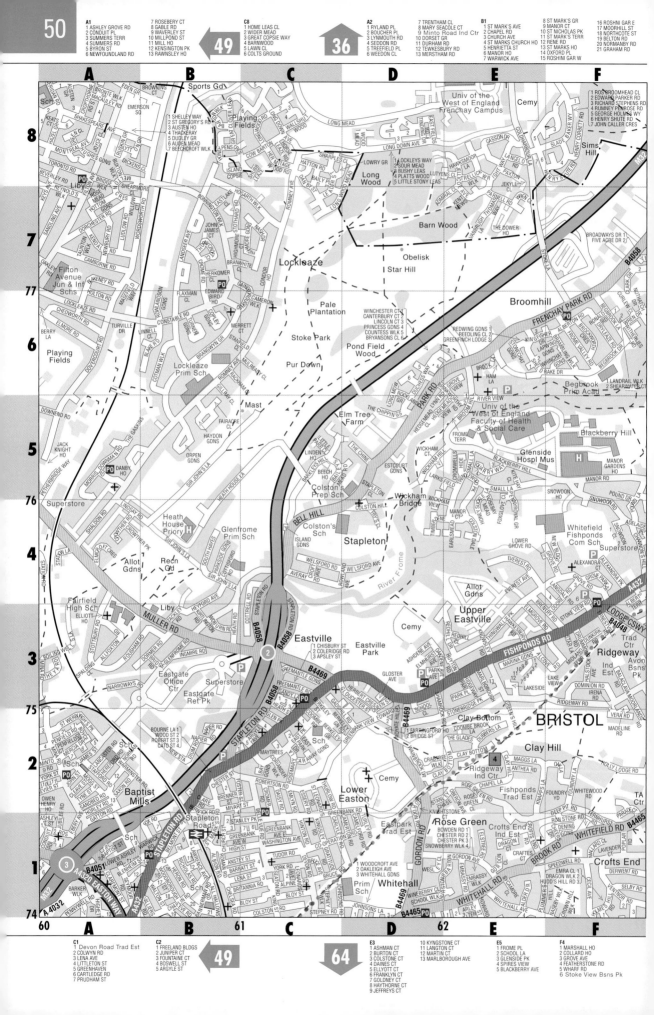

A1
1 ASHLEY GROVE RD
2 CONDUIT PL
3 SUMMERS TERR
4 SUMMERS RD
5 BYRON ST
6 NEWFOUNDLAND RD

7 ROSEBERY CT
8 GABLE RD
9 WAVERLEY ST
10 MILLPOND ST
11 MILL HO
12 KENSINGTON PK
13 RAWNSLEY HO

C8
1 HOME LEAS CL
2 WIDER MEAD
3 GREAT COPSIE WAY
4 BARNWOOD
5 LAWN CL
6 COLTS GROUND

49 **36**

A2
1 RYLAND PL
2 BOUCHER CT
3 LYNMOUTH RD
4 SEDDON RD
5 TREEFIELD PL
6 WEEDON CL

7 TRENTHAM CL
8 MARY SEACOLE CT
9 MINTO ROAD IND CTR
10 DORSET GR
11 DURHAM RD
12 TEWKESBURY RD
13 MERSTHAM RD

B1
1 ST MARK'S AVE
2 CHAPEL RD
3 CHURCH AVE
4 ST MARKS CHURCH HO
5 HENRIETTA ST
6 MANOR HO
7 WARWICK AVE

8 ST MARK'S GR
9 MANOR CT
10 ST NICHOLAS PK
11 ST MARK'S TERR
12 RENE
13 ST MARKS HO
14 OXFORD PL
15 ROSHINI GAR W

16 ROSHNI GAR E
17 MOORHILL ST
18 NORTHCOTE ST
19 BELTON RD
20 NORMANBY CT
21 GRAHAM RD

1 ROSEBROOMHEAD CL
2 EDWARD PARKER RD
3 RICHARD STEPHENS RD
4 RUMNEY PENROSE RD
5 GEORGE HOLMES WY
6 HENRY SHUTE RD
7 JOHN CALLER CRES

C1
1 DEVON ROAD TRAD EST
2 COLWYN RD
3 LENA AVE
4 LITTLETON ST
5 GREENHAVEN
6 CARTLEDGE RD
7 PRUDHAM ST

C2
1 FREELAND BLDGS
2 JUNIPER CT
3 FOUNTAINE CT
4 BOSWELL ST
5 KERSGYLE ST

E3
1 ASHMAN CT
2 BURTON CT
3 COLSTONE CT
4 DAINES CT
5 ELLYOTT CT
6 FRANKLYN CT
7 GOLDNEY CT
8 HAYTHORNE CT
9 JEFFREYS CT

10 KYNGSTONE CT
11 LANGTON CT
12 MARTIN CT
13 MARLBOROUGH AVE

E5
1 FROME PL
2 SCHOOL LA
3 GLENSIDE PK
4 SPIRES VIEW
5 BLACKBERRY AVE

F4
1 MARSHALL HO
2 COLLARD HO
3 GROVE AVE
4 FEATHERSTONE RD
5 WHARF RD
6 STOKE VIEW BSNS PK

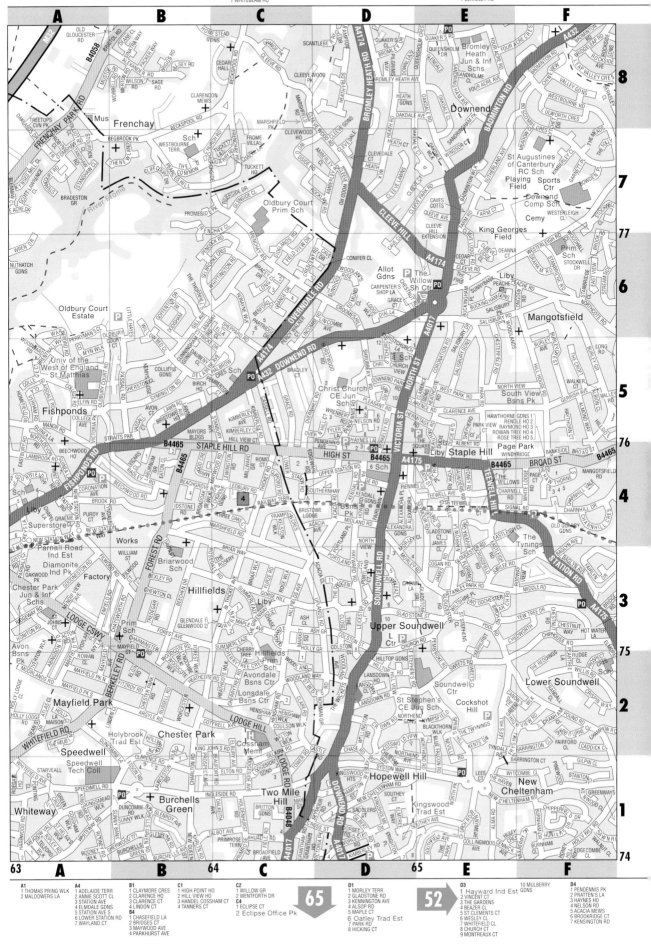

52

A7
1 WAKEFORD RD
2 WESTBOURNE CL

C7
1 MEADOWSWEET RD
2 FOXGLOVE RD
3 WALNUT WAY
4 PRIMROSE RD
5 YARROW CL
6 CARNATION RD

51

38

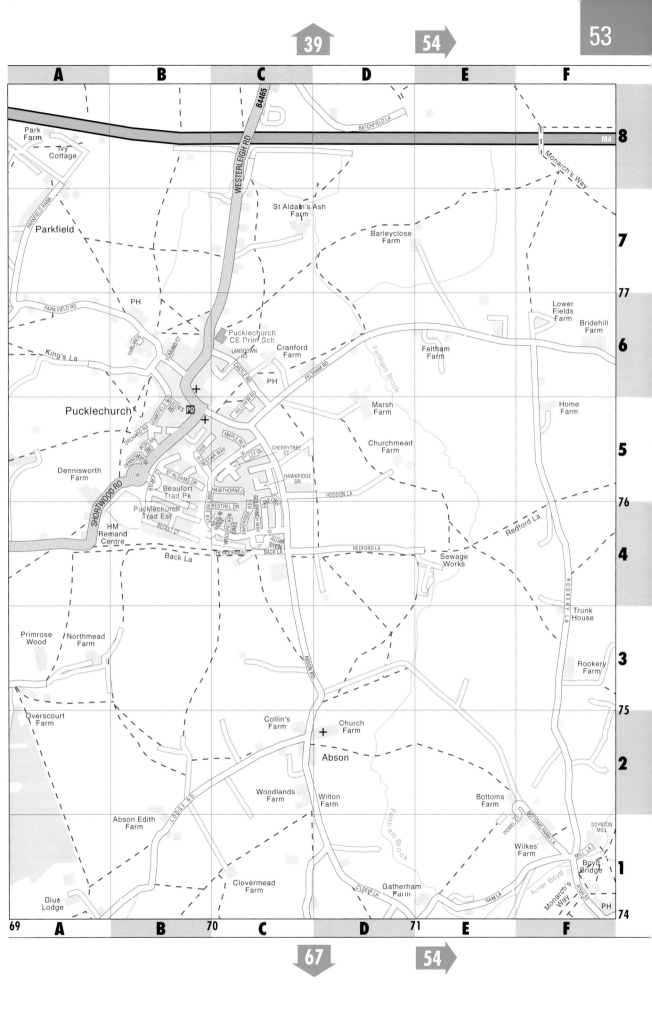

Park Farm
Ivy Cottage
PARKFIELD RANK
Parkfield
PARK FIELD RD
King's La
PH
FARLANDS
EDMUND CT
Pucklechurch CE Prim Sch
LANSDOWN RD
CASTLE RD
Cranford Farm
PH
WESTERLEIGH RD
B4465
St Aldam's Ash Farm
BATCHFIELD LA
M4
Monarch's Way
Barleyclose Farm
Lower Fields Farm
Bridehill Farm
Feltham Farm
FELTHAM RD
Feltham Brook
Pucklechurch
HOMEFIELD
QUEEN'S RD
PO
ORCHARD RD
POPLAR
DENNIS WK
DR
BECKS CT
ST ALDAMS DR
Dennisworth Farm
SHORTWOOD RD
Beaufort Trad Pk
Pucklechurch Trad Est
BECKET CT
HM Remand Centre
HILLVIEW RD
MAPLE WK
LILY CL
HO
CEDAR WAY
HAWTHORNE CL
OAK TREE AVE
KESTREL DR
MERLIN RIDGE
WOODPECKER CRES
PARTRIDGE RD
GOLDFINCH WAY
DV
BITHAM VIEW
BACK LA
THE MOORINGS
CHERRYTREE CT
PH
HLDR
JUB
HO
ELM DR
PF CRES
HAWKRIDGE DR
HODDON LA
Marsh Farm
Churchmead Farm
Home Farm
REDFORD LA
Sewage Works
Redford La
ROOKERY LA
Trunk House
Rookery Farm
Back La
Primrose Wood
Northmead Farm
ABSON RD
Overscourt Farm
Collin's Farm
Church Farm
Abson
Woodlands Farm
Wilton Farm
Bottoms Farm
POWEL LA
BOTTOMS FARM LA
DOYNTON MILL
MILL LA
Wilkes' Farm
Boyd Bridge
TRINITY ST
PH
Abson Edith Farm
LODGE RD
Feltham Brook
Clovermead Farm
CLEEVE LA
Gatherham Farm
HAM LA
River Boyd
Monarch's Way
Blue Lodge

69 A B 70 C D 71 E F 74
8 7 77 6 5 76 4 3 75 2 1

A B C D E F

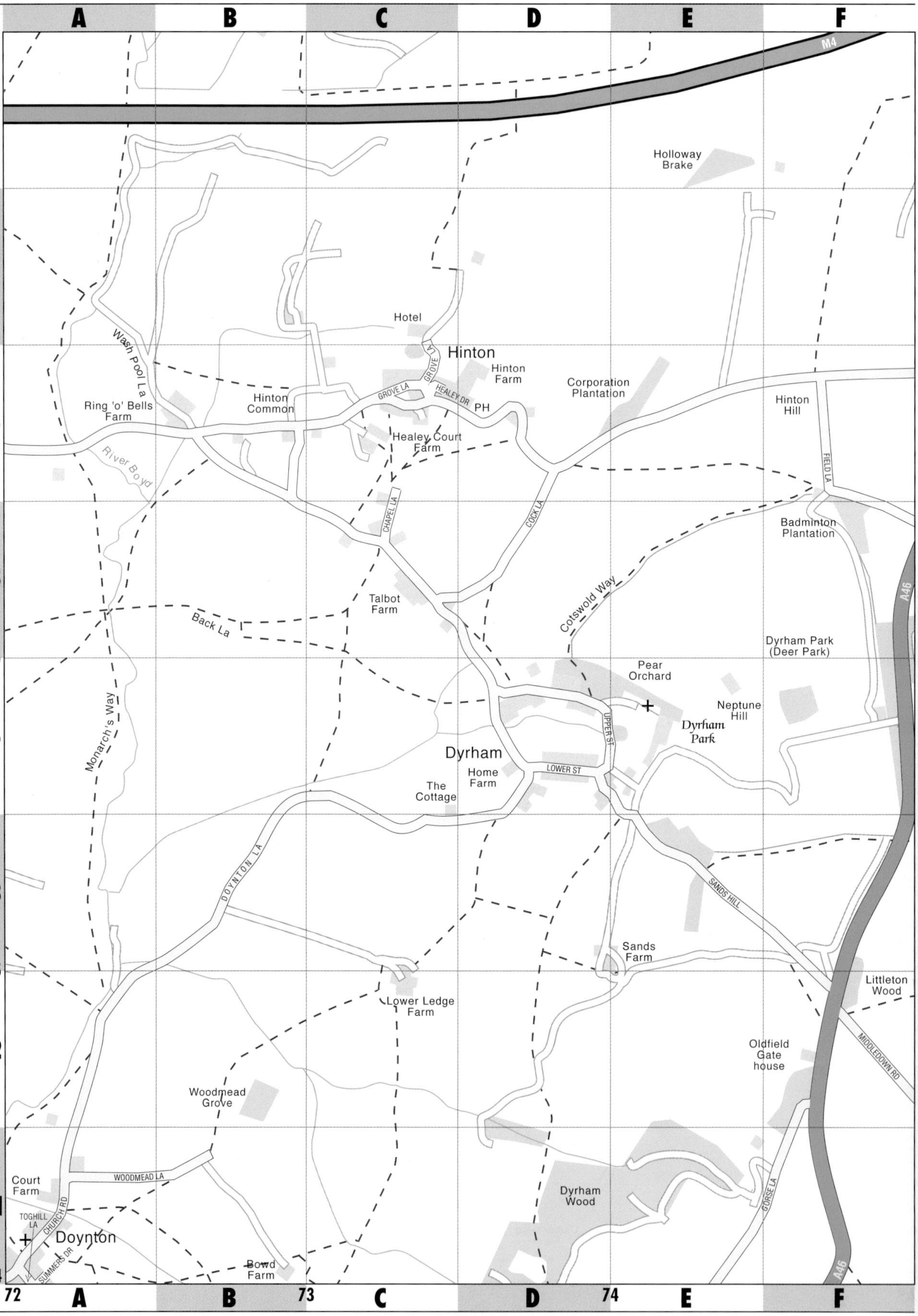

8

M4

Holloway
Brake

7

77

Hotel

Hinton

Hinton
Farm

Corporation
Plantation

Hinton
Hill

GROVE LA

HEALEY DR PH

Ring 'o' Bells
Farm

Hinton
Common

Healey Court
Farm

6

Wash Pool La

River Boyd

CHAPEL LA

COCK LA

Badminton
Plantation

FIELD LA

A46

5

Talbot
Farm

Cotswold Way

Dyrham Park
(Deer Park)

Back La

76

Pear
Orchard

Neptune
Hill

Monarch's Way

Dyrham
Park

4

Dyrham

Home
Farm

LOWER ST

UPPER ST

The
Cottage

DOYNTON LA

Sands Hill

3

Sands
Farm

75

Littleton
Wood

Lower Ledge
Farm

Oldfield
Gate
house

MIDDLEDOWN RD

2

Woodmead
Grove

Dyrham
Wood

GORSE LA

Court
Farm

WOODMEAD LA

1

TOGHILL LA

CHURCH RD

Doynton

SUMMERS DR

Bowd
Farm

A46

74

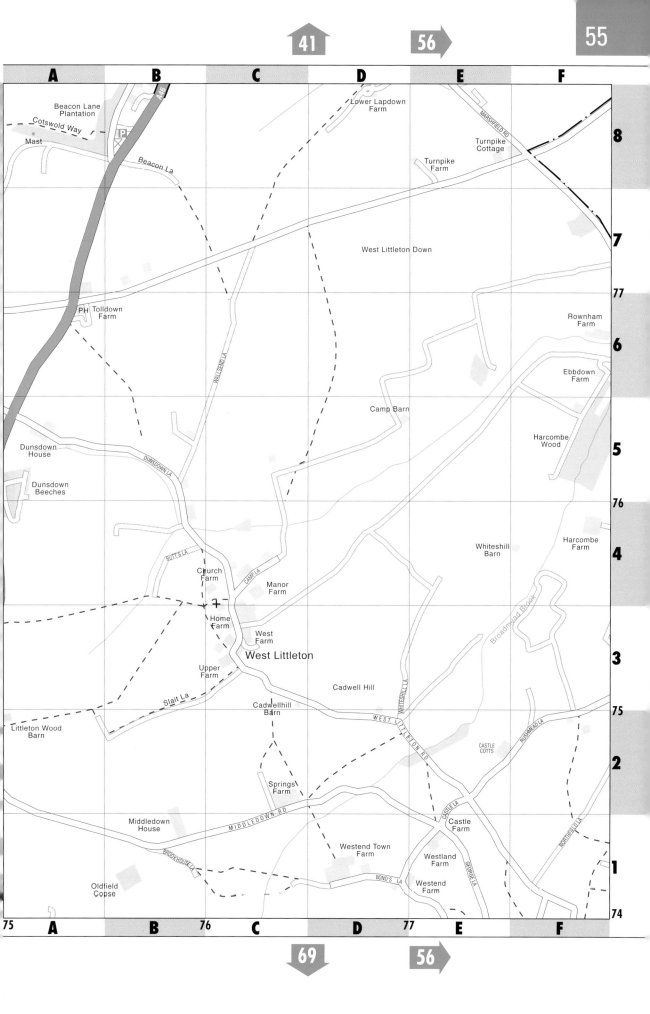

A   B   C   D   E   F

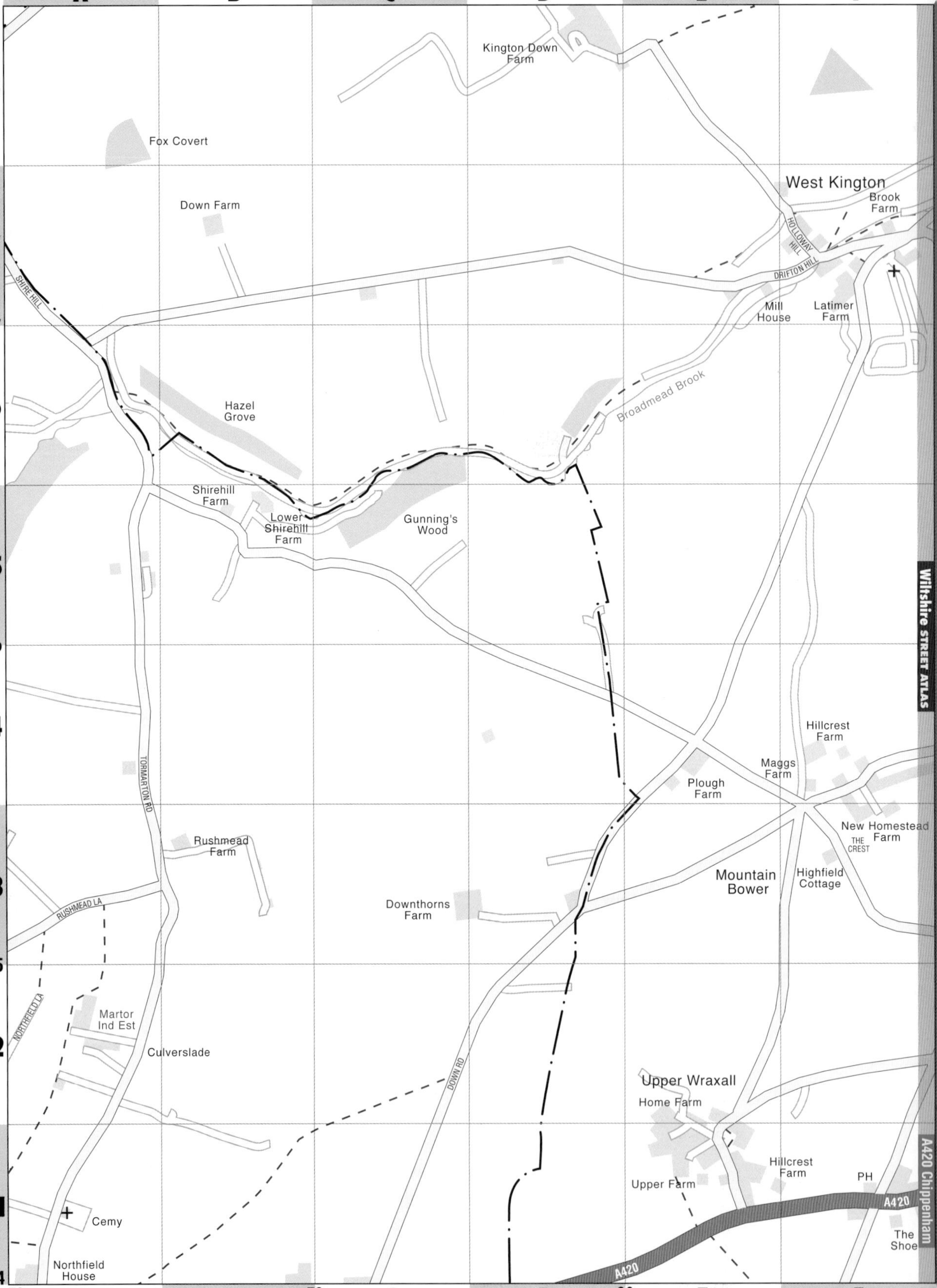

8

Kington Down
Farm

Fox Covert

West Kington

Brook
Farm

Down Farm

7

SHIRE HILL

HOLLOWAY HILL

DRIFTON HILL

Mill
House

Latimer
Farm

77

Hazel
Grove

Broadmead Brook

6

Shirehill
Farm

Lower
Shirehill
Farm

Gunning's
Wood

5

TORMARTON RD

76

4

Hillcrest
Farm

Maggs
Farm

Rushmead
Farm

Plough
Farm

New Homestead
Farm

THE
CREST

3

RUSHMEAD LA

Downthorns
Farm

Mountain
Bower

Highfield
Cottage

75

NORTHFIELD LA

Martor
Ind Est

Culverslade

2

DOWN RD

Upper Wraxall

Home Farm

Hillcrest
Farm

PH

1

Cemy

Upper Farm

A420

A420

The
Shoe

74

78   A   B   79   C   D   80   E   F

Northfield
House

CLEVEDON

B1
1 CRAWFORD CL
2 SANDFORD CL
3 HEDGES CL
4 SOUTHERN RING PATH
5 LADYCROFT
6 LONGACRE
7 GARSTONS
8 BAKER CL

C1
1 Carey Developments
2 Tweed Rd Ind Est
3 St John the
  Evangelist
  CE Prim Sch

C2
1 Speedwell Ind Est
2 COLERIDGE VALE RD W
3 WAINS CL
4 HANSON'S WAY
5 CHURCHILL CL
6 COPPACK HO
7 GARLAND HO
8 SHOPLAND HO
9 BRIDGE HO

10 CLIFTON CT

D2
1 COLERIDGE VALE RD E
2 MELBOURNE TERR
3 PENNYWELL EST

E1
1 OTTER RD
2 TIVERTON RD
3 PORLOCK CL
4 PLUMERS CL

F3
1 STREAMSIDE
2 WOODVIEW
3 GREENWAY PK
4 MAYNARD CL
5 HOLLYMAN WLK
6 FRESHMOOR

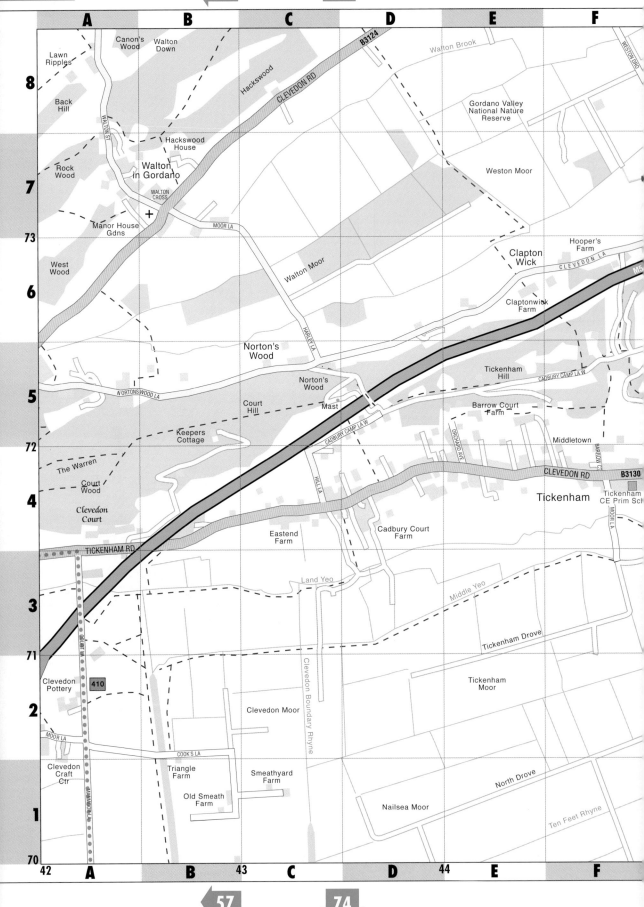

A   B   C   D   E   F

8

Lawn Ripples
Canon's Wood
Walton Down
Hackswood
CLEVEDON RD
B3124
Walton Brook

Back Hill

WALTON ST

Hackswood House

7
Rock Wood
Walton in Gordano
WALTON CROSS

Gordano Valley National Nature Reserve

Weston Moor

WESTON DRO

73
Manor House Gdns
MOOR LA

West Wood
Walton Moor

Clapton Wick
Hooper's Farm
CLEVEDON LA
M5

6
HARLEY LA

Claptonwick Farm

Norton's Wood

NORTONS WOOD LA

Norton's Wood

Tickenham Hill
CADBURY CAMP LA W

5
Court Hill
Mast
CADBURY CAMP LA W

Barrow Court Farm
Middletown
BARROW CT

Keepers Cottage

72

HILL LA

ORCHARD AVE

CLEVEDON RD
B3130

The Warren

Court Wood

Tickenham

Tickenham CE Prim Sch

4
Clevedon Court

Eastend Farm

Cadbury Court Farm

MOOR LA

TICKENHAM RD

3

Land Yeo

Middle Yeo

71

GALLOP LA

Clevedon Pottery
410

Tickenham Drove

Clevedon Moor

Clevedon Boundary Rhyne

Tickenham Moor

2
MOOR LA

COOK'S LA

Clevedon Craft Ctr

Triangle Farm

Smeathyard Farm

North Drove

HAMMOND LA

1
Old Smeath Farm

Nailsea Moor

Ten Feet Rhyne

70

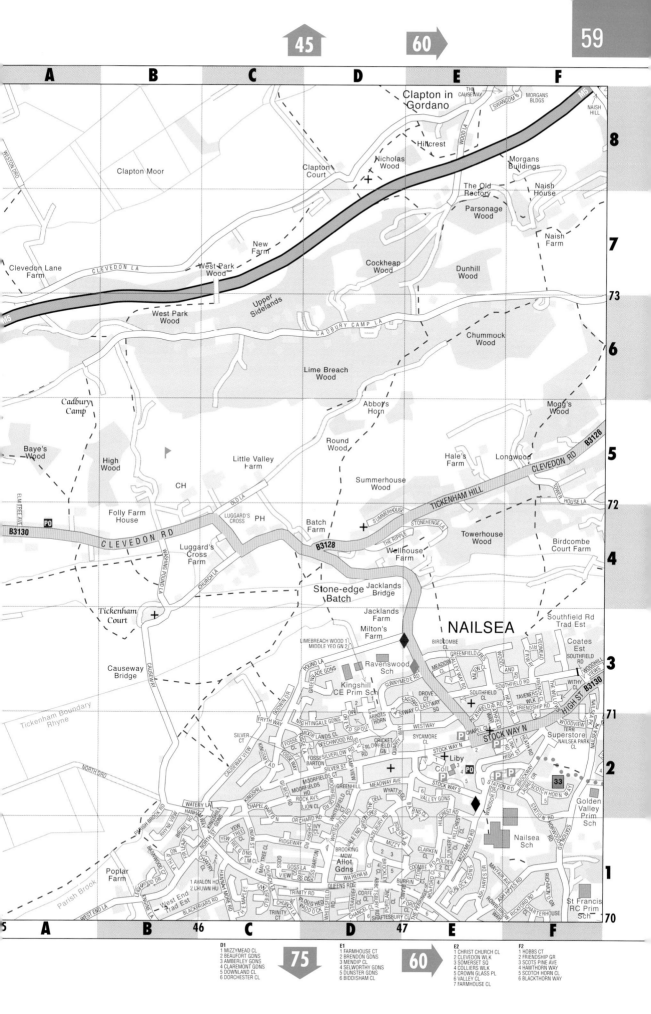

A B C D E F

8
7
73
6
5
72
4
3
71
2
1
70

Clapton in Gordano

Clapton Moor

Clevedon Lane Farm

West Park Wood

CLEVEDON LA

West Park Wood

Upper Sidelands

CADBURY CAMP LA

Cadbury Camp

Baye's Wood

High Wood

CH

Little Valley Farm

OLD LA

Folly Farm House

Luggard's Cross

PH

B3130

PO

CLEVEDON RD

WASHING POUND LA

Luggard's Cross Farm

CHURCH LA

Tickenham Court

CAUSEWAY

Causeway Bridge

Tickenham Boundary Rhyne

NORTH DRO

Poplar Farm

Parish Brook

WEST END LA

New Farm

Nicholas Wood

Clapton Court

Hillcrest

THE CAUSEWAY

SWANGOM'S

MORGANS BLDGS

NAISH HILL

Morgans Buildings

The Old Rectory

Parsonage Wood

Naish House

Naish Farm

Cockheap Wood

Dunhill Wood

WOOD LA

Chummock Wood

Lime Breach Wood

Abbot's Horn

Round Wood

Summerhouse Wood

Hale's Farm

Longwood

Mogg's Wood

B3128

CLEVEDON RD

TICKENHAM HILL

TOWER HOUSE LA

Summerhouse Wood

STONEHENGE LA

THE RIPPLE

B3128

Batch Farm

Wellhouse Farm

Towerhouse Wood

Birdcombe Court Farm

Stone-edge Batch

Jacklands Bridge

Jacklands Farm

Milton's Farm

LIMEBREACH WOOD 1
MIDDLE YEO GN 2

Ravenswood Sch

NAILSEA

Southfield Rd Trad Est

Coates Est

SOUTHFIELD RD

WOODHILL VIEWS

BIRDCOMBE CL

GREENFIELD CRES

MEADOW

VALLEY WAY RD

NYLON CL

SOUTHFIELD RD

WITHY CL

B3130

HIGH ST

Kingshill CE Prim Sch

Sunnymede Rd

EASTWAY

DROVE

CLEASTWAY

ST WAY

ABBOTS HORN

SOUTHFIELD CL

TAVENERS WLK

FRIENDSHIP RD

THE WILLOWS

Superstore

NAILSEA PK

WOODVIEW TERR

NAILSEA PARK CL

POUND LA

GREENSLADE GDNS

GOODWIN DR

ERYTH WAY

NIGHTINGALE GDNS

SPOUT

Cricket Gd

WESTWAY

SYCAMORE

STOCK WAY N

STOCK WAY N

SILVER CT

FOSSE CL

MOOR LANDS CL

BEECHWOOD RD

SILVERLOW RD

SILVER ST

CAMP VIEW

ARLOW FIELD

QUARRY

STOCK WAY N

HIGH ST

P

P

Liby

Coll

P

PO

33

KINGSHILL

FOSSE WAY

FOSSE LA

Silverdown Barton

Greenhill

THE DELL

MEADWAY AVE

ST WAY S

BA

STOCK WAY S

STATION RD

P

P

P

WINDSOR DR

BROCKWAY

SCOTCH HORN WAY

Golden Valley Prim Sch

WATERY LA

CAUSEWAY VIEW

Moorfields Ho

MOORFIELDS

GILBER RD

LION CL

ORCHARD RD

WYATT CL

VALLEY GDNS

HILLCREST

HEATHER CL

STATION RD

HORWOOD RD

Nailsea Sch

PARISH BROOK RD

RHYNE VIEW

BRUNEL WAY

NORTH ST

HANNAH MORE RD

CHAPEL BARTON

ROCK AVE

WHITESFIELD RD

GREENFIELD

IVY CL

CHERRY

HALE END

HAZELBURY RD

MIZZY

BROCK LA

CLARKEN

DUNKERRY

POLDEN

POLLOCK CL

MAYTREE AVE

ASH HAYES RD

ASH HAYES DR

RICHMOND RD

St Francis RC Prim Sch

West End Trad Est

YEW TREE CL

YEW TREE GDNS

MAY TREE CL

ELM CL

GOSS VIEW

GOSS LA

GOSS BARTON

RIDGEWAY

BROOKING

MDW

Allot Gdns

WAREHAM CL

COOMBE

BURRIN

ASH HAYES RD

ROWBERROW

CHARTERHOUSE

1 AVALON HO
2 CROWN HU

1 FILLA

CHANTRY DR

FIR LEAZE

MAPLE

CHURCH LA

CHURCH TOWN

TRINITY CT

TRINITY RD

CHURCH LA

PLOUGH

WHITESFIELD

PADDOCK

QUEENS RD

CORFE

STRAWBERRY

CHANCEL CL

SHAFTESBURY CL

BARTON CL

ABBEY CL

BRISTOL RD

COMBE

RICKFORD RD

TRENDLEWOOD WAY

5 A B 46 C D 47 E F

D1
1 MIZZYMEAD CL
2 BEAUFORT GDNS
3 AMBERLEY GDNS
4 CLAREMONT GDNS
5 DOWNLAND CL
6 DORCHESTER CL

E1
1 FARMHOUSE CT
2 BRENDON GDNS
3 MENDIP CL
4 SELWORTHY GDNS
5 DUNSTER GDNS
6 BIDDISHAM CL

E2
1 CHRIST CHURCH CL
2 CLEVEDON WLK
3 SOMERSET SQ
4 COLLIERS WLK
5 CROWN GLASS PL
6 VALLEY CL
7 FARMHOUSE CL

F2
1 HOBBS CT
2 FRIENDSHIP GR
3 SCOTS PINE AVE
4 HAWTHORN WAY
5 SCOTCH HORN CL
6 BLACKTHORN WAY

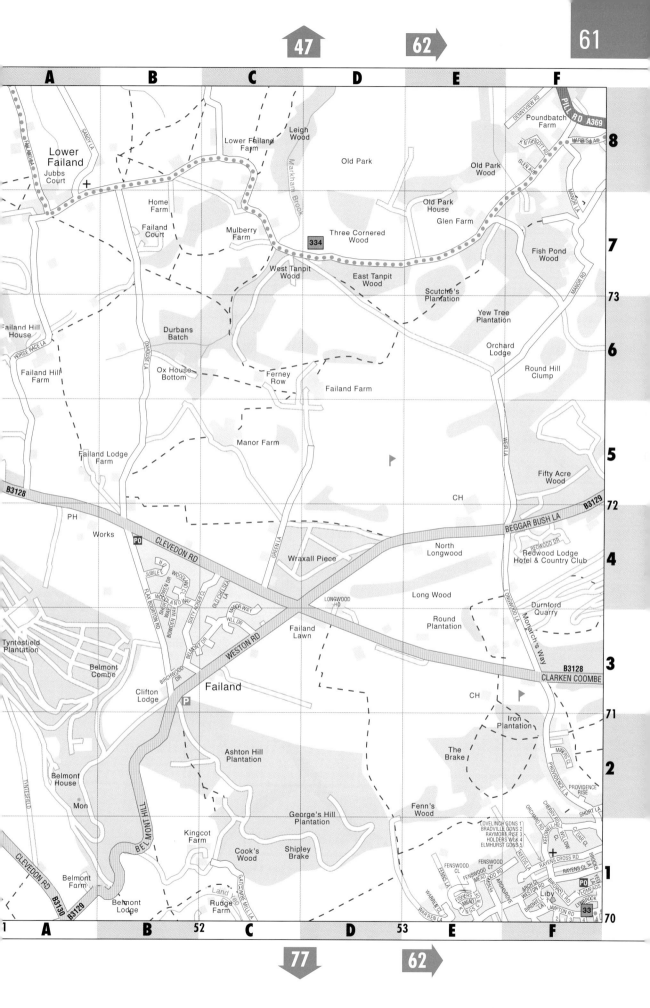

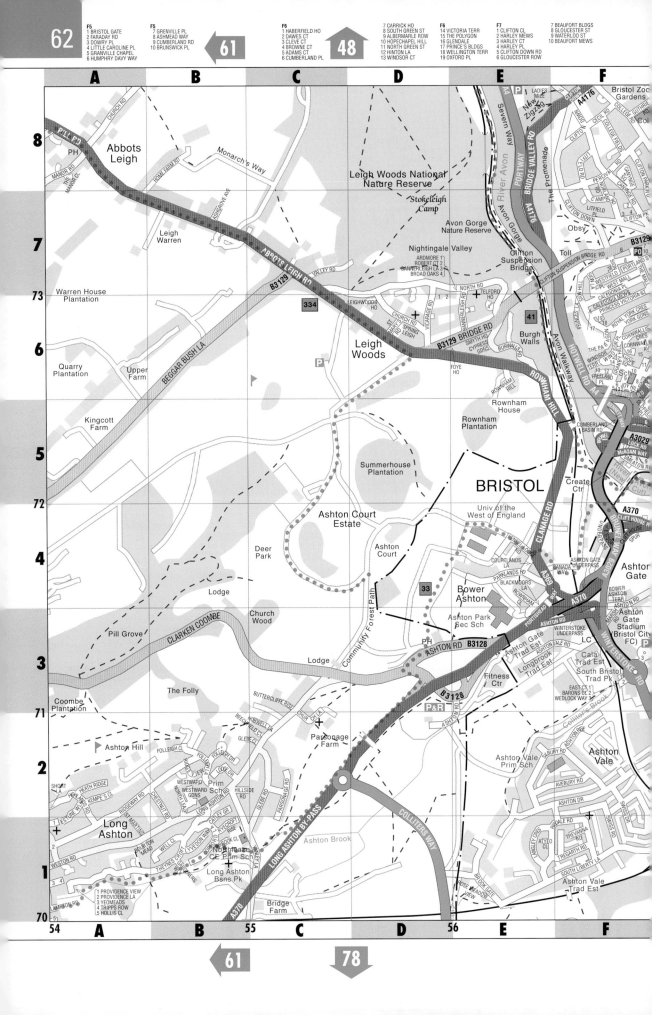

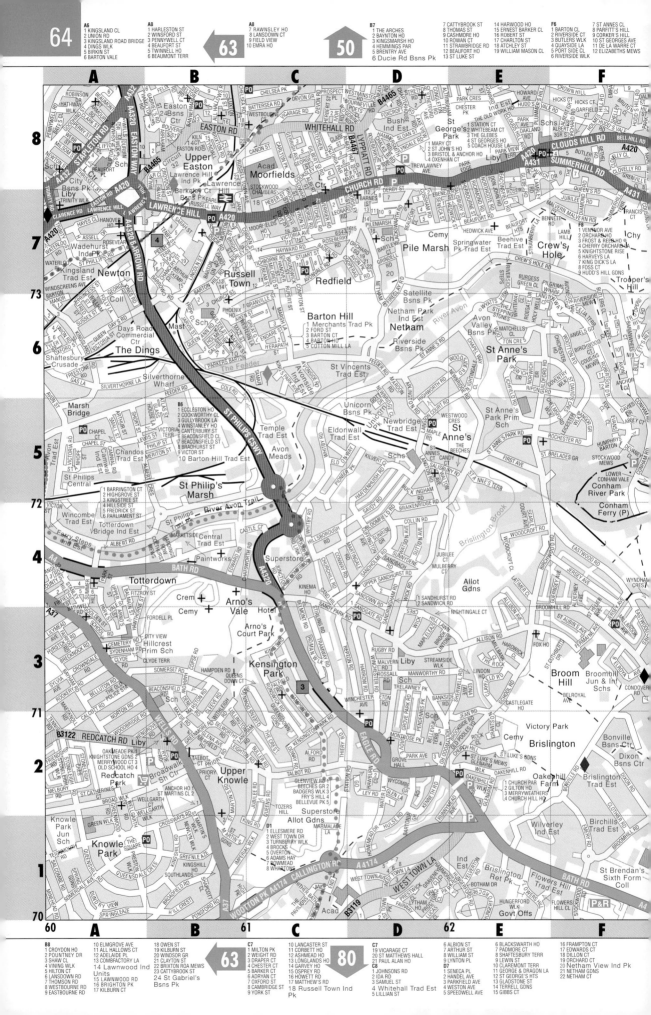

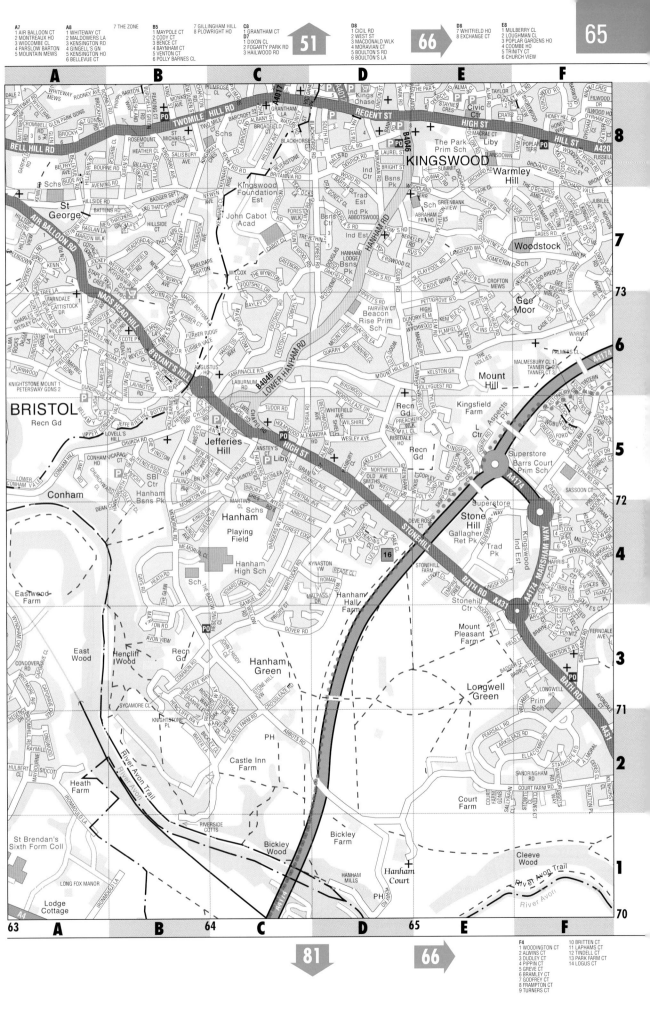

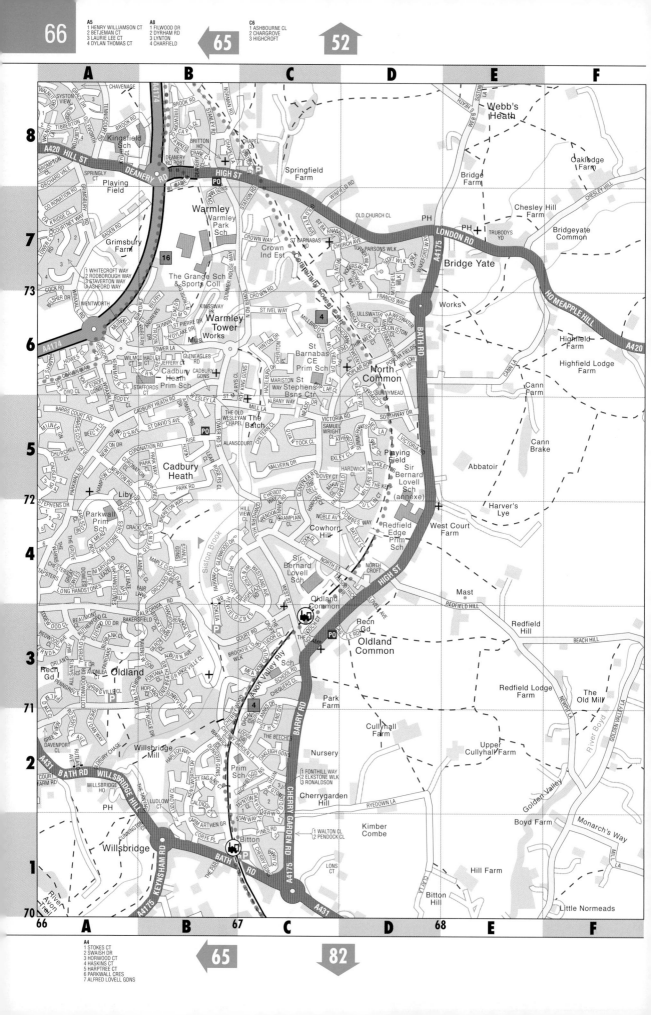

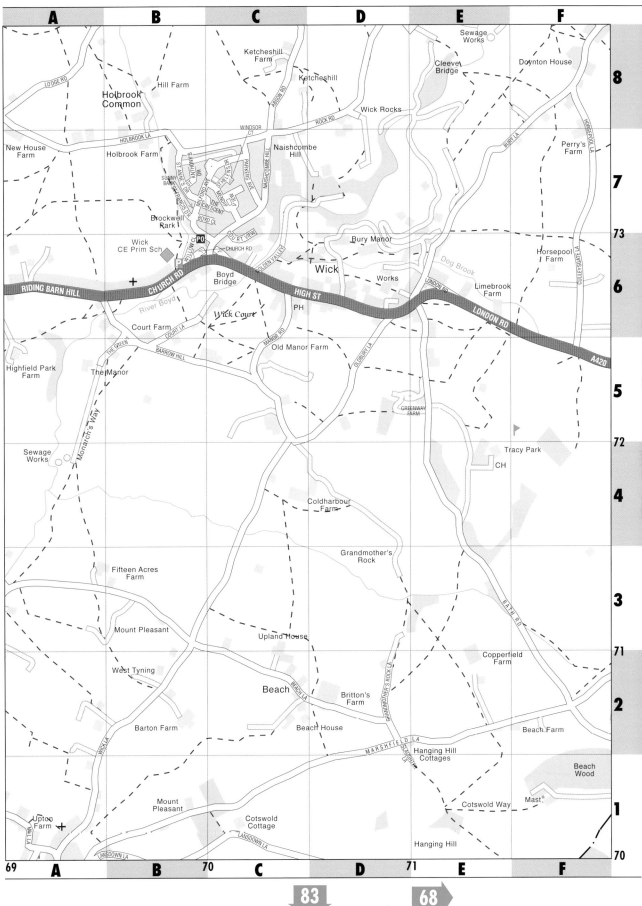

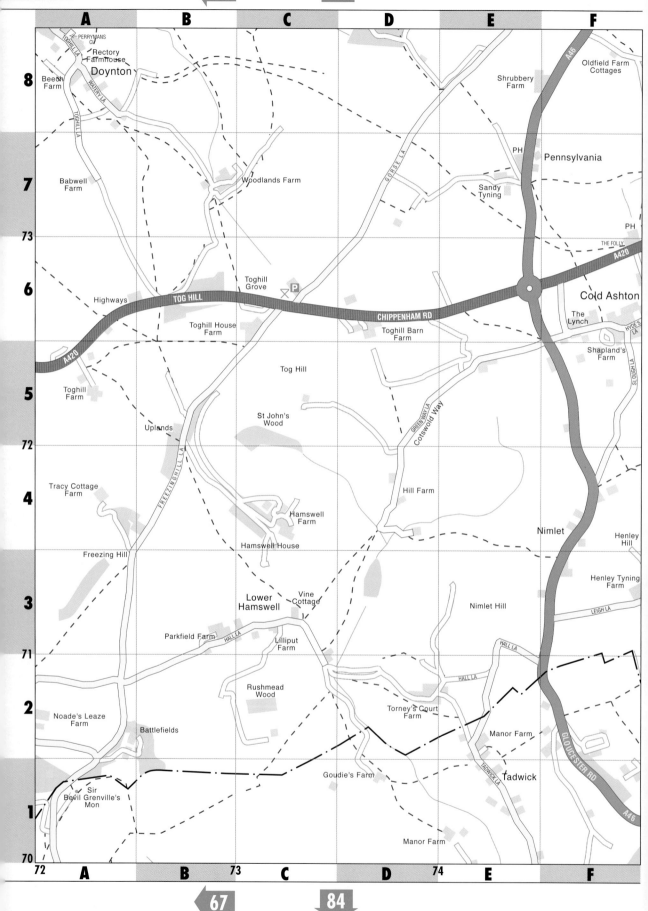
8 Beech Farm PERRYMANS CV Rectory Farmhouse Doynton Shrubbery Farm Oldfield Farm Cottages

7 Babwell Farm Woodlands Farm PH Pennsylvania Sandy Tyning

73 PH THE FOLLY A420

6 Highways TOG HILL Toghill Grove P CHIPPENHAM RD Cold Ashton The Lynch

Toghill House Farm Toghill Barn Farm Shapland's Farm HYDE S LA

A420 SLOUGH LA

5 Toghill Farm Tog Hill

Uplands St John's Wood

72 GREEN WAY LA Cotswold Way

4 Tracy Cottage Farm Hamswell Farm Hill Farm Nimlet Henley Hill

Freezing Hill Hamswell House Henley Tyning Farm

FREEZINGHILL LA

3 Lower Hamswell Vine Cottage Nimlet Hill LEIGH LA

Parkfield Farm HALL LA Lilliput Farm HALL LA

71 HALL LA

2 Noade's Leaze Farm Battlefields Rushmead Wood Torney's Court Farm Manor Farm GLOUCESTER RD

TADWICK LA Tadwick

1 Sir Bevil Grenville's Mon Goudie's Farm Manor Farm A46

70 72 73 74

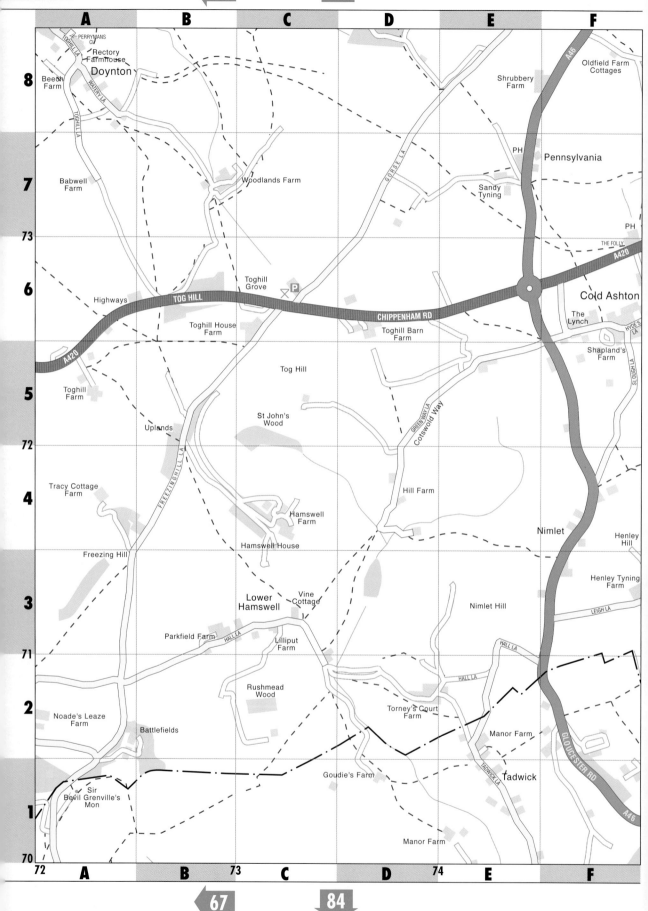

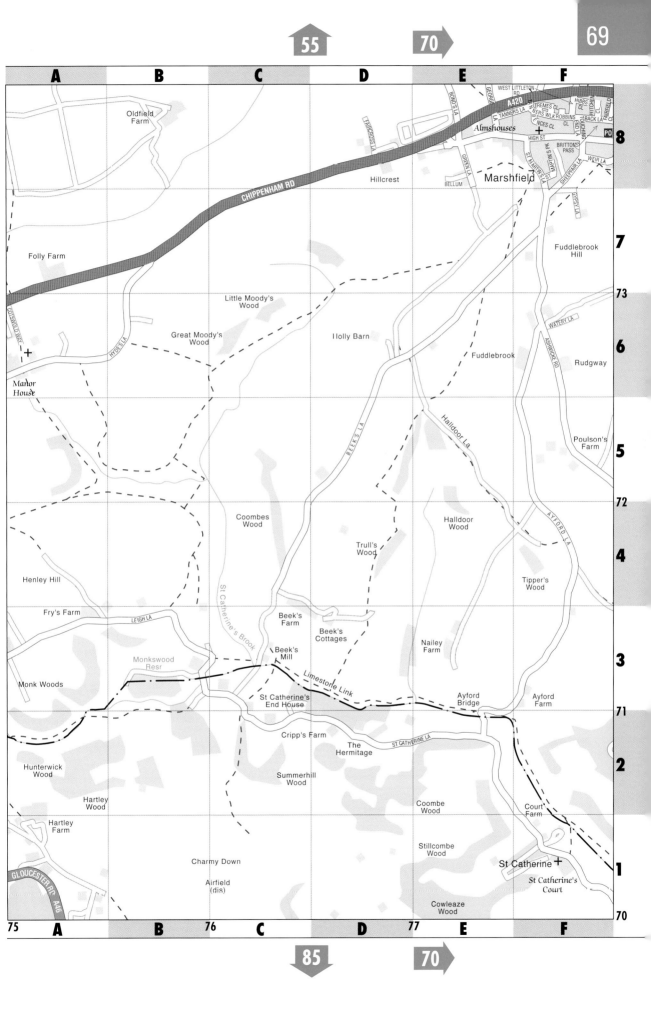

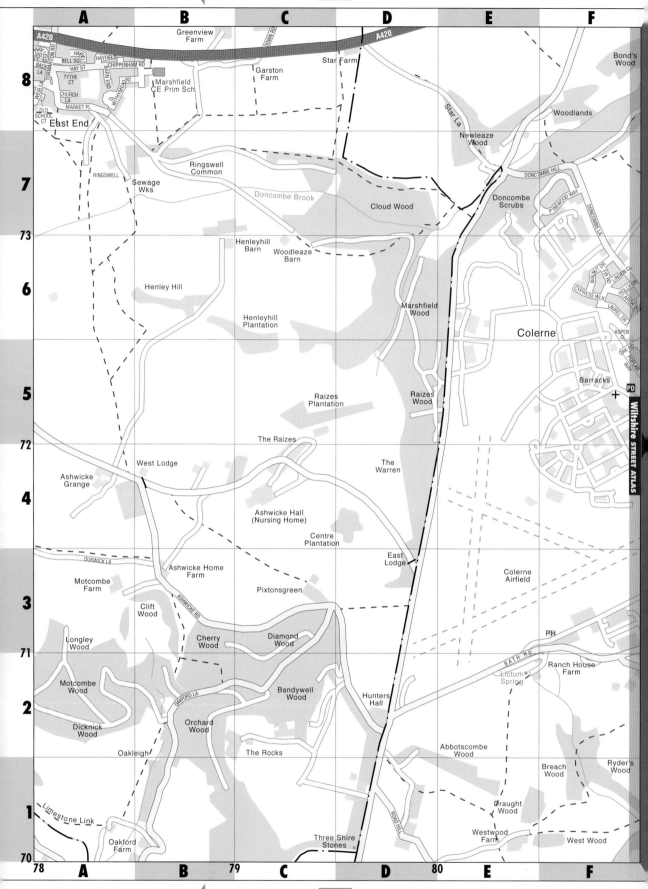

East End

Greenview Farm

A420

DOWN RD

CHIPPENHAM RD

Garston Farm

Star Farm

Bond's Wood

Woodlands

Newleaze Wood

Star La

Doncombe Scrubs

DONCOMBE HILL

PINEWOOD WAY

DONCOMBE LA

Marshfield CE Prim Sch

HAYFIELD

BELL SQ

HAY ST

BARN END

WITHYMEAD RD

TYTHE CT

CHURCH LA

MARKET PL

OLD SCHOOL CT

WELL LA

BACKS LA

Ringswell Common

Ringswell

Sewage Wks

Doncombe Brook

Cloud Wood

Henleyhill Barn

Woodleaze Barn

Henley Hill

Henleyhill Plantation

Marshfield Wood

Colerne

WALNUT DR

LINDEN CL

CYPRESS WLK

LARCH RD

HOLLY DR

LAUREL DR

ASPEN CL

OAK RD

POPLAR WAY

Barracks

PO

Raizes Plantation

Raizes Wood

The Raizes

West Lodge

The Warren

Ashwicke Grange

DUNKICK LA

Ashwicke Home Farm

Pixtonsgreen

Centre Plantation

Ashwicke Hall (Nursing Home)

East Lodge

Colerne Airfield

Motcombe Farm

ASHWICKE RD

Clift Wood

Cherry Wood

Diamond Wood

PH

BATH RD

Lictum Spring

Ranch House Farm

Longley Wood

Motcombe Wood

OAKFORD LA

Bandywell Wood

Hunters Hall

Abbotscombe Wood

Dicknick Wood

Orchard Wood

The Rocks

Breach Wood

Ryder's Wood

Oakleigh

ROAD HILL

Draught Wood

Westwood Farm

West Wood

Limestone Link

Oakford Farm

Three Shire Stones

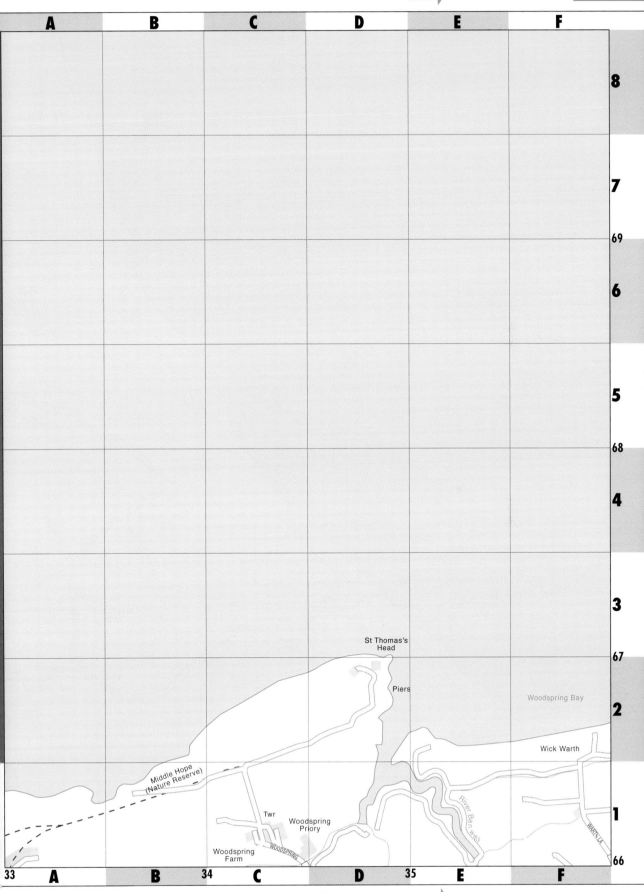

8

7

69

6

5

68

4

3

67

St Thomas's
Head

Piers

Woodspring Bay

2

Wick Warth

Middle Hope
(Nature Reserve)

River Ban web

1

Twr

Woodspring
Priory

WOODSPRING

Woodspring
Farm

66

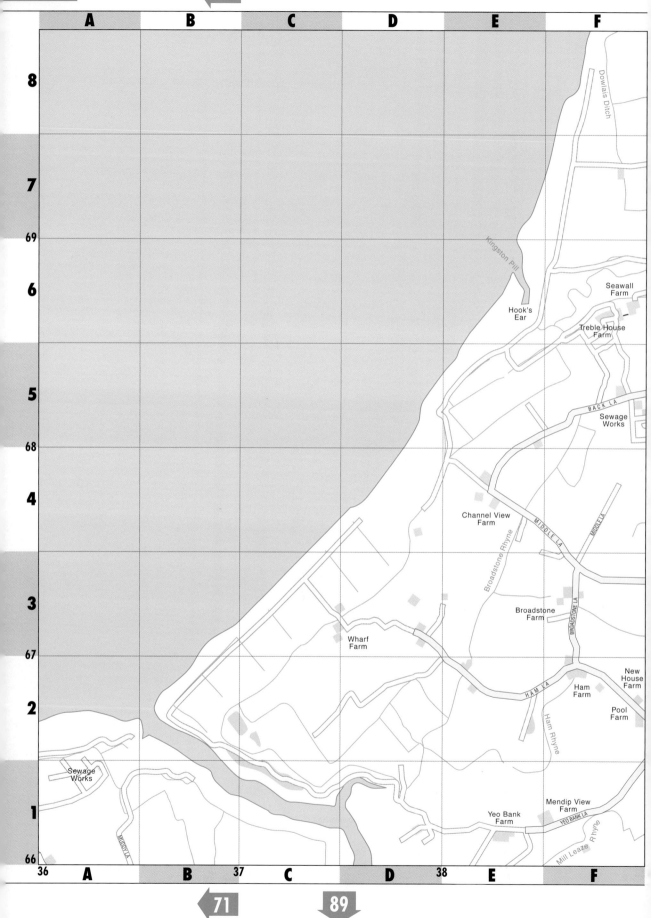

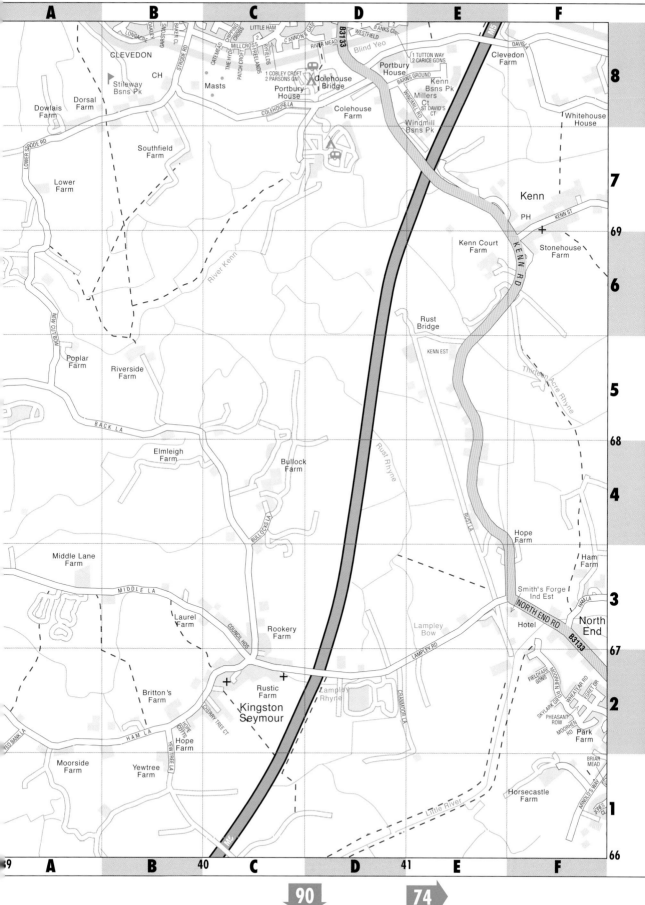

73
58

A
B
C
D
E
F
8
7
69
6
5
68
4
3
67
2
1
66
42
43
44
Blind Yeo
Ten Feet Rhyne
DAVIS LA
410
NAILSEA WALL
Kenn Pier Farm
River Kenn
Moorside Farm
Parish Brook
BREACH LA
West End
NAILSEA MOOR LA
WEST END LA
NAILSEA WALL LA
OLD CHAPEL LA
PH
NETHERTON WOOD LA
Yew Tree Farm
KENN ST
DUCK LA
West End Farm
Elm Tree Farm
Myrtle Farm
Western Drainage Rhyne
Kenn Moor
Lilypool Dro
Blackditch Rhyne
Decoypool Rhyne
Eastern Dro
Manor Farm
Meadmoor Rhyne
Mawkin's Bridge
KENN MOOR RD
Decoypool Dro
River Kenn
CLAVERHAM DRO
Say's Rhyne
26
Barberry Farm
Little River
Kenn Moor Gate
Laurel Bank
HAM LA
Claverham Court
Moorstreet Bow
LOWER CLAVERHAM
MUD LA
LC
Lower Claverham
Chestnut Farm
Chestnut Farm
MOOR RD
Stowey Rhyne
Hillsea
JASMINE LA
Horsecastle
NORTH END
The Grange
Laurel Farm
BROCKLEY WAY
DAIRY CL
GRANGE FARM RD
Claverham
WITHYMEAD
Manor Farm
STREAMCROSS
Market Ind Est
B3133
HORSECASTLE FARM RD
HORSECASTLE CL
MOOR RD
BRAMBLEWOOD
SOUTH VIEW TERR
STATION RD
DUNSTERS RD
HIGH ST
KLIN'S WAY
FRAN
ANVIL RD
ORCHARD CT
BROADCROFT AVE
CHESTNUT DR
BROADCROFT CL
CLAVERHAM RD
CHAPEL LA
BISHOPS RD
CLAVERHAM PK
Court-de-Wyck Prim Sch
Claverham Farm
Yatton
LAUREL TERR
HIGH ST
THE PARK
PARK AVE
ATLAY CT
FARM RD
STOWEY RD
URBAN WAY
THE LAWNS
AVALON CL
WEMBERHAM LA
WEMBERHAM CRES
THE WOOD KILNS
WAKE D
JONES CL
BRIAR MEAD
MEADOWLAND
GREGORY MEAD
HAWTHORN CRES
ARNOLD'S WAY
MACQUARIE FARM CL

73
91

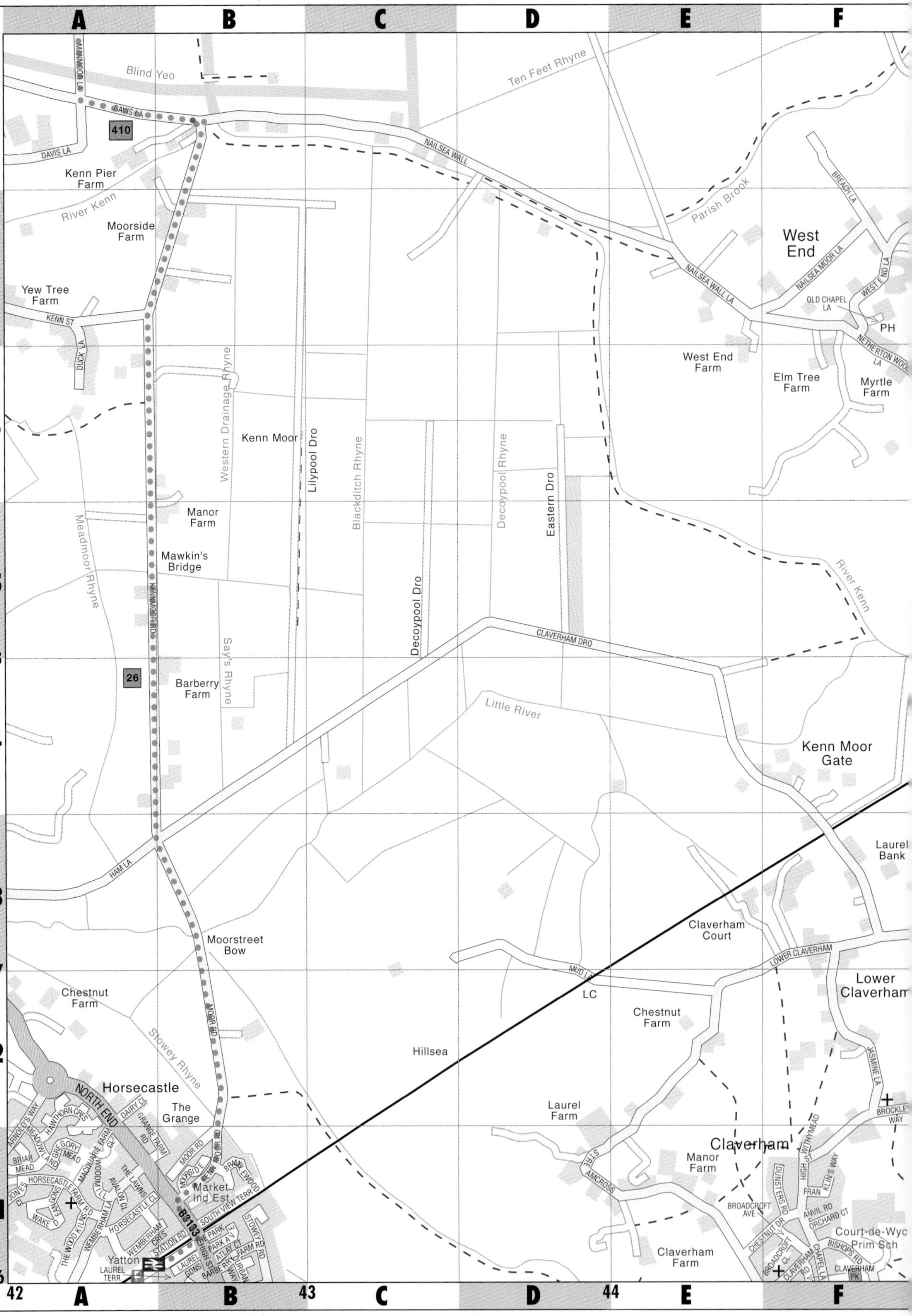

A   B   C   D   E   F

8

Birdlip Cl
Trendle Wood
Chelvey Way
St Austell Cl
Fowey Cl
Truro Cl
Inchbroke
Avening Cl
Bucklands View
Buck Lanes View

Dibden's Farm

Schrubbets Farm

Cider House

Backwell Common

Backwell Common

Depot
LC

Flax Bourton
CE Prim Sch

Priory Farm

Church Lane End

Castle Cl

Church La

Parsonage La

The Grange

7

Moorside Farm

Cheltfield Rd
Chovedge
Combe Side
Waverley Rd
The Avenue
Allister Cl
Austin Cl
Binsley Cl
Kidner Cl
Tamblyn Cl

Woolleys Farm

Hunts Farm

Backwell Green

Farleigh

Chapel Hill
George La
Fairfield Mead

MAIN RD

A370

Flax Bourton

Bourton Combe

69

Moor La
Morfield Rd
Long Thorn
Westfield
Westfield Dr
The Crescent
Meadow Cl
Westhaven Cl

Backwell Sch

Fairfield Cl
Uncombe Cl

Backwell House

Stancombe La

6

West Leigh Inf Sch

A6
1 Marl Pits
2 Slades Ct

Westfield Cl
Mariners Cl
Mariners Dr
Embercourt Dr
Orchard Rd
Car Russel
Earls Russel
Rodney Rd

L Ctr

Liby

PO

Backwell

Fairfield Sch

The Wedge
Line M
Gre Cl

Backwell Down

Farleigh Combe Manor

Cherry Wood

Bourton Combe

5

Rushmoor La
Bramley Dr
Betts Cl
Lawnside
St Andrews Rd
St John's Rd
St Margarets Dr
Summerlands
Park La
Hill Dale Rd

WEST TOWN RD

Backwell CE Sch

Church Town

Church La
Church Town

Quarry

The Conygar

68

A370
PH

Keliway
Robinson's
Hillside Rd
Pit La
Karen Gd
Oakleigh Cl
Rope Wlk
Karen Gd

Chelvey Farm

Pit La

Chesian Combe

Water Catch Farm

4

Chelvey Batch

Mast

Quarry

Backwell Hill

Backwell Hill Rd

The Spinney

3

Backwell Hill House

Backwell Hill

Hyatt's Wood

Hyattswood Farm

67

Home Farm

Long La

Spinnings Dro

Quarry

Hyatts Wood Rd

2

Healls Scars

Edson's Farm

Oatfield Pool

Brockley Wood

Brockley Combe Rd

Willis's Batch

Downside Rd

Oatfield Farm

Oatfield Wood

1

The Batch

Downside House Farm

The Batch

Oatfield

66

Warren Plantation

Downside

A B C D E F

8
7
69
6
5
68
4
3
67
2
1
66

HOLLIS CL
FENSHURST GDNS
Birdwell Prim Sch

LONG ASHTON BY-PASS

A370

Yanley Farm

Yanley

YANLEY LA

Hanging Hill Wood

Colliter's Brook

A4174

Crem

Mast

Cemy

Elm Farm

A38

BRUNEL WAY
LANGFORD RD
YATTON CL

Bedminster Down Sch

COLLITERS WAY

Yewtree Fram

MARTHA'S ORCH

PIPPIN CT RD
MARGUERITE RD
DONALD RD
ALEXANDRA RD

DINGL

OLDMEAD WLK

ROSE MEARE GDNS

KINGS WLK

LOCK GD

KING'S HEAD LA

GREYLANDS RD

GARDINER RD

WESTWARD RD

Highridge

Castle Farm

BRIDGWATER RD

CH

Ridings Wood

CLOVERHILL WAY

WINSTONES RD

The Wild Country

Colliter's Brook Farm

Motel

Highridge Farm

BRISTOL

D'ANCEY MEAD

SPARTLEY WLK

SPARTLEY DR

HAYES

WATCH RD

SANDHOLME CL

ROWS LA

MARLEPIT GR

GEOFFREY CL

ESLBERT DR

HIGHRIDGE GN

LAMINGTON CL

WATCHILL CL

VICARAGE RD

Highridge Inf Sch
St Peter's CE Prim Sch

FERNSTEED RD

MONARCH'S WAY

Barrow Big Wood

YANLEY LA

Highridge Common

OAKTREE GDNS

COLDPARK GDNS

COLDPARK RD

KING GEORGE'S RD

SOLON

GILLON WLK

SHUTER RD

BROADWAY RD

SPINNEY CROFT

Winford Arms (PH)
WINFORD TERR

Community Forest Path

PEART RD

GREENDRIDGE CL

MILLFORD

ELMTREE DR

TEMPLELAND RD

THREE WELLS RD

QUEENS RD

The Peart

BUMBLEBE

HUNTINGHAM RD

WATERBRI

PAYBRIDGE RD

LEYLAND WLK

P

COWLER WLK

BROAD OAK RD

Barrow Common

Valley View Farm

Highridge Farm
CHALCROFT WLK

HIGHMEAD GDNS

PEART DR

THISTLECATE AVE

STILLMAN

Four Acres Prim Sch

FOUR ACRES

RUSHAM

LONGMEAD CROFT

BEARPIT

TAYLOR GDNS

COBHORN DR

TIPPIE

Greenditch Farm

DUNDRY LA

Lower Grove Farm

Highridge

HERSEY GDNS

HAM LA

MALAGO

ROSPOOL RD

FARMER RD

SHERRIN WAY

BILLAND CL

REDFORD CRES

STRAWBERRY LA

Grove Farm

Masts

Dundry CE Prim Sch

HILL RD

BEECHAM

Castle Farm

Dundry Down

CASTLE FARM LA

Masts

THE MEAD

DOWNS RD

CHURCH RD

ANDRUSS DR

Dundry Inn

Dundry

WEST DUNDRY LA

OXLEAZE LA

EAST DUNDRY LA

ELWELL LA

WINFORD LA

LITTLETON LA

Elwell Farm

CRABTREE LA

CRABTREE CL

Samaritans Way South West

WELLS RD

PH

Maiden Head

UPTON LA

Watercress Farm

Mast

Upton Farm

54 A B 55 C D 56 E F

77

95

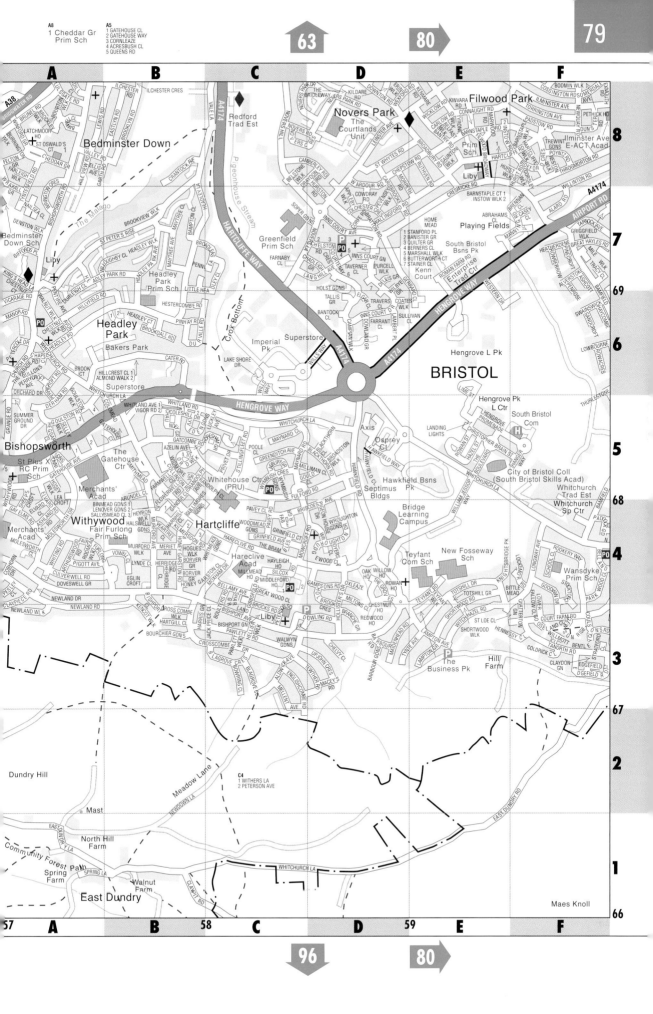

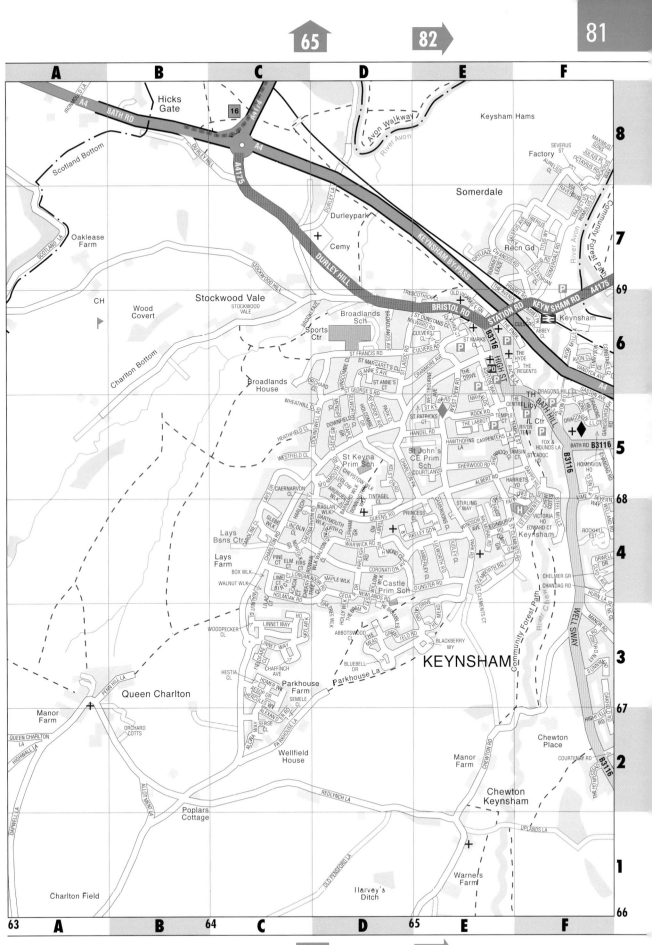

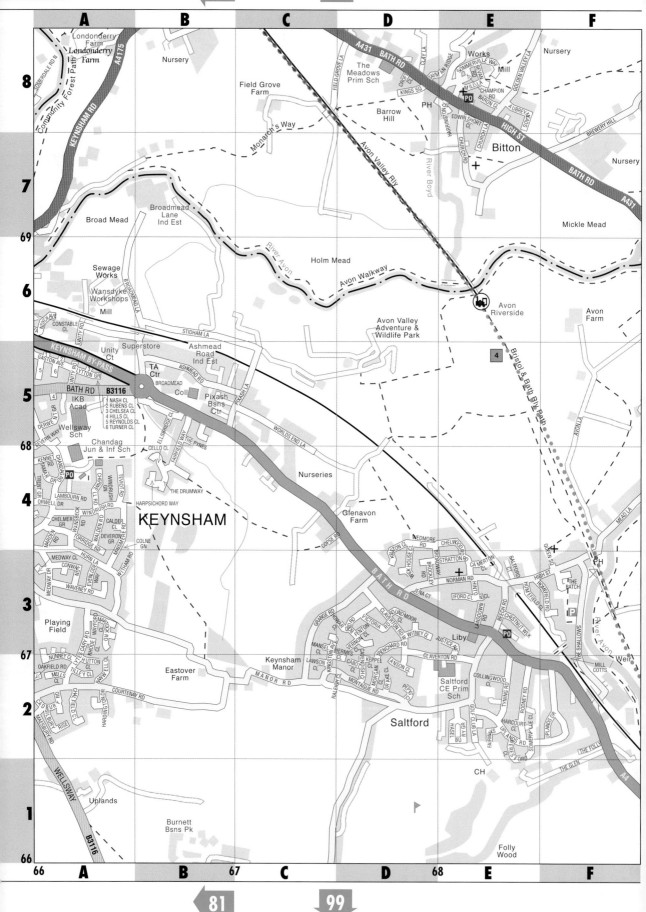

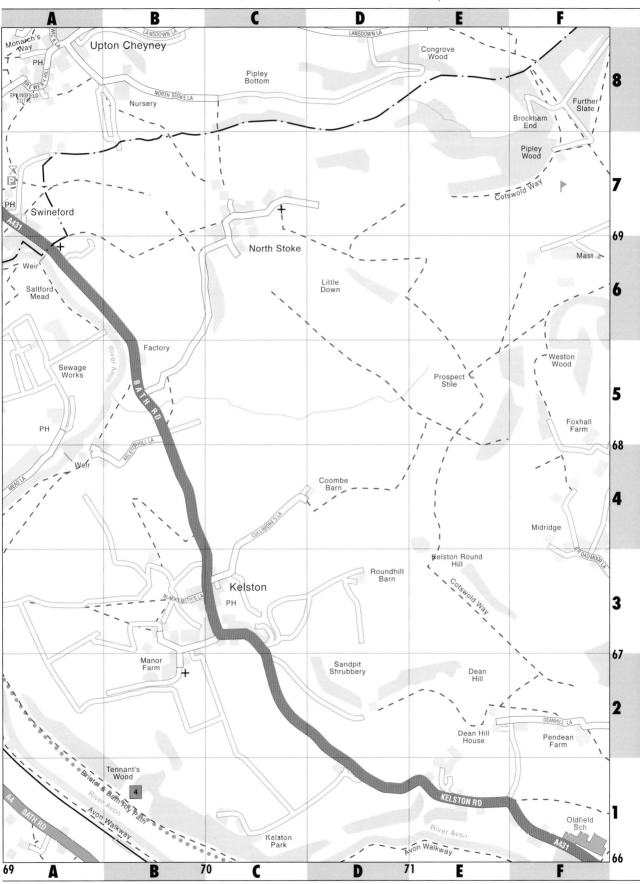

83
68

A B C D E F

8

Midfields
The Grove
Court Farm
Langridge House
LANGRIDGE LA
Upper Langridge
Langridge
Ashcombe Farm
Ashcombe House
TYNING LA

7
Upper Farm
Upper Langridge Farm
Aldermoor Wood
TADWICK LA
Lam Brook
Hall

69
Lansdown Hill
CH
Lansdown
Bath Racecourse
PH
Upper Langridge Farm
Mill Farm

6
HIGH ST
CHURCH
Woolley
WOOLLEY LA

5
Heather Cottage
Charlcombe Grove Farm
Ravenswell House
Soper's Wood

68
Aldermead
P&R

4
Heather Farm
LANSDOWN LA
Kingswood Sch Upper Sports Fields
Abbot Alphege Acad
Kingswood
Beckford's Twr & Museum
CORNISHMEN'S RD
PENNSYLVANIA W
CHELSCOMBE C
WALLER GDNS
FAIRWAYS
BECKFORD DR
ENSLEIGH AVE
GRANVILLE RD
HOPTON WY
BATTLE WK
View Point Farm
COLLIERS LA

3
Upper Weston
Upper Weston Farm
Cemy
HAMILTON HO
STONELEIGH CT
LANSDOWN PK
Charlcombe
NAPIER RD
FALCONER RD
LEIGH RD
KINBER CL
DUNCAN GDNS
BERESFORD GDNS
BROADMOOR LA
DOMOOR
HEATHFIELD CL
HAVILAND GR
GREENLANDS
THE MACES
LANSDOWN RD
CHARLCOMBE LA

67
Weston All Saints CE Prim Sch
Dean Hill
Nursery
OSBORNE'S RD
PRIESTHOOD PK
WESTMEAD GDNS
DEA NHILL LA
BROADMOOR PK
HOLCOMBE GN
MICHAELS MEAD
EASTFIELD AVE
MORTIMER CL
SIX STREAMS
WEAL TERR
THE WEAL
Rohannon Farm
BLIND LA
FAIRFIELD PARK RD
CHARLCOMBE WAY
CHARLCOMBE RI

2
Upper Weston
WESTMEAD GDNS
HOLCOMBE GN
BOOKFIELD PK
WELLINGTON
LYNGFIELD PK
PURLEWENT DR
1 BROOKSIDE HO
2 KNIGHTSTONE PL
3 SHEPPARDS GDNS
4 THE OLD BREWHOUSE
5 GAINSBOROUGH CT
6 CHELSCOMBE
7 EDGECOMBE MEWS
8 PROSPECT PL
BATH
FONTHILL RD
Kingswood Sch
VAN DIEMEN'S LA
The Royal High School Bath
HAMILTON RD
Lansdown
NEWLAND
LANSDOWN HO
NORTHFIELDS
NORTHFIELD HO
CHARLCOTE
CHARLCOTE RD
RICHMOND
RICHMOND CL
Prim Sch
RICHMOND HTS

1
Cotswold Way
Penn Hill
St Mary's RC Prim Sch
BELTON CT
BIBURY HO
HARCOURT BLDGS
HIGH ST
Liby
CHURCH ST
Weston Park
Primrose Hill
MOUNTAIN ASH
PRIMROSE HILL
Summerhill Park
Kingswood Prep Sch
HOCKLEY CT
Bath Spa Univ Art and Design
Sion Hill
WALDEGRAVE RD
HERMITAGE RD
SOMERSET LA
Beacon Hill
St Stephen's
SPRINGFIELD PL
RICHMOND RD

66
Sch
WESTMEAD GDNS
EAST LEA RD
PENN HILL RD
CHANDLER CL
FRANKLAND CL
Bernard Ireland Ho
Royal United
MANOR RD
ANCHOR RD
FELDEN GDNS
CROWN HILL
CHURCH RD
LUCKLANDS RD
ST CLEMENTS RD
THE GROVE
WOODLAND
THE ELMS
WESTON PK
WESTON PK
SUMMERHILL RD
MONTROSE COTTS
The Royal High School Bath Jun Sch
MANOR VILLAS
THE GRANGE
SION HILL
WINIFRED'S LA
SOMERSET LA
UPPER LANSDOWN MEWS
RICHMOND PL

72 A B 73 C D 74 E F

83
101

F1
1 LANSDOWN PL W
2 LANSDOWN CRES
3 MOUNT BEACON PL

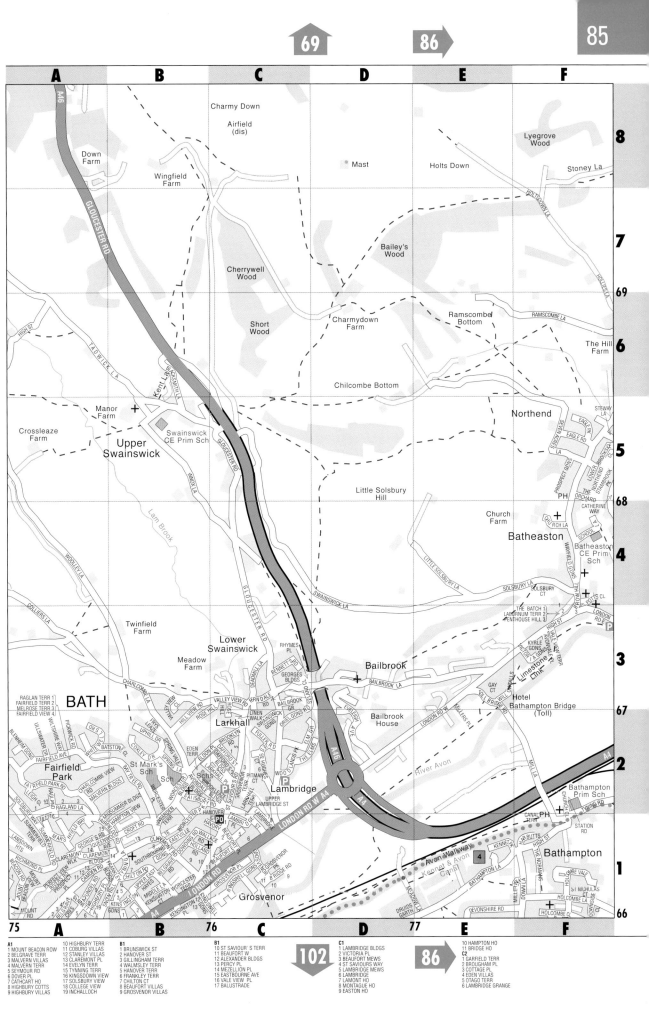

102 86

A1
1 MOUNT BEACON ROW
2 BELGRAVE TERR
3 MALVERN VILLAS
4 MALVERN TERR
5 SEYMOUR RD
6 DOVER PL
7 CATHCART HO
8 HIGHBURY COTTS
9 HIGHBURY VILLAS
10 HIGHBURY TERR
11 COBURG VILLAS
12 STANLEY VILLAS
13 CLAREMONT PL
14 EVELYN TERR
15 TYNNING TERR
16 KINGSDOWN VIEW
17 SOLSBURY VIEW
18 COLLEGE VIEW
19 INCHALLOCH

B1
1 BRUNSWICK ST
2 HANOVER ST
3 GILLINGHAM TERR
4 WALMSLEY TERR
5 HANOVER TERR
6 FRANKLEY TERR
7 CHILTON CT
8 BEAUFORT VILLAS
9 GROSVENOR VILLAS

B1
10 ST SAVIOUR'S TERR
11 BEAUFORT W
12 ALEXANDER BLDGS
13 PERCY PL
14 MEZELLION PL
15 EASTBOURNE AVE
16 VALE VIEW PL
17 BALUSTRADE

C1
1 LAMBRIDGE BLDGS
2 VICTORIA PL
3 BEAUFORT MEWS
4 ST SAVIOURS WAY
5 LAMBRIDGE MEWS
6 LAMBRIDGE
7 LAMONT HO
8 MONTAGUE HO
9 EASTON HO
10 HAMPTON HO
11 BRIDGE HO

C2
1 GARFIELD TERR
2 BROUGHAM PL
3 COTTAGE PL
4 EDEN VILLAS
5 OTAGO TERR
6 LAMBRIDGE GRANGE

A **B** **C** **D** **E** **F**

8

The Oaks Farm

Road Hill

Stoney La

Rodney Farm

Alcombe Manor

Upper Northend Farm

Mast

Alcombe

7

Grubbins Wood

69

Oldhouse Farm

ST WAY LA

Lower Shockerwick Farm

6

Banner Down

Starfall Farm

SHOCKERWICK FARM LA

Shockerwick House

HOLLIES LA

Limestone Link

St Catherine's Brook

Sheep Sleight

Shockerwick Farm

Shockerwick

BATH RD

BROOKSIDE CL

STAMBROOK PK

CATHERINE WAY

5

The Mount

HIGH BANNERDOWN

BANNERDOWN RD

SHOCKERWICK LA

LOWER SHOCKERWICK LA

A4

68

WHITEMORE CT

ELMHURST EST

FOSSE LA

DAMSON PATH

BANNERDOWN CL

HIGH BANNERDOWN

WHITEFIELD

Sheylor's Farm

COALPIT RD

AVON CL

DEN PARK DR

KEEP PARK CL

COURT GDNS

BANK RD

BARNFIELD WAY

MORRIS LA

MEADOW PK

EASTWOODS

Box Bridge

Ashley House

WOODCLIFFE LA

4

LONDON RD E

WEST VIEW RD

BATHAMPTON DOWN

WESTWOODS

BOX RD

A SHLEY RD

3

By Brook

Ashley Wood Farm

Kingsdown

67

PH

A363

Mill

Bannerdown View Farm

LOWER KINGSDOWN RD

KINGSDOWN GR

Bathampton Farm

BATHFORD HILL

DOVERS LA

TITAN BARROW

MILL LA

High St

MOTSON

CHRIST LA

PROSPECT PL

PLEASANT PL

2

TYNING RD

River Avon

BRADFORD RD

CHURCH RD

OSTLINGS LA

PH

CHURCH ST

BATHFORD MANOR

MANOR PK

DOVERS LA

MANOR RD

MOUNTAIN WOOD

CHAPEL ROW

High St

Ashley Wood

LC

Bathford CE Prim Sch

COURT LA

PUMP LA

Bathford

FARLEIGH RISE

P

Limestone Link

Kennet & Avon Canal

WARLEIGH LA

A363

Warleigh Lodge

Brown's Folly

Brown's Folly Nature Reserve

FARLEIGH RISE

FARLEIGH RISE

Avon Walkway

1

4

HOLCOMBE LA

66

78 **A** **B** 79 **C** **D** 80 **E** **F**

Sand Point

BS22 9

Swallow Cliff

Middle Hope (Nature Reserve)

66 32   E   F   33

Sand Bay

BEACH RD

KEWSTOKE RD

Worlebury Hill

Weston Woods

Mast
Wr Twr

WORLEBURY HILL RD

Bathing Cove

Spring Cove

Birnbeck Island

Pier (dis)

IRB Sta

CAPRI VILLAS

Worlebury

Anchor Head

LB Sta

FORELANDS 1
CAMP RD N 2

BIRKETT RD

UPPER KEWSTOKE RD

MATTHEW PK

CLAREMONT CRES

BIRNBECK RD

MADEIRA

DRAGON CT

MANILLA RD

HIGHBURY RD

ATLANTIC RD

ATLANTIC VIEW CT

ATLANTIC RD S

SHRUBBERY RD

SPRINGFIELD RD

TRINITY PL

THE RETREAT

SOUTH RD

Knightstone CT

SHRUBBERY AVE

ST MATTHEW'S CL

PETER'S AVE

ST JOHN'S CL

UPPER CHURCH RD

VICTORIA PK

TOWER WLK E

GROVE PARK RD

GROVE PARK

DENSE RD

ALL SAINTS RD

ST JOSEPH'S RD

1 GLENWOOD MANS
2 SHRUBBERY WLK W
3 STUART HO
4 COACH HOUSE MEWS
5 KNIGHTSTONE CT
6 WOODLANDS

1 KINGSHOLME CT
2 EASTERN HO
3 SYCAMORES

HIGHCROFT

TICHBORNE KEW RD

CECIL RD

LEEWOD CL

LANDEMANN CIR

ARUNDELL RD

TREWARTHA PK

COOMBE RD

MONTPELIER E

ALBANY

EASTFIELD PK

BRISTOL ROAD LOWER

EASTCOMBE GDNS

EASTFIELD

SEDGEMOOR RD

DUNKERY RD

Cemy

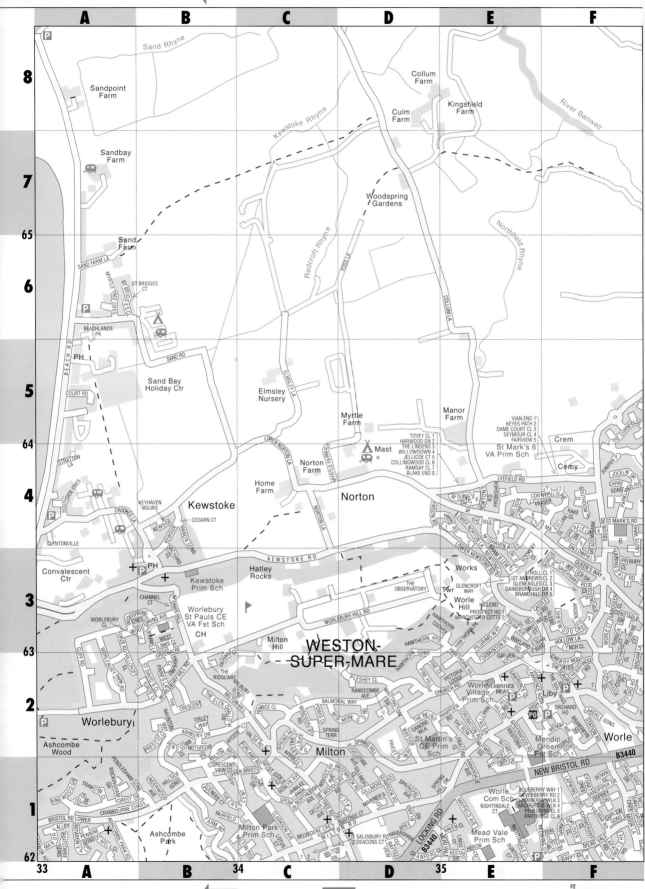

A B C D E F

8

Sandpoint Farm

Sand Rhyne

Collum Farm

Kewstoke Rhyne

Culm Farm

Kingsfield Farm

River Banwell

7

Sandbay Farm

Woodspring Gardens

Northfield Rhyne

65

Sand Farm

Redcroft Rhyne

FOSS LA

6

SAND FARM LA

MYRTLE TREE CRES

ST BRIDGES CT

ST BRIDGES CL

COLLUM LA

BEACHLANDS PK

PH

SAND RD

Sand Bay Holiday Ctr

5

BEACH RD

COURT RD

ELMSLEY LA

Elmsley Nursery

Manor Farm

VIAN END 1
KEYES PATH 2
DAME COURT CL 3
SEYMOUR CL 4
FAIRVIEW 5

Crem

64

STRATTON LA

LOWER NORTON LA

Myrtle Farm

TOVEY CL 1
HARWOOD GN 2
THE LINDENS 3
WILLOWDOWN 4
JELLICOE CT 5
COLLINGWOOD CL 6
RAMSAY CL 7
BLAKE END 8

St Mark's VA Prim Sch

Cemy

MYRTLE FARM RD

Mast

4

SOUTHSIDE CRES

CROOKS LA

KEYHAVEN BGLWS

KEWSIDE

CEDARN CT

Kewstoke

Norton Farm

Home Farm

NORTON LA

Norton

LOWER NORTON LA

NEWTONS RD

THE DELL

FRASER

CORNWALLIS CL

DRAKE

MA CLELLAN

COPPERFIELD

GLYNTONVILLE

MANOR GDNS

ORCHARD

ANSON RD

WAKE RD

MIDHAVEN RISE

ROCKERY

FALLOWFIELD

Convalescent Ctr

PH

Kewstoke Prim Sch

CHANNEL CT

Hatley Rocks

KEWSTOKE RD

Works

THE OBSERVATORY

Twr

Glencroft Way

Worle Hill

HILLEND
PROSPECT HO 1
MANCHESTER COTTS 2

ATHOLL CL 1
ST ANDREWS CL 2
GLENEAGLES CL 3
GAINSBOROUGH DR 4
BRAMSHILL DR 5

QUEEN'S WAY

3

CLIFF RD

WORLEBURY PARK RD

FURZE RD

Worlebury St Pauls CE VA Fst Sch

CH

Milton Hill

WORLEBURY HILL RD

HAWTHORN

HAWTHORN HTS

PILGRIMS WAY

FRIAR AVE

ST MARTINS

CASTLE

GLEBE WOOD CRES

63

Worlebury

Ashcombe Wood

THE RIDGEWAY

MILBURY

MILTON HILL

PLESHEY CL

RANSCOMBE AVE

WHITTING RD

BALMORAL WAY

VICTORIA LODGE

PINE HILL

CHURCH RD

Worle Village Prim Sch

Milton

St Martin's CE Prim Sch

Mendip Green Fst Sch

Worle

2

ASHCOMBE PARK RD

PRESCOT CT

TIRLEY WAY

ASHBURY DR

PRINCE CL

SPRING TERR

THE END

CANONS WLK

ORCHARD GDNS

B3440

Ashcombe Park

HILLSIDE GDNS

CAVENDISH

THE CRES

Milton Park Prim Sch

UPPER BRISTOL RD

MARINER'S WAY

NEW BRISTOL RD

Worle Com Sch

Mead Vale Prim Sch

1

BRISTOL RD LOWER

CRANBOURNE CHASE

FAIRFIELD

BELVEDERE CRES

SALISBURY RD
DEACONS CT

LOCKING RD

B3440

BLUEBERRY WAY 1
SILVERBERRY RD 2
ELDERBERRY WLK 3
CRABGROVE WLK 4
PEREGRINE CL 5
PARTRIDGE CL 6

62

33 A 34 B C D 35 E F

WESTON-SUPER-MARE

A B C D E F

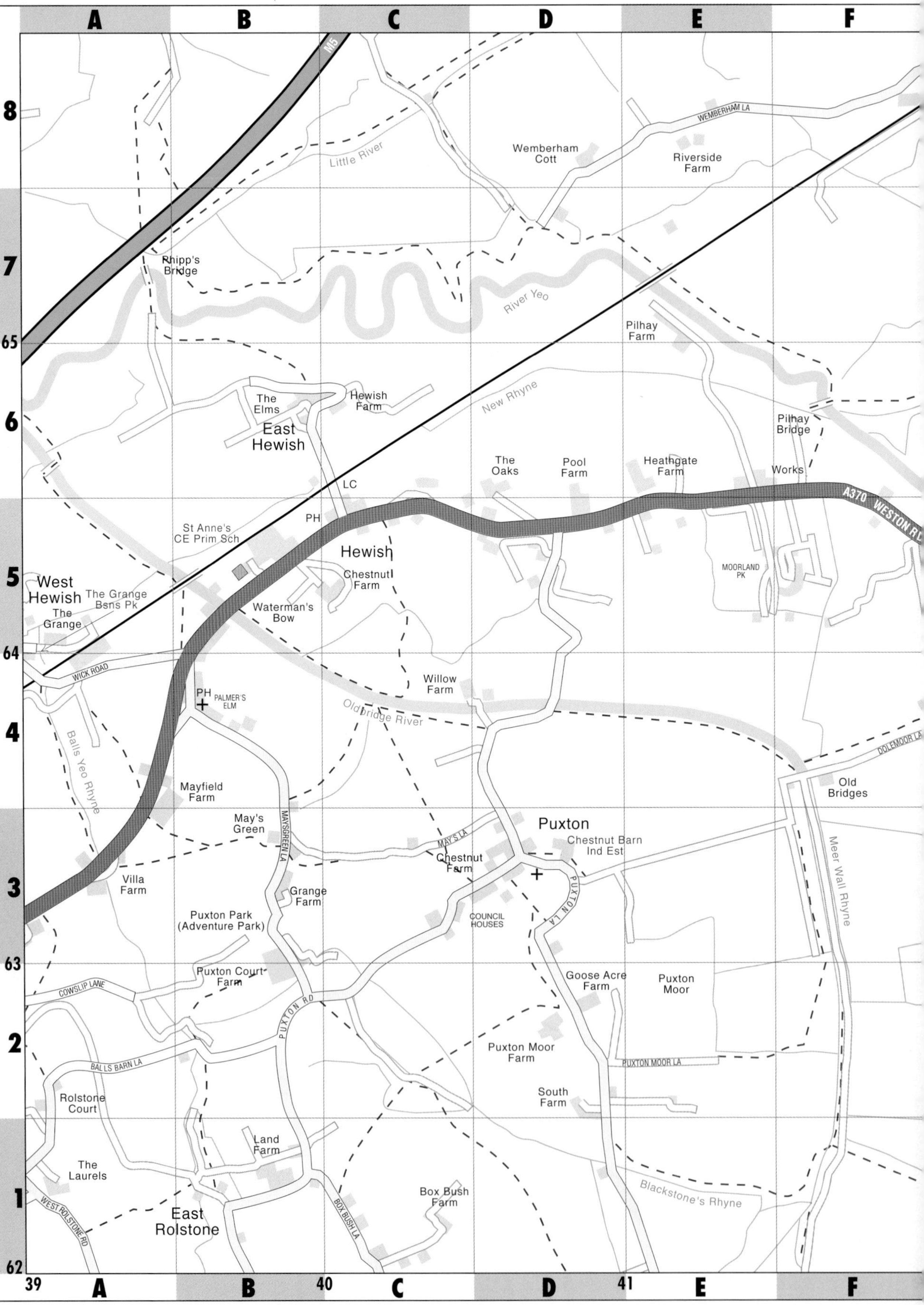

8

M5

Little River

Wemberham Cott

WEMBERHAM LA

Riverside Farm

7

Rhipp's Bridge

River Yeo

Pilhay Farm

65

New Rhyne

6

The Elms

East Hewish

Hewish Farm

Pilhay Bridge

The Oaks

Pool Farm

Heathgate Farm

Works

LC

St Anne's CE Prim Sch

PH

Hewish

A370 WESTON RD

MOORLAND PK

5

West Hewish

The Grange Bsns Pk

The Grange

Chestnut Farm

Waterman's Bow

64

WICK ROAD

Willow Farm

Old Bridge River

Balls Yeo Rhyne

4

PH PALMER'S ELM

Old Bridges

DOLEMOOR LA

Mayfield Farm

May's Green

MAY'S GREEN LA

MAY'S LA

Puxton

Chestnut Barn Ind Est

Meer Wall Rhyne

Villa Farm

Grange Farm

Chestnut Farm

PUXTON LA

3

Puxton Park (Adventure Park)

COUNCIL HOUSES

63

Puxton Court Farm

COWSLIP LANE

Goose Acre Farm

Puxton Moor

PUXTON RD

2

BALLS BARN LA

Puxton Moor Farm

PUXTON MOOR LA

Rolstone Court

South Farm

Land Farm

The Laurels

BOX BUSH LA

Box Bush Farm

Blackstone's Rhyne

1

WEST ROLSTONE RD

East Rolstone

62

39 A B 40 C D 41 E F

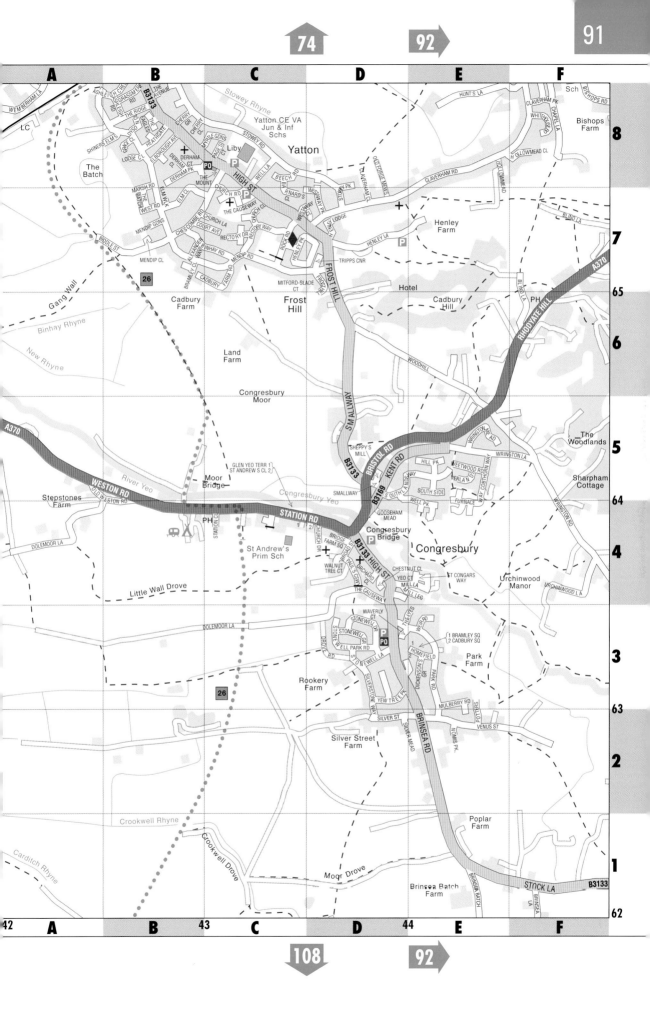

91
75

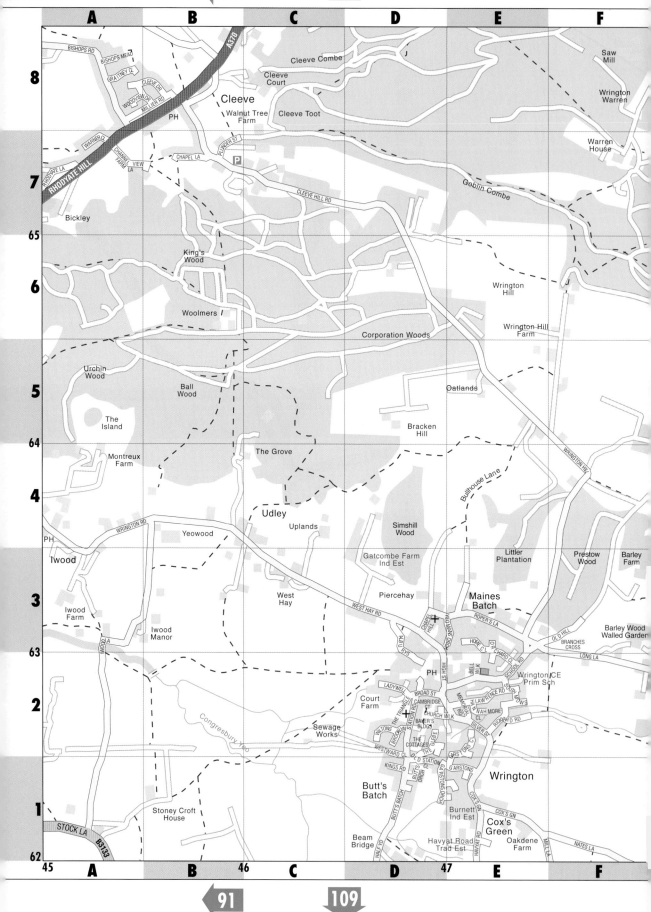

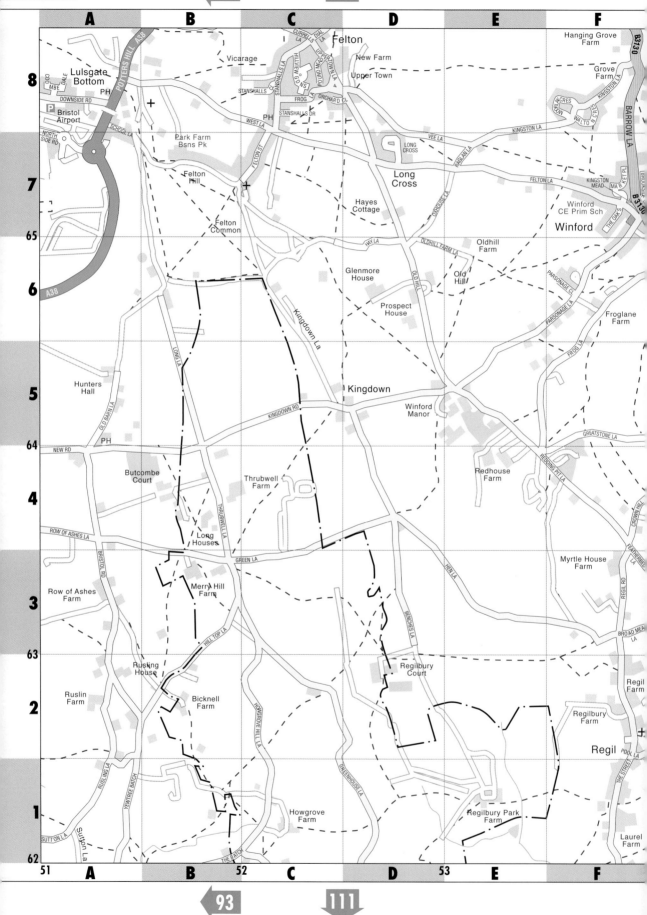

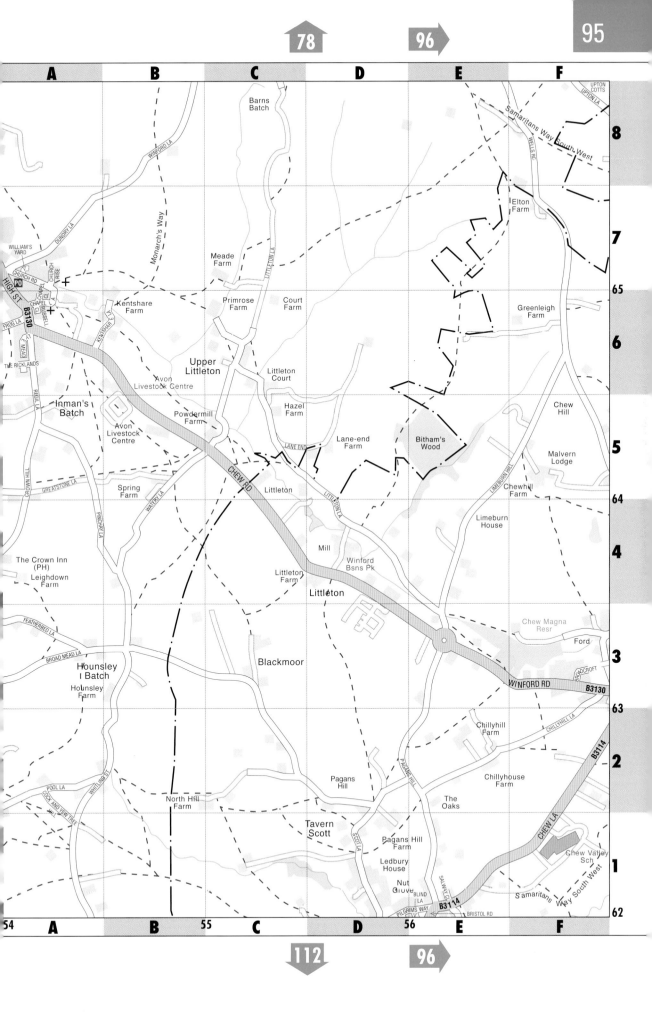

95 79

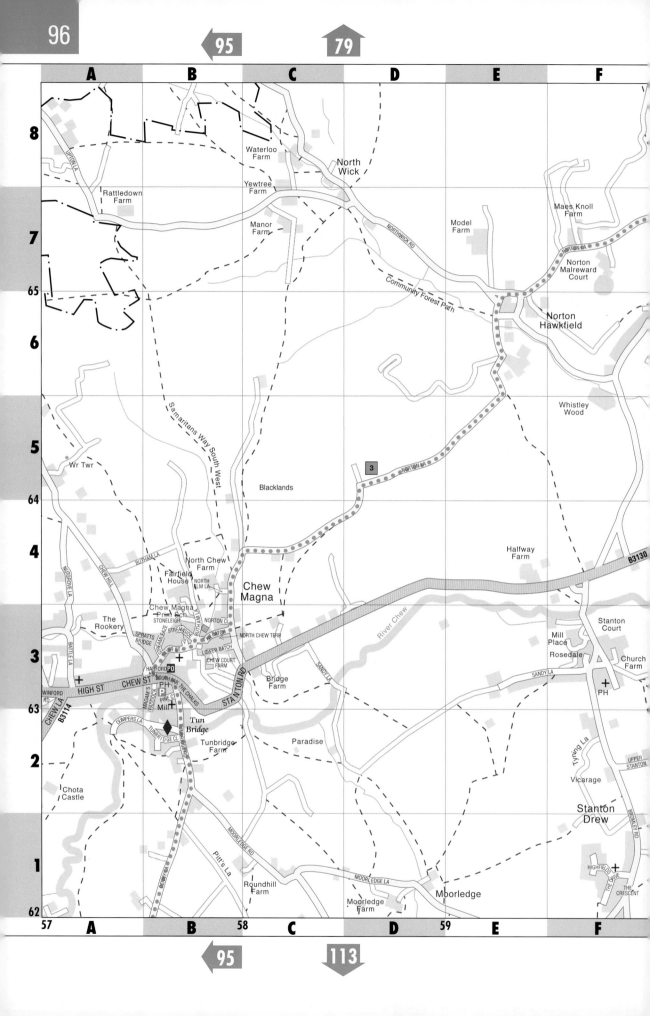

95 113

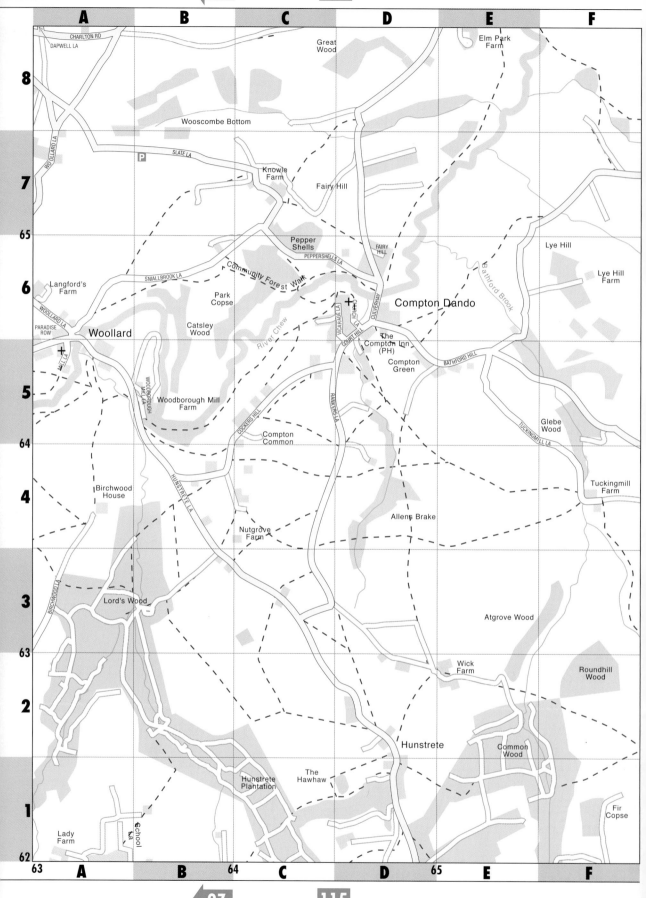

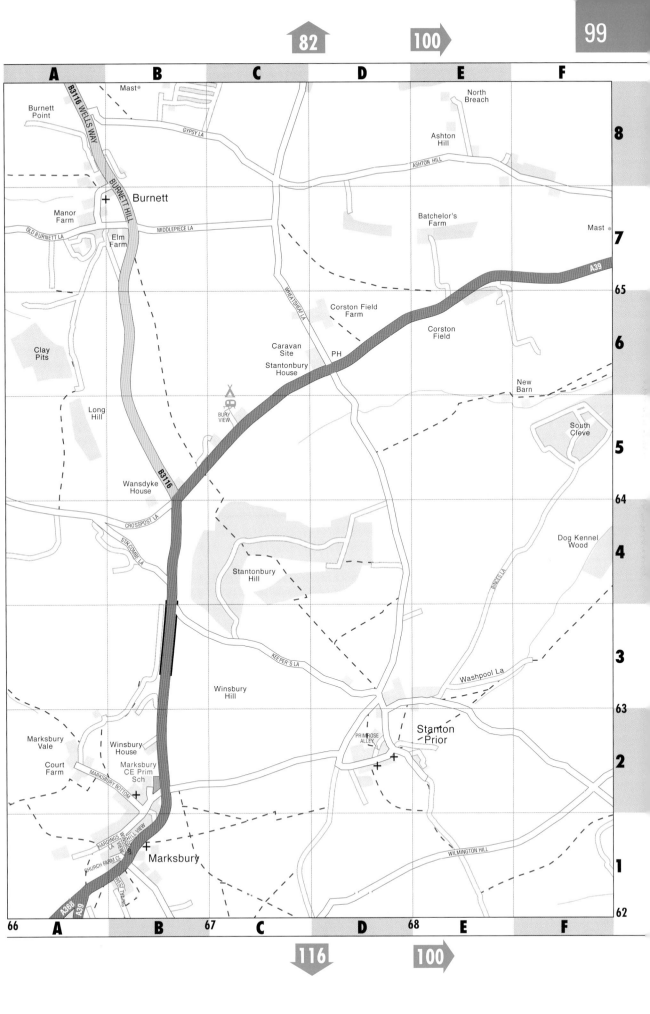

A B C D E F

8

7

65

6

5

64

4

3

63

2

1

62

Burnett Point

Mast

B3116 WELLS WAY

GYPSY LA

North Breach

Ashton Hill

ASHTON HILL

Burnett

BURNETT HILL

Manor Farm

OLD BURNETT LA

Elm Farm

MIDDLEPIECE LA

Batchelor's Farm

Mast

A39

Clay Pits

Long Hill

WHEATSHEAF LA

Corston Field Farm

PH

Corston Field

New Barn

Caravan Site

Stantonbury House

BURY VIEW

South Cleve

Wansdyke House

B3116

CROSSPOST LA

STALCOMBE LA

Stantonbury Hill

Dog Kennel Wood

BINCE'S LA

KEEPER'S LA

Washpool La

Winsbury Hill

Stanton Prior

PRIMROSE ALLEY

Marksbury Vale

Court Farm

Winsbury House

Marksbury CE Prim Sch

MARKSBURY BOTTOM

HARDINGS LA

WINSBURY VIEW

WINSBURY VIEW

WEST STRAND

WILMINGTON HILL

CHURCH FARM CL

Marksbury

A368

A39

99
83

A B C D E F

8

A4

BATH RD

Avon Walkway

4

PH
P&R

New
Bridge

A431
KELSTON RD

NEWBRIDGE RD

Avon Walkway

A4

HOMEMEAD

GOOLD CL

CORSTON LA

THE ORCHARD

Newton
Bridge

BRISTOL RD

Corston

LOWER FARM LA

PO

THE PADDOCK
MEADLANDS

THE BARTON

ASHTON HILL

Church
Farm
Bsns Pk

WELLS RD

COTTON MEAD

BROOK
COTTS

A39

A4

BRISTOL RD

A4

A36

A36

CARRSWOOD
VIEW

LOWER BRISTOL RD

7

PH

Long
Shrub

Seven Acre
Wood

Camp
Site

Mill

REDL PK

PENNYQUICK
VIEW

REDL
AVE
REDL

65

Corston Brook

WALING LA

DAV CRES

HINTON
CL

CLEEV
GN

Sch

6

Woodenhouse
Covert

CHURCH
COTTS

WORKSHOP LA

PO

VILLAGE RD

Home
Farm

Newton
St Loe

PENNYQUICK

CLAYS END LA

Clays
End

NEWTON RD

CAMELEY GN

CAMELEY GN

SHAW'S WAY

Sch

Newton
Park

CLAYSEND

KEEPERS HILL

Claysend
Farm

B LOYCE
CL

TANNERS
WLK

LONG
CL

SHERIDAN RD

GARRICK RD

WEDGWOOD RD

POOLE MEAD RD

PO

5

Bath Spa
University Coll
(Newton Park
Campus)

P

PENNYQUICK HILL

ALEC RICKETTS CL 1
KELSTON VIEW 2
POOLE HO 3
GARRE HO 4

WHITEWAY RD

64

Park
Wood

Whiteway

4

St Loe's
Castle

Whistling
Copse

Ashery
Gully

Newton Brook

Haycombe
Farm

Crem

Cemy

HAYCOMBE LA

3

Park
Farm

TWELVE O'CLOCK LA

Pennsylvania
Farm

Nursery

63

WILMINGTON HILL

WASHPOOL LA

2

Wilmington
Farm

Manor
Farm

RECTORY FARM LA

Tithe
Barn

INN OX GR

Englishcombe

1

Wilmington

Wilmington La

62

69 A B 70 C D 71 E F

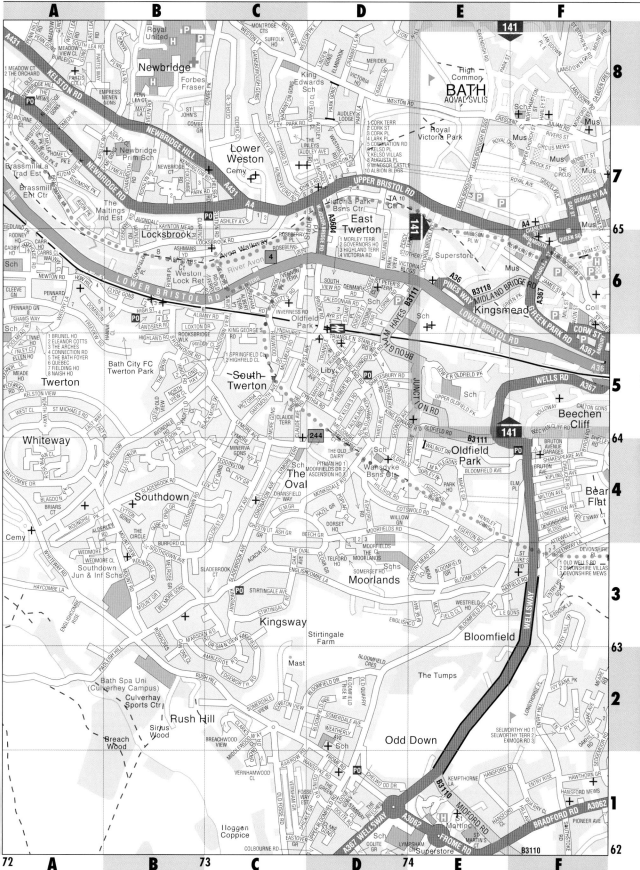

For full street detail of the highlighted area see page 141.

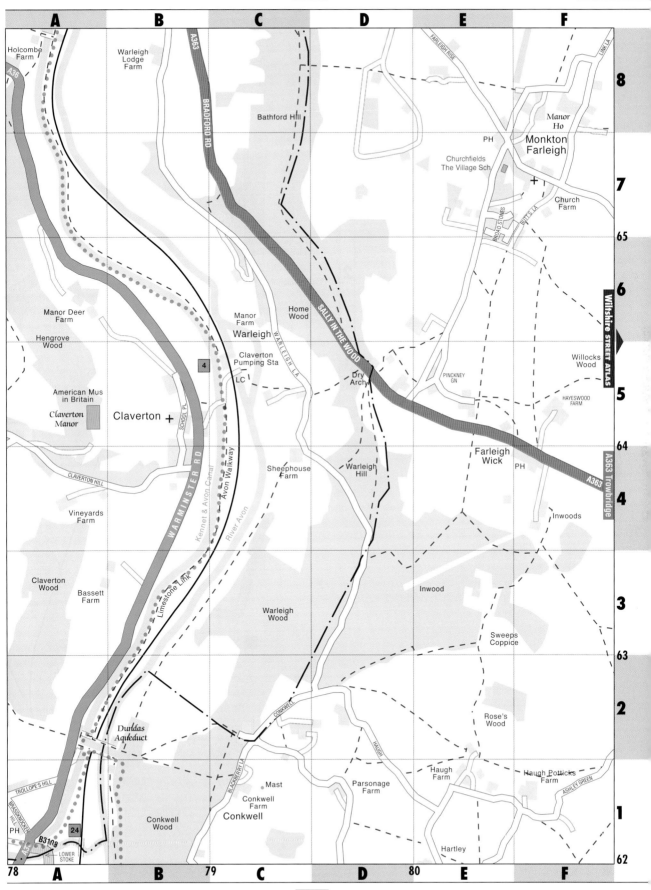

A B C D E F

8
7
65
6
5
64
4
3
63
2
1
62

78 A B 79 C D 80 E F

Holcombe Farm
A36
Warleigh Lodge Farm
A363
BRADFORD RD
Bathford Hill
FARLEIGH RISE
LINK LA
Manor Ho
Monkton Farleigh
PH
Churchfields The Village Sch
Church Farm
BROAD STONES
BUTTS LA

Manor Deer Farm
Hengrove Wood
Manor Farm
Home Wood
Warleigh
SALLY IN THE WOOD
WARLEIGH LA
Willocks Wood
PINCKNEY GN
HAYESWOOD FARM

American Mus in Britain
Claverton Manor
Claverton
Claverton Pumping Sta
LC
4
SCHOOL PL
Dry Arch
Farleigh Wick
PH
A363 Trowbridge

Claverton Hill
WARMINSTER RD
Kennet & Avon Canal
Avon Walkway
Sheephouse Farm
River Avon
Warleigh Hill
Inwoods

Vineyards Farm
Limestone Link
Warleigh Wood
Inwood
Sweeps Coppice

Claverton Wood
Bassett Farm
Rose's Wood

Dundas Aqueduct
CONKWELL
HAUGH
Haugh Farm
Haugh Potticks Farm
ASHLEY GREEN

TROLLOPE'S HILL
BRASSKNOCKER HILL
PH
B3108
24
BLACKBERRY LA
Mast
Conkwell Wood
Conkwell Farm
Conkwell
Parsonage Farm
Hartley
A36
LOWER STOKE

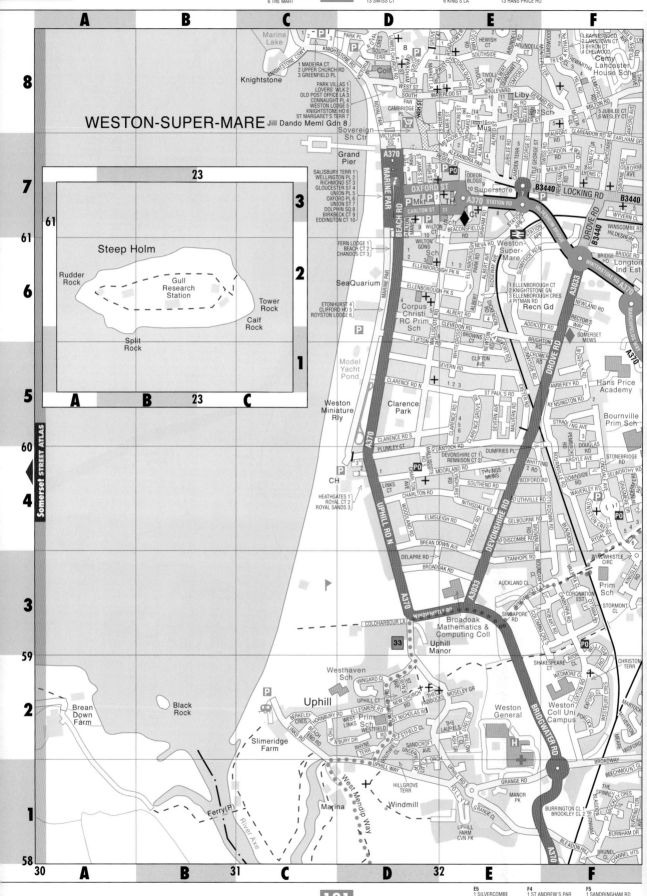

WESTON-SUPER-MARE

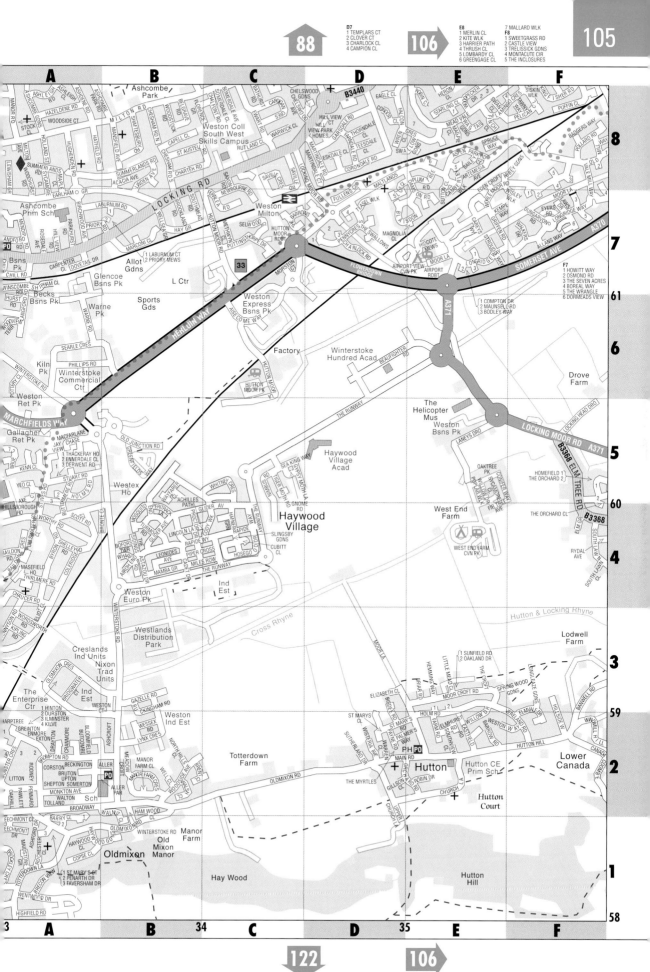

105
89

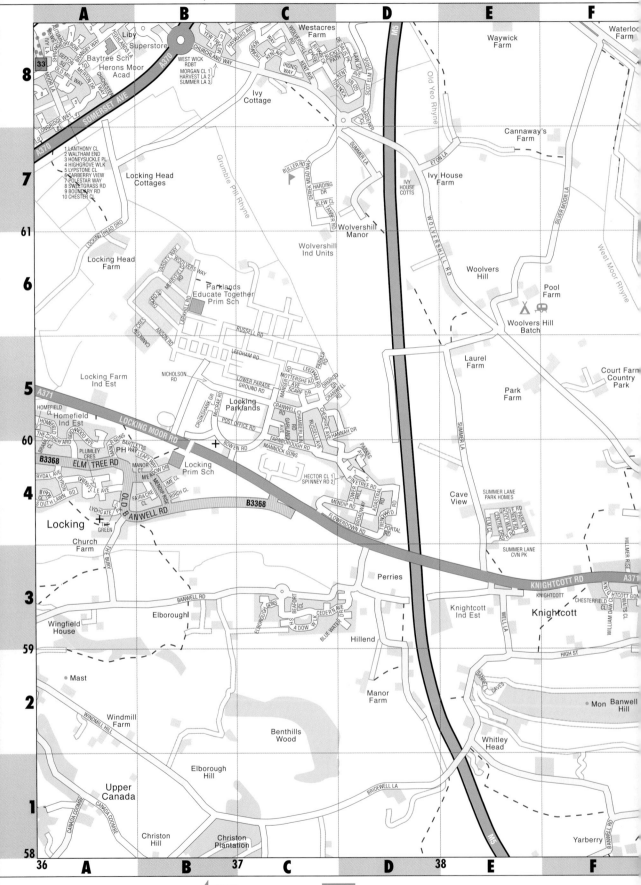

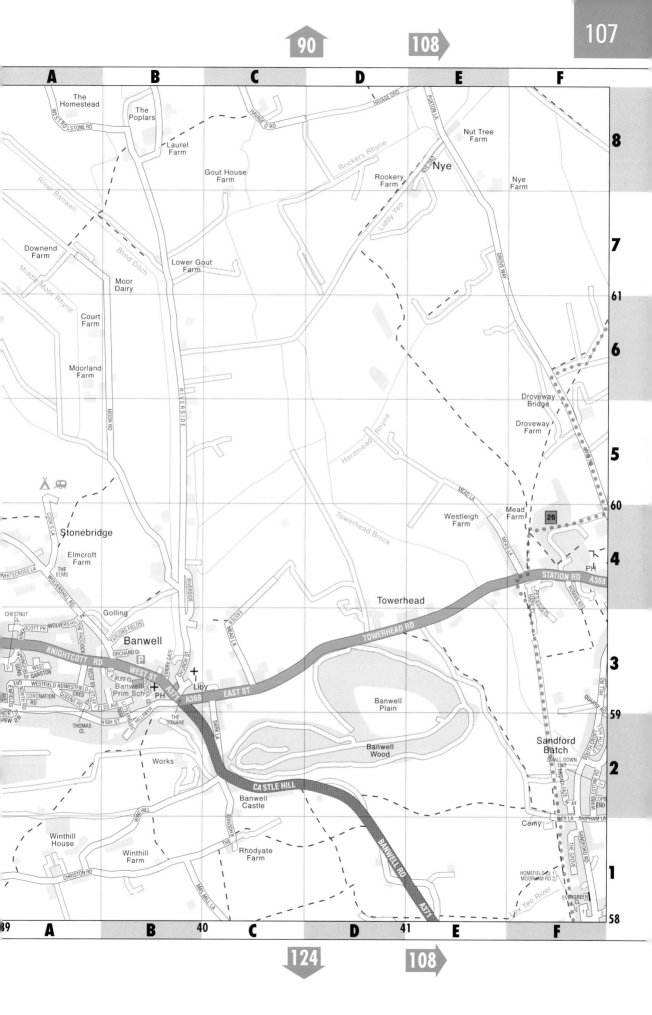

107
91

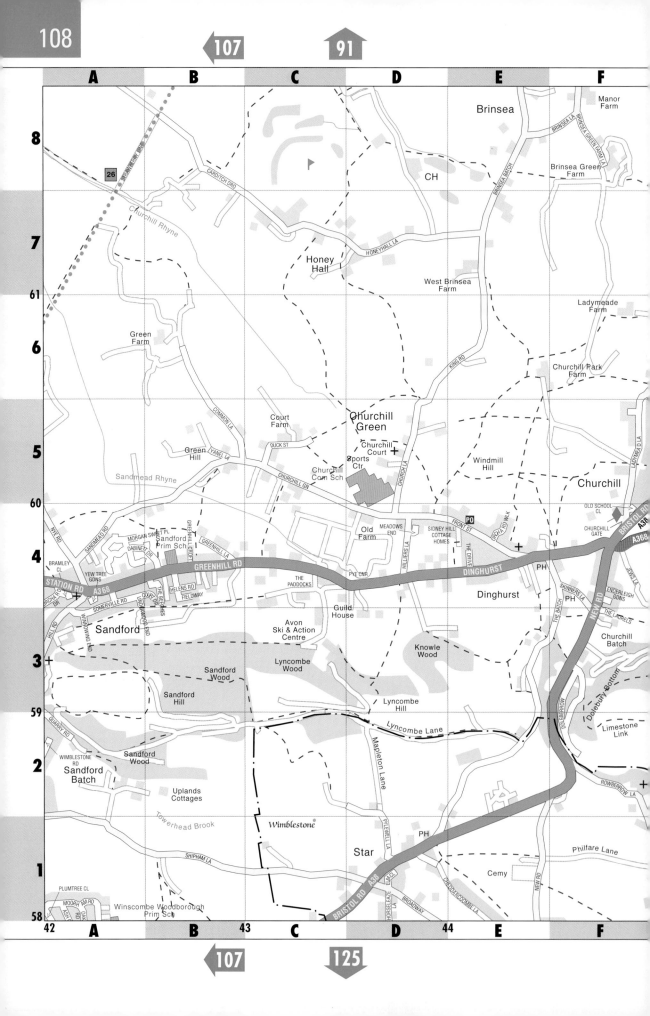

109
93

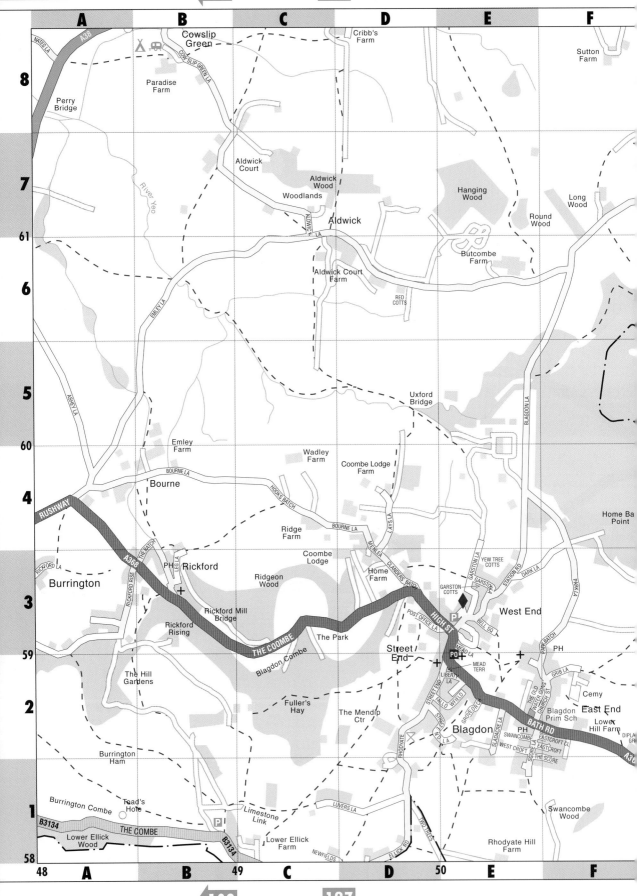

109
127

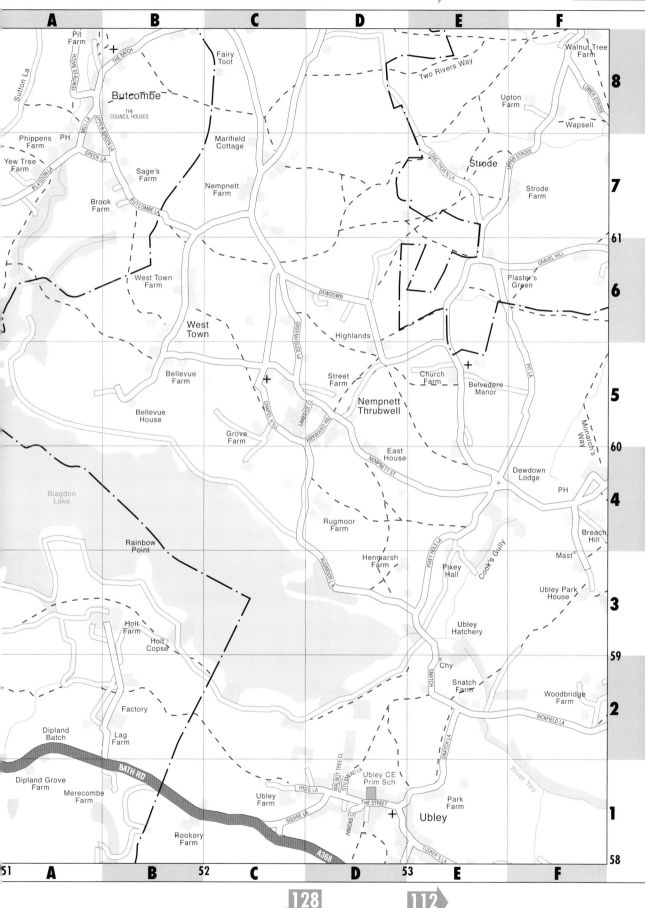

96
114

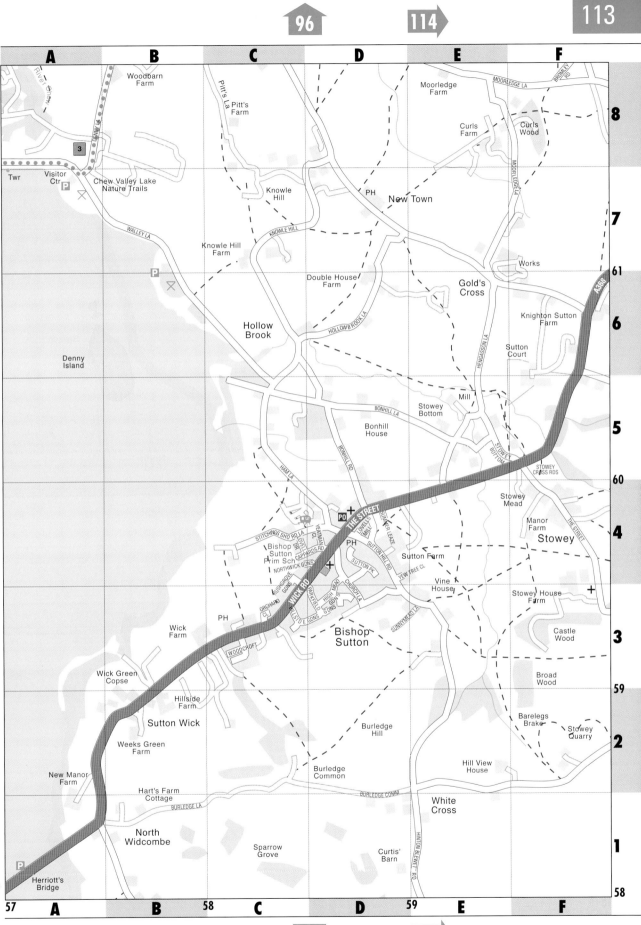

130
114

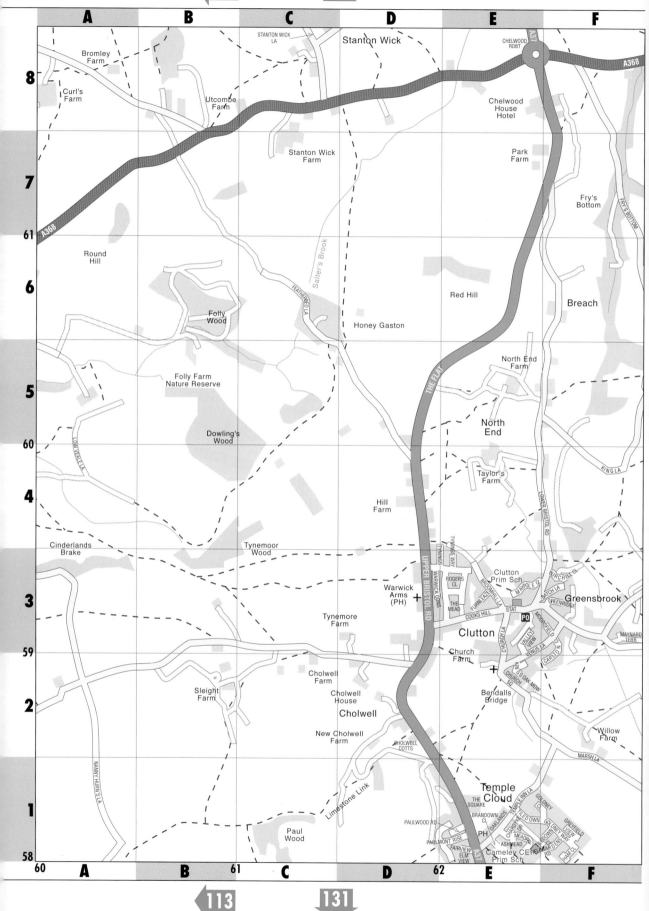

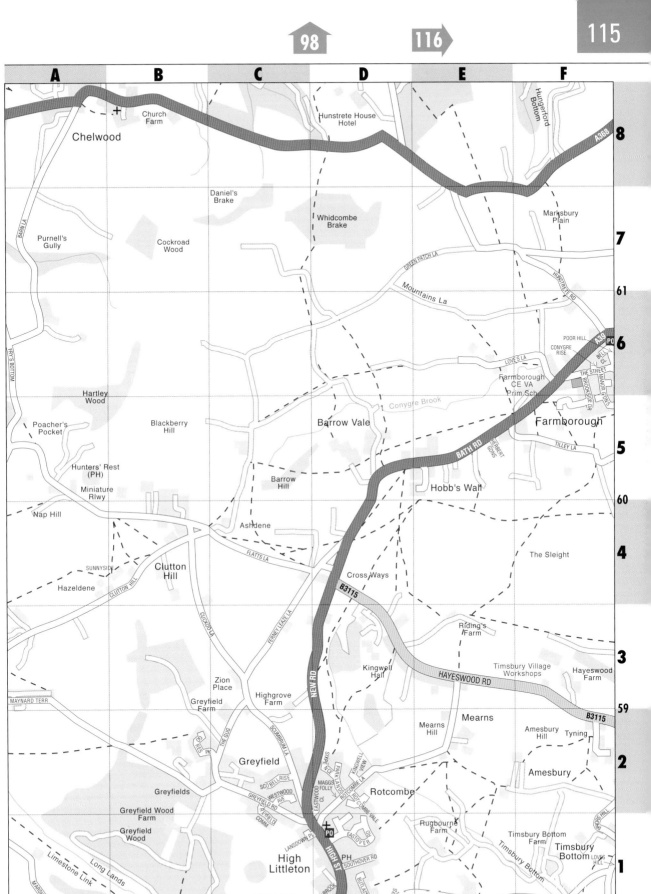

98
116
132
116

Chelwood

Church Farm

Hunstrete House Hotel

Hungerford Bottom

A368

Daniel's Brake

Whidcombe Brake

Marksbury Plain

Purnell's Gully

BARN LA

Cockroad Wood

Green Patch La

Mountains La

HUNSTRETE RD

FRY'S BOTTOM

Hartley Wood

Blackberry Hill

Barrow Vale

Conygre Brook

LOVE'S LA

POOR HILL

CONYGRE RISE

A39

PO

BELL CL

MANOR GDNS

THE STREET

BROOKSIDE DR

Farmborough CE VA Prim Sch

Farmborough

Poacher's Pocket

Hunters' Rest (PH)

Miniature Rlwy

Barrow Hill

BATH RD

HERBERT GDNS

Hobb's Wall

TILLEY LA

Nap Hill

Ashdene

The Sleight

SUNNYSIDE

FLATTIS LA

CLUTTON HILL

Clutton Hill

Hazeldene

Cross Ways

B3115

Riding's Farm

Timsbury Village Workshops

Hayeswood Farm

CUCKOO LA

FERNEY LEAZE LA

NEW RD

Kingwell Hall

HAYESWOOD RD

MAYNARD TERR

Zion Place

Highgrove Farm

Mearns

B3115

Greyfield Farm

THE GUG

SOLSBURY LA

Mearns Hill

Amesbury Hill

Tyning

Greyfield

SCD

BELL RISE

SNIPE NEST

PARK LANE

KINGWELL VIEW

Amesbury

Greyfields

GREYFIELD RD

WESTWOOD AVE

MAGGS FOLLY

EASTWOOD CL

ROTCOMBE LA

COMBE VALE

Rotcombe

Rugbourne Farm

Timsbury Bottom Farm

Timsbury Bottom

Greyfield Wood Farm

Greyfield Wood

ALFRED CL

COMM

LANSDOWN PL

EASTOVER

PO

Timsbury Bottom

LOVE'S HILL

Limestone Link

Long Lands

High Littleton

HIGH ST

PH

SOUTHOVER RD

MARSH LA

High Littleton CE Prim Sch

ASH BROOK

A39

BUTTS CL

TIMSBURY RD

GOOSARD LA

LANGFORD'S

BUNGAY'S HILL

BROOM HILL LA

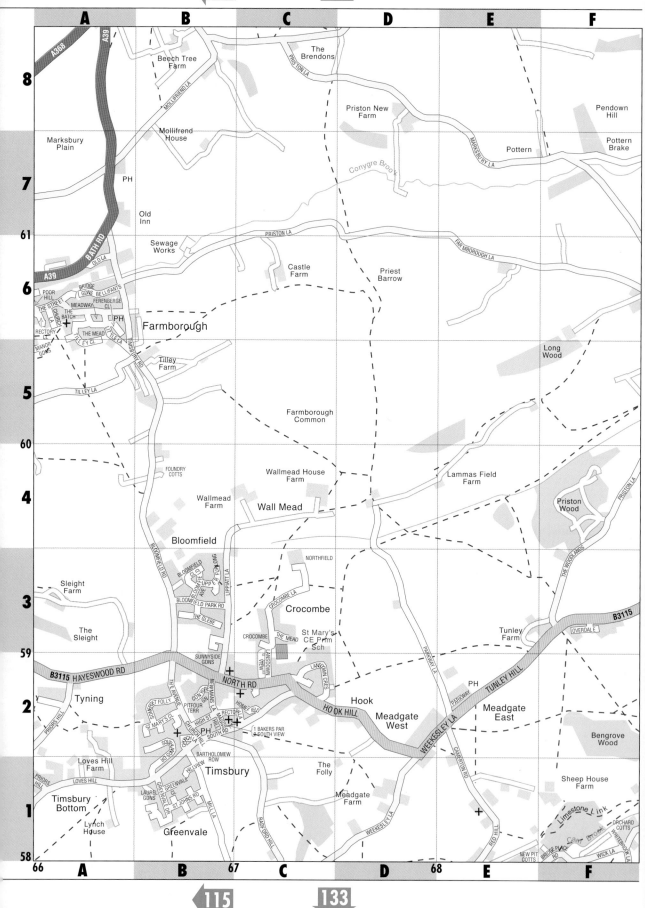

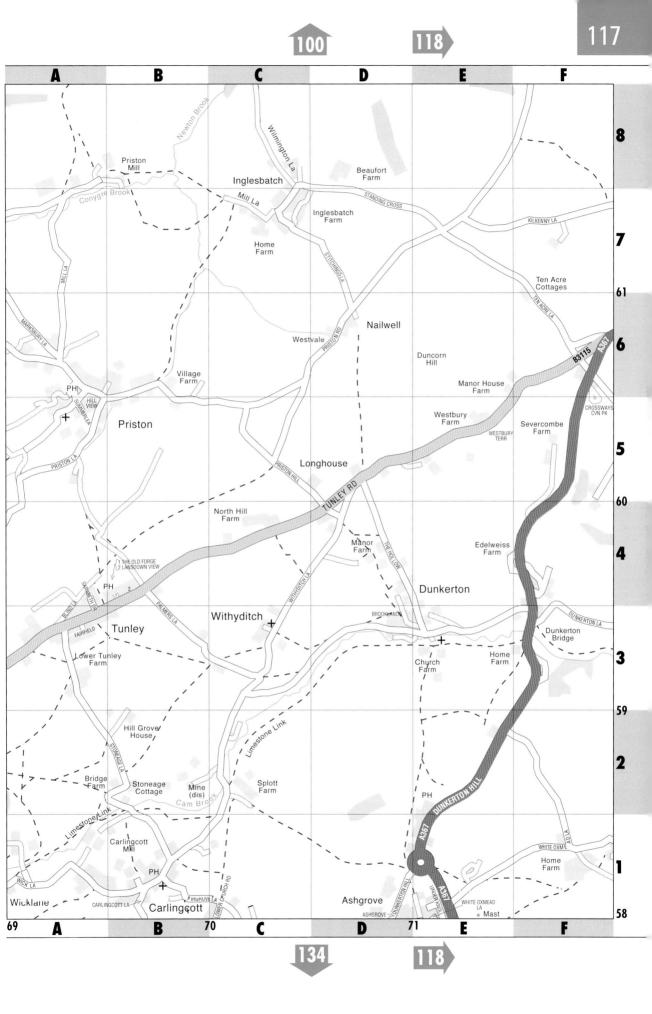

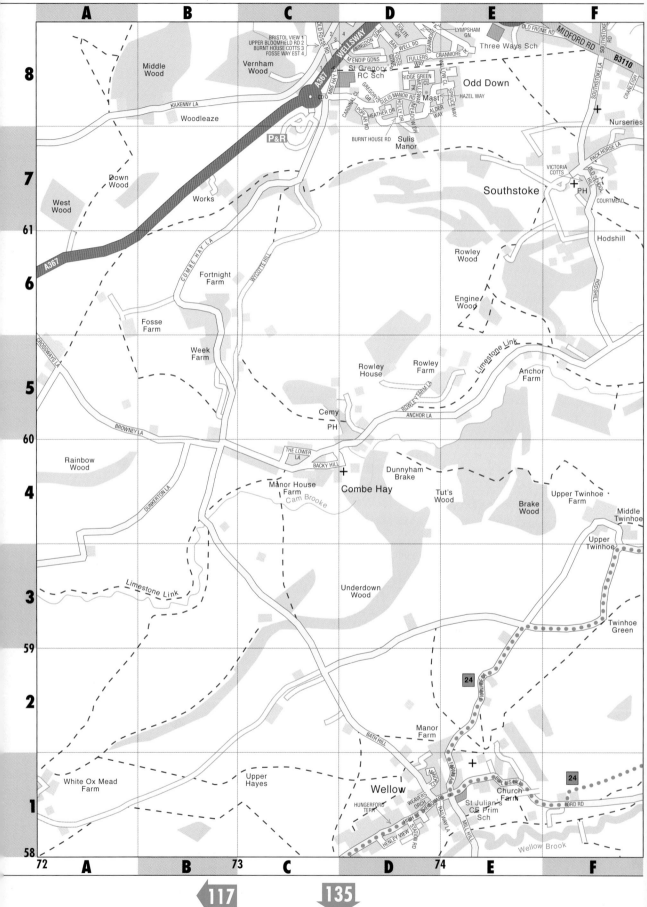

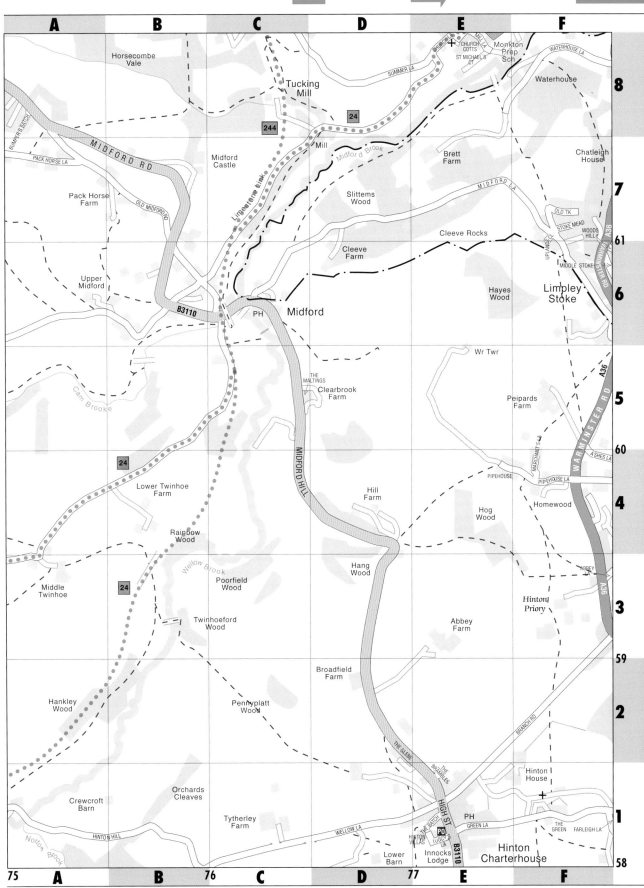

119
103

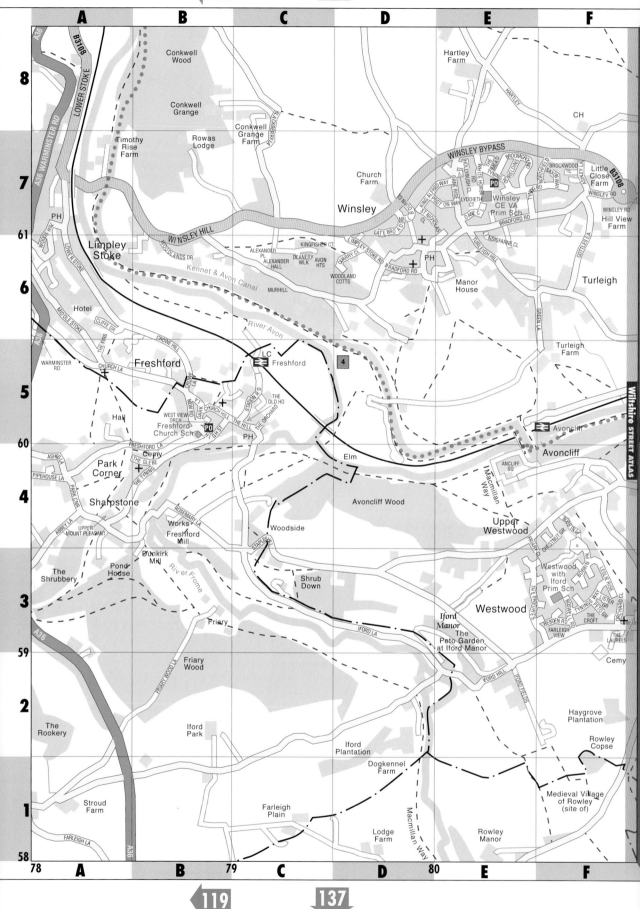

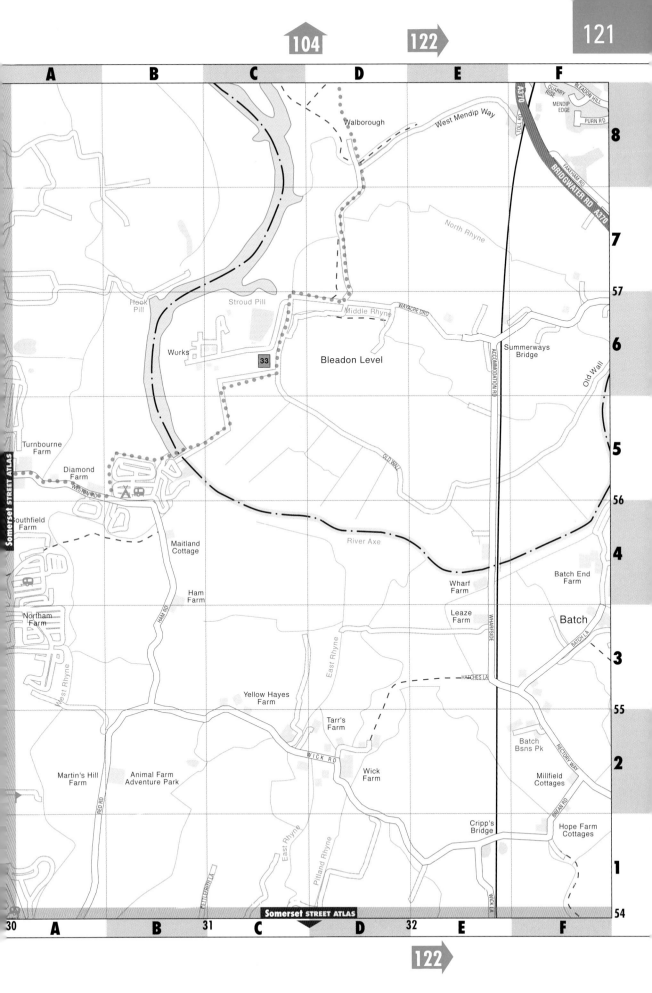

A B C D E F

8
7
57
6
5
56
4
3
55
2
1
54

Somerset STREET ATLAS

West Mendip Way

Walborough

BLEADON HILL
QUARRY RISE
MENDIP EDGE
PURN RD

TOLL RD A370
FAKEHAM RD
BRIDGWATER RD A370

North Rhyne

Hook Pill

Stroud Pill

Middle Rhyne

WAYACRE DRO

Summerways Bridge

Old Wall

Works

33

Bleadon Level

ACCOMMODATION RD

Turnbourne Farm

Diamond Farm

WESTON RD

OLD WALL

Southfield Farm

Maitland Cottage

River Axe

Batch End Farm

Ham Farm

HAM RD

Wharf Farm

Leaze Farm

Batch

WHARFSIDE

BATCH LA

Northam Farm

West Rhyne

East Rhyne

HATCHES LA

RECTORY WAY

Yellow Hayes Farm

Tarr's Farm

Batch Bsns Pk

Martin's Hill Farm

RED RD

Animal Farm Adventure Park

WICK RD

Wick Farm

Millfield Cottages

BREAN RD

East Rhyne

Pitland Rhyne

Cripp's Bridge

WICK LA

Hope Farm Cottages

PETTLEBRIDGE LA

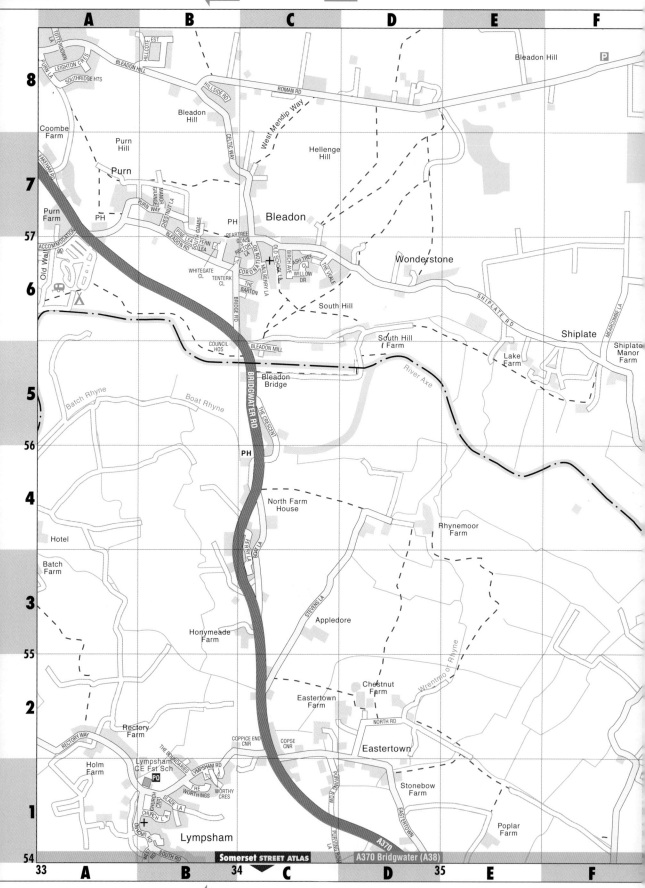

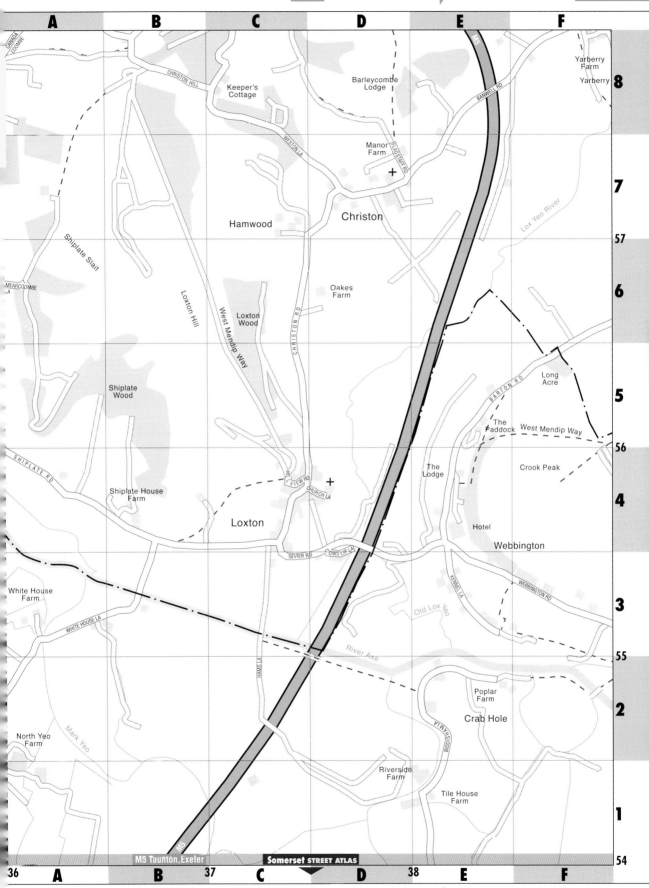

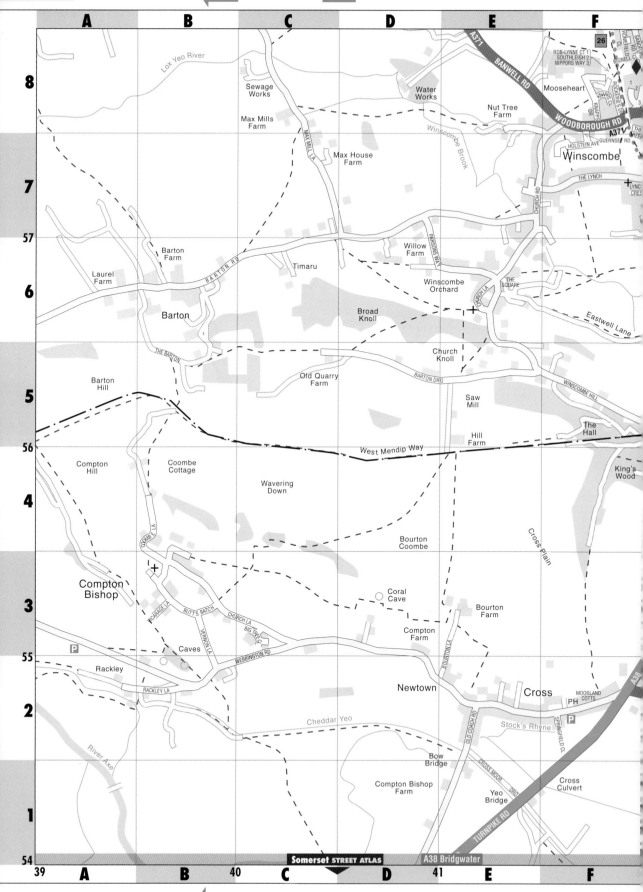

125
109

A **B** **C** **D** **E** **F**

8

ROWBERROW LA

Holloway La

Riding Sch

Rowberrow Warren

Black Down

West Twin Brook

East Twin Brook

LIPPIATT LA

7

Blackdown Farm

57

Longbottom Farm

6

Longbottom

LONGBOTTOM

West Mendip Way

Tyning's Farm

Trots Corner

5

Tyning's Gate

GB Cave

Long House Barn

56

Tyning's Gate

Ashridge Farm

Charterhouse Farm

WARRENS HILL RD

4

The Perch

Race Track (Vehicular)

Milkway Barn

Piney Sleight Farm

Batts Combe Quarry

3

55

Batt's Coombe

Piney Sleight

Fore Cliffs

2

SHIPHAM RD

Chelm's Coombe

Structural Test Ctr

Cheddar Gorge

Horseshoe Bend

THE CLIFFS

B3135

Warrens Hill

VENNS GATE

P

AXBRIDGE RD

Cheddar Cliffs

Samaritans Way South West

West Mendip Way

Cliff Plantation

1

B3135

MEWSWELL DR

Hamfield Farm

TUTTORS HILL

P

UPPER NEW RD

A371

Round Oak Farm

THE BAG RD

WARREN'S HILL

THE CHESTNUTS 1

MENDIP VILLAS 2

HAN WAY RD

KENT ST

A35

OAK RD

CUFIC LA

Somerset STREET ATLAS

54

45 **A** 46 **B** **C** 47 **D** **E** **F**

125

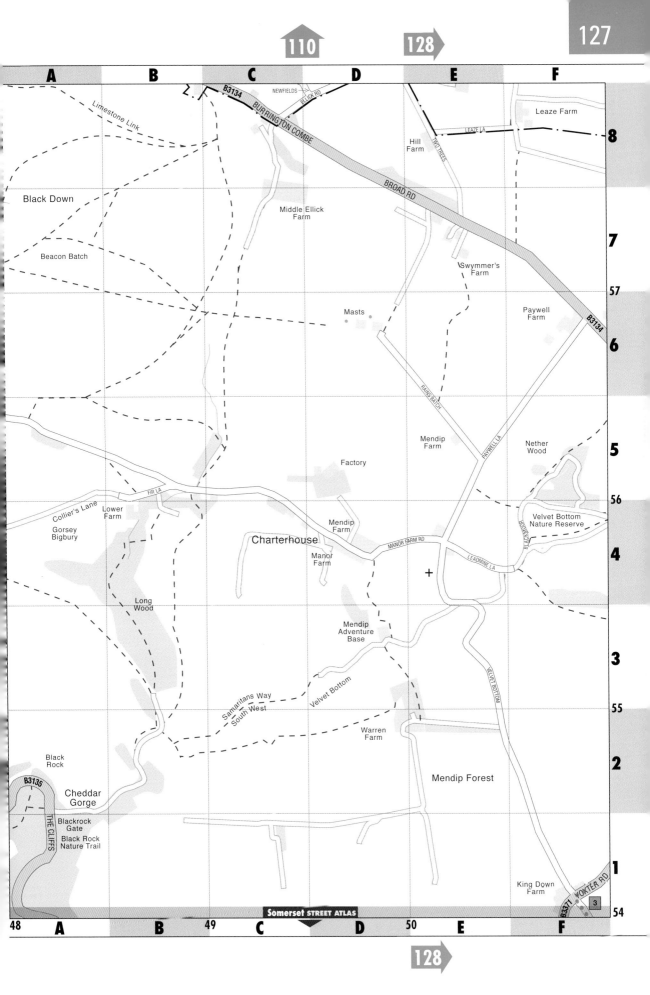

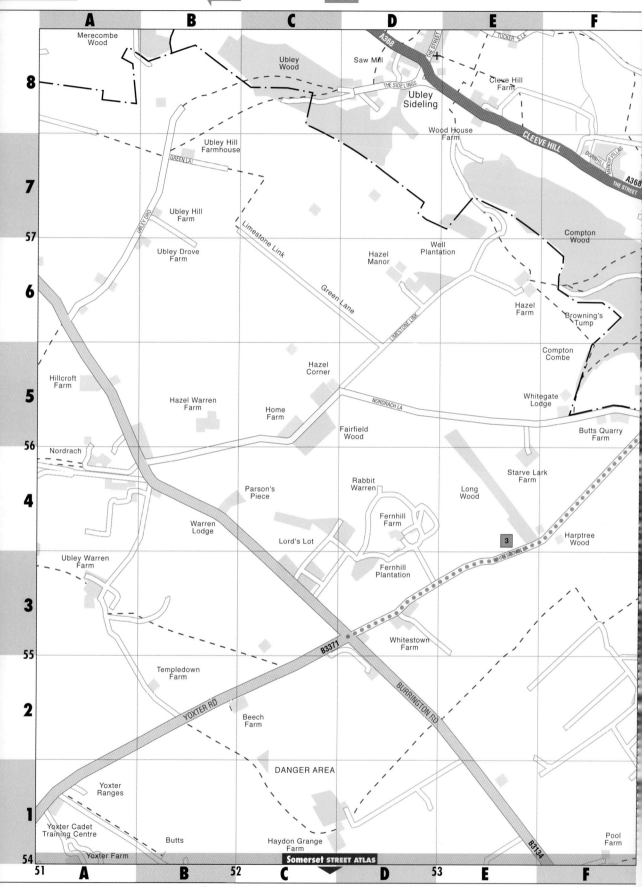

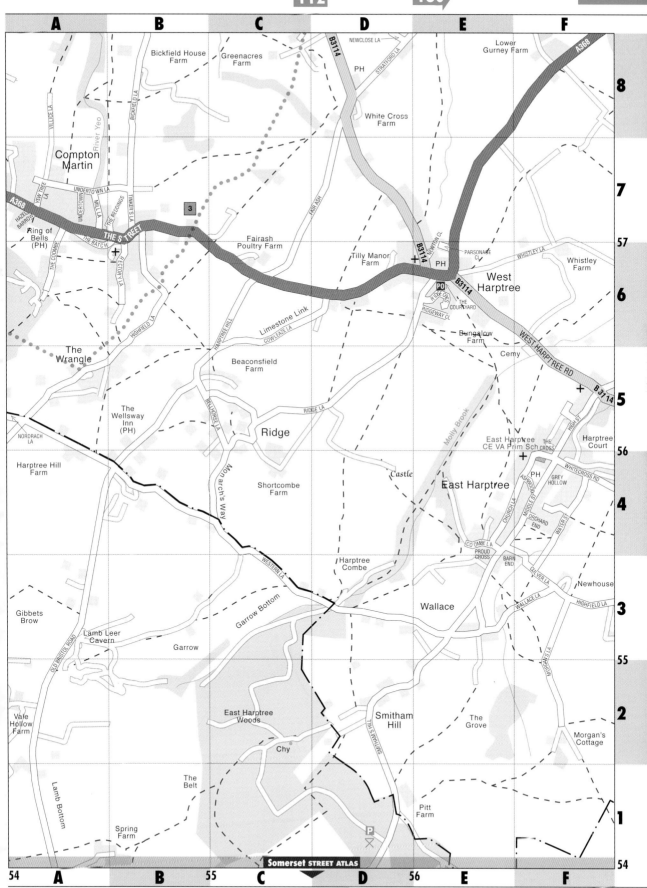

129
113

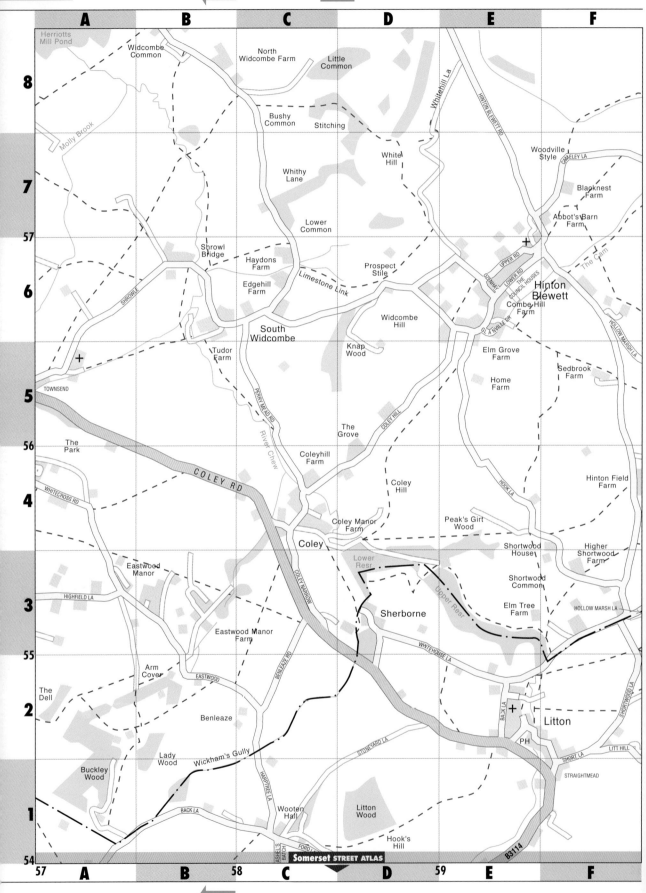

Herriotts Mill Pond

Molly Brook

Widcombe Common

North Widcombe Farm

Little Common

Bushy Common

Stitching

Whithy Lane

White Hill

Whitehill La

Woodville Style

Cameley La

Blacknest Farm

Abbot's Barn Farm

The Cam

Lower Common

Shrowl Bridge

Haydons Farm

Limestone Link

Prospect Stile

Hinton Blewett

Edgehill Farm

SHROWLE

South Widcombe

Widcombe Hill

Combe Hill Farm

THE COUNCIL HOUSES

UPPER RD

LOWER RD

OZENHAY

GLEBVILLE DR

HOLLOW MARSH LA

Tudor Farm

Knap Wood

Elm Grove Farm

Home Farm

Sedbrook Farm

TOWNSEND

The Park

River Chew

COLEY RD

The Grove

Coleyhill Farm

COLEY HILL

Coley Hill

HOOK LA

Hinton Field Farm

WHITECROSS RD

Coley Manor Farm

Peak's Girt Wood

Higher Shortwood Farm

HIGHFIELD LA

Coley

Lower Resr

Shortwood House

Shortwood Common

Elm Tree Farm

HOLLOW MARSH LA

Eastwood Manor

Sherborne

Upper Resr

COLEY NARROW

PERRY MEAD RD

BENLEAZE RD

Eastwood Manor Farm

WHITEHOUSE LA

Arm Cover

EASTWOOD

SHORTWOOD LA

The Dell

Benleaze

STONEYARD LA

BACK LA

Litton

PH

LITT HILL

SHORT LA

Lady Wood

Wickham's Gully

HARPTREE LA

STRAIGHTMEAD

Buckley Wood

BACK LA

Wooten Hall

Litton Wood

ASHELS BATCH

FORD LA

Hook's Hill

B3114

129

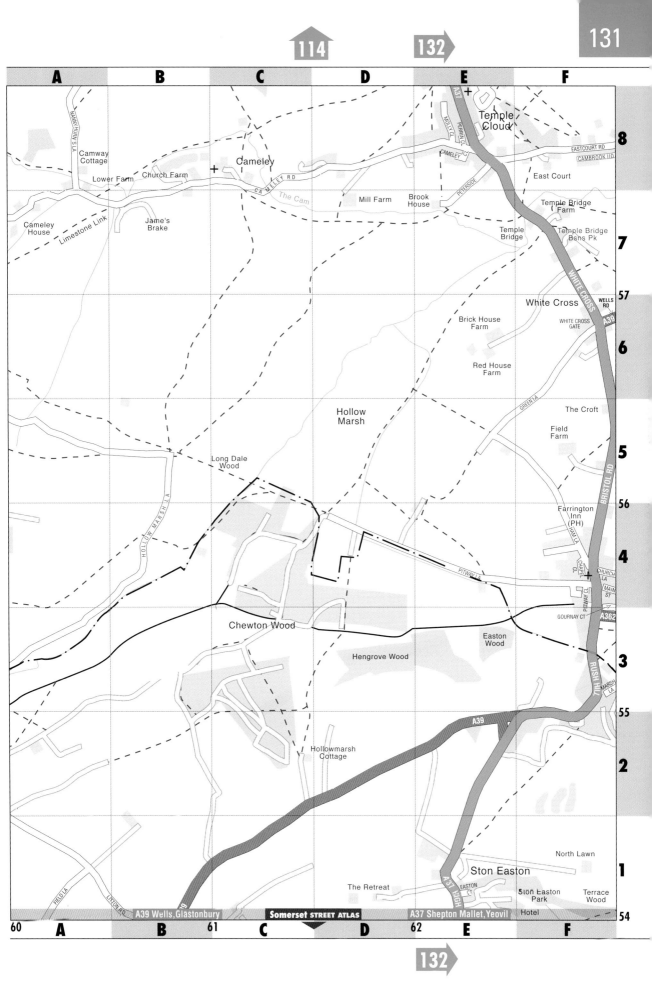

A B C D E F

8
7
57
6
5
56
4
3
55
2
1
54

MANN HURN S LA
Camway
Cottage
Lower Farm
Church Farm
Cameley
CAMELEY RD
The Cam
Mill Farm
Brook
House
MOLLY CL
PERRIN CL
CAMELEY
PETERSIDE
A37
Temple
Cloud
EASTCOURT RD
CAMBROOK RD
East Court
Temple Bridge
Farm
Temple
Bridge
Temple Bridge
Bsns Pk
Cameley
House
Limestone Link
Jame's
Brake

WHITE CROSS

White Cross
WELLS
RD
A39
WHITE CROSS
GATE

Brick House
Farm

Red House
Farm

HOLLOW MARSH LA

Hollow
Marsh

GREEN LA
The Croft
Field
Farm

BRISTOL RD

Long Dale
Wood

Farrington
Inn
(PH)
HAM LA

CHAPEL CL
CHURCH
LA
MAIN
ST

Chewton Wood
PITWAY LA
Easton
Wood
PITWAY CL
GOURNAY CT
A362

Hengrove Wood
RUSH HILL
MARSH
LA

A39

Hollowmarsh
Cottage

North Lawn

A37 HIGH
EASTON
CT
Ston Easton
The Retreat
Ston Easton
Park
Terrace
Wood

Hotel

FIELD LA
LITTON RD

60 A 61 B C 62 D E F

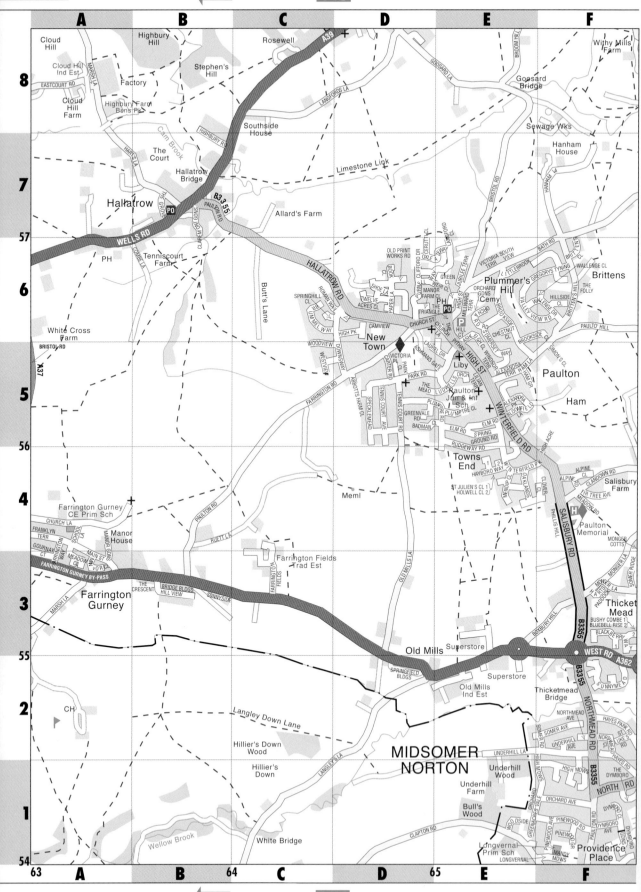

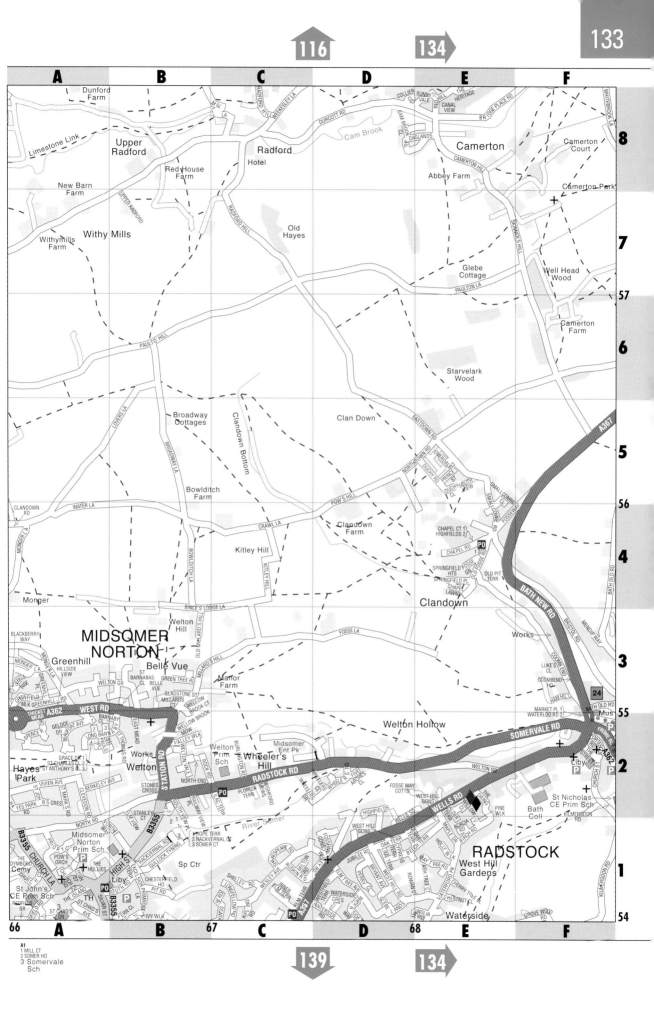

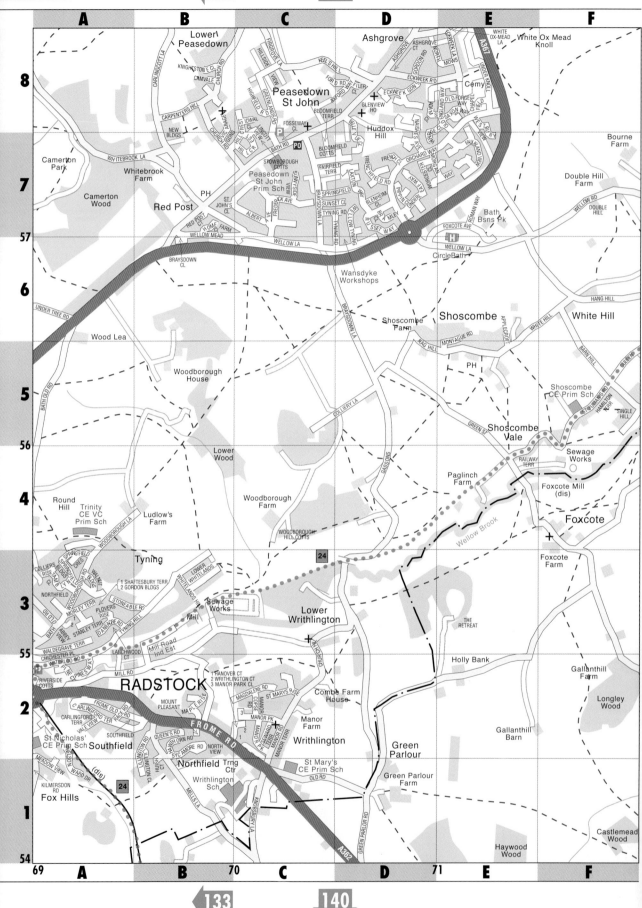

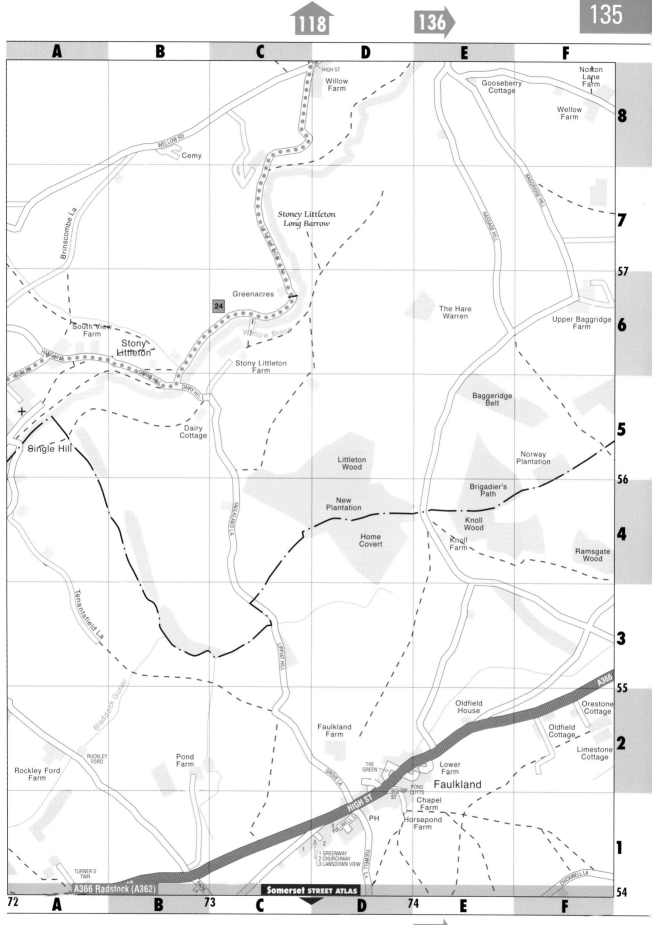

A   B   C   D   E   F

8
7
57
6
5
56
4
3
55
2
1
54

HIGH ST
Willow Farm
Norton Lane Farm
Gooseberry Cottage
Wellow Farm

WELLOW RD
Cemy

Stoney Littleton Long Barrow

BAGGRIDGE HILL

HASSAGE HILL

Brinscombe La

Greenacres
24
Wellow Brook
The Hare Warren
Upper Baggridge Farm

South View Farm
Stony Littleton
Stony Littleton Farm

Baggeridge Belt

Dairy Cottage
Littleton Wood
Norway Plantation

Single Hill

FAULKLAND LA

New Plantation
Home Covert
Brigadier's Path
Knoll Wood
Knoll Farm
Ramsgate Wood

Tenantsfield La

Bladdock Gutter

LIPPIAT HILL

A366
Oldfield House
Orestone Cottage
Oldfield Cottage
Limestone Cottage

RUCKLEY FORD
Pond Farm
Faulkland Farm
GROVE LA
THE GREEN
Lower Farm
Faulkland
Rockley Ford Farm

BISHOP ST
POND COTTS
Chapel Farm
Horsepond Farm

HIGH ST
PH
FULWELL LA
FULWELL CL
1 GREENWAY
2 CHURCHWAY
3 LANSDOWN VIEW

TURNER'S TWR
PARK LA
CHICKWELL LA

72   A   73   B   C   73   D   74   E   F

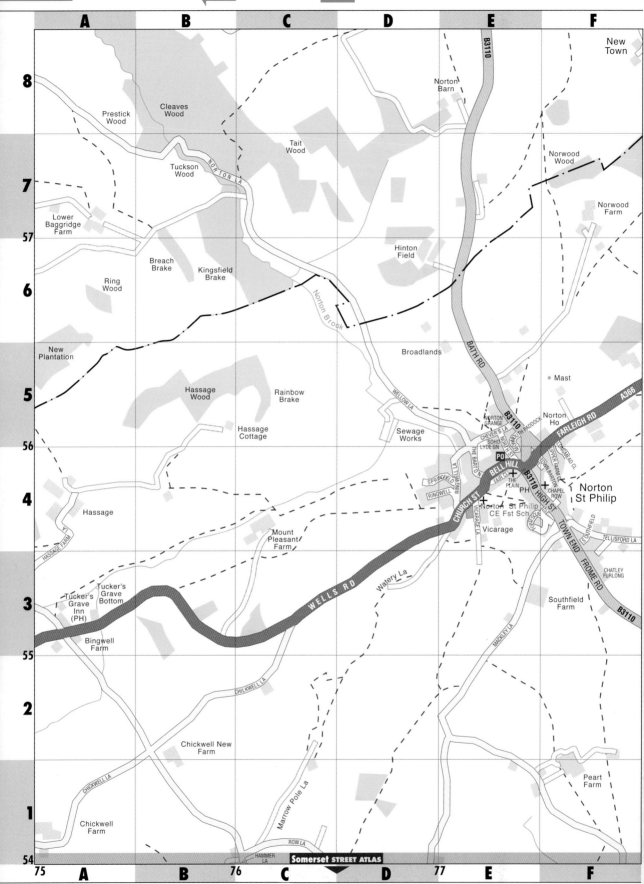

New Town

Norton Barn

Norwood Wood

Prestick Wood

Cleaves Wood

Tait Wood

Norwood Farm

Tuckson Wood

NORTON LA

Lower Baggridge Farm

Breach Brake

Kingsfield Brake

Hinton Field

Ring Wood

Norton Brook

New Plantation

Broadlands

BATH RD

Mast

Hassage Wood

Rainbow Brake

WELLOW LA

Norton Grange

B3110

Norton Ho

FARLEIGH RD

A366

Hassage Cottage

Sewage Works

CHEVER'S LA

SOHO LYDE GN

SOUTH PADDOCK

LONGMEAD CL

PO

BELL HILL

Norton St Philip

Hassage

SPRINGWELL LA

RINGWELL LA

THE BARTON

FAIR CL

THE PLAIN

B3110 HIGH ST

CHAPEL ROW

PH

RINGWELL

Norton St Philip CE Fst Sch

SOUTHFIELD

Mount Pleasant Farm

VICARAGE LA

Vicarage

TOWN END

TELLISFORD LA

HASSAGE FARM

Watery La

CHATLEY FURLONG

WELLS RD

MACKLEY LA

Southfield Farm

Tucker's Grave Inn (PH)

Tucker's Grave Bottom

FROME RD

B3110

Bingwell Farm

CHILKWELL LA

Chickwell New Farm

MARROW POLE LA

Peart Farm

CHICKWELL LA

Chickwell Farm

ROW LA

HAMMER LA

Somerset STREET ATLAS

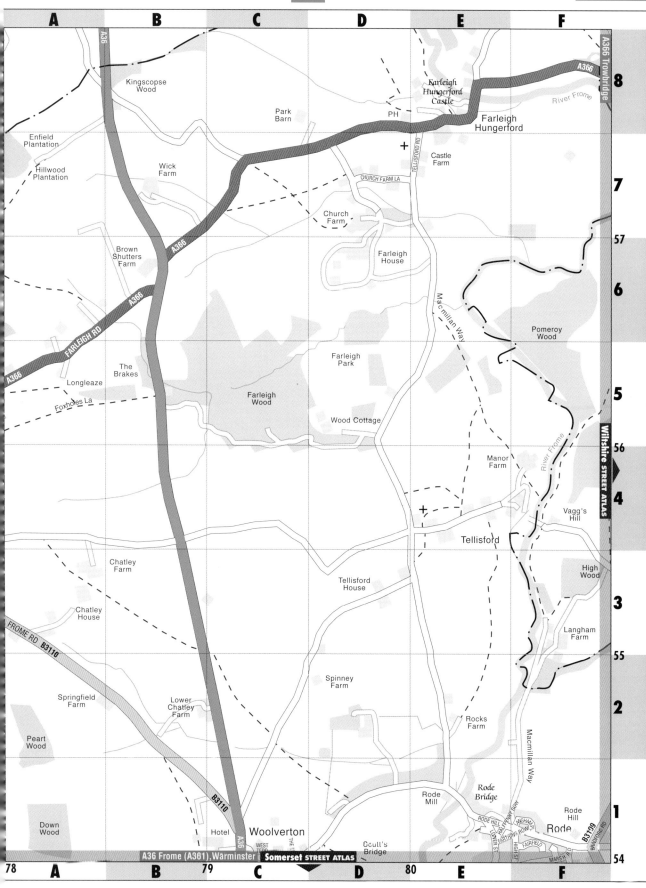

Kingscope Wood

Enfield Plantation

Hillwood Plantation

Wick Farm

Park Barn

PH

Farleigh Hungerford Castle

Farleigh Hungerford

River Frome

A366 Trowbridge

Castle Farm

CHURCH FARM LA

Church Farm

Farleigh House

Brown Shutters Farm

A366

A366

FARLEIGH RD

Macmillan Way

Pomeroy Wood

Longleaze

The Brakes

Foxholes La

Farleigh Wood

Farleigh Park

Wood Cottage

River Frome

Wiltshire STREET ATLAS

Manor Farm

Tellisford

Vagg's Hill

Chatley Farm

High Wood

Chatley House

Tellisford House

FROME RD B3110

Langham Farm

Spinney Farm

Springfield Farm

Lower Chatley Farm

Rocks Farm

Macmillan Way

Peart Wood

Down Wood

B3110

Hotel

Woolverton

WEST

THE

Scull's Bridge

Rode Mill

Rode Bridge

Rode Hill

Rode

RODE HILL

HALFPENNY ROW

FAIRFIELD

LOWER ST

HIGH ST

LANGHAM PL

MARSH RD

B3109

BRADFORD RD

A36

A366

57

56

55

54

8

7

6

5

4

3

2

1

78 A B 79 C D 80 E F

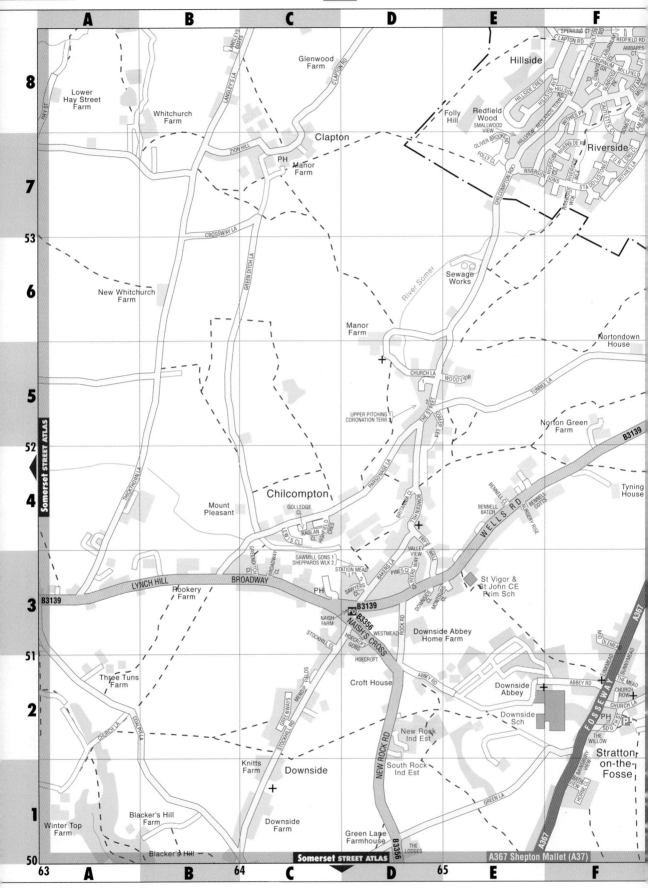

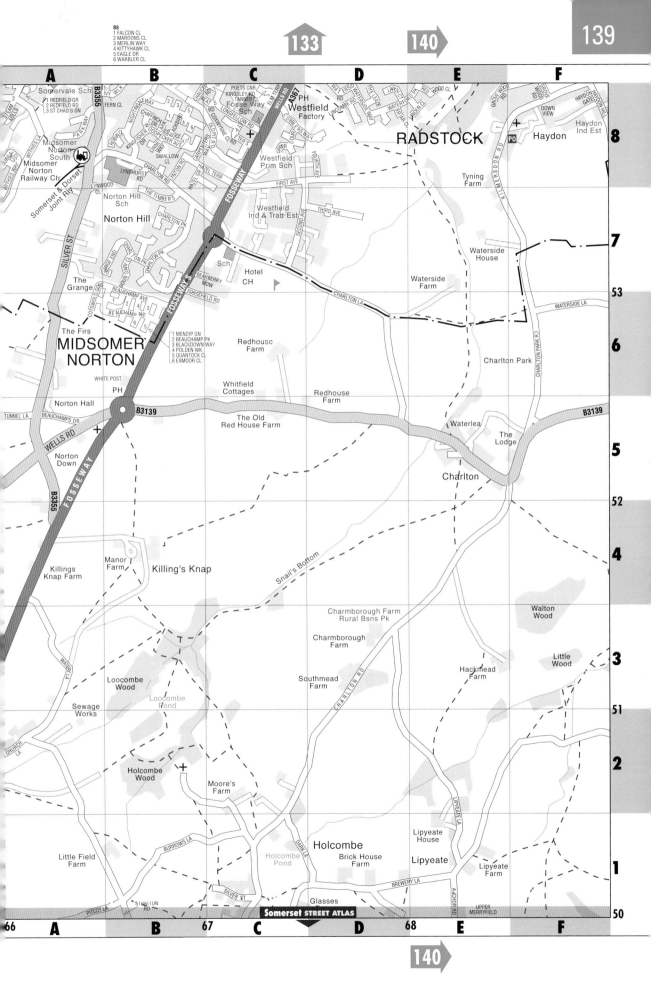

B8
1 FALCON CL
2 MARDONS CL
3 MERLIN WAY
4 KITTYHAWK CL
5 EAGLE DR
6 WARBLER CL

A   B   C   D   E   F

Somervale Sch

1 REDFIELD GR
2 REDFIELD RD
3 ST CHAD'S GN

FERN CL
B3355
SILVER ST
PARKWAY
WITHIES LA
STEAM MILLS
JUBILEE WAY
WITHIES WAY

NIGHTINGALE WAY
CHAFFINCH DR
WREN CL
WOODPECKER AVE
ROBIN CL
KINGFISHER WAY
SWALLOW CL

CHALICE WAY
CHARLTON RYNTON RD

POETS CNR
KINGSLEY RD
Fosse Way Sch
LONGFELLOW RD

WELLS RD
A367
PH
Westfield
Factory

RADSTOCK

WAY RD
UNCOMBE RD
WATERSIDE WAY
THE LEAZE
LARK CT
WATERFORD PK
RED WOOD CL
GROVE WOOD RD
GROVE WOOD RD

DOWN VIEW
HAYDON GATE
HAYDON HILL

Haydon
KILMERSDON RD
PO
Haydon Ind Est

Midsomer Norton South
Midsomer Norton Railway Ctr

Somerset & Dorset Joint Rly

LYNWOOD CL
LYNDHURST RD
THE TIMBERS
Norton Hill Sch
CHARLTON PK

Norton Hill

GRANGE END

The Grange

Sch
BEARBERRY MDW
Hotel
CH
FOSSEFIELD RD

Upper FIRST AVE

Westfield Prim Sch
Westfield Ind & Trad Est
SECOND AVE
THIRD AVE
FOURTH AVE

Tyning Farm

Waterside House

53

The Firs

BEAUCHAMP AVE
BEAUCHAMP AVE

MIDSOMER NORTON

1 MENDIP GN
2 BEAUCHAMP PK
3 BLACKDOWN WAY
4 POLDEN WK
5 QUANTOCK CL
6 EXMOOR CL

Redhouse Farm

Whitfield Cottages

Redhouse Farm

CHARLTON LA
Waterside Farm

WATERSIDE LA

Charlton Park

CHARLTON PARK RD

7

6

WHITE POST
PH

Norton Hall
BEAUCHAMPS DR
TUNNEL LA
WELLS RD

B3139

The Old Red House Farm

Waterlea
The Lodge

B3139

Norton Down
B3355
FOSSEWAY

Charlton

5

52

Killings Knap Farm

Manor Farm

Killing's Knap

Snail's Bottom

Walton Wood

4

WATER LA

Loocombe Wood
Loocombe Pond

Charmborough Farm Rural Bsns Pk

Charmborough Farm

Hackmead Farm

Little Wood

3

Sewage Works

Southmead Farm

CHARLTON RD

51

CHURCH LA

Holcombe Wood

Moore's Farm

2

BURROWS LA

Holcombe Pond

DARK LA

Holcombe

Brick House Farm

Lipyeate House

Lipyeate

LIPYEATE LA

Lipyeate Farm

Little Field Farm

SILVER ST

Glasses

BREWERY LA

A367 RD

UPPER MERRYFIELD

1

STRATTON RD
PITCOT LA

50

66   A   67   B   C   68   D   E   F

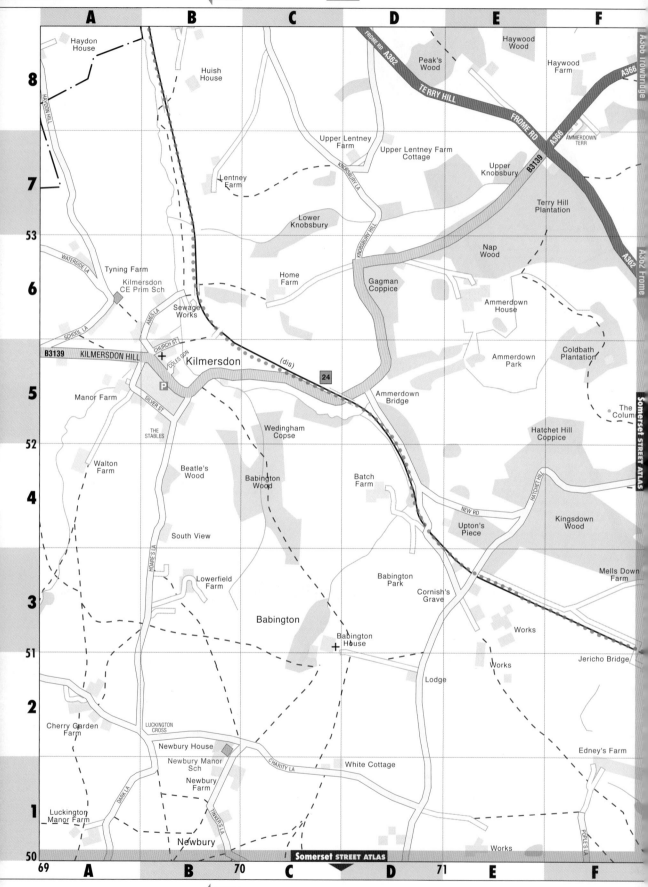

A B C D E F

8
Haydon House
Huish House
Haywood Wood
Peak's Wood
Haywood Farm
HAYDON HILL
A362
FROME RD
TERRY HILL
A366
A3o5 Trowbridge
AMMERDOWN TERR

7
Upper Lentney Farm
Upper Lentney Farm Cottage
Upper Knobsbury
KNOBSBURY LA
B3139
A366
Lentney Farm

53
Lower Knobsbury
Terry Hill Plantation
WATERSIDE LA
KNOBSBURY HILL
A362 Frome

6
Tyning Farm
Kilmersdon CE Prim Sch
Home Farm
Gagman Coppice
Nap Wood
Ammerdown House
SCHOOL LA
AMS LA
Sewage Works
CHURCH ST

5
B3139 KILMERSDON HILL
Kilmersdon
(dis)
24
Ammerdown Bridge
Ammerdown Park
Coldbath Plantation
The Colum
Manor Farm
SILVER ST
COLES GDN
THE STABLES
P
Somerset STREET ATLAS

52
Wedingham Copse
Hatchet Hill Coppice

4
Walton Farm
Beatle's Wood
Babington Wood
Batch Farm
New Rd
Upton's Piece
Kingsdown Wood
HATCHET HILL
HOARE'S LA
South View
Mells Down Farm

3
Lowerfield Farm
Babington Park
Cornish's Grave
Works
Jericho Bridge
Babington

51
Babington House
Works
Lodge
Works

2
Cherry Garden Farm
LUCKINGTON CROSS
DARK LA
Edney's Farm

1
Luckington Manor Farm
Newbury House
Newbury Manor Sch
Newbury Farm
CHARITY LA
White Cottage
TINKER'S LA
POPE'S LA

50
Newbury
Somerset STREET ATLAS
Works

69 A B 70 C D 71 E F

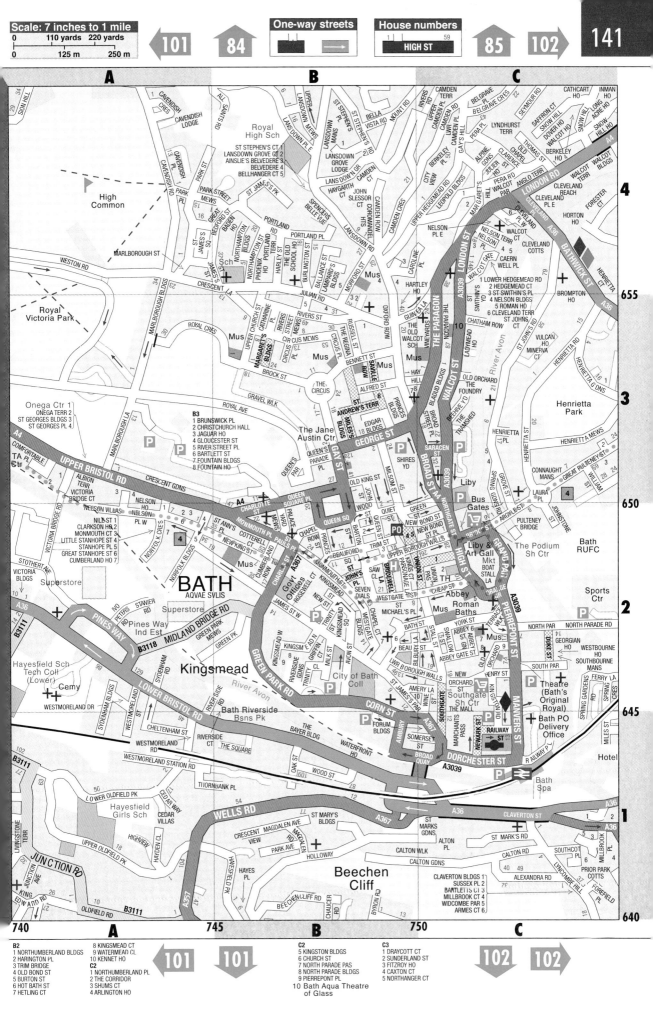

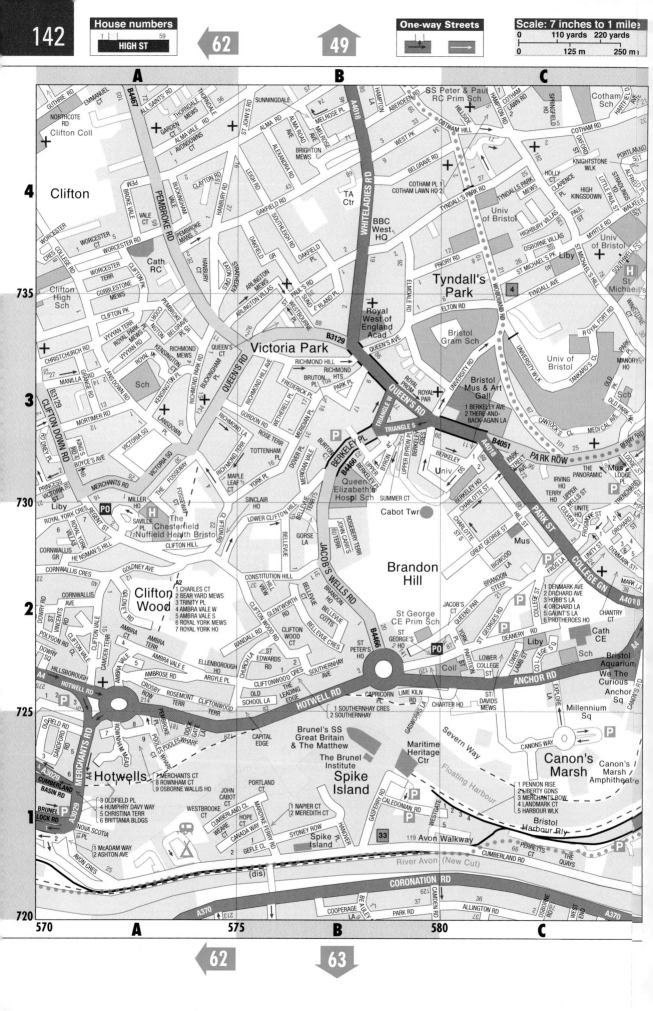

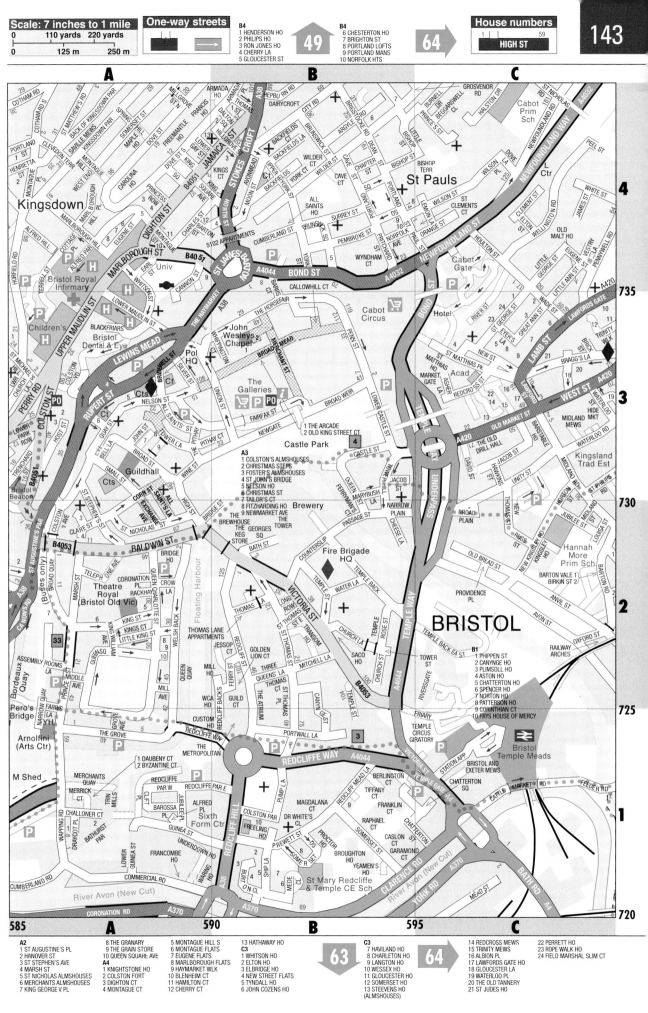

Index

Place name May be abbreviated on the map ○——→ **Church Rd** **6** Beckenham BR2.....**53** C6

Location number Present when a number indicates the place's position in a crowded area of mapping ○

Locality, town or village Shown when more than one place has the same name ○

Postcode district District for the indexed place ○

Page and grid square Page number and grid reference for the standard mapping ○

Cities, towns and villages are listed in CAPITAL LETTERS

Public and commercial buildings are highlighted in magenta   **Places of interest** are highlighted in blue with a star★

Abbreviations used in the index

Acad	**Academy**	Comm	**Common**	Gd	**Ground**	L	**Leisure**	Prom	**Promenade**
App	**Approach**	Cott	**Cottage**	Gdn	**Garden**	La	**Lane**	Rd	**Road**
Arc	**Arcade**	Cres	**Crescent**	Gn	**Green**	Liby	**Library**	Recn	**Recreation**
Ave	**Avenue**	Cswy	**Causeway**	Gr	**Grove**	Mdw	**Meadow**	Ret	**Retail**
Bglw	**Bungalow**	Ct	**Court**	H	**Hall**	Meml	**Memorial**	Sh	**Shopping**
Bldg	**Building**	Ctr	**Centre**	Ho	**House**	Mkt	**Market**	Sq	**Square**
Bsns, Bus	**Business**	Ctry	**Country**	Hospl	**Hospital**	Mus	**Museum**	St	**Street**
Bvd	**Boulevard**	Cty	**County**	HQ	**Headquarters**	Orch	**Orchard**	Sta	**Station**
Cath	**Cathedral**	Dr	**Drive**	Hts	**Heights**	Pal	**Palace**	Terr	**Terrace**
Cir	**Circus**	Dro	**Drove**	Ind	**Industrial**	Par	**Parade**	TH	**Town Hall**
Cl	**Close**	Ed	**Education**	Inst	**Institute**	Pas	**Passage**	Univ	**University**
Cnr	**Corner**	Emb	**Embankment**	Int	**International**	Pk	**Park**	Wk, Wlk	**Walk**
Coll	**College**	Est	**Estate**	Intc	**Interchange**	Pl	**Place**	Wr	**Water**
Com	**Community**	Ex	**Exhibition**	Junc	**Junction**	Prec	**Precinct**	Yd	**Yard**

Index of towns, villages, streets, hospitals, industrial estates, railway stations, schools, shopping centres, universities and places of interest

510–Ale

5102 Apartments BS1 143 B4

A

Abbey Church Yd **10**
  BA1 . . . . .141 C2
Abbey Cl BS31 . . . . 81 F6
Abbey Ct
  Bath BA2 . . . . .102 B7
  Bristol BS4 . . . . 64 F5
Abbeydale BS36 . . . . 37 E6
Abbeyfield Ho BS37 . . 28 C1
Abbey Gate St BA1 . .141 C2
Abbey Gdns BS22 . . . . .105 E8
Abbey Gn BA1 . . . . .141 C2
Abbey Ho **5** BS37 . . . . . . .39 D7
Abbey La
  Hinton Charterhouse
    BA2 . . . . .120 A4
  Thornbury BS35 . . . . . . .15 D6
Abbey Mews GL12 . . . . . 11 F4
Abbey Pk BS31 . . . . 81 F6
Abbey Rd
  Bristol BS9 . . . . .48 F7
  Chilcompton BA3 . . . . .138 D2
  Stratton-on-t-F BA3 . . . .138 F2
Abbey St
  Bath BA1 . . . . .141 C2
  Kingswood GL12 . . . . 11 F5
Abbey View
  Bath BA2 . . . . .102 B5
  Radstock BA3 . . . . .134 A3
Abbey View Gdns BA2 .102 B5
Abbeywood Dr BS9 . . .48 C5
Abbeywood Pk BS34 . .36 C2
Abbey Wood Ret Pk
  BS34 . . . . .36 C2
Abbot Alphege Acad
  BATH BA1 . . . . .84 E4
  Charlcombe BA1 . . . . . .84 D4
Abbots Ave BS15 . . . . . .65 C6
Abbotsbury Rd BS48 . .59 D1
Abbots Cl BS14 . . . . . .80 A3
Abbot's Cl BS22 . . . . . .89 A3
Abbotsford Rd BS6 . . . .49 B1

Abbots Horn BS48 . . . . .59 D2
ABBOTSIDE 9 F2
ABBOTS LEIGH 62 A8
Abbots Leigh Rd BS8 . .62 C7
Abbots Rd BS15 . . . . . . .65 C2
Abbots Way
  Bristol BS9 . . . . .49 E6
  Longwell Green BS30 . . . .65 F2
Abbotswood
  Bristol BS15 . . . . .65 D7
  Yate BS37 . . . . .39 D7
Abbotswood Cl BS31 . .81 D3
Abbotswood Prim Sch
  BS37 . . . . .39 D6
Abbott Rd BS35 . . . . 22 A5
Abbotts Farm Cl BS39 132 D5
Aberdeen Rd BS6 . . . . .142 B4
Abingdon Gdns BA2 . .118 D8
Abingdon Rd BS16 . . . . . 51 A3
Ableton Ct BS35 . . . . . . 22 A6
Ableton La
  Hallen BS10 . . . . .34 A8
  Severn Beach BS35 . . . .22 A5
Ableton Wlk BS9 . . . . . . 48 C5
Abon Ho BS9 . . . . .48 C4
Abraham Cl BS5 . . . . . . .64 B8
Abraham Fry Ho BS15 . .65 E7
Abrahams Cl BS4 . . . . . .79 F7
ABSON 53 D2
Abson Rd
  Pucklechurch BS16 . . . . .53 C3
  Wick BS30 . . . . .67 C8
Acacia Ave
  Bristol BS16 . . . . .51 D4
  Weston-s-M BS23 . . . . .105 B8
Acacia Cl BS16 . . . . 51 D3
Acacia Ct BS31 . . . . .81 C4
Acacia Gr BA2 . . . . .101 C3
Acacia Mews **5** BS16 . .51 D4
Acacia Rd
  Bristol BS16 . . . . .51 D4
  Radstock BA3 . . . . .133 E1
Access 18 BS11 . . . . . . .33 D3
Accommodation Rd
  BS24 . . . . .121 E6
Acer Cres BS32 . . . . 24 E5
Acer Village BS14 . . . . .80 C7
Aconite Cl BS22 . . . . . . .89 B5
Acorn Dr BS16 . . . . .52 C8

Acorn Gr BS13 . . . . 78 E6
Acorns The BS37 . . . . 27 B5
Acraman's Rd **7** BS3 . . 63 C4
Acresbush Cl BS13 . . . . .79 A5
Acton Rd BS16 . . . . .51 A3
ACTON TURVILLE 42 F6
Acton Turville Rd GL9 . . 42 B4
Adams Cl BA2 . . . . .134 D8
Adams Ct **5** BS8 . . . . . . 62 F6
Adams Hay **6** BS4 . . . . .64 D1
Adams Land BS36 . . . . . .38 C7
Adastral Rd BS24 . . . . .106 D4
Adderly Gate BS16 . . . . . 52 B7
Addicott Rd BS23 . . . . .104 E6
Addiscombe Rd
  Bristol BS14 . . . . .80 B5
  Weston-s-M BS23 . . . . .104 E4
Addison Rd BS3 . . . . .63 E3
Adelaide Pl
  Bristol, Fishponds BS16 . .50 F4
  12 Bristol, Upper Easton
    BS5 . . . . .64 B8
Adelaide Terr **1** BS16 . .51 A4
Adelante Cl BS34 . . . . . .37 A4
Admiral Cl BS16 . . . . . . .50 E7
Admiral's Wlk BS20 . . . . 45 B5
Adryan Ct **6** BS5 . . . . . .64 C7
Aelfric Mdw BS20 . . . . . 45 F4
Aesop Dr BS31 . . . . .81 C3
Agate St BS3 . . . . .63 B3
Aiken St BS5 . . . . .64 B6
Ainslie's Belvedere
  BA1 . . . . .141 B4
Aintree Dr BS16 . . . . 37 F1
Air Balloon Ct **1** BS5 . .65 A7
Air Balloon Hill Jun & Inf
  Schs BS5 . . . . .65 A7
Air Balloon Rd BS5 . . . .65 A7
Airoh End BS24 . . . . . . .105 B4
Airport Rd BS14 . . . . . . .80 A8
Airport Rdbt BS24 . . . . .105 E7
Airport View Cvn Pk
  BS24 . . . . .105 D7
Aisecome Way BS22 . . .105 C6
Akeman Way BS11 . . . . . 47 C8
Alanscourt BS30 . . . . . . .66 B5
Alard Rd BS4 . . . . .79 F7
Albany BS23 . . . . .87 F1
Albany Ct **6** BA1 . . . . .101 B6

Albany Gate BS34 . . . . . . 36 E5
Albany Rd
  Bath BA2 . . . . .101 C6
  Bristol BS6 . . . . .49 F1
Albany St BS15 . . . . .65 C8
Albany Way BS30 . . . . . .66 C5
Albemarle Row **10** BS8 62 F6
Albemarle Terr **7** BS8. 62 F6
Albert Ave
  Peasedown St John
    BA2 . . . . .134 C7
  Weston-s-M BS23 . . . . .104 E6
Albert Cres BS2 . . . . 64 B5
Albert Ct BS23 . . . . .104 E6
Albert Gr BS5 . . . . 64 F8
Albert Gr S BS5 . . . . .64 F8
Albert Ho BS1 . . . . .143 B2
Alberton Rd BS16 . . . . . .50 F6
Albert Par BS5 . . . . .64 D8
Albert Park Pl BS6 . . . . .49 F1
Albert Pk BS6 . . . . .49 F1
Albert Pl
  Bath BA2 . . . . .102 C1
  1 Bristol, Bedminster
    BS3 . . . . .63 C3
  Bristol, Eastfield BS9 . . .49 A7
  Portishead BS20 . . . . . .45 D4
Albert Quadrant BS23 .104 E8
Albert Rd
  Bristol, Hanham BS15 . .65 D5
  Bristol, St Philip's Marsh
    BS2 . . . . .64 A4
  Bristol, Staple Hill BS16 . 51 E4
  Clevedon BS21 . . . . .57 E3
  Keynsham BS31 . . . . 81 E5
  Portishead BS20 . . . . . .45 D5
  Severn Beach BS35 . . . .22 A6
  Weston-s-M BS23 . . . . .104 E6
Albert St BS5 . . . . 64 C8
Albert Terr
  Bath BA2 . . . . .101 C6
  Bristol BS16 . . . . .50 F4
Albion Bldgs BA1 . . . . .101 D7
Albion Cl BS16 . . . . 51 F5
Albion Pl
  Bath BA1 . . . . .141 A3
  16 Bristol BS2 . . . . . . .143 C3
Albion Rd BS5 . . . . 50 B1
Albion St **6** BS5 . . . . . .64 C8

Albion Terr
  Bath BA1 . . . . .141 A3
  Bristol BS34 . . . . .24 B1
Alburys BS40 . . . . 92 D3
Alcina Way BS31 . . . . . . .81 C2
ALCOMBE 86 F7
Alcove Rd BS16 . . . . .50 F3
Alden Ho BS36 . . . . .37 D4
Aldercombe Rd BS9 . . . .48 C8
Alder Ct BS14 . . . . .80 B5
Alderdown Cl BS11 . . . . .48 A8
Alder Dr BS5 . . . . 50 E1
Alderley Rd BA2 . . . . . .101 B4
Aldermoor Way BS30 . .65 E4
Alderney Ave BS4 . . . . . .64 F4
Alders The BS16 . . . . 37 B1
Alder Terr BA3 . . . . .133 E2
ALDERTON 31 F2
Alderton Rd
  Bristol BS7 . . . . .49 E8
  Burton SN14 . . . . .43 D6
Alder Way BA2 . . . . .118 D8
ALDWICK 110 D7
Aldwick Ave BS13 . . . . . .79 C3
Aldwick La BS40 . . . . . . .110 C7
Alec Ricketts Cl BA2 . .100 F5
Alexander Bldgs **12**
  BA1 . . . . .85 B1
Alexander Ct **4** BS3 . . .63 A2
Alexander Hall BA2 . . .120 C6
Alexander Ho **5** BS23 104 F4
Alexander Hosea Prim Sch
  GL12 . . . . .18 B5
Alexander Mews **5**
  BS23 . . . . .104 E7
Alexander Pl BA2 . . . . .120 C6
Alexander Rd BS31 . . . . .81 C2
Alexander Way BS49 . . .91 B7
Alexandra Apartments
  BS6 . . . . .49 C2
Alexandra Cl BS16 . . . . . 51 D4
Alexandra Ct
  Bristol BS16 . . . . .50 F4
  Clevedon BS21 . . . . .57 E4
Alexandra Gate BS8 . . .142 B4
Alexandra Gdns BS16 . . 51 D4
Alexandra Par BS23 . . .104 E7
Alexandra Pk
  Bristol, Cotham BS6 . . . .49 C2

Ale–Ave 145

Alexandra Pk *continued*
Bristol, Ridgeway BS16 .. 50 F4
Paulton BS39 .... 132 E5
Alexandra Pl
Bath BA2 .... 102 C1
Bristol BS16 .... 51 D4
Alexandra Rd
Bath BA2 .... 141 C1
Bristol BS8 .... 142 B4
Bristol, Eastfield BS10 .. 49 C8
Bristol, Hanham BS15 ... 65 D5
Bristol, Highridge BS13 .. 78 F7
Clevedon BS21 .... 57 E4
Frampton Cotterell BS36 38 D7
Alexandra Terr BS39 .. 132 E5
Alexandra Way BS35 .... 8 B3
Alford Rd BS4 .... 64 C2
Alfred Ct 4 BS23 ..... 104 E7
Alfred Hill BS2 .... 143 A4
Alfred Lovell Gdns 7
BS30 .... 66 A4
Alfred Par BS2 .... 143 A4
Alfred Pl BS2 .... 142 C4
Alfred Rd
Bristol, Westbury Park
BS6 .... 49 A4
Bristol, Windmill Hill BS3 63 D3
Alfred St
Bath BA1 .... 141 B3
Bristol, Moorfields BS5 .. 64 D8
Bristol, Newton BS2 .... 64 A6
Weston-s-M BS23 ..... 104 E8
Algars Dr BS37 .... 26 E3
Algiers St BS3 .... 63 D3
Alison Gdns BS48 ...... 76 A7
Allanmead Rd BS14 .... 80 B8
Allans Way BS24 ...... 105 F7
Allengrove La SN14 .... 31 C3
Allens La BS25 .... 125 F8
Aller BS24 .... 105 B2
Aller Par BS24 .... 105 B2
Allerton Cres BS14 .... 80 B4
Allerton Gdns BS14 .... 80 B5
Allerton Rd BS14 ...... 80 B4
Allfoxton Rd BS7 ...... 50 A3
All Hallows Ct 11 BS5 .. 64 B8
All Hallows Rd BS5 ..... 64 B8
Allington Dr BS30 ..... 65 F4
Allington Gdns BS48 ... 75 C8
Allington Rd BS3 ..... 142 C1
Allison Ave BS4 .... 64 E4
Allison Rd BS4 .... 64 E3
Allotment La
Keynsham BS31 .... 81 B2
Keynsham BS31 .... 81 B2
All Saints Cl BS30 ..... 66 A3
All Saints' Ct BS1 .... 143 A3
All Saints East Clevedon
CE Prim Sch BS21 .... 57 H4
All Saints Ho BS2 ..... 143 B4
All Saints La BS21 ..... 57 H4
All Saints' La BS1 .... 143 A2
All Saints Pl BA2 ..... 102 E4
All Saints Rd BA1 ..... 141 B4
All Saints' Rd
Bristol BS8 .... 142 A4
Weston-s-M BS23 ...... 87 E1
All Saints' St BS1 .... 143 A3
Alma Cl BS15 .... 65 E8
Alma Ct BS8 .... 49 B1
Alma Rd
Bristol BS8 .... 142 B4
Bristol, Kingswood BS15 51 E1
Alma Road Ave BS8 ... 142 B4
Alma St
Bristol BS8 .... 49 B1
Weston-s-M BS23 ..... 104 E7
Alma Vale Rd BS8 ..... 142 A4
Almeda Rd BS5 .... 65 A6
Almond Cl BS22 .... 89 A1
ALMONDSBURY 24 B5
Almondsbury Bsns Ctr
BS32 .... 24 D3
Almondsbury CE Prim Sch
BS32 .... 24 A4
Almondsbury Intc BS32. 24 E4
Almond Way BS16 ...... 51 F5
Almorah Rd BS3 .... 63 E3
Almshouses SN14 ...... 69 E8
Alonzo Pl BS21 .... 57 F4
Alpha Ctr The BS37 .... 27 C3
Alpha Rd BS3 .... 63 D4
Alpine Cl BS39 .... 132 F4
Alpine Gdns BA1 ...... 141 C4
Alpine Rd
Bristol BS5 .... 50 C1
Paulton BS39 .... 132 F4
Alsop Rd 4 BS15 .... 51 D1
Alton Pl BA2 .... 141 C1
Alton Rd BS7 .... 49 F5
Altringham Rd BS5 ..... 64 D8
Alverstoke BS14 .... 79 F7
ALVESTON 15 B4
ALVESTON DOWN 14 F5
Alveston Hill BS35 ..... 15 A6
Alveston Rd BS32 ...... 14 D3
Alveston Wlk BS9 ...... 48 B7
Alwins Ct 2 BS30 ...... 65 F4
Ambares Ct BA3 ...... 138 F8
Amberey Rd BS23 ..... 104 F5
Amberlands Cl BS48 ... 76 A7
Amberley Cl
Bristol BS16 .... 51 D7
Keynsham BS31 .... 81 E4
Amberley Gdns 3
BS48 .... 59 D1
Amberley House Sch
BS8 .... 49 A1
Amberley Rd
Bristol, Kingswood
BS16 .... 51 D7
Bristol, Patchway BS34 .. 36 B8
Amberley Way GL12 .... 18 B4
Amble Cl BS15 .... 65 F7
Ambleside Ave BS10 ... 35 B2
Ambleside Rd BA2 .... 101 C2
Ambra Ct BS8 .... 142 A2
Ambra Terr BS8 ...... 142 A2
Ambra Vale BS8 ...... 142 A2
Ambra Vale E BS8 .... 142 A2
Ambra Vale S 5 BS8 .. 142 A2
Ambra Vale W 4 BS8 .. 142 A2
Ambrose Rd BS8 ...... 142 A2
Ambury BA1 .... 141 B1
Amercombe Wlk BS14 .. 80 D7
American Mus in Britain*
BA2 .... 103 A5
Amery La BA1 .... 141 C2
AMESBURY 115 F2
Amesbury Dr BS24 .... 122 B6
Ames La BA3 .... 140 B6
Ammerdown Terr BA3 140 F7
Anchor Cl BS5 .... 64 F6
Anchor Ho BS4 .... 64 B2
Anchor La BA2 .... 118 D5
Anchor Rd
Bath BA1 .... 84 B1
Bristol BS1 .... 142 C2
Bristol, Kingswood BS15 52 A2
Anchor Way BS20 ...... 47 D4
Ancliff Sq BA15 ...... 120 E4
Andalusia Acad BS2 .. 143 C4
Andereach Cl BS14 ..... 80 B8
Andover Rd BS4 .... 63 F2
Andrew Millman Ct
BS37 .... 27 F1
Andruss Dr BS41 ...... 78 D2
Angels Gd BS4 .... 64 F6
Angers Rd BS4 .... 64 A4
Anglesea Pl 15 BS8 .... 49 A2
Anglo Terr BA1 .... 141 C4
Animal Farm Adventure
Pk* TA8 .... 121 B2
Ankatel Cl BS23 ...... 105 A5
Annandale Ave BS22 ... 88 E1
Annie Scott Cl 2 BS16 . 51 A4
Anson Cl BS31 .... 82 D2
Anson Rd
Locking BS24 .... 106 B6
Weston-s-M BS22 ...... 88 D4
Anstey Rd BS37 .... 27 D6
Ansteys Cl BS15 .... 65 B5
Anstey's Ct BS15 ...... 65 C5
Anstey's Rd BS15 ...... 65 C5
Anstey St BS5 .... 50 B1
Anthea Rd BS5 .... 50 E2
Antona Ct BS11 .... 47 D7
Antona Dr BS11 .... 47 D7
Antrim Rd BS9 .... 49 B6
Anvil Rd BS49 .... 74 F1
Anvil St BS2 .... 143 C2
Apex Ct BS32 .... 24 D3
Apollo Pk BS37 .... 27 C3
Apperley Cl BS37 ...... 39 E8
Appleby Wlk BS4 ...... 79 D7
Applecroft BA2 ...... 134 E6
Appledore 4 BS22 ..... 88 F2
Appledore Cl BS14 .... 80 B8
Apple Farm La BS24 .... 89 C1
Applegate BS10 .... 35 B3
Appleridge La GL13 ..... 3 C4
Appletree Ct BS22 ..... 89 B2
Apple Tree Dr BS25 ... 125 A8
Appletree Mews BS22 .. 89 B2
Applin Gn BS16 .... 52 C6
Appsley Cl BS22 ...... 88 C1
Apseleys Mead BS32 ... 24 C2
Apsley Cl BA1 .... 101 B7
Apsley Garden Apartments
BS6 .... 49 E2
Apsley Mews BS8 ...... 49 A2
Apsley Rd
Bath BA1 .... 101 A7
Bristol BS8 .... 49 A1
Apsley St BS5 .... 50 C3
Arbutus Dr BS9 .... 48 C8
Arbutus Wlk BS9 ...... 34 D1
Arcade The BS1 ...... 143 B3
Arcadius Way BS31 .... 81 F8
Arch Cl BS41 .... 61 F1
Archer Ct
Bristol BS30 .... 65 F3
Clevedon BS21 .... 57 F4
Archer Wlk BS14 ...... 80 E6
Arches The
Bath BA2 .... 101 A6
1 Bristol BS5 .... 64 B7
Archfield Ct BS6 ...... 49 C1
Archfield Rd BS6 ...... 49 C1
Archgrove BS41 .... 61 F1
Archway St BA2 ...... 102 B5
Ardagh Ct BS7 .... 49 F7
Arden Cl
Bristol BS32 .... 36 E6
Weston-s-M BS22 ...... 88 F3
Ardenton Wlk BS10 .... 35 A3
Ardern Cl BS9 .... 48 B8
Ardmore BS8 .... 62 D7
Argus Ct 4 BS3 .... 63 C2
Argus Rd BS3 .... 63 C3
Argyle Ave
Bristol BS5 .... 50 C2
Weston-s-M BS23 ..... 104 F4
Argyle Dr BS37 .... 27 E4
Argyle Pl BS8 .... 142 A2
Argyle Rd
Bristol BS2 .... 143 B4
Bristol, Chester Park
BS16 .... 51 B2
Clevedon BS21 .... 57 F6
Argyle St
Bath BA2 .... 141 C2
5 Bristol, Eastville BS5 . 50 C2
6 Bristol, Southville BS3 63 C4
Argyle Terr BA2 ...... 101 C6
Arkells Ct GL12 .... 18 A6
Arley Cotts 5 BS6 ..... 49 D1
Arley Ct 4 BS6 .... 49 D1
Arley Hill BS6 .... 49 D1
Arley Pk BS6 .... 49 D1
Arley Terr BS5 .... 50 E1
Arlingham Way BS34 ... 23 F1
Arlington Ho 4 BA1 .. 141 C2
Arlington Mans BS8 ... 142 B4
Arlington Rd
4 Bath BA2 .... 101 D5
Bristol BS4 .... 64 D5
Arlington Villas BS8 .. 142 B3
Armada Ho BS2 .... 143 A4
Armada Pl BS1 .... 143 B4
Armes Ct BA2 .... 141 C1
Armidale Ave 4 BS6 ... 49 E1
Armidale Cotts 5 BS6 . 49 E1
Armoury Sq BS5 .... 64 A8
Armstrong Cl BS35 .... 15 D7
Armstrong Ct BS37 .... 27 C3
Armstrong Dr BS30 .... 66 B5
Armstrong Way BS37 ... 27 B3
Arnall Dr BS10 .... 34 F1
Arncliffe BS10 .... 49 C8
Arneside Rd BS10 ..... 35 C1
Arnold Ct BS37 .... 28 B1
Arnold Rd BS16 .... 52 B3
Arnolds Field Trad Est
GL12 .... 18 A5
Arnold's Way BS49 .... 74 A2
Arnolfini (Arts Ctr)*
BS1 .... 143 A1
Arnor Cl BS22 .... 89 A4
Arno's St BS4 .... 64 A3
ARNO'S VALE 64 B4
Arrowfield Cl BS14 .... 80 A2
Artemesia Ave BS22 .. 105 E8
Arthur Ball Way BS10 .. 21 F2
Arthurs Cl BS16 .... 52 C6
Arthur Skemp Cl BS5 ... 64 B7
Arthur St
7 Bristol, Moorfields
BS5 .... 64 C8
Bristol, St Philip's Marsh
BS2 .... 64 A5
Arthurswood Rd BS13 .. 79 A4
Arundel Cl BS13 .... 79 B5
Arundel Ct BS7 .... 49 D3
Arundell Ct BS23 ..... 104 E8
Arundell Rd BS23 ...... 87 E1
Arundel Rd
Bath BA1 .... 85 A1
Bristol BS7 .... 49 D3
Clevedon BS21 .... 57 F3
Arundel Wlk BS31 ...... 81 D5
Ascension Ho BA2 .... 101 D4
Ascot Cl BS16 .... 37 F1
Ascot Rd BS10 .... 35 E2
Ashbourne Cl 1 BS30 .. 66 C6
Ash Brook BS39 ...... 115 D1
Ashbrooke House Sch
BS23 .... 104 D6
Ashburton Rd BS10 .... 35 C1
Ashbury Dr BS22 ...... 88 B2
Ash Cl
Bristol, Hillfields BS16 .. 51 C3
Bristol, Little Stoke BS34 36 D7
Weston-s-M BS22 ...... 89 D2
Winscombe BS25 ..... 108 A1
Yate BS37 .... 27 D3
Ashcombe Cres BS30 .. 66 D6
Ashcombe Ct 1 BS23 . 104 F7
Ashcombe Gdns BS23 . 105 A8
Ashcombe Park Rd
BS23 .... 88 A1
Ashcombe Pl 4 BS23 . 104 F7
Ashcombe Prim Sch
BS23 .... 105 A7
Ashcombe Rd BS23 ... 104 F7
Ashcott BS14 .... 79 F7
Ashcroft BS24 .... 105 B2
Ashcroft Ave BS31 ..... 81 D5
Ashcroft Rd BS9 .... 48 C7
Ash Ct BS14 .... 80 A6
Ashdene Ave BS5 ...... 50 D3
Ashdene Rd BS23 .... 105 A8
Ashdown Ct BS9 .... 48 F8
Ashdown Rd BS20 ...... 45 A6
Asher La BS2 .... 143 C3
Ashes La BA2 .... 120 A4
Ashey La BS40 ...... 110 A5
Ashfield Pl BS6 .... 49 F1
Ashfield Rd BS3 ...... 63 B3
Ashfield Terr 9 BS3 ... 63 B3
Ashford Dr BS24 ..... 105 A1
Ashford Rd
Bath BA2 .... 101 D4
Bristol BS34 .... 36 A7
Redhill BS40 .... 93 E4
Ashford Way BS15 ..... 66 A7
Ash Gr
Bath BA2 .... 101 C4
Bristol BS16 .... 51 D3
Clevedon BS21 .... 57 G4
Weston-s-M BS23 ..... 104 E2
ASHGROVE 134 D8
Ashgrove
Peasedown St John
BA2 .... 134 D8
Thornbury BS35 .... 8 C1
Ashgrove Ave
Abbots Leigh BS8 ...... 62 B7
Bristol BS7 .... 49 F4
Ashgrove Cl BS7 ...... 49 F4
Ashgrove Ct BA2 ..... 134 D8
Ashgrove Rd
Bristol, Ashley Down
BS7 .... 49 F4
Bristol, Bedminster BS3 . 63 B3
Ash Hayes Dr BS48 .... 59 E1
Ash Hayes Rd BS48 .... 59 F1
Ash La BS32 .... 23 D2
Ashland Rd BS13 ...... 79 A4
Ashleigh Cl
Paulton BS39 .... 132 E6
Weston-s-M BS23 .... 105 A8
Ashleigh Cres BS49 .... 91 B8
Ashleigh Rd
Weston-s-M BS23 .... 105 A8
Yatton BS49 .... 91 B8
Ashley BS15 .... 65 F8
Ashley Ave BA1 ...... 101 C7
Ashley Cl
Bristol BS7 .... 49 F4
Winscombe BS25 ..... 125 A7
Ashley Court Rd 2 BS7 49 F2
Ashley Ct 1 BS2 ...... 49 F1
ASHLEY DOWN 49 E4
Ashley Down Jun & Inf
Schs BS7 .... 49 F5
Ashley Down Rd BS7 ... 49 F4
Ashley Green BA15 ... 103 F1
Ashley Grove Rd
7 Bristol BS2 .... 49 F2
1 Bristol BS2 .... 50 A1
Ashley Hill BS6, BS7 .... 49 F2
Ashley Ho BS34 .... 23 F1
Ashley La BA15 ...... 120 F7
Ashley Par BS2 .... 49 F2
Ashley Pk BS6 .... 49 F3
Ashley Rd
Bathford BA1, SN13 .... 86 D2
Bristol BS6 .... 49 E1
Clevedon BS21 .... 57 D1
Ashley St BS2 .... 50 A1
Ashley Terr 1 BA1 ... 101 C7
Ashley Trad Est 6 BS2 . 49 F2
Ashman Cl BS5 .... 64 A8
Ashman Ct 1 BS16 .... 50 E3
Ashmans Ct BA1 ..... 101 B6
Ashmans Gate BS39 .. 132 E5
Ashmans Yd BA1 ..... 101 B6
Ashmead BS39 .... 114 E1
Ashmead Ho 12 BS5 ... 64 C7
Ashmead Way 8 BS1 .. 62 F5
Ash Rd
Banwell BS29 .... 106 E4
Bristol BS7 .... 49 E5
Ash Ridge Rd BS32 .... 24 B3
Ashton BS16 .... 37 C1
Ashton Ave BS1 ...... 142 A1
Ashton Cl BS21 .... 57 D1
Ashton Court Estate*
BS41 .... 62 C4
Ashton Cres BS48 ..... 59 D1
Ashton Dr BS3 .... 62 F2
ASHTON GATE 62 F4
Ashton Gate Prim Sch
BS3 .... 63 A4
Ashton Gate Rd BS3 ... 63 A4
Ashton Gate Stadium
(Bristol City FC) BS3 .. 62 F3
Ashton Gate Terr 4
BS3 .... 63 A4
Ashton Gate Trad Est
BS3 .... 62 E3
Ashton Gate Underpass
BS3 .... 62 F3
Ashton Hill BA2 ...... 100 A7
Ashton Park Sch BS3 .. 62 E3
Ashton Rd
Bristol BS3 .... 62 D2
Bristol, Ashton Gate BS3 . 62 F4
Bristol, Bower Ashton
BS3 .... 62 D3
Ashton Rise BS3 .... 62 F2
ASHTON VALE 62 F2
Ashton Vale Prim Sch
BS3 .... 62 F2
Ashton Vale Rd BS3 .... 62 E3
Ashton Vale Trad Est
BS3 .... 62 F1
Ashton Way BS31 ...... 81 E6
Ash Tree Cl BS24 ..... 122 C6
Ash Tree Ct BA3 ..... 133 E1
Ashvale Cl BS48 .... 60 A2
Ashville Pk BS35 ...... 15 B7
Ashville Rd BS3 .... 63 A4
Ashways Ho BS39 .... 114 E1
Ashwell Cl BS14 .... 80 E6
Ashwicke BS14 .... 80 A6
Ashwicke Rd SN14 ..... 70 B3
Ash Wlk BS10 .... 35 B3
Ashwood BS40 .... 129 F4
Aspects L Pk BS15 ..... 65 E5
Aspen Cl SN14 .... 70 F6
Aspen Dr BS10 .... 35 B5
Aspen Park Rd BS22 .. 105 E8
Assembly Rooms*
BA1 .... 141 B3
Assembly Rooms La
BS1 .... 143 A2
Astazou Dr BS24 ..... 105 B4
Aster Cres BS16 .... 52 D8
Aston Ho 4 BS1 ...... 143 B1
Astry Cl BS11 .... 34 A1
Atchley St 18 BS5 ..... 64 B7
Athena Ct 3 BS7 ...... 49 F4
Atherston BS30 .... 66 D5
Athlone Wlk BS4 ...... 63 E1
Atholl Cl BS22 .... 88 F3
Atkins Cl BS14 .... 80 E6
Atlantic Rd
Bristol BS11 .... 47 C8
Weston-s-M BS23 ...... 87 C1
Atlantic Rd S BS23 .... 87 C1
Atlantic View Ct BS23 .. 87 C1
Atlas Cl BS5 .... 51 A2
Atlas Rd BS3 .... 63 E3
Atlas St BS2 .... 64 B5
Atlay Ct BS49 .... 74 B1
Atrium The
Bristol BS1 .... 143 B2
Bristol BS2 .... 143 C2
Attewell Ct BA2 ..... 101 F4
Atwell Dr BS32 .... 24 B1
Atwood Dr BS11 .... 34 B2
Atyeo Cl BS3 .... 62 E1
Aubretia Rd BS16 ..... 52 E7
Aubrey Ho 10 BS3 ..... 63 B3
Aubrey Meads BS30 .... 82 E8
Aubrey Rd BS3 .... 63 B3
Auburn Ave BS30 ...... 66 B3
Auburn Rd BS6 .... 49 B1
Auckland Cl BS23 .... 104 F3
Auden Mead BS7 ...... 50 A8
Audley Ave BA1 ...... 101 D7
Audley Cl
Bath BA1 .... 101 D7
Rangeworthy BS37 ..... 27 A8
Audley Gr BA1 .... 101 C7
Audley Lodge BA1 .... 101 D7
Audley Park Rd BA1 .. 101 C7
Audrey Wlk BS9 .... 49 D7
Augusta Pl BA1 ...... 101 D7
Augustine's Cl BS20 .... 44 E4
Augustus Ho BS15 ..... 65 B6
Aurelius Cl BS31 ...... 81 F8
AUST 13 A6
Austen Dr BS22 .... 89 B4
Austen Gr BS7 .... 50 A8
Austen Ho BS7 .... 50 A8
Austen Pl BS11 .... 47 E7
Aust La BS9 .... 49 A8
Aust Rd
Northwick BS35 .... 12 D3
Olveston BS35 .... 13 F5
Autumn Mews BS24 ... 106 A8
Avalon Cl BS49 .... 74 A1
Avalon Ho BS48 .... 59 C1
Avalon La BS5 .... 65 B6
Avalon Rd BS5 .... 65 B6
Avebury Rd BS3 .... 62 F2
Avening Cl BS48 .... 76 A8
AVENING GREEN 10 D8
Avening Rd BS15 ...... 65 A8
Avenue Pl BA2 .... 102 B1
Avenue The
Backwell BS48 .... 76 A7
Bath, Bushey Norwood
BA2 .... 102 E5
Bath, Combe Down BA2 102 C1
Bristol, Ashley Down BS7 49 E3
Bristol, Clifton BS8 .... 49 A1
Bristol, Crew's Hole BS5 . 64 F8
Bristol, Frenchay BS16 .. 36 E1

Avenue The continued
Bristol, Little Stoke BS34 **36** C6
Bristol, Patchway BS34 . . **24** B2
Bristol, Sneyd Park BS9 . . **48** E3
Clevedon BS21. . . . . **57** G6
Keynsham BS31 . . . . **81** E6
Timsbury BA2. . . . .**116** B2
Weston-s-M BS22 . . . . . **89** C3
Winscombe BS25. . . . . .**125** C8
Yate BS37. . . . .**27** D1
Yatton BS49 . . . . **91** B8
Averay Rd BS16. . . . . **50** C4
Averill Ct BS21. . . . . **57** F4
Avonbank Ind Est BS11. **47** B7
Avon Bsns Pk BS16. . . . . **51** A3
Avon Cl
Bristol BS5. . . . . **64** F6
Keynsham BS31. . . . . . . **81** F6
Weston-s-M BS23 . . . . .**104** F2
AVONCLIFF. **120** F4
Avoncliff Halt BA15 . . .**120** F5
Avon Cres
Bristol BS1. . . . .**142** A1
Wickwar GL12 . . . . **18** B6
Avon Ct
Batheaston BA1. . . . . . . **86** A4
Bristol, Clifton BS8 . . . . **49** A1
Bristol, Fishponds BS16. **51** B5
Avondale Bldgs BA1. . . . **85** B3
Avondale Bsns Ctr
BS15. . . . . **51** C2
Avondale Ct
Bath BA1. . . . .**101** B7
Bristol BS9. . . . . **48** D3
Bristol, Oldland BS30. . . **65** F3
Avondale Rd BA1 . . . . .**101** B6
Avondown Cl BS10 . . . . **35** D1
Avondown Ct 5 BS3 . . . **63** C2
Avondown Ho BA2 . . . .**101** B5
Avondowns Ct BS8 . . . .**142** A4
Avon Gorge Ind Est
BS11. . . . . **47** C7
Avon Gorge Nature
Reserve* BS8 . . . . **62** E7
Avon Gr BS9. . . . . **48** D2
Avon Hts BA2 . . . .**120** C6
Avon La BS31 . . . . **82** F5
Avonlea
Bristol BS15. . . . . **65** C5
Yate BS37. . . . . **39** D8
Avonlea Ct BS30 . . . . . . **66** A3
Avonleaze BS9. . . . . **48** B5
Avonleigh Ct 4 BS3. . . **63** B2
Avonleigh Rd BS3 . . . . . **63** B2
Avonmead BS2 . . . .**143** B4
Avon Meads BS2. . . . . . **64** C5
Avon Mill La BS31 . . . . . **81** F6
AVONMOUTH. **33** D2
Avonmouth CE Prim Sch
BS11. . . . . **47** C8
Avonmouth Rd
Avonmouth BS11 . . . . . . **33** B1
Bristol BS11. . . . . **47** C8
Avonmouth Sta BS11. . . **33** B1
Avonmouth Way
Avonmouth BS11 . . . . . . **33** D1
Bristol BS10. . . . . **34** E3
Avonmouth Way W
BS11. . . . . **33** B1
AVONPARK. **120** C6
Avon Pk
Bath BA1 . . . .**101** A7
Bristol BS5. . . . . **64** D7
Avon Prim Sch BS11 . . **47** D8
Avon Rd
Bristol BS13. . . . . **79** A6
Charfield GL12. . . . . **11** A4
Keynsham BS31. . . . . . . **81** F5
Pill BS20. . . . . **47** C5
Avon Rise SN14 . . . . **31** E4
Avon Riverside Est
BS11. . . . . **47** B7
Avon Riverside Sta*
BS30. . . . . **82** E6
Avonside Ind Est BS2. . **64** C6
Avonside Rd BS2. . . . . . **64** C6
Avonside Way BS4 . . . . **64** F6
Avon Ski Centre*
BS25. . . . .**108** C3
Avonsmere Residential Pk
BS34. . . . . **36** C3
Avon St
Bath BA1 . . . .**141** B2
Bristol BS2. . . . .**143** C2
Avon Trad Est BS2. . . . . **64** A5
Avon Vale BS9. . . . . **48** D4
Avonvale Pl BA1 . . . . . . **85** F3
Avonvale Rd BS5. . . . . . **64** C7
Avon Valley Bsns Pk
BS4. . . . . **64** E6
Avon Valley Ctry Pk*
BS31. . . . . **82** E6
Avon Valley Farm Bsns Pk
BS31. . . . . **82** D5

Avon Valley Rly*
Bitton BS30. . . . .**82** D7
Bristol BS30. . . . . **66** C3
Avon View BS15. . . . . . . **65** B3
Avon Way
Bristol BS9. . . . . **48** C4
Bristol, Southmead BS10 **49** D7
Portishead BS20. . . . . . . **45** C5
Thornbury BS35. . . . . . . **15** D7
Avonwood Cl BS11 . . . . **47** E6
Awdelett Cl BS11 . . . . . **34** B1
AWKLEY. **23** E8
Awkley La BS32. . . . . . . **23** E8
Awkward Hill BA40. . . .**111** D5
AXBRIDGE. **125** B1
Axbridge Bypass BS26 **125** A3
Axbridge CE Fst Sch
BS26. . . . .**125** C1
Axbridge Cl BS48. . . . . **75** E8
Axbridge Moor Dro
BS26. . . . .**125** C1
Axbridge Rd
Bath BA2. . . . .**102** A2
Bristol BS4. . . . . **63** F2
Cheddar BS27 . . . .**125** F2
Axe Cl BS23 . . . .**105** A5
Axe Ct BS35 . . . . **15** C8
Axford Way BA2. . . . . .**134** D8
Axis BS14. . . . . **79** D5
Aycote Cl BS22 . . . . **88** C2
Ayford La SN14 . . . . **69** F4
Aylesbury Cres BS3 . . . **63** B1
Aylesbury Rd BS3 . . . . . **63** B1
Aylmer Cres BS14. . . . . **80** B6
Aylminton Wlk BS11. . . **34** B2
Ayr St BA2. . . . .**101** D6
Azalea Rd BS22 . . . . **89** A5
Azelin Ave BS13. . . . . . . **79** B5
Aztec Ctr The BS32. . . . **24** A2
Aztec West BS32. . . . . . **24** A2

B

BABINGTON. **140** C3
Backfield Farm BS37. . . **26** F5
Backfields BS2. . . . .**143** B4
Backfields Ct BS2. . . . .**143** B4
Backfields La BS2. . . . .**143** B4
Back La
Axbridge BS26 . . . .**125** C2
Chewton Mendip BA3 . . .**130** B1
Keynsham BS31. . . . . . . **81** E6
Kingston Seymour BS21. . **73** A5
Litton BA3. . . . .**130** E2
Marshfield SN14 . . . . . . **69** F8
Pill BS20. . . . . **47** C5
Pucklechurch BS16. . . . . **53** C4
Rowberrow BS25. . . . . .**109** A1
Wickwar GL12. . . . . **18** A5
Back Of Kingsdown Par
BS6. . . . .**143** A4
Back Rd BS3. . . . . **63** A4
Back St
Hawkesbury Upton GL9. . **20** A3
Weston-s-M BS23 . . . . .**104** E7
Back Stoke La BS9 . . . . **48** F6
BACKWELL. **76** B6
Backwell Bow BS48 . . . . **60** C1
Backwell CE Jun Sch
BS48. . . . . **76** C5
Backwell Comm BS48 . . **76** B8
BACKWELL COMMON . **76** B8
Backwell Down BS48. . . **76** D8
BACKWELL GREEN. . . . **76** D8
Backwell Hill BS48. . . . . **76** B3
Backwell Hill Rd BS48. . **76** E5
Backwell Sch BS48. . . . . **76** B6
Backwell Wlk BS13. . . . . **78** F8
Backy Hill BA2. . . . .**118** C4
Badenham Gr BS11 . . . . **47** F8
Baden Hill Rd GL12. . . . **16** C6
Baden Ho BA1 . . . .**141** B4
Baden Rd
Bristol, Kingswood
BS15. . . . . **66** A7
Bristol, Redfield BS5. . . . **64** C7
Bader Cl BS37 . . . . **27** D3
Badger Cl BS30. . . . . . . **65** F3
Badger Rd BS35 . . . . **8** D3
Badger Rise BS20. . . . . **44** F3
Badgers Cl BS32. . . . . . . **24** D3
Badger Sett BS5 . . . . . . **65** B7
Badgers Holt BS14. . . . . **80** C6
Badger's La BS32 . . . . . **23** C3
Badgers Rise BS10. . . . . **35** E4
Badgers The BS22. . . . . **89** D3
Badgers Way BS24. . . .**105** F8
Badgers Wlk BS4 . . . . . . **64** D2
Badgeworth BS37. . . . . . **39** D6
Badman Cl BS39. . . . . . .**132** D5
BADMINTON. **30** F2
Badminton BS16. . . . . . . **37** C1
Badminton Ct
17 Weston-s-M BS23. . . **87** C1
Yate BS37. . . . . **27** C2
Badminton Ctr The
BS37. . . . . **27** C2
Badminton Gdns BA1 .**101** C8

Badminton Rd
Bristol, Downend BS16 . . **51** E7
Bristol, Montpelier BS2 . . **49** F1
Chipping Sodbury BS37 . . **41** B7
Frampton Cotterell BS36,
BS37. . . . . **38** C6
Badminton Road Trad Est
BS37. . . . . **27** B1
Badminton Sch BS9 . . . . **49** A5
Badminton Wlk BS16. . . **51** E7
Badock's Wood Prim Sch
BS10. . . . . **35** B3
Baggridge Hill BA2. . . .**135** F7
Baglyn Ave
Bristol BS15. . . . . **51** F3
Mangotsfield BS15. . . . . **50** F3
Bagnell Cl BS14. . . . . . . **80** E5
Bagnell Rd BS14. . . . . . . **80** E5
BAGSTONE. **17** A3
Bagstone Rd BS37, GL12 **17** A2
Bagworth Dr BS30 . . . . . **65** F3
BAILBROOK. **85** D3
Bailbrook Gr BA1. . . . . . **85** C3
Bailbrook La BA1. . . . . . **85** D3
Baildon Cres BS23 . . . .**105** A4
Baildon Ct 2 BS23. . . . .**104** F4
Baildon Rd BS23 . . . . . .**105** A4
Bailey Cl BS22 . . . .**105** E8
Bailey Ct BS20 . . . . **45** F6
Bailey's Court Prim Sch
BS32. . . . . **36** F6
Baileys Court Rd BS32. . **36** F6
Baileys Ct BS32. . . . . . . **36** F6
Baileys Mead Rd BS16. . **50** C5
Bailiffs Cl BS26 . . . .**125** C1
Bailiff's Wall BS26 . . . .**125** B1
Baily Pl BS7 . . . . **50** C8
Bainsbury View BA3 . . .**138** F1
Baker Cl 7 BS21. . . . . . . **57** D1
Baker's Bldgs BS40 . . . . **92** D2
Bakersfield BS30. . . . . . **66** B3
Bakers Ground BS34 . . . **37** A5
Bakers La
Chilcompton BA3 . . . . . .**138** D3
Lower Langford BS40 . . .**109** C8
Bakers Par BA2. . . . . . .**116** B2
Bakers Pk BS13. . . . . . . **79** B6
Baker St BS23 . . . .**104** E8
Balaclava Ind Est BS4. . **50** F3
Balaclava Rd BS16. . . . . **50** F3
Baldwin Chambers 6
BS1. . . . .**143** A2
Baldwin Lofts BS1 . . . .**143** A2
Baldwin St BS1 . . . .**143** A2
Balfour Rd BS3 . . . . **63** B3
Ballance St BA1. . . . . . .**141** B4
Ballast La BS11. . . . . **33** E2
Balls Barn La BS24 . . . . **90** A2
Balmain St BS4. . . . . **64** A4
Balmoral Cl BS34 . . . . . . **36** D4
Balmoral Ct BS16 . . . . . **52** A5
Balmoral Ho BS1. . . . . .**142** C1
Balmoral Mans 3 BS7 . **49** F2
Balmoral Rd
Bristol, Longwell Green
BS30 . . . . **65** F2
Bristol, Montpelier BS7 . . **49** F2
Keynsham BS31. . . . . . . **81** E4
Balmoral Way BS22 . . . . **88** D2
Baltic Pl BS20. . . . . **47** D4
Balustrade 17 BA1 . . . . **85** B1
Bamfield BS14. . . . . **80** A6
Bampton 5 BS22 . . . . . . **88** F2
Bampton Cl
Bristol, Emerson's Green
BS16. . . . . **52** C6
Bristol, Headley Park
BS13. . . . . **79** B7
Bampton Croft BS16 . . . **52** C6
Bampton Dr BS16. . . . . . **37** D1
Banfield Cl BS11. . . . . . . **48** A8
Bangor Gr BS4. . . . . **64** F5
Bangrove Wlk BS11 . . . . **47** E8
Banister Gr BS4. . . . . . . **79** D7
Bank Leaze Prim Sch
BS11. . . . . **34** B2
Bank Pl BS20 . . . . **47** D4
Bank Rd
Avonmouth BS11 . . . . . . **33** D7
Bristol BS15. . . . . **65** D8
Pilning BS35. . . . . **22** E6
Banks Cl BS21. . . . . **73** D8
Bankside BS16. . . . . **51** F4
Bankside Rd BS4. . . . . . **64** D3
Bannerdown Cl BA1. . . . **86** B4
Bannerdown Dr BA1 . . . **86** A4
Bannerdown Rd BA1 . . . **86** C5
Bannerleigh La BS8. . . . **62** E6
Bannerleigh Rd BS8. . . . **62** E6
Bannerman Rd BS5 . . . . **64** B8
Bannerman Road Com Sch
BS5. . . . . **50** B1
Banner Rd BS6. . . . . **49** E1
Bannetts Tree Cres
BS35. . . . . **15** A5
Bantock Cl BS14. . . . . . . **79** D6
Bantry Rd BS4. . . . . **79** E8
BANWELL. **107** B3
Banwell Caves BS26. . .**106** C3

Banwell Cl
Bristol BS13. . . . . **79** A8
Keynsham BS31. . . . . . . **82** A2
Banwell Prim Sch
BS29. . . . .**107** B3
Banwell Rd
Banwell BS26, BS29. . . .**123** E8
Bath BA2. . . . .**118** D8
Bristol BS3. . . . . **63** A3
Locking BS24. . . . .**106** A3
Winscombe BS25, BS29 **124** E8
Banyard Rd BS20. . . . . . **46** E5
BAPTIST MILLS. **50** A2
Baptist St BS5 . . . . **50** A1
Baranwheel Ct BS5 . . . . **64** F6
Barberry Farm Rd
BS49. . . . . **74** B1
Barbour Gdns BS13. . . . **79** D3
Barbour Rd BS13. . . . . . **79** D3
Barcroft Cl BS15 . . . . . . **65** C8
Barker Ct
5 Bristol BS5. . . . . **64** C7
Long Ashton BS41 . . . . . **61** E1
Barkers Mead BS37 . . . . **27** F4
Barker Wlk BS5. . . . . **50** A1
Barkleys Hill BS16. . . . . **50** D5
Barlands Ho BS10. . . . . . **34** F3
Barley Cl
Bristol BS16. . . . . **52** A6
Frampton Cotterell BS36 **38** C8
Barley Close Com Prim
Sch BS16. . . . . **52** A6
Barley Croft BS9 . . . . . . **48** F5
Barley Cross BS22. . . . . **89** A5
Barleyfields BS2 . . . . . .**143** C2
Barley Fields BS35. . . . . . **8** B3
Barley Wood Walled
Garden* BS40 . . . . **92** F3
Barnabas Cl BS26 . . . . .**125** D2
Barnabas St 9 BS2 . . . . **49** E1
Barnaby Cl BA3. . . . . . .**133** B2
Barnack Trad Est BS3 . . **63** C1
Barnard's Cl BS49. . . . . **91** C7
Barnard Wlk BS31. . . . . **81** D4
Barn Cl BS16. . . . . **52** B6
Barn End
East Harptree BS40. . . . .**129** E3
Marshfield SN14 . . . . . . **70** A8
Barnes Ct BS34. . . . . **36** B3
Barnes St BS5 . . . . **64** D8
Barnfield Way BA1. . . . . **86** B3
Barnhill Cl BS37 . . . . **28** A4
Barnhill Rd BS37. . . . . . . **28** B1
Barn La BS39 . . . .**115** A7
Barn Owl Way BS34 . . . . **36** F5
Barn Pool BS25 . . . .**125** F8
Barns Cl
Barrow Gurney BS48. . . . **77** E4
Nailsea BS48. . . . . **59** E2
Barns Ground BS21 . . . . **73** E8
Barnstaple Ct BS4 . . . . . **79** E8
Barnstaple Rd BS4 . . . . . **79** E8
Barnstaple Wlk BS4 . . . . **79** F8
Barnwood 4 BS7 . . . . . . **50** C8
Barnwood Ct BS48 . . . . . **59** B1
Barnwood Rd BS37. . . . . **39** C7
Baron Cl BS30. . . . . **82** E8
Barons Cl BS3 . . . . **62** F3
Barossa Pl BS1 . . . .**143** A1
Barrack's La BS11. . . . . . **47** D8
Barratt St BS5 . . . . **50** C1
Barrington Cl BS15. . . . . **51** F2
Barrington Ct
Bristol BS4. . . . . **64** A4
11 Bristol, Knowle BS2 . . **63** F4
Bristol, New Cheltenham
BS15. . . . . **51** E1
BARROW COMMON. . . . **78** B4
Barrow Court La BS19 . . **77** B5
Barrow Ct
Barrow Gurney BS48. . . . **77** A5
Tickenham BS21. . . . . . . **58** F3
BARROW GURNEY **77** E5
Barrow Hill BS30. . . . . . . **67** B5
Barrow Hill Cres BS11. . **47** C7
Barrow Hill Rd BS11. . . . **47** D6
Barrow La BS40. . . . . **77** L1
Barrowmead Dr BS11 . . **47** F7
Barrow Rd
Bath BA2. . . . .**101** C1
Bristol BS2. . . . . **64** A7
Hutton BS24. . . . .**105** E2
Barrow St BS48. . . . . **77** D5
Barrows The
Cheddar BS27 . . . .**126** A1
Weston-s-M BS22 . . . . .**105** C7
BARROW VALE. **115** D5
Barrs Court Ave BS30 . . **66** A5
Barrs Court Prim Sch
BS30. . . . . **65** F5
Barrs Court Rd BS30 . . . **66** A5
Barrs La GL11. . . . . **5** E4
Barry Cl
Bristol BS30. . . . . **66** C1
Weston-s-M BS24 . . . . .**105** A1
Barry Rd BS30 . . . . **66** C2
Barstaple Ho BS2 . . . . .**143** C3
Barter Cl BS15 . . . . **65** D8

Bartholomew Row
BA2. . . . .**116** B2
Bartholomew Sq BS7. . . **49** F7
Bartletts Ct BA2 . . . . . .**141** C1
Bartlett's Rd BS3 . . . . . . **63** C2
Bartlett St 6 BA1. . . . . .**141** B3
Bartletts Way BS24. . . .**106** A4
Bartley Ct BS5 . . . . **64** D7
Bartley St BS3 . . . . **63** D4
BARTON. **124** B6
Barton Bldgs BA1. . . . . .**141** B3
Barton Cl
Alveston BS35 . . . . **15** A5
1 Bristol BS4 . . . . **64** F6
Winterbourne BS36. . . . . **37** E5
Barton Ct BS5 . . . . **64** C6
Barton Dro BS25 . . . . . .**124** D5
Barton Gn BS5. . . . . **64** B7
BARTON HILL. **64** C6
Barton Hill Prim Sch
BS5. . . . . **64** B6
Barton Hill Rd BS5 . . . . . **64** B7
Barton Hill Trad Est 10
BS5. . . . . **64** B6
Barton Ho BS5. . . . . **64** C6
Bartonia Gr BS4. . . . . . . **64** D1
Barton Manor BS2 . . . . . **64** A6
Barton Rd
Bristol BS2. . . . .**143** C2
Winscombe BS26. . . . . .**124** C6
Barton St
Bath BA1 . . . .**141** B2
Bristol BS1. . . . .**143** A4
Barton The
Barton BS25. . . . .**124** B5
Bleadon BS24. . . . .**122** C6
Bristol BS15. . . . . **65** C4
Compton Martin BS40 . .**129** B7
Corston BA2. . . . .**100** A7
Hawkesbury Upton GL9 . . **19** D1
Norton St Philip BA2 . . .**136** E4
Barton Vale
6 Bristol BS2. . . . . **64** A6
Bristol BS2. . . . .**143** C2
Barton Wlk BS7. . . . . . . **50** B8
Barwick Ho BS11 . . . . . . **47** E7
Barwood Cl BS15 . . . . . . **65** F8
BATCH. **121** F3
Batch Bsns Pk BS24. . . .**121** F2
Batches The BS3 . . . . . . **63** B2
Batchfield La BS16,
BS37. . . . . **53** D8
Batch La
Clutton BS39. . . . .**114** F3
Lympsham BS24. . . . . . .**121** F3
Batch The
Backwell BS48. . . . . **76** D1
Batheaston BA1. . . . . . . **85** F3
Burrington BS40 . . . . . .**110** B3
Butcombe BS40 . . . .**111** B8
Chew Magna BS40. . . . . **96** B3
Churchill BS25 . . . .**108** F4
Compton Martin BS40 . .**129** A6
Farmborough BA2 . . . . .**116** A2
Hinton Charterhouse
BA2. . . . .**119** E1
Saltford BS31. . . . . **82** F3
Yatton BS49. . . . . **91** B7
Bates Cl BS5. . . . . **64** A8
BATH. **141** B3
Bath Abbey* BA1. . . . .**141** C2
Bath Acad BA1. . . . .**141** B3
BATHAMPTON. **85** F1
Bathampton La BA2. . . . **85** F1
Bathampton Prim Sch
BA2. . . . . **85** F2
Bath Bldgs BS6 . . . . **49** E1
Bath Bridge Rdbt
BS1. . . . .**143** C1
Bath Chew Valley
Caravan Pk BS39 . . . .**113** C4
Bath Coll BA3. . . . .**133** F2
BATHEASTON. **85** F4
Batheaston CE Prim Sch
BA1 . . . . **85** F4
BATHFORD. **86** C1
Bathford CE Prim Sch
BA1 . . . . **86** C1
Bathford Hill
Bathford BA1. . . . . **86** B2
Compton Dando BS39 . . **98** E5
Bathford Manor BA1 . . . **86** C2
Bath Foyer The BA2 . . .**101** A6
Bath Hill
Keynsham BS31. . . . . . . **81** F5
Wellow BA2. . . . .**118** D2
Bathings The 1 BS35. . . **15** C8
Bath La GL9 . . . . **19** E2
Bath New Rd BA3. . . . . .**133** F4
Bath Old Rd BA3 . . . . . .**133** F4
Bath Postal Mus*
BA1. . . . .**141** C2
Bath Race Course*
BA1. . . . . **84** A6
Bath Rd
Bitton BS30 . . . . **82** D8
Blagdon BS40. . . . .**111** B1
Bristol BS2, BS4. . . . . . .**143** C1
Bristol, Brislington BS4 . . **64** F1

Bath Rd *continued*
Bristol, Longwell Green BS30 65 F3
Bristol, North Common BS30 66 D6
Bristol, Totterdown BS4 64 B4
Bristol, Upper Knowle BS4 64 D2
Bristol, Willsbridge BS30 66 C1
Chipping Sodbury BS37, GL9 41 C4
Colerne SN14 70 E2
Farmborough BA2 115 E5
Kelston BA1, BS30 83 B6
Kingsdown SN13 86 F5
Norton St Philip BA2 136 E5
Paulton BS39 132 F6
Peasedown St John BA2 134 C7
Saltford BS31 82 D3
Thornbury BS35 15 B8
Upper Langford BS40 109 D3
Wick BS30 67 E4
Bath Spa Sta BA1 141 C1
Bath Spa Univ Art and Design BA1 84 E1
Bath Spa University Coll (Newton Pk Campus) BA2 100 B5
Bath St
Bath BA1 141 C2
Bristol BS1 143 B2
Bristol, Ashton Gate BS3 63 A4
Bristol, Staple Hill BS16 51 E4
Bathurst Par BS1 143 A1
Bathurst Rd BS22 105 C8
Bath View BA3 138 F1
Bathwell Rd BS4 64 A3
BATHWICK 102 B7
Bathwick Hill BA2 102 C6
Bathwick Rise BA2 102 B7
Bathwick St Mary CE Prim Sch BA2 102 C8
Bathwick St BA1, BA2 141 C4
Batley Ct BS30 66 D4
Batstone Cl BA1 85 B2
Batt Cl BS32 24 E5
Battenburg Rd BS5 65 A8
Batten Ct BS37 28 C1
Batten's La BS5 65 A6
Battens Rd BS5 65 B7
Battersby Way BS10 34 E2
Battersea Rd BS5 64 C8
Battery La BS20 45 D7
Battery Rd BS20 45 D6
Battle La BS40 96 A3
Battle Wk BA1 84 E4
Battson Rd BS14 80 E4
Baugh Gdns BS16 37 E1
Baugh Rd BS16 37 E1
Baxter Cl BS15 65 F8
Bayer Bldg The BA2 141 B1
Bay Gdns BS5 50 C2
Bayham Rd BS4 64 A3
Bayleys Dr BS15 65 C6
Baynham Ct 4 BS15 65 B5
Baynton Ho 2 BS5 64 B7
Baynton Mdw BS16 52 C6
Baynton Rd BS3 63 A4
Bay Rd BS21 57 F6
Bayswater Ave BS6 49 B3
Bayswater Rd BS7 49 F7
Bay Tree Cl BS34 35 F7
Baytree Ct BS22 88 D1
Baytree Rd BS22 88 C1
Bay Tree Rd
Bath BA1 85 B2
Clevedon BS21 57 G1
Baytree Sch BS24 106 A8
Baytree View BS22 88 D1
Bay Tree View BS22 88 D1
Bay Willow Dr BS6 49 B2
BEACH 67 C2
Beach Ave
Clevedon BS21 57 E2
Severn Beach BS35 22 A7
Beach Ct BS23 104 D6
Beach End Rd BS23 104 C2
Beachgrove Gdns BS16 51 C4
Beachgrove Rd BS16 51 B4
Beach Hill
Bristol BS30 66 F3
Portishead BS20 45 C6
Beach La BS30 67 C2
Beachlands Pk BS22 88 A6
Beachley Wlk BS11 47 D7
Beach Mews BS21 57 E4
Beach Rd
Severn Beach BS35 21 F7
Weston-s-M BS23 104 D6
Weston-s-M, Kewstoke BS22 88 A5
Beach Rd E BS20 45 D6
Beach Rd W BS20 45 C6
Beach The BS21 57 E4
BEACON HILL 84 F1
Beacon La BS16 37 C6
Beaconlea BS15 65 D6
Beacon Rd BA1 85 A1
Beacon Rise Prim Sch BS15 65 D6
Beaconsfield Cl 6 BS2 64 B6
Beaconsfield Rd
Bristol, Clifton BS8 49 A1
Bristol, Crew's Hole BS5 64 E7
Bristol, Kensington Park BS4 64 B3
Clevedon BS21 57 G3
Weston-s-M BS23 104 E7
Beaconsfield St 7 BS5 64 B6
Beafort Cl BS24 106 C3
Beale Cl BS14 80 E6
Beam St BS5 64 C7
Bean Acre The BS11 47 D8
Beanhill Cres BS35 15 A5
Beanwood Pk (Cvn Site) BS37 39 E3
Bearbridge Rd BS13 78 F4
BEAR FLAT 101 F4
Bear Yard Mews 2 BS8 142 A2
Beauchamp Ave BA3 139 B6
Beauchamp Pk BA3 139 B6
Beauchamp Rd BS7 49 D4
Beauchamps Dr BA3 139 A5
Beauford Sq BA1 141 B2
Beaufort BS16 37 C1
Beaufort Ave
Midsomer Norton BA3 133 A2
Yate BS37 27 D2
Beaufort Bldgs 7 BS8 62 F7
Beaufort Cl BS5 64 D7
Beaufort Cres BS34 36 E4
Beaufort Ct
Bristol BS16 52 A8
Clevedon BS21 57 E5
Beaufort E BA1 85 C1
Beaufort Gdns 2 BS48 59 D1
Beaufort Ho 12 BS5 64 B7
Beaufort Hts BS5 64 E7
Beaufort Mews
3 Bath BA1 85 C1
11 Bristol BS8 62 F7
Chipping Sodbury BS37 28 B1
Beaufort Pl
Bath BA1 85 C1
Bristol, Frenchay BS16 37 B1
Bristol, Upper Easton BS5 64 A8
Beaufort Rd
Bristol, Clifton BS8 49 A1
Bristol, Horfield BS7 49 F6
Bristol, Kingswood BS15 51 C1
Bristol, Pile Marsh BS5 64 E7
Bristol, Staple Hill BS16 51 E5
Bristol, Vinney Green BS16 52 A8
Frampton Cotterell BS36 38 A8
Weston-s-M BS23 104 F7
Yate BS37 27 D2
Beaufort St
2 Bristol, Bedminster BS3 63 C2
4 Bristol, Upper Easton BS5 64 A8
Beaufort Trad Pk BS16 53 B5
Beaufort View SN14 31 E4
Beaufort Villas 8 BA1 85 B1
Beaufort W 11 BA1 85 B1
Beaufort Way BS10 49 D8
Beauley Rd BS3 63 B4
Beaumont BA1 84 F1
Beaumont Cl
Bristol BS30 66 A3
Weston-s-M BS23 104 F4
Beaumont St BS5 64 A8
Beaumont Terr 6 BS5 64 A8
Beau St BA1 141 B2
Beaver Cl BS36 37 F7
Beazer Cl 4 BS16 51 D3
Beck Cl BS16 52 C7
Becket Ct BS16 53 B5
Becket Dr BS22 89 A3
Becket Prim Sch BS22 89 A2
Becket Rd BS22 89 A4
Becket's La BS48 75 E8
Beckford Ct BA2 102 B7
Beckford Dr BA1 84 E4
Beckford Gdns
Bath BA2 102 B8
Bristol BS14 80 A3
Beckford Rd BA2 102 B7
Beckford's Twr & Mus* BA1 84 D4
Beckhampton Rd BA2 101 D5
Beck Ho BS34 36 A8
Beckington BS24 105 A2
Beckington Rd BS3 63 F2
Beckington Wlk BS3 63 F2
Becks Bsns Pk BS23 105 A7
Beckspool Rd BS16 37 C1
Bedford Cres BS7 49 F5
Bedford Ct 9 BA1 102 B8
Bedford Rd BS23 104 E4
Bedford St
Bath BA1 102 B8
6 Bathwick BA2 102 B8
BEDMINSTER 63 C3
BEDMINSTER DOWN 79 B8
Bedminster Down Rd BS3, BS13 63 B1
Bedminster Down Sch
Bristol BS13 78 F7
Bristol BS13 79 A7
Bedminster Par BS3 63 D4
Bedminster Pl 9 BS3 63 D4
Bedminster Rd BS3 63 C2
Bedminster Sta BS3 63 D3
Bedwin Cl BS20 44 F4
Beechacres BS35 8 C1
Beech Ave BA2 102 E5
Beech Cl
Alveston BS35 15 A5
Bristol BS30 66 A5
Shipham BS25 125 F8
Beechcroft BS41 78 D2
Beech Croft BS14 80 B5
Beechcroft Wlk BS7 50 A8
Beech Ct BS14 80 A5
Beech Dr
Nailsea BS48 60 A3
Shipham BS25 125 E8
BEECHEN CLIFF 141 B1
Beechen Cliff Rd BA2 141 B1
Beechen Cliff Sch BA2 102 A4
Beechen Cliff Villas BA2 141 B1
Beechen Dr BS16 51 B3
Beeches Gr BS4 64 D2
Beeches Ind Est BS37 27 B2
Beeches The
Bath BA2 101 D1
Bristol BS9 48 D3
Bristol, Bradley Stoke BS32 36 D8
Bristol, Frenchay BS16 37 B1
Bristol, Oldland Common BS30 66 C2
Bristol, St Anne's BS4 64 E5
Sandford BS25 108 B4
Beechfield Cl BS41 62 C2
Beechfield Gr BS9 48 C8
Beech Gr BA2 101 D4
BEECH HILL 39 B7
Beech Ho
Bristol BS16 50 C5
Clevedon BS21 57 F4
Beech Leaze BS35 15 A5
Beechmont Dr BS24 105 A1
Beechmount Cl BS24 104 F1
Beechmount Ct BS14 80 B8
Beechmount Gr BS14 80 B8
Beech Rd
Bristol BS7 49 E5
Saltford BS31 82 E3
Shipham BS25 125 F8
Yatton BS49 91 C8
Beech Terr BA3 133 E1
Beechwood Ave
Bristol BS15 65 D5
Locking BS24 106 A5
Beechwood Cl BS14 80 C8
Beechwood Dr BS20 44 E5
Beechwood Ho BS16 51 A4
Beechwood Rd
Bath BA2 102 B1
Bristol BS16 51 B4
Easton-in-G BS20 47 A4
Nailsea BS48 59 D2
Portishead BS20 44 E5
Beehive Trad Est BS5 64 E7
Beehive Yd BA1 141 C3
Beek's La SN14, BA1 69 D5
Bees Ho BS21 57 E2
Beesmoor Rd BS36 38 B6
Begbrook Dr BS16 50 F6
Begbrook La BS16 50 F6
Begbrook Pk BS16 51 A7
Begbrook Prim Acad BS16 50 F6
Beggar Bush La BS8 62 B6
Beggarswell Cl BS2 143 C4
Belfast Wlk BS4 79 E8
Belfields La BS16 37 C1
Belfry BS30 66 B6
Belfry Ave BS5 65 A8
Belgrave Cres BA1 141 C4
Belgrave Hill 5 BS8 49 A2
Belgrave Ho BS8 142 A3
Belgrave Pl
Bath BA1 141 C4
Bristol BS8 142 A3
Belgrave Rd
Bath BA1 85 B1
Bristol BS8 142 B4
Weston-s-M BS22 105 B8
Belgrave Terr 1 BA1 85 A1
Bellamy Ave BS13 79 C4
Bellamy Cl BS15 65 A5
Belland Dr BS14 79 F4
Bell Ave BS1 143 A1
Bella Vista Rd BA1 141 B4
Bell Barn Rd BS9 48 D6
Bell Cl
Bristol BS10 49 E7
Farmborough BA2 115 F6
Belle Ct 7 BS2 63 F4
Bellevue BS8 142 B2
BELLE VUE 133 B3
Belle Vue BA3 133 B3
Bellevue Cl BS15 65 E7
Belle Vue Cl BA2 134 D7
Bellevue Cotts
Bristol, Brandon Hill BS8 142 B2
5 Bristol, Eastfield BS9 49 A7
Bellevue Cres BS8 142 B2
Bellevue Ct
Bristol, Brandon Hill BS8 142 B2
6 Bristol, St George BS5 65 A8
Clevedon BS21 57 F4
Bellevue Mans BS21 57 F4
Bellevue Pk BS4 64 D2
Bellevue Rd
Bristol, Kingswood BS15 65 F7
Bristol, St George BS5 65 A8
6 Bristol, Windmill Hill BS2 63 F4
Clevedon BS21 57 F4
Belle Vue Rd BS5 50 C1
Bellevue Terr
Bristol BS8 142 B2
Bristol, Brislington BS4 64 D2
Bristol, Windmill Hill BS2 63 F4
Bell Field The SN14 31 E4
Bellflower Cl BS16 52 D8
Bellhanger Ct BA1 141 B4
Bell Hill
Bristol BS16 50 C4
Norton St Philip BA2 136 E4
Bell Hill Rd BS5 64 F8
Bellhorse La BS40 129 C5
Bellhouse Wlk BS11 34 B1
Bellifants BA2 116 A6
Bell La BS1 143 A3
Bell Language Sch The BA1 101 C8
Bellotts Rd BA2 101 C6
Bell Pit Brow BS48 60 B2
Bell Rd BS36 38 C6
Bell Sq
Blagdon BS40 110 E3
Marshfield SN14 70 A8
Bellum SN14 69 E8
BELLUTON 97 D6
Belluton La BS39 97 D5
Belluton Rd BS4 64 A3
Belluton Villas BS39 97 D5
Bell Wlk BS40 92 E2
Belmont Dr
Bristol BS34 36 E5
Failand BS8 61 B3
Belmont Hill BS48 61 B1
Belmont Pk BS7 35 F1
Belmont Rd
Bath BA2 102 C1
Bristol, Arno's Vale BS4 64 C3
Bristol, Montpelier BS6 49 E2
Winscombe BS25 125 A8
Belmont St BS5 50 B1
Belmont The BS21 57 F3
Belmore Gdns BA2 101 B3
Beloe Rd BS7 49 E5
Belroyal Ave BS4 64 F3
Belsher Dr BS15 66 A6
Belstone Wlk BS4 79 C8
Belton Ct BA1 84 B2
Belton Rd
Bristol BS5 64 B8
Portishead BS20 45 A6
Belvedere BA1 141 B4
Belvedere Cl BS34 36 B5
Belvedere Cres BS22 88 C1
Belvedere Rd BS6 49 B3
Belvoir Rd
6 Bath BA2 101 D5
Bristol BS6 49 E2
Bence Ct 3 BS15 65 B5
Bence Rd BS37 27 E5
Bences Cl SN14 69 F8
Benches La BS40 94 D3
Bendalls Bridge BS39 114 E2
Benford Cl BS16 51 C6
Benleaze Rd BS40 130 C2
Bennell Batch BA3 138 E4
Bennell Cl BA3 138 E4
Bennell Cotts BA3 138 E4
Bennett La BA1 85 A1
Bennett Rd BS5 64 F7
Bennett's Ct BS37 28 A1
Bennett's Rd BA1 85 C3
Bennett St BA1 141 B3
Bennetts Way BS21 57 G5
Bennett Way BS1, BS8 62 F5
Bensaunt Gr BS10 35 D4
Bentley Cl BS14 79 F3
Bentley Rd BS22 89 B3
Benville Ave BS9 48 C8
Berchel Ho 4 BS3 63 D4
Berenda Dr BS30 66 B3
Beresford Cl BS31 82 E2
Beresford Gdns BA1 84 A3
Berkeley Ave
Bristol BS8 142 C3
Bristol, Bishopston BS7 49 D3
Midsomer Norton BA3 133 A2
Berkeley Cl
Bristol BS16 52 A8
Charfield GL12 11 A5
Berkeley Cres
Bristol BS8 142 B3
Weston-s-M BS23 104 C2
Berkeley Ct
Bath BA2 102 C6
Bristol, Bishopston BS7 49 D3
Berkeley Ct Bsns Pk BS5 64 B7
Berkeley Gdns BS31 81 E4
Berkeley Gn BS16 37 B1
Berkeley Gn Rd BS5 50 D2
Berkeley Gr BS5 50 C2
Berkeley Ho
Bath BA1 141 C4
Bristol BS1 142 C3
7 Bristol, Staple Hill BS16 51 D5
Berkeley Pl
Bath BA1 141 C4
Bristol, Brandon Hill BS8 142 B3
Bristol, Windmill Hill BS3 63 D2
Berkeley Rd
Bristol, Bishopston BS7 49 D3
Bristol, Kingswood BS15 65 D7
Bristol, Mayfield Park BS16 51 B2
Bristol, Staple Hill BS16 51 D5
Bristol, Westbury Park BS6 49 B4
Berkeleys Mead BS34 37 A6
Berkeley Sq BS8 142 C3
Berkeley St BS5 50 C3
Berkeley Way BS16 52 B7
Berkshire Rd BS7 49 D3
Berlington Ct BS1 143 B1
Bernard Ireland Ho BA1 84 B1
Berners Cl BS4 79 D7
Berrow Lodge 7 BS23 104 E5
Berrows Mead BS37 27 A8
Berrow Wlk BS3 63 E2
Berry Croft 5 BS3 63 D4
Berry Hill Cl BS10 35 D1
Berry La BS7 49 F6
BERWICK 34 D6
Berwick Cl BS10 34 E8
Berwick Ct BS10 34 B5
Berwick Dr BS10 34 E5
Berwick La BS10 34 D7
Berwick Rd BS5 50 B2
Beryl Gr BS14 80 C8
Beryl Rd BS3 63 B3
Besom La BS37 39 D5
Bethel Rd BS5 64 F8
Betjeman Ct 2 BS30 66 A5
Betts Gn BS16 52 C7
Bevan Ct BS34 35 F2
Bevan Rd BS30 82 E8
Beverley Ave BS16 37 F1
Beverley Cl BS5 65 B6
Beverley Ct BS7 49 F8
Beverley Gdns BS9 48 D7
Beverley Rd BS7 49 F8
Beverstone BS15 65 C8
Beverston Gdns BS11 34 B2
BEVINGTON 2 F6
Bevington Cl BS34 23 E1
Bevington La GL13 2 F7
Bevington Wlk BS34 23 E1
Bewdley Rd BA2 102 B4
Bexley Rd BS16 51 B3
BIBSTONE 10 C3
Bibstone BS15 66 A8
Bibury Ave BS34 36 B8
Bibury Cl
Bristol BS9 49 D7
Nailsea BS48 60 A1
Bibury Cres
Bristol, Hanham BS15 65 C5
Bristol, Henleaze BS9 49 D7
Bibury Ho BA1 84 B2
Bickerton Cl BS10 34 F3
Bickfield La
Compton Martin BS40 129 B8
Ubley BS40 111 F2
Bickford Cl BS30 66 A6
Bickley Cl BS15 65 C2
Biddestone Rd BS7 35 E1
Biddisham Cl 6 BS48 59 E1
Biddle St BS49 91 B7
Bideford Cres BS4 79 F8
Bideford Rd BS22 88 F2
Bidwell Cl BS10 35 B3
Bifield Cl BS14 80 F5
Bifield Gdns BS14 80 E5
Bifield Rd BS14 80 F5
Bignell Cl BS25 124 F8

Big Tree Cl BS26 . . . . **124** C3
Bigwood La BS1 . . . . **142** C2
Bilberry Cl BS9 . . . . 48 C8
Bilbie Cl
  Bristol BS10 . . . . **49** E7
  Chew Stoke BS40 . . . . . **112** E8
Bilbie Rd
  Chew Stoke BS40 . . . . . **112** E8
  Weston-s-M BS22 . . . . . . 89 B3
Bilbury La BA1 . . . . **141** B2
Billand Cl BS13 . . . . 78 E3
Bilsham La BS35 . . . . . . 12 F2
Binces La BA2 . . . . 99 E3
Bince's Lodge La BA3 . **133** B3
Bindon Dr BS10 . . . . 35 D4
Binhay Rd BS49 . . . . . . 91 C7
Binley Gr BS41 . . . . 80 D5
Binmead Gdns BS13 . . . . 79 B4
Birbeck Rd BS9 . . . . 48 E5
Birchall Rd BS6 . . . . 49 C4
Birch Ave
  Bleadon BS24 . . . . **122** C6
  Clevedon BS21 . . . . 57 G4
Birch Cl
  Bristol BS34 . . . . 35 E7
  Locking BS24 . . . . **106** B4
Birch Croft BS14 . . . . . . 80 A3
Birch Ct
  Keynsham BS31 . . . . 81 C4
  Weston-s-M BS22 . . . . . . 89 C2
  Yate BS37 . . . . 27 D2
Birchdale Rd BS14 . . . . . 80 A8
Birchdene BS48 . . . . 60 A2
Birch Dr
  Alveston BS35 . . . . 14 F4
  Churchill BS40 . . . . **109** A5
  Pucklechurch BS16 . . . . 53 B5
Birches The BS48 . . . . . . 60 A2
Birch Gr BS20 . . . . 45 C4
Birch Ho BS16 . . . . 51 B5
Birchills Trad Est BS4 . 64 F1
Birch Rd
  Bristol, Kingswood
    BS15 . . . . 51 E3
  Bristol, Southville BS3 . . 63 B4
  Radstock BA3 . . . . **133** E1
  Yate BS37 . . . . 27 D2
Birchwood Ave BS23 . . **105** A7
Birchwood Ct BS4 . . . . . 64 F6
Birchwood Dr BS8 . . . . . 61 B3
Birchwood La BS39 . . . . 97 F2
Birchwood Rd BS4 . . . . . 64 F2
Birdale Cl BS10 . . . . 34 E3
Birdcombe Cl BS48 . . . . 59 E3
Birdlip Cl BS48 . . . . 60 A1
Birds Bush La GL12 . . . . 18 B1
Birdwell La BS41 . . . . . . 61 F1
Birdwell Prim Sch
  BS41 . . . . 78 A8
Birdwell Rd BS41 . . . . . . 61 F1
Birdwood BS15 . . . . 65 D6
Birgage Rd GL9 . . . . 19 F2
Birkdale
  Bristol BS30 . . . . 66 B6
  Yate BS37 . . . . 39 E8
Birkett Rd BS23 . . . . 87 B1
Birkin St BS2 . . . . 64 A6
Birnbeck Ct BS23 . . . . . **104** D7
Birnbeck Rd BS23 . . . . . 87 C1
Biscay Dr BS20 . . . . 45 F6
Bisdee Rd BS24 . . . . . . **105** D2
Bishop Ave BS22 . . . . . . 89 A3
Bishop La BS7 . . . . 49 E4
Bishop Manor Rd BS10 49 D7
Bishop Rd
  Bristol, Bishopston BS7 . 49 D4
  Bristol, Emerson's Green
    BS16 . . . . 52 C6
Bishop Road Prim Sch
  BS7 . . . . 49 D4
Bishops Cl BS9 . . . . 48 E3
Bishops Cove BS13 . . . . 78 F5
Bishops Ct BS9 . . . . 48 C3
Bishops Knoll BS9 . . . . . 48 C3
Bishops Mead BS49 . . . . 92 A8
Bishops Rd BS49 . . . . . . 92 A8
Bishop St
  Bristol BS2 . . . . **143** B4
  Faulkland BA3 . . . . **135** D2
BISHOPSTON 49 C3
BISHOP SUTTON **113** D3
Bishop Sutton Prim Sch
  BS39 . . . . **113** D4
Bishop's Wood BS32 . . 24 C6
BISHOPSWORTH 79 A5
Bishopsworth CE Jun Sch
  BS13 . . . . 78 F6
Bishopsworth Rd BS13 . 79 A7
Bishop Terr BS2 . . . . . . **143** C4
Bishopthorpe Rd BS10 . 49 E7
Bishport Ave BS13 . . . . . 79 C3
Bishport Cl BS13 . . . . . . 79 B4
Bishport Gn BS13 . . . . . 79 C3
Bisley BS37 . . . . 39 C7
Bissex Mead BS16 . . . . . 52 B5
Bittern Cl BS22 . . . . . . 88 F1

Bitterwell Cl BS36 . . . . . . 38 D3
Bittlemead BS13 . . . . . . 79 F4
BITTON 82 E7
Bitton Sta★ BS30 . . . . . 66 B1
Blackacre BS14 . . . . 80 C4
Blackberry Ave 5 BS16 50 E5
Blackberry Cl 5 BS37 . . 27 F4
Blackberry Dr
  Frampton Cotterell
    BS36 . . . . 38 C6
  Weston-s-M BS22 . . . . . . 89 A2
Blackberry Hill BS16 . . . 50 E5
Blackberry Hill Hospl
  BS16 . . . . 50 F5
Blackberry La
  Portishead BS20 . . . . . . 44 F2
  Winsley BA2 . . . . **120** C8
Blackberry Way BA3 . **132** F3
Blackbird Cl BA3 . . . . . **139** B8
Blackcurrant Dr BS41 . . 77 E8
Blackdown Ct BS14 . . . . 80 B5
Blackdown Rd BS20 . . . . 45 B5
Blackdown Way BA3 . . **139** B6
Blackfriars BS1 . . . . **143** A3
Blackfriars Rd BS48 . . . . 59 B1
BLACKHORSE 52 A7
Blackhorse Ct BS16 . . . . 52 A8
Blackhorse Ct BS15 . . . . 65 C8
Blackhorse Hill BS35,
  BS10 . . . . 35 B8
Blackhorse La BS16 . . . . 52 A8
Blackhorse Pl BS16 . . . . 52 A6
Blackhorse Prim Sch
  BS16 . . . . 52 A8
Blackhorse Rd
  Bristol, Kingswood
    BS15 . . . . 65 D8
  Bristol, Mangotsfield
    BS16 . . . . 52 A7
Black La BS26 . . . . **125** E2
BLACKMOOR
  Chew Stoke 95 C3
  Lower Langford **109** D6
Blackmoor
  Charterhouse BS40 . . . **127** F4
  Clevedon BS21 . . . . 57 F1
  Lower Langford BS40 . . **109** C6
  3 Weston-s-M BS22 . . . . 88 F2
Blackmoor Cl BS40 . . . **109** C6
Blackmoor Rd BS8 . . . . . 47 E2
Blackmoors La BS3 . . . . 62 E4
Blackmore Dr BA2 . . . . **101** C5
Black Nore Point BS20 . 44 F5
BLACKROCK 97 E8
Blackrock La BS39 . . . . . 97 E7
Black Rock Nature Trail★
  BA5 . . . . **127** A1
Blackrock Villas BS20 . . 45 B1
Blacksmith La BA1 . . . . 85 B6
Blacksmith's La BA1 . . . 83 B3
Blacksworth Ho 6 BS5 64 D7
Blacksworth Rd BS5 . . . . 64 D7
Blackthorn Cl BS13 . . . . 79 D5
Blackthorn Dr
  Bristol BS32 . . . . 36 D7
  Portishead BS20 . . . . . . 45 E5
Blackthorn Gdns BS22 . 89 A1
Blackthorn Rd BS13 . . . . 79 D5
Blackthorn Sq BS21 . . . . 57 F1
Blackthorn Terr BS22 . . 89 A1
Blackthorn Way BS48 . . 60 A2
Blackthorn Wlk BS15 . . 51 E2
Bladen Cl 1 BS20 . . . . . 45 E4
Bladud Bldgs BA1 . . . . **141** C3
BLAGDON **110** F1
Blagdon Cl
  Bristol BS3 . . . . 63 E2
  Weston-s-M BS24 . . . . . **104** F1
Blagdon La BS40 . . . . . **110** F6
Blagdon Pk BA2 . . . . . **101** A4
Blagdon Prim Sch
  BS40 . . . . **110** E2
Blagrove Cl BS13 . . . . . . 79 C3
Blagrove Cres BS13 . . . . 79 C3
Blaisdon
  Weston-s-M BS22 . . . . . **105** D7
  Yate BS37 . . . . 39 E7
Blaisdon Cl BS10 . . . . . . 35 A1
Blaise Castle Mus★
  BS10 . . . . 34 E2
Blaisedell View BS10 . . 34 D3
Blaise Hamlet BS11 . . . 34 D2
Blaise Prim Sch BS10 . . 34 F2
Blaise Wlk BS9 . . . . 48 C6
Blake End BS22 . . . . 88 E4
Blakeney Gr BS48 . . . . . 75 C8
Blakeney Mills BS37 . . . 27 E1
Blakeney Rd
  Bristol BS34 . . . . 23 E1
  Bristol, Horfield BS7 . . . . 50 A7
Blake Rd BS7 . . . . 50 B6
Blakes Rd BS35 . . . . 8 B1
Blanchards BS37 . . . . . . 40 D8
Blanchards Cotts BS37 . 40 D8
Blandford Cl
  2 Bristol BS9 . . . . 49 B6
  Nailsea BS48 . . . . 59 E1
Blandmour Way BS10 . . 35 D2
Blands Row BS35 . . . . . . 12 B1

BLEADON **122** C7
Bleadon Hill BS23,
  BS24 . . . . **122** A8
Bleadon Mill BS24 . . . . **122** C5
Bleadon Rd BS24 . . . . . **122** B7
Blenheim Cl
  Peasedown St John
    BA2 . . . . **134** D7
  Weston-s-M BS22 . . . . . . 89 A2
Blenheim Ct
  10 Bristol, Kingsdown
    BS1 . . . . **143** A4
  Bristol, Patchway BS32 . **24** C3
Blenheim Dr
  Bristol BS34 . . . . 36 B4
  Yate BS37 . . . . 27 D3
Blenheim Gdns BA1 . . . 85 A2
Blenheim Rd BS6 . . . . . . 49 B3
Blenheim St BS5 . . . . . . 50 A1
Blenheim Way BS20 . . . . 45 E5
Blenman Cl BS16 . . . . . . 51 A7
Blethwin Cl BS10 . . . . . . 34 F1
Blew Cl BS29 . . . . **106** C7
Blind La
  Bath BA1 . . . . 84 C2
  Chew Stoke BS40 . . . . . **112** E8
  Congresbury BS49 . . . . . 91 F6
  Tunley BA2 . . . . **117** A4
  Yatton BS49 . . . . 91 F7
BLOOMFIELD
  Bath **101** E3
  Timsbury **116** B4
Bloomfield
  Hallatrow BS39 . . . . . . **132** A6
  Weston-s-M BS24 . . . . . **105** A2
Bloomfield Ave
  Bath BA2 . . . . **101** E4
  Timsbury BA2 . . . . **116** B3
Bloomfield Cl BA2 . . . . **116** B3
Bloomfield Cotts BA2 . **134** C7
Bloomfield Cres BA2 . . **101** D2
Bloomfield Dr BA2 . . . . **101** D2
Bloomfield Gr BA2 . . . . **101** E3
Bloomfield La BS39 . . . **132** E5
Bloomfield Park Rd
  BA2 . . . . **116** B3
Bloomfield Pk BA2 . . . . **101** E3
Bloomfield Rd
  Bath BA2 . . . . **101** E3
  Bristol BS4 . . . . 64 D4
  Timsbury BA2 . . . . **116** B3
Bloomfield Rise BA2 . . **101** D2
Bloomfield Rise N
  BA2 . . . . **101** D2
Bloomfield Road Link
  BS4 . . . . 64 C4
Bloomfield Terr BA2 . . **134** C7
Bloy St BS5 . . . . 50 C1
Bluebell Cl
  Bristol BS9 . . . . 48 B6
  2 Goose Green BS37 . . 27 F5
Bluebell Rd BS22 . . . . . . 89 A6
Bluebell Dr BS31 . . . . . . 81 D3
Bluebell Rise BA3 . . . . **132** F3
Bluebells The BS32 . . . . 36 F7
Bluebell Way BS16 . . . . 38 C1
Blueberry Way BS22 . . . 88 F1
Blue Falcon Rd BS15 . . 51 E1
Blue Iris Rd BS16 . . . . . 52 D8
Blue Water Dr BS24 . . **106** D3
Blythe Gdns BS22 . . . . . 89 A3
Boardinghouse La
  BS35 . . . . 23 C5
Boat La BS24 . . . . **122** C3
Boat Stall La BA2 . . . . **141** C2
Bobbin La BA15 . . . . . . **120** F4
Bobbin Pk BA15 . . . . . . **120** F3
Bockenem Cl BS35 . . . . 15 D7
Bodey Cl BS30 . . . . 66 A5
Bodley Way BS24 . . . . . **105** E7
Bodmin Wlk BS4 . . . . . . 79 F8
Bodyce Rd 4 BS35 . . . . 15 A5
Bofors Twr BS23 . . . . . **105** B4
Boiling Wells La BS2 . . . 50 A3
Bolingbroke Way BS34 . 36 B5
Bolton Rd BS7 . . . . 49 E3
Bond St BS16 . . . . 14 C8
Bond's La SN14 . . . . 69 E8
Bond St BS1 . . . . **143** B4
Bonhill La BS39 . . . . . . **113** D5
Bonhill Rd BS39 . . . . . . **113** D5
Bonnington Wlk BS7 . . . 50 B7
Bonville Bsns Ctr BS4 . . 64 F2
Bonville Rd BS4 . . . . 64 F2
Boon Villas BS11 . . . . . . 47 E7
Booth Rd BS3 . . . . 63 C4
Boot La BS3 . . . . 63 D4
Bordesley Rd BS14 . . . . 80 A3
Boreal Way 4 BS24 . . **105** F7
Borgie Pl BS22 . . . . 88 F3
Borkley St BS7 . . . . 36 A7
Borleyton Wlk BS13 . . . 78 F4
Borver Gr BS13 . . . . 79 B4
Boscombe Cres BS16 . . 51 F7
Boston Rd BS7 . . . . 49 F8
Boswell Rd BA15 . . . . . **120** F3
Boswell St 4 BS5 . . . . . 50 C2
Botham Cl BS22 . . . . . . 89 A4

Botham Dr BS4 . . . . 64 E1
Bottoms Farm La BS30 . 53 F1
Boucher Pl 2 BS2 . . . . . 50 A2
Boulevard BS23 . . . . . . **104** E8
Boulters Rd BS13 . . . . . 79 C4
Boulton's La 5 BS15 . . . 65 D8
Boulton's Rd 5 BS15 . . 65 D8
Boundaries The BS24 . . **122** B1
Boundary Cl
  Kingswood G12 . . . . . . 11 E4
  Midsomer Norton BA3 . **139** B7
  Weston-s-M BS23 . . . . . **104** E3
Boundary Rd
  Avonmouth BS11 . . . . . 33 D3
  Frampton Cotterell BS36 38 D7
  Weston-s-M BS24 . . . . . **106** A7
Bourchier Gdns BS13 . . 79 B3
BOURNE **110** B4
Bourne Cl
  Bristol BS15 . . . . 65 B8
  Winterbourne BS36 . . . . 37 E7
Bourne La
  Blagdon BS40 . . . . **110** C4
  Bristol BS5 . . . . 50 B2
  Burrington BA3 . . . . . . **110** B4
Bourne Rd BS15 . . . . . . 65 A8
Bourneville Rd BS5 . . . . 64 D8
BOURNSTREAM 5 F2
Bournville Com Inf Sch
  BS23 . . . . **105** A4
Bournville Jun Sch
  BS23 . . . . **104** F5
Bournville Rd BS23 . . . **104** F4
Boursland Cl BS32 . . . . . 24 D2
BOURTON 89 C6
Bourton Ave BS34 . . . . . 36 C8
Bourton Cl BS34 . . . . . . 36 C8
Bourton Combe BS48 . . 76 F7
Bourton La
  Cross BS26 . . . . **124** E3
  Weston-s-M BS22 . . . . . . 89 D4
Bourton Mead
  Flax Bourton BS48 . . . . . 76 F8
  Long Ashton BS41 . . . . . 62 A1
Bourton Wlk BS13 . . . . . 79 A8
Bouverie St BS5 . . . . 64 B8
Boverton Rd BS34 . . . . . 36 B4
Bow Cotts BS20 . . . . 47 C4
Bowden Cl BS9 . . . . 48 C8
Bowden Hill BA3 . . . . . **138** D4
Bowden Pl BS16 . . . . . . 51 F7
Bowden Rd BS5 . . . . 50 E1
Bowden Way BS8 . . . . . . 61 B3
Bowen Rd BS24 . . . . . . **106** C5
BOWER ASHTON 62 E4
Bower Ashton Terr BS3 . 62 F4
Bower Ct BS3 . . . . 63 A2
Bowerleaze BS9 . . . . 48 C5
Bower Rd BS3 . . . . 63 A3
Bower Wlk BS3 . . . . 63 E3
Bowland Cl BS24 . . . . . . 24 D1
Bowlditch La BA3 . . . . **133** B4
Bowling Hill BS37 . . . . . 28 A1
Bowling Hill Bsns Pk
  BS37 . . . . 28 A1
Bowling Rd BS37 . . . . . . 40 B8
Bowmead 7 BS4 . . . . . . 64 D1
Bowood BS16 . . . . 37 C1
Bowring Cl BS13 . . . . . . 79 C3
Bowsland BS32 . . . . 24 E2
Bowsland Green Prim Sch
  BS32 . . . . 24 E2
Bowsland Way BS32 . . . 24 D2
Bowstreet La BS35 . . . . 35 A8
Boxbury Hill BS39 . . . . **132** F3
Box Bush La BS24 . . . . . 90 C1
Boxhedge Farm La
  BS36 . . . . 38 E3
Box Rd BA1 . . . . 86 C3
Box Wlk BS31 . . . . 81 C4
Boyce Cl BA2 . . . . **100** F5
Boyce Dr BS2 . . . . 50 A2
Boyce's Ave BS8 . . . . . **142** A3
Boyd Cl BS30 . . . . 67 B7
Boyd Rd BS31 . . . . 82 D3
Brabazon Rd BS34 . . . . . 36 B2
Bracewell Gdns BS10 . . 35 C4
Bracey Dr BS16 . . . . 51 C6
Brackenbury Dr BS34 . . 36 F5
Brackendene BS32 . . . . 24 D3
Brackenwood Rd BS21 . 57 G6
Bracton Dr BS14 . . . . . . 80 A5
Bradeston Gr BS16 . . . . 51 A7
Bradford Cl BS21 . . . . . . 57 E1
Bradford Pk BA2 . . . . . **102** A2
Bradford Rd
  Bath BA2 . . . . **102** A1
  Bathford BA1 . . . . 86 B2
  Winsley BA15 . . . . **120** E7
  Winsley, Avonpark
    BA15 . . . . **120** D6
Bradhurst St 8 BS5 . . . 64 B6
BRADLEY 11 F8
Bradley Ave
  Bristol BS11 . . . . 47 E6
  Winterbourne BS36 . . . . 37 E5
Bradley Cres BS11 . . . . . 47 E6
Bradley Ct BS16 . . . . 51 C5
BRADLEY GREEN 11 E7

Bradley Pavilions BS32 24 C2
Bradley Rd
  Bristol BS34 . . . . 23 F1
  Portbury BS20 . . . . 46 E5
BRADLEY STOKE 36 F8
Bradley Stoke Com Sch
  BS32 . . . . 36 E8
Bradley Stoke Way
  BS32 . . . . 36 F7
Bradstone Rd BS36 . . . . 37 D5
Bradville Gdns BS41 . . . 77 F8
Bradwell Gr BS10 . . . . . 49 C8
Braemar Ave BS7 . . . . . 35 F1
Braemar Cres BS7 . . . . . 35 F1
Braemor Ct BS9 . . . . . . 49 A8
Brae Rd BS25 . . . . **125** B8
Brae Rise BS25 . . . . **125** A8
Bragg's La BS2 . . . . **143** C3
Braikenridge Cl BS21 . . 57 E1
Braikenridge Rd BS4 . . 64 D4
Brainsfield BS9 . . . . 48 F6
Brake Cl
  Bristol, Bradley Stoke
    BS32 . . . . 36 E7
  Bristol, Warmley Hill
    BS15 . . . . 65 F7
Brake The
  Frampton Cotterell
    BS36 . . . . 38 C5
  Yate BS37 . . . . 27 E5
Brakewell Gdns BS14 . . 80 A4
Bramble Cl BS16 . . . . . . 52 D7
Bramble Dr BS9 . . . . . . 48 D3
Bramble La BS9 . . . . 48 C3
Brambles The
  Bristol BS13 . . . . 79 C4
  Hinton Charterhouse
    BA2 . . . . **119** E1
  Keynsham BS31 . . . . 81 D3
  Weston-s-M BS22 . . . . . . 89 D2
Bramble Way BA2 . . . . **102** B1
Bramblewood BS49 . . . . 74 B1
Bramblewood Rd BS22 . 88 E3
Brambling Wlk BS16 . . 50 F6
Bramley Cl
  Kingswood GL12 . . . . . . 11 F4
  Locking BS24 . . . . **106** A5
  Olveston BS35 . . . . 14 A3
  Peasedown St John
    BA2 . . . . **134** D7
  Pill BS20 . . . . 47 C4
  Sandford BS25 . . . . **108** A4
  Yatton BS49 . . . . 91 B7
Bramley Copse BS41 . . . 77 E8
Bramley Ct 6 BS30 . . . 65 F4
Bramley Dr BS48 . . . . . . 76 A5
Bramley Sq BS49 . . . . . . 91 E3
Bramleys The
  Nailsea BS48 . . . . 75 B8
  Portishead BS20 . . . . . . 45 F5
Bramling Ave BS20 . . . . 46 A6
Brampton Ho 4 BS20 . . 45 E4
Brampton Way BS20 . . . 45 E4
Bramshill Dr BS22 . . . . . 88 F3
Branche Gr BS13 . . . . . . 79 D3
Branches Cross BS40 . . 92 E3
Branch Rd BA2 . . . . **119** F2
Brandash Rd BS37 . . . . . 28 C1
Brandon Cotts BS1 . . . . **142** C2
BRANDON HILL **142** B2
Brandon Ho BS8 . . . . . **142** B2
Brandon St BS1 . . . . . . **142** C2
Brandon Steep BS1 . . . **142** C2
Brandown Cl BS39 . . . . **114** E1
Brangwyn Gr BS7 . . . . . 50 B6
Brangwyn Sq BS22 . . . . 88 F2
Branksome Cres BS34 . . 36 B3
Branksome Dr
  Bristol BS34 . . . . 36 B3
  Winterbourne BS36 . . . . 37 E6
Branksome Rd BS6 . . . . 49 B3
Bransby Way BS24 . . . . **106** A8
Branscombe Ct BS3 . . . 63 D2
Branscombe Rd BS9 . . . 48 C4
Branscombe Wlk BS20 . 44 F3
Branwhite Cl BS7 . . . . . 50 B7
BRASSKNOCKER **102** F2
Brassknocker Hill BA2 **102** F2
Brassmill Ent Ctr BA1 **101** A7
Brassmill La BA1 . . . . . **101** A7
Brassmill Lane Trad Est
  BA1 . . . . **101** A7
Bratton Rd BS4 . . . . 79 D7
Braunton Rd BS3 . . . . . . 63 C3
Braydon Ave BS32 . . . . . 36 D7
Brayne Ct BS30 . . . . 65 F3
Braysdown Cl BA2 . . . . **134** B6
Braysdown La BA2 . . . . **134** C7
BREACH **114** F6
Breaches Gate BS32 . . . 36 F6
Breaches The BS20 . . . . 47 B5
Breach Hill Comm
  BS40 . . . . **112** A5
Breach Hill La BS40 . . . **112** C6
Breach La BS48 . . . . 74 F7
Breach Rd BS3 . . . . 63 A3
Breachwood View
  BA2 . . . . **101** C2
BREAN **121** A5

Brean Down Ave
Bristol BS9. . . . . .49 B5
Weston-s-M BS23 . . . . .104 E4
Brean Gdns BS3 . . . . . . .63 E2
Brean Rd BS24. . . . . . . .121 F1
Brecknock Rd BS4 . . . . .64 A3
Brecon Cl BS9 . . . . .49 B6
Brecon Ct BS16 . . . . . . .36 D1
Brecon Rd BS9 . . . . .49 B6
Brecon View BS24. . . . .105 A1
Bredon BS37. . . . . .39 D7
Bredon Cl BS15. . . . . . . .65 F7
Bredon Nook Rd BS10. .49 C7
Bree Cl BS22. . . . . .89 A4
Brendon Ave BS23. . . . .104 F8
Brendon Cl BS30. . . . . . .66 C4
Brendon Gdns 2 BS48 . .59 E1
Brendon Rd
Bristol BS3. . . . . .63 D3
Portishead BS20 . . . . . . .45 A5
Brennan Cl BS4. . . . . . . .79 F7
Brenner St BS5 . . . . .50 B2
Brent Cl BS24. . . . . . . .105 B2
Brent Rd BS7. . . . . .49 F5
BRENTRY. 35 B2
Brentry Ave 5 BS5. . . . .64 B7
Brentry La BS10. . . . . . . .35 B3
Brentry Lo BS10. . . . . . . .35 A3
Brentry Prim Sch BS10. .35 B4
Brentry Rd BS16. . . . . . . .50 F3
Brereton Way BS30. . . . .66 B4
Brewerton Cl BS10. . . . . .35 C3
Brewery Ct BS3. . . . . . . .63 A4
Brewery Hill BS30. . . . . .82 F7
Brewery La BS3. . . . . . .139 D1
Brewhouse The BS1. . . .143 B2
Briar Cl
Nailsea BS48 . . . . .60 A2
Radstock BA3. . . . . . . .139 D8
Briar Ct BS20. . . . . .47 C4
Briarfield Ave BS15 . . . . .65 C5
Briarlands Office Pk
BS35. . . . . .15 A2
Briarleaze BS35. . . . . . . .14 F2
Briar Mead BS49. . . . . . .74 A1
Briar Rd BS24. . . . . . . .105 E3
Briars Ct BA2. . . . . . . .101 A4
Briarside Ho BS10 . . . . . .35 D3
Briarside Rd BS10. . . . . .35 D3
Briars The BS48. . . . . . . .75 F7
Briar Way BS16 . . . . .51 C3
Briar Wlk BS16 . . . . .51 C3
Briarwood BS9 . . . . .48 F6
Briarwood Sch BS16 . . . .51 B3
Briary Rd BS20. . . . . . . .45 C5
Briavels Gr BS6. . . . . . . .49 F2
Brick Cotts BS35. . . . . . . .6 E1
Brick Hill Way BS34. . . . .35 E6
Brick St BS2. . . . . .143 C3
Bridewell La
Bath BA1. . . . . .141 B2
Hutton BS24, BS26,
BS29 . . . . .106 D1
Bridewell St BS1. . . . . .143 A3
Bridge Access Rd BS35 .13 A7
Bridge Bldgs BS39 . . . .132 B3
Bridge Cl BS14. . . . . . . .80 C4
Bridge Farm Cl BS14 . . .80 A3
Bridge Farm Prim Sch
Bristol BS14. . . . . .80 A4
Bristol BS14. . . . . .80 A4
Bridge Farm Sq BS49. . . .91 D4
Bridge Farm Wlk BS16 . .52 B3
Bridge Gdns BA2. . . . . .116 A6
Bridge Ho
Alveston BS35 . . . . .14 F5
11 Bath BA1. . . . . .85 C1
Bristol BS1. . . . . .143 A2
9 Clevedon BS21. . . . . .57 E2
Weston-s-M BS23 . . . . .104 F6
Bridgeleap Rd BS16. . . . .51 F8
Bridge Place Rd BA2. . .133 E8
Bridge Rd
Bath BA2. . . . . .101 C5
Bleadon BS24. . . . . . . .122 B6
Bristol, Eastville BS5. . . . .50 B3
Bristol, Lower Soundwell
BS15. . . . . .52 A3
Bristol, Shortwood BS16 .52 C4
Leigh Woods BS8 . . . . . .62 E6
Weston-s-M BS23 . . . . .104 F6
Yate BS37. . . . . .27 A2
Bridge Road Ind Est
BS15. . . . . .52 A3
Bridges Ct 2 BS16. . . . .51 B4
Bridges Dr 3 BS16. . . . .51 C6
Bridge St
Bath BA2. . . . . .141 C2
Bristol BS1. . . . . .143 A2
Bristol, Eastville BS5. . . . .50 C2
Bridge Valley Rd BS8 . . .62 E8
Bridge Way BS36. . . . . . .38 B8
Bridge Wlk BS7. . . . . . . .50 A8
BRIDGE YATE. 66 E7
Bridgman Gr BS34. . . . . .36 B3
Bridgwater Ct BS24. . . .105 A3
Bridgwater Rd
Dundry BS41, BS13,
BS48 . . . . .78 D6

Bridgwater Rd *continued*
Felton BS48. . . . . .94 A8
Lympsham BS24. . . . . .122 C4
Weston-s-M BS23, BS24 .104 F2
Winscombe BS25. . . . . .125 A5
Bridle Ave BS14. . . . . . .80 D3
Bridle Way BS35. . . . . . .14 F4
Bridleway Cl BA3 . . . . .138 E8
Briercliffe Rd BS9. . . . . .48 D7
Brierly Furlong BS34. . . .36 D3
Briery Leaze Rd BS14. . . .80 A4
Brighton Cres BS3 . . . . . .63 B2
Brighton Mews BS8 . . . .142 B4
Brighton Pk 16 BS5 . . . . .64 B8
Brighton Pl BS15. . . . . . .51 D1
Brighton Rd
Bristol, Patchway BS34 . . .35 F8
Bristol, Redland BS6 . . . . .49 C1
Weston-s-M BS23 . . . . .104 E6
Brighton St
12 Bristol BS2 . . . . .49 E1
7 Bristol BS2 . . . . .143 B4
Brighton Terr 9 BS3 . . . .63 B2
Bright St
Bristol, Kingswood
BS15. . . . . .65 D8
Bristol, Russell Town BS5 .64 B7
Brigstocke Rd BS2. . . . .143 B4
Brimbles The BS7 . . . . . .36 B2
Brimbleworth La BS22 . . .89 C3
Brimridge Rd BS25. . . . .125 A8
Brimsham Green Sch
BS37. . . . . .27 D4
Brimsham Park Sh Ctr
BS37. . . . . .27 F4
Brinkmarsh La GL12. . . . . .9 D2
Brinkworth Rd BA2 . . . .102 B2
Brinkworthy Rd BS16. . . .50 E6
Brinmead Wlk BS13. . . . .78 F3
Brins Cl BS34. . . . . .36 F4
BRINSEA. 108 E8
Brinsea Batch BS49. . . .108 E8
Brinsea Green Farm La
BS49. . . . . .108 F8
Brinsea La BS49 . . . . . .108 F8
Brinsea Rd BS49 . . . . . . .91 E2
Brinsham La BS37. . . . . . .28 A6
Brinsmead Cres BS20 . . .47 D4
Briscoes Ave BS13. . . . . .79 D4
BRISLINGTON 64 E2
Brislington Hill BS4 . . . . .64 E2
Brislington Ret Pk BS4. . .64 E1
Brislington Trad Est
BS4. . . . . .64 F2
Bristol & Anchor Ho
BS5. . . . . .64 D8
Bristol and Exeter Mews
BS1. . . . . .143 C2
Bristol Beacon BS1. . .143 A3
Bristol Bsns Pk BS16. . . .36 E1
Bristol Cathedral Sch
BS1. . . . . .142 C2
Bristol Dental Hospl
BS1. . . . . .143 A3
Bristol Eye Hospl BS1 .143 A3
Bristol Gate 1 BS8 . . . .62 F5
Bristol Gateway Sch The
BS2. . . . . .50 A2
Bristol General Hospl
BS1. . . . . .143 A1
Bristol Gram Sch BS8 .142 C3
Bristol Harbour Rly
BS1. . . . . .142 C1
Bristol Hill BS4 . . . . .64 D2
Bristol Hippodrome The
BS1. . . . . .142 C2
Bristol Homeopathic Hospl
BS6. . . . . .142 C4
Bristol Ind Mus BS1 .143 A1
Bristol International
Airport BS48 . . . . .93 E7
Bristol Old Vic Theatre Sch
BS8. . . . . .49 A1
Bristol Parkway N BS34 .37 A5
Bristol Parkway Sta
BS34. . . . . .36 E4
Bristol Rd
Bristol BS16. . . . . .37 C2
Chew Stoke BS40. . . . . .112 E8
Churchill BS25. . . . . . . .109 A5
Congresbury BS49. . . . . .91 D5
Cromhall GL12. . . . . .17 B7
Farrington Gurney BS39 .131 F5
Frampton Cotterell BS36 .26 B3
Keynsham BS31. . . . . . .81 E6
Luckington SN14 . . . . . .31 E3
Newton St Loe BA2 . . . .100 D7
Paulton BS39. . . . . . . .132 E7
Pensford BS39. . . . . . . .97 D6
Portishead BS20 . . . . . . .45 E4
Radstock BA3. . . . . . . .133 F3
Redhill BS40. . . . . .94 A3
Thornbury BS35. . . . . . . .15 B8
Weston-s-M BS22 . . . . . .89 C2
Whitchurch BS14 . . . . . . .80 D3
Winscombe BS25. . . . . .125 C8
Winterbourne BS16 . . . . .37 D4
Wraxall BS48. . . . . .60 D4

Bristol Rd By-pass
BS40. . . . . .109 C5
Bristol Rd Lower BS23. . .87 F1
Bristol Royal Hospl for
Children BS1. . . . . . .143 A3
Bristol Royal Infmy
BS2. . . . . .143 A4
Bristol Southend BS3 . . .63 D2
Bristol Steiner Waldorf
Sch BS6 . . . . .49 B2
Bristol Temple Meads Sta
BS1. . . . . .143 C1
Bristol Vale Trad Est
BS3. . . . . .63 B1
Bristol View BA2. . . . . .118 C8
Bristol Zoo Gdns BS8. .48 F1
Bristow Broadway
BS11. . . . . .33 C1
Bristowe Ho BS16. . . . . .51 B5
Bristowe Lodge BS16. . . .51 C4
Britannia Bldgs BS8. . . .142 A1
Britannia Cl
4 Bristol BS16. . . . . . . .37 F1
Chilcompton BA3 . . . . . .138 D4
Britannia Cres BS34. . . . .36 D5
Britannia Ct 1 BS16. . . . .51 D5
Britannia Ho BS34 . . . . . .35 F2
Britannia Rd
Bristol, Kingswood
BS15. . . . . .65 C8
Bristol, Lower Easton
BS5. . . . . .50 C1
Bristol, Patchway BS34 . . .35 E7
Britannia Way BS21. . . . .57 E1
British Rd BS3. . . . . .63 C3
British The BS37. . . . . . . .27 B4
Brittan Pl BS20. . . . . .46 E3
Britten Cl 10 BS30 . . . . . .65 F4
BRITTENS. 132 E6
Brittens BS39. . . . . .132 F6
Britten's Cl BS39. . . . . .132 F6
Britten's Hill BS39. . . . .132 F6
Britton Bottom GL9 . . . . .20 B1
Britton Gdns BS15. . . . . .51 C1
Britton Ho BS15. . . . . . . .66 B8
Brittons Pass SN14. . . . . .69 F8
Brixham Rd BS3 . . . . .63 C1
Brixton Rd BS5. . . . . .64 B8
Brixton Road Mews 22
BS5. . . . . .64 B8
Broadbury Rd BS4 . . . . . .79 E8
Broad Cft BS34. . . . . .35 F6
Broadcroft BS40. . . . . . . .95 F3
Broad Croft BS32. . . . . . .24 C2
Broadcroft Ave BS49. . . . .74 F1
Broadcroft Cl BS49. . . . . .74 F1
Broadfield Ave BS15. . . . .51 C1
Broadfield Ct BS15. . . . . .65 C8
Broadfield Rd
Bristol BS4. . . . . .64 B1
Bristol BS4. . . . . .80 A8
Broad La
Henfield BS36 . . . . .38 D5
Westerleigh BS37 . . . . . . .39 A4
Yate BS37. . . . . .27 C4
Broadlands BS21. . . . . . . .57 H3
Broadlands Ave BS31. . . .81 D6
Broadlands Dr BS11. . . . . .34 A1
Broadlands Sch BS31 . . . .81 D6
Broadleas BS13. . . . . .79 C7
Broad Leaze 5 BS34 . . . .35 F7
Broadleaze Way BS25. . .107 F2
Broadleys Ave BS9 . . . . . .49 C7
Broadmead BS1 . . . . . . .143 B3
Broadmead La BS31. . . . .82 A6
Broad Mead La BS40. . . . .95 A3
Broadmead Lane Ind Est
BS31. . . . . .82 B7
Broadmoor La BA1. . . . . .84 A3
Broadmoor Pk BA1. . . . . .84 B2
Broadmoor Vale BA1. . . . .84 A3
Broadoak Hill BS41. . . . . .78 F2
Broadoak Mathematics &
Computing Coll
BS23. . . . . .104 E3
Broadoak Rd
Churchill BS40. . . . . . . .109 A5
Weston-s-M BS23 . . . . .104 D3
Broad Oak Rd BS13 . . . . .78 F4
Broad Oaks BS8. . . . . . . .62 E6
Broadoak Wlk BS16. . . . . .51 B4
Broad Plain BS2 . . . . . . .143 C2
Broad Quay
Bath BA1. . . . . .141 C1
Bristol BS1. . . . . .143 A2
Broad Rd
Blagdon BS40. . . . . . . .127 D8
Bristol BS15. . . . . .51 C1
Broad St
Bath BA1. . . . . .141 C3
Bristol BS1. . . . . .143 A3
Bristol, Staple Hill BS16 . .51 F4
Chipping Sodbury BS37 . .28 B1
Congresbury BS49. . . . . .91 D4
Wrington BS40. . . . . . . .92 D2
Broadstone La BS21. . . . . .72 F3
Broadstones BA15 . . . . .103 E7
Broadstone Wlk BS13 . . . .79 D5

Broad Street Pl BA1. . .141 C3
Broadwalk Sh Ctr BS4. . .64 D2
Broadway
Bath BA2. . . . . .102 B6
Chilcompton BA3 . . . . . .138 C3
Locking BS24. . . . . .106 D4
Saltford BS31. . . . . .82 D3
Shipham BS25. . . . . . . .125 E8
Weston-s-M BS24 . . . . .105 A2
Yate BS37. . . . . .27 F2
Broadway Acres BS27 .125 F1
Broadway Ave BS9 . . . . . .49 D6
Broadway Cl BA3 . . . . . .138 C3
Broadway Inf Sch
BS37. . . . . .27 F2
Broadway La BA3 . . . . . .133 B5
Broadway Rd
Bristol, Bishopston BS7. . .49 D3
Bristol, Bishopsworth
BS13. . . . . .78 F5
Broadways Dr BS16. . . . . .50 F7
Broadway The GL11 . . . . . .5 F8
Broad Weir BS1. . . . . . .143 B3
Broad Wlk BS4. . . . . .64 A2
Brock End BS20. . . . . . . .44 F3
Brockeridge Inf Sch
BS36. . . . . .38 C7
Brockhurst Gdns BS15 . . .65 A8
Brockhurst Rd BS15. . . . .65 A8
BROCKLEY. 75 C2
Brockley Cl
Bristol BS34. . . . . .36 C7
Nailsea BS48 . . . . .59 D1
Weston-s-M BS24 . . . . .104 F1
Brockley Combe Rd
BS48. . . . . .76 B1
Brockley Cres BS24. . . . .104 F1
Brockley La BS48 . . . . . . .75 D4
Brockley Mini Farm
(Open Farm) BS48 . .92 F7
Brockley Rd BS31. . . . . . .82 D3
Brockley Way BS49. . . . . .75 B3
Brockley Wlk BS13 . . . . . .79 A8
Brockridge La BS36. . . . . .38 C7
Brocks 4 BS4. . . . . .64 D1
Brocks La BS41. . . . . .61 F1
Brocks Rd BS13. . . . . . . .79 C3
Brock St BA1. . . . . .141 B3
Brockway BS48. . . . . .59 F2
Brockwood BA15. . . . . .120 F7
Brockworth BS37. . . . . . . .39 C6
Brockworth Cres BS16 . . .50 F6
Bromfield Wlk BS16. . . . . .52 B7
Bromley Dr BS16. . . . . . . .51 D8
Bromley Farm BS16. . . . . .37 D1
BROMLEY HEATH. 37 D1
Bromley Heath Ave
BS16. . . . . .51 D8
Bromley Heath Jun & Inf
Schs BS16. . . . . .51 E8
Bromley Heath Rd
BS16. . . . . .51 D8
Bromley Heath Rdbt
BS16. . . . . .37 D1
Bromley Rd
Bristol BS7. . . . . .49 F5
Stanton Drew BS39 . . . . .96 F1
Brompton Cl BS15. . . . . . .66 A8
Brompton Ho BA2. . . . . .141 C4
Brompton Rd BS24. . . . . .105 A2
Broncksea Rd BS7. . . . . . .35 F1
Bronte Cl BS23. . . . . . . .105 B4
Bronte Wlk BS7. . . . . . . .50 A8
Brook Cl BS41. . . . . .62 B1
Brookcote Dr BS34. . . . . .36 D6
Brook Cotts BA2. . . . . . .100 B7
Brook Ct BS13. . . . . .79 A6
Brookdale Rd BS13. . . . . .79 B6
Brook End SN14. . . . . . . .31 F5
Brookfield Ave BS7 . . . . . .49 D3
Brookfield Cl BS37. . . . . . .28 C2
Brookfield La 2 BS6 . . . . .49 D2
Brookfield Pk BA1. . . . . . .84 B2
Brookfield Rd
3 Bristol, Montpelier
BS6. . . . . .49 D2
Bristol, Patchway BS34 . . .36 B8
Brookfield Wlk
Bristol BS30. . . . . .66 C3
Clevedon BS21. . . . . . . .57 H3
Brook Gate BS3. . . . . . . .62 E1
Brook Gdns BS40. . . . . .109 A5
Brook Hill BS6. . . . . .49 F1
Brook Ho
Bristol BS34. . . . . .36 C8
3 Thornbury BS35. . . . . .15 C8
Brookhouse La SN14. . . . .55 B1
Brook La
Bristol, Montpelier BS6. . .49 F1
Bristol, Stapleton BS16. . .50 F6
Brookland Rd
Bristol BS6. . . . . .49 D5
Weston-s-M BS23 . . . . .105 B7
Brooklands BA2. . . . . . .117 D3
Brooklea BS30. . . . . .66 B3
Brookleaze BS9. . . . . .48 C5
Brookleaze Bldgs BA1. . .85 B2
Brook Lintons BS4. . . . . .64 D3
Brooklyn BS40. . . . . .92 D2

Brooklyn Rd
Bath BA1. . . . . .85 C2
Bristol BS13. . . . . .79 B8
Brookmead BS35. . . . . . . .15 D7
Brook Office Pk BS16. . . .38 B2
Brook Rd
Bath BA2. . . . . .101 D6
Bristol, Hillfields BS16. . . .51 B4
Bristol, Mangotsfield
BS16. . . . . .51 F6
Bristol, Montpelier BS6. . .49 F1
Bristol, Southville BS3. . . .63 D4
Bristol, Speedwell BS5. . .50 F1
Bristol, Warmley BS5. . . .66 B8
Brookridge Ct 6 BS16. . .51 D4
Brookridge Ho BS10 . . . . .34 F3
Brookside
Paulton BS39. . . . . . . .132 E6
Pill BS20. . . . . .47 D3
Winford BS40. . . . . .94 F7
Brookside Cl
Batheaston BA1. . . . . . . .85 F5
Paulton BS39. . . . . . . .132 E6
Brookside Dr
Farmborough BA2 . . . . .115 F6
Frampton Cotterell BS36 .38 B8
Brookside Ho BA1. . . . . . .84 B1
Brookside Rd BS4. . . . . . .64 E2
Brook St BS5. . . . . .64 C7
Brookthorpe BS37 . . . . . .39 D8
Brookthorpe Ave BS11. . .34 A1
Brookthorpe Ct BS37. . . . .39 D8
Brookview Wlk BS13 . . . . .79 B7
Brook Way BS32. . . . . . . .36 D8
Broom Farm Cl BS48 . . . .75 E8
Broomground BA15. . . . .120 E7
BROOMHILL. 50 E6
BROOM HILL. 64 F3
Broom Hill BS16. . . . . . . .50 E5
Broomhill Inf Sch BS4. . . .64 F3
Broomhill Jun Sch BS4. . .64 F3
Broomhill La BS39 . . . . .114 E3
Broom Hill La BS39 . . . .132 E8
Broomhill Rd BS4. . . . . . .65 A2
Brooms The BS16 . . . . . . .38 A1
Brotherswood Ct BS32. . .24 D4
Brougham Hayes BA2. . .101 D6
Brougham Pl 2 BA1. . . . .85 C2
Broughton Ho BS1. . . . . .143 B1
Brow Hill BA2. . . . . .85 F4
Browne Ct 4 BS8. . . . . . .62 F6
Browney La BS24. . . . . .118 A5
Browning Ct BS7. . . . . . . .50 B8
Brownlow Rd BS23. . . . .104 E4
Browns Ct BS23. . . . . . .104 E6
Brown's Folly Nature
Reserve BA15 . . . . . . .86 D1
Brow The
Bath BA2. . . . . .101 B5
Bath, Combe Down BA2 .102 C1
Broxholme Wlk BS11. . . . .47 F8
Bruce Ave BS5. . . . . .50 C1
Bruce Rd BS5. . . . . .50 C1
Brue Cl BS23 . . . . .105 A5
Brummel Way BS39 . . . .132 C6
Brunel Cl
Bristol BS30. . . . . .66 C7
Weston-s-M BS24 . . . . .104 F1
Brunel Ct
Portishead BS20 . . . . . . .45 D6
Yate BS37. . . . . .27 C2
Brunel Ho BA2. . . . . . . .101 A6
Brunel Lock Rd BS1. . . . . .62 F5
Brunel Rd
Bristol BS13. . . . . .79 A8
Nailsea BS48 . . . . .59 B1
Brunel Way
Bristol BS1, BS3. . . . . . . .62 F4
Thornbury BS35. . . . . . . .15 B7
Brunswick Pl
1 Bath BA1. . . . . .141 B3
10 Bristol BS1. . . . . . . .62 F5
Brunswick Sq BS2 . . . . .143 B4
Brunswick St
1 Bath BA1. . . . . .85 B1
3 Bathwick BA2. . . . . .102 B8
Bristol BS2. . . . . .143 B4
Bristol, Redfield BS5. . . . .64 C7
Bruton Cl BS5. . . . . .105 A2
Bruton Ave
Bath BA2. . . . . .101 F4
Portishead BS20 . . . . . . .45 A5
Bruton Avenue Garages
BA2. . . . . .101 F4
Bruton Cl
Bristol BS5. . . . . .64 F8
Nailsea BS48. . . . . .75 E8
Bruton La GL12 . . . . .11 F5
Bruton Pl BS8 . . . . .142 B3
Bryansons Cl BS16. . . . . .50 D6
Bryant Ave BA3 . . . . . . .133 D1
Bryant Gdns BS21. . . . . . .57 E1
Bryants Cl BS16. . . . . . . .37 C1
Bryant's Hill BS5. . . . . . . .65 B6
Brynland Ave BS7. . . . . . .49 E4
Brynland Ct BS7 . . . . .49 E5

Buckingham Ct BS32....24 D3
Buckingham Dr BS34..36 D5
Buckingham Gdns
BS16.................51 E6
Buckingham Ho BS34..35 F2
Buckingham Lodge **1**
BS31.................81 F6
Buckingham Par **11**
BS35.................8 B1
Buckingham Pl
Bristol BS8..........142 A3
Bristol, Mangotsfield
BS16.................51 E6
Buckingham Rd
Bristol BS4..........64 D5
Weston-s-M BS24....105 B2
Buckingham St **1** BS3.63 C2
Buckingham Vale BS8.142 A4
Buckland Gn BS22....89 A5
Bucklands Batch BS48.75 F8
Bucklands Dr BS48....76 A8
Bucklands End BS48...75 F8
Bucklands Gr BS48....75 F8
Bucklands La BS48....75 F8
Bucklands View BS48..76 A8
Bucklewell Cl BS11....47 F6
Buckleys Rd BS34.....36 A7
BUCKOVER.............9 B1
Buckthorn Ct **3** BS37..27 F5
Bude Ave BS5.........65 A8
Bude Cl BS48.........60 B1
Bude Rd BS34.........36 B4
Building of Bath Mus*
BA1.................141 C3
Bullens Cl BS32......24 D2
Buller Rd
Bristol BS4..........64 C2
Locking BS29........106 C7
Bullfinch Cl BS34....36 B6
Bull La
Bristol BS5..........64 F6
Pill BS20............47 C4
Bullocks Size BS21...73 C4
Bull's Hill BA2......118 E1
Bully La BS37.........17 D1
Bumper's Batch BA2..119 A8
Bungalows The BS26..125 C2
Bungay's Hill BA2,
BS39................115 E1
Bunting Ct BS22......88 E1
Burbank Cl BS30......66 A3
Burchells Ave BS15...51 B1
BURCHELLS GREEN...51 B1
Burchells Green Cl
BS15................51 B1
Burchells Green Rd
BS15................51 B1
Burchill Cl BS39.....114 F3
Burcombe Cl BS36....38 D6
Burcott Rd BS11......33 D5
Burden Cl BS32.......36 F6
Burdock Rd BS16......52 D7
Burdock Way BS16.....52 D8
Burfoote Gdns BS14...80 E4
Burfoot Rd BS14......80 E4
Burford Ave BS34.....36 C8
Burford Cl
Bath BA2............101 B3
Portishead BS20......45 E4
Burford Gr BS11......47 F5
Burgage Cl BS37......40 B8
Burgess Green Cl BS4..64 E7
Burghill Rd BS10.....35 A1
Burghley Ct BS36.....37 E5
Burghley Rd BS6......49 E2
Burgis Rd BS14.......80 D6
Burledge Comm BS39 113 B1
Burleedge La BS39....113 D1
Burleigh Gdns BA1...101 A8
Burleigh Way GL12....18 B5
Burley Ave BS16......51 F5
Burley Crest BS16....51 F5
Burley Gr BS16.......51 F5
Burlington Ct
9 Bristol BS6.......49 B2
Portishead BS20......45 E6
Burlington Rd
Bristol BS6..........49 B2
Midsomer Norton BA3.133 C2
Portishead BS20......45 E7
Burlington St
Bath BA1............141 B4
15 Weston-s-M BS23..104 E8
Burltons The GL12....10 B2
Burnbush Cl BS14.....80 E6
Burnbush Prim Sch
BS14................80 D5
Burnell Dr BS2.......143 C4
Burneside Cl BS10....35 C2
BURNETT.............99 B7
Burnett Bsns Pk BS31..82 B1
Burnett Hill BS31....99 B8
Burnett Ind Est BS40..92 E1
Burney Way BS30.....66 A3
Burnham Cl
Bristol BS15.........51 F1

Burnham Cl continued
Weston-s-M BS24....104 F1
Burnham Dr
Bristol BS15.........51 F1
Weston-s-M BS24....104 F1
Burnham Rd
Bath BA2............101 C6
Bristol BS11.........47 D6
Burnt House Cotts
BA2................118 C8
Burnt House Rd BA2..118 D8
BURRINGTON.........109 F3
Burrington Ave BS24..104 F1
Burrington CE Prim Sch
BS40................109 F3
Burrington Cl
Nailsea BS48.........59 E1
Weston-s-M BS24....104 F1
Burrington Combe
BS40................127 C8
Burrington Coombe*
BS40................110 A1
Burrington La
Burrington BS40.....110 A3
Burrington BS40.....110 A3
Burrington Rd BS40..128 D2
Burrington Wlk BS13..79 A8
Burrough Way BS36...37 E6
Burrows La BA3.......139 B1
Burrows The BS22....89 D3
BURTON.............43 B3
Burton Cl BS1........143 B1
Burton Ct
Bristol BS8..........142 B3
2 Bristol, Upper Eastville
BS16................50 E3
Burton Farm Cl SN14..43 B3
Burton Rd GL9........42 F6
Burton St **5** BA1....141 B2
Burwalls Rd BS8......62 E6
Burycourt Cl BS11....34 A1
Bury Hill BS36.......37 F3
Bury Hill La BS37....28 A8
Bury Hill View BS16..37 E1
Bury La BS30.........67 F7
Bury The BS24........106 A3
Bury View BA2........99 C5
Bushacre Bsns Pk
BS22................105 C8
Bush Ave BS34........36 D5
Bush Ct
Alveston BS32........14 F5
10 Bristol BS2......63 F4
Bushes La BS37.......29 A6
BUSHEY NORWOOD....102 F6
Bush Ind Est BS5.....64 D8
Bushy Combe BA3....132 F3
Bushy Ho BS2........63 F3
Bushy Leas BS16......50 D8
Bushy Pk BS2........63 F3
Bushy Rd BS34.......36 A7
Bushy Thorn Rd BS40.112 E8
Business Pk The BS13..79 E3
BUTCOMBE............111 B8
Butcombe BS24.......105 A2
Butcombe La BS40....111 B7
Butcombe Wlk BS14...80 B5
Butham La
Chew Magna BS40....96 B3
Chew Magna BS40....96 B4
Buthay La GL12.......18 A5
Buthay The GL12......18 A5
Butlass Cl BS39......115 D1
Butler Ho BS5........64 F7
Butlers Cl BS5.......64 F7
Butlers Wlk **3** BS5...64 F6
Buttercliffe Rise BS41..62 C3
Buttercup Cres BS16..52 D7
Buttercup Rd BS35....8 B3
Butterfield Cl
Bristol BS10.........49 E7
Frampton Cotterell
BS36................38 B6
Butterfield Pk BS21..57 E1
Butterfield Rd BS10..49 E7
Buttermere Rd BS23..105 A5
Butterworth Ct BS4...79 D7
Butt La BS35.........8 C3
Button Cl BS14.......80 A6
Butts Batch BS26....124 B3
BUTT'S BATCH........92 D1
Butt's Batch BS40....92 D1
Butt's La SN14.......55 B4
Butts Orch BS40......92 D1
Buxton Wlk BS7......50 A8
Bye Mead BS16.......52 B8
Byfield BA2..........102 B1
Byfield Pl BA2.......102 B1
Byfields BS21........73 C8
Byron Cl BS24........106 A4
Byron Ct BS23........104 F8
Byron Pl
Bristol BS8..........142 B3
Bristol, Staple Hill BS16.51 E4
Byron Rd
Bath BA2............101 F4
Locking BS24........106 A4
Weston-s-M BS23....105 A4

Byron St
Bristol, Moorfields BS5..64 C7
Bristol, St Pauls BS2..50 A1
5 Bristol, St Pauls BS2..50 A1
Byways Cvn Pk BS21...57 E1
Byzantine Ct BS1.....143 A1

C

Cabot Cl
Bristol BS15.........65 C7
Saltford BS31........82 D2
Yate BS37............27 F1
Cabot Ct BS7.........35 F1
Cabot Gn BS5.........64 B7
Cabot Ho **6** BS35....15 C8
Cabot Pk BS11........33 B6
Cabot Prim Sch BS2..143 C4
Cabot Rise BS20......45 A5
Cabot Twr* BS8.......142 B2
Cabot Way
Bristol BS8..........62 F5
Pill BS20............47 D3
Weston-s-M BS22.....89 A3
Cabstand BS20........45 D6
Cadbury Camp La BS20 59 D6
Cadbury Camp La W
BS21................58 C5
Cadbury Farm Rd BS49 91 C7
Cadbury Gdns BS30...66 B6
Cadbury Halt BS20....44 F1
CADBURY HEATH......66 B5
Cadbury Heath Prim Sch
BS30................66 B6
Cadbury Heath Rd
BS30................66 B5
Cadbury Ho **5** BS20..45 E4
Cadbury La BS20......44 F1
Cadbury Rd
Keynsham BS31......82 A2
Portishead BS20......45 E4
Cadbury Sq BS49.....91 E3
Cadby Ho BA2........101 A6
Caddick Cl BS15......51 F2
Cade Cl
Bristol, Kingswood
BS15................65 F6
Bristol, Stoke Gifford
BS34................36 E5
Cadet Dr BS24........105 B4
Cadogan Gr BS48.....76 B6
Cadogan Rd BS14.....80 A8
Caen Rd BS3.........63 D3
Caernarvon Rd BS31..81 C4
Caern Well Pl BA1....141 C4
Caine Rd BS7.........49 F7
Cains Cl BS15........65 E6
Cairn Cl BS48........60 A1
Cairn Gdns BS36.....37 E4
Cairns' Cres **12** BS2..49 F1
Cairns Cl BS6........49 C4
Cairns Rd BS6........49 C4
Cairo Ct **18** BS23....87 C1
Caitlin Ct BS14......80 D6
Cala Trad Est BS3....62 F3
Calcott Rd BS4.......64 A3
Caldbeck Cl BS10.....35 D2
Calder Cl BS31.......82 A4
Caldicot Cl
Bristol, Lawrence Weston
BS11................34 C2
Bristol, Willsbridge BS30 66 B2
Caledonia Mews BS8..62 F6
Caledonian Rd
Bath BA2............101 D6
Bristol BS1..........142 B1
Caledonia Pl BS8.....62 F7
California Rd BS30....66 B3
Callicroft Prim Sch
BS10................35 F8
Callicroft Rd BS34...36 A7
Callington Rd BS4....64 D1
Callowhill Ct BS1....143 B3
Calluna Cl BS22......89 A5
Calton Gdns BA2.....141 C1
Calton Rd BA2.......141 C1
Calton Wlk BA2......141 B1
Calves Gdn BS34.....35 F7
Camberley Dr BS36...37 F8
Camberley Rd BS4....79 D8
Camberley Wlk BS22..105 E8
Camborne Rd BS7....50 A7
Cambrian Dr BS37....27 E3
CAMBRIDGE BATCH...77 C8
Cambridge Cres BS9..49 A7
Cambridge Ct BS40...92 D2
Cambridge Gr BS21...57 F5
Cambridge Pk BS6....49 B3
Cambridge Pl
Bath BA2............102 B5
Weston-s-M BS23....104 D8
Cambridge Rd
Bristol BS7..........49 C4
Clevedon BS21.......57 F5
Cambridge St
8 Bristol, Redfield
BS5................64 C4
Bristol, Windmill Hill BS3..63 F4
Cambridge Terr BA2..102 B5

Cam Brook Cl BA2....133 D8
Cambrook Ho BS39...131 F8
Camden Cres BA1....141 B4
Camden Cl BA1.......141 B4
Camden Rd
Bath BA1............85 A1
Bristol BS3..........142 B1
Camden Row BA1.....141 B4
Camden Terr
Bath BA1............141 C4
Bristol BS3..........142 A2
Weston-s-M BS23....104 E7
CAMELEY............131 C8
Cameley CE Prim Sch
BS39................114 E1
Cameley Cl BS39.....131 E8
Cameley Gn BA2......100 F6
Cameley La BS39.....130 F7
Cameley Rd BS39.....131 C8
Camelford Rd BS5....50 D1
Camellia Dr BS32....24 D5
Cameron Wlk BS7....50 C6
Cameroons Cl BS31...81 E4
CAMERTON...........133 E8
Camerton Cl BS31....82 E3
Camerton Hill BA2...133 E8
Camerton Rd
Bristol BS5..........50 D1
Timsbury BA2........116 E1
Camomile Wlk BS20..45 F5
Campbell Ct BS11....33 F1
Campbell Farm BS11..33 F1
Campbell Farm Dr
BS11................33 F1
Campbell St BS2......49 E1
Campian Wlk BS4....79 D6
Campion Cl
Thornbury BS35......8 D2
4 Weston-s-M BS22..105 D7
Campion Dr BS32.....24 D2
Camp La SN14........55 C4
Camplins BS21.......57 E1
Camp Rd
Bristol BS8..........62 F7
Oldbury-on-S BS35...7 B6
Weston-s-M BS23.....87 C1
Camp Rd N BS23.....87 B1
Camps La BS37.......29 B3
Camp View
Nailsea BS48.........59 D2
Winterbourne BS36...37 E4
Camvale BA2.........134 B8
Camview BS39........132 D6
Camwal Ind Est BS2..64 A5
Camwal Rd BS2.......64 A5
Canada Coombe BS24 106 A1
Canada Way BS1......142 B1
Canal Terr BA2.......85 F1
Canal View BA2......133 E8
Canberra Cres BS24..106 B6
Canberra Gr BS34....36 B4
Canberra Rd BS23....104 F3
Candy Ct BS4........64 D5
Canford La BS9......48 E8
Canford Rd BS9......48 F8
Cannan Ct BA2.......102 A2
Cannans Cl BS36.....37 E7
Cann La BS30.........66 E6
Cannons Gate BS21...73 C8
CANNON'S MARSH....142 C1
Cannon St
Bristol BS1..........143 A4
Bristol, Southville BS3..63 C4
Canons Cl BA2.......101 B2
Canons Rd BS1.......142 C1
Canon St BS5.........64 C8
Canons Way BS1.....142 C1
Canons Wlk BS22....88 D2
Canon's Wlk BS15....51 F2
Canowie Rd BS6......49 B3
Cantell Gr BS14......80 F5
Canterbury Cl
Weston-s-M BS22.....89 B3
Yate BS37............27 E3
Canterbury Ct BS16..50 E6
Canterbury Rd BA2...101 D5
Canterbury St **5** BS5..64 B6
Canters Leaze GL12...18 B4
Cantock's Cl BS8....142 C3
Canvey Cl BS10......49 E7
Canynge Ho **2** BS1..143 B1
Canynge Rd BS8......62 F8
Canynge Sq BS8.....62 F8
Canynge St BS1......143 B2
Capel Cl BS15........66 B8
Capell Cl BS22.......105 B8
Capel Rd BS11........34 B1
Capenor Cl BS20.....45 C4
Capgrave Cl BS4.....65 A3
Capgrave Cres BS4...65 A3
Capital Edge BS8.....142 B1
Caple La BS40........112 B5
Cappards Rd BS39...113 D4
Capricorn Pl BS8.....142 B2
Capri Villas BS23....105 A8
Caraway Gdns BS5....50 C2
Carberry View BS24..106 A8
Cardigan Cres BS22..105 C8

Cardigan Mews BS9...49 B5
Cardigan Rd BS9.....49 B6
Cardill Cl BS13.......79 A8
Cardinal Cl BA2......118 C8
Carditch Dro BS49...108 B8
Carey Developments **1**
BS21................57 E1
Carey's Cl BS21......57 H4
Careys Way BS24.....105 E7
Carfax Ct BS6........49 A3
Carice Gdns BS21....73 D8
Carisbrooke Lodge BS6 49 A3
Carisbrooke Rd BS4..79 D7
CARLINGCOTT........117 B1
Carlingcott La
Carlingcott BA2......117 B1
Peasedown St John BA2 134 B8
Carlingford Terr BA3..134 A2
Carlingford Terrace Rd
BA3................134 A2
Carlow Rd BS4.......79 E8
Carlton Cl BS39......114 F3
Carlton Ct
1 Bristol, Ashley Down
BS7................49 F4
3 Bristol, Eastfield BS9..49 A7
Carlton Ho **2** BS9...49 A7
Carlton Mans BS23...104 D7
Carlton Pk BS5.......64 C8
Carlton St BS23......104 D7
Carlyle Rd BS5.......50 C1
Carmarthen Cl BS37..27 F4
Carmarthen Gr BS30..66 B1
Carmarthen Rd BS9...49 A5
Carnarvon Rd BS6....49 B2
Carnation Rd **6** BS16.52 C7
Carolina Ho BS2......143 A4
Caroline Bldgs BA2..102 B5
Caroline Cl
Chipping Sodbury BS37..28 B2
Keynsham BS31.......81 C4
Caroline Pl BA1......141 B4
Carousel La BS24....105 E2
Carpenter Cl BS23...105 A7
Carpenters Hill BA2..134 B8
Carpenters La BS31...81 E5
Carpenter's Shop La
BS16................51 E6
Carpenters Way BA3..139 B8
Carre Gdns BS22.....88 F4
Carr Ho
Bath BA2............101 A6
3 Bristol BS2.......49 F1
Carriage Dr BS10.....35 B2
Carrick Ho **8** BS8...62 F6
Carrington Rd BS3....63 A3
Carroll Ct BS16......36 E1
Carrs Cl BA2.........101 A6
Carsons Rd BS16.....52 B2
Carter Rd BS39......132 D5
Carters Bldgs **12** BS8..62 F7
Carters Way BA3.....138 D3
Carter Wlk BS32.....36 D8
Cartledge Rd **6** BS5..50 C1
Cary Ct **2** BS2......49 F1
Casey Cl BS4.........79 F7
Cashmore Ho **9** BS5..64 B7
Caslon Ct BS1........143 B1
Cassell Rd BS16......51 C5
Cassey Bottom La BS5..65 A7
Casson Dr BS16......50 D4
Castle Batch Com Prim
Sch BS22............89 A5
Castle Cl
Bristol BS10.........34 E2
Flax Bourton BS48....76 F7
Castle Coombe BS35...8 C1
Castle Cotts SN14....55 E2
Castle Ct
Bristol BS34.........37 A4
Bristol, Arno's Vale BS4..64 C4
Thornbury BS35......8 B1
Castle Farm La BS41..78 B2
Castle Farm Rd BS15..65 C2
Castlegate Ho BS4....64 E3
Castle Gdns BA2.....101 E3
Castle Hill BS29.....107 C2
Castle La SN14.......55 E2
Castlemead Sh Ctr
BS22................89 A5
Castle Prim Sch BS31..81 D4
Castle Rd
Bristol, Kingswood
BS15................51 D2
Bristol, Oldland Common
BS30................66 D3
Clevedon BS21.......57 G6
Pucklechurch BS16...53 C6
Weston-s-M BS22.....88 E3
Castle Sch Sixth Form Ctr
The BS35............8 B1
Castle Sch The BS35..8 B2
Castle St
Bristol BS1..........143 B3
Thornbury BS35......8 B1
Castle View **2** BS23..105 F8
Castle View Rd BS21..57 F5
Castlewood Cl BS21..57 F4
Caswell Hill BS20....46 B1

Caswell La BS20 . . . . 46 B2
CATBRAIN. 35 B6
Catbrain Hill BS10 . . . . 35 B6
Catbrain La BS10 . . . . . . 35 B6
Catchpot La BS37 . . . . . 41 A6
Catemead BS21 . . . . 73 C8
Cater Dr BS37 . . . . 27 D6
Cater Rd BS13 . . . . 79 B6
Catharine Pl BA1 . . . . . . 85 A1
Cathcart Ho **6** BA1 . . . . 85 A1
Cathedral Church of The
Holy & Undivided
Trinity★ BS1. . . . . .142 C2
Cathedral Wlk BS1. . . . .142 C1
Catherine Ct **14** BS6. . . . 49 E1
Catherine Hill BS35 . . . . 13 F2
Catherine Mead St BS3 63 D4
Catherine St BS11. . . . . 47 C8
Catherine Way BA1 . . . . 86 A5
Cathorn La BS48 . . . . 77 C6
Catley Gr BS41. . . . . 62 B2
Cato St BS5. . . . . 50 B2
Catsbrain La BS35 . . . . . . 8 D5
Cattistock Dr BS5. . . . . . 65 A6
Cattle Market Rd BS1 . .143 B1
Cattybrook Rd BS16. . . .52 D5
Cattybrook Rd N BS16. .52 D6
Cattybrook St
7 Bristol BS5 . . . . .64 B7
23 Bristol BS5 . . . . .64 B8
Caulfield Rd BS22. . . . . . 89 B4
Causeway BS48 . . . . 59 B3
Causeway The
Congresbury BS49. . . . .91 D4
Frampton Cotterell BS36 38 D7
Yatton BS49. . . . . .91 C7
Causeway View BS48 . . .59 C2
Causley Dr BS30 . . . . . . 66 A5
Cautletts Cl BA3 . . . . . .138 F8
Cavan Wlk BS4 . . . . 63 D1
Cave Cl BS16 . . . . 51 D6
Cave Ct BS2 . . . . .143 B4
Cave Dr BS16 . . . . 51 D6
Cave Gr BS16 . . . . 52 B7
Cavell Ct BS21 . . . . 57 E1
Cavendish Cl
Saltford BS31. . . . . 82 D2
Tormarton GL9. . . . . . . 41 E2
Cavendish Cres BA1. . . .141 A4
Cavendish Gdns BS9 . . 48 C4
Cavendish Lodge BA1 141 A4
Cavendish Pl BA1 . . . . .141 A4
Cavendish Rd
Bath BA1. . . . . .141 A4
Bristol, Henleaze BS9 . .49 A5
Bristol, Patchway BS34 . .35 F8
Caveners Ct BS22. . . . . . 88 B1
Caversham Dr BS48 . . . 60 A2
Caves Cotts BS16 . . . . . 51 E7
Cave St BS2 . . . . .143 B4
Caxton Ct **4** BA2 . . . .141 C3
Cecil Ave BS5. . . . . 50 F1
Cecil Rd
Bristol, Clifton BS8 . . . .62 F8
Bristol, Kingswood BS15 65 D8
Weston-s-M BS23 . . . . . 87 E1
Cedar Ave BS22. . . . . 88 C1
Cedar Cl
Bristol, Oldland BS30. . .66 B4
Bristol, Patchway BS34. .35 F7
Long Ashton BS41 . . . . . 61 F1
Cedar Ct
Bristol BS9. . . . . .48 C4
Bristol, Combe Dingle
BS9 . . . . .48 D7
Bristol, Mangotsfield
BS16. . . . . 51 E6
Bristol, Westbury on T
BS9 . . . . .48 F8
Cedar Dr BS31. . . . . 81 D4
Cedar Gr
Bath BA2 . . . . .101 D3
Bristol BS9. . . . . .48 D5
Cedar Hall BS16 . . . . . . 51 C8
Cedarhurst Rd BS20. . . 44 E4
Cedarn Ct BS22. . . . . . . 88 B4
Cedar Pk BS9. . . . . 48 D5
Cedar Row BS11 . . . . . . 47 F6
Cedars The
Bristol BS9. . . . . .48 D3
Chew Stoke BS40. . . . .112 D8
Cedars Way BS36 . . . . . 37 D5
Cedar Terr BA3 . . . . . . .133 D1
Cedar Villas BA2 . . . . . .141 A1
Cedar Way
Bath BA2 . . . . .141 A1
Nailsea BS48 . . . . 60 A2
Portishead BS20 . . . . . . 45 C4
Pucklechurch BS16 . . . . 53 C5
Cedern Ave BS24. . . . . .106 C3
Cedric Cl BA1. . . . . .101 C7
Cedric Rd BA1. . . . . . . .101 C8
Celandine Cl BS16 . . . . 50 E5
Celandine Ct **5** BS37 . . 27 F5
Celestine Rd BS37 . . . . 27 C3
Celia Terr BS4 . . . . 64 F6
Cello Cl BS31 . . . . 82 B4
Celtic Way BS24 . . . . . .122 B7
Cemetery Rd BS4 . . . . . 64 A3

Cennick Ave BS15. . . . . 51 E1
Centaurus Rd BS34. . . . 35 D7
Central Ave
Bristol BS15. . . . . 65 C5
Dyer's Common BS35 . .22 D2
Severn Beach BS10 . . . .22 A3
Central Pk BS14 . . . . . . 80 B7
Central Trad Est BS4 . . 64 B4
Central Way
Bristol BS10. . . . . 49 E8
Clevedon BS21. . . . . . . 57 G1
Centre Dr BS29 . . . . . .106 E4
Centre Quay BS20. . . . . 45 E7
Centre The
Keynsham BS31. . . . . . . 81 F5
10 Weston-s-M BS23. . .104 E7
Centre Wlk BS40. . . . . . 30 F2
Ceres Cl BS30. . . . . 65 F2
Cerimon Gate BS34 . . . 36 E5
Cerney Gdns BS48 . . . . 60 A2
Cerney La BS11. . . . . . . 47 E5
Cerutti Cl BS39 . . . . . .132 D6
Cesson St BS37 . . . . 40 C8
Chadleigh Gr BS4 . . . . . 79 D7
Chaffinch Ave BS31 . . . 81 C3
Chaffinch Dr BA3 . . . . .139 B8
Chaffins The BS21. . . . . 57 G2
Chaingate La BS37 . . . . 27 A6
Chakeshill Cl BS10 . . . . 35 C3
Chakeshill Dr BS10. . . . 35 C4
Chalcombe Cl BS34 . . . 36 C8
Chalcroft Ho **2** BS3. . . 63 A4
Chalcroft Wlk BS13 . . . 78 E4
Chalet The BS10 . . . . . . 34 F3
Chalfield Cl BS31 . . . . . 82 A2
Chalfont Rd BS22 . . . . .105 C8
Chalfont Cl BS37 . . . . . 39 D8
Chalk Farm Cl BS39 . . . 97 A7
Chalks Rd BS5 . . . . 64 D8
Chalks The BS40 . . . . . . 96 B3
Challender Ave BS10 . . 34 F2
Challoner Ct BS1. . . . . .143 A1
Challow Dr BS22 . . . . . . 88 B2
Champion Rd
Bitton BS30. . . . . 82 E8
Bristol BS15. . . . . 52 A2
Champneys Ave BS10 . . 34 F3
Champs Sur Marne
BS32. . . . . 36 E8
Chancel Cl
Bristol BS9. . . . . .48 D3
Nailsea BS48 . . . . 59 D1
Chancellor's Pound
BS40. . . . . 93 D3
Chancery St BS5 . . . . . . 64 B7
Chandag Inf Sch BS31. .82 A4
Chandag Jun Sch BS31 82 A4
Chandag Rd BS31. . . . . 82 A4
Chandler Cl BA1 . . . . . . 84 B1
Chandos BS6 . . . . 49 C2
Chandos Ct BS23. . . . . .104 D6
Chandos Ho **7** BA1 . . .141 B2
Chandos Rd
Bristol BS6. . . . . .49 C1
Keynsham BS31. . . . . . . 81 E7
Chandos Trad Est BS2 . 64 A5
Channel Ct BS22. . . . . . . 88 B3
Channel Hts BS24. . . . .104 C1
Channell's Hill BS9 . . . 49 A8
Channel Rd BS21 . . . . . 57 G5
Channel View Cres
BS20. . . . . 45 B5
Channel View Farm La
BS49. . . . . 92 A4
Channel View Rd BS20. 45 B5
Channon's Hill BS16 . . .50 F4
Chantry Cl BS48 . . . . . . 59 C1
Chantry Ct BS1 . . . . . . .142 C2
Chantry Dr BS22 . . . . . . 89 A4
Chantry Gr BS11 . . . . . . 34 C2
Chantry La BS16 . . . . . . 37 F1
Chantry Mead Rd BA2 101 E3
Chantry Rd
Bristol BS8. . . . . .49 B1
Thornbury BS35. . . . . . . 8 B2
Chapei Way BS10 . . . . . 49 D8
Chapel Barton
7 Bristol BS3 . . . . . . .63 B2
Nailsea BS48 . . . . 59 C2
Chapel Cl
Bristol BS15. . . . . 66 B8
Chew Stoke BS40. . . . .112 E8
Farrington Gurney BS39 131 F4
Nailsea BS48 . . . . 59 C2
Winford BS40. . . . . 95 A6
Chapel Ct
8 Bath BA1 . . . . . . .141 B2
Bristol, Brentry BS10 . . .35 D3
Bristol, St Philip's Marsh
BS2 . . . . 64 A5
Clandown BA3 . . . . . . .133 E4
Clevedon BS21. . . . . . . 57 F3
Chapel Field BA2 . . . . .134 E8
Chapel Gdns BS10 . . . . 35 A1
Chapel Green La BS6. . .49 B2
Chapel Hill
Backwell BS48. . . . . . . .76 D7
Clevedon BS21. . . . . . . 57 F3
Newport GL13 . . . . 4 B7

Chapel Hill continued
Ubley BS40. . . . . .111 C5
Wrington BS40. . . . . . . 92 D3
Chapel La
Acton Turville GL9 . . . . .43 A6
Bristol, Clay Hill BS5 . . . 50 E2
Bristol, Fishponds BS16. . 51 A4
Bristol, Frenchay BS16 . .51 C7
Bristol, Lawrence Weston
BS11. . . . . .34 C2
Bristol, Warmley BS15. . .66 B8
Chew Stoke BS40. . . . .112 D8
Chipping Sodbury BS37. .41 A7
Claverham BS49. . . . . . . 91 F8
Cleeve BS49. . . . . 92 B7
Hillesley GL12 . . . . .19 E8
Hinton SN14. . . . . 54 C5
Thornbury BS35. . . . . . . 9 A1
Winford BS40. . . . . 95 A6
Chapel Lawns BA3 . . . .133 E4
Chapel Orch BS37. . . . . 27 C2
Chapel Pill La BS20 . . . 47 E4
Chapel Rd
Bristol, Bishopsworth
BS13 . . . . .79 A6
Bristol, Hanham BS15 . .65 C5
2 Bristol, Lower Easton
BS5 . . . . 50 B1
Clandown BA3 . . . . . . .133 E4
Oldbury-on-S BS35. . . . . 7 C5
Chapel Row
Bath BA1 . . . . .141 B2
Bathford BA1. . . . . .86 C2
Clandown BA3 . . . . . . .133 E4
Luckington SN14 . . . . . . 31 E4
Norton St Philip BA2 . . .136 F4
Pill BS20. . . . . 47 C4
Chapel St
Bristol BS2. . . . . .64 A5
Thornbury BS35. . . . . . . 15 B8
Chapel Way BS4 . . . . . . 64 E6
Chaplains Wood BS20. . 44 E5
Chaplin Rd BS5 . . . . 50 B1
Chapter St BS2 . . . . . . .143 B4
Chapter Wlk BS6. . . . . . 49 B3
Charbon Gate BS34 . . . 36 F5
Charborough Ct
Bristol BS34. . . . . 35 F2
Bristol BS34. . . . . 36 A2
Charborough Rd BS34. . 35 F2
Charborough Road Prim
Sch BS34. . . . . 35 F2
Charbury Wlk BS11 . . . . 47 E5
Chard Cl BS48 . . . . 75 F8
Chard Ct BS14 . . . . 80 B6
Chard Rd BS21. . . . . 57 G1
Chardstock Ave BS9. . . 48 C8
Char Dyke Dr BS39 . . . .114 E1
CHARFIELD 11 B4
Charfield **4** BS15. . . . . 66 A8
CHARFIELD GREEN . . . 11 B5
CHARFIELD HILL. 10 F5
Charfield Prim Sch
GL12. . . . . 10 F5
Charfield Rd
Bristol BS10. . . . . 35 D1
Kingswood GL12 . . . . . . 11 E5
Chargrove
2 Bristol BS30. . . . . .66 C6
Yate BS37. . . . . 39 D7
Charis Ave BS10 . . . . . . 49 C7
Charity La BA11. . . . . . .140 C1
CHARLCOMBE 84 E3
Charlcombe La BA1 . . . 84 F3
Charlcombe Pk BS20. . . 44 D3
Charlcombe Rise BA1 . . 84 F2
Charlcombe View Rd
BA1. . . . . 85 A2
Charlcombe Way BA1 . . 84 F2
Charlcome Rise BS20 . . 44 D3
Charlecombe Ct BS9 . . 48 F6
Charlecombe Rd BS9. . 48 F6
Charlecote BA1. . . . . . . 84 F1
Charles Ave BS34 . . . . . 36 E4
Charles Cl BS35. . . . . . . 8 C3
Charles Ct **1** BS8. . . . .142 A2
Charles England Ho **1**
BS34. . . . . 35 F7
Charles Pl BS8. . . . . . . .142 A2
Charles Rd
Bristol BS34. . . . . 36 B3
Yate Rocks BS37 . . . . . . 27 E5
Charles St
Bath BA1 . . . . .141 B2
Bristol BS1. . . . . .143 A4
Charles Wesley Ct BS5 . 65 A6
Charleton Ho **8** BS2. . .143 C3
Charlock Cl **3** BS22. . .105 D7
Charlock Rd BS22. . . . .105 D7
Charlotte St S BS1 . . . .142 C2
Charlotte St
Bath BA1 . . . . .141 B2
Bristol, Brandon Hill
BS1 . . . . .142 C3
CHARLTON. 139 E5
Charlton Ave
Bristol BS34. . . . . 35 F2
Weston-s-M BS23 . . . . .104 D4
Charlton Bvd BS34 . . . . 36 A7

Charlton Comm BS10 . . 35 D4
Charlton Ct BS34. . . . . . 23 F1
Charlton Dr BS48 . . . . . 60 C7
Charlton Gdns BS10 . . . 35 D4
Charlton La
Bristol BS10. . . . . 35 A3
Radstock BA3. . . . . . . .139 D6
Charlton Leaze BS10 . . 35 A6
Charlton Mead Ct BS10 35 D3
Charlton Mead Dr BS10 35 D3
Charlton Park Rd BA3 139 F6
Charlton Pk
Keynsham BS31. . . . . . . 81 D5
Midsomer Norton BA3. .139 B8
Charlton Pl BS10. . . . . . 35 D4
Charlton Rd
Bristol, Brentry BS10. . .35 C3
Bristol, Kingswood BS15 51 B1
Holcombe BA3. . . . . . .139 D3
Keynsham BS31, BS14. . .81 C3
Midsomer Norton BA3. .139 B8
Weston-s-M BS23 . . . . .104 D4
Charlton St **17** BS5. . . . 64 B7
Charlton View BS20 . . . 45 C5
Charmborough Farm Rural
Bsns Pk BA3 . . . . .139 D3
Charminster Rd BS16 . . 51 B3
Charmouth Ct BS3 . . . . 63 D1
Charmouth Rd BA1 . . . .101 B7
Charnell Rd BS16 . . . . . 51 E4
Charnhill Brow BS16. . . 52 A4
Charnhill Cres BS16. . . 51 F4
Charnhill Dr BS16. . . . . 51 F4
Charnhill Ridge BS16. . 52 A4
Charnhill Vale BS16 . . . 51 F4
Charnwood BS16. . . . . . 52 A4
Charnwood Rd BS14 . . . 80 B4
Charter Ho BS1 . . . . . . .142 B2
CHARTERHOUSE 127 C4
Charterhouse Cl BS48. . 59 F1
Charterhouse Rd BS5 . . 64 D8
Charter Rd BS22 . . . . . .105 B8
Charter Wlk BS14. . . . . 80 A6
Chartley BS9 . . . . 48 D2
Chasefield La **1** BS16. .51 B4
Chase La GL12 . . . . 18 C6
Chase Rd BS15. . . . . 51 D2
Chase The BS16 . . . . . . 51 C3
Chatcombe BS37. . . . . . 39 E7
Chatford Ho BS8. . . . . . 62 F8
Chatham Pk BA2. . . . . .102 C6
Chatham Row BA1 . . . .141 C3
Chatley Furlong BA2 . .136 F3
Chatsworth Pk BS35 . . . 8 C3
Chatsworth Rd
Bristol, Arno's Vale BS4 . .64 C4
Bristol, Hillfields BS16. . .51 B3
Chattenden Ho BS9 . . . 48 F3
Chatterton Gn BS14 . . . 79 F3
Chatterton Ho **5** BS1. .143 A1
Chatterton Rd BS37 . . . 27 D1
Chatterton Sq BS1. . . . .143 C1
Chatterton St BS1. . . . .143 C1
Chaucer Rd
Bath BA2 . . . . .101 F4
Midsomer Norton BA3. .139 B8
Weston-s-M BS23 . . . . .105 A4
Chaundey Gr BS13 . . . . 79 B5
Chavenage BS15. . . . . . 52 A1
Cheapside BS2 . . . . . . .143 C4
Cheapside St **8** BS3 . . 63 F4
Cheap St BA1. . . . . .141 C2
Cheddar Cl BS48 . . . . . 75 F8
Cheddarcoombe La
BS25. . . . . .108 D1
Cheddar Gorge★
BS27 . . . . .126 E1
Cheddar Gr BS13. . . . . . 79 A8
Cheddar Grove Prim Sch
BS13. . . . . 79 A8
Cheddar Gr Prim Sch
BS13. . . . . 79 A8
Cheddar Rd BS26 . . . . .125 E2
Chedworth
Bristol BS15. . . . . 51 F3
Yate BS37. . . . . 39 B7
Chedworth Cl BA2 . . . .102 F3
Chedworth Rd BS7. . . . 50 A6
Cheers Dr BS5. . . . . 50 F1
Cheese La BS2. . . . . . . .143 B2
Chelford Gr BS34 . . . . . 36 B8
Chelmer Gr BS31 . . . . . 81 F4
Chelmsford Wlk BS4 . . 64 F5
Chelscombe BA1. . . . . . 84 B1
Chelscombe Cl BA1 . . . 84 E4
Chelsea Cl BS31 . . . . . . 82 A5
Chelsea Ho BA1. . . . . . .141 C4
Chelsea Pk BS5. . . . . . . 64 C8
Chelsea Rd
Bath BA1 . . . . .101 C7
Bristol BS5. . . . . .50 B1
Chelsfield BS48 . . . . . . 76 A7
Chelston Rd BS4 . . . . . . 79 D7
Chelswood Ave BS22 . .105 C8
Chelswood Gdns
BS22. . . . . .105 D8
Cheltenham Cres **2**
BS6. . . . . 49 D1
Cheltenham La BS6. . . . 49 D2

Cheltenham Rd BS6. . . 49 E1
Cheltenham St BA2 . . .141 A1
CHELVEY. 75 D5
Chelvey Batch BS48 . . . 75 F3
Chelvey La BS48 . . . . . . 75 E4
Chelvey Rd BS48 . . . . . 75 D5
Chelvey Rise BS48 . . . . 60 A1
Chelvy Cl BS13. . . . . 79 D3
CHELWOOD 115 A8
Chelwood BS23 . . . . . .104 F8
Chelwood Dr BA2 . . . . .101 D1
Chelwood Rd
Bristol BS11. . . . . 47 D7
Saltford BS31. . . . . 82 E4
Chelwood Rdbt BS39 . .114 E8
Chepstow Pk BS16 . . . . 37 F1
Chepstow Rd BS4 . . . . . 79 D8
Chepstow Wlk BS31. . . 81 D5
Chequers Cl BS30. . . . . 66 C3
Chequers Ct BS34. . . . . 37 A6
Cherington
Bristol BS15. . . . . 65 B5
Yate BS37. . . . . 39 D6
Cherington Rd
Bristol BS10. . . . . 49 D7
Nailsea BS48 . . . . 60 A2
Cheriton Pl
Bristol, Eastfield BS9. . .49 B5
Bristol, Warmley BS30. . 66 C6
Cherry Ave BS21 . . . . . . 57 G2
Cherry Banks BS16. . . . 38 C1
Cherry Cl BS49. . . . . . . 91 B8
Cherry Ct **12** BS1. . . . .143 A4
Cherry Garden La BS30. 66 B2
Cherry Garden Prim Sch
BS30. . . . . 66 C2
Cherry Garden Rd BS30 66 C1
Cherry Gdns BS30. . . . . 66 C1
Cherry Gr
Bristol BS16. . . . . 52 A6
Yatton BS49. . . . . 91 B8
Cherry Hay BS21. . . . . . 57 F1
Cherry La **4** BS1. . . . . .143 B4
Cherry Orchard La
4 Bristol BS5. . . . . . .64 F8
Luckington SN14 . . . . . . 31 C5
Cherry Rd
Chipping Sodbury BS37. .28 A1
Long Ashton BS41 . . . . . 61 F1
Nailsea BS48 . . . . 59 D1
Cherry Tree Cl
Bristol BS16. . . . . 51 C2
Keynsham BS31. . . . . . . 81 C4
Radstock BA3. . . . . . . .133 E1
Cherrytree Cres BS16 . . 51 C2
Cherrytree Ct BS16. . . . 53 C5
Cherry Tree Ct BS21 . . . 73 C2
Cherrytree Rd BS16 . . . 51 C2
Cherry Wood BS30 . . . . 66 B2
Cherrywood Rd BS22. . . 88 F2
Cherrywood Rise BS22. . 88 F2
Chertsey Rd BS6. . . . . . 49 B1
Cherwell Cl BS35 . . . . . 15 C7
Cherwell Rd BS31. . . . . 82 A4
Chescombe Rd BS49. . . 91 B7
Chesham Rd N BS22 . . .105 B8
Chesham Rd S BS22 . . .105 B8
Chesham Way BS15 . . . 51 D1
Cheshire Cl BS37 . . . . . 27 E3
Chesle Cl BS20. . . . . . . 44 E3
Cheslefield BS20. . . . . . 44 E3
Chesle Way BS20 . . . . . 44 E3
Chesley Hill BS30. . . . . 66 F7
Chessel Cl BS32. . . . . . . 24 C2
Chessel Ct **6** BS3. . . . . 63 B2
Chessel Dr BS34 . . . . . . 36 A7
Chessell Ave BS35 . . . . 22 C7
Chessel Mews **8** BS3 . 63 C3
Chessel St BS3 . . . . 63 B3
Chessington Ave BS14. . 80 B5
Chester Cl BS24. . . . . . .106 A8
Chester Ct **4** BS5. . . . . 64 C7
Chesterfield Ave BS6. . . 49 E2
Chesterfield Bldgs
BS8. . . . . .142 A3
Chesterfield Cl BS29 . .106 F3
Chesterfield Ho
Bristol BS10. . . . . 34 F1
Midsomer Norton BA3. .133 B1
Chesterfield Hospl
BS8. . . . . .142 A2
Chesterfield Ho
Bristol, Mangotsfield
BS16. . . . . 51 E5
Bristol, Montpelier BS6. . 49 E2
Chestermaster Cl BS32 24 A5
CHESTER PARK. 51 B2
Chester Park Jun & Inf
Schs BS16. . . . . 51 A3
Chester Park Rd BS16. . 51 B2
Chester Pk BS5. . . . . . . 50 E1
Chester Rd BS5. . . . . . . 50 E1
Chesters BS30. . . . . 66 A4
Chester St BS5 . . . . 50 B2
Chesterton Dr BS48. . . 60 A2
Chesterton Ho **6** BS2 143 B4

Chestertons The BA2 . . 102 F8
Chestnut Ave
  Axbridge BS26 . . . . . . .125 C2
  Weston-s-M BS22 . . . . . .89 A1
Chestnut Barn Ind Est
  BS24 . . . . .90 D3
Chestnut Chase BS48. . .60 A3
Chestnut Cl
  Acton Turville GL9 . . . . . .43 A6
  Banwell BS29 . . . . .107 A3
  Bristol BS14 . . . . .80 F5
  Congresbury BS49 . . . . . .91 D4
  Paulton BS39 . . . . .132 E6
  Radstock BA3. . . . . . . .133 E1
Chestnut Ct
  Bristol BS13 . . . . .79 A7
  Bristol, Hillhouse BS16 . .52 A5
Chestnut Dr
  Chipping Sodbury BS37 . .28 A1
  Claverham BS49. . . . . . .74 F1
  Thornbury BS35 . . . . .8 C1
Chestnut Gr
  Bath BA2 . . . . .101 C4
  Clevedon BS21. . . . . . . .57 G4
  Westwood BA15 . . . . . .120 F4
Chestnut Ho BS13. . . . . .79 D3
Chestnut La BS24 . . . . .122 B7
Chestnut Park Est GL12 . 11 F4
Chestnut Park Prim Sch
  BS49 . . . . .73 F2
Chestnut Pk G12 . . . . . . 11 F4
Chestnut Rd
  Bristol, Lower Soundwell
    BS15 . . . . .51 F3
  Bristol, Mangotsfield
    BS16 . . . . .51 D6
  Long Ashton BS41 . . . . . .62 B2
Chestnut Springs BS37 . 27 F4
Chestnuts The
  Cheddar BS27 . . . . .126 A1
  Winscombe BS25. . . . . .125 A7
Chestnut Way BS15 . . . . 51 F3
Chestnut Wlk
  Bristol BS13 . . . . .79 A6
  Saltford BS31. . . . . .82 E3
Chetwode Cl BS10 . . . . .35 D3
Chetwood Ho BS5. . . . . .64 C6
Chevening Cl BS34. . . . .36 D4
Chever's La BA2 . . . . . .136 E5
Cheviot Dr BS35 . . . . . . 15 E8
Cheviot Way BS30. . . . . .66 C5
Chew Cotts BS31. . . . . . 81 F5
Chew Court Farm BS40. 96 B3
Chew Hill BS40 . . . . . . .96 A4
Chew La BS40 . . . . .95 F1
CHEW MAGNA 96 C4
Chew Magna Prim Sch
  BS40 . . . . .96 B3
Chew Rd BS40 . . . . .95 C5
Chew St BS40 . . . . .96 A3
CHEW STOKE 112 D8
Chew Stoke CE Prim Sch
  BS40. . . . . .112 D8
Chewton Cl BS16 . . . . . .51 B3
CHEWTON KEYNSHAM . 81 E2
Chewton Rd BS31. . . . . .81 F2
Chew Valley Lake Nature
  Trails ★ BS39. . . . . . .113 B7
Chew Valley Lake Visitor
  Ctr ★ BS39. . . . . .113 A7
Chew Valley Sch BS40. . 95 F1
Cheyne Rd BS9 . . . . . . .48 D6
Chichester Ho BS4. . . . .64 F6
Chichester Pl BA3 . . . . .134 A2
Chichester Way
  Weston-s-M BS24 . . . . .106 A8
  Yate BS37. . . . . .27 D3
Chickwell La BA3 . . . . .136 A1
CHILCOMPTON 138 C4
Chilcompton Rd BA3 . .138 E7
Chilkwell La BA3. . . . . .136 C2
Chillwood Cl BS37 . . . . .26 E3
Chillyhill La BS40 . . . . .95 F2
Chiltern Cl
  Bristol BS14. . . . . .80 B4
  Bristol, Warmley BS30. . .66 C5
Chiltern Pk BS35. . . . . . 15 E8
Chilton Ct **7** BA1 . . . . .85 B1
Chilton Rd
  Bath BA1. . . . . .85 B1
  Bristol BS4. . . . . .80 A8
Chilwood Cl BS37 . . . . .26 E3
Chimes The BS48 . . . . . .75 C8
Chimney Steps BS2 . .143 C2
Chine The BS16 . . . . . . .50 D5
Chine View BS16 . . . . . . 51 F8
Chiphouse Rd BS15 . . . . 51 F3
Chippenham Rd
  Doynton BS30 . . . . .68 D6
  Marshfield SN14 . . . . . . .69 C2
  Marshfield SN14 . . . . . . .70 A8
Chipperfield Dr BS15. . .51 F1
Chipping Cross BS21 . . .73 C8
Chipping Edge Est
  BS37. . . . . .28 C1
CHIPPING SODBURY . . .28 D1

Chipping Sodbury Sch
  BS37 . . . . .40 B8
Chippings The BS16 . . . .50 D5
Chipping The GL12 . . . . 11 F4
Chisbury St BS5 . . . . . . .50 C3
Chittening Ind Est
  BS11 . . . . .33 D7
Chittening Rd BS11 . . . .33 E7
Chivers St BA2 . . . . . . .102 A2
Chock La BS9 . . . . .49 A7
CHOLWELL 114 D2
Cholwell Cotts BS39. . .114 D2
Christchurch Ave BS16 . 51 D5
Christ Church CE Inf Sch
  BS16. . . . . .51 D5
Christ Church CE Jun Sch
  BS16. . . . . .51 D5
Christ Church CE Prim Sch
  BS8. . . . . .142 A3
Christ Church CE Prim Sch
  BS3. . . . . .63 A3
Christ Church CE Prim Sch
  BS23. . . . . .104 E8
Christ Church Cl **1**
  BA1. . . . . .59 E2
Christchurch Hall **2**
  BA1 . . . . .141 B3
Christ Church Hanham CE
  Prim Sch BS15 . . . . . .65 B4
Christchurch La BS16 . . .51 D5
Christ Church Path S **12**
  BS23. . . . . .104 E8
Christchurch Rd BS8. .142 A3
Christian Cl BS22 . . . . .89 A3
Christina Terr BS8. . . . .142 A1
Christmas St **7** BS1. .143 A3
Christmas Steps **3**
  BS1. . . . . .143 A3
Christmas Tree BS34 . . .35 D6
CHRISTON 123 D7
Christon Hill BS26 . . . .123 B8
Christon Rd
  Banwell BS29 . . . . .107 A1
  Loxton BS26. . . . . .123 C6
Christon Terr BS23 . . . .104 F2
Christ the King RC Prim
  Sch BS35. . . . . .8 D1
Christy Cl BS36 . . . . . . .38 B6
Chubb Cl BS30. . . . . . . .65 F5
Church Ave
  Bristol BS9 . . . . .48 E4
  3 Bristol, Upper Easton
    BS5 . . . . .50 B1
  Bristol, Warmley BS30. . .66 D7
  Falfield GL12 . . . . .9 E7
Church Cl
  Bathampton BA2 . . . . . .85 F2
  Bathford BA1. . . . . .86 B2
  Bristol BS10. . . . . .34 E2
  Clevedon BS21. . . . . . . .57 C2
  Frampton Cotterell BS36 . 38 B8
  Portishead BS20 . . . . . . .45 D5
  Yatton BS49 . . . . .91 C7
Church Cnr BS24. . . . . .122 B1
Church Cotts
  Monkton Combe BA2 . . .119 E8
  Newton St Loe BA2 . . . .100 B6
Church Ct
  8 Bristol BS16 . . . . . .51 D5
  Midsomer Norton BA3. .133 A1
  Redhill BS40. . . . . .93 D3
Churchdown Wlk BS11 . 47 E5
Church Dr
  Bristol BS5. . . . . .64 E8
  Congresbury BS49. . . . . .91 D4
CHURCHEND 10 F3
Churchend La GL12 . . . . 10 F3
Church Farm Bsns Pk
  BA2 . . . . .100 A7
Churchfarm Cl BS37. . . .27 F3
Church Farm Cl BA2 . . .99 B1
Church Farm La BA2 . .137 D7
Church Farm Rd BS16. . .52 C6
Churchfields The Village
  Sch BA15 . . . . .103 E7
Church Hayes Cl BS48. .75 E8
Church Hayes Dr BS48 . 75 E8
Church Hill
  Bristol BS4. . . . . .64 E2
  Burton SN14 . . . . .43 B3
  Freshford BA2 . . . . .120 B5
  Oldbury-on-S BS35. . . . . .7 B5
  Olveston BS35 . . . . .13 F3
  Radstock BA3. . . . . . . .134 C3
  Timsbury BA2. . . . . . . .116 B2
Church Hill Rd BS4 . . . .64 E2
Church Ho BS7 . . . . . . .49 F8
CHURCHILL 108 F5
Churchill Ave BS21. . . . .57 E2
Churchill Bsns Pk
  BS23. . . . . .105 A7
Churchill CE VA Prim Sch
  BS40. . . . . .109 A5
Churchill Cl
  Bristol BS30. . . . . .66 A5
  5 Clevedon BS21. . . . .57 E2
Churchill Com Sch & Sixth
  Form Ctr BS25 . . . . . .108 D5
Churchill Dr BS9. . . . . . .48 D7

Churchill Gate BS25. . .108 F4
Churchill Gdns BS37 . . .27 E4
Churchill Gn BS25. . . . .108 C5
CHURCHILL GREEN . . .108 D5
Churchill Rd
  Bristol BS4. . . . . .64 C4
  Weston-s-M BS23 . . . . .105 A7
Churchill Sch & Sixth Form
  Ctr BS25 . . . . .108 D5
Church La
  Axbridge BS26 . . . . . . .125 C2
  Backwell BS48. . . . . . . .76 C5
  Badminton GL9. . . . . . . .30 E5
  Bath BA2 . . . . .102 C4
  Batheaston BA1. . . . . . .85 F4
  Bishop Sutton BS39 . . .113 D4
  Bitton BS30 . . . . .82 E7
  Bristol BS1. . . . . .143 B2
  Bristol, Bromley Heath
    BS16 . . . . .37 F1
  Bristol, Clifton Wood
    BS8 . . . . .142 B2
  Bristol, Dundry Hill BS14 80 B3
  Bristol, Henbury BS10 . . .34 E2
  Bristol, Southville BS3 . . .63 D3
  Chew Stoke BS40. . . . . .112 D8
  Chilcompton BA3 . . . . .138 D5
  Chipping Sodbury BS37 . .41 B8
  Churchill BS25. . . . . . . .108 D5
  Clutton BS39 . . . . .114 E3
  Compton Bishop BS26 . .124 B3
  Compton Dando BS39 . . .98 D6
  Cromhall GL12 . . . . .10 A1
  Downside BA3. . . . . . . .138 A2
  East Harptree BS40. . . .129 E4
  Farmborough BA2 . . . . .116 A6
  Farrington Gurney BS39 132 A4
  Flax Bourton BS48. . . . . .76 F7
  Frampton Cotterell BS36 . 38 C6
  Hambrook BS16. . . . . . . .37 E2
  Hutton BS24. . . . . .105 E2
  Limpley Stoke BA2. . . . .120 A5
  Long Ashton BS41 . . . . . .62 C2
  Loxton BS26. . . . . .123 D4
  Lympsham BS24. . . . . . .122 B1
  Marshfield SN14 . . . . . . .70 A8
  Midsomer Norton BA3. .133 A1
  Monkton Combe BA2 . . .119 E8
  Nailsea BS48. . . . . .59 C1
  Paulton BS39 . . . . .132 E6
  Portbury BS20 . . . . .46 E3
  Rangeworthy BS37 . . . . . 16 F1
  Stratton-on-t-F BA3 . . .138 F2
  Tickenham BS21 . . . . . . .59 C4
  Timsbury BA2. . . . . . . .116 B2
  Wickwar GL12 . . . . .18 A6
  Winscombe BS25. . . . . .124 C6
  Winterbourne BS36 . . . .37 C6
  Yatton BS49 . . . . .91 C7
Churchlands Rd **8** BS3. 63 B2
Churchland Way BS22 106 B8
Church Lane End BS48. .76 F8
Church Leaze BS11. . . . .47 D6
Church Mdws BS14 . . . .80 C4
Church Par BS4. . . . . . . .64 E2
Church Path Rd BS20 . .47 C4
Church Pl BS20. . . . . . . .47 C4
Church Rd
  Abbots Leigh BS8. . . . . .62 A4
  Almondsbury BS32. . . . . .24 A5
  Alveston BS35 . . . . .15 A1
  Bath, Combe Down BA2 102 C1
  Bath, Weston Park BA1 . .84 C1
  Bitton BS30 . . . . .82 E7
  Bristol BS9. . . . . .48 D3
  Bristol, Bedminster BS3 . .63 C3
  Bristol, Bishopsworth
    BS13 . . . . .79 A6
  Bristol, Filton BS34 . . . . .36 A3
  Bristol, Frenchay BS16 . . .51 C7
  Bristol, Hanham BS15 . . .65 B5
  Bristol, Horfield BS7 . . . . .49 F8
  Bristol, Kingswood BS15 65 E8
  Bristol, Moorfields BS5 . .64 D8
  Bristol, Stoke Gifford
    BS34 . . . . .36 E4
  Bristol, Upper Soundwell
    BS16 . . . . .51 E3
  Bristol, Westbury on Trym
    BS9 . . . . .49 A7
  Doynton BS30 . . . . .54 A1
  Dundry BS41 . . . . .78 D2
  Easter Compton BS35 . . .23 A1
  Easton-in-G BS20. . . . . .47 A4
  Frampton Cotterell BS36 38 C8
  Leigh Woods BS8. . . . . . .62 D6
  Luckington SN14 . . . . . . .31 F4
  Lympsham BS24. . . . . . .122 B1
  Oldbury-on-S BS35. . . . . .7 B5
  Peasedown St John BA2 134 B8
  Pensford BS39. . . . . . . .97 A7
  Pilning BS35. . . . . .22 B7
  Redhill BS40. . . . . .93 D3
  Severn Beach BS35. . . . .22 A6
  Thornbury BS35. . . . . . . .8 B2
  Tormarton GL9. . . . . . . .41 D2
  Weston-s-M BS22 . . . . . .88 E2
  Whitchurch BS14 . . . . . .80 C4
  Wick BS30 . . . . .67 B6

Church Rd continued
  Winford BS40. . . . . .95 A7
  Winscombe BS25. . . . . .124 E7
  Winterbourne BS36 . . . . .37 E4
  Yate BS37. . . . . .27 E3
  Yate BS37. . . . . .27 F2
  Yatton BS49 . . . . .91 C7
Church Rd N BS20 . . . . .45 D5
Church Rd S BS20 . . . . .45 D4
Church Rise BS40. . . . . .95 A7
Church Row BA3 . . . . . .138 F2
Churchside BS16. . . . . . .51 B7
Church Sq
  Clutton BS39 . . . . .114 E2
  Midsomer Norton BA3. .133 A1
Church St
  Banwell BS29 . . . . .107 B3
  6 Bath BA1. . . . . . . .141 C2
  Bathford BA1. . . . . .86 B2
  Bath, Weston Park BA1 . .84 B1
  Bath, Widcombe BA2. . .102 B4
  Blagdon BS40. . . . . . . .110 F2
  Bristol BS1. . . . . .143 B2
  Bristol, Lower Easton
    BS5. . . . . .50 B1
  Bristol, Russell Town BS5 64 B6
  Kilmersdon BA3. . . . . . .140 B5
  Norton St Philip BA2. . .136 E4
  Paulton BS39 . . . . .132 D6
  Pensford BS39. . . . . . . .97 A4
  Radstock BA3. . . . . . . .133 F2
  Woolley BA1. . . . . .84 F6
CHURCH TOWN 76 C5
Church Town BS48. . . . .76 C5
Church View
  Almondsbury BS32. . . . . .23 F4
  6 Bristol BS15. . . . . . .65 E8
  Bristol, Filton BS34 . . . . .36 A3
  Hillesley GL12 . . . . .19 D8
  Newport GL13 . . . . .4 C8
  Thornbury GL13. . . . . . . .8 E7
  Wraxall BS48. . . . . .60 B2
Churchward Cl BS15 . . .65 B5
Churchward Rd
  Weston-s-M BS22 . . . . . .89 B3
  Yate BS37. . . . . .27 B3
Churchway BA3. . . . . . .135 D1
Churchways BS14 . . . . .80 C4
Churchways Ave BS7. . .49 E6
Churchways Cres BS7 . .49 E6
Church Wlk
  Pill BS20. . . . . .47 C4
  Wrington BS40. . . . . . . .92 D2
Churston Cl BS14. . . . . .80 A3
Cicil Rd **1** BS15 . . . . . .65 D8
Cider Mill La BS16 . . . . .52 A2
Circle The BA2 . . . . . . .101 B3
Circuit 32 BS5 . . . . .64 B8
Circular Rd BS9. . . . . . .48 E2
Circus Mews BA1 . . . . .141 B3
Circus Pl BA1 . . . . .141 B3
Circus The BA1 . . . . . . .141 B3
City Academy Bristol The
  BS5. . . . . .64 C8
City Bsns Pk BS5. . . . . .64 A8
City Mus & Art Gall ★
  BS8 . . . . .142 C3
City of Bath Coll BA1. .141 B2
City of Bristol Coll
  BS1. . . . . .142 C2
City of Bristol Coll, Ashley
  Down Ctr BS7. . . . . . . .49 F4
City of Bristol Coll,
  Bedminster Ctr BS3 . .63 E2
City of Bristol Coll,
  Downend Ctr BS16 . . .52 A8
City of Bristol College
  Lawrence Weston Ctr
  BS11. . . . . .34 B1
City of Bristol Coll (Folly
  La Ctr) BS2 . . . . .64 A6
City of Bristol Coll
  (Hartcliffe Ctr) BS13. .79 D4
City of Bristol Coll
  (Kingswood Ctr) BS15 65 E8
City of Bristol Coll,
  Parkway Transport Tech
  Ctr BS34. . . . . .36 D3
City of Bristol Coll,
  Soundwell Ctr BS16 . .51 E2
City Rd BS2. . . . . .143 B4
City View
  Bath BA1 . . . . .141 C4
  Bristol BS4. . . . . .64 A4
Clamp The BS30 . . . . . .66 C3
Clanage Rd BS3. . . . . . .62 E4
Clanders Batch BS40. .110 D3
CLANDOWN 133 E4
Clandown Rd BS39. . . .132 F4
Clan Ho BA2. . . . . .102 C7
CLAPTON 138 C7
Clapton Dro BS20. . . . . .45 D1
**CLAPTON IN
  GORDANO** 45 E1
Clapton La BS20 . . . . . .45 E2
Clapton Rd
  Midsomer Norton BA3. .132 D1
  Stone GL13. . . . . .2 B8

CLAPTON WICK 58 E6
Clapton Wlk BS9. . . . . . .48 C5
Clara Cross La BA2. . . .101 E1
Clare Ave BS7 . . . . .49 C3
Clare Gdns BA2 . . . . . .101 D1
Claremont Ave BS7 . . . .49 D3
Claremont Bldgs BA1 . .85 A1
Claremont Cres BS23. . .87 B1
Claremont Ct BS9. . . . . .49 C5
Claremont Gdns
  Clevedon BS21. . . . . . . .57 G1
  Hallatrow BS39 . . . . . . .132 B7
  4 Nailsea BS48. . . . . .59 D1
Claremont Hall BS21 . .57 G4
Claremont Pl **12** BA1. . .85 A1
Claremont Rd
  Bath BA1 . . . . .85 B1
  Bristol BS7. . . . . .49 D3
Claremont Specl Sch
  BS9. . . . . .49 C5
Claremont St BS5 . . . . .50 A1
Claremont Terr **10** BS5 . .64 B7
Claremont Wlk BA1 . . . .85 A1
Clarence BS24 . . . . . . .105 E7
Clarence Ave BS16 . . . . 51 C5
Clarence Ct **3** BS15. . . .51 B1
Clarence Gdns BS16. . . .51 B1
Clarence Grove Rd
  BS23. . . . . .104 E5
Clarence Ho **2** BS15 . . .51 B1
Clarence Pl
  Bath BA1 . . . . .101 B6
  Bristol BS2. . . . . .142 C4
Clarence Rd
  Bristol BS1. . . . . .143 B1
  Bristol, Kingswood BS15 . 51 B1
  Bristol, Newton BS2. . . . .64 A7
  Bristol, Staple Hill BS16 . 51 C5
Clarence Rd E BS23 . . .104 E5
Clarence Rd N BS23 . . .104 D5
Clarence Rd S BS23 . . .104 D5
Clarence St BA1 . . . . . .141 C4
Clarence Terr BA2. . . . .102 D5
Clarendon Mews BS16 . 51 B8
Clarendon Rd
  Bath BA2 . . . . .102 B5
  Bristol BS6. . . . . .49 C2
  Weston-s-M BS23 . . . . .104 F8
Clarendon Villas BA2. .102 B5
Clare Rd
  Bristol, Cotham BS6. . . . .49 D1
  Bristol, Kingswood BS15 . 51 C2
  Bristol, Lower Easton
    BS5 . . . . .50 B2
Clare St
  Bristol BS1. . . . . .143 A2
  Bristol, Moorfields BS5 . .64 C8
Clare Wlk BS35 . . . . .8 B2
Clark Cl BS48. . . . . .60 B2
Clark Dr
  Bristol BS16. . . . . .50 F7
  Yate Rocks BS37. . . . . . .27 D6
Clarken Cl BS48. . . . . . .59 E1
Clarken Coombe BS41. .62 B3
Clarke St BS3. . . . . .63 D4
Clarkson Ave BS22 . . . .88 C1
Clarkson Ho BA1. . . . . .141 A2
Clark St BS5. . . . . .64 A8
Clarks Way BA2 . . . . . .101 C2
Clatworthy Dr BS14 . . .80 A7
Claude Ave BA2 . . . . . .101 C5
Claude Terr BA2 . . . . . .101 C5
Clavell Rd BS10. . . . . . .34 F2
CLAVERHAM 74 E1
Claverham Cl BS49. . . . .91 D7
Claverham Dro BS49 . . .74 D5
Claverham Pk BS49 . . . .91 E8
Claverham Rd
  Bristol BS16. . . . . .51 A5
  Yatton BS49 . . . . .91 E8
CLAVERTON 103 B5
Claverton Bldgs BA2 . .141 C1
Claverton Ct BA2 . . . . .102 E4
CLAVERTON DOWN . . .102 F3
Claverton Down Rd
  BA2 . . . . .102 F3
Claverton Dr BA2 . . . . .102 F3
Claverton Hill BA2 . . . .103 A4
Claverton Lodge BA2. .102 C5
Claverton Pumping Sta ★
  BA2. . . . . .103 C5
Claverton Rd BS31 . . . .82 E2
Claverton Rd W BS31. . .82 D3
Claverton St BA2. . . . . .141 C1
Clay Bottom BS5. . . . . .50 E2
Claydon Gn BS14. . . . . .79 F3
Clayfield BS37. . . . . . . .27 E5
Clayfield Rd BS4. . . . . . .64 E3
CLAY HILL 50 E2
Clay Hill BS5. . . . . .50 E2
Clayhill Dr BS37 . . . . . .27 F5
Clay La
  Bitton BS30 . . . . .82 D8
  Bristol, Little Stoke BS34 36 C7
  Bristol, Willsbridge BS30 66 D1
  Thornbury BS35. . . . . . . .8 B2
Claymore Cres **1** BS15. 51 B1
Claypiece Rd BS13. . . . .79 A4
Clay Pitch BS37 . . . . . . .29 C3

Claypit Hill BS37 . . . . . . 40 B7
Claypit Rd BS41. . . . . 79 B1
Clay Pit Rd BS6 . . . . . . 49 A3
Claypool Rd BS15 . . . . . 65 E7
Claysend BA2 . . . . 100 D5
CLAYS END 100 D6
Clays End La BA2 . . . . 100 D6
Clayton Cl BS20 . . . . . . 45 E4
Clayton Rd
  Bristol BS3 . . . . 63 A1
  Clifton BS8 . . . . 63 A4
Clayton St
  Avonmouth BS11 . . . . . . 33 A1
  21 Bristol BS5 . . . . . . 64 B8
Cleave St BS2 . . . . 50 A2
CLEEVE 92 B8
Cleeve Ave BS16 . . . . . 51 E7
Cleeve Ct BS16 . . . . . . 51 D7
Cleevedale Rd BA2 . . . . 102 A1
Cleeve Dr BS49 . . . . . . 92 B8
Cleeve Gdns BS16 . . . . . 51 D7
Cleeve Gn BA2 . . . . 101 A6
Cleeve Gr BS31 . . . . . . 81 D5
Cleeve Hill
  Bristol BS16 . . . . 51 D7
  Ubley BS40 . . . . 128 E8
Cleeve Hill Extension
  BS16 . . . . 51 E6
Cleeve Hill Rd BS40 . . . . 92 C7
Cleeve La BS30 . . . . . . 53 D1
Cleeve Lawns BS16 . . . . 51 D7
Cleeve Lodge Cl BS16 . . . 51 E6
Cleeve Lodge Rd BS16 . 51 E6
Cleeve Park Rd BS16 . . . 51 E7
Cleeve Pl BS48 . . . . 60 A1
Cleeve Rd
  Bristol BS4 . . . . 64 B3
  Bristol, Frenchay BS16 . . 51 C8
  Bristol, Mangotsfield
    BS16 . . . . 51 E6
  Yate BS37 . . . . 27 E1
Cleeves Ct BS30 . . . . . . 65 F2
Cleeve Wood Pk BS16 . . 51 C8
Cleeve Wood Rd BS16 . . 51 D7
Clematis Rd BS16 . . . . . 38 D1
Clement St BS2 . . . . . . 143 C4
Clermont Cl BS34 . . . . . 35 F8
Cleve Ct
  3 Bristol, Clifton Wood
    BS8 . . . . 62 F6
  Bristol, Filton BS34 . . . . 36 B4
Clevedale BS16 . . . . . . 51 D7
Clevedale Ct BS16 . . . . . 51 D7
CLEVEDON 57 D3
Clevedon Court★ BS21 58 A4
Clevedon Craft Ctr★
  BS21 . . . . 58 A1
Clevedon Hospl BS21 . . 57 G3
Clevedon La BS21 . . . . . 59 C7
Clevedon Min Rly★
  BS21 . . . . 57 D3
Clevedon Pier★ BS21 . . 57 E4
Clevedon Rd
  Bristol BS7 . . . . 49 D4
  Flax Bourton BS48 . . . . . 60 F2
  Midsomer Norton BA3 . . 133 A2
  Nailsea BS48 . . . . 60 B4
  Portishead BS20 . . . . . . 45 D3
  Tickenham BS21 . . . . . . 59 B4
  Weston-s-M BS23 . . . . 104 E6
  Wraxall BS48 . . . . 60 D6
Clevedon Sch BS21 . . . 57 H5
Clevedon Terr BS6 . . . . 143 A4
Cleve House Sch BS4 . . 64 B3
Cleveland Cl BS35 . . . . . 15 E8
Cleveland Cotts BA1 . . 141 C4
Cleveland Ct BA2 . . . . . 102 C6
Cleveland Pl BA1 . . . . . 141 C4
Cleveland Pl E BA1 . . . 141 C4
Cleveland Pl W BA1 . . . 141 C4
Cleveland Reach BA1 . . 141 C4
Cleveland Row BA1 . . . 102 B8
Cleveland Terr BA1 . . . 141 C4
Cleveland Wlk BA2 . . . 102 C6
Cleve Rd BS34 . . . . 36 A4
Clevewood Ho BS16 . . . 51 C7
Clewson Rise BS14 . . . . 79 F3
Cliff Court Dr BS16 . . . 51 B7
Cliffe Dr BA2 . . . . 120 A6
Clifford Gdns BS11 . . . 47 E6
Clifford Ho BS23 . . . . . 104 D6
Clifford Rd BS16 . . . . . 51 C4
Cliff Rd BS22 . . . . 88 A2
Cliffs The
  Charterhouse BA5 . . . . 127 A1
  Cheddar BS27 . . . . 126 E1
Clift House Rd BS3 . . . . 63 A4
Clift House Spur BS3 . . 62 F4
CLIFTON 142 A4
Clifton Arc BS8 . . . . . . 142 A3
Clifton Ave BS23 . . . . . 104 E5
Clifton Cl **1** BS8 . . . . . 62 F7
Clifton Coll BS8 . . . . . 142 A4
Clifton College Prep Sch
  BS8 . . . . 48 F1
Clifton Ct **10** BS21 . . . . 57 E2
Clifton Down BS8 . . . . . 62 F7
Clifton Down Rd BS8 . . 142 A3

Clifton Down Sh Ctr **11**
  BS8 . . . . 49 B1
Clifton Down Sta BS8 . . 49 B1
Clifton High Gr BS9 . . . 48 E5
Clifton High Sch BS8 . . 142 A4
Clifton Hill BS8 . . . . . . 142 A2
Clifton Metro **10** BS8 . . 49 B1
Clifton Park Rd BS8 . . . 62 F8
Clifton Pk BS8 . . . . 142 A3
Clifton Pl BS5 . . . . 64 A8
Clifton Rd
  Bristol BS8 . . . . 142 A2
  Weston-s-M BS23 . . . . 104 E5
Clifton St
  Bristol, Bedminster BS3 . 63 C3
  Bristol, Upper Easton
    BS5 . . . . 64 A8
  Portishead BS20 . . . . . . 45 C2
Clifton Suspension
  Bridge★ BS8 . . . . 62 E7
Clifton Suspension Bridge
  Rd BS8 . . . . 62 F7
Clifton Vale BS8 . . . . . 142 A2
Clifton Vale Cl BS8 . . . 142 A2
Clifton View
  Bristol, Bedminster Down
    BS13 . . . . 63 A1
  1 Bristol, Windmill Hill
    BS3 . . . . 63 F4
CLIFTON WOOD 142 A2
Cliftonwood Cres BS8 142 B2
Clifton Wood Ct BS8 . 142 B2
Clifton Wood Rd BS8 . 142 B2
Cliftonwood Terr BS8 . 142 A2
Clift Pl BS1 . . . . 143 A1
Clift Rd BS3 . . . . 63 A4
Clinton Rd BS3 . . . . 63 C2
Clive Rd BS14 . . . . 80 C8
Clockhouse Mews
  BS20 . . . . 45 D6
Cloisters Ct BS16 . . . . . 37 E6
Cloisters Ct BS36 . . . . . 37 E6
Cloisters Rd BS36 . . . . . 37 F6
Cloisters The BS6 . . . . . 49 C3
Clonmel Rd BS4 . . . . . . 63 D1
Closemead BS21 . . . . . . 57 F1
Close The
  Bristol BS16 . . . . 36 F1
  Bristol, Henbury BS10 . . 35 A5
  Bristol, Little Stoke BS34 36 C6
  Bristol, Patchway BS32 . 24 C1
  Bristol, Upper Soundwell
    BS16 . . . . 51 D3
  Frampton Cotterell BS36 38 C6
  Portishead BS20 . . . . . . 44 F1
  Thornbury BS35 . . . . . . 15 B8
Clothier Rd BS4 . . . . . . 64 F2
Cloud Hill Ind Est
  BS39 . . . . 132 A8
Clouds Hill Ave BS5 . . . 64 E8
Clouds Hill Rd BS5 . . . . 64 F8
Clovelly Cl BS5 . . . . 64 F8
Clovelly Rd
  Bristol BS5 . . . . 64 F8
  Weston-s-M BS22 . . . . . 89 A2
Clover Cl
  Clevedon BS21 . . . . 57 H3
  Paulton BS39 . . . . 132 E4
Clover Ct **2** BS20 . . . . 105 D7
Cloverdale Dr BS30 . . . 66 A3
Clover Ground BS9 . . . . 49 B7
Clover Hill Way
  Barrow Gurney BS48 . . . . 77 F7
  Bristol BS48 . . . . 78 A6
Cloverlea Bsns Ctr
  BS36 . . . . 38 C3
Cloverlea Rd BS30 . . . . 66 C5
Clover Leaze BS34 . . . . 36 D6
Clover Rd
  Lyde Green BS16 . . . . . . 52 C8
  Thornbury BS35 . . . . 8 B4
  Weston-s-M BS22 . . . . . 89 A6
CLUTTON 114 E3
CLUTTON HILL 115 B4
Clutton Hill BS39 . . . . . 115 B4
Clutton Prim Sch
  BS39 . . . . 114 E3
Clyde Ave BS31 . . . . . . 81 F4
Clyde Ct **2** BS3 . . . . . . 63 C3
Clyde Gdns
  Bath BA2 . . . . 101 B6
  Bristol BS5 . . . . 65 B6
Clyde Gr BS34 . . . . 35 F2
Clyde Ho **7** BS35 . . . . . 15 C8
Clyde La BS6 . . . . 49 C2
Clyde Mews **3** BS6 . . . 49 C2
Clyde Rd
  Bristol, Redland BS6 . . . 49 B2
  Bristol, Totterdown BS4 . 64 A3
  Frampton Cotterell BS36 38 B8
Clydesdale Cl BS14 . . . 80 A6
Clyde Terr
  Bristol, Bedminster BS3 . 63 C3
  Bristol, Totterdown BS4 . 64 A3
Clynder Gr BS21 . . . . . . 57 G6
Clyntonville BS22 . . . . . 88 A4
Coach House La BS5 . . . 64 E8
Coach House Mews
  BS23 . . . . 87 D1

Coalbridge Cl BS22 . . . . 88 F2
Coaley Rd BS11 . . . . 47 D5
COALPIT HEATH 38 D6
Coalpit La BA3 . . . . 138 A2
Coalpit Rd BA1 . . . . 86 A4
Coalsack La BS36 . . . . . 38 B3
Coalville Rd BS36 . . . . . 38 D7
Coape Rd BS14 . . . . 80 F5
Coast Cvn Pk BS21 . . . . 44 B1
Coates Est BS48 . . . . . . 59 F3
Coates Gr BS48 . . . . 60 A2
Coates Wlk BS4 . . . . 79 D6
Cobblestone Mews
  BS8 . . . . 142 A4
Cob Ct BS34 . . . . 36 C3
Cobden Ctr The BS16 . . 38 B2
Cobden St BS5 . . . . 64 C7
Coberley BS15 . . . . 65 C6
Cobhorn Dr BS13 . . . . . 78 F4
Cobley Croft BS21 . . . . 73 C8
Cobourg Rd BS6 . . . . . . 49 F2
Cobthorn Way BS49 . . . 91 E5
Coburg Villas **10** BA1 . . 85 A1
Cock And Yew Tree Hill
  BS40 . . . . 95 A2
Cockers Hill BS39 . . . . . 98 C5
Cock La SN14 . . . . 54 D5
Cock Rd BS15 . . . . 65 F6
Cockshute La
  Greenways GL11 . . . . 4 D8
  Greenways GL13 . . . . 2 D8
CODRINGTON 40 C2
Codrington Pl BS8 . . . . 142 A3
Codrington Rd BS7 . . . . 49 D3
Cody Ct **2** BS15 . . . . . . 65 B5
Cogan Rd BS16 . . . . 51 E3
Cogsall Rd BS14 . . . . . . 80 F6
Coity Pl BS21 . . . . 57 E4
Coker Rd BS22 . . . . 89 B2
Colbourne Rd BA2 . . . . 101 D1
Colburn Rd BS7 . . . . 49 F7
Colchester Cres BS4 . . . 79 D7
COLD ASHTON 68 F6
Coldharbour La
  Bristol BS16 . . . . 50 E8
  Weston-s-M BS23 . . . . 104 D3
Coldharbour Rd BS6 . . . 49 B4
Coldpark Gdns BS13 . . . 78 E5
Coldpark Rd BS13 . . . . . 78 E5
Coldrick Cl BS14 . . . . . . 79 F3
Colebrook Rd BS15 . . . . 65 C8
Coleford Rd BS10 . . . . . 35 D1
Colehouse La BS21 . . . . 73 C8
Colemead BS13 . . . . 79 B5
Cole Rd BS2 . . . . 64 B6
Coleridge Ct **10** BS3 . . 63 C3
Coleridge Ho BS34 . . . . 24 A1
Coleridge Rd
  Bristol BS5 . . . . 50 C3
  Clevedon BS21 . . . . 57 F2
  Weston-s-M BS23 . . . . 105 A4
Coleridge Vale Rd E **1**
  BS21 . . . . 57 F2
Coleridge Vale Rd N
  BS21 . . . . 57 E2
Coleridge Vale Rd S
  BS21 . . . . 57 F2
Coleridge Vale Rd W **2**
  BS21 . . . . 57 F2
COLERNE 70 E6
Colesborne Cl BS37 . . . 39 E8
Coles Gdns BA3 . . . . . . 140 B5
Coleshill Dr BS13 . . . . . 79 B5
COLEY 130 C4
Coley Hill BS40 . . . . . . 130 D5
Coley Narrow BS40 . . . 130 C4
Coley Rd BS40 . . . . 130 B4
Colin Cl BS35 . . . . 8 C1
Collard Ho **2** BS16 . . . 50 F4
College Ave BS16 . . . . . 51 A5
College Ct
  Bristol BS8 . . . . 142 A4
  Bristol, Fishponds BS16 . 51 A5
College Fields BS8 . . . . 62 F8
College Gn BS1 . . . . . . 142 C2
College Mews BS9 . . . . 49 A7
College Park Dr BS10 . . 34 F1
College Rd
  Bath BA1 . . . . 84 E1
  Bristol, Clifton BS8 . . . . 62 F8
  Bristol, Fishponds BS16 . 51 A5
  Bristol, Westbury on Trym
    BS9 . . . . 49 A7
College Sq BS1 . . . . . . 142 C2
College St BS1 . . . . 142 C2
College View **17** BA1 . . 85 A1
College Way BS34 . . . . . 36 A4
Collet Cl BS22 . . . . 89 C4
Collett Cl BS15 . . . . 65 B5
Collett Ho BS36 . . . . . . 37 D4
Collett Way BS37 . . . . . 27 C3
Collier Cl BA2 . . . . 133 D4
Colliers Break BS16 . . . 52 B5
Colliers Gdns
  Backwell BS48 . . . . 75 F7
Colliers La BA1 . . . . 84 F4
Colliers Rise BA3 . . . . . 134 A3
Colliers Way BA3 . . . . . 139 F8

Collcrs Wlk **4** BS48 . . . 59 E2
Colliery La BA2 . . . . . . 134 D5
Collingwood Ave BS15 . 51 E1
Collingwood Cl
  Saltford BS31 . . . . 82 E2
  Weston-s-M BS22 . . . . . 88 E4
Collingwood Rd **4** BS6. 49 B1
Collin Rd BS4 . . . . 64 D4
Collins Ave BS34 . . . . . . 36 C6
Collins Dr BS35 . . . . 22 C3
Collinson Rd BS13 . . . . 79 B5
Collins St BS11 . . . . 47 B8
Colliter Cres BS3 . . . . . 63 B2
Colliters Way
  Bristol BS13 . . . . 78 D7
  Bristol BS3 . . . . 62 D1
Collum La BS22 . . . . 88 E6
Colne Gn BS31 . . . . 82 A4
Coln Sq BS35 . . . . 15 C8
Colombo Cres BS23 . . . 104 E3
Colston Ave BS1 . . . . . 143 A3
Colston Cl
  Bristol BS16 . . . . 51 D3
  Winterbourne BS36 . . . . 37 E4
Colston Ct BS7 . . . . 49 D3
Colston Dale BS16 . . . . 50 E4
Colstone Ct **3** BS16 . . 50 E3
Colston Fort **2** BS2 . . 143 A4
Colston Hill BS16 . . . . . 50 D4
Colston Mews BS6 . . . . 49 E1
Colston Par BS1 . . . . . . 143 B1
Colston Rd BS5 . . . . 50 C1
Colston's Almshouses **1**
  BS1 . . . . 143 A3
Colston's Prep Sch
  BS16 . . . . 50 D5
Colston's Sch BS16 . . . 50 C4
Colston St
  Bristol BS1 . . . . 143 A3
  Bristol, Upper Soundwell
    BS16 . . . . 51 D3
Colston Yd BS1 . . . . . . 143 A3
Colthurst Dr BS15 . . . . 65 E5
Colthurst Mews BS2 . . . 64 B4
Colts Gn BS37 . . . . 40 E8
COLT'S GREEN 40 E8
Colts Ground **6** BS7 . . 50 C8
Columbus Ho BA2 . . . . 102 D8
Colwyn Rd **2** BS5 . . . . 50 C1
Colyton **11** BS22 . . . . . 89 A2
Colyton Ct BS3 . . . . 63 D1
Combe Ave BS20 . . . . . 45 C6
COMBE DOWN 102 B1
Combe Down CE Prim Sch
  BA2 . . . . 102 B1
Combe Down CEVC Prim
  Sch BA2 . . . . 102 B1
Combe Fields BS20 . . . . 45 C6
Combe Gr BA1 . . . . 101 B8
COMBE HAY 118 D4
Combe Hay La BA2 . . . 118 B6
Combe La BS39 . . . . . . 132 B6
Combe Pk BA1 . . . . 101 C8
Combe Rd
  Bath BA2 . . . . 102 B1
  Portishead BS20 . . . . . . 45 D5
Combermere BS35 . . . . 15 D8
Combe Road Cl **3**
  BA2 . . . . 102 B1
Combeside BA2 . . . . . . 102 A3
Combe Side BS48 . . . . . 76 A7
Combe The BS40 . . . . . 109 F2
Combfactory La **13** BS5. 64 B8
Comb Paddock BS9 . . . 49 B7
Comfortable Pl BA1 . . . 141 A3
Commercial Rd BS1 . . . 143 A1
Commercial Way BS22 . 89 B2
Common (East) The
  BS32 . . . . 24 C1
Commonfield Rd BS11 . 34 B1
Common La
  Aust BS35 . . . . 13 A6
  Churchill BS25 . . . . 108 B5
  Easton-in-G BS20 . . . . . 47 B2
Commonmead La BS37. 40 F8
Common Mead La
  BS16 . . . . 37 A1
Common Rd
  Bristol BS15 . . . . 65 B3
  Winterbourne BS36 . . . . 37 F7
Common The
  Bristol, Frenchay BS16 . . 51 B7
  Bristol, Patchway BS32 . . 24 C1
  Olveston BS35 . . . . 13 F3
Como Ct BS20 . . . . 45 C6
COMPTON BISHOP . . . 124 A3
COMPTON COMMON . . 98 C5
COMPTON DANDO 98 D6
Compton Dr
  Bristol BS9 . . . . 48 C7
  Weston-s-M BS24 . . . . . 105 E7
Compton Gn BS31 . . . . . 81 E4
COMPTON
  GREENFIELD 34 F8
Compton La BS26 . . . . . 125 B1
Compton Lodge **3** BS6. 49 B1
COMPTON MARTIN . . . 129 A7
Compton St BS5 . . . . . . 64 C7
Comrade Ave BS25 . . . . 125 E8

Comyn Wlk BS16 . . . . . . 51 A5
Concorde Dr
  Bristol BS10 . . . . 35 B1
  Clevedon BS21 . . . . 57 D1
Concorde Ho BS34 . . . . 35 F2
Concorde Rd BS34 . . . . 35 E7
Condor Cl BS22 . . . . . . 105 D8
Condor Ho BS7 . . . . 50 C7
Condover Rd BS4 . . . . . 65 A3
Conduit Pl **2** BS2 . . . . 50 A1
Conduit Rd BS2 . . . . 50 A1
Cone The BS10, BS34 . . 35 C6
Coneygrce BS13 . . . . . . 78 F6
Conference Ave BS20 . . 45 F5
Conference Cl BS20 . . . 45 F4
Congleton Rd BS5 . . . . . 64 D8
CONGRESBURY 91 E4
CONHAM 65 A5
Conham Hill BS15 . . . . . 65 A5
Conham Ho BS15 . . . . . 65 A5
Conham Rd BS4, BS5,
  BS15 . . . . 64 F5
Conifer Cl
  Bristol BS16 . . . . 51 D6
  Frampton Cotterell BS36 . 26 A1
Conifer Way BS24 . . . . . 105 E5
Coniston Ave BS9 . . . . . 48 E6
Coniston Cl BS30 . . . . . 66 D6
Coniston Cres BS23 . . . 104 F4
Coniston Prim Sch
  BS34 . . . . 23 F1
Coniston Rd BS34 . . . . . 23 F1
CONKWELL 103 C1
Conkwell BA15 . . . . 103 C2
Connaught Mans BA2 . 141 C3
Connaught Pl BS23 . . . 104 D8
Connaught Prim Sch
  BS4 . . . . 79 E8
Connaught Rd BS4 . . . . 79 E8
Connection Rd BA2 . . . 101 A6
Constable Cl BS31 . . . . 81 F6
Constable Dr BS22 . . . . 88 F3
Constable Rd BS7 . . . . . 50 B6
Constantine Ave BS34 . . 36 E5
Constitution Hill BS8 . . 142 B2
Contemporis BS8 . . . . . 142 A3
Convent Cl BS10 . . . . . . 34 D3
Convocation Ave BA2 . 102 E5
Conway Gn BS31 . . . . . . 82 A3
Conway Rd BS4 . . . . 64 C4
Conygar Cl BS21 . . . . . . 57 H5
Conygre Gn BA2 . . . . . 116 B2
Conygre Gr BS34 . . . . . 36 C3
Conygre Rd BS34 . . . . . 36 B3
Conygre Rise BA2 . . . . 115 F6
Cook Cl BS30 . . . . 66 C4
Cooke's Dr BS35 . . . . . . 23 A1
Cooks Bridle Path
  BS48 . . . . 93 D8
Cooks Cl BS32 . . . . 24 D3
Cook's Folly Rd BS9 . . . 48 D3
Cooks Gdns BS48 . . . . . 60 A2
Cooks Hill
  Clutton BS39 . . . . 114 E3
  Clutton BS39 . . . . 114 E3
Cooks La BS36 . . . . 38 D3
Cook's La
  Banwell BS29 . . . . 107 A4
  Clevedon BS21 . . . . 58 B2
Cooksley Rd BS5 . . . . . . 64 C8
Cook St BS11 . . . . 47 C8
Cookworthy Cl **2** BS5 . 64 B6
Coombe Ave BS35 . . . . . 8 B2
Coombe Bank Mews
  BS23 . . . . 87 D1
Coombe Bridge Ave
  BS9 . . . . 48 D6
Coombe Brook La BS5 . 50 E2
Coombe Cl BS10 . . . . . . 34 D3
Coombe Dale
  Backwell BS48 . . . . 94 A8
  Bristol BS9 . . . . 48 C6
COOMBE DINGLE 48 C8
Coombe Gdns BS9 . . . . 48 E6
Coombe Ho **4** BS15 . . 65 E8
Coombe La
  Bristol BS9 . . . . 48 E6
  Compton Bishop BS26 . 124 B4
  East Harptree BS40 . . . 129 E4
  Easton-in-G BS20 . . . . . 47 A2
Coomb End BA3 . . . . . 133 F3
Coombend Ho BA3 . . . 133 F3
Coombend Rise BA3 . . 133 F3
Coombe Rd
  Bristol BS5 . . . . 50 C2
  Nailsea BS48 . . . . 59 E1
  Weston-s-M BS23 . . . . . 87 E1
Coombes Way BS30 . . . 66 D4
Coombe The
  Blagdon BS40 . . . . 110 C3
  Compton Martin BS40 . 129 A6
Coombe Way BS10 . . . . 34 F1
Coomb Rocke BS9 . . . . 48 D6
COOMB'S END 41 A6
Cooperage La BS3 . . . . 142 B1
Cooperage Rd BS5 . . . . 64 D7

Co-operation Rd BS5 . . 50 C1
Cooper Rd
  Bristol BS9 . . . . 48 F7
  Thornbury BS35 . . . . 15 B7
Coopers Dr BS37 . . . . . . 27 F5
Coots The BS14 . . . . 80 E6
Copeland Dr BS14 . . . . . 80 B5
Copford La BS41 . . . . 62 B1
Copley Ct BS15 . . . . 65 E5
Copley Gdns
  Bristol BS7 . . . . 50 B6
  Weston-s-M BS22 . . . . . 88 F2
Coppack Ho **6** BS21 . . 57 E2
Copperfield Dr BS22 . . . 88 F4
Coppice End Cnr
  BS24 . . . . 122 C2
Coppice Mews BS21 . . . . 57 E4
Coppice The
  Bristol, Bradley Stoke
    BS32 . . . . 36 E7
  Bristol, Highridge BS13 . . 78 E4
Copse Cl BS24 . . . . 105 A1
Copse Cnr BS24 . . . . . . 122 C2
Copse End BS25 . . . . . . 107 F2
Copseland BA2 . . . . 102 D5
Copse Rd
  Bristol BS4 . . . . 64 B3
  Clevedon BS21 . . . . 57 E4
  Keynsham BS31 . . . . 82 C4
Copse The BS22 . . . . 89 D2
Copthorne Cl BS14 . . . . 80 B5
Copthorn La BS40 . . . . 109 F6
Coralberry Dr BS22 . . . . 88 F1
Corbet Cl BS11 . . . . 34 C2
Corbett Cl **1** BS37 . . . . 27 F4
Corbett Ho **11** BS5 . . . . 64 C7
Cordwell Wlk BS10 . . . . 49 D7
Corey Cl **6** BS2 . . . . 49 F1
Corfe Cl BS48 . . . . 59 D1
Corfe Cres BS31 . . . . . . 81 E4
Corfe Pl BS30 . . . . 66 B1
Corfe Rd BS4 . . . . 79 D7
Coriander Dr BS34 . . . . . 37 A7
Coriander Wlk BS5 . . . . 50 C2
Corinthian Ct **9** BS1 . 143 B1
Corinum Cl BS16 . . . . . . 52 C6
Corker's Hill **9** BS5 . . . 64 F6
Cork Pl BA1 . . . . 101 D7
Cork St BA1 . . . . 101 D7
Cork Terr BA1 . . . . 101 D7
Cormorant Cl BS22 . . . . 88 F1
Corner Croft BS21 . . . . . 57 E1
Cornfield Cl BS32 . . . . . 24 C1
Cornfields The BS22 . . . . 88 F5
Cornhill Dr BS14 . . . . . . 80 A7
Cornishmen's Rd BA1 . . 84 E4
Cornish Rd BS14 . . . . . . 80 E6
Cornish Wlk BS14 . . . . . 80 E6
Cornleaze BS13 . . . . 79 A5
Corn St
  Bath BA1 . . . . 141 B2
  Bristol BS1 . . . . 143 A3
Cornwall Cres BS37 . . . . 27 F3
Cornwallis Ave
  Bristol BS8 . . . . 142 A2
  Weston-s-M BS22 . . . . . 88 F4
Cornwallis Cres BS8 . . . 62 F6
Cornwallis Gr BS8 . . . . 142 A2
Cornwallis Ho BS8 . . . . 142 A2
Cornwall Rd BS7 . . . . . . 49 D4
Coromandel Hts BA1 . . 141 B4
Coronation Ave
  Bath BA2 . . . . 101 C4
  Bristol BS16 . . . . 51 A4
  Keynsham BS31 . . . . 81 D4
Coronation Cl BS30 . . . . 66 A5
Coronation Est BS23 . . 104 F3
Coronation Pl BS1 . . . . 143 A2
Coronation Rd
  Banwell BS29 . . . . 107 A3
  Bath BA1 . . . . 101 D7
  Bleadon BS24 . . . . 122 C6
  Bristol BS3 . . . . 142 B1
  Bristol, Cadbury Heath
    BS30 . . . . 66 B5
  Bristol, Mangotsfield
    BS16 . . . . 51 E5
  Bristol, Warmley BS15 . . 66 A4
  Weston-s-M BS22 . . . . . 88 E2
Coronation Terr BA3 . . 138 D5
Corondale Rd BS22 . . . 105 D8
Corpus Christi RC Prim
  Sch BS23 . . . . 104 D6
Corridor The **2** BA1 . . 141 C2
Corsley Wlk BS4 . . . . . . 79 F8
CORSTON 100 B7
Corston BS24 . . . . 105 A2
Corston Dr BA2 . . . . . . 100 B6
Corston La BA2 . . . . . . 100 A8
Corston View BA2 . . . . 101 C4
Corston Wlk BS11 . . . . . 47 F7
Cossham Cl BS35 . . . . . . 8 C2
Cossham Memorial Hospl
  BS16 . . . . 51 C2

Cossham Rd BS5 . . . . . . 64 D7
Cossham St BS16 . . . . . 52 B5
Cossham Wlk BS5 . . . . . 51 A1
Cossington Rd BS4 . . . . 79 F8
Cossins Rd BS6 . . . . 49 B3
Costers Cl BS35 . . . . 15 A5
Costiland Dr BS13 . . . . . 78 F6
Cote Bank Ho BS9 . . . . . 49 B7
Cote Dr BS9 . . . . 49 A4
Cote House La BS9 . . . . 49 A5
Cote La BS9 . . . . 49 A5
Cote Lea Pk BS9 . . . . . . 49 B7
Cote Paddock BS9 . . . . . 48 F4
Cote Pk BS9 . . . . 48 E6
Cote Rd BS9 . . . . 49 A4
COTHAM 49 C1
Cotham Brow BS6 . . . . . 49 D1
Cotham Gardens Prim Sch
  BS6 . . . . 49 D1
Cotham Gdns **15** BS6 . . 49 D1
Cotham Gr BS6 . . . . 49 D1
Cotham Gram Sch
  (Charnwood Annex)
  BS6 . . . . 49 C1
Cotham Hill BS6 . . . . . . 49 C1
Cotham Lawn Ho BS6 . 142 C4
Cotham Lawn Rd
  Bristol BS6 . . . . 49 C1
  Bristol BS6 . . . . 142 C4
Cotham Pk BS6 . . . . 49 C1
Cotham Pk N BS6 . . . . . 49 C1
Cotham Pl BS6 . . . . 142 C4
Cotham Rd BS6 . . . . . . 142 C4
Cotham Rd S BS6 . . . . 143 A4
Cotham Sch BS6 . . . . . 142 C4
Cotham Side BS6 . . . . . . 49 D1
Cotham Vale BS6 . . . . . . 49 C1
Cotman Wlk
  Bristol BS7 . . . . 50 B6
  1 Weston-s-M BS22 . . 88 F2
Cotrith Gr BS10 . . . . 34 E3
Cotswold Cl **3** BS20 . . 45 E4
Cotswold Ct
  Bristol BS16 . . . . 36 F1
  Chipping Sodbury BS37 . . 28 B1
Cotswold Ed Ctr The
  BS34 . . . . 35 F2
Cotswold Gdns BA3 . . . 139 A6
Cotswold La BS37 . . . . . 41 A8
Cotswold Rd
  Bath BA2 . . . . 101 B4
  Bristol BS3 . . . . 63 D3
  Chipping Sodbury BS37 . . 40 B8
Cotswold View
  Bath BA2 . . . . 101 B5
  Bristol, Filton BS34 . . . . . 36 A3
  Bristol, Kingswood BS15 . 51 D2
  Charfield GL12 . . . . 11 B5
  Wickwar GL12 . . . . 18 B3
Cotswold Way SN14 . . . 69 A6
Cottage Gdns BS5 . . . . . 65 A7
Cottage Pl
  3 Bath BA1 . . . . 85 C2
  Bristol BS2 . . . . 143 A4
Cottages The BS40 . . . . . 92 D2
Cotterell Ct BA1 . . . . . . 141 B2
Cottington Ct BS15 . . . . 65 E5
Cottisford Rd BS5 . . . . . 50 B4
Cottle Gdns BS14 . . . . . 80 F6
Cottle Rd BS14 . . . . 80 F6
Cottles La BA15 . . . . . . 120 F6
Cottongrass Rd BS16 . . . 52 D7
Cotton Mead BA2 . . . . 100 B7
Cotton Mill La BS5 . . . . 64 C6
Cottonwood Dr BS30 . . . 66 A4
Cottrell Ave BS15 . . . . . 51 C2
Cottrell Rd BS5 . . . . 50 C3
Coulson Dr BS22 . . . . . . 89 B3
Coulson Ho **2** BS7 . . . . 49 F4
Coulson's Cl BS14 . . . . . 80 A3
Coulson's Rd BS14 . . . . 80 A3
Coulson Wlk BS15 . . . . . 51 C2
Council Hos
  Bleadon BS24 . . . . 122 B5
  Kingston Seymour BS21 . 73 C3
  Wick St L BS22 . . . . 89 B8
Council Hos The BS40 . 111 B8
Council Houses BS24 . . . 90 C3
Council Houses The
  BS39 . . . . 130 E6
Counterpool Rd BS15 . . 65 C7
Countership BS1 . . . . . 143 B2
Countership Gdns BS14 80 C6
Countess Wlk BS16 . . . . 50 D6
County Bridge BA3 . . . 133 F2
County St BS4 . . . . 64 A4
County Way BS34 . . . . . 37 A4
Court Ave
  Bristol BS34 . . . . 36 F5
  Yatton BS49 . . . . 91 C7
Court Cl
  Backwell BS48 . . . . 76 C5
  Bristol BS7 . . . . 49 E7
  Portishead BS20 . . . . 45 D4
Court Cotts BS37 . . . . . . 29 D6
Court-de-Wyck Prim Sch
  BS49 . . . . 74 F1
Court Dr BS25 . . . . 108 B4
Courtenay Cres BS4 . . . . 79 D7

Courtenay Rd BS31 . . . . 82 B2
Courtenay Wlk BS22 . . . 89 A3
Court Farm Gdns BS30 . 65 E2
Court Farm Park★
  BS29 . . . . 106 F5
Court Farm Rd
  Bristol BS14 . . . . 79 F3
  Bristol, Longwell Green
    BS30 . . . . 65 E2
Courtfield Gr BS16 . . . . . 51 A4
Court Gdns
  Batheaston BA1 . . . . 86 A4
  Yate BS37 . . . . 39 E8
Court Hay BS20 . . . . 47 A4
Court Hill BS39 . . . . 98 D5
Court Ho BS26 . . . . 125 B2
Court La
  Bathford BA1 . . . . 86 B2
  Clevedon BS21 . . . . 58 A3
  Shipham BS25 . . . . 125 F8
  Wick BS30 . . . . 67 B6
Courtlands
  Bristol BS32 . . . . 24 C1
  Keynsham BS31 . . . . 81 E5
Courtlands La BS3 . . . . . 62 E4
Court Mdw GL13 . . . . 3 E3
Courtmead BA2 . . . . . . 118 F7
Court Mead GL13 . . . . . . 3 E3
Courtney Prim Sch
  BS15 . . . . 65 E7
Courtney Rd BS15 . . . . . 65 E7
Courtney Way BS15 . . . . 66 A7
Court Pl BS22 . . . . 88 F2
Court Rd
  Bristol, Horfield BS7 . . . . 49 F6
  Bristol, Kingswood BS15 . 65 D7
  Bristol, Oldland Common
    BS30 . . . . 66 C3
  Frampton Cotterell BS36 . 37 F8
  Weston-s-M BS22 . . . . . 88 A5
Courtside Mews BS6 . . . 49 C1
Court View BS30 . . . . . . 67 C6
Court View Cl BS32 . . . . 24 A5
Courtyard The BS40 . . . 129 E6
Courville Cl BS35 . . . . . . 15 A4
Cousins Cl BS10 . . . . 34 D3
Cousins La BS5 . . . . 64 F8
Cousins Mews BS4 . . . . 64 F6
Cousins Way BS16 . . . . . 52 B8
Couzens Cl BS37 . . . . . . 28 B2
Couzens Pl BS34 . . . . . . 36 F5
Coventry Wlk BS4 . . . . . 64 F6
Cow Barton BS7 . . . . . . 50 C8
Cowdray Rd BS4 . . . . . . 79 D7
COWHILL 7 B3
Cowhorn Hill BS30 . . . . 66 C4
Cow Leaze BS36 . . . . . . 38 B6
Cowleaze La BS40 . . . . 129 C6
Cowler Wlk BS13 . . . . . . 78 F4
Cowling Dr BS14 . . . . . . 80 C5
Cowling Rd BS14 . . . . . . 80 D5
Cowper Rd BS6 . . . . 49 C1
Cowper St BS5 . . . . 64 C7
Cowship La GL12 . . . . . . 17 D6
Cowslip Cres BS16 . . . . . 52 C8
COWSLIP GREEN 110 B8
Cowslip La BS26 . . . . . . 123 D3
Cowslip Way G12 . . . . . . 11 B5
Cox Ct BS30 . . . . 65 F4
Coxgrove Hill BS16 . . . . 52 F7
Coxley Dr BA1 . . . . 85 B2
Cox's Gn BS40 . . . . 92 E1
COX'S GREEN 92 E1
Coxway BS21 . . . . 57 H2
Coxwynne Cl BA3 . . . . 139 C8
CRAB HOLE 123 E2
Crabtree Cl BS41 . . . . . . 78 D1
Crabtree La BS41 . . . . . . 78 D2
Crabtree Wlk BS5 . . . . . 50 D2
Cradock Cl BS30 . . . . . . 66 B4
Craftes Ct BS5 . . . . 50 E1
Cranberry Wlk BS9 . . . . 48 C8
Cranbourne Chase
  BS23 . . . . 88 A1
Cranbourne Rd BS34 . . . 35 F7
Cranbrook Rd BS6 . . . . . 49 C3
Crandale Rd **3** BA2 . . 101 D5
Crandell Cl BS10 . . . . . . 34 F4
Crane Cl BS15 . . . . 66 B8
Cranesbill Cres G12 . . . . 11 B5
Cranford Cl BS22 . . . . . . 88 D1
Cranford Ct **1** BS9 . . . . 49 B6
Cranham BS37 . . . . 39 C7
Cranham Cl BS15 . . . . . . 51 F2
Cranham Dr BS34 . . . . . 24 C1
Cranham Rd BS10 . . . . . 49 C8
Cranhill Rd BA1 . . . . . . 101 D8
Cranleigh BA2 . . . . 118 F8
Cranleigh Court Inf Sch
  BS37 . . . . 27 D3
Cranleigh Court Rd
  BS37 . . . . 27 D2
Cranleigh Gdns BS9 . . . 48 E4
Cranleigh Rd BS14 . . . . 80 B5
Cranmoor Gn BS35 . . . . 22 D6
Cranmoor La BS49 . . . . 73 D2
Cranmore BS24 . . . . . . 105 A2
Cranmore Ave BS31 . . . . 81 E6
Cranmore Cres BS10 . . . 35 D1

Cranmore Pl BA2 . . . . . 118 E8
Cranside Ave BS6 . . . . . 49 C4
Cransley Cres BS9 . . . . . 49 C7
Crantock Ave BS13 . . . . 79 B8
Crantock Dr BS32 . . . . . 24 B5
Crantock Rd BS37 . . . . . 27 D1
Cranwell Gr BS14 . . . . . 80 A5
Cranwell Rd
  Locking BS24 . . . . 106 C5
  Locking BS24 . . . . 106 C5
Cranwells Pk BA1 . . . . . 101 D8
Crates Cl BS15 . . . . 65 E8
Craven Cl BS30 . . . . 65 E8
Craven Way BS30 . . . . . 65 F5
Crawford Cl **1** BS21 . . 57 D1
Crawl La BA3 . . . . 133 C4
Craydon Gr BS14 . . . . . . 80 D4
Craydon Rd BS14 . . . . . . 80 D5
Craydon Wlk BS14 . . . . . 80 D5
Create Ctr★ BS1 . . . . . . 62 F5
Crediton **5** BS22 . . . . . 89 A2
Crediton Cres BS4 . . . . . 63 F1
Crescent Gdns BA1 . . . 141 A3
Crescent La BA1 . . . . . . 141 B4
Crescent Place Mews
  BA2 . . . . 101 D1
Crescent Rd BS16 . . . . . 51 C6
Crescent The
  Backwell BS48 . . . . 76 A6
  Bristol BS16 . . . . 36 F1
  Bristol, Frenchay BS16 . . 36 F1
  Bristol, Henleaze BS9 . . . 49 C6
  Bristol, Sea Mills BS9 . . . 48 C6
  Bristol, Upper Soundwell
    BS16 . . . . 51 D3
  Farrington Gurney BS39 132 B3
  Lympsham BS24 . . . . . . 122 C5
  Olveston BS35 . . . . 14 C4
  Stanton Drew BS39 . . . . 96 F1
  Weston-s-M BS22 . . . . . 88 B1
  Wick BS30 . . . . 67 C7
Crescent View BA2 . . . . 141 D1
Crescent View Ct BS22 . 88 B1
Creslands Ind Units
  BS24 . . . . 105 A3
Cresswell Cl BS22 . . . . . 89 A2
Crest The
  Bristol BS4 . . . . 64 C2
  West Kington SN14 . . . . 56 F3
Creswicke Ave BS15 . . . 65 C5
Creswicke Ho **12** BS1 . 143 A3
Creswicke Rd BS4 . . . . . 79 E7
Crewkerne Cl BS48 . . . . 60 B1
CREW'S HOLE 64 E7
Crew's Hole Rd BS5 . . . 64 C7
CRIBBS CAUSEWAY . . . 35 D6
Cribbs Causeway Ctr
  BS34 . . . . 35 A6
Cribbs Causeway Ret Pk
  BS10 . . . . 35 C6
Cribbs Cswy BS10 . . . . . 35 A6
Cribb's La BS40 . . . . 93 D1
Crickback La
  Chew Magna BS40 . . . . . 96 A2
  Chew Magna BS40 . . . . . 96 A3
Cricket Field Gn BS48 . . 59 D2
Cricket La BS10 . . . . 49 A8
Cricklade Ct BS48 . . . . . 60 A1
Cricklade Rd BS7 . . . . . . 49 E4
Cripps Rd BS3 . . . . 63 D3
Crispin La **4** BS35 . . . . . 8 B1
Crispin Way BS15 . . . . . 51 F2
Crockerne CE Prim Sch
  BS20 . . . . 47 C4
Crockerne Dr BS20 . . . . 47 C3
Crockerne Ho BS20 . . . . 47 C4
CROCOMBE 116 C3
Crocombe BA2 . . . . 116 C3
Crocombe La BA2 . . . . 116 C3
Crocus Rd BS16 . . . . 52 D7
Croft Ave BS16 . . . . 50 C4
Croft Cl BS30 . . . . 82 D8
Crofters Wlk BS32 . . . . . 36 D8
Crofton Ave BS7 . . . . . . 49 F6
Crofton Fields BS36 . . . . 37 E6
Crofton Mews BS15 . . . . 65 E7
Croft Rd BA1 . . . . 85 B1
CROFTS END 50 F1
Crofts End Ind Est BS5 . 50 E1
Crofts End Rd BS5 . . . . . 50 E1
Croft The
  Backwell BS48 . . . . 76 A7
  Bristol, Mangotsfield
    BS16 . . . . 51 F5
  Bristol, Oldland Common
    BS30 . . . . 66 C3
  Clevedon BS21 . . . . 57 H4
  Hutton BS24 . . . . 105 A3
  Monkton Combe BA2 . . . 102 E1
  Westwood BA15 . . . . . . 120 F3
Croft View BS9 . . . . 49 C6
Crokeswood Wlk BS11 . . 34 A1
Cromer Ct BS21 . . . . 57 F5
Crome Rd BS7 . . . . 50 B7
Cromer Rd
  Bristol BS5 . . . . 50 C2
  Weston-s-M BS23 . . . . . 104 E5
CROMHALL 10 A1
Cromhall La GL12 . . . . . . 9 D1

Cromwell Ct BS15 . . . . . 65 E5
Cromwell Dr BS22 . . . . . 89 A4
Cromwell Rd
  Bristol, Montpelier BS6 . . 49 C2
  Bristol, St George BS5 . . . 65 A8
Cromwells Hide BS16 . . . 50 E5
Cromwell St BS3 . . . . . . 63 C3
Cromwell View BS6 . . . . 49 E2
Crookes La BS22 . . . . . . 88 A4
Croomes Hill BS16 . . . . . 51 D6
Cropthorne Rd BS7 . . . . 36 A1
Cropthorne Road S
  BS7 . . . . 50 A8
Crosby Hall BS23 . . . . . 104 D8
Crosby Row BS8 . . . . . . 142 A2
CROSS 124 E2
Crosscombe Dr BS13 . . . 79 C3
Cross Combe Wlk BS13 . 79 B3
Cross Cotts GL13 . . . . 2 C3
Cross Elms La BS9 . . . . . 48 E5
Cross Field **9** BS34 . . . 35 F7
Crossfield Rd BS16 . . . . 51 E5
Cross Hands Rd BS35 . . 22 D7
Cross La BS26 . . . . 125 A2
Cross Lanes BS20 . . . . . 47 C4
Crossleaze Rd BS15 . . . . 65 C3
Crossley Cl BS36 . . . . . . 37 F7
Crossley Farm Bsns Ctr
  BS36 . . . . 37 E7
Crossman Ave BS36 . . . . 37 E5
Crossman Rd BS37 . . . . 27 D6
Crossman Wlk BS21 . . . . 57 H2
Cross Moor Dr BS26 . . 125 B1
Cross Moor Dro BS26 . 124 E1
Cross Moor Rd BS26 . . 125 B1
Crosspost La BA2 . . . . . . 99 B4
Cross St
  Bristol BS15 . . . . 51 D1
  Keynsham BS31 . . . . 81 F7
  3 Weston-s-M BS23 . . 104 E7
Cross The BS40 . . . . 129 F4
Cross Tree Gr BS32 . . . . 36 D8
Crossway La BA3 . . . . . 138 B7
CROSSWAYS 8 F2
Crossways Cvn Pk
  BA2 . . . . 117 F5
Crossways Jun & Inf Schs
  BS35 . . . . 8 D1
Crossways La
  Combe Hay BA2 . . . . . . 118 A3
  Crossways BS35 . . . . 8 E2
Crossways Rd
  Bristol BS4 . . . . 64 A1
  Thornbury BS35 . . . . 8 D1
Cross Wlk BS14 . . . . 80 A6
Crowe Hill BA2 . . . . . . 120 B5
Crowe La BA2 . . . . 120 B5
CROWELL BROOK 5 F6
Crow La
  Bristol BS1 . . . . 143 A2
  Bristol, Henbury BS10 . . . 34 F2
Crowley Way BS11 . . . . . 33 B1
Crow Mdw GL12 . . . . . . 11 F4
Crowndale Rd BS4 . . . . . 64 A3
Crown Gdns BS30 . . . . . 66 B7
Crown Glass Pl **5** BS48 59 E2
Crown Hill
  Bath BA1 . . . . 84 C1
  Bristol BS5 . . . . 64 F8
  Winford BS40 . . . . 95 A5
Crown Ho
  Bristol BS1 . . . . 143 A2
  Nailsea BS48 . . . . 59 C1
Crown Ind Est BS30 . . . . 66 C7
Crown La BS16 . . . . 51 D3
Crownleaze BS16 . . . . . . 51 D3
Crown Rd
  Bath BA1 . . . . 84 B1
  Bristol, Upper Soundwell
    BS15 . . . . 51 D2
  Bristol, Warmley BS30 . . . 66 C6
Crown Way BS30 . . . . . . 66 C7
Crows Gr BS32 . . . . 24 D3
Crowther Pk BS7 . . . . . . 50 A4
Crowther Rd BS7 . . . . . . 50 A4
Crowthers Ave BS37 . . . 27 E3
Crowther St **4** BS3 . . . 63 B3
Croydon Ho **1** BS5 . . . 64 B8
Croydon St BS5 . . . . 64 B8
Cruikshank Gr BS24 . . . 106 B5
Crunnis The BS32 . . . . . 36 E6
Crusader Ho **4** BS1 . . 143 A2
Crusty La BS20 . . . . 47 C5
Crystal Way BS32 . . . . . 36 E8
Cuck Hill BS25 . . . . 125 E7
Cuckoo La
  High Littleton BS39 . . . 115 B3
  Winterbourne BS36 . . . . 37 F3
  Wraxall BS48 . . . . 60 A6
Cuffington Ave BS4 . . . . 64 D4
Culleysgate La BS30 . . . 67 F6
Cullimore's La BA1 . . . . 83 C4
Culver La BS39 . . . . 98 D6
Culverhay BS39 . . . . 98 D6
Culverhay Sch BA2 . . . . 101 B2
Culverhill Rd BS37 . . . . . 28 A1
Culverhill Sch BS37 . . . . 39 D7
Culver La BS40 . . . . 129 C3

Culvers Cl BS31........81 E6
Culvers Rd BS31........81 E6
Culver St BS1.........142 C2
Culvert Ave BS37.......27 B1
Culvert The BS32........36 D8
Culverwell Rd BS13......79 A4
Culvery La BS39.........97 D4
Cumberland Basin Rd
BS8..................62 F5
Cumberland Cl BS1......142 A1
Cumberland Gr **5** BS6. 49 F2
Cumberland Ho BA1 ....141 A2
Cumberland Pl **6** BS8 . 62 F6
Cumberland Rd BS1.....142 A1
Cumberland Row BA1 141 B2
Cumberland St BS2.....143 B4
Cumbria Cl BS35.........8 E1
Cunningham Gdns
BS16.................51 B5
Cunnington Cl BS30......66 B1
Curland Gr BS14........80 B5
Curlew Cl BS16.........50 F6
Curlew Gdns BS22.......88 F1
Curlew Pl BS20.........45 F6
Currells La BS40........77 B1
Curtis La BS34..........37 A4
Cussons St BA2........102 C8
Custom Cl BS14.........80 A7
Custom Ho BS1.........143 A1
Cutler Rd BS13..........78 F6
Cutters Row BS3.........63 E4
Cuttsheath Rd GL12......16 C8
Cutts Heath Rd BS35.....9 A1
Cygnet Cres BS22.......88 F1
Cylde Pk BS6...........49 B2
Cynder Way BS16........38 A1
Cynthia Rd BA2........101 D5
Cypress Ct BS9.........48 D3
Cypress Gdns BS8.......62 E6
Cypress Gr BS9.........49 C6
Cypress Terr BA3.......133 D1
Cypress Wlk SN14.......70 F2
Cyrus Ct BS16..........52 B7

D

Dabinett Dr BS25 .....108 A4
Daffodil Way BS16.......52 D8
Dafford's Bldgs BA1.....85 C2
Dafford St BA1.........85 C2
Daglands The BA2......133 E8
Daines Ct **4** BS16.....50 E3
Dairy Cl BS49..........74 A2
Dairycroft BS2........143 B4
Dairy Hill BA2.........135 B5
Daisy Bank BA2........102 B4
Daisy Green La GL12....5 D2
Daisy Rd BS5..........50 C2
Dakin Cl BS4..........63 E1
Dakota Dr BS14........80 A4
Dalby Ave BS3.........63 D4
Daldry Gdns BS35......14 A3
Dale St BS5............64 F8
Dalkeith Ave BS15......51 C1
Dalrymple Rd **10** BS2... 49 E1
Dalston Rd BS3.........63 B4
Dalton Sq BS2.........143 B4
Dalwood **12** BS22.....89 A2
Dame Court Cl BS22.....88 F4
Damery La
Stone GL13............3 F3
Woodford GL13.........4 A3
Damery Works GL13.....4 B3
Dampier Rd BS3.........63 A3
Damson Cl BS36........38 A3
Damson Rd BS22.......105 E7
Danbury Cres BS10......35 C1
Danbury Wlk BS10.......35 C1
Danby Ho BS7..........50 A5
Danby St BS7..........50 C6
Dancey Mead BS13......78 F6
Dandy's Mdw BS20......45 E4
Daneacre Rd BA3.......134 A3
Dane Cl BA15.........120 E7
Dane Rise BA15........120 E7
Dangerfield Ave BS13 ..78 F6
Daniel Cl BS21.........57 H3
Daniel Mews BA2......102 B7
Daniel St BA2.........102 B7
Dapps Hill BS31.........81 F5
Dapwell La BS14, BS31..81 A1
Dark La
Backwell BS48.........76 B5
Banwell BS29.........107 C2
Bathampton BA2........85 F1
Blagdon BS40.........110 E3
Chew Magna BS40......95 F3
Freshford BA2.........120 B5
Holcombe BA3........139 C1
Kilmersdon BA11.......140 A1
Darley Cl BS10.........34 D3
Darlington Mews BA2 102 B7
Darlington Pl BA2.....102 B6
Darlington Rd BA2.....102 B8
Darlington St BA2.....102 B7
Darmead BS24..........89 B1

Darnley Ave BS7........49 F6
Dart Cl BS35...........15 B8
Dartmoor St BS3........63 B3
Dartmouth Ave BA2 ...101 C5
Dartmouth Cl BS22.....89 A2
Dartmouth Wlk BS31...81 D4
Dart Rd BS21..........57 F1
Daubeny Cl BS16.......51 B5
Daubeny St BS1.......143 A1
Davenport Cl BS30......66 A2
Daventry Rd BS4........63 F1
Davey St BS2...........49 F1
Davey Terr **8** BS2.....49 F1
Davids Cl BS35.........15 A4
David's La BS35.........15 A4
Davidson Rd BS10......35 D2
David's Rd
Bristol BS14...........80 C6
Thornbury BS35.........8 C1
David St BS2.........143 C3
David Thomas Ho BS6.. 49 E2
Davies Dr BS4..........64 F5
Davin Cres BS20........47 C3
Davis Cl BS30..........65 F5
Davis Ct BS35...........8 C2
Davis La BS21..........73 F8
Davis St BS11..........47 B8
Davron Ct BS3.........63 E4
Dawes Cl BS21.........57 F1
Dawes Ct **2** BS8......62 F6
Dawley Cl BS36.........37 E7
Dawlish Rd BS3.........63 D2
Dawn Rise BS15........52 A1
Daws Cl BS16..........51 B4
Day Cres BA2.........100 F6
Day House La GL12.....19 C8
Day's Rd BS2..........64 A6
Days Road Commercial Ctr
BS2..................64 A7
Deacon Cl BS36.........37 E5
Deacons Cl BS22.......88 E2
Deacons Ct BS22.......88 C1
Deadmill La BA1........85 C3
Dean Ave BS35..........8 C2
Dean Cl
Bristol BS15...........65 B4
Weston-s-M BS22.......89 B3
Dean Cres
8 Bristol BS3........63 C4
1 Bristol BS3........63 D4
Dean Ct BS37..........27 C3
Deanery Cl BS15........66 B8
Deanery Rd
Bristol BS1..........142 C2
Bristol, Warmley BS15..66 B8
Deanery Rd Rdbt BS15 . 66 B8
Deanery Wlk BS20.....120 C6
Deanhill La BA1.........84 A2
Dean La BS3...........63 C4
Deanna Ct BS16.........51 E6
Dean Rd
Avonmouth BS11........33 C5
Yate BS37.............27 C3
Dean's Cl BS1.........142 C2
Dean's Dr BS5..........51 A2
Deans Mead BS11.......48 A8
Dean St
Bristol BS2..........143 B4
Bristol, Southville BS3 ..63 C4
Deans The BS20.........45 B4
Debecca's La BS20......47 B4
De Clifford Rd BS11.....34 C2
Deep Coombe Rd BS3.. 63 A2
Deep Pit Rd BS5........50 F2
Deep St BS1..........143 A3
Deerhurst
Bristol BS15...........51 E3
Yate BS37.............39 C8
Deering Cl BS11........34 B1
Deerleap BS25........125 F8
Deer Mead BS21........57 D1
Deer Pk BS35...........8 B3
Deerswood BS15........52 A2
Delabere Ave BS16......51 B5
Delapre Rd BS23.......104 D3
De La Warre Ct **11** BS4 . 64 F6
Delius Gr BS4..........79 D7
Dell The
Bristol, Bradley Stoke
BS32.................36 E7
Bristol, Oldland Common
BS30.................66 C5
Bristol, Westbury on T
BS9..................48 F5
Nailsea BS48..........59 D2
Weston-s-M BS22.......88 E4
Delvin Rd BS10.........49 C8
De Montalt Pl BA2.....102 B1
Denbigh St BS2.........49 F1
Dene Cl BS31..........81 F3
Dene Rd BS14..........80 C4
Dening Gdns BS5.......50 F1
Denleigh Cl BS14.......80 A4
Denmark Ave BS1.....142 C2
Denmark Pl BS7........49 E3
Denmark Rd BA1.......101 D6
Denmark St BS1......142 C2
Denning Ct BS22........89 B4
Dennisworth BS16......53 B5

Dennor Pk BS14........80 B7
Denny Cl BS20.........45 A5
Denny Isle Dr BS35.....22 A6
Denny La BS40.........96 B1
Denny View BS20.......45 A5
Dennyview Rd BS8......61 F8
Denston Dr BS20.......45 E4
Denston Wlk BS13......79 A7
Denton Patch BS16.....52 B7
Dentwood Gr BS9.......48 B8
Denys Ct BS35..........14 A3
Derby Rd BS7..........49 E3
Derby St BS5..........64 D7
Derek Mead Way
BS29................106 C7
Derham Cl BS49........91 B8
Derham Cres BS37......27 E6
Derham Pk BS49........91 B8
Derham Rd BS13........79 A5
Dermot St **11** BS2.....49 F1
Derrick Rd BS15........65 E4
Derrick Rd BS15........65 D8
Derry Rd BS3..........63 B2
Derwent Cl BS34........36 A8
Derwent Ct BS35.......15 D8
Derwent Gr BS31.......82 A5
Derwent Rd
Bristol BS5............50 F1
Weston-s-M BS23......105 A5
Devaney Cl BS4........64 F5
Deveron Gr BS31.......82 A4
De Verose Ct BS15......65 E4
Devil's La GL12.........11 A2
Devon Gr BS5..........64 C8
Devon Rd BS5..........50 C1
Devon Road Trad Est **1**
BS5..................50 C1
Devonshire Bldgs
Bath BA2............101 F4
Bristol BS3............63 E4
Devonshire Ct BS23...104 E4
Devonshire Dr BS20....44 F5
Devonshire Mews
BA2.................101 F3
Devonshire Pl BA2....101 F4
Devonshire Rd
Bathampton BA2........85 E1
Bristol BS6............49 B4
Weston-s-M BS23.....104 E4
Devonshire Villas BA2 101 F3
Dewfalls Dr BS32.......24 D1
Dial Hill Rd BS21.......57 F4
Dial La
Bristol BS16...........51 D6
Felton BS40............77 D1
Diamond Batch BS24...89 B1
Diamond Rd BS5........64 F7
Diamond St BS3.........63 C3
Diamonite Ind Pk BS16 51 A3
Diana Gdns BS32........36 E8
Dibden Cl BS16.........52 A8
Dibden La BS16.........52 B7
Dibden Rd BS16........52 A7
Dickens Cl BS7.........50 A8
Dickenson Rd BS23...104 E6
Dickenson's Gr BS49 ...91 E3
Dickinsons Fields BS3...63 D2
Didsbury Cl BS10.......34 F1
Dighton Ct **3** BS2....143 A4
Dighton Gate BS34.....36 E5
Dighton St BS2........143 A4
Dillon Ct **18** BS5.....64 D7
Dinder Cl BS48.........75 E8
DINGHURST...........108 E4
Dinghurst Rd BS25....108 E4
Dingle Cl BS9..........48 C6
Dingle Ct BS13.........78 F7
Dingle Rd BS9.........48 D7
Dingle The
Bristol BS9............48 D7
Winterbourne BS36.....37 F3
Yate BS37.............27 F4
Dingle View BS9........48 C7
Dinglewood Cl BS9.....48 D7
Dingley La BS37........27 F5
DINGS THE............64 A6
Dings Wlk **4** BS2.....64 A6
Dipland Gr BS40.......110 F2
Dirac Rd BS7..........49 F4
District Ctr BS32.......36 D8
Dixon Bsns Ctr BS4.....64 F2
Dixon Cl **1** BS15.....65 D5
Dixon Gdns BA1........84 F1
Dixon Rd BS4..........64 F2
Dobunni Cl BS14.......80 D3
Dock Gate La BS8.....142 A1
DODINGTON............40 F5
Dodington Ash BS37....41 B2
Dodington La BS37......40 D5
Dodington Rd
Chipping Sodbury BS37 .40 B7
Yate BS37.............39 F7
Dodisham Wlk BS16....51 B6
Dogwood Rd BS32.....24 D5
Doleberrow BS25......108 D5
Dolebury Warren Nature
Reserve* BS40.......109 A3
DOLEMEADS..........102 B5

Dolemoor La
Congresbury BS49.....91 C3
Puxton BS49..........91 A4
Dolman Cl BS10........34 F3
Dolman Ct BS37........27 D1
Dolphin Sq BS23......104 D7
Dominion Rd
Bath BA2............101 A6
Bristol BS16...........50 F3
Donald Rd BS13........78 F7
Donal Early Way BS7...49 E8
Doncaster Rd BS10.....49 C8
Doncombe Hill SN14...70 F7
Doncombe La SN14....70 F7
Donegal Rd BS4........63 D1
Dongola Ave BS7.......49 E4
Dongola Rd BS7........49 E4
Don John Ho BS5.......64 E8
Donnington Wlk BS31..81 D4
Donns Cl BS34..........36 A7
Doone Rd BS7..........49 F8
Dorcas Ave BS34........36 F5
Dorchester Cl **6** BS48.. 59 D1
Dorchester Rd BS7.....50 A7
Dorchester St BA1.....141 C1
Dorester Cl BS10.......35 C4
Dorian Cl BS7..........49 E7
Dorian Rd BS7.........49 E7
Dorian Way BS7........49 E8
Dormeads View **6**
BS24................105 F7
Dormer Cl BS36........38 D6
Dormer Rd BS5.........50 B3
Dorset Cl BA2.........101 D6
Dorset Gr **10** BS2.....50 A2
Dorset Ho BA2........101 D3
Dorset Rd
Bristol, Kingswood
BS15.................51 D1
Bristol, Westbury on Trym
BS9..................49 B6
Dorset St
Bath BA2............101 D6
6 Bristol BS3.......63 B3
Dorset Way BS37......28 A3
Double Hill BA2.......134 F7
Doudney Ct BS3........63 E4
Douglas Ct **3** BS23 ...104 F5
Douglas Rd
Bristol, Horfield BS7 ....49 F7
Bristol, Kingswood BS15 65 D7
Weston-s-M BS23.....104 F5
Douglas Road Ind Pk
BS15.................65 D7
Doulton Way BS14......80 B5
Dovecote BS37.........39 E7
Dovedale BS35.........15 D8
Dove La
Bristol BS2..........143 C4
Bristol, Russell Town BS5 64 C7
Dovercourt Rd BS7.....50 A6
Dover Ho BA1.........141 C4
Dover Pl
5 Bath BA1........85 A1
Bristol BS8..........142 B3
Dover Place Cotts
BS8.................142 B3
Dovers La BA1.........86 C2
Dovers Pk BA1.........86 C2
Dove St S BS2.........143 A4
Dove St BS2..........143 A4
Doveswell Gr BS13.....79 A4
Dovetail Dr BS23......105 A7
Dovey Ct BS30.........66 C5
Dowdeswell Cl BS10 ...34 F3
Dowding Cl BS37.......28 C2
Dowding Rd BA1........85 B1
Dower Ho The BS16....50 E7
Dowland **13** BS22....89 A2
Dowland Gr BS4........79 D6
Dowling Rd BS13.......79 D3
Down Ave BA2........102 A1
Down Cl BS20..........44 F4
DOWNEND.............51 E8
Downend Comp Sch
BS16.................51 F7
Downend Park Rd
BS16.................51 D5
Downend Pk BS7.......49 F5
Downend Rd
Bristol, Fishponds BS16..51 C5
Bristol, Horfield BS7 ....49 F5
Bristol, Kingswood BS15 51 D1
Down Farm Ho BS36 ...37 D6
Downfield
Bristol BS9............48 C7
Keynsham BS31........81 D5
Downfield Cl **1** BS35 ...15 A5
Downfield Dr BS36......38 B8
Downfield Lodge BS8 . 49 A1
Downfield Rd BS8......49 A1
Down La BA2..........85 F1
Downland Cl **5** BS48.. 59 D1
Downleaze
Bristol, Downend BS16 ..51 D8
Portishead BS20.......45 A5
Stoke Bishop BS9......48 F3
Down Leaze **2** BS35 ..15 A5
Downleaze Dr BS37....40 B8

Downleaze Rd BS9.....48 F3
Downman Rd BS7......50 A5
Down Rd
Alveston BS35.........15 A5
Marshfield SN14.......56 C2
Portishead BS20.......44 F4
Winterbourne BS36.....37 F4
Downs Cl
3 Alveston BS35......15 A5
Weston-s-M BS22......88 F1
Downs Cote Ave BS9...48 F6
Downs Cote Dr BS9....48 F6
Downs Cote Gdns BS9..49 A6
Downs Cote Pk BS9....49 A6
Downs Cote View BS9 ..49 A6
Downs Ct BS9.........49 B6
DOWNSIDE
Chilcompton.........138 C1
Nailsea..............76 D1
Downside BS20........45 C5
Downside Abbey*
BA3.................138 E2
Downside Cl
Bathampton BA2.......85 F1
Bristol BS30...........65 F5
Chilcompton BA3......138 D3
Downside Rd
Backwell BS48.........93 E8
Bristol BS8............49 A1
Weston-s-M BS23.....104 F4
Downside Sch BA3....138 E2
Downs Pk E BS6........49 A4
Downs Pk W BS6......49 A4
Downs Rd
Bristol BS9............49 A6
Dundry BS41...........78 D2
Downs Sch The BS48 ...60 C8
Downs The
Portishead BS20.......45 B4
Wickwar GL12.........17 F7
Downsview Ct BS8......49 A1
Downsway BS39.......132 D6
Down The
Alveston BS35.........14 F5
Tockington BS32.......14 D3
Downton Rd BS4........63 D1
Down View
Bristol BS7............49 F3
Radstock BA3........139 F8
Dowry Pl **3** BS8......62 F5
Dowry Rd BS8.........142 A2
Dowry Sq BS8........142 A2
Dowsell Way BS37......27 E6
DOYNTON..............54 A1
Doynton La SN14, BS30.. 54 E3
Doynton Mill BS30......53 F1
Dragon Ct BS5..........50 E1
Dragonfly Cl BS15......65 D7
Dragon Rd BS36........37 D5
Dragons Hill Cl BS31....81 F5
Dragons Hill Ct BS31....81 F5
Dragons Hill Gdns
BS31.................81 F5
Dragonswell Rd BS10 ..35 A2
Dragon Wlk BS5........50 F1
Drake Ave BA2........101 F2
Drake Cl
Saltford BS31.........82 D2
Weston-s-M BS22......88 F4
Drake Rd BS3..........63 A3
Drakes Way BS20.......45 B5
Dram La BS5...........65 A6
Dramway Rdbt BS16....52 D6
Dransfield Way BA2...101 C4
Draper Ct **3** BS5......64 C7
Draycot Ct **1** BA2....141 C3
Draycott Pl BS1.......143 A1
Draycott Rd BS7........49 F5
Draydon Rd BS4........79 D8
Drayton BS24.........105 A2
Drayton Cl BS14........80 B8
Drayton Rd BS9........48 C8
Drifton Hill SN14.......56 F7
Dring The BA3........133 E2
Drive The
Bristol BS14...........80 C6
Bristol, Henleaze BS9 ...49 B5
Churchill BS25.......108 E4
Keynsham BS31........81 E6
Shipham BS25.......125 E8
Stanton Drew BS39.....96 F1
Weston-s-M BS23.....104 F8
Drove Ct BS48.........59 E3
Drove Rd
Congresbury BS49.....91 D3
Weston-s-M BS23.....104 F5
Drovers Way BS37......28 B2
Drove The BS26........70 D6
Drove Way BS24, BS25 107 C2
Druetts Cl BS10.........49 E6
Druid Cl BS9...........48 E5
Druid Hill BS9..........48 E5
Druid Rd BS9..........48 D4
Druids Garth BA2.......85 D1
Druid Stoke Ave BS9...48 D5
Druid Woods BS9......48 C5

Drumhead Way The
BS25 . . . .**125** E8
Drummond Ct BS30 . . . . **65** F4
Drummond Rd
Bristol, Fishponds BS16 . . **50** F3
Bristol, St Pauls BS2 . . . . **49** E1
Drumway The BS31 . . . . **82** B4
Dr White's Cl BS1 . . . . **143** B1
DRY HILL **45** C6
Dryleaze
Keynsham BS31 . . . . **81** E7
Yate BS37 . . . . **27** E5
Dryleaze Rd BS16 . . . . . **50** F6
Drysdale Cl BS22 . . . . . . **88** D1
Dubbers La BS5 . . . . **50** E2
Dublin Cres BS9 . . . . **49** B6
Duchess Rd BS8 . . . . **49** A1
Duchess Way BS16 . . . . . **50** D6
Duchy Cl BA3 . . . . **133** C5
Duchy Rd BA3 . . . . **133** C5
Ducie Cl GL12 . . . . **10** B2
Ducie Cl BS16 . . . . **51** E4
Ducie Rd
Bristol, Russell Town
BS5 . . . . **64** B7
Bristol, Staple Hill BS16 . . **51** E5
Ducie Rd Bsns Pk 6
BS5 . . . . **64** B7
Duckett Fields BS10 . . . . **49** D7
DUCKHOLE **8** C5
Duck La
Churchill BS40 . . . . **109** A8
Kenn BS21 . . . . **74** A6
Duckmoor Rd BS3 . . . . . **63** A4
Duckmoor Road Ind Est
BS3 . . . . **63** A4
Ducks La BS22 . . . . **89** A8
Duck St
Churchill BS25 . . . . **108** C5
Tytherington GL12 . . . . . . **16** C5
Dudley Cl BS31 . . . . **81** E4
Dudley Ct 3 BS30 . . . . . **65** F4
Dudley Gr BS7 . . . . **50** A8
Dugar Wlk BS6 . . . . **49** C3
Duke St BA2 . . . . **141** C2
Dukwick La SN14 . . . . . . **67** A3
Dulverton Rd BS7 . . . . . . **49** D4
Dumaine Ave BS34 . . . . . **36** E5
Dumfries Pl BS23 . . . . . **104** E5
Dumpers La BS40 . . . . . . **96** B2
Duncan Gdns BA1 . . . . . . **84** A3
Duncan Ho BS8 . . . . **142** A4
Duncombe La BS15 . . . . . **51** B2
Duncombe Rd BS15 . . . . . **51** B1
Dundas Cl BS10 . . . . **34** E2
Dundonald Rd BS6 . . . . . **49** B3
Dundridge Gdns BS5 . . . . **65** A6
Dundridge La BS5 . . . . . . **65** A6
DUNDRY **78** D2
Dundry CE Prim Sch
BS41 . . . . **78** D2
Dundry Cl BS15 . . . . **65** D6
DUNDRY HILL **80** B3
Dundry La
Dundry BS41 . . . . **78** C3
Winford BS40 . . . . **95** A4
Dundry View BS4 . . . . . . **64** A1
Dunedin Way BS22 . . . . . **89** C4
Dunford Rd BS3 . . . . **63** D3
Dungarvon Rd BS24 . . . . **105** F7
Dunkeld Ave BS34 . . . . . **35** F2
Dunkerry Rd BS3 . . . . . . **63** D3
DUNKERTON **117** E4
Dunkerton Hill BA2 . . . **117** E2
Dunkerton La
Combe Hay BA2 . . . . **118** B4
Dunkerton BA2 . . . . **117** F3
Dunkery Cl BS48 . . . . **59** E1
Dunkery Rd BS23 . . . . . . **87** F1
DUNKIRK **20** B1
Dunkirk Rd BS16 . . . . **50** F3
Dunlin Dr BS20 . . . . **45** F6
Dunmail Rd BS10 . . . . . . **35** C2
Dunmore St 3 BS2 . . . . **63** F4
Dunmurry BS9 . . . . **48** D3
Dunsdown La SN14 . . . . . **55** B5
Dunsford Pl BA2 . . . . . . **102** B6
Dunster Cres BS24 . . . . **105** A2
Dunster Ct BS25 . . . . . . **125** A8
Dunster Gdns
Bristol BS30 . . . . **66** B2
5 Nailsea BS48 . . . . **59** E1
Dunster Ho BA2 . . . . . . **102** A2
Dunster Rd
Bristol BS4 . . . . **79** F8
Keynsham BS31 . . . . **81** E4
Dunsters Rd BS49 . . . . . . **74** F1
Durban Rd BS34 . . . . **35** F8
Durban Way BS49 . . . . . . **74** B1
Durbin Park Rd
BS21 . . . . **57** F5
Durbin Wlk BS5 . . . . **64** A8
Durcott La BA2 . . . . **133** D8
Durdham Ct BS6 . . . . **49** A3
Durdham Pk BS6 . . . . **49** A3
Durham Gr BS31 . . . . **81** D4

Durham Rd
11 Bristol BS2 . . . . **50** A2
Charfield GL12 . . . . **11** A5
Durleigh Cl BS13 . . . . **79** A7
Durley Hill BS31 . . . . **81** C7
Durley La BS31 . . . . **81** D7
Durley Pk BA2 . . . . **101** E4
Durnford Ave BS3 . . . . . . **63** A4
Durnford St BS3 . . . . **63** A4
Durnhill BS40 . . . . **128** F7
Dursley Cl BS37 . . . . **27** E1
Dursley Rd BS11 . . . . **47** E5
Durston BS24 . . . . **105** A2
Durville Rd BS13 . . . . **79** B6
Durweston Wlk BS14 . . . . **80** C8
Dutton Cl BS14 . . . . **80** D6
Dutton Rd BS14 . . . . **80** D6
Dutton Wlk BS14 . . . . . . **80** D6
Dye House Rd GL12 . . . . . **11** F5
Dyers BS13 . . . . **79** D4
DYER'S COMMON **22** C3
Dyer's La BS37 . . . . **27** A4
Dylan Thomas Ct 4
BS30 . . . . **66** A5
Dymboro Ave BA3 . . . . . **132** F1
Dymboro Cl BA3 . . . . . . **132** F1
Dymboro Gdns BA3 . . . . **132** F1
Dymboro The BA3 . . . . . **132** F1
DYRHAM **54** D4
Dyrham BS16 . . . . **37** C1
Dyrham Cl
Bristol, Henleaze BS9 . . . . **49** D6
Bristol, Kingswood BS15 . . **65** F8
Pucklechurch BS16 . . . . . . **53** C4
Thornbury BS35 . . . . **8** C3
Dyrham Par BS34 . . . . . . **36** C8
Dyrham Park SN14 . . . . **54** F5
Dyrham Rd BS15 . . . . **65** F8
Dyrham View BS16 . . . . . **53** C4
Dyson Cl BS49 . . . . **91** B8

E

Eagle Cl BS22 . . . . **105** D8
Eagle Cres BS16 . . . . **53** C5
Eagle Dr
Bristol BS34 . . . . **35** E8
5 Radstock BA3 . . . . . . **139** B8
Eagle Pk BA1 . . . . **85** F5
Eagle Rd
Batheaston BA1 . . . . **85** F5
Bristol BS4 . . . . **64** D2
Eagles The BS49 . . . . **91** B8
Eagles Wood BS32 . . . . . **24** D3
Eagles Wood Bsns Pk
BS32 . . . . **24** C3
Eamoth Ground BS34 . . . **35** E6
Earlesfield BS48 . . . . **59** C1
Earlham Gr BS23 . . . . . . **105** A7
Earl Russell Way BS5 . . . **64** B7
Earlsmead BS16 . . . . **50** E4
Earl St BS1 . . . . **143** A4
Earlstone Cl BS30 . . . . . . **66** A4
Earlstone Cres BS30 . . . . **66** A4
EARTHCOTT GREEN **25** E7
Earthcott Rd BS35 . . . . . **15** F1
Easedale BS10 . . . . **35** D2
Eastbourne Ave 15 BA1 . . **85** B1
Eastbourne Rd 9 BS5 . . . **64** B8
Eastbury Cl BS35 . . . . **8** C1
Eastbury Rd
Bristol BS16 . . . . **51** A4
Thornbury BS35 . . . . **8** C1
East Cl BA2 . . . . **101** A5
EAST CLEVEDON **57** H3
East Clevedon Triangle
BS21 . . . . **57** H3
Eastcliff BS20 . . . . **45** E7
Eastcombe Gdns BS23 . . . **87** F1
Eastcombe Rd BS23 . . . . . **87** F1
Eastcote Pk BS14 . . . . **80** B5
Eastcourt Rd BS39 . . . . . **131** F4
Eastcroft BS40 . . . . **110** E2
East Croft BS9 . . . . **49** C7
Eastcroft Cl BS40 . . . . . **110** E2
East Ct BS3 . . . . **62** F3
Eastdown Pl BA3 . . . . . **133** E5
Eastdown Rd BA3 . . . . . **133** D5
EAST DUNDRY **79** A1
East Dundry La BS41 . . . . **79** A1
East Dundry Rd BS13,
BS14 . . . . **79** F2
EAST END
Blagdon **110** E2
Marshfield **70** A4
Nailsea **60** A1
EASTER COMPTON **23** A2
Easter Ct BS37 . . . . **27** B1
Eastermead La BS29 . . . **107** C3
Eastern Ho BS23 . . . . **87** E1
EASTERTOWN **122** D2
Eastertown BS24 . . . . . . **122** D1
EASTFIELD **49** B7
Eastfield BS9 . . . . **49** B7
Eastfield Ave BA1 . . . . . . **84** B2
Eastfield Dr BS37 . . . . . . **27** E4
Eastfield Gdns BS23 . . . . **87** F1
Eastfield La BS35 . . . . . . **12** E3

Eastfield Pk BS23 . . . . . . **87** F1
Eastfield Rd
Bristol, Eastfield BS9 . . . . **49** B7
Bristol, Montpelier BS6 . . . **49** D2
Bristol, Westbury on Trym
BS9 . . . . **49** A7
Hutton BS24 . . . . **105** E2
East Fields Rd BS16 . . . . . **50** D8
Eastfield Terr BS9 . . . . . . **49** B7
Eastgate Office Ctr BS5 **50** B3
Eastgate Ret Pk BS5 . . . . **50** B3
East Gr BS6 . . . . **49** F1
EAST HARPTREE **129** E4
East Harptree CE VA Prim
Sch BS40 . . . . **129** F4
EAST HEWISH **90** B6
East Hill BS9 . . . . **49** B7
East Hill Cl BS9 . . . . **49** B6
Eastlake Cl BS7 . . . . **50** B7
Eastland Ave BS35 . . . . . . **8** C2
Eastland Rd BS35 . . . . **8** C2
Eastlea BS21 . . . . **57** D1
East Lea Rd BA1 . . . . . . **101** A8
Eastleigh Cl BS16 . . . . . . **51** E4
Eastleigh Rd
Bristol, Brentry BS10 . . . . **35** D1
Bristol, Staple Hill BS16 . . **51** E3
Eastley Cl GL12 . . . . **9** E7
Eastlyn Rd BS13 . . . . **79** B8
East Mead BA3 . . . . **133** B2
Eastmead Ct BS9 . . . . **48** E4
Eastmead La BS9 . . . . **48** E4
Eastnor Rd BS14 . . . . **80** A3
Easton Bsns Ctr BS5 . . . . **64** B8
Easton CE Prim Sch
BS5 . . . . **64** A8
Easton Ct BA3 . . . . **131** E1
Easton Gdns BA1 . . . . **85** F5
Easton Hill Rd BS35 . . . . . **8** D1
Easton Ho 9 BA1 . . . . . . **85** C1
EASTON-IN-
GORDANO **47** A4
Easton Rd
Bristol, Newton BS5 . . . . . **64** A7
Bristol, Upper Easton
BS5 . . . . **64** B8
Pill BS20 . . . . **47** C4
Easton Way BS5 . . . . **64** A8
Eastover Cl BS9 . . . . **49** A8
Eastover Gr BA2 . . . . . . **101** C1
Eastover Rd BS39 . . . . . **115** D1
East Par BS9 . . . . **48** C6
East Park Dr BS5 . . . . **50** C2
Eastpark Trad Est BS5 . . . **50** D1
East Pk BS5 . . . . **50** C2
East Priory Cl BS9 . . . . . . **49** A7
East Ridge Dr BS13 . . . . . **78** F5
EAST ROLSTONE **90** B1
East Shrubbery 3 BS6 . . **49** B2
East St
Avonmouth BS11 . . . . **33** A1
Banwell BS29 . . . . **107** C3
Bristol, Southville BS3 . . . **63** D4
EAST TWERTON **101** D6
East View BS16 . . . . **51** F6
EASTVILLE **50** C3
Eastville BA1 . . . . **85** B1
Eastway BS48 . . . . **59** E3
East Way BA2 . . . . **101** A5
Eastway Cl BS48 . . . . **59** D2
Eastway Sq BS48 . . . . **59** E3
Eastwell La BS25 . . . . . . **124** E6
East Wlk BS37 . . . . **27** E1
Eastwood
Bath BA2 . . . . **102** F6
Sherborne BS40 . . . . **130** B2
Eastwood Cl BS39 . . . . . **115** C1
Eastwood Cres BS4 . . . . . **64** F3
East Wood Pl BS20 . . . . . **45** E7
Eastwood Rd BS4 . . . . . . **64** F4
Eastwoods BA1 . . . . **86** B3
Eaton Cl
Bristol BS14 . . . . **80** E5
Bristol, Fishponds BS16 . . **51** B4
Eaton Cres BS8 . . . . **142** A4
Eaton St 14 BS3 . . . . **63** C3
Ebden Lo 15 BS22 . . . . . **89** A2
EBDON **89** B6
Ebdon La BS22 . . . . **89** C5
Ebdon Rd BS22 . . . . **88** F4
Ebenezer La BS9 . . . . **48** E5
Ebenezer St BS5 . . . . **64** D7
Ebenezer Terr BA2 . . . . **141** C1
Eccleston Ho 1 BS5 . . . . **64** B6
Eckweek Gdns BA2 . . . . **134** D8
Eckweek La BA2 . . . . . . **134** E8
Eckweek Rd BA2 . . . . . . **134** D8
Eclipse Ct 1 BS16 . . . . . **51** C4
Eclipse Office Pk 2
BS16 . . . . **51** C4
Eddington Ct BS23 . . . . **104** D7
Eden Croft BS22 . . . . . . **105** E8
Eden Gr BS7 . . . . **36** A1
Eden Office Pk BS20 . . . . **47** E4
Eden Park Cl BA1 . . . . . . **86** A4
Eden Park Dr BA1 . . . . . . **86** A4
Eden Terr BA1 . . . . **85** B2
Eden Villas 4 BA1 . . . . . **85** C2
Edgar Bldgs BA1 . . . . . **141** B3

Edgarley Ct BS21 . . . . . . **57** E5
Edgecombe Ave BS22 . . **88** D2
Edgecombe Cl BS15 . . . . **51** F1
Edgecombe Mews BA1 . . **84** B1
Edgecombe Rd BS6 . . . . **49** D2
Edgecorner La SN14 . . . . **43** A3
Edgefield Cl BS14 . . . . . . **79** F3
Edgefield Rd BS14 . . . . . . **79** F3
Edgehill Rd BS21 . . . . . . **57** F6
Edgeware Rd
Bristol, Southville BS3 . . . **63** C4
Bristol, Staple Hill BS16 . . **51** D4
Edgewood Cl
Bristol BS14 . . . . **80** B8
Bristol, Longwell Green
BS30 . . . . **66** A3
Edgeworth BS37 . . . . **39** C6
Edgeworth Rd BA2 . . . . **101** C2
Edinburgh Pl 1 BS23 . . **104** E8
Edinburgh Rd BS31 . . . . . **81** E4
Edington Gr BS10 . . . . . . **35** A2
Edmund Cl BS16 . . . . **51** D6
Edmund Ct BS16 . . . . **53** B6
Edna Ave BS4 . . . . **64** E3
Edward Bird Ho BS7 . . . . **50** B6
Edward Cl BS22 . . . . **88** F4
Edward Rd BS31 . . . . **81** F4
Edward Parker Rd BS16 **50** F8
Edward Rd
Bristol, Kingswood
BS15 . . . . **65** E8
Bristol, Totterdown BS4 . . **64** B4
Clevedon BS21 . . . . **57** G5
Edward Rd S BS21 . . . . . . **57** G5
Edward Rd W BS21 . . . . . **57** G6
Edwards Ct 17 BS5 . . . . . **64** D7
Edward St
Bath, Bathwick BA2 . . . . **102** B7
Bath, Lower Weston
BA1 . . . . **101** C7
Bristol, Eastville BS5 . . . . **50** D2
Bristol, Moorfields BS5 . . . **64** C7
Edwin Short Cl BS30 . . . . **82** E8
Effingham Rd BS6 . . . . . . **49** E2
Egerton Brow BS7 . . . . . . **49** D4
Egerton Ct BS7 . . . . **49** E4
Egerton Rd
Bath BA2 . . . . **101** E4
Bristol BS7 . . . . **49** D4
Eggshill La BS37 . . . . **27** D1
Eglin Croft BS13 . . . . **79** B4
Egret Dr BS49 . . . . **73** F2
Eighteen Acre Dr
Bristol BS34 . . . . **35** F6
Little Stoke BS34 . . . . **36** A7
Eighth Ave
Bristol BS14 . . . . **80** A7
Bristol, Filton BS7 . . . . . . **36** B1
Eirene Terr BS20 . . . . **47** D4
ELBERTON **14** A6
Elberton BS15 . . . . **66** A8
Elberton Rd
Bristol BS9 . . . . **48** B7
Elberton BS35 . . . . **13** F5
Elborough Ave BS49 . . . . **91** B8
Elborough Gdns BS24 . . **106** C3
Elbridge Ho 3 BS2 . . . . **143** C3
Elbury Ave BS15 . . . . **51** C2
Elbury View GL12 . . . . . . **11** B5
Elderberry Way BS32 . . . **24** E5
Elderberry Wlk
Bristol BS10 . . . . **35** C3
Weston-s-M BS22 . . . . . . **88** F1
Elderflower Dr BS16 . . . . **38** D1
Elderwood Dr BS30 . . . . . **66** A3
Elderwood Rd BS14 . . . . . **80** B7
Eldon Pl BA1 . . . . **85** B2
Eldon Terr BS3 . . . . **63** D3
Eldonwall Trad Est BS4 . . **64** C5
Eldon Way BS4 . . . . **64** C5
Eldred Cl BS9 . . . . **48** D5
Eleanor Cl BA2 . . . . **101** A5
Eleanor Cotts BA2 . . . . **101** A6
Eleventh Ave BS7 . . . . . . **36** B1
Elfin Rd BS16 . . . . **51** A5
Elgar Cl
Bristol BS4 . . . . **79** D6
Clevedon BS21 . . . . **57** G1
Elgin Ave BS7 . . . . **35** F1
Elgin Pk BS6 . . . . **49** B2
Elgin Rd BS16 . . . . **51** B2
Eliot Cl
Bristol BS7 . . . . **36** A1
Weston-s-M BS23 . . . . . **105** A3
Elizabeth Cl
Hutton BS24 . . . . **105** D3
Thornbury BS35 . . . . **15** D8
Elizabeth Cres BS34 . . . . **36** E4
Elizabeths Mews 12
BS4 . . . . **64** F6
Elizabeth Way BS16 . . . . **52** B3
Elkstone Wlk BS30 . . . . . **66** C2
Ella Cl BS16 . . . . **51** C6
Ellacombe Rd BS30 . . . . . **65** F2
Ellan Hay Rd BS34 . . . . . **37** A6
Ellbridge Cl BS9 . . . . **48** D5
Ellenborough Cres
BS23 . . . . **104** E6
Ellenborough Ct BS23 **104** E6
Ellenborough Ho BS8 **142** A2

Ellenborough Park Rd
BS23 . . . . **104** E6
Ellenborough Pk N
BS23 . . . . **104** D6
Ellenborough Pk S
BS23 . . . . **104** D6
Ellen Ho BA2 . . . . **101** A5
Ellerncroft Rd GL12 . . . . . **11** F8
Ellesmere BS35 . . . . **15** C8
Ellesmere Rd
1 Bristol BS4 . . . . **64** D1
Weston-s-M BS23 . . . . . **104** D2
Ellfield Cl BS13 . . . . **78** A5
Ellick Rd BS40 . . . . **110** D1
Ellicks Cl BS32 . . . . **24** E2
Ellicott Rd BS7 . . . . **49** F5
Elliinghurst Cl BS10 . . . . **35** A2
Elliott Ave BS16 . . . . **37** C5
Elliott Ho BS7 . . . . **50** A3
Ellis Ave BS13 . . . . **79** A8
Ellis Pk BS22 . . . . **89** C4
Elliston Dr BA2 . . . . **101** B4
Elliston La BS6 . . . . **49** C2
Elliston Rd BS6 . . . . **49** C2
Ellsworth Rd BS10 . . . . . . **34** F2
Ellyott Ct 5 BS16 . . . . . . **50** E3
Elmbrook BA1 . . . . **101** D8
Elm Cl
Banwell BS29 . . . . **106** E4
Bristol, Lawrence Weston
BS11 . . . . **33** F1
Chipping Sodbury BS37 . . **28** A1
Nailsea BS48 . . . . **59** C1
Star BS25 . . . . **108** D1
Yatton BS49 . . . . **91** B7
Elmcroft Cres BS7 . . . . . . **50** A4
Elm Ct
Bristol BS14 . . . . **80** A6
Bristol, Redland BS6 . . . . **49** B2
Keynsham BS31 . . . . **81** C4
Elmdale Cres BS35 . . . . . . **8** C1
Elmdale Gdns 4 BS16 . . . **51** A4
Elmdale Rd
Bristol BS8 . . . . **142** B3
Bristol, Bedminster BS3 . . **63** B2
Elm Farm BS48 . . . . **60** A2
Elmfield BS15 . . . . **65** E6
Elmfield Cl BS15 . . . . **65** E6
Elmfield Rd BS9 . . . . **49** A8
Elmfield Sch for Deaf
Children BS10 . . . . **49** B8
Elm Gr
Bath, Larkhill BA1 . . . . . . **85** C2
Bath, The Oval BA2 . . . . **101** C4
Locking BS24 . . . . **105** F4
Elmgrove Ave 10 BS5 . . . **64** B8
Elmgrove Dr BS37 . . . . . . **27** F2
Elmgrove Pk 1 BS6 . . . . **49** D1
Elmgrove Rd
Bristol, Fishponds BS16 . . **50** E3
Bristol, Redland BS6 . . . . **49** D1
Elmham Way BS24 . . . . . **89** B1
Elm Hayes BS13 . . . . **78** F6
Elm Hayes Rd BS34 . . . . . **35** F7
Elmhirst Gdns BS37 . . . . **28** A2
Elmhurst Ave BS5 . . . . . . **50** D3
Elmhurst Est
Batheaston BA1 . . . . **86** A4
Bathford BA1 . . . . **86** A4
Elmhurst Gdns BS41 . . . . **77** F8
Elmhurst Rd BS24 . . . . . **105** E2
Elmhyrst Rd BS23 . . . . . **104** F8
Elming Down Cl BS32 . . . **36** D6
Elm La BS6 . . . . **49** B2
Elmlea Ave BS9 . . . . **48** F5
Elmlea Jun & Inf Schs
BS9 . . . . **48** F5
Elmleigh Ave BS16 . . . . . **52** B5
Elmleigh Cl BS16 . . . . **52** B5
Elmleigh Rd BS16 . . . . . . **52** B5
Elm Lodge Rd BS48 . . . . . **60** B2
Elmore
Bristol BS15 . . . . **51** F2
Yate BS37 . . . . **39** C8
Elmore Rd
Bristol BS34 . . . . **23** F1
Bristol, Horfield BS7 . . . . **50** A6
Elm Park Prim Sch
BS36 . . . . **37** E6
Elm Pk BS34 . . . . **36** A2
Elm Pl BA2 . . . . **101** F4
Elm Rd
Bristol, Horfield BS7 . . . . **49** E5
Bristol, Kingswood BS15 . . **65** E6
Paulton BS39 . . . . **132** E5
Elms Gr BS34 . . . . **24** B1
Elmsleigh Rd BS23 . . . . **104** E4
Elmsley La BS22 . . . . **88** C5
Elms The
Banwell BS29 . . . . **107** A4
Bath, Lambridge BA1 . . . . **85** C2
Bath, Weston Park BA1 . . **84** C1
Bristol, Frenchay BS16 . . . **37** B1
Bristol, Henbury BS10 . . . **34** F2
Tockington BS32 . . . . **14** B2
Elmswood BS23 . . . . **104** F8
Elm Terr BA3 . . . . **139** C8
Elmtree Ave BS16 . . . . . . **52** A7

Elm Tree Ave
Nailsea BS21 . . . . .59 A4
Radstock BA3 . . . . .133 D1
Elmtree Cl BS15 . . . . .51 D1
Elmtree Dr BS13 . . . . . . .78 F5
Elm Tree Pk BS20 . . . . . .46 D3
Elm Tree Rd
Clevedon BS21 . . . . .57 F2
Locking BS24 . . . . .106 A4
Elmtree Way BS15 . . . . . .51 D1
Elmvale Dr BS24 . . . . . .105 F3
Elm View
Midsomer Norton BA3 . .133 B1
Temple Cloud BS39 . . .114 E1
Elm Wlk
Portishead BS20 . . . . . . .45 C4
Yatton BS49 . . . . .91 B7
Elm Wood BS37 . . . . .39 E8
Elsberd Dr BS13 . . . . . . .78 E6
Elstree Rd BS5 . . . . .50 E1
Elton Ho
Bristol, Clifton BS8 . . . .142 A4
2 Bristol, Newton BS2 143 C3
Elton La BS7 . . . . .49 D2
Elton Mans **5** BS7 . . . .49 D2
Elton Rd
Bristol BS8 . . . . .142 A4
Bristol, Bishopston BS7 . .49 D2
Bristol, Kingswood BS15 .51 C1
Clevedon BS21 . . . . .57 E3
Weston-s-M BS22 . . . . . .89 A4
Elton St BS2 . . . . .143 C4
Elvard Cl BS13 . . . . .79 A4
Elvard Rd BS13 . . . . .79 A4
Elvaston Rd BS3 . . . . .63 E3
Elwell La BS40, BS41 . . . .78 A1
Ely Gr BS9 . . . . .48 B7
Embassy Rd BS5 . . . . . . .50 E1
Embassy Wlk BS5 . . . . . .50 E1
Embercourt Dr BS48 . . . .76 A6
Embleton Rd BS10 . . . . . .35 C2
EMERSON'S GREEN 52 C6
Emersons Green La
BS16 . . . . .52 B6
Emersons Green Prim Sch
BS16 . . . . .52 B7
Emerson Sq BS7 . . . . . . .50 A8
Emerson Way BS16 . . . . .52 C7
Emery Gate BS29 . . . . .107 B3
Emery Rd BS4 . . . . .64 F1
Emet Gr BS16 . . . . .52 B6
Emet La BS16 . . . . .52 B6
Eminence BS1 . . . . .143 B1
Emley La BS40 . . . . .110 B6
Emlyn Cl **6** BS22 . . . . . .89 B4
Emlyn Rd BS5 . . . . .50 C2
Emma-Chris Way BS34 36 C2
Emmanuel Ct BS8 . . . . .142 A4
Emmett Wood BS14 . . . .80 B3
Empire Cres BS15 . . . . . .65 E4
Empress Menen Gdns
BA1 . . . . .101 A8
Emra Cl BS5 . . . . .50 F1
Emra Ho **10** BS5 . . . . . .64 A8
Enderleigh Gdns BS25 108 F4
Enfield Rd BS16 . . . . .51 A3
ENGINE COMMON 27 B5
Engine Common La
BS37 . . . . .27 C5
Engine La BS48 . . . . .75 B4
England's Cres BS36 . . . .37 E7
ENGLISHCOMBE 100 F2
Englishcombe La BS41 101 D3
Englishcombe Rd BS13 79 C3
Englishcombe Rise
BA2 . . . . .101 A3
Englishcombe Tithe Barn★
BA2 . . . . .100 F2
Englishcombe Way
BA2 . . . . .101 E3
Enmore BS24 . . . . .105 A2
Ennerdale Cl BS23 . . . . .105 A5
Ennerdale Rd BS10 . . . . .35 D2
Ensleigh Ave BA1 . . . . . .84 E4
Enterprise Ctr The
BS24 . . . . .105 A3
Enterprise Trade Ctr
BS4 . . . . .79 E7
Entry Hill BA2 . . . . .101 F2
Entry Hill Dr BA2 . . . . . .101 F3
Entry Hill Gdns BA2 . . . .101 F3
Entry Hill Pk BA2 . . . . . .101 F2
Entry Rise BA2 . . . . .101 F1
Epney Cl BS34 . . . . .23 F1
Epsom Cl BS16 . . . . .37 F1
Epworth Rd BS10 . . . . . .35 A3
Equinox BS32 . . . . .24 C3
Erin Wlk BS4 . . . . .79 D8
Ermine Way BS11 . . . . . .47 C7
Ermleet Rd **1** BS6 . . . . .49 C2
Ernest Barker Cl **15**
BS5 . . . . .64 B7
Ernestville Rd BS16 . . . . .50 F3
Ervine Terr BS2 . . . . . . .143 C4
Esgar Rise BS22 . . . . . . .88 E3
Eskdale BS35 . . . . .15 D7
Eskdale Cl BS22 . . . . . . .105 D8
Esmond Gr BS21 . . . . . . .57 F4
Esplanade Rd BS20 . . . .45 C7

Essery Rd BS5 . . . . .50 C2
Esson Rd BS15 . . . . .51 B1
Estcourt Gdns BS16 . . . .50 D5
Estoril BS37 . . . . .27 F1
Estuary Ho BS20 . . . . . . .45 E7
Estune Wlk BS41 . . . . . . .62 A2
Etloe Rd BS6 . . . . .49 A4
Etonhurst BS23 . . . . . . .104 D6
Eton La BS29 . . . . .106 E7
Eton Rd BS4 . . . . .64 D3
Ettlingen Way BS21 . . . . .57 H2
Ettricke Dr BS16 . . . . . . .51 B5
Eugene Flats **7** BS2 . .143 A4
Eugene St
Bristol, Kingsdown
BS2 . . . . .143 A4
Bristol, St Pauls BS2,
BS5 . . . . .143 C4
Evans Cl BS4 . . . . .64 F5
Evans Rd BS6 . . . . .49 B2
Eveleigh Ave BA1 . . . . . .85 D3
Evelyn Rd
Bath BA1 . . . . .101 B8
Bristol BS10 . . . . .49 C7
Evelyn Terr **13** BA1 . . . .85 A1
Evenlode Gdns BS11 . . . .47 F5
Evenlode Way BS31 . . . . .82 A3
Evercreech Rd BS14 . . . .80 B4
Eve Rd BS5 . . . . .50 B1
Everest Ave BS16 . . . . . .50 E4
Everest Rd BS16 . . . . . . .50 E4
Evergreen Cl BS25 . . . . .107 F1
Ewart Rd BS22 . . . . .105 C8
Ewell Rd BS14 . . . . .80 B6
Exbourne **10** BS22 . . . . .89 A2
Excelsior St BA2 . . . . . . .102 B5
Excelsior Terr BA3 . . . . .133 B1
Exchange Ave BS1 . . . . .143 A2
Exchange Ct **8** BS15 . . .65 D8
Exeter Bldgs BS6 . . . . . .49 B2
Exeter Rd
Bristol BS3 . . . . .63 B4
Portishead BS20 . . . . . .45 E4
Weston-s-M BS23 . . . .104 E5
Exford Cl BS23 . . . . .104 F2
Exley Cl BS30 . . . . .66 D5
Exmoor Rd BA3 . . . . . . .139 B4
Exmoor Rd BA2 . . . . . . .101 F2
Exmoor St BS3 . . . . .63 B3
Exmouth Rd BS4 . . . . . . .63 F1
Explore La BS1 . . . . .142 C2
Exton BS24 . . . . .105 A2
Exton Cl BS14 . . . . .80 B5
Eyer's La BS2 . . . . .143 C3
Eyers Rd BS24 . . . . .105 F7

F

Faber Gr BS13 . . . . .79 C4
Fabian Dr BS34 . . . . .36 E5
Factory Rd BS36 . . . . . . .37 F7
FAILAND 61 C3
Failand Cres BS9 . . . . . . .48 C5
Failand La
Easton-in-G BS8 . . . . . . .47 A1
Portbury BS20 . . . . .46 F2
Failand Wlk BS9 . . . . . . .48 C6
Fairacre Cl
Bristol BS7 . . . . .50 B5
Locking BS24 . . . . .106 B4
Fairacres Cl BS31 . . . . . .81 F5
Fair Ash BS40 . . . . .129 C7
Fair Cl BA2 . . . . .136 E4
Faircross La SN14 . . . . . .69 D8
Fairfax St BS1 . . . . .143 B3
Fairfield
Rode BA11 . . . . .137 F1
Tunley BA2 . . . . .117 A3
Fairfield Ave BA1 . . . . . .85 A2
Fairfield Cl
Backwell BS48 . . . . .76 D7
Marshfield SN14 . . . . . .69 F8
Weston-s-M BS22 . . . . .88 B1
Fairfield High Sch
Bristol BS5, BS7 . . . . . .50 A3
Bristol BS6 . . . . .49 F2
Fairfield Mead BS48 . . . .76 D7
FAIRFIELD PARK 85 A2
Fairfield Park Rd BA1 . .85 A2
Fairfield Pl BS3 . . . . .63 B4
Fairfield Pneu Sch
BS48 . . . . .76 C6
Fairfield Rd
Bath BA1 . . . . .85 B1
Bristol, Montpelier BS6 . .49 F2
Bristol, Southville BS3 . .63 B4
Fairfield Terr
Bath BA1 . . . . .85 A1
Peasedown St John
BA2 . . . . .134 C7
Fairfield View BA1 . . . . . .85 A2
Fairfield Way
Backwell BS48 . . . . .76 C6
Saltford BS31 . . . . .82 B4
Fairfoot Rd BS4 . . . . .64 A3
Fairford Cl BS15 . . . . . . .51 F2
Fairford Cres BS34 . . . . .36 C8
Fairford Rd BS11 . . . . . . .47 D7

Fair Furlong BS13 . . . . . .79 A4
Fair Furlong Prim Sch
Bristol BS13 . . . . .79 B4
Bristol BS13 . . . . .79 A4
Fairhaven BS37 . . . . .27 F1
Fairhaven Rd BS6 . . . . . .49 C4
Fair Hill BS25 . . . . .125 F8
Fairlawn BS16 . . . . .51 D4
Fair Lawn BS30 . . . . .66 B4
Fairlawn Ave
Bristol BS34 . . . . .35 F5
Bristol BS34 . . . . .36 A3
Filton BS34 . . . . .36 A3
Fairlawn Rd BS6 . . . . . . .49 F2
Fairlyn Dr BS15 . . . . .51 F3
Fairoaks BS30 . . . . .66 A3
Fairseat Ind Unit
BS40 . . . . .112 E7
Fairview BS22 . . . . .88 F4
Fairview Ct BS15 . . . . . . .65 D6
Fair View Dr BS6 . . . . . . .49 C2
Fairview Ho BS9 . . . . . . .48 F8
Fairview Rd BS15 . . . . . .65 F8
Fairway BS4 . . . . .64 D1
Fairway Cl
Bristol BS30 . . . . .66 B4
Weston-s-M BS22 . . . . .88 B2
Yate BS37 . . . . .28 C2
Fairway Ind Ctr BS34 . . .35 F3
Fairways
Charlcombe BA1 . . . . . .84 E4
Saltford BS31 . . . . .82 E2
Fairy Hill BS39 . . . . .98 D6
Fakeham Rd BS24 . . . . .121 F8
Falcon Cl
Bristol, Patchway BS34 . .35 E8
Bristol, Westbury on T
BS9 . . . . .48 F8
Portishead BS20 . . . . . .45 D4
1 Radstock BA3 . . . . .139 B8
Falcon Cres BS22 . . . . . .105 D8
Falcon Ct BS9 . . . . .49 A7
Falcondale Rd BS9 . . . . .48 F7
Falcondale Wlk BS9 . . . .49 A8
Falcon Dr BS34 . . . . .35 E8
Falconer Rd BA1 . . . . . . .84 A3
Falcon Rd G12 . . . . .11 A5
Falcons Gate BS37 . . . . .27 C3
Falcon Way BS35 . . . . . . .8 D2
Falcon Wlk BS34 . . . . . . .23 E1
FALFIELD 9 E7
Falfield Rd BS4 . . . . .64 C3
Falfield Wlk BS10 . . . . . .49 C8
Falkland Rd **4** BS6 . . . .49 F2
Fallodon Ct BS9 . . . . .49 B5
Fallodon Way BS9 . . . . . .49 B5
Fallowfield
Blagdon BS40 . . . . .110 E2
Bristol BS30 . . . . .66 D5
Weston-s-M BS22 . . . . .88 F3
Falmouth Cl BS48 . . . . . .60 A1
Falmouth Rd BS7 . . . . . . .49 E4
Fane Cl BS10 . . . . .35 A3
Fanshawe Rd BS14 . . . . .80 A7
Faraday Rd **2** BS8 . . . . .62 F5
Farendell Rd BS16 . . . . . .38 B1
Far Handstones BS30 . . .66 A4
Farington Rd BS10 . . . . . .49 D7
Farlands BS16 . . . . .53 B6
FARLEIGH 76 D7
Farleigh Ct BS48 . . . . . . .77 B8
FARLEIGH
HUNGERFORD 137 E8
Farleigh Hungerford
Castle★ BA2 . . . . .137 E8
Farleigh Rd
Backwell BS48 . . . . .76 C6
Clevedon BS21 . . . . .57 D1
Keynsham BS31 . . . . . . .81 D4
Norton St Philip BA2 . .136 F5
Farleigh Rise BA15 . . . . .86 E1
Farleigh View BA15 . . . .120 F3
FARLEIGH WICK 103 E4
Farleigh Wlk BS13 . . . . .79 A8
Farler's End BS48 . . . . . .75 F8
FARLEY 44 B1
Farley Cl BS34 . . . . .36 C7
FARMBOROUGH 116 B6
Farmborough CE VA Prim
Sch BA2 . . . . .115 F6
Farmborough La BA2 .116 E6
Farm Cl
Bristol BS16 . . . . .52 B6
Weston-s-M BS22 . . . . .89 C4
Farmcote GL12 . . . . .19 D8
Farm Ct BS16 . . . . .51 E7
Farmer Rd BS13 . . . . . . .78 F4
Farmers Wlk BS35 . . . . . .8 B4
Farmhouse Cl **7** BS48 . .59 E1
Farmhouse Ct **1** BS48 . .59 E1
Farm La
Easter Compton BS35 . . .22 E2
Wellow BA2 . . . . .118 E1
Farm Lees GL12 . . . . . . .11 A6

Farm Rd
Bristol BS16 . . . . .51 E7
Hutton BS24 . . . . .105 E2
Weston-s-M BS22 . . . . .88 B1
Farmwell Cl BS13 . . . . . .79 B5
Farnaby Cl BS4 . . . . .79 C7
Farnborough Rd BS24 106 C4
Farndale BS5 . . . . .65 A6
Farndale Rd BS22 . . . . . .105 D8
Farne Cl BS9 . . . . .49 B5
Farrant Cl BS4 . . . . .79 D6
Farrier Wy BS14 . . . . . . .80 D3
Farringford Ho BS5 . . . . .50 D2
Farrington Fields
BS39 . . . . .132 C3
Farrington Fields Trad Est
BS39 . . . . .132 C3
FARRINGTON
GURNEY 132 A3
Farrington Gurney By-Pass
BS39 . . . . .132 A3
Farrington Gurney CE Prim
Sch BS39 . . . . .132 A3
Farrington Rd BS39 . . . .132 C5
Farrington Way BS39 . .132 A3
Farrs La BA2 . . . . .102 B2
Farr's La BS1 . . . . .143 A2
Farr St BS11 . . . . .47 B8
Farthing Combe BS26 125 D2
Farthing Row BA11 . . . .137 E1
FAULKLAND 135 E2
Faulkland La BA2, BA3 135 C4
Faulkland Rd BA2 . . . . . .101 D5
Faulkland View BA2 . . . .134 E7
Faversham Dr BS24 . . . .105 A1
Fawkes Cl BS15 . . . . .66 B8
Featherbed La
Chew Stoke BS40 . . . . .95 A3
Clutton BS39 . . . . .114 C6
Oldbury-on-S BS35 . . . . .7 B6
Featherstone Rd **4**
BS16 . . . . .50 F4
Fedden Village BS21 . . . .44 F5
Feeder Rd BS2 . . . . .64 A5
Felix Rd BS5 . . . . .64 B8
Felstead Rd BS10 . . . . . .35 E1
Feltham Ct BS34 . . . . . . .35 F2
Feltham Rd BS16 . . . . . . .53 C6
Feltmakers La BS37 . . . .27 B6
FELTON 94 D8
Felton Gr BS13 . . . . .79 A8
Felton La BS40 . . . . .94 E7
Felton St BS40 . . . . .94 C7
Fenbrook Cl BS16 . . . . . .37 B1
Feniton **6** BS22 . . . . . . .89 A2
Fennel Dr BS34 . . . . .37 A7
Fennel La BS26 . . . . .125 C2
Fennell Gr BS10 . . . . .35 A2
Fenners BS22 . . . . .89 B4
Fenns La BS41 . . . . .61 E1
Fenshurst Gdns BS41 . . .77 F8
Fenswood Cl BS41 . . . . . .61 F1
Fenswood Rd BS41 . . . . .61 E1
Fenswood Mead BS41 . .61 E1
Fenton Cl BS31 . . . . .82 D3
Fenton Ct BS7 . . . . .49 D4
Fenton Rd BS7 . . . . .49 D4
Ferenberge Cl BA2 . . . . .116 A6
Fermaine Ave BS4 . . . . . .64 F3
Fernbank Ct **2** BS6 . . . .49 C2
Fernbank Rd BS6 . . . . . . .49 C2
Fernbrook Cl BS16 . . . . . .37 B1
Fern Cl
Bristol BS10 . . . . .35 B3
Midsomer Norton BA3 . .133 B1
Ferncliffe BS8 . . . . .62 E7
Ferndale Ave BS30 . . . . .66 A3
Ferndale Cl BS32 . . . . . . .24 D7
Ferndale Rd
Bath BA1 . . . . .85 C3
Bristol BS34 . . . . .36 A2
Portishead BS20 . . . . . .45 D6
Ferndene BS32 . . . . .24 C2
Ferndown BS37 . . . . .27 E1
Ferndown Cl BS11 . . . . . .48 A7
Ferndown Grange BS9 . .49 B6
Ferney Leaze La BS39 .115 C3
Fern Gr
Bristol BS32 . . . . .36 D8
Nailsea BS48 . . . . .75 C8
Fernhill BS32 . . . . .24 C7
Fernhill Ct
Bristol BS11 . . . . .34 B1
Tockington BS32 . . . . . .24 C7
Fernhill La BS11 . . . . .34 B1
Fernhurst Rd BS5 . . . . . .50 F1
Fern Lea BS24 . . . . .122 B6
Fernlea Gdns BS20 . . . . .47 B4
Fernlea Rd BS22 . . . . . .105 C7
Fernlea Ho BS36 . . . . . . .38 C6
Fernleigh Ct **1** BS6 . . . .49 B2
Fern Lodge BS23 . . . . . .104 D6
Fern Rd BS16 . . . . .51 D5
Fernside BS48 . . . . .76 A7
Fern St BS2 . . . . .49 F1
Fernsteed Rd BS13 . . . . .78 F6
Fernville Est BS21 . . . . . .57 F2
Ferry Ct BA2 . . . . .102 B6

Ferry La
Bath BA2 . . . . .102 B6
Lympsham BS24 . . . . . .122 C3
Ferryman's Ct BS2 . . . .143 B2
Ferry Rd BS15 . . . . .65 D1
Ferry St BS1 . . . . .143 B2
Ferry Steps Ind Est BS2 64 A4
Fersfield BA2 . . . . .102 B3
Feynman Way Central
BS16 . . . . .52 C8
Feynman Way N BS16 . .38 C1
Fiddes Rd BS6 . . . . .49 C4
Fiddlers Wood La BS32 . .36 E8
Fielders The BS22 . . . . . .89 B4
Fieldfare BS16 . . . . .38 A2
Fieldfare Ave BS20 . . . . .46 A6
Fieldfare Cl BS31 . . . . . . .81 C3
Fieldfare Gdns BS49 . . . .73 F2
Field Farm Cl BS34 . . . . .36 F4
Field Grove La BS30 . . . .82 C8
Fielding Ho BA2 . . . . . . .101 A6
Fielding's Rd BA2 . . . . . .101 C6
Fieldins BA15 . . . . .120 E7
Field La
Bristol BS30 . . . . .65 F3
Dyrham SN14 . . . . .54 F6
Littleton-u-S BS35 . . . . .14 A8
Tytherington BS35 . . . . .15 E3
Field Marshal Slim Ct **24**
BS2 . . . . .143 C4
Field Rd BS15 . . . . .51 C1
Fields The BS22 . . . . .89 D2
Field View **9** BS5 . . . . . .64 A8
Field View Dr BS16 . . . . .51 C6
Fieldway BS25 . . . . .108 A4
Fiennes Cl BS16 . . . . .51 E4
Fifth Ave
Bristol BS14 . . . . .80 B7
Bristol, Filton BS7 . . . . .36 A1
Fifth Way BS11 . . . . .33 E2
Filby Dr BS34 . . . . .36 C8
Filer Cl BA2 . . . . .134 D8
FILTON 36 B3
Filton Abbey Wood Sta
BS34 . . . . .36 B1
Filton Ave
Bristol, Filton BS34 . . . .36 B3
Bristol, Horfield BS7,
BS34 . . . . .50 A7
Filton Avenue Jun & Inf
Schs BS7 . . . . .50 A7
Filton Coll BS34 . . . . .36 A4
Filton Coll (WISE Campus)
BS34 . . . . .36 D3
Filton Gr BS7 . . . . .49 F6
Filton High Sch BS34 . . .36 D3
Filton Hill Prim Sch
BS34 . . . . .36 B4
Filton La BS34 . . . . .36 D2
Filton Rd
Bristol, Frenchay BS16 . .36 F6
Bristol, Harry Stoke BS34 36 D2
Bristol, Horfield BS7 . . . .49 F8
Filton Rdbt BS34 . . . . . . .36 A2
Filton Road Avon Ring Rd
BS16 . . . . .37 C1
Filwood Broadway BS4 .79 E8
Filwood Ct BS16 . . . . . . .51 B3
Filwood Dr BS15 . . . . . . .65 F8
Filwood Ho BS15 . . . . . . .65 F8
FILWOOD PARK 79 E8
Filwood Rd BS16 . . . . . . .51 A3
Finch Cl
Thornbury BS35 . . . . . . .8 C2
Weston-s-M BS22 . . . . .105 E8
Finches The BS20 . . . . . .45 F6
Finch Rd BS37 . . . . .40 A8
Finisterre Par BS20 . . . . .45 F6
Finmere Gdns BS22 . . . . .89 A4
Fircliff Pk BS20 . . . . .45 D7
Fireclay Rd BS5 . . . . .64 D6
Fire Engine La BS36 . . . .38 D7
Fire Station La BS11 . . . .33 B2
Firework Cl BS15 . . . . . . .66 B8
Firfield St BS4 . . . . .64 A4
Firgrove Cres BS37 . . . . .28 A2
Firgrove La BA2 . . . . . . .117 B1
Fir La BS40 . . . . .127 B5
Fir Leaze BS48 . . . . .59 B1
Fir Rd SN14 . . . . .70 F1
Firs Ct BS31 . . . . .81 C4
First Ave
Bath BA2 . . . . .101 E4
Bristol BS14 . . . . .80 A7
Bristol, St Anne's BS4 . .64 E5
Portbury BS20 . . . . .46 E5
Radstock BA3 . . . . .139 C8
First Field Way BS34 . . .35 E6
Firs The
Bath BA2 . . . . .102 B1
Bristol BS16 . . . . .51 E6
Limpley Stoke BA2 . . . .120 A5
First Way BS11 . . . . .33 C1
Fir Tree Ave
Paulton BS39 . . . . .132 F4

Fir Tree Ave continued
Weston-s-M BS24 . . . . **105** E4
Fir Tree CI BS34 . . . . **35** F7
Fir Tree La BS5 . . . . **65** A7
Fisher Ave BS15 . . . . . . **52** A1
Fisher Rd BS15 . . . . . . **52** A1
Fishers Mead BS41 . . . . **61** E1
FISHPONDS **51** A5
Fishponds Rd BS5 . . . . . **50** D3
Fishponds Trad Est
BS5 . . . . **50** E2
Fishpool Hill BS10 . . . . . **35** B4
Fitchett Wlk BS10 . . . . . **34** F3
Fitzgerald Rd BS3 . . . . . **63** F3
Fitzgerald St BS34 . . . . . **35** F5
Fitzharding Ho 8
BS1 . . . . **143** A3
Fitzharding Rd BS20 . . . **47** E3
Fitzroy Circ BS20 . . . . . **46** F6
Fitzroy Ho 3 BA2 . . . . **141** C3
Fitzroy Rd BS16 . . . . . . **51** B2
Fitzroy St BS4 . . . . **64** A4
Fitzroy Terr 7 BS6 . . . . **49** B2
Five Acre Dr BS16 . . . . . **51** A7
Five Arches BA3 . . . . . **133** D2
Five C Bsns Ctr BS21 . . . **57** D1
Flagstaff Rd BS3 . . . . . **123** D7
Flamingo Cres BS22 . . **105** E8
Flat The BS39 . . . . **114** D5
Flatts La BS39 . . . . **115** C4
Flatwoods Cres BA2 . . . **102** F3
Flatwoods Rd BA2 . . . . **102** F3
FLAX BOURTON **76** F7
Flax Bourton CE Prim Sch
BS48 . . . . **76** F8
Flax Bourton Rd BS8 . . . **61** B3
Flaxman CI BS7 . . . . **50** B6
FLAXPITS **37** E5
Flaxpits La BS36 . . . . . . **37** E5
Fletcher Rd BS37 . . . . . . **27** E6
Florence Brown Com Sch
BS4 . . . . **79** D8
Florence Gr BS22 . . . . **105** B8
Florence Pk
Almondsbury BS32 . . . . . **24** C5
Bristol BS6 . . . . **49** B4
Florence Rd BS16 . . . . . **51** E3
Florida Terr BA3 . . . . . **133** C2
Flowerdown Bridge
BS22 . . . . **105** D7
Flowerdown Rd BS24 . . **106** D4
Flowers Hill BS4 . . . . . . **64** E1
Flowers Hill CI BS4 . . . . **64** E1
Flowers Hill Trad Est
BS4 . . . . **64** E1
Flowerwell Rd BS13 . . . . **79** B5
Fogarty Park Rd 2
BS15 . . . . **65** D5
Folleigh CI BS41 . . . . . . **62** B2
Folleigh Dr BS41 . . . . . . **62** B2
Folleigh La BS41 . . . . . . **62** B2
Folliot CI BS16 . . . . **51** A7
Folly Bridge CI BS37 . . . **27** D2
Folly Brook Rd BS16 . . . **38** B1
Folly CI BA3 . . . . **138** E7
Folly Farm Nature
Reserve* BS39 . . . . . **114** B5
Folly La
Bristol BS2 . . . . **64** A6
Shipham BS25 . . . . **125** E7
Weston-s-M BS23 . . . . . **104** E1
Folly Rd
Latteridge BS37 . . . . **26** A5
North Corner BS37 . . . . . **25** F4
Folly The
Bristol BS16 . . . . **51** F7
Cold Ashton SN14 . . . . . . **68** F6
Paulton BS39 . . . . **132** F6
Saltford BS31 . . . . **82** F2
Fontana CI BS30 . . . . . . **66** B3
Fonthill Prim Sch BS10 . **35** E2
Fonthill Rd
Bath BA1 . . . . **84** E2
Bristol BS10 . . . . **35** D2
Fonthill Way BS30 . . . . . **66** C2
Fontmell Ct BS14 . . . . . . **80** D7
Fontwell Dr BS16 . . . . . . **37** F1
Footes La BS36 . . . . **38** B7
Footshill CI BS15 . . . . . . **65** C6
Footshill Dr BS15 . . . . . . **65** C7
Footshill Rd BS15 . . . . . . **65** C6
Forde CI BS30 . . . . **65** F5
Fordell PI BS4 . . . . **64** A3
Ford La BS16 . . . . **52** B6
Ford Rd
Peasedown St John
BA2 . . . . **134** D8
Wellow BA2 . . . . **118** F1
Ford St BS5 . . . . **64** C6
Forefield PI BA2 . . . . . **141** C1
Forefield Rise BA2 . . . . **102** B4
Forefield Terr BA2 . . . . **102** A4
Forelands BS23 . . . . **87** B1
Forest Ave BS16 . . . . . . **51** B3
Forest Dr
Bristol BS10 . . . . **35** C3

Forest Dr continued
Weston-s-M BS23 . . . . . . **88** A1
Forest Edge BS15 . . . . . **65** C4
Forester Ave BA2 . . . . **102** B8
Forester Ct BA2 . . . . . **141** C4
Forester La BA2 . . . . . **102** B8
Forester Rd
Bath BA2 . . . . **102** B8
Portishead BS20 . . . . **45** D4
Forest Hills BS32 . . . . . . **24** B5
Forest Rd
Bristol, Fishponds BS16 . . **51** B4
Bristol, Kingswood BS15 . **65** D7
Forest Wlk
Bristol, Fishponds BS16 . . **51** B2
Bristol, Kingswood BS15 . **65** C7
Forge End BS20 . . . . **46** E3
Forgetmenot Way BS16 . **38** C1
Fortescue Rd BA3 . . . . **133** F2
Fortfield Rd BS14 . . . . . . **80** B5
Forth Ave BS20 . . . . **45** F6
FORTHAY **5** E5
Forty Acre La BS35 . . . . . **15** B3
Forum Bldgs BA1 . . . . . **141** C1
Foss CI 8 BS5 . . . . **64** F8
Fosse Barton BS48 . . . . . **59** D2
Fosse CI BS48 . . . . **59** C2
Fossedale Ave BS14 . . . . **80** C6
Fossefield Rd BA3 . . . . **139** B6
Fosse Gdns BA2 . . . . . **118** D8
Fosse Gn BA3 . . . . **133** C4
Fosse La
Batheaston BA1 . . . . **86** A4
Clandown BA3 . . . . **133** D3
Nailsea BS48 . . . . **59** D2
Fosseway
Clandown BA3 . . . . **133** E4
Clevedon BS21 . . . . **57** E2
Midsomer Norton BA3 . . **139** A5
Radstock BA3 . . . . **139** C8
Fosse Way BS48 . . . . **59** C2
Fosseway CI BA2 . . . . . **134** C7
Fosse Way Cotts BA3 . . **133** D2
Fosseway Ct BS8 . . . . . **142** A2
Fosse Way Est BA2 . . . **101** D1
Fosseway Gdns BA3 . . . **133** E1
Fosseway S BA3 . . . . . . **139** B7
Fosse Way Sch BA3 . . . **139** C8
Fosseway The BS8 . . . . **142** A3
Foss La
Norton BS22 . . . . **88** D6
Oldbury-on-S BS35 . . . . . . **7** E6
Foster's Almshouses 4
BS1 . . . . **143** A3
Foster St BS5 . . . . **50** B2
Foundry Cotts BA2 . . . . **116** B4
Foundry La BS5 . . . . **50** F2
Foundry The BA1 . . . . . **141** C3
Foundry Yd BS5 . . . . **50** F2
Fountain Bldgs 7
BA1 . . . . **141** B3
Fountain Ct
Bristol BS32 . . . . **24** C3
2 Yate BS37 . . . . **39** D7
Fountaine Ct 3 BS5 . . . **50** C2
Fountain Ho 8 BA1 . . . **141** B3
Fountain La BS25 . . . . . **125** B7
Fountains Dr BS30 . . . . . **65** F6
Four Acre Ave BS16 . . . . **51** E8
Four Acre Cres BS16 . . . . **37** E1
Four Acre Rd BS16 . . . . . **51** E8
Four Acres BS13 . . . . . . **78** E4
Four Acres CI
Bristol BS13 . . . . **78** F4
Nailsea BS48 . . . . **75** E8
Four Acres Prim Sch
BS13 . . . . **78** E4
Four Seasons Sq BS37 . . **27** E1
Fourth Ave
Bristol BS14 . . . . **80** B7
Bristol, Filton BS7 . . . . . . **36** A1
Radstock BA3 . . . . **139** D8
Fourth Way BS11 . . . . . . **33** B1
Fowey CI BS48 . . . . **76** A8
Fowey Rd BS22 . . . . **89** A4
Fox and Hounds La
BS31 . . . . **81** F5
Fox Ave BS37 . . . . **27** D2
Foxborough Gdns BS32 . **24** D2
Fox CI
Bristol BS4 . . . . **64** F5
Hawkesbury Upton GL9 . . **19** F3
Thornbury BS35 . . . . **8** D3
Foxcombe Rd
Bath BA1 . . . . **101** B7
Bristol BS14 . . . . **80** B4
FOXCOTE **134** F4
Foxcote BS15 . . . . **65** F7
Foxcote Ave BA2 . . . . . **134** C7
Foxcote Rd BS3 . . . . **63** A3
Foxcroft CI BS32 . . . . **36** F6
Foxcroft Rd BS5 . . . . **64** D8
Fox Ct BS30 . . . . **65** F3
Fox Den Rd BS34 . . . . . . **36** D3
Foxe Rd BS36 . . . . **38** B8
Foxfield Ave BS32 . . . . . **24** D3
Foxglove CI
Bristol BS16 . . . . **50** E5
Thornbury BS35 . . . . **8** D2

Foxglove CI continued
Weston-s-M BS22 . . . . . . **89** A5
Foxglove Rd 2 BS16 . . . **52** C7
FOX HILL **102** A2
Fox Hill BA2 . . . . **102** A2
Foxhill Ho BA2 . . . . **102** A1
FOX HILLS **134** A1
Fox Ho
Bristol, Broom Hill BS4 . . **64** E3
Bristol, Victoria Park
BS8 . . . . **142** A3
Foxholes La BS32 . . . . . . **14** C4
Foxhol La G12 . . . . **10** D1
Fox La BS25 . . . . **125** A7
Fox Rd BS5 . . . . **50** B1
Foye Ho BS8 . . . . **62** E6
Fraley Rd BS9 . . . . **49** A7
FRAMPTON
COTTERELL **38** B7
Frampton Cotterell CE
Prim Sch BS36 . . . . . . **38** A8
Frampton Cres BS16 . . . . **51** C4
Frampton Ct
8 Bristol, Longwell Green
BS30 . . . . **65** F4
16 Bristol, Pile Marsh
BS5 . . . . **64** D7
FRAMPTON END **38** D8
Frampton End Rd BS37 . . **26** D2
France La GL9 . . . . **20** B2
Frances Greeves Ct
BS10 . . . . **34** F1
Frances Mews 12 BS3 . . **63** C4
Francis Fox Rd 7
BS23 . . . . **104** E7
Francis Gr BA2 . . . . **102** A2
Francis Ho BS2 . . . . **143** A4
Francis PI BS30 . . . . **65** F4
Francis Rd
Bristol, Bedminster BS3 . **63** C2
Bristol, Westbury on Trym
BS10 . . . . **49** C8
Yate Rocks BS37 . . . . **27** E6
Francis Way BS30 . . . . . . **66** D6
Francombe Gr BS10 . . . . **49** E6
Francombe Ho BS1 . . . . **143** A1
Frankcom Ho BA2 . . . . **102** B7
Frankford Mans 7
BS23 . . . . **87** C1
Frankland CI BA1 . . . . . . **84** B1
Frankley Bldgs BA1 . . . . **85** B1
Frankley Terr 6 BA1 . . . **85** B1
Franklin Ct BS1 . . . . **143** B1
Franklin's Way BS49 . . . . **74** F1
Franklyn Ct 6 BS16 . . . . **50** E3
Franklyn La 10 BS2 . . . . **49** F1
Franklyn St BS2 . . . . **49** F1
Franklyn Terr BS39 . . . . **132** A4
Fraser CI BS22 . . . . **88** F4
Fraser St BS3 . . . . **63** D3
Frayne Rd BS3 . . . . **63** A4
Frederick Ave BA2 . . . . **134** C7
Frederick PI BS8 . . . . . . **142** B3
Fredericks Way SN14 . . . **43** B3
Fredrick St BS4 . . . . **64** A4
Freeland Bldgs 1 BS5 . **50** C2
Freeland PI BS8 . . . . **62** F6
Freelands BS21 . . . . **73** C8
Freeling Ho BS1 . . . . . . **143** B1
Freemans La BS48 . . . . . **77** B2
Freemantle Gdns BS5 . . **50** C3
Freemantle Ho BS2 . . . . **143** A4
Freemantle Rd BS5 . . . . **50** C3
Freestone Rd BS2 . . . . . . **64** A6
Freeview Rd BA2 . . . . . **101** A5
Freezinghill La BS30 . . . . **68** B4
Fremantle La 9 BS6 . . . . **49** B1
Fremantle Rd BS6 . . . . . **49** D1
Fremantle Sq BS6 . . . . . **49** D1
FRENCHAY **51** B8
Frenchay CE Prim Sch
BS16 . . . . **51** B7
Frenchay CI BS16 . . . . . . **51** B7
Frenchay Hill BS16 . . . . . **51** B7
Frenchay Park Rd BS16 . **50** F6
Frenchay Rd
Bristol BS16 . . . . **51** C6
Weston-s-M BS23 . . . . . **104** E4
Frenchay Village Mus*
BS16 . . . . **51** A8
French CI
Nailsea BS48 . . . . **59** C4
Peasedown St John
BA2 . . . . **134** D7
Frenchfield Rd BA2 . . . **134** D7
FRESHFORD **120** B5
Freshford Church Sch
BA2 . . . . **120** B5
Freshford La BA2 . . . . . **120** A4
Freshford Sta BA2 . . . . **120** C5
Freshland Way BS15 . . . . **65** B8
Freshmoor 6 BS21 . . . . . **57** H3
Friar Ave BS22 . . . . **88** E3
Friars Ho 4 BS37 . . . . . . **39** D7
Friary BS1 . . . . **143** C1
Friary CI
Clevedon BS21 . . . . **57** E5
Westwood BA15 . . . . . . **120** E4

Friary Grange Pk BS36 . **37** E6
Friary Rd
Bristol BS7 . . . . **49** D4
Portishead BS20 . . . . **45** B5
Friary Wood La BA2 . . . **120** B2
Friendly Row BS20 . . . . . **47** C5
Friendship Gr 2 BS48 . . **59** F2
Friendship Rd
Bristol BS4 . . . . **64** A2
Nailsea BS48 . . . . **59** F3
Friezewood Rd BS3 . . . . **63** A4
Fripp CI BS5 . . . . **64** B6
Frith La GL12 . . . . **17** F3
Frobisher Ave BS20 . . . . **45** B5
Frobisher CI
Portishead BS20 . . . . **45** A5
Weston-s-M BS22 . . . . . . **88** E4
Frobisher Rd BS3 . . . . . . **63** A3
Frog La
Bristol BS1 . . . . **142** C2
Felton BS40 . . . . **94** C8
Frampton Cotterell BS36 . **38** E7
North Nibley GL11 . . . . . . **5** C5
Ubley BS40 . . . . **111** D1
Winford BS40 . . . . **94** F5
Frogmore St BS1 . . . . . **142** C2
Frome Bank Gdns BS36 . **37** E3
Fromebank Jun Sch
BS37 . . . . **27** D3
Frome Ct BS35 . . . . **15** C8
Frome Glen BS36 . . . . . . **37** E4
Frome Old Rd BA3 . . . . **134** A2
Frome PI 1 BS16 . . . . . . **50** E5
Frome Rd
Bath BA2 . . . . **101** D1
Chipping Sodbury BS37 . . **28** C1
Norton St Philip BA2 . . . **136** F3
Radstock BA3 . . . . **134** B2
Radstock BA3 . . . . **140** E8
Fromeside Pk BS16 . . . . . **51** B7
Frome Terr BS16 . . . . **50** E5
Frome Valley Rd BS16 . . **50** F6
Frome View BS36 . . . . . . **38** B7
Frome Villas BS16 . . . . . . **51** C7
Frome Way BS36 . . . . **37** E5
Front Home CI BS34 . . . . **35** E6
Front St BS25 . . . . **108** E4
Froomshaw Rd BS16 . . . . **51** A7
FROST HILL **91** C6
Frost Hill BS49 . . . . **91** D7
Frost & Reed Ho 3
BS5 . . . . **64** F8
Fry Ct 2 BS3 . . . . **63** C4
Fry's Bottom
Breach BS39 . . . . **114** F7
Chelwood BS39 . . . . **115** A6
Fry's CI BS16 . . . . **50** D4
Frys Hill BS15 . . . . **51** E2
Fry's Hill BS4 . . . . **64** D2
Frys House of Mercy 10
BS1 . . . . **143** B1
Fry's La BS40 . . . . **109** F3
Frys Leaze BA1 . . . . **85** B2
Fry's Well BA3 . . . . **138** D3
Fryth Ho BS48 . . . . **60** D3
Fryth Way BS48 . . . . **59** C2
Fuchsia CI BS16 . . . . **52** D8
Fuddlebrook Cotts
SN14 . . . . **69** F6
Fulford Rd BS13 . . . . **79** C5
Fulford Wlk BS13 . . . . . . **79** B5
Fullens CI BS22 . . . . **105** D7
Fuller Rd BA1 . . . . **85** C2
Fullers La BS25 . . . . **125** A6
Fullers Way BA2 . . . . . . **118** D8
Fullwell CI BA3 . . . . **135** D1
Fulmar CI BS35 . . . . **8** D2
Fulmar Rd BS22 . . . . **88** F1
Fulwell La BA3 . . . . **135** D1
Furber Ct BS5 . . . . **65** B6
Furber Rd BS5 . . . . **65** B6
Furber Ridge BS5 . . . . . . **65** B6
Furber Vale BS5 . . . . **65** B6
Furland Rd BS22 . . . . **88** C2
Furlong CI BA3 . . . . **138** F7
Furlong PI BS26 . . . . . . **125** C1
Furlong The BS6 . . . . **49** D6
Furnace Way BS49 . . . . . **91** E4
Furnleaze BS39 . . . . **114** E3
Furnwood BS5 . . . . **65** A6
Furze CI BS22 . . . . **88** B2
Furze Rd
Bristol BS16 . . . . **51** C3
Weston-s-M BS22 . . . . . . **88** A1
Furzewood Rd BS15 . . . . **65** F8
Fussell Ct BS15 . . . . **65** F8
Fylton Croft BS14 . . . . . . **80** B3

Friary Grange Pk BS36 . **37** E6

G

Gable CI BS35 . . . . **23** A2
Gable Rd 8 BS5 . . . . **50** A1
Gables CI BS29 . . . . **107** B3
Gadshill Dr BS34 . . . . . . **36** E5
Gadshill Rd BS5 . . . . **50** C2
Gages CI BS15 . . . . **65** F7
Gages Rd BS15 . . . . **65** F7
Gainsborough Ct BA1 . . **84** B1

Gainsborough Dr BS22 . . **88** F3
Gainsborough Gdns
BA1 . . . . **101** C8
Gainsborough Mews
BS10 . . . . **35** B2
Gainsborough Rd BS31 . **81** F5
Gainsborough Sq BS7 . . **50** B7
Galingale Way BS20 . . . . **45** F5
Gallagher Ret Pk
Bristol BS30 . . . . **65** E4
Weston-s-M BS23 . . . . . **105** A5
Galleries The BS1 . . . . . **143** B3
Gallivan CI BS34 . . . . **36** B8
Galway Rd BS4 . . . . **63** E1
Gambril La GL12 . . . . **9** F5
Gander CI BS13 . . . . **79** B5
Gannet Rd BS22 . . . . **88** F1
Garamond Ct BS1 . . . . . **143** B1
Garden CI
Bristol BS9 . . . . **48** C5
Weston-s-M BS22 . . . . . . **88** E2
Garden Ct BS8 . . . . **142** A4
Gardeners Wlk BS41 . . . . **62** B1
Gardens Rd BS21 . . . . . . **57** E4
Gardens The
Bristol, Frenchay BS16 . . . **36** F1
3 Bristol, Upper Soundwell
BS16 . . . . **51** B3
Gardner Ave BS13 . . . . . . **78** F7
Gardner Rd BS20 . . . . **45** D6
Garfield Ct BS5 . . . . **64** F8
Garfield Rd BS5 . . . . **65** A8
Garfield Terr 1 BA1 . . . **85** C2
Garland Ho 7 BS21 . . . . **57** E2
Garner Ct 4 BS22 . . . . . **89** A4
Garnet St BS3 . . . . **63** B3
Garnett PI BS16 . . . . **51** F7
Garonor Way BS20 . . . . . **46** F5
Garre Ho BA2 . . . . **100** F5
Garrett Dr BS32 . . . . **36** D7
Garrick Rd BA2 . . . . **100** F5
Garsdale Rd BS22 . . . . . **105** D8
Garston Cotts BS40 . . . **110** E3
Garston La BS40 . . . . . . **110** E3
Garstons
Bathford BA1 . . . . **86** D2
6 Clevedon BS21 . . . . . . **57** D1
Wrington BS40 . . . . **92** E1
Garstons CI
Backwell BS48 . . . . **75** F6
Wrington BS40 . . . . **92** E1
Garstons Orch BS40 . . . . **92** D1
Garstons The BS20 . . . . . **45** D4
Garth Rd BS13 . . . . **79** A8
Garton Ho 3 BS16 . . . . . **51** D5
Garvey Ho 14 BS5 . . . . . **64** C7
Gascoigns Way BS34 . . . **36** A7
Gaskins The BS7 . . . . **50** A5
Gas La BS2 . . . . **64** A6
Gassons BA2 . . . . **134** D4
Gaston Ave BS31 . . . . **81** F6
Gastons The BS11 . . . . . . **48** A8
Gasworks La BS1 . . . . . . **142** B1
Gatcombe Dr BS34 . . . . . **36** E4
Gatcombe Farm Ind Est
BS40 . . . . **92** D3
Gatcombe La BS48 . . . . . **77** D8
Gatcombe Mill La BS48 . **61** C1
Gatcombe Rd BS13 . . . . . **79** B5
Gatehouse Ave BS13 . . . . **79** A5
Gatehouse CI BS13 . . . . . **79** A5
Gatehouse Ct BS13 . . . . . **79** B5
Gatehouse Ctr The
BS13 . . . . **79** B5
Gatehouse Way BS13 . . . **79** A5
Gatesby Mead BS34 . . . . **36** E5
Gateway Terr BS21 . . . . . **57** B1
Gathorne Cres BS37 . . . . **27** D2
Gathorne Rd BS3 . . . . **63** B4
Gatton Rd BS2 . . . . **50** A1
GAUNT'S EARTHCOTT . . . **25** B5
Gaunts Earthcott La
BS32 . . . . **25** B5
Gaunt's La BS1 . . . . **142** C2
Gaunts Rd BS37 . . . . **40** B8
Gauting Rd BS34 . . . . **35** E6
Gay Ct BA1 . . . . **85** E3
Gay Elms Prim Sch
BS13 . . . . **79** A4
Gay Elms Rd BS13 . . . . . . **79** A4
Gayner Rd BS7 . . . . **36** A1
Gay's Hill BA1 . . . . **141** C4
Gays Rd BS15 . . . . **65** B4
Gay St BA1 . . . . **141** B3
Gaywood Ho 7 BS3 . . . . **63** B3
Gazelle Rd BS24 . . . . . . **105** B3
Gazzard CI BS36 . . . . **37** E2
Gazzard Rd BS36 . . . . **37** E2
GEE MOOR **65** F6
Gee Moors BS15 . . . . **65** F7
Gefle CI BS1 . . . . **142** B1
Geldof Dr BA3 . . . . **133** A2
Gentian CI BS16 . . . . **52** C8
Geoffrey CI BS13 . . . . **78** E6
George CI BS48 . . . . **76** D7
George Ct 12 BS6 . . . . . . **49** B1
George & Dragon La 11
BS5 . . . . **64** D7

George Holmes Wy
BS16 50 E8
George Jones Rd BS2 64 A6
George La SN14 55 E1
Georges Bldgs BA1 85 C3
Georges Ho BA2 102 B6
George's Pl BA2 102 B6
George's Rd BA1 85 A1
Georges Sq BS1 143 B2
George St
Bath BA1 141 B3
Bath, Bathwick BA2 102 B6
Bristol BS5 64 C8
Portishead BS20 45 C2
Weston-s-M BS23 104 E7
Georgian Ho BA2 141 C2
Georgian House (Mus)★
BS1 142 C2
Georgian View BA2 101 C2
Gerald Rd BS3 63 A3
Gerard Rd BS23 104 F8
Gerrard Bldgs BA2 102 B7
Gerrard Cl BS4 79 D7
Gerrish Ave
Bristol, Moorfields BS5 64 C8
Bristol, Staple Hill BS16 51 F5
Gibbet La BS14 80 D1
Gibbets Brow BS40 129 A3
Gibbs Ct 15 BS5 64 D7
Gibbsfold Rd BS13 79 C4
Gibbs La BS37 40 B4
GIBB THE 43 F3
Gibson Rd BS6 49 D1
Giffard Ho BS34 36 D6
Gifford Cl BS37 27 A8
Gifford Cres BS34 36 C6
Gifford Ct BS34 36 D2
Gifford Rd BS10 34 F4
Giffords Pl BS13 79 A7
Gilbeck Rd BS48 59 C2
Gilbert Rd
Bristol, Kingswood
BS15 51 D1
Bristol, Moorfields BS5 64 C8
Gilberyn Dr BS22 89 A3
Gilda Cl BS14 80 C5
Gilda Cres BS14 80 B6
Gilda Par BS14 80 C5
Gilda Sq W BS14 80 B5
Gillard Cl BS15 65 B8
Gillard Rd BS15 65 B8
Gill Ave BS16 51 B6
Gillebank Cl BS14 80 D5
Gillham Ho 4 BS7 49 D2
Gillingham Hill 7 BS15 65 B5
Gillingham Terr 3 BA1 85 B1
Gillingstool BS35 15 C8
Gillingstool Prim Sch
BS35 15 B8
Gill Mews BS22 89 B4
Gillmore Cl BS22 88 D1
Gillmore Rd BS22 88 D1
Gillray Cl BS7 50 B6
Gillson Cl BS24 105 D2
Gilpin Cl BS15 51 F1
Gilroy Cl BS30 66 B3
Gilslake Ave BS10 35 B3
Gilton Ho BS4 64 E2
Gimblet Rd BS22 89 B4
Gingell's Gn 4 BS5 65 A8
Gipsy Patch La BS34 36 C6
Glades The BS5 50 E2
Gladstone Ct
Bath BA2 102 C2
Bristol BS16 51 E4
Gladstone Dr BS16 51 E3
Gladstone La BS36 38 C7
Gladstone Pl BA2 102 C2
Gladstone Rd
Bath BA2 102 C2
Bristol BS14 80 B6
2 Bristol, Kingswood
BS15 51 D1
Gladstone St
Bristol, Bedminster BS3 63 B3
Bristol, Kingswood BS16 51 D3
13 Bristol, Pile Marsh
BS5 64 D7
Midsomer Norton BA3 133 B3
Glaisdale Rd BS16 51 A5
Glamis BS24 105 E7
Glanville Dr BS39 130 E6
Glanville Gdns BS15 65 E7
Glass House La BS2 64 B5
Glastonbury Cl
Bristol BS30 65 F5
Nailsea BS48 60 B1
Glastonbury Way BS22 89 A2
Glebe Ave BS20 45 E4
Glebe Cl BS41 62 C2
Glebe Field BS32 24 A5
Glebe Ho
Bath BA2 102 B5
Portishead BS20 45 E4
Weston-s-M BS22 88 F3
Glebe Inf Sch The
BS49 91 C4
Glebelands BA3 133 D1
Glebelands Rd BS34 36 A3
Glebe Rd
Bath BA2 101 B4
Bristol BS5 64 E8
Clevedon BS21 57 E2
Long Ashton BS41 62 C2
Portishead BS20 45 E4
Weston-s-M BS23 104 E8
Glebes The BS5 64 E8
Glebe The
Freshford BA2 120 B4
Hinton Charterhouse
BA2 119 D2
Pilning BS35 22 C7
Timsbury BA2 116 B3
Wrington BS40 92 D2
Glebe Wlk BS31 81 C4
Gledemoor Dr BS36 38 D7
Glena Ave BS4 64 B2
Glenarm Rd BS4 64 E2
Glenarm Wlk BS4 64 E2
Glen Ave BS8 61 F8
Glenavon Ct BS9 48 C4
Glenavon Pk BS9 48 C4
Glen Brook BS9 48 D4
Glenburn Rd BS15 51 B1
Glencairn Ct BA2 102 B6
Glencoe Bsns Pk
BS23 105 A7
Glencoyne Ct 1 BS10 35 C2
Glencoyne Sq BS10 35 C2
Glencroft Way BS22 88 E3
Glendale
17 Bristol BS8 62 F6
Bristol, Downend BS16 51 E8
Bristol, Hillfields BS16 51 C3
Glendare St BS5 64 C6
Glendevon Rd BS14 80 A3
Glendower Ho BS8 62 F7
Glen Dr BS9 48 D5
Gleneagles BS37 27 E1
Gleneagles Cl
Nailsea BS48 60 A1
Weston-s-M BS22 88 F3
Gleneagles Dr BS10 34 D3
Gleneagles Rd BS30 66 B6
Glenfall BS37 39 D7
Glenfrome Prim Sch
BS5 50 B4
Glenfrome Rd BS2 50 B3
Glen Hospl The BS6 49 A2
Glen La BS4 64 D2
Glen Park Gdns BS5 65 A8
Glen Pk
Bristol, Eastville BS5 50 C2
Bristol, St George BS5 65 A8
Glenroy Ave BS15 51 B1
Glenside Cl BS16 51 C7
Glenside Hospl Mus★
BS16 50 E5
Glenside Pk 3 BS16 50 E5
Glen The
Bristol, Hanham BS15 65 B4
Bristol, Redland BS6 49 B3
Saltford BS31 82 F1
Weston-s-M BS22 88 B2
Yate BS37 27 E2
Glentworth Ct 19 BS23 87 C1
Glentworth Rd
Bristol BS8 142 B2
Bristol, Redland BS6 49 C2
Glenview Ho BA2 134 D8
Glenview Rd BS4 64 D2
Glenwood BS16 51 C3
Glenwood Dr BS30 66 B4
Glenwood Mans BS23 87 D1
Glenwood Rd BS10 49 C7
Glenwood Rise BS20 44 F5
Glen Yeo Terr BS49 91 C4
Glevum Cl BS16 52 C7
Glider Ave BS24 105 B4
Gloster Ave BS5 50 D3
Gloucester Cl BS34 36 D5
Gloucester Ho 11 BS2 143 C3
Gloucester La 18 BS2 143 C3
Gloucester Pl 2 BS2 143 A3
Gloucester Rd
Almondsbury BS32,
BS35 24 C6
Avonmouth BS11 33 A1
Bath BA1 85 C3
Bristol BS32 24 A3
Bristol, Bishopston BS7 49 E4
Bristol, Patchway BS34 36 B7
Bristol, Staple Hill BS16 51 E3
Stone GL13 3 F3
Thornbury BS35 8 C3
Upper Swainswick BA1 85 A7
Gloucester Rd N BS7,
BS34 36 A4
Gloucester Row
6 Bristol BS8 62 F7
Kingswood GL12 11 F8
Gloucestershire Cty
Cricket Club★ BS7 49 F4
Gloucester St
4 Bath BA1 141 B3
5 Bristol BS2 143 B4
9 Bristol, Clifton BS8 62 F7
Bristol, Eastville BS5 50 D3
Gloucester St *continued*
Weston-s-M BS23 104 D7
Gloucester Terr 12 BS35 8 B1
Glovers Field BS25 125 F7
Glyn Vale BS3 63 E1
Gnome Rd BS24 105 C5
Goddard Dr BS22 89 B4
Goddard Way BS10 35 A1
Godfrey Ct 7 BS30 65 F4
Godwin Dr BS48 59 C3
Goffenton Dr BS16 51 B6
Goldcrest Rd BS37 39 F7
Goldcrest Way
Dyer's Common BS35 22 C3
Portishead BS20 45 F6
GOLDEN HILL 49 D5
Golden Hill BS6 49 C5
Golden La GL12 11 F4
Golden Lion Ct BS1 143 B2
Goldenrod Rd BS16 52 D8
Golden Valley BS30 67 C6
Golden Valley La
Bitton BS30 82 E8
Upton Cheyney BS30 66 F2
Golden Valley Prim Sch
BS48 59 F2
Goldfinch Way BS16 53 C4
Goldney Ave
Bristol BS8 142 A2
Bristol, Warmley BS30 66 C7
Goldney Cl BS39 114 F1
Goldney Ct 7 BS16 50 E3
Goldney Rd BS8 142 A2
Goldney Way BS39 114 F1
Goldsbury Wlk BS11 34 A1
GOLD'S CROSS 113 E6
Golf Club La BS31 82 E2
Golf Course La BS34 35 F3
Golf Course Rd BA2 102 D6
Golledge Cl BA3 138 C4
Gooch Ct BS30 66 C3
Gooch Way BS22 89 B3
Goodeve Pk BS9 48 D3
Goodeve Rd BS9 48 D3
Goodhind St BS5 64 A8
Goodneston Rd BS16 51 A3
Goodrich Cl BS37 27 B1
Goodring Hill BS11 34 A1
Good Shepherd Cl BS7 49 C4
Goodwin Dr BS14 79 F4
Goodwood Gdns BS16 37 F1
Goold Cl BA2 100 A8
Goolden St BS4 64 A3
Goosard La BS39 132 E8
Goose Acre BS32 36 F6
Goosefoot Rd BS16 52 D7
Goose Gn
Bristol BS30 52 C1
Frampton Cotterell BS36 38 C8
Yate BS37 27 E3
GOOSE GREEN
Bristol 52 C1
Yate 27 E3
Goose Green Way BS37 27 E4
Gooseham Mead BS49 91 D4
Gooseland Cl BS14 79 F3
Goosey La BS22 89 C2
Gordano Ct BS20 45 E5
Gordano Gate Bsns Pk
BS20 45 E5
Gordano Gdns BS20 47 B4
Gordano Rd BS20 46 D7
Gordano Sch BS20 45 D3
Gor Dano View BS20 45 C5
Gordano Way BS20 46 F5
Gordon Ave BS5 50 E1
Gordon Bldgs BA3 134 A3
Gordon Cl BS5 50 E1
Gordon Rd
Bath BA2 102 B5
Bristol BS8 142 B3
14 Bristol, St Pauls BS2 49 F1
Bristol, Whitehall BS5 50 D1
Peasedown St John
BA2 134 D8
Weston-s-M BS23 104 F7
Gore Rd BS3 63 A3
Gore's Marsh Rd BS3 63 A2
Gores Pk BS39 115 B2
Gorham Cl BS11 34 C2
Gorlands Rd BS37 28 C1
Gorlangton Cl BS14 80 A7
Gorse Cover Rd BS35 22 A7
Gorse Hill BS16 51 C3
Gorse La
Bristol BS8 142 B2
Cold Ashton BS30, SN14 68 D7
Gosford Mans 6 BS23 87 C1
Gosforth Cl BS10 35 B1
Gosforth Rd BS10 35 B1
Goslet Rd BS14 80 E5
Goss Barton BS48 59 D1
Goss Cl BS48 59 C1
Goss La BS48 59 C1
Goss View BS48 59 C1
Gotley Rd BS4 64 D2
Gott Dr BS4 64 D5
Goulston Rd BS13 79 A5
Goulston Wlk BS13 79 A5
Goulter St BS5 64 B6
Gournay Ct BS39 132 A3
Gourney Cl BS11 34 B2
Governors Ho 2 BA2 101 D6
Gover Rd BS15 65 C3
Govier Way BS35 22 C4
Grace Cl
Chipping Sodbury BS37 28 C1
Yatton BS49 91 B8
Grace Ct BS16 51 D6
Grace Dr
Bristol BS15 66 A8
Midsomer Norton BA3 133 A2
Gracefield Sch BS16 51 C5
Grace Park Rd BS4 64 D1
Grace Rd
Bristol BS16 51 C5
Weston-s-M BS22 89 B4
Gradwell Cl BS22 89 B3
Graeme Cl BS16 51 A4
Graham Rd
3 Bristol, Bedminster
BS3 63 C3
Bristol, Downend BS16 51 F6
21 Bristol, Upper Easton
BS5 50 B1
Weston-s-M BS23 104 E7
Grainger Ct BS11 47 E7
Grain Loft The 9 BS1 143 A2
Graitney Cl BS49 92 A8
Grampian Cl BS30 66 C4
Granary The 8 BS1 143 A2
Granby Ct 18 BS8 62 F6
Granby Hill BS8 62 F6
Grandmother's Rock La
BS30 67 D2
Grand Par BA2 141 C2
Grand Pier★ BS23 104 D7
Granfield Gdns BS40 109 A5
Grange Ave
Bristol, Hanham BS15 65 D5
Bristol, Little Stoke
BS34 36 C6
Grange Bsns Pk The
BS24 90 A5
Grange Cl
Bristol, Patchway BS32 24 C2
Bristol, Stoke Gifford
BS34 37 A4
Weston-s-M BS23 104 E1
Grange Cl N BS9 49 B6
Grange Court Rd BS9 49 A6
Grange Ct
Bristol BS15 65 D5
Bristol, Henleaze BS9 49 B6
Bristol, Westbury on Trym
BS9 49 A8
Grange Dr BS16 51 C6
Grange End BA3 139 B7
Grange Farm Rd BS49 74 A1
Grange Pk
Bristol, Frenchay BS16 51 C8
Bristol, Westbury on Trym
BS9 49 B6
Grange Rd
Bristol BS8 142 A3
Bristol, Bishopsworth
BS13 79 A5
Saltford BS31 82 C3
Weston-s-M BS23 104 E1
Grange Sch & Sports Coll
The BS30 66 B7
Grange The
Bath BA1 84 C1
Bristol, Coombe Dingle
BS9 48 D7
Bristol, Sneyd Park BS9 48 F3
Flax Bourton BS48 76 F7
Limpley Stoke BA2 120 B5
Grangeville Cl BS30 66 B3
Grangewood Cl 4
BS16 51 C6
Granny's La BS15 65 E6
Grantham Ct 1 BS15 65 C8
Grantham Ho BS15 51 C1
Grantham La BS15 65 C8
Grantham Rd BS15 51 C1
Grantson Cl BS4 64 E2
Granville Cl BS15 65 B3
Granville Rd BA1 84 E4
Granville St BS5 64 C6
Grasmere Cl BS10 49 A8
Grasmere Dr BS23 104 F4
Grassington Dr BS37 40 A8
Grass Meers Dr BS14 80 A4
Grassmere Gdns BS30 66 D6
Grassmere Rd BS49 91 B8
Gratitude Rd BS5 50 C1
Gravel Hill BS40 112 B7
Gravel Hill Rd N BS37 28 A5
Graveney Cl BS4 64 D1
Gray Cl BS10 34 E2
Grayle Rd BS10 35 A2
Grayling Ho BS9 48 F7
Gray Rd BS34 35 E6
Grays Hill BA2 135 B5
Great Ann St BS2 143 C3
Great Bedford St BA1 141 B4
Great Brier Leaze BS34 35 E7
Great Britain S.S.★
BS1 142 B1
Great Brockeridge BS9 48 F6
Great Clover Leaze BS7 50 B8
Great Copsie Way 3
BS7 50 C8
Great Dowles BS30 66 A4
Great George St
Bristol, Brandon Hill
BS1 142 C2
Bristol, St Pauls BS2 143 C3
Great Hayles Rd BS14 80 A6
Great Leaze BS30 66 A4
Great Mdw BS34 37 A6
Great Meadow Rd BS32 36 F6
Great Park Rd BS32 24 C3
Great Pease Pk BS34 35 F6
Great Pulteney St
BA2 141 C3
Great Stanhope St
BA1 141 A2
GREAT STOKE 36 F5
Great Stoke BS34 37 A5
Great Stoke Way
Bristol, Great Stoke
BS34 37 A5
Bristol, Harry Stoke BS34 36 D3
Greatstone La BS40 94 F5
Great Swanmoor Cl
BS34 36 C3
Great Western Bsns Pk
BS37 27 B3
Great Western Ct BS34 36 F4
Great Western La BS5 64 C6
Great Western Rd BS21 57 F2
Great Wood Cl BS13 79 C4
Greenacre BS22 88 B2
Green Acre Rd BS14 80 A3
Greenacres
Bath BA1 84 B3
Bristol BS9 48 E7
Midsomer Norton BA3 132 E1
Greenacres Park Homes
BS36 38 E5
Greenbank Ave E BS5 50 C1
Greenbank Ave W BS5 50 C1
Greenbank Gdns BA1 84 B1
Greenbank Rd
Bristol, Hanham BS15 65 D5
Bristol, Lower Easton
BS5 50 D2
Bristol, Southville BS3 63 A4
Greenbank View
Bristol, Kingswood
BS15 65 E7
Bristol, Lower Easton
BS5 50 D2
Green Cl
Bristol BS7 50 A8
Paulton BS39 132 E6
Green Cotts BA2 102 C2
Green Croft BS5 51 A1
Green Ct BS35 14 A2
Greendale Rd
Bristol, Lower Knowle
BS3 63 E2
Bristol, Redland BS6 49 B3
Green Dell Cl BS10 34 D3
Greenditch Ave BS13 79 C5
Greenditch Cl BA3 138 C3
Green Ditch La BA3 138 B6
Greenditch St BS35 13 D1
Greendown BS5 65 A7
Greendown Pl BA2 102 A1
Green Dragon Rd BS36 37 D5
Greenfield Ave BS10 49 D8
Greenfield Cres BS48 59 E3
Greenfield Ct BS10 35 D1
Greenfield Pk BS20 45 C3
Greenfield Pl BS23 104 C8
Greenfield Prim Sch
BS4 79 C7
Greenfield Rd BS10 35 D1
Greenfields Ave BS29 107 A3
Greenfields Way BS23 105 B4
Greenfield Wlk BA3 133 A3
Greenfinch Lodge BS16 50 E6
Greengage Cl 6 BS22 105 E8
Greenhaven 5 BS5 50 C1
Greenhayes BS37 40 C8
GREENHILL 133 A3
Greenhill BS35 15 A4
Green Hill BS35 15 A4
Greenhill Cl
Nailsea BS48 59 D2
Weston-s-M BS22 89 A3
Greenhill Croft BS25 108 B4
Greenhill Down BS35 15 A5
Greenhill Gdns BS35 15 A4
Greenhill Gr BS3 63 A2
Greenhill La
Alveston BS35 14 F4
Bristol BS11 34 C1
Sandford BS25 108 B4
Greenhill Par 5 BS35 15 A5
Greenhill Pl BA3 133 A3

Greenhill Rd
Alveston BS35 . . . .**15** A5
Midsomer Norton BA3 . .**133** A3
Sandford BS25 . . . .**108** B4
Greenhouse La
Nempnett Thrubwell
 BS40 . . . .**111** C6
Regil BS40 . . . .**94** D1
Green La
Avonmouth BS11 . . . .**33** B1
Bristol BS11 . . . .**47** B8
Butcombe BS40 . . . .**111** A7
Failand BS8 . . . .**61** C4
Farrington Gurney BS39 **131** F6
Felton BS40 . . . .**94** C3
Hinton Charterhouse
 BA2 . . . .**119** E1
Marshfield SN14 . . . .**69** E8
Priddy BS40 . . . .**128** B7
Rangeworthy BS37, GL12 **17** B2
Severn Beach BS35 . . . . .**22** B8
Stratton-on-t-F BA3 . . . .**138** E1
Tytherington GL12 . . . . . .**16** B8
Winsley BA15 . . . .**120** F6
Winterbourne BS36 . . . . .**37** C7
Greenland Rd BS22 . . . .**88** D1
Greenlands Rd BA2 . . . .**134** C8
Greenlands Way BS10 . .**34** F4
Greenleaze BS4 . . . .**64** B1
Greenleaze Ave BS16 . . .**37** D1
Greenleaze Cl BS16 . . . .**37** D1
Greenmore Rd BS4 . . . . .**64** B2
Greenore BS15 . . . .**65** C7
Green Paddock BS34 . . .**35** E6
Green Park Mews
 BA1 . . . .**141** A2
Greenpark Rd BS10 . . . .**35** E1
Green Park Rd BA1 . . . .**141** B2
Green Park Station
 BA1 . . . .**141** B2
GREEN PARLOUR **134** D2
Green Parlour Rd BA3 **134** D1
Green Pastures Rd
 BS48 . . . .**60** B2
Green Patch La BA2 . . .**115** E7
Green Pk BA1 . . . .**141** B2
Greenridge BS39 . . . . . .**114** F3
Greenridge BS13 . . . . . .**78** E4
Green Sands Rd 3
 BS34 . . . .**35** F7
Greensbrook BS39 . . . .**114** F3
Green's Hill BS16 . . . . . .**50** E3
Green Side BS16 . . . .**52** A6
Greenside Cl BS10 . . . . .**34** D3
Greenslade Gdns BS48 . .**59** D3
Greensplott Rd BS11 . . .**33** C7
Green St
 Bath BA1 . . . .**141** C2
 Bristol BS3 . . . .**63** F4
 Shoscombe BA2 . . . . . .**134** E5
Green The
 Backwell BS48 . . . .**76** A5
 Bath BA2 . . . .**101** D1
 Bristol, New Cheltenham
 BS15 . . . .**51** E2
 Bristol, Stoke Gifford
 BS34 . . . .**36** E4
 Chipping Sodbury BS37 . .**41** A8
 Cromhall GL12 . . . .**17** B8
 Faulkland BA3 . . . .**135** D2
 Hinton Charterhouse
 BA2 . . . .**119** F1
 Iron Acton BS37 . . . .**26** D4
 Locking BS24 . . . .**106** A4
 Luckington SN14 . . . . . .**31** E4
 Olveston BS35 . . . .**14** A2
 Pill BS20 . . . .**47** D4
 Wick BS30 . . . .**67** B5
 Winscombe BS25 . . . . . .**125** A4
Green Tree Rd BA3 . . . .**133** B3
GREENVALE **116** B1
Greenvale BA2 . . . .**116** B1
Greenvale Cl BA2 . . . . . .**116** B1
Greenvale Dr BA2 . . . . . .**116** B1
Greenvale Rd BS39 . . . .**132** D5
Greenview BS30 . . . .**66** A2
Greenway BA3 . . . .**135** C1
Greenway Bush La
 BS3 . . . .**63** B4
Greenway Ct BA2 . . . . . .**101** F4
Greenway Dr BS10 . . . . .**49** D8
Greenway Farm BS30 . . .**67** E5
Greenway Ho 10 BS6 . . .**49** B2
Greenway La
 Bath BA2 . . . .**102** A4
 Cold Ashton SN14 . . . . . .**68** D5
Greenway Pk
 Bristol BS10 . . . .**49** D8
 3 Clevedon BS21 . . . . .**57** H3
Greenway Rd BS6 . . . . . .**49** B2
Greenways
 Bristol BS15 . . . .**52** A1
 Chilcompton BA3 . . . . . .**138** C2
Greenways Rd 4 BS37 . .**27** E3
Greenway The BS16 . . . .**51** C3
Greenwell La BS40 . . . .**109** C7

Greenwich Apartments
 BS6. . . . .**49** C3
Green Wlk BS4 . . . .**64** A1
Greenwood Cl BS7 . . . . .**49** E7
Greenwood Dr BS35. . . .**14** F4
Greenwood Rd
 Bristol BS4. . . . .**64** A1
 Weston-s-M BS22 . . . . . .**88** E2
Gregory Ct BS30 . . . .**66** A4
Gregory Mead BS49 . . . .**74** A1
Gregorys Gr BA2 . . . . . .**118** D8
Gregorys Tyning BS39 .**132** F6
Greinton BS24 . . . .**105** A2
Grenville Ave BS24 . . . .**106** A4
Grenville Chapel 5
 BS8. . . . .**62** F5
Grenville Cl BS5 . . . .**64** F8
Grenville Pl 7 BS1. . . . .**62** F5
Grenville Rd BS6 . . . .**49** E3
Greve Ct 5 BS30. . . . . . .**65** F4
Greville Rd BS3 . . . .**63** B4
Greville St BS3. . . . .**63** C4
GREYFIELD **115** C2
Greyfield Comm BS39 . .**115** C2
Greyfield Rd BS39. . . . . .**115** C2
Greyfield View BS39. . . .**114** F1
Grey Gables BS35 . . . . . .**14** A3
Grey Hollow BS40. . . . . .**129** F4
Greylands Rd BS13 . . . . .**78** F7
Greystoke Ave BS10 . . . .**35** C1
Greystoke Bsns Ctr
 BS20. . . . .**45** D4
Greystoke Gdns BS10. . .**49** A8
Greystones BS16 . . . .**37** E1
Grib La BS40 . . . .**110** F2
Griffen Rd BS24 . . . .**105** E7
Grindell Rd BS5. . . . .**64** D7
Grinfield Ave BS13 . . . . .**79** C4
Grinfield Ct BS13 . . . . . .**79** C4
Grittleton Rd BS7 . . . .**49** E8
GROSVENOR **85** C1
Grosvenor Bridge Rd
 BA1 . . . .**85** C1
Grosvenor Ct 2 BS6 . . . .**49** B1
Grosvenor Pk BA1 . . . . . .**85** C1
Grosvenor Pl BA1 . . . .**85** C1
Grosvenor Rd
 Bristol BS2. . . . .**49** F1
 Bristol BS2. . . . .**143** C4
Grosvenor Terr BA1 . . . . .**85** C2
Grosvenor Villas 9
 BA1 . . . .**85** B1
Grove Ave
 Bristol BS1. . . . .**143** A1
 Bristol, Coombe Dingle
 BS9 . . . .**48** C7
 3 Bristol, Fishponds
 BS16 . . . .**50** F4
Grove Bank BS16 . . . .**37** C1
Grove Ct BS9 . . . .**48** E5
Grove Dr BS22 . . . .**88** C1
Grove Hall BS4 . . . .**64** D2
Grove Ho BA2. . . . .**102** B6
Grove Ind Est The BS34 .**36** B8
Grove Jun Sch BS48. . . . .**75** D8
Grove La
 Faulkland BA3 . . . .**135** D2
 Hinton SN14 . . . .**54** C6
 Weston-s-M BS23 . . . . .**104** D8
Grove Leaze BS11 . . . . . .**47** D6
Grove Mews The BS36 . .**37** E7
Grove Orch BS40. . . . . .**110** D2
Grove Park Ave BS4 . . . . .**64** D2
Grove Park Ct BS23 . . . . .**87** D1
Grove Park Rd
 Bristol BS4. . . . .**64** D2
 Weston-s-M BS23 . . . . . .**87** D1
Grove Park Terr BS16. . . .**50** F4
Grove Pk
 Bristol, Brislington BS4 . .**64** D2
 Bristol, Redland BS6 . . . .**49** C2
Grove Rd
 Banwell BS29 . . . .**106** E4
 Bristol, Coombe Dingle
 BS9 . . . .**48** D8
 Bristol, Fishponds BS16. .**50** F4
 Bristol, Redland BS6 . . . .**49** A2
 Weston-s-M BS23 . . . . .**104** D8
 Weston-s-M, Milton BS22 **88** C1
Grovesend Rd BS35 . . . .**15** D8
Grove St BA2 . . . .**141** C3
Groves The BS13 . . . .**79** D4
Grove The
 Bath BA1 . . . .**84** C1
 Bristol BS1. . . . .**143** A1
 Bristol, Oldland BS30. . . .**66** A4
 Bristol, Patchway BS34 . .**36** B7
 Hallatrow BS39 . . . .**132** B7
 Rangeworthy BS37 . . . . .**27** A8
 Winscombe BS25 . . . . . .**107** F1
 Wraxall BS48. . . . .**60** C3
Grove View BS16 . . . .**50** E6
Grove Wood Rd BA3. . . .**133** F1

Guardian Ct 8 BS8 . . . . .**62** F7
Guernsey Ave BS4. . . . . .**64** F4
Guernsey Rd BS25 . . . .**124** F7
Guest Ave BS16 . . . .**52** B7
Gug The BS39. . . . .**115** C2
Guild Ct BS1. . . . .**143** B2
Guildford Rd BS4 . . . .**64** E6
Guildhall The★
 Bath BA1 . . . .**141** C2
 Bristol BS1. . . . .**143** A3
Guinea La
 Bath BA1 . . . .**141** C3
 Bristol BS16. . . . .**51** A4
 Bristol, Fishponds BS16. .**51** A5
Guinea St BS1. . . . .**143** A1
Gullen BA2 . . . .**135** A6
Gulliford's Bank BS21 . .**57** H2
Gullimores Gdns BS13. . .**79** B4
Gullivers Pl BS37 . . . .**40** A8
Gullock Tyning BA3 . . . .**133** B1
Gullons Cl BS13. . . . .**79** A6
Gullon Wlk BS13 . . . .**78** F5
Gullybrook La 3 BS5 . . . .**64** B6
Gully La BS35. . . . .**8** E7
Gully The BS36. . . . .**37** F7
Gumhurn La BS35. . . . . . .**22** E7
Gunning Cl BS15. . . . .**65** D6
Gunter's Hill BS5 . . . .**65** A6
Guthrie Rd BS8 . . . .**142** A4
Gwilliam St BS3 . . . .**63** D3
Gwyn St BS2. . . . .**49** E1
Gypsy La
 Keynsham BS31. . . . .**99** B8
 Marshfield SN14 . . . .**69** F7
Gypsy Moth La BS24. . . .**105** C5

H

Haberfield Hill BS8 . . . . .**47** E2
Haberfield Ho 1 BS8 . . . .**62** F6
Hacket Hill BS35 . . . .**15** F8
Hacket La BS35. . . . .**15** F8
Haddrell Ct BS35. . . . .**14** F5
Hadley Ct BS30 . . . .**66** B6
Hadley Rd BA2 . . . .**102** B2
Hadrian Cl BS9 . . . .**48** C4
Hadrians Wlk BS16 . . . . . .**52** C6
Hadwells Rd 7 BS34 . . . .**35** F7
Haig Cl BS9. . . . .**48** B7
Hailwood Rd 8 BS15. . . . .**65** D5
Halbrow Cres BS16. . . . . .**51** C5
Haldon Cl BS3 . . . .**63** D1
Hale Cl BS15. . . . .**65** D4
Hales Horn Cl BS32 . . . . .**36** D6
Half Acre Cl BS14 . . . .**80** A3
Halfacre La BS14. . . . .**80** B4
Halfpenny Row BA11. . .**137** E1
Halfway Gdn BS34 . . . . . .**35** E7
Half Yd BS40. . . . .**109** D8
Halifax Rd BS37. . . . .**27** D4
Hallam Ct BS21 . . . .**57** E4
Hallam Rd BS21 . . . .**57** E4
Hallards Cl BS11 . . . .**47** F8
HALLATROW **132** B7
Hallatrow Bsns Pk
 BS39. . . . .**132** A6
Hallatrow Rd BS39 . . . . .**132** C6
HALLEN **34** C5
Hallen Cl
 Bristol, Emerson's Green
 BS16 . . . .**52** C6
 Bristol, Henbury BS10 . . .**34** D3
HALL END **17** D2
Hall End La BS37. . . . .**17** D2
Hallen Dr BS9 . . . .**48** C7
Hallen Ind Est BS10 . . . . .**34** A7
Hallen Rd BS10. . . . .**34** D4
Halletts Way BS20. . . . . . .**45** D5
Halliwell Rd BS20. . . . .**44** D4
Hall La
 Cold Ashton BA1 . . . .**68** B3
 Horton BS37 . . . .**29** E5
Halls Gdns BS34. . . . .**37** A4
Halls Rd BS15. . . . .**65** D8
Hall St BS3 . . . .**63** C2
Hall The BS20. . . . .**44** F5
Halsbury Rd BS6. . . . .**49** B4
Halstock Ave BS16 . . . . . .**50** F3
Halston Dr BS2 . . . .**143** C4
Halswell Gdns BS13 . . . . .**79** B4
Halswell Rd BS21 . . . .**57** F1
Halt End BS14 . . . .**80** C3
Halwyn Cl BS9 . . . .**48** D5
HAM **132** F5
Hamble Cl BS35. . . . .**15** C8
Hambledon Ho BS6 . . . .**142** C4
Hambledon Rd BS22 . . . . .**89** C4
HAMBROOK **37** C3
Hambrook La BS34. . . . . . .**37** A3
Hambrook Prim Sch
 BS16. . . . .**37** D3
Ham Cl BS39 . . . .**114** F1
Ham Farm La BS16. . . . . .**52** B6
Ham Gn BS20. . . . .**47** D3
Ham Gr BS39 . . . .**132** E5
HAM GREEN **47** E4
Ham Hill BA3 . . . .**133** F3
Hamilton Ct 11 BS1. . . . .**143** A4

Hamilton Ho BA1 . . . .**84** E3
Hamilton Rd
 Bath BA1 . . . .**84** E2
 Bristol, Southville BS3 . . .**63** B4
 Bristol, Upper Easton
 BS5 . . . .**64** B8
 8 Weston-s-M BS23 . . . .**87** C1
Hamilton Terr BA2 . . . . .**134** F5
Ham La
 Bishop Sutton BS39 . . . .**113** C5
 Bristol BS16. . . . .**50** E6
 Doynton BS30 . . . .**53** E1
 Dundry BS41. . . . .**78** D3
 Farrington Gurney BS39 .**131** F5
 Kingston Seymour BS21. . .**73** B2
 Oldbury-on-S BS35 . . . .**7** C7
 Paulton BS39 . . . .**132** E5
 Wraxall BS48. . . . .**60** B4
 Yatton BS49 . . . .**74** A3
Hamlet The BS48. . . . .**60** A3
Ham Link BS40 . . . .**109** F3
Hammersmith Rd BS5. . . .**64** D8
Hammond Cl BS4 . . . .**64** E1
Hammond Gdns BS9 . . . . .**48** E7
Hammond Rd BS34. . . . . . .**35** F7
Hampden Cl BS37. . . . .**27** D4
Hampden Rd
 Bristol BS4. . . . .**64** B3
 Weston-s-M BS22 . . . .**88** E2
Hampshire Way 3
 BS37. . . . .**27** F4
Hampstead Rd BS4. . . . . .**64** C3
Hampton Cl BS30 . . . .**66** A5
Hampton Cnr BS11. . . . . . .**47** E6
Hampton Ct BS6 . . . .**49** B1
Hampton Hall BA2 . . . . .**102** D8
Hampton Ho 10 BA1. . . . .**85** C1
Hampton La
 17 Bristol BS6. . . . .**49** B1
 Bristol BS6. . . . .**142** B4
Hampton Pk BS6. . . . .**49** B1
Hampton Rd BS6. . . . .**49** B1
Hampton Row BA2 . . . . .**102** B8
Hampton St BS15 . . . .**51** D1
Hampton View BA1. . . . . .**85** B1
Ham Rd BS24, TA8 . . . . . .**121** B3
Hams La BS26 . . . .**123** C3
Hams Rd BS31. . . . .**81** F7
HAMWOOD **123** C7
Ham Wood Cl BS24. . . . . .**105** B2
Hanbury Cl BS15. . . . .**65** D5
Hanbury Ct BS8. . . . .**142** A4
Hanbury Rd BS8 . . . .**142** A4
Handel Ave 2 BS5 . . . . . .**64** D7
Handel Cossham Ct 3
 BS15. . . . .**51** C1
Handel Rd BS31. . . . .**81** E5
Handford Way BS30 . . . . .**66** B3
Hanford Ct BS14 . . . .**80** D7
Hang Hill BA2 . . . .**135** A6
HANHAM **65** C4
Hanham Abbots Jun Sch
 BS15. . . . .**65** C4
Hanham Bsns Pk BS15 . .**65** B5
HANHAM GREEN **65** C3
Hanham High Sch BS15 **65** C4
Hanham La BS39. . . . .**132** F7
Hanham Lodge BS15. . . . .**65** D7
Hanham Mills BS15 . . . . .**65** D1
Hanham Rd BS15 . . . .**65** D7
Hanham Way BS48 . . . . . .**59** B2
Hanna Cl BA2 . . . .**101** B6
Hannah More Cl BS40. . . .**92** E4
Hannah More Inf Sch
 BS48. . . . .**75** D8
Hannah More Prim Sch
 BS2. . . . .**143** C2
Hannah More Rd BS48 . . .**75** D8
Hannay Rd BS27 . . . .**126** B1
Hanover Cl BS22 . . . .**89** A4
Hanover Ct
 Bath BA1 . . . .**85** B2
 Bristol, Filton BS34 . . . . .**36** A3
 Radstock BA3. . . . .**134** C2
Hanover Ho
 Bristol BS2. . . . .**64** A7
 Portishead BS20 . . . .**45** B5
Hanover Pl
 Bath BA1 . . . .**102** B8
 4 Bathwick BA2. . . . . . .**102** B8
 Bristol BS1. . . . .**142** B1
Hanover St
 2 Bath BA1 . . . .**85** B1
 2 Bristol BS1 . . . .**143** A2
 Bristol, Russell Town BS5 **64** C7
Hanover Terr 5 BA1 . . . . .**85** B1
Hansford Cl BA2. . . . .**101** E1
Hansford Mews BA2. . . . .**101** F1
Hansford Sq BA2. . . . . . .**101** E1
Hanson's Way 4 BS21 . . .**57** C2
Hans Price Cl 18 BS23 **104** E8
Hans Price Ho 18
 BS23. . . . .**104** E8
Hantone Hill BA2 . . . . . .**102** F8
Happerton La BS20 . . . . . .**47** D2
Hapsburg Cl BS22 . . . .**89** A4
Harbour Cres BS20. . . . . . .**45** E5
Harbour Ho BS8 . . . .**142** A1
Harbour Rd BS20 . . . .**45** D6

Harbour Road Trad Est
 BS20. . . . .**45** F6
Harbours Edge BS8 . . . .**142** B2
Harbour Wall BS9. . . . . . .**48** B4
Harbour Way BS1. . . . . .**142** C1
Harbour Wlk BS1 . . . . . .**142** C1
Harbury Rd BS9. . . . .**49** C7
Harbutts BA2 . . . .**85** F1
Harcombe Hill BS36. . . . . .**37** C4
Harcombe Rd BS36 . . . . . .**37** D5
Harcourt Ave BS5 . . . .**65** A6
Harcourt Cl BS31 . . . .**82** E2
Harcourt Gdns BA1 . . . . . .**84** B2
Harcourt Hill BS6 . . . .**49** C3
Harcourt Rd BS6. . . . .**49** B3
Hardenhuish Rd BS4 . . . . .**64** D5
Harden Rd BS14 . . . .**80** E5
Harding Dr BS29. . . . .**106** C7
Harding Rd BS16. . . . .**36** F2
Hardings La BA2 . . . .**99** A1
Hardings Row BS2 . . . . . .**64** B4
Hardington Dr BS31. . . . . .**82** A2
Hardwick Cl
 Bristol, Broom Hill BS4 . .**64** E3
 Bristol, North Common
 BS30. . . . .**66** D5
Hardwicke BS37 . . . .**39** C7
Hardwick Rd BS20. . . . . . .**47** C5
Hardy Ave BS3. . . . .**63** A4
Hardy Ct BS30 . . . .**65** F5
Hardy La BS32. . . . .**14** A1
Hardy Rd BS3. . . . .**63** B2
Harebell Rd BS16 . . . .**52** D8
Hareclive Prim Sch
 BS13. . . . .**79** C4
Hareclive Rd BS13 . . . . . .**79** C4
Harefield Cl BS15. . . . .**65** C2
Harescombe BS37 . . . .**39** E7
Harewood Ho BS6 . . . .**49** A3
Harewood Rd BS5. . . . .**51** A4
Harford Cl BS9. . . . .**48** C7
Harford Dr BS16 . . . .**37** C1
Harford Sq BS40 . . . .**96** B3
Harington Pl 2 BA1 . . . . .**141** B2
Harlech Way BS30 . . . .**66** B2
Harleston St 1 BS5 . . . . . .**64** A8
Harley Ct 3 BS8 . . . .**62** F7
Harley La BS21. . . . .**58** C6
Harley Mews 2 BS8 . . . . .**62** F7
Harley Pl 4 BS8. . . . .**62** F7
Harmer Cl BS10. . . . .**34** F3
Harmony Dr BS20 . . . .**44** F4
Harnhill Cl BS13 . . . .**79** B4
Harolds Way BS15. . . . . . .**65** C6
Harpsichord Way
 BS31. . . . .**82** B4
Harptree BS24 . . . .**105** A2
Harptree Cl BS48 . . . .**75** D8
Harptree Ct 5 BS30. . . . . .**66** A4
Harptree Gr BS3 . . . .**63** B2
Harptree Hill BS40 . . . . . .**129** B5
Harptree La BA3 . . . .**130** C1
Harrier Path 3 BS22 . . . .**105** E8
Harriets Yd BS31. . . . .**81** F5
Harrington Ave BS14 . . . . .**80** E6
Harrington Cl BS30 . . . . . .**82** E8
Harrington Gr BS14 . . . . . .**80** E6
Harrington Rd BS14 . . . . . .**80** E6
Harrington Wlk BS14. . . . .**80** E6
Harris Barton BS36. . . . . .**38** B7
Harris Ct BS30 . . . .**65** F4
Harris Gr BS13 . . . .**79** B3
Harris La BS8 . . . .**61** F8
Harrison Cl BS16. . . . .**52** B6
Harrowdene Rd BS4. . . . . .**64** B3
Harrow Rd BS4 . . . .**64** D3
HARRY STOKE **36** E2
Harry Stoke Rd BS34. . . . .**36** E2
Hart Cl BS20. . . . .**47** E4
HARTCLIFFE **79** C4
Hartcliffe Engineering
 Com Coll BS13 . . . .**79** E4
Hartcliffe Rd BS4 . . . .**79** E8
Hartcliffe Way BS3, BS4,
 BS13. . . . .**79** C7
Hartcliffe Wlk BS4 . . . . . .**79** F8
Hartfield Ave BS6 . . . . . .**142** C4
Hartgill Cl BS13. . . . .**79** B3
Hartington Pk BS6 . . . .**49** C2
Hartland 14 BS22 . . . .**89** A2
Hartland Ho BS5 . . . .**64** C6
Hartley Cl BS37 . . . .**28** C1
Hartley Ho BA1 . . . .**141** B3
Harts Croft BS37 . . . .**27** F4
Hart's La BS39 . . . .**132** B7
Harts Paddock BA3 . . . . .**132** F3
Harvest Cl BS32 . . . .**24** D1
Harvest La BS22 . . . .**106** B8
Harvest Way
 Thornbury BS35. . . . .**8** B3
 Weston-s-M BS22 . . . .**89** A5
Harvey Cl BS22 . . . .**89** A4
Harvey's La 6 BS5. . . . . . .**64** F8
Harwood Gn BS22. . . . . . .**88** E4
Harwood Ho 14 BS5 . . . . .**64** B7
Harwood Sq BS7. . . . .**49** E5
Haselbury Gr BS31. . . . . . .**82** E2
Haskins Ct 4 BS30. . . . . . .**66** A4

Haslemere Ind Est
BS11. . . . . .33 C2
Hassage Farm La BA3 136 A3
Hassage Hill BA2 . . . . .135 E7
Hassell Dr BS2. . . . . . . .64 A7
Hastings Cl BS3. . . . . . . .63 C1
Hastings Rd BS3 . . . . . . .63 C1
Hatches La BS24 . . . . . .121 E3
Hatchet Hill BA3, BA11 140 E4
Hatchet La BS34 . . . . . . .36 E4
Hatchet Rd BS34. . . . . . .36 E5
Hatchmere BS35. . . . . . .15 D8
Hatfield Bldgs BA2. . . .102 B5
Hatfield Rd
  Bath BA2 . . . . .101 F3
  Weston-s-M BS23 . . . .105 A8
Hathaway Ho 13 BS2 . .143 A4
Hatherley BS37 . . . . .39 E7
Hatherley Rd BS7. . . . . .49 E4
Hathway Wlk BS5. . . . . .64 A8
Hatters' La BS37 . . . . . . .28 C1
Hatton Rd BS7. . . . . .50 C8
Haugh BA15 . . . . .103 D2
Haven The BS15. . . . . . . .51 E1
Haversham Cl BS22 . . . .88 D1
Haverstock Rd BS4. . . . .64 A3
Haviland Gr BA1 . . . . . . .84 B3
Haviland Ho 7 BS2 . . .143 C3
Haviland Pk BA1. . . . . . .84 B2
Havory BA1. . . . . .85 C1
Havyat Rd BS40 . . . . . .109 E8
Havyat Road Trad Est
  BS40. . . . . .92 E1
HAVYATT GREEN. . . .109 F7
Hawarden Terr BA1 . . . .85 B1
Hawburn Cl BS4 . . . . . . .64 D2
Haweswater BS10. . . . . .35 B2
Haweswater Cl BS30. . . .66 D6
Hawke Rd BS22 . . . . . . .88 E4
HAWKESBURY. 19 D2
Hawkesbury CE Prim Sch
  GL9. . . . . .19 F3
Hawkesbury Grange
  GL9. . . . . .20 A2
Hawkesbury Rd
  Bristol BS16. . . . . .50 E3
  Hillesley GL12 . . . . . . .19 D6
HAWKESBURY UPTON. 20 A3
Hawkesley Dr BS34. . . . .36 D6
Hawkesworth Rd BS37 . 27 C3
Hawkfield Bsns Pk
  BS14. . . . . .79 D5
Hawkfield Cl BS14 . . . . .79 D5
Hawkfield Rd BS13. . . . .79 D5
Hawkfield Way BS14 . . .79 D5
Hawkins Cl BS30 . . . . . .66 C5
Hawkins Cres BS32. . . . .36 E8
Hawkins St BS2. . . . . . .143 C3
Hawkley Dr BS32. . . . . . .24 D3
Hawkridge Dr BS16. . . . .53 C5
Hawksmoor Cl BS14. . . .80 A6
Hawksmoor La BS16. . . .50 E8
Hawksworth Dr
  Bristol BS15. . . . . .65 B5
  Weston-s-M BS22 . . . .89 C4
Haw La BS35. . . . . .14 B3
Hawley's La G12. . . . . . .10 D2
Hawthorn Ave BS15 . . . .65 B5
Hawthorn Cl
  Bristol BS34. . . . . .35 E7
  Charfield GL12. . . . . . . .11 A4
  Portishead BS20 . . . . . .44 F5
Hawthorn Coombe
  BS22. . . . . .88 E3
Hawthorn Cres
  Thornbury BS35. . . . . . .8 C2
  Yatton BS49. . . . . .74 A2
Hawthorne Cl BS16. . . . .53 C5
Hawthorne Gdns BS16 . 51 F4
Hawthorne Rise BS10. . .35 C3
Hawthorne St BS5 . . . . .64 A3
Hawthornes The BS16. . .51 F4
Hawthorn Gdns BS22. . .88 D2
Hawthorn Gr BA2 . . . . .102 A1
Hawthorn Hill BS22 . . . .88 E2
Hawthorn Hts BS22. . . . .88 D3
Hawthorn Pk BS22 . . . . .88 E3
Hawthorn Rd BA3. . . . .134 B2
Hawthorns La BS31 . . . .81 E5
Hawthorns The BS21 . . .57 E3
Hawthorn Way
  Bristol BS34. . . . . .36 E5
  Lyde Green BS16 . . . . .52 C8
  Nailsea BS48. . . . . .60 A2
Haybob Rd BS35. . . . . . . .8 B3
Hayboro Way BS39. . . . .132 E4
Haybow BS24 . . . . .89 E2
Haycombe BS14 . . . . . . .79 F6
Haycombe Dr BA2. . . . .101 A4
Haycombe La BA2 . . . . .101 A3
Haycroft La GL13. . . . . . .4 C6
Haycroft Rd BS34 . . . . . .36 A3
Hayden Cl BA2. . . . . . . .141 A1
HAYDON. 139 F8
Haydon Ct 12 BS8 . . . . .49 A2
Haydon Gate BA3 . . . . .139 F8
Haydon Gdns BS7. . . . . .50 B5

Haydon Hill BA3 . . . . . .140 A8
Haydon Ind Est BA3. . . .139 F8
Hayeley Dr BS32. . . . . . .36 E6
Hayes Cl BS2 . . . . .64 A7
Hayes Ct BS34 . . . . .36 A7
Hayesfield Pk BA2 . . . . .141 B1
Hayesfield School Tech
  Coll (Upper) BA2 . . . .141 A1
Hayesfield Sch Tech Coll
  (Lower) BA2 . . . . .101 D6
Haye's La GL9 . . . . .30 F2
HAYES PARK. 133 A2
Hayes Park Rd BA3. . . .132 F2
Hayes Pl BA2 . . . . .141 B1
Hayes Rd BA3. . . . . . . .132 F1
Hayes Way BS34 . . . . . . .36 A6
Hayeswood Farm
  BA15. . . . . .103 F5
Hayeswood Rd BA2 . . . .115 E3
Hayfield SN14 . . . . .70 A8
Hay Fields BS35. . . . . . . .8 C3
Haygarth Ct BA1. . . . . .141 B4
Hay Hill BA1. . . . . .141 B3
Hay La BS40 . . . . .94 D6
Hay Leaze BS37. . . . . . . .27 D4
Hayleigh Ho BS13. . . . . .79 C4
Haymarket The BS1 . . .143 A3
Haymarket Wlk 9
  BS1. . . . . .143 A4
Haynes Ho 3 BS16. . . . .51 D4
Haynes La BS16. . . . . . . .51 D5
Hay St
  Farrington Gurney
    BA3 . . . . .138 A8
  Marshfield SN14 . . . . . .70 A8
Hayter Ct BS10. . . . . . . .35 D3
Haythorn Ct BS16 . . . . .51 F5
Haythorne Ct 8 BS16 . .50 D4
Haytor Pk BS9 . . . . .48 D6
Hayward Cl BS5 . . . . . . .64 C7
Hayward Ind Est 1
  BS16. . . . . .51 D3
Hayward Rd
  Bristol, Russell Town
    BS5 . . . . .64 C7
  Bristol, Staple Hill BS16 .51 D3
Haywood Cl BS24 . . . . .105 A1
Haywood Gdns BS24 . .105 B1
Hazel Ave BS6 . . . . .49 B2
Hazel Barrow BS40. . . .129 A7
Hazelbury Dr BS30. . . . .66 C6
Hazelbury Rd
  Bristol BS14. . . . . .80 C7
  Nailsea BS48. . . . . .59 D1
Hazel Cl BS37. . . . . .27 F5
Hazel Cote Rd BS14. . . .80 A4
Hazel Cres BS35. . . . . . . .8 D1
Hazeldene Rd
  Bristol BS34. . . . . .36 A7
  Weston-s-M BS23 . . . .105 A8
Hazel Gdns BS35. . . . . . .15 A4
Hazel Gr
  Bath BA2 . . . . .101 D4
  Bristol BS7. . . . . .50 A8
  Midsomer Norton BA3. .139 B8
Hazelgrove BS36. . . . . . .37 E5
Hazel La BS32, BS35 . . . .14 E3
Hazell Cl BS21. . . . . .57 G1
Hazel St BS14. . . . . .79 E5
Hazel Terr BA3. . . . . . . .139 C8
Hazelton Rd BS7. . . . . . .49 D3
Hazel Way BA2 . . . . . . .118 D6
Hazelwood Ct BS9. . . . .48 D3
Hazelwood Rd BS9. . . . .48 D3
Hazleton Gdns BA2 . . .102 F3

Heathfield Rd BS48 . . . .59 E3
Heathfields BS16. . . . . . .51 D8
Heathfield Way BS48. . . .59 E2
Heathgate BS49. . . . . . . .91 B8
Heathgates BS23. . . . . .104 D4
Heath Gdns
  Bristol BS16. . . . . .51 D8
  Frampton Cotterell BS36 38 C5
Heath House La BS7,
  BS16. . . . . .50 C5
Heath House Priory Hospl
  BS16. . . . . .50 B4
Heath Rd
  Bristol, Downend BS16 . .51 D8
  Bristol, Eastville BS5 . . .50 B3
  Bristol, Hanham BS15 . .65 B4
  Nailsea BS48. . . . . .59 F3
Heath Ridge BS41. . . . . .62 A2
Heath Rise BS30 . . . . . . .66 B5
Heath St BS5 . . . . .50 C3
Heath The BS9. . . . . .48 E3
Heath Wlk BS16. . . . . . .51 D7
Hebden Rd BA15. . . . . .120 F3
Heber St BS5 . . . . .64 C7
Hebron Ct BS3. . . . . .63 C3
Hebron Rd BS3 . . . . .63 C3
Hedgemead Cl BS16. . . .50 D5
Hedgemead Ct BA1. . . .141 C4
Hedgemead View BS16. .50 E5
Hedgerows 2 BS32. . . . .24 D1
Hedgers Cl BS3. . . . . . . .63 A2
Hedges Cl 3 BS21. . . . .57 D1
Hedges The BS22 . . . . . .89 C3
Hedwick Ave BS5. . . . . .64 E7
Hedwick St BS5. . . . . . . .64 E7
Heggard Cl BS13. . . . . . .79 A5
Helens Rd BS25. . . . . . .108 B4
Heligan Wlk BS24. . . . .105 E7
Hellier Wlk BS13. . . . . . .79 C3
Helston Rd BS48. . . . . . .60 A1
Hemmings Par 4 BS5. .64 B7
Hemming Way BS24. . . .105 E3
Hemplow Cl BS14. . . . . .80 D7
Hempton Field Dr BS34 36 A7
Hempton La BS32. . . . . .24 B2
Henacre Rd BS11. . . . . .47 F8
HENBURY 34 E2
Henbury Court Prim Sch
  BS10. . . . . .34 F3
Henbury Ct BS10. . . . . . .34 E3
Henbury Gdns BS10 . . . .34 E2
Henbury Hill
  Bristol BS9. . . . . .34 F1
  Bristol BS9. . . . . .48 F8
Henbury Ho BA2 . . . . . .102 E4
Henbury Rd
  Bristol BS9. . . . . .48 F8
  Bristol, Hanham BS15 . .65 B5
  Bristol, Henbury BS10 . .34 F2
  Bristol, Westbury on Trym
    BS9 . . . . .49 A8
Henbury Sch BS10. . . . . .34 E3
Hencliffe Rd BS14. . . . . .80 D7
Hencliffe Way BS15 . . . .65 B3
Henderson Ho 1 BS2 143 B4
Henderson Rd BS15. . . .65 B5
Hendre Rd BS3. . . . . . . .63 A2
Heneage La GL12 . . . . . .9 F8
HENFIELD. 38 D3
Henfield Bsns Pk BS36 . 38 D2
Henfield Cres BS30. . . . .66 B3
Henfield Rd BS36 . . . . . .38 C4
Hengasson La BS39 . . . .113 E6
Hengaston St BS3. . . . . .63 B2
HENGROVE. 80 B6
Hengrove Ave BS14 . . . .80 B8
Hengrove Com Arts Coll
  BS14. . . . . .80 B7
Hengrove La BS14 . . . . .80 B8
Hengrove Rd BS4. . . . . .64 A2
Hengrove Way BS14. . . .79 E6
Hen La BS40 . . . . .94 E3
HENLEAZE 49 C6
Henleaze Ave BS9. . . . . .49 A5
Henleaze Gdns BS9 . . . .49 A5
Henleaze Jun & Inf Schs
  BS9. . . . . .49 B6
Henleaze Park Dr BS9. . .49 C5
Henleaze Pk BS9 . . . . . .49 C5
Henleaze Rd BS9 . . . . . .49 B6
Henleaze Terr BS9 . . . . .49 B7
Henley Gr BS9 . . . . .49 B5
Henley Grove Ct BS9 . . .49 B5
Henley La BS49 . . . . .91 D7
Henley Lodge BS49 . . . .91 D7
Henley Pk BS49. . . . . . . .91 C7
Henley View BA2. . . . . .118 D1
Hennessy Cl BS14. . . . . .79 F3
Henrietta Ct BA2. . . . . .141 C4
Henrietta Gdns BA2 . . .141 C3
Henrietta Mews BA2 . . .141 C3
Henrietta Pl BA2. . . . . .141 C3
Henrietta Rd BA2 . . . . .141 C3
Henrietta St
  Bath BA2 . . . . .141 C3
  Bristol BS2. . . . . .143 A4
  5 Bristol, Lower Easton
    BS5 . . . . .50 B1
Henrietta Villas BA2 . . .141 C3

Henry Butt Ho 11
  BS23. . . . . .104 E8
Henry Corbett Rd
  BS16. . . . . .50 F8
Henry Shute Rd
  Lockleaze BS16 . . . . . . .50 E8
  Lockleaze BS16 . . . . . . .50 F8
Henry St
  Bath BA1 . . . . .141 C2
  Bristol BS3. . . . . .63 F4
Henry Williamson Ct 1
  BS30. . . . . .66 A5
Henshaw Cl BS15 . . . . . .51 C2
Henshaw Rd BS15. . . . . .51 C2
Henshaw Wlk BS15 . . . .51 C2
Hensley Gdns BA2. . . . .101 E4
Hensley Rd BA2 . . . . . . .101 E3
Hensman's Hill BS8 . . . .142 A2
Hepburn Rd BS2 . . . . . .143 B4
Herald Cl BS9. . . . . .48 D5
Herapath St BS5 . . . . . . .64 C6
Herbert Cres BS5 . . . . . .50 D3
Herbert Gdns BA2. . . . .115 E5
Herbert Rd
  Bath BA2 . . . . .101 D5
  Clevedon BS21. . . . . . . .57 F4
Herbert St
  Bristol, Moorfields BS5 . .64 C8
  Bristol, Southville BS3 . .63 D4
Hercules Cl BS34 . . . . . .36 D6
Hercules Wy BS31. . . . . .81 C3
Hereford Rd BS2. . . . . . .50 A2
Hereford St BS3 . . . . . . .63 D3
Heritage Cl BA2. . . . . . .134 D8
Heritage The BA2 . . . . .133 E8
Herkomer Cl BS7 . . . . . .50 B7
Herluin Way BS22,
  BS23. . . . . .105 B6
Hermes Cl BS31. . . . . . . .82 D2
Hermitage Cl BS11 . . . . .47 E7
Hermitage Rd
  Bath BA1 . . . . .84 E1
  Bristol BS16. . . . . .51 E5
Hermitage Wood Rd
  BS7. . . . . .50 C8
Hern La BS48. . . . . .77 E5
Heron Cl BS22 . . . . .105 E8
Heron Ct BS21 . . . . .57 E2
Heron Gdns BS20 . . . . . .45 E4
Heron Rd BS5. . . . . .50 B1
HERONS GREEN 112 C3
Herons Green La
  BS40. . . . . .112 C4
Herons Moor Acad
  BS24. . . . . .106 A8
Heron Way BS37 . . . . . . .40 A8
Heron Wlk BS21 . . . . . . .44 B1
Herridge Cl BS13 . . . . . .79 B4
Herridge Rd BS13. . . . . .79 B4
Hersey Gdns BS13. . . . . .78 E3
Hesding Cl BS15 . . . . . . .65 C3
Hestercombe Cl BS24 . .105 E7
Hestercombe Rd BS13. . .79 B6
Hester Wood BS37 . . . . .27 F4
Hestia Cl BS31. . . . . .81 C3
Hetling Ct 10 BA1. . . . .141 B2
Hewish Ct BS23. . . . . . .104 E8
Hewland Ct BS11 . . . . . .34 C2
Hexagon The BA2. . . . . .101 E1
Heyford Ave BS5. . . . . . .50 B4
Heyron Wlk BS13. . . . . . .79 B4
Heywood Rd BS20. . . . . .47 C4
Heywood Terr BS20 . . . .47 C4
Hibbs Cl SN14 . . . . .69 F8
Hicking Ct 8 BS15. . . . .51 D1
Hickory La BS32. . . . . . . .24 D5
Hicks Ave BS16 . . . . .52 B8
HICKS COMMON. 37 F5
Hicks Common Rd
  BS36. . . . . .37 E5
Hicks Ct
  Bristol, Crofts End BS5 . .64 E8
  Bristol, Stone Hill BS30 . 65 F4
HICKS GATE 81 B8
Hidcote Mews BS24 . . .105 E7
Hide Mkt BS2. . . . . .143 C3
Higgs Cl BS37 . . . . .27 F5
Higham St 4 BS2 . . . . .63 F4
High Acre BS39. . . . . . .132 F4
High Bannerdown
  Batheaston BA1. . . . . . . .86 B4
  Shockerwick BA1. . . . . . .86 B5
Highbury Cotts 7 BA1. 85 A1
Highbury Ct 15 BS23 . .87 C1
Highbury Farm Bsns Pk
  BS39. . . . . .132 A8
Highbury Par BS23. . . . .87 C1
Highbury Pl BA1. . . . . . .85 A1
Highbury Rd
  Bristol, Bedminster BS3 .63 C2
  Bristol, Horfield BS7 . . .49 E7
  Hallatrow BS39 . . . . . .132 B7
  Weston-s-M BS23 . . . . .87 C1
Highbury Terr 9 BA1. . .85 A1
Highbury Villas
  8 Bath BA1 . . . . .85 A1
  Bristol BS2. . . . . .142 C4
High Cnr BS10. . . . . .34 F1

Has–Hig 161

Highcroft
  3 Bristol BS30 . . . . . . .66 C6
  Weston-s-M BS23 . . . . .87 F1
Highdale Ave BS21. . . . . .57 G3
Highdale Cl BS14. . . . . . .80 B4
Highdale Cl BS21 . . . . . .57 F3
Highdale Rd BS21. . . . . .57 G3
High Down Jun & Inf Schs
  BS20. . . . . .45 A4
High Elm BS15. . . . . .65 E6
Highett Dr BS5 . . . . .50 A1
Highfield Ave BS15. . . . .65 D5
Highfield Cl BA2 . . . . . .101 B5
Highfield Cres BA3. . . . .138 C4
Highfield Dr BS20. . . . . .44 E3
Highfield Gdns BS30 . . .66 C2
Highfield Gr BS7. . . . . . .49 D5
Highfield La
  Compton Martin BS40 . .129 B6
  East Harptree BS40. . . .130 A3
  Horton BS37, GL9. . . . . .29 E7
Highfield Rd
  Chipping Sodbury BS37 . 28 A1
  Keynsham BS31 . . . . . . .81 F2
  Peasedown St John
    BA2. . . . . .134 C8
  Weston-s-M BS24 . . . . .105 A1
Highfields
  Clandown BA3 . . . . . . .133 E4
  Hawkesbury Upton GL9. .19 F2
  Stanton Drew BS39 . . . .96 F1
High Fields BA3. . . . . . .133 D2
Highfields Cl BS34 . . . . .36 F3
High Gr BS9 . . . . .48 B7
Highgrove St BS4 . . . . . .64 A4
Highgrove Wlk BS24 . . .106 A8
High Kingsdown BS2. . .142 C4
High La BS36 . . . . .37 C8
Highland Cl BS22 . . . . . .88 B2
Highland Cres 3 BS8 . .49 A2
Highland Pl 13 BS8. . . . .49 A2
Highland Rd BA2. . . . . .101 B5
Highlands Dr GL11. . . . . .5 E4
Highlands La BS24 . . . .106 A8
Highland Sq 4 BS8 . . . .49 A2
Highlands Rd
  Long Ashton BS41. . . . . .62 A2
  Portishead BS20 . . . . . .45 B5
Highland Terr 3 BA2. .101 D6
Highleaze Rd BS30. . . . .66 C4
High Leaze Rd 8 BS34 . 35 F7
HIGH LITTLETON 115 C1
High Littleton CE VA Prim
  Sch BS39. . . . . .115 C1
High Mdws BS23. . . . . .132 F1
Highmead Gdns
  Bishop Sutton BS39 . . . .113 D3
  Bristol BS13. . . . . .78 E4
Highmore Ct BS7 . . . . . .50 B7
Highmore Gdns BS7. . . .50 C7
Highnam Cl BS34 . . . . . .24 B1
High Pk
  Bristol BS14. . . . . .64 B1
  Paulton BS39 . . . . .132 D6
High Point Ho 1 BS15 . 51 C1
HIGHRIDGE
  Bristol 78 F7
  Dundry. 78 D3
Highridge Cres BS13. . . .78 F5
Highridge Gn BS13. . . . .78 E6
Highridge Inf Sch BS13. 78 F6
Highridge Pk BS13. . . . .78 F6
Highridge Rd
  Bristol, Bedminster BS3 .63 B2
  Bristol, Withywood BS13,
    BS41. . . . . .78 E4
Highridge Wlk BS13. . . .78 E7
High Six Gdns BS34 . . . .35 F6
High St
  Axbridge BS26 . . . . . . .125 B2
  Badminton GL9. . . . . . . .30 E2
  Banwell BS29. . . . . . . .107 A2
  Bath BA1 . . . . .141 C2
  Bathampton BA2 . . . . . .85 F1
  Batheaston BA1. . . . . . . .85 F3
  Bathford BA1. . . . . .86 D2
  Bath, Twerton BA2 . . . .101 B6
  Bath, Weston BA1 . . . . . .84 B1
  Bitton BS30 . . . . .82 E8
  Blagdon BS40. . . . . . . .110 E3
  Bristol BS1. . . . . .143 A2
  Bristol, Clifton BS8 . . . .49 A2
  Bristol, Jefferies Hill
    BS15. . . . . .65 C5
  Bristol, Kingswood BS15 65 E8
  Bristol, Lower Easton
    BS5 . . . . .50 B1
  Bristol, Oldland Common
    BS30 . . . . .66 D4
  Bristol, Shirehampton
    BS11. . . . . .47 E6
  Bristol, Staple Hill BS16 .51 D4
  Bristol, Warmley BS15. . .66 B8
  Bristol, Westbury on Trym
    BS9 . . . . .49 A7
  Chew Magna BS40. . . . .96 A3

High St continued
Chipping Sodbury BS37. . **28** B1
Claverham BS49. . . . . **74** F1
Congresbury BS49. . . . . . **91** D4
Doynton BS30 . . . . **53** F1
East Harptree BS40. . . . **129** F5
Faulkland BA3 . . . . **135** D1
Freshford BA2. . . . . **120** B5
Hawkesbury Upton GL9. . **19** F3
High Littleton BS39 . . . . **115** D1
Hillesley GL12 . . . . **19** D8
Hinton Charterhouse
 BA2. . . . . **119** C1
Iron Acton BS37. . . . . **26** D4
Keynsham BS31. . . . . **81** E6
Kingswood GL12 . . . . **11** F4
Marshfield SN14 . . . . **69** F8
Midsomer Norton BA3. . **133** B1
Nailsea BS48. . . . . **59** F3
Norton St Philip BA2. . . **136** E4
Paulton BS39 . . . . **132** E5
Paulton, Plummer's Hill
 BS39 . . . . **132** E6
Pensford BS39. . . . . **97** E4
Portbury BS20. . . . . **46** E3
Portishead BS20 . . . . **45** D5
Saltford BS31. . . . . **82** F3
Thornbury BS35. . . . . **15** B8
Timsbury BA2. . . . . **116** B2
Tormarton GL9. . . . . **41** D2
Wellow BA2. . . . . **118** D1
Weston-s-M BS23 . . . . . **104** D8
Weston-s-M, Worle BS22 **88** E2
Wick BS30 . . . . **67** D6
Wickwar GL12 . . . . **18** A5
Winford BS40. . . . . **95** A7
Winterbourne BS36. . . . . **37** D6
Woolley BA1. . . . . **84** F6
Wrington BS40. . . . . **92** D2
Yatton BS49. . . . . **91** C8
High View BS20. . . . . **45** A4
Highview Rd BS15 . . . . . . **51** F2
Highwall La BS14, BS31. **80** F1
Highway BS37 . . . . **27** F2
Highwood Bsns Pk
 BS34. . . . . **35** E7
Highwood La BS10,
 BS34. . . . . **35** D7
Highwood Pk Cvn Site
 BS34. . . . . **35** E6
Highwood Rd BS34. . . . . . **35** F7
Highworth Cres BS37. . . **39** D8
Highworth Rd BS4. . . . . . **64** D6
Hildesheim Bridge
 BS23. . . . . **104** F7
Hildesheim Cl BS23 . . . . **104** F6
Hildesheim Ct 9
 BS23. . . . . **104** E7
Hilhouse BS9. . . . . **48** C6
HILL. **2** D3
Hill Ave
 Bath BA2. . . . . **101** F1
 Bristol BS3. . . . . **63** E3
Hillbrook Rd 5 BS35. . **15** D8
Hill Burn BS9. . . . . **49** C6
Hillburn Rd BS5. . . . . **65** A8
Hill Cl BS16. . . . . **52** B8
Hillcote BS24. . . . . **122** B8
Hillcrest
 Peasedown St John
 BA2. . . . . **134** C7
 Pensford BS39. . . . . **97** E3
 Thornbury BS35. . . . . **8** B1
Hill Crest BS4. . . . . **64** B1
Hillcrest Cl BS48. . . . . . . **59** E1
Hillcrest Dr BA2 . . . . . . **101** C4
Hillcrest Prim Sch BS4 **64** A3
Hillcrest Rd
 Nailsea BS48. . . . . **59** E1
 Portishead BS20 . . . . . . **44** E4
Hillcroft Cl
 Bristol BS15. . . . . **65** E4
 Weston-s-M BS22 . . . . . **88** A2
Hill Ct BS39. . . . . **132** E6
Hilldale Rd BS48. . . . . . . **76** B5
Hill Dr BS8. . . . . **61** C3
Hillend BS22. . . . . **88** E3
Hill End Dr BS10. . . . . . . **34** D3
HILLESLEY. **19** E8
Hillesley CE Prim Sch
 GL12. . . . . **19** E8
Hillesley Rd GL12 . . . . . . **11** F4
HILLFIELDS. **51** B3
Hillfields Ave BS16. . . . . **51** C3
Hillfields Prim Sch
 BS16. . . . . **51** C2
Hill Gay Cl BS20. . . . . **44** F4
Hill Gr BS9. . . . . **49** C6
Hillgrove St BS2. . . . . . . **143** B4
Hillgrove Terr BS23. . . . **104** D1
HILLHOUSE. **52** A5
Hill House Rd BS16 . . . . . **51** F5
Hillier's La BS25. . . . . . **108** C4
Hill La
 Chipping Sodbury BS37. . **41** B7
 Clevedon BS21. . . . . **58** C4

Hill La continued
 Portishead BS20 . . . . . . **44** F1
 Rowberrow BS25. . . . . . **109** A1
 Thornbury BS35, GL13. . . **2** A2
Hill Lawn BS4. . . . . **64** D3
Hillmead BS40. . . . . **109** A5
Hillmer Rise BS29. . . . . **106** F3
Hill Moor BS21. . . . . **57** G2
Hillpath BS29. . . . . **107** B2
Hill Pk BS49. . . . . **91** E5
Hill Rd
 Clevedon BS21. . . . . **57** F4
 Dundry BS41. . . . . **78** D2
 Sandford BS25. . . . . **108** A3
 Weston-s-M BS23 . . . . . **104** F8
 Weston-s-M, Worle BS22 **88** E2
Hill Rd E BS22. . . . . **88** E2
Hill's Barton BS13. . . . . . **63** A1
Hillsborough BS8 . . . . . . **142** A2
Hillsborough Ho BS23 . . **105** A4
Hillsborough Rd BS4. . . . **64** C4
Hills Cl BS31. . . . . **82** A5
Hillsdon Rd BS9. . . . . **48** F8
HILLSIDE. **138** E8
Hillside
 Axbridge BS26. . . . . . . **125** C2
 Bristol BS6. . . . . **142** C4
 Bristol, Mangotsfield
 BS16. . . . . **52** A5
 Burton SN14. . . . . **43** A4
 Portbury BS20. . . . . **46** D3
Hillside Ave
 Bristol BS5. . . . . **65** C8
 Midsomer Norton BA3. . **138** F8
Hillside Cl
 Frampton Cotterell
 BS36. . . . . **38** C7
 Paulton BS39. . . . . **132** F6
Hillside Cres BA3. . . . . . **138** E8
Hillside Ct BS5. . . . . **65** B7
Hillside Fst Sch BS22. . . **88** E2
Hillside Gdns
 Bishop Sutton BS39. . . . **113** C3
 Weston-s-M BS22 . . . . . **88** B1
Hillside Ho 6 BS6. . . . . . **49** D1
Hillside La BS36. . . . . **38** C7
Hillside Rd
 Backwell BS48. . . . . **76** A4
 Bath BA2. . . . . **101** D4
 Bleadon BS24. . . . . **122** B8
 Bristol BS5. . . . . **65** A7
 Clevedon BS21. . . . . **57** F3
 Long Ashton BS41. . . . . . **62** B2
 Midsomer Norton BA3. . **138** F8
 Portishead BS20 . . . . . . **44** D4
Hillside St BS4. . . . . **64** A4
Hillside View
 Midsomer Norton BA3. . **133** A3
 Peasedown St John
 BA2. . . . . **134** C8
Hillside W BS24. . . . . . . **105** F2
Hill St
 Bristol BS1. . . . . **142** C2
 Bristol, Kingswood BS15 . **65** F8
 Bristol, St George BS5. . . **64** F8
 Bristol, Windmill Hill BS3 **63** F4
Hill The
 Almondsbury BS32. . . . . . **24** B4
 Freshford BA2. . . . . **120** C5
Hill Top BS20. . . . . **45** A4
Hilltop Gdns
 Bristol, St George BS5. . . **65** A7
 Bristol, Upper Soundwell
 BS16. . . . . **51** D2
Hilltop Rd BS16. . . . . **51** D2
Hill Tops BS20. . . . . **35** F6
Hilltop View BS5. . . . . . . **65** A7
Hillview
 Midsomer Norton BA3. . **138** E7
 Timsbury BA2. . . . . **116** B1
Hill View
 Bristol BS8. . . . . **142** B2
 Bristol, Blackhorse BS16 **52** A8
 Bristol, Filton BS34. . . . . **36** A3
 Bristol, Henleaze BS9 . . **49** C6
 Bristol, Upper Soundwell
 BS16. . . . . **51** D2
 Farrington Gurney BS39 **132** B3
 Marksbury BA2. . . . . **99** B1
 Priston BA2. . . . . **117** A5
Hillview Ave BS21. . . . . . **57** F2
Hill View Cl BS30. . . . . . . **66** C6
Hill View Ct
 Bristol BS16. . . . . **51** C5
 Weston-s-M BS22 . . . . . **105** D8
Hill View Cvn Pk BS40 . . **77** B1
Hillview Gdns BS40 . . . . . **94** C8
Hill View Ho 2 BS15 . . . . **51** C1
Hill View Park Homes
 BS22. . . . . **105** D8
Hillview Rd
 Loxton BS26. . . . . **123** C4
 Pucklechurch BS16. . . . . **53** C5
Hill View Rd
 Bath BA1. . . . . **85** B2
 Bristol BS13. . . . . **79** A8
 Weston-s-M BS23 . . . . . **105** A7
Hillyfield Rd BS13. . . . . . **79** A6

Hillyfields BS25 . . . . . . **125** B8
Hillyfields Way BS25 . . . **125** A8
Hilton Cl 5 BS5 . . . . **64** B8
Hinckley Cl BS22. . . . . . . **89** C4
Hind Pitts BS25. . . . . . . **125** F7
HINTON. **54** D6
Hinton BS24. . . . . **105** A2
HINTON BLEWETT **130** F6
Hinton Blewett Rd
 Hinton Blewett BS39. . . **130** E8
 Sutton Wick BS39. . . . . **113** E1
**HINTON
 CHARTERHOUSE** **119** E1
Hinton Cl
 Bath BA2. . . . . **100** F6
 Saltford BS31. . . . . **82** E3
Hinton Dr BS30. . . . . **66** C6
Hinton Hill BA2. . . . . . . **119** A1
Hinton La 13 BS8. . . . . . **62** F6
Hinton Rd
 Bristol, Fishponds BS16. . **51** A4
 Bristol, Lower Easton
 BS5. . . . . **50** C1
Hinton Villas BS4. . . . . . **119** E1
Hippisley Dr BS26. . . . . **125** D2
Hiscocks Dr BA2. . . . . . . **101** E4
Hitchen Cl SN14. . . . . **69** F8
Hitchings Leaze BS34 . . . **36** A7
Hither Bath Bridge BS4 **64** C1
Hither Gn BS21. . . . . **57** H2
Hither Green Ind Est
 BS21. . . . . **57** H2
Hither Mead BS36. . . . . . **38** B6
Hoare's La BA11. . . . . . . **140** B3
Hobart Rd BS23. . . . . . . **104** F3
Hobbiton Rd BS22. . . . . . **89** A4
Hobbs Ct 1 BS48. . . . . . . **59** F2
Hobbs La
 Barrow Gurney BS48. . . . **77** E3
 Bristol BS30. . . . . **52** B1
Hobb's La BS1. . . . . **142** C2
HOBB'S WALL **115** E5
Hobhouse Cl BS9 . . . . **49** C7
Hobwell La BS41. . . . . . . **62** C2
Hockeys La BS16. . . . . . . **51** A4
Hockley Ct BA1. . . . . **84** D1
Hoddon La BS16. . . . . **53** D5
Hodshill BA2. . . . . **118** F6
Hoecroft BA3. . . . . **138** D8
Hoecroft Gdns BA3. . . . . **138** D3
Hogarth Mews BS22. . . . **89** A3
Hogarth Wlk
 Bristol BS7. . . . . **50** C7
 Weston-s-M BS22 . . . . . **89** A3
Hogues Wlk BS13. . . . . . . **79** B4
Holbeach Way BS14. . . . . **80** A2
HOLBROOK COMMON . . **67** B8
Holbrook Cres BS13. . . . . **79** D4
Holbrook La BS30. . . . . . . **67** B7
Holburne Mus of Art★
 BA2. . . . . **102** B7
Holburne Pk BA2. . . . . . **102** C8
HOLCOMBE. **139** D1
Holcombe BS14. . . . . **80** A5
Holcombe Cl BA2. . . . . . . **85** F1
Holcombe Gn BA1. . . . . . . **84** B2
Holcombe Gr BS31. . . . . . **81** D5
Holcombe La BA2. . . . . . . **85** F1
Holcombe Vale BA2. . . . . **85** F1
Holdenhurst Rd BS15 . . . **51** C1
Holders Wlk BS41. . . . . . . **77** F8
Holford Cl BS48. . . . . **59** E1
Holford Ct BS14. . . . . **80** B5
Holland Rd
 Bath BA1. . . . . **85** B1
 Clevedon BS21. . . . . **57** D1
Holland St BS23 . . . . **105** A8
Hollidge Gdns 3 BS3 . . **63** D4
Hollies La BA1. . . . . **86** A6
Hollies The
 Bristol BS15. . . . . **65** E6
 Midsomer Norton BA3. . **133** A1
Hollis Ave BS20. . . . . **45** C3
Hollis Cl BS41. . . . . **78** A8
Hollis Cres BS20 . . . . **45** C3
Hollister's Dr BS13. . . . . . **79** D4
Holloway BA2. . . . . **141** B1
Holloway Hill SN14. . . . . . **56** F7
Holloway Rd BS35. . . . . . . **22** C5
HOLLOW BROOK. **113** C6
Hollowbrook La BS39,
 BS40. . . . . **113** D6
Hollow La BS22. . . . . **88** F3
Hollow Marsh La BA3,
 BS39. . . . . **131** B4
Hollowmead BS49. . . . . . . **91** E8
Hollow Mead 6 BS4. . . . . **35** F7
Hollowmead Cl BS49. . . . . **91** F8
Hollow Rd
 Almondsbury BS32. . . . . . **24** A4
 Bristol BS15. . . . . **65** E8
 Shipham BS25 . . . . **125** F8
Hollows The BS36. . . . . . . **38** D2
Hollow The
 Bath BA2. . . . . **101** B4
 Dunkerton BA2. . . . . . . **117** D4
Hollway Cl BS14. . . . . **80** E5
Hollway Rd BS14. . . . . . . **80** E5

Hollybrook Pk BS15. . . . . **51** B2
Hollybush Cl
 Acton Turville GL9. . . . . . **43** A6
 Winsley BA15. . . . . **120** E7
Hollybush La
 Bristol BS9. . . . . **48** E5
 Bristol BS9. . . . . **48** F4
Holly Cl
 Alveston BS35. . . . . **14** F4
 Bristol BS5. . . . . **51** A2
 Nailsea BS48. . . . . **60** A3
 Pucklechurch BS16. . . . . **53** C5
 Weston-s-M BS22 . . . . . **89** A1
Holly Cres BS15. . . . . **51** E1
Holly Ct BS2. . . . . **142** C4
Holly Dr
 Bath BA2. . . . . **118** D8
 Colerne SN14. . . . . **70** F6
Holly Gdns BS34. . . . . **36** A7
Holly Gn BS15. . . . . **52** A1
Holly Gr BS16. . . . . **51** C3
Hollyguest Rd BS15. . . . . **65** E6
Holly Hill BS37. . . . . **26** C3
Holly Hill Rd BS15. . . . . . **51** F1
Holly Ho BS11. . . . . **34** C2
Holly La BS21. . . . . **57** H6
Hollyleigh Ave BS34. . . . **35** F2
Holly Lodge Cl BS5. . . . . **51** A2
Holly Lodge Rd BS5. . . . . **50** F2
Hollyman Wlk 5 BS21 . **57** H3
Hollymead La BS9 . . . . . . **48** E4
Holly Mews 4 BS37. . . . . **27** F5
Hollymead La BS14. . . . . . **80** C6
Holly Ridge BS20. . . . . . . **45** A5
Holly Wlk
 Keynsham BS31. . . . . **81** D4
 Radstock BA3. . . . . **133** E1
Hollywood La BS10,
 BS35. . . . . **35** A7
Hollywood Rd BS4. . . . . . **64** D2
Holmdale Rd BS34. . . . . . **36** C3
Holmes Ct BS9. . . . . **49** B5
Holmesdale Rd BS3 . . . . . **63** E3
Holmes Gr BS9. . . . . **49** B5
Holmes Hill Rd BS5. . . . . **64** F8
Holmes St BS5. . . . . **64** B6
Holm La BS35. . . . . **13** B2
Holmlea BS20. . . . . **45** F5
Holmoak Rd BS31. . . . . . . **81** C4
Holm Rd BS24. . . . . **105** E2
Holms Rd BS23 . . . . **105** A5
Holmwood BS15. . . . . **65** C5
Holmwood Cl BS36. . . . . . **37** D6
Holmwood Gdns BS9. . . . **49** B8
Holroyd Ho BS3. . . . . **63** D3
Holsom Cl BS14. . . . . **80** F6
Holsom Rd BS14. . . . . **80** F6
Holstein Ave BS25. . . . . **124** F7
Holst Gdns BS4. . . . . **79** D7
Holton Rd BS7. . . . . **50** A6
Holtsdown La BA1. . . . . . . **85** F7
Holwell Cl BS39. . . . . . . **132** E4
Holybrook Trad Est
 BS15. . . . . **51** B2
Holy Cross RC Prim Sch
 BS3. . . . . **63** C4
Holy Family RC Prim Sch
 BS34. . . . . **36** B8
Holymead Inf Sch BS4 **64** D2
Holymead Jun Sch BS4 **64** D3
Holyrood Cl BS34. . . . . . . **36** D4
Holy Trinity Prim Sch
 BS32. . . . . **24** C2
Holy Well Cl BS4. . . . . **64** F6
Homeapple Hill BS30. . . . **66** F6
Homeavon Ho BS31. . . . . **81** F5
Home Cl
 Bristol BS10. . . . . **35** E2
 Wrington BS40. . . . . **92** E3
Home Farm Cl BA2. . . . . **134** B7
Home Farm Ct BS22. . . . . **89** C3
Home Farm Rd BS8 . . . . . **62** B8
Home Farm Way BS35. . . **23** A1
Homefield
 Congresbury BS49. . . . . . **91** E3
 Locking BS24. . . . . **106** A5
 Thornbury BS35. . . . . **15** D8
 Timsbury BA2. . . . . **116** B1
 Yate BS37. . . . . **27** E3
Homefield Cl
 Locking BS24. . . . . **106** A5
 Saltford BS31. . . . . **82** E3
 Winscombe BS25. . . . . **107** F1
Homefield Dr BS16. . . . . . **51** A5
Homefield Ind Est
 BS24. . . . . **106** A5
Homefield Rd
 Pucklechurch BS16. . . . . **53** B5
 Saltford BS31. . . . . **82** E3
Homeground
 Bristol BS16. . . . . **52** B6
 Clevedon BS21. . . . . **57** H2
Home Ground
 Bristol, Eastfield BS9. . . . **49** B7
 Bristol, Shirehampton
 BS11. . . . . **47** D7
Homelea Pk E BA1. . . . . **101** A7
Homelea Pk W BA1. . . . . **101** A7

Home Leas Cl 1 BS7. . . **50** C8
Homeleaze Rd BS10. . . . . **35** D3
Homemead BA2. . . . . . . **100** A8
Home Mead
 Bristol, Cadbury Heath
 BS30. . . . . **66** A4
 Bristol, Filwood Park BS4 **79** E7
Homemead Dr BS4. . . . . . **64** D1
Home Orch
 Chew Stoke BS40. . . . . **112** D8
 Yate BS37. . . . . **27** D2
Homer Wk BS31. . . . . **81** C3
Homestead BS20. . . . . . . **44** E3
Homestead Cl BS36. . . . . **38** C8
Homestead Gdns BS16 . . **51** B8
Homestead Rd BS34. . . . . **36** A3
Homestead The
 Clevedon BS21. . . . . **57** E3
 Keynsham BS31. . . . . **81** E7
Homestead Way BS25 . . **125** A8
Honeyborne Way GL12 . . **18** B5
Honey Garston Cl BS13 . **79** B4
Honey Garston Rd BS13 **79** B4
HONEY HALL. **108** C7
Honeyhall La BS49. . . . . **108** C7
Honey Hill Rd BS15. . . . . **65** F8
Honeylands BS20 . . . . . . **45** C3
Honeymead BS14. . . . . . . **80** C6
Honey Pens Cres BS7. . . **50** B8
Honeysuckle Cl BS32. . . . **24** E2
Honey Suckle La BS16. . . **50** E5
Honeysuckle Pl BS24. . **106** A4
Honeysuckle Rd BS16. . . **52** D7
Honey Way BS15. . . . . . . **65** F8
Honeywick Cl BS3. . . . . . . **63** C2
Honister Ho BS34. . . . . . . **36** A8
Honiton 9 BS22. . . . . **89** A4
Honiton Rd
 Bristol BS16. . . . . **51** A3
 Clevedon BS21. . . . . **57** G1
HOOK. **116** D2
Hook Hill BA2. . . . . **116** D2
Hook La BS40, BA3. . . . . **130** E4
Hooks Batch BS40. . . . . **110** C4
Hooper Rd BS14. . . . . **80** D5
Hoopers Wlk BS30. . . . . . **65** E3
Hoover's La BS36, BS37. . **26** C2
Hopechapel Hill 11
 BS8. . . . . **62** F6
Hope Cote Lodge BA2 **102** C1
Hope Cotts BS21. . . . . **73** B2
Hope Ct BS1. . . . . **142** B1
Hope Rd
 Bristol BS3. . . . . **63** C2
 Yate BS37. . . . . **27** A2
Hope Sq BS8. . . . . **62** F6
Hope Terr BA3. . . . . **133** B1
Hopetoun Rd BS2. . . . . . . **49** F3
Hopewell Gdns BS11. . . . **47** F7
HOPEWELL HILL. **51** D1
Hopkin Cl BS35. . . . . **15** D7
Hopkins Ct 13 BS6. . . . . **49** B1
Hopkins St BS23. . . . . . **104** E8
Hopland Cl BS30. . . . . **66** B3
Hopp's Rd BS15. . . . . **65** D7
Hopton Wy BA1. . . . . **84** E4
Horesham Gr BS13. . . . . . **79** C5
HORFIELD. **49** F6
Horfield CE Prim Sch
 BS10. . . . . **49** D7
Horfield Ct BS7. . . . . **49** E4
Horfield Rd BS2. . . . . . . **143** A4
Horley Rd BS2. . . . . **50** A2
Hornbeam Ho 5 BS16. . . **51** C6
Hornbeams The BS16. . . . **37** B4
Horne Cl BA3. . . . . **138** F1
Horn's La BS26 . . . . **125** B2
HORSECASTLE. **74** A2
Horsecastle Cl BS49. . . . . **74** A1
Horsecastle Farm Rd
 BS49. . . . . **74** A1
Horsecombe Brow
 BA2. . . . . **102** A1
Horsecombe Gr BA2. . . . **102** A1
Horsecombe Vale
 BA2. . . . . **102** A1
Horsecroft Gdns BS30. . . **66** A6
Horsefair The BS1. . . . . **143** B3
Horse La BS35. . . . . **8** D5
Horseleaze La BS25. . . . **108** D1
Horse Leaze Rd BS7. . . . . **50** C8
Horsepool La BS30. . . . . . **67** F8
Horsepool Rd BS13 . . . . . **78** E3
Horse Race La BS8. . . . . . **61** A6
Horseshoe Ct BS36. . . . . . **38** D7
Horseshoe Dr BS9. . . . . . **48** C4
Horseshoe La BS37 . . . . . **28** L1
Horseshoe Wlk BA2. . . . **102** B5
Horse St BS37. . . . . **28** C1
Horse World★ BS14. . . . . **80** D3
Horsford Rd GL12. . . . . . . **11** B5
Horstmann Cl 2 BA1. . . **101** B4
Hortham La BS32. . . . . . . **24** E5
HORTON. **29** B6
Horton CE Prim Sch
 BS37. . . . . **29** C5
Horton Hill BS37. . . . . **29** C5
Horton Ho BA2. . . . . **141** C4

Horton Rd
Chipping Sodbury BS37 . .28 C2
Chipping Sodbury, Little
 Sodbury End BS37. . . . . .28 D4
Horton St BS2 . . . . .143 C3
Horwood Ct **3** BS30 . . . .66 A4
Horwood La GL12 . . . . . . .18 B4
Horwood Rd BS48. . . . . . .59 F1
Hosey Wlk BS13 . . . . .79 A5
Hospital Rd BS48 . . . . . . .77 F7
Host St BS1. . . . . .143 A3
Hot Bath St **9** BA1. . . . .141 B2
Hottom Gdns BS7. . . . . . .50 A7
Hot Water La BS15 . . . . . .52 A3
Hotwell Hts BS8 . . . . . . .142 A2
Hotwell Rd BS8. . . . . . . .142 B1
HOTWELLS. 142 A1
Hotwells Ho BS8. . . . . . .142 A2
Hotwells Prim Sch BS8. 62 F6
Houlgate Way BS26 . . . .125 B1
Houlton St BS2 . . . . .143 C4
Hounds Cl BS37. . . . . . . .28 B1
Hounds Rd BS37 . . . . . . .28 B1
HOUNSLEY BATCH 95 A3
Howard Ave BS5 . . . . . . .64 E8
Howard Cl BS31. . . . . . . .82 D3
Howard Rd
Bristol, Southville BS3 . . .63 C4
Bristol, Staple Hill BS16 .51 D4
Bristol, Westbury Park
 BS6 . . . . .49 B4
Thornbury BS35. . . . . .8 C2
Howard St BS5. . . . . .50 E1
Howard Wlk BS30 . . . . . .66 D7
Howecroft Ct BS9. . . . . .48 E4
Howecroft Gdns BS9. . . .48 E4
Howells Mead BS16. . . . .52 B7
Howes Cl BS30. . . . . .66 A6
Howett Rd **16** BS5. . . . .64 C7
Howgrove Hill La BS40 . .94 C2
How Hill BA2 . . . . .101 A6
Howitt Way **1** BS24 . .105 F7
HOWLEY 5 E1
Howsmoor La
Bristol, Lyde Green
 BS16 . . . . .52 C8
Bristol, New England
 BS16 . . . . .52 B8
Hoylake BS37 . . . . .39 E8
Hoylake Dr BS30 . . . . . . .66 B6
Huckford La BS36. . . . . . .38 A4
Huckford Rd BS36. . . . . .37 E5
Huckley Way BS32 . . . . . .36 F6
Hudds Hill Gdns **9** BS5 64 E8
Hudd's Hill Rd BS5. . . . . .64 E8
Hudd's Vale Rd BS5 . . . . .64 E8
Hudson Ave BS10 . . . . . .34 B8
Hudson Cl BS37. . . . . . . .39 F8
Hughenden Rd
Bristol, Clifton BS8 . . . . .49 A2
Bristol, Horfield BS7 . . . . .49 E5
Weston-s-M BS23 . . . . . .105 A4
Hughes Gdns BS7. . . . . . .50 A8
Huish Ct BA3 . . . . .134 B2
Hulbert Cl BS4. . . . . .65 A2
Hulse Rd BS4. . . . . .64 D1
Humberstan Wlk BS11 . .47 E8
Humber Way BS11 . . . . . .33 D5
Humphry Davy Way 6
 BS8. . . . . .62 F5
Humphrys Barton BS4. .64 F5
Hungerford Cl BS4. . . . . .80 E8
Hungerford Cres BS4. . . .64 E1
Hungerford Gdns BS4. . .80 E8
Hungerford Rd
Bath BA1 . . . . .101 C7
Bristol BS4. . . . . .80 E8
Hungerford Terr BA2 . .118 D3
Hungerford Wlk BS4 . . . .64 E1
Hung Rd BS11 . . . . .47 E5
HUNSTRETE 98 D2
Hunstrete Rd BA2. . . . .115 F7
Hunters Cl BS15 . . . . . . .65 C5
Hunters Dr BS15 . . . . . . .51 F1
Hunters Mead GL9 . . . . .20 A2
Hunters Rd BS15. . . . . . .65 C5
Hunters Rd E BS15 . . . . .65 C4
**Hunters Rest Miniature
 Rlwy** ★ BS39 . . . . .115 A5
Hunter's Way BS34. . . . .36 B3
HUNTINGFORD 10 F8
Huntingham Rd BS13. . .78 F4
Huntley Gr BS48 . . . . . . .60 A1
Hunts Ground Rd BS34 .36 F4
Hunts La BS7 . . . . .49 E6
Hunt's La BS49 . . . . .91 E8
Hurle Cres BS8 . . . . .49 B1
Hurle Rd BS8 . . . . .49 B1
Hurlingham Rd BS7 . . . .49 F2
Hurn La BS31 . . . . .82 A3
Hurn Rd BS21. . . . . .57 H2
Hursley Hill
Bristol BS14, BS39. . . . . . .97 D8
Whitchurch BS14. . . . . . . .80 D1
Hursley La BS14 . . . . . . .80 E1
Hurston Rd BS4. . . . . . . .79 D7
Hurst Rd
Bristol BS4. . . . . .79 F8
Weston-s-M BS23 . . . . . .105 A6

Hurst Wlk BS4 . . . . .79 F8
Hurstwood Rd BS16. . . . .51 D5
HUTTON 105 E2
Hutton CE Prim Sch
 BS24. . . . . .105 E2
Hutton Cl
Bristol BS9 . . . . .48 E7
Keynsham BS31. . . . . . . .82 A2
Hutton Hill BS24 . . . . . .105 F2
Hutton Moor La BS22,
 BS24. . . . . .105 C6
Hutton Moor Pk BS24 .105 C6
Hutton Moor Rd BS22 .105 C7
Hutton Moor Rdbt
 BS22. . . . . .105 C7
Huyton Rd BS5. . . . . .50 E3
Hyacinth Cl BS16. . . . . . .52 D7
Hyacinth Way BS16 . . . . .52 D7
Hyatts Wood Rd BS48 . .76 E1
Hyde Apartments BS6. . .49 C3
Hyde Ave BS35. . . . . .8 B3
Hyde's La SN14 . . . . .69 A6
Hydes The BS31. . . . . . . .81 F6
Hyde The BS21. . . . . .73 C8
Hyland Gr BS9 . . . . .48 F8
HYSTFIELD 3 B5

I

ICELTON 89 C8
Ida Rd **2** BS5. . . . . .64 C8
Iddesleigh Rd BS6 . . . . . .49 B3
Idstone Rd BS16 . . . . . . .51 B4
Idwal Cl BA2. . . . . .134 C8
Iford Cl BS31 . . . . .82 E3
Iford Fields BA15 . . . . . .120 E2
Iford Hill BA15 . . . . .120 E2
Iford La BA2, BA15. . . . .120 C3
IKB Academy BS31. . . . . .82 A5
Ilchester Cres BS13 . . . . .63 B1
Ilchester Rd BS13 . . . . . .79 B8
Iles Cl BS15. . . . . .65 D4
Ilex Ave BS21 . . . . .57 G2
Ilex Cl BS13. . . . . .78 F6
Ilex La BS25 . . . . .107 F1
Ilminster BS24 . . . . .105 A2
Ilminster Ave BS4 . . . . . .79 F8
Ilminster Ave E-ACT Acad
 BS4. . . . . .79 F8
Ilminster Avenue Prim Sch
 BS4. . . . . .80 A8
Ilminster Cl
Clevedon BS21. . . . . .57 G2
Nailsea BS48 . . . . .75 D8
Ilsyn Gr BS14 . . . . .80 D7
Imber Court Cl BS14 . . . .80 B8
Imperial Arc 11 BS3. . .63 D4
Imperial Pk BS13 . . . . . . .79 C6
Imperial Rd
Bristol BS14. . . . . .80 C8
 8 Bristol, Clifton BS8 . .49 B1
Imperial Wlk BS14 . . . . . .64 B1
Inchalloch **18** BA1. . . . .85 A1
Inclosures The 5
 BS22. . . . . .105 F8
INGLESBATCH 117 C8
Ingleside Rd BS15. . . . . . .51 C1
Inglestone Rd GL12 . . . . .18 B8
Ingleton Dr BS22. . . . . . .89 A4
Ingmire Rd BS5. . . . . .50 B3
INGST 13 C4
Ingst Hill BS35. . . . . .13 B3
Ingst Rd BS35. . . . . .13 D4
Inkerman Cl BS7. . . . . . . .49 E7
Inman Ho BA1 . . . . .141 C4
INMAN'S BATCH 95 A5
Inn Cotts BS11. . . . . .48 A7
Inner Down The BS32 . .14 D3
Inner Elm Terr BA3 . . . .133 C1
Innicks Est GL11. . . . . .5 D4
Innox Gdns BS13. . . . . . .79 A5
Innox Gr BA2 . . . . .100 F2
Innox La BA1 . . . . .85 B5
Innox Rd BA2. . . . . .101 B5
Inns Court Ave BS4. . . . .79 D7
Inns Court Dr BS4. . . . . .79 D6
Inns Court Gn BS4. . . . . .79 D7
Instow **7** BS22 . . . . . . .89 A2
Instow Rd BS4. . . . . .79 E8
Instow Wlk BS4. . . . . . . .79 E8
**International Helicopter
 Mus** ★ BS24. . . . . .105 E5
International Trad Est
 BS11. . . . . .33 B2
Interplex 16 BS32. . . . . .24 C3
Inverness Rd BA2 . . . . .101 C6
IO Ctr BS11. . . . . .33 F5
Ipswich Dr BS4. . . . . .64 E6
Irby Rd BS3. . . . . .63 A3
Ireland Rd BS16. . . . . . . .50 F3
Ireton Rd BS3. . . . . .63 B3
IRON ACTON 26 D4
Iron Acton CE Prim Sch
 BS37. . . . . .26 E4
Iron Acton Way BS37 . . .27 B3
Ironchurch Rd BS11. . . . .33 C5
Iron Hogg La GL12 . . . . . .9 C3

Ironmould La
Bristol BS4. . . . . .65 A1
Keynsham BS31 . . . . .81 A8
Irving Cl
Bristol BS16. . . . . .51 E4
Clevedon BS21. . . . . .57 H3
Irving Ho BS1. . . . . .142 C3
I.S.F. Rd BS11. . . . . .33 C3
Island Copsie BS7. . . . . . .50 B8
Island Gdns BS16 . . . . . .50 C4
Island The BA3. . . . . . . .133 A1
Island Trad Pk BS11. . . . .33 C1
Isle Of Rhé GL11 . . . . .5 C5
Isleys Ct BS30. . . . . .65 F3
Islington Rd BS3 . . . . . . .63 C4
Ison Hill Rd BS10. . . . . . .34 D3
ITCHINGTON 15 F2
Itchington Rd
Alveston BS35, GL12 . . . .15 F4
Tytherington GL12 . . . . . .16 B4
Ivo Peters Rd BA2. . . . .141 A2
Ivor Rd BS5. . . . . .64 C8
Ivy Ave BA2. . . . . .101 C4
Ivy Bank Pk BA2 . . . . . .101 F2
Ivy Cl BS48 . . . . .59 D1
Ivy Ct BS20 . . . . .44 F5
Ivy Gr BA2. . . . . .101 C4
Ivy House Cotts BS29. .106 C3
Ivy La
Bristol BS16. . . . . .51 A3
Weston-s-M BS24 . . . . . .106 A8
Ivy Lodge **4** BS9. . . . . .49 A7
Ivy Pl BA2 . . . . .101 C4
Ivy Terr BS37. . . . . .39 B4
Ivywell Rd BS9. . . . . .48 E3
Ivy Wlk
Banwell BS29. . . . . .106 E4
Midsomer Norton BA3 . .139 B8
IWOOD 92 A3
Iwood La BS40 . . . . .92 A2

J

Jack Knight Ho BS7. . . . .49 F5
Jack Price Cl BS13. . . . . .79 C3
Jackson Cl BS35 . . . . .22 D7
Jacob Ct BS2 . . . . .143 C3
Jacobs Bldg The BS8. .142 B3
Jacob's Ct BS1 . . . . .142 C2
Jacobs Mdw BS20. . . . . .45 F4
Jacob St
Bristol BS2. . . . . .143 B3
Bristol BS2. . . . . .143 C3
Jacob's Wells Rd BS8 .142 B2
Jaguar Ho **3** BA1. . . . .141 B4
Jamaica St BS2 . . . . . . .143 B4
James Cl BS16. . . . . .51 E4
James Counsell Way
 BS16. . . . . .36 F2
James Rd BS16 . . . . .51 E3
James St W BA1 . . . . . .141 B2
James St
Bristol BS5. . . . . .143 C4
Bristol, Baptist Mills BS2 .50 A2
Janes Gr BA2. . . . . .102 A2
Jane St BS5. . . . . .64 B7
Jarrets Rd BS10. . . . . . . .35 D2
Jarvis St BS5 . . . . .64 B6
Jasmine Cl BS22. . . . . . . .89 A1
Jasmine Ct **8** BS23. . .104 E8
Jasmine Gr BS11 . . . . . . .34 C2
Jasmine La BS49. . . . . . . .74 F2
Jasmine Way BS24. . . . . .89 A1
Jasper St BS3 . . . . .63 B3
Jays The GL12 . . . . .16 B6
Jay View BS23 . . . . .105 A5
Jean Rd BS4 . . . . .64 E2
JEFFERIES HILL 65 C5
Jefferies Hill Bottom
 BS15. . . . . .65 B5
Jeffery Ct BS30. . . . . .66 B6
Jeffreys Ct **9** BS16 . . . .50 E3
Jekyll Cl BS16. . . . . .50 E8
Jellicoe Ave BS16. . . . . . .50 E8
Jellicoe Ct BS22 . . . . .88 E4
Jena Ct BS31 . . . . .82 D3
Jenkinson Wy G12 . . . . . . .9 E8
Jenner Bvd BS16. . . . . . .38 C1
Jenner Cl BS37 . . . . .40 D8
Jennings Ct **1** BS3 . . . .63 A4
Jersey Ave BS4 . . . . .64 F4
Jesmond Rd
Clevedon BS21. . . . . .57 E3
Weston-s-M BS22 . . . . . . .89 C4
Jesse Hughes Ct BA1. . .85 C2
Jessop Cres BS10 . . . . . . .35 A1
Jessop Cl BS1 . . . . .143 B2
Jessop Underpass BS3 . 62 F4
Jews La
Bath BA2 . . . . .101 C6
Churchill BS25 . . . . .108 F4
Jim O'Neil Ho BS11. . . . .47 D7
Jinty La BS16 . . . . .52 B2
Jobbins Cl BS37 . . . . .40 A8
Jocelin Dr BS22. . . . . .88 F4
Jocelyn Rd BS7. . . . . .49 F7
Jockey La BS5 . . . . .65 A7

John Cabot Acad BS15 .65 C7
John Cabot Ct BS1. . . . .142 A1
John Caller Cres BS16. . .50 E8
John Carr's Terr BS8 . . .142 B2
John Chiddy Cl BS15. . . .65 C3
John Cozens Ho 6
 BS2. . . . . .143 C3
John James Ct BS7. . . . . .50 B7
John Repton Gdns
 BS10. . . . . .35 B2
John Slessor Ct BA1 . . .141 B4
Johnson Dr BS30 . . . . . . .65 F5
Johnson Rd BS16 . . . . . . .52 C5
Johnsons La BS5. . . . . . . .50 D1
Johnsons Rd
Bristol BS5. . . . . .50 C1
 1 Bristol, Moorfields
 BS5 . . . . .64 C8
John St
Bath BA1 . . . . .141 B3
Bristol BS1. . . . . .143 A3
Bristol, Baptist Mills BS2 50 A2
Bristol, Two Mile Hill
 BS15 . . . . .65 C8
Johnstone St BA2. . . . . .141 C2
John Wesley Ct 10
 BS16. . . . . .51 D5
John Wesley Rd BS5 . . .65 B6
John Wesleys Chapel ★
 BS1 . . . . .143 B3
Jones Cl BS49. . . . . .74 A1
Jonny Ball La BS2. . . . . .143 A3
Jordan Wlk BS32. . . . . . .36 D8
Jorrocks Ind Est BS37. . .39 C4
Joyce Cl BS7 . . . . .50 A8
Joy Hill BS8 . . . . .62 F6
Jubilee Cres BS16. . . . . . .52 A6
Jubilee Ct
Bristol BS4. . . . . .64 D4
Weston-s-M BS23 . . . . . .104 F8
Jubilee Dr
Failand BS8 . . . . .61 B4
Thornbury BS35 . . . . .8 D1
Jubilee Gdns BS37 . . . . . .28 A2
Jubilee Ho BS34 . . . . .36 C8
Jubilee La
Churchill BS40 . . . . .109 A6
Cromhall GL12. . . . . .17 B7
Jubilee Path BS22 . . . . . .88 C3
Jubilee Pl
Bristol BS1. . . . . .143 A1
Bristol, Woodstock BS15 .65 F7
Clevedon BS21. . . . . .57 F1
Jubilee Rd
Axbridge BS26. . . . . . . .125 C2
Bristol, Baptist Mills BS2 50 A1
Bristol, Crew's Hole BS5 .64 F7
Bristol, Staple Hill BS15 .51 E3
Bristol, Upper Knowle
 BS4 . . . . .64 C2
Radstock BA3. . . . . .133 D1
Weston-s-M BS23 . . . . . .104 F8
Jubilee St BS2 . . . . .143 C2
Jubilee Terr BS39 . . . . . .132 E6
Jubilee Way
Avonmouth BS11. . . . . . .33 B2
Elberton BS35. . . . . .14 B8
Weston-s-M BS22 . . . . .89 C3
Julian Cl BS9 . . . . .48 E3
Julian Rd
Bath BA1 . . . . .141 B3
Bristol BS9. . . . . .48 E3
Julier Ho BA1 . . . . .141 C4
Julius Cl BS16 . . . . .52 C6
Julius Pl BS31 . . . . .81 F8
Julius Rd BS7 . . . . .49 D3
Junction Ave BA2 . . . . .141 A1
Junction Rd
Bath BA2 . . . . .141 A1
Bristol BS4. . . . . .64 C4
Junction Way BS15,
 BS16. . . . . .52 B3
Juniper Ct **2** BS5. . . . . .50 C2
Juniper Pl BS22. . . . . . . .88 F4
Juniper Way BS34. . . . . .37 A7
Jupiter Rd BS34 . . . . .35 E7
Justice Ave BS31. . . . . . .82 E3
Justice Rd BS16 . . . . .51 A3
Jutland Rd BS11 . . . . . . .33 B1

K

Karelean Ct BS10 . . . . . . .35 D3
Karen Cl BS48. . . . . .76 A4
Karen Dr BS48. . . . . .76 A5
Kathdene Gdns BS7. . . . .49 F3
Katherine Cl GL12. . . . . .11 A5
**Katherine Lady Berkeley's
 Sch** GL12. . . . . .11 F6
Kaynton Mead BA1. . . .101 B7
Keats Ct BS7 . . . . .50 A8
Keats Ho **4** BS23 . . . . .104 F4
Keats Rd BA3 . . . . .139 C8
Keble Ave BS13 . . . . .78 F5
Keeds La BS41 . . . . .61 F1
Keedwell Hill BS41. . . . . .61 F1
Keel Cl BS5. . . . . .64 F6

Keel's Hill BA2 . . . . .134 C8
Keene's Way BS21 . . . . . .57 E2
Keen's Gr BS35 . . . . .22 C7
Keepers Hill BA2. . . . . . .100 C5
Keepers La BS7 . . . . .49 F3
Keeper's La BA2 . . . . .99 C3
Keep The
Bristol BS10. . . . . .66 D5
Weston-s-M BS22 . . . . . . .89 A3
Keg Store The BS1 . . . . .143 B2
Keinton Wlk BS10 . . . . . .35 A2
Kelbra Cres BS36. . . . . . .38 B6
Kellaway Ave BS7. . . . . . .49 D5
Kellaway Cres BS9 . . . . . .49 D6
Kellaway Ct BS6 . . . . .49 D5
Kellaway La BA2 . . . . . . .102 A2
Kellways BS48 . . . . .76 A4
Kelso Pl BA1 . . . . .101 D7
Kelso Villa BA1. . . . . . . .101 D7
KELSTON 83 C3
Kelston Cl
Saltford BS31. . . . . .82 D4
Yate BS37 . . . . .39 D7
Kelston Gdns
Bristol BS10. . . . . .49 D8
Weston-s-M BS22 . . . . . . .89 B5
Kelston Gr BS15 . . . . .65 E6
Kelston Hill La BA1 . . . . .83 B4
Kelston Rd
Bath BA1 . . . . .83 E1
Bristol BS10. . . . . .49 D8
Keynsham BS31 . . . . .81 D5
Weston-s-M BS22 . . . . . . .89 B5
Kelston View BA2 . . . . . .101 A5
Kelston Wlk BS16 . . . . . .51 C4
Kelting Gr BS21 . . . . .57 H2
Kemble Cl
Bristol BS15. . . . . .65 E6
Nailsea BS48 . . . . .60 A1
Kemble Gdns BS11. . . . . .47 F5
Kemble Ho BS34 . . . . . . .23 F1
Kemperleye Way BS32. .36 D7
Kempe's Cl BS41. . . . . . . .62 A2
Kempe Way BS24 . . . . . .105 E7
Kempthorne La BA2. . . .101 E1
Kempton Cl
 2 Bristol BS16 . . . . . . .37 F1
Thornbury BS35. . . . . .8 B3
Kencot Wlk BS13 . . . . . . .79 B3
Kendall Gdns BS16. . . . . .51 D4
Kendall Rd BS16 . . . . . . .51 D4
Kendal Rd BS7. . . . . .50 A7
KENDLESHIRE 38 A4
Kendon Dr BS10 . . . . . . .49 D7
Kendon Way BS10. . . . . .49 D8
Kenilworth BS37 . . . . . . .39 F8
Kenilworth Cl BS31. . . . .81 D4
Kenilworth Ct
 1 Bath BA1 . . . . .102 B8
 1 Bathwick BA2. . . . . .102 B8
Kenilworth Dr BS30 . . . .66 B2
Kenilworth Rd BS6. . . . . .49 C1
Kenmare Rd BS4 . . . . . . .63 E1
Kenmeade Cl BS25 . . . .125 E8
Kenmore Cres BS7. . . . . .35 E1
Kenmore Dr BS7 . . . . . . .35 E1
Kenmore Gr BS7. . . . . . . .35 E1
KENN 73 F7
Kennard Cl BS15. . . . . . . .65 C7
Kennard Rd BS15. . . . . . .65 C8
Kennard Rise BS15. . . . . .65 C8
Kennaway Rd BS21. . . . . .57 G2
Kenn Bsns Pk BS21. . . . .73 E8
Kenn Cl BS23 . . . . .105 A5
Kenn Court BS4. . . . . .79 E7
Kennedy Ho BS37 . . . . . .27 F1
Kennedy Way BS37. . . . .27 F1
Kennel Dr GL9 . . . . .30 E2
Kennel La BS21 . . . . .123 E3
Kennel Lodge Rd BS3 . .62 E4
Kenn Est BS21 . . . . .73 E5
Kenneth Rd BS4 . . . . .64 D2
Kennet Pk BA2. . . . . .85 E1
Kennet Rd BS31. . . . . . . .82 A4
Kennet Way **4** BS35 . . .15 D8
Kennford **6** BS22. . . . . .88 F2
Kennington Ave
Bristol, Bishopston BS7 . .49 F4
 3 Bristol, Two Mile Hill
 BS15 . . . . .51 D1
Kennington Rd BA1 . . . .101 B7
Kennion Rd BS5. . . . . . . .65 A7
Kennmoor Cl BS30 . . . . .66 A6
Kennmoor Dr BS21 . . . . .57 G1
KENN MOOR GATE 74 A6
Kennmoor Rd BS21 . . . . .74 A6
Kenn Moor Rd RS49 . . . .74 B1
Kenn Rd
Bristol BS5. . . . . .65 A7
Clevedon BS21. . . . . .73 F6
Kenn St BS21. . . . . .73 F7
Kensal Ave BS3. . . . . .63 E3
Kensal Rd BS3 . . . . .63 E3
Kensington BS24. . . . . . .105 E7
Kensington Apartments
 BS6. . . . . .49 C3

Kensington Cl BS35 ..... 8 B2
Kensington Ct
  Bath BA1 .... 85 B2
  Bristol BS8 .... 142 A3
Kensington Gdns BA1 .. 85 B1
Kensington Ho **5** BS5.. 65 A8
KENSINGTON PARK 64 C3
Kensington Park Rd
  BS4 .... 64 C2
Kensington Pk **12** BS5.. 50 A1
Kensington Pl
  Bath BA1 .... 85 B1
  8 Bathwick BA2 ... 102 B8
  Bristol BS8 .... 142 A3
Kensington Rd
  Bristol, Redland BS6 .. 49 C1
  3 Bristol, St George
    BS5 .... 65 A8
  7 Bristol, Staple Hill
    BS16 .... 51 D4
  Weston-s-M BS23 .. 104 F5
Kent Ave BS37 .... 27 F3
Kent Cl BS34 .... 36 D4
Kent Mews BS5 .... 50 E7
Kenton Ho BS34 ...... 23 F1
Kenton Mews BS9..... 49 C5
Kent Rd
  Bristol BS7 .... 49 E4
  Congresbury BS49.... 91 D5
Kents Gn BS15........ 51 E2
Kentshare La BS40 .... 95 B6
Kent St
  Bristol BS3 .... 63 C3
  Cheddar BS27 ...... 126 B1
Kent Way BS22........ 89 B4
Kenwood Cl BS15 ..... 51 F1
Keppel Cl BS31 .... 82 D2
Kerry Rd BS4 .... 63 E1
Kersteman Rd BS6 .... 49 C3
Kestrel Cl
  Bristol BS34......... 35 E8
  Chipping Sodbury BS37 . 39 F8
  Thornbury BS35...... 8 D2
Kestrel Dr
  Pucklechurch BS16 ... 53 C4
  Weston-s-M BS22 .... 88 E1
Kestrel Rd G12........ 11 A5
Keswick Wlk BS10 .... 35 C2
Ketch Rd BS3 .... 63 F3
Kewhaven Bglws BS22 . 88 B4
Kew Rd BS23 .... 87 E1
Kewside BS22 .... 88 B4
KEWSTOKE 88 B4
Kewstoke Prim Sch
  BS22................ 88 B3
Kewstoke Rd
  Bath BA2 .... 102 A2
  Bristol BS9.......... 48 E4
  Weston-s-M BS22 .... 88 C3
Kew Wlk BS4 .... 80 C8
Keyes Path BS22 ...... 88 F4
KEYNSHAM 81 E3
Keynsham By-Pass
  BS31................ 81 E7
Keynsham Hospl BS31 . 81 F4
Keynsham Prim Sch
  BS31................ 81 D5
Keynsham Rd BS30,
  BS31................ 82 A8
Keynsham Sta BS31 ... 81 F6
Keys Ave BS7 .... 49 F7
Kidney Hill
  Westerleigh BS37 .... 39 A3
  Westerleigh BS37 .... 39 A3
Kielder Dr BS22....... 88 F3
Kilbirnie Rd BS14 ..... 80 A3
Kilburn Ct **17** BS5 .... 64 B8
Kilburn St **19** BS5 ..... 64 B8
Kildare BA2 .... 102 B7
Kildare Rd BS4 .... 63 D1
Kilkenny La BA2 ...... 118 B8
Kilkenny Pl BS20...... 45 C6
Killcott Rd GL12 ...... 19 E8
KILLING'S KNAP 139 B4
KILMERSDON 140 B5
Kilmersdon CE Prim Sch
  BA3 .... 140 A6
Kilmersdon Hill BA3 .. 140 A5
Kilmersdon Rd
  Bristol BS13......... 79 B4
  Radstock BA3........ 139 E8
Kilminster Cl BS34.... 36 D7
Kilminster Rd BS11 ... 47 D7
Kiln Cl BS15 .... 51 B2
Kiln Ct BS5 .... 64 B8
Kiln Pk BS23......... 105 A6
Kilve BS24........... 105 A2
Kilvert Cl BS4........ 64 D5
Kimberley Ave BS16 .. 51 C5
Kimberley Cl BS16 .... 51 F7
Kimberley Cres BS16.. 51 C5
Kimberley Rd
  Bristol, Fishponds BS16 . 51 C5
  Bristol, Kingswood BS15 51 D1
  Clevedon BS21........ 57 E2

Kinber Cl BA1 .... 84 A3
Kinema Ho BS4 .... 64 C4
King Alfred Way BA15 120 D7
Kingcott Mill Farm Cvns
  BS48................ 77 B8
King Dick's La **7** BS5 .. 64 F8
KINGDOWN 94 D5
Kingdown Rd BS40.... 94 C5
King Edward Cl BS14.. 80 A6
King Edward Rd BA2 .. 101 D5
King Edward's Pre-Prep
  Sch BA1............ 101 C8
King Edwards Sch
  BA1 .... 101 C8
King Edward's Sch
  BA2 .... 102 C7
Kingfisher Cl
  Bristol BS32......... 24 E2
  Thornbury BS35...... 8 D2
Kingfisher Ct BA2 .... 120 C1
Kingfisher Dr
  Bristol BS16......... 50 E6
  Midsomer Norton BA3 . 139 B8
Kingfisher Rd
  Chipping Sodbury BS37 . 40 A8
  Portishead BS20 ..... 46 A6
  Weston-s-M BS22 ... 105 F8
King George's Rd
  Bath BA2 .... 101 C6
  Bristol BS13......... 78 F5
  Bristol BS13......... 78 F5
King George V Pl BS2 . 143 A2
King John's Hunting
  Lodge★ BS26...... 125 C2
King John's Rd BS15 .. 51 B2
King La
  Clutton BS39........ 114 F4
  Horton BS37......... 29 A7
King Rd
  Bristol BS4.......... 64 C1
  Churchill BS49....... 108 E6
King Road Ave BS11... 33 B2
Kingrove Cres BS37 ... 40 C8
Kingrove La BS37 ..... 40 C7
Kings Ave BS15 ...... 65 B4
King's Ave BS6, BS7 .. 49 C4
Kings Chase BS15..... 65 D8
Kingscote BS37 ...... 39 D6
Kingscote Pk BS5 .... 65 B6
Kingscourt Cl BS14 ... 80 A4
Kings Croft BS41..... 61 E1
Kings Ct
  Bath BA1 .... 141 B2
  Bristol BS1.......... 143 A2
  Bristol, Little Stoke
    BS34 .... 36 C6
  Bristol, St Pauls BS1 . 143 B4
  Bristol, Southville BS3 . 63 C4
  2 Bristol, Withywood
    BS13 .... 78 F4
  8 Nailsea BS48 ..... 59 E2
KINGSDOWN
  Bathford............ 86 F3
  Bristol 143 A4
Kingsdown Gr SN13... 86 F3
Kingsdown Par BS6 .. 143 A4
Kingsdown View **15**
  BA1 .... 85 A1
Kings Dr
  Bristol, Hanham BS15 . 65 B4
  Bristol, Stoke Gifford
    BS34 .... 37 A4
King's Dr BS7........ 49 C4
Kingsfield BA2........ 101 C3
Kingsfield La
  Bristol, Longwell Green
    BS15 .... 65 E5
  Bristol, Mount Hill BS30 . 65 E4
Kingsfield Rdbt BS15.. 65 E5
Kings Fields BS37..... 27 A8
Kingsfield Sch BS15... 66 A8
King's Forest Prim Sch
  BS15................ 51 F2
Kingsgate BS37 ...... 39 E8
KINGSGATE PARK 39 F8
King's Head La BS13 .. 78 F7
Kingshill BS48 .... 59 C2
Kingshill CE Prim Sch
  BS48................ 59 D3
Kingshill Gdns BS48... 59 C1
Kingshill Ho BS4...... 64 B1
Kingshill La BS40 .... 112 C4
Kingshill Rd BS4...... 64 B1
Kingsholme Ct BS23 .. 87 E1
Kingsholme Rd BS15.. 51 D1
Kingsholm Rd BS10 .. 49 D8
King's La
  Clevedon BS21....... 57 F5
  6 Weston-s-M BS23 . 104 E8
Kingsland Cl **1** BS2... 64 A6
Kingsland Rd BS2 .... 64 A6
Kingsland Road Bridge **3**
  BS2................. 64 A6
Kingsland Trad Est
  Bristol BS2.......... 143 C3
  Bristol, Newton BS2.. 64 A7
Kingsleigh Ct BS15... 65 F7
Kingsleigh Gdns BS15. 65 F7
Kingsleigh Pk BS15 ... 65 F7

Kingsley Ho
  Bristol BS2.......... 143 C2
  Bristol, Westbury on Trym
    BS9 .... 49 A8
Kingsley Pl **1** BS3 .... 63 C4
Kingsley Rd
  Bristol, Lower Easton
    BS5 .... 50 C1
  Bristol, Montpelier BS6 . 49 C2
  Clevedon BS21....... 57 F2
  Radstock BA3........ 133 C1
  Weston-s-M BS23 ... 104 F3
Kingsmarsh Ho **3**
  BS5................. 64 B7
KINGSMEAD 141 B2
Kingsmead BS48...... 59 C2
Kingsmead Ct **12** BA1 . 141 B2
Kingsmead N BA1..... 141 B2
Kingsmead Rd BS5.... 51 A1
Kingsmead Sq BA1 ... 141 B2
Kingsmead St BA1 ... 141 B2
Kingsmead Wlk BS5.. 51 A1
Kingsmill BS9 .... 48 D5
Kings Oak Mdw BS39. 114 E2
King's Parade Ave **1**
  BS8................. 49 B1
King's Parade Mews
  BS8................. 49 A1
Kings Park Ave BS2 ... 64 C6
King Sq BS2 .... 143 A4
King Square Ave BS2 . 143 A4
Kings Quarter
  Apartments **14** BS2 . 143 A4
Kings Rd BS40........ 92 D1
King's Rd
  Bristol BS8 .... 142 A3
  Bristol, Kensington Park
    BS4 .... 64 C3
  Clevedon BS21....... 57 F5
  Portishead BS20 ..... 44 F4
  Saltford BS31........ 82 C3
Kings Sq BS30........ 82 D8
King St
  Avonmouth BS11 .... 33 A1
  Bristol BS1.......... 143 A2
  Bristol, Lower Easton
    BS5 .... 50 C1
  Bristol, St George BS15. 65 B8
Kingston Ave
  Clevedon BS21....... 57 G3
  Saltford BS31........ 82 C3
Kingston Bldgs **5**
  BA1 .... 141 C2
Kingston Cl BS16 ..... 52 A7
Kingston Dr
  Bristol BS16......... 52 A7
  Nailsea BS48 .... 75 C8
Kingston La BS40 .... 94 F8
Kingston Mead BS40 . 94 F7
Kingston Rd
  Bath BA2 .... 141 C2
  Bristol BS3.......... 63 C4
  Nailsea BS48 .... 75 C8
KINGSTON SEYMOUR . 73 C2
Kingston Way BS48 .. 75 C8
Kingstree St BS4...... 64 A4
KINGSWAY 101 C3
Kingsway
  Bath BA2 .... 101 C3
  Bristol, Little Stoke BS34 36 C6
  Bristol, St George BS5.. 65 B7
  Portishead BS20 ..... 44 F4
Kingsway Ave BS15 .. 65 B8
Kingsway Cres BS15.. 65 C8
Kingsway Pk BS30 ... 66 B6
Kingsway Sh Prec BS5 . 65 B7
Kingswear **3** BS22.... 89 A2
Kingswear Rd BS3 .... 63 D2
Kings Weston Ave
  BS11................ 47 E8
Kingsweston Down Nature
  Res★ BS9, BS11...... 34 C1
Kings Weston La
  Avonmouth BS11 .... 33 E3
  Bristol BS11......... 48 A8
Kings Weston Rd BS11,
  BS10................ 47 E8
Kingsweston Sch BS11. 48 A8
Kings Wlk BS13....... 78 E7
KINGSWOOD
  Bristol 65 E8
  Wotton-under-Edge .. 11 E4
Kingswood Abbey
  Gatehouse★ GL12.... 11 F5
Kingswood Douglas Ind Est
  BS15................ 65 D7
Kingswood Foundation Est
  BS15................ 65 C8
Kingswood Heritage
  Mus★ BS30.......... 66 B6
Kingswood Hts BS15.. 51 D1
Kingswood Ind Est
  BS30................ 65 F4
Kingswood Prep Sch
  BA1 .... 84 E1
Kingswood Prim Sch
  GL12................ 11 F5
Kingswood Rd GL12... 19 D8
Kingswood Sch BA1.. 84 E2

Kingswood Sch Upper
  Sports Fields
  BATH BA1........... 84 D4
  Bristol BS15......... 84 D4
Kingswood Trad Est
  BS15................ 51 D1
KINGTON 7 E1
Kington La BS35...... 7 E1
Kington Rd BS35 ..... 7 E1
Kingwell View BS39... 115 D2
King William Ave BS1 . 143 A2
King William St BS3... 63 B4
Kinsale Rd BS14 ..... 80 C7
Kinsale Wlk BS4 ..... 63 E1
Kinvara Rd BS4 ...... 79 E8
Kipling Ave BA2...... 101 F4
Kipling Rd
  Bristol BS7.......... 36 B1
  Radstock BA3........ 133 C1
  Weston-s-M BS23 ... 105 A3
Kirkby Rd BS11 ...... 34 A1
Kirkstone Gdns BS10. 35 C2
Kirkstone Ho BS34 ... 36 A8
Kirtlington Rd BS5.... 50 B3
Kite Hay Cl BS16..... 50 E5
Kites Cl BS32 .... 24 C2
Kite Wlk **3** BS22..... 105 E8
Kitland La BS40 ...... 109 C8
Kitley Hill BA3 .... 133 C4
Kittyhawk Cl **4** BA3.. 139 B8
Knapp La GL12........ 10 B3
Knapp Rd BS35 ...... 8 D1
Knapps Cl BS25...... 124 F8
Knapps Dr BS25...... 124 F8
Knapps La BS5........ 50 E2
KNAPP THE 8 F3
Knapp The BS37 ..... 27 F5
Kneller Cl BS11 ...... 48 A8
Knight Cl BS22....... 89 A5
KNIGHTCOTT 106 F3
Knightcott BS29 ..... 106 F3
Knightcott Gdns BS29 106 F3
Knightcott Ind Est
  BS29................ 106 E3
Knightcott Pk BS29 .. 107 F3
Knightcott Rd
  Abbots Leigh BS8..... 61 F8
  Banwell BS29........ 106 F3
Knighton Rd BS10.... 35 E1
Knightsbridge Pk
  BS13................ 79 E4
Knights Cl BS9....... 49 B6
Knightstone Cl
  Axbridge BS26....... 125 C1
  Peasedown St John
    BA2 .... 134 B8
Knightstone Cswy
  BS23................ 104 C8
Knightstone Ct
  Bristol BS5.......... 50 D2
  Clevedon BS21....... 57 F1
  Weston-s-M BS23 .... 87 D1
Knightstone Gdns
  BS4................. 64 B2
Knightstone Gn BS23. 104 E6
Knightstone Ho
  1 Bristol BS2....... 143 A4
  Weston-s-M BS23 ... 104 D8
Knightstone Lodge
  BS6................. 49 D1
Knightstone Mount
  BS5................. 65 A6
Knightstone Pk **4**
  BS23................ 104 E5
Knightstone Pl
  Bath BA1 .... 84 B1
  Bristol BS5.......... 65 B2
  7 Weston-s-M BS22 . 88 F2
Knightstone Rd BS23 . 104 C8
Knightstone Rise **5**
  BS5................. 64 F8
Knightstone Sq BS14. 80 D7
Knightstone Wlk BS2. 142 C4
Knightwood Rd BS34. 36 F5
Knobsbury Hill BA3 .. 140 D6
Knobsbury La BA3 ... 140 C7
Knole Cl BS32 .... 23 F4
Knole Ct BS10 .... 35 A3
Knole La BS10 .... 35 B3
Knole Pk BS32 .... 23 F3
Knoll Cl BS9......... 48 D3
Knoll Hill BS9........ 48 D3
Knoll The BS20....... 45 D7
Knovill Cl BS11 ...... 34 B2
KNOWLE 63 F3
KNOWLE HILL BS40.. 113 C7
KNOWLE PARK 64 A1
Knowle Park Jun Sch
  BS4................. 64 A1
Knowle Rd BS2 ...... 63 F3
Knowles Rd BS21 .... 57 E2
Knowsley Rd BS16 ... 50 E3
Kyght Cl BS15 .... 66 A8
Kylross Ave BS14..... 80 B5
Kynaston View BS15. 65 D4
Kynges Mill Cl BS16.. 51 A7
Kyngstone Ct **10**
  BS16................ 50 D2
Kyrle Gdns BA1 ...... 85 F3

L

Labbott The BS31 .... 81 E5
Laburnum Cl BA3 ... 138 F8
Laburnum Ct BS23 .. 105 B7
Laburnum Gr
  Bristol BS16......... 51 B5
  Midsomer Norton BA3 . 138 F8
Laburnum Rd
  Bristol BS15......... 65 C5
  Weston-s-M BS23 ... 105 B7
Laburnum Terr BA1 .. 85 F3
Lacey Rd BS14....... 80 F6
Lacock Dr BS30...... 65 F5
Ladd Cl BS15 .... 65 F7
Ladden Ct BS35...... 15 C8
Laddon Mead BS37... 27 D4
Ladies Mile BS8...... 48 F1
Ladman Gr BS14 ..... 80 E6
Ladman Rd BS14..... 80 E5
Ladycroft **4** BS21.... 57 D1
Ladye Bay BS21...... 57 F2
Ladye Wake BS22.... 88 F4
Ladymead BS20...... 45 F5
Ladymead Ho BA1 ... 141 C3
Ladymead La BS40 .. 108 F5
Ladysmith Rd BS6.... 49 B4
Ladywell BS40 .... 92 D2
Laggan Gdns BA1 .... 84 E1
Laggan Ho BA1 ...... 84 E1
Lakemead Gdns **3**
  BS13................ 78 F4
Lakemead Gr BS13 ... 78 F6
Lake Rd
  Bristol BS10......... 49 C8
  Portishead BS20 ..... 45 D7
Lakeside BS16 .... 50 E3
Lakeside Cl BS40..... 111 D5
Lakeside Ct BS24 .... 89 B1
Lake View BS16 ...... 50 F3
Lake View Rd BS5 .... 64 D8
Lakewood Cres BS10. 49 B8
Lakewood Rd BS10... 49 B8
La Maison BS5........ 51 A2
Lambert Pl BS4....... 79 C4
Lamb Hill BS5........ 64 F7
Lambley Rd BS5 ..... 64 E8
Lambourn Cl BS3 .... 63 D3
Lambourne Way BS20 . 45 F5
Lambourn Rd BS31... 82 A4
Lambretta Scooter Mus★
  BS23................ 104 E8
LAMBRIDGE 85 C2
Lambridge **6** BA1.... 85 C1
Lambridge Bldgs **1**
  BA1 .... 85 C1
Lambridge Grange **6**
  BA1 .... 85 C1
Lambridge Mews **5**
  BA1 .... 85 C1
Lambridge Pl BA1.... 85 C1
Lambridge St BA1 ... 85 C1
Lambrook Rd BS16... 51 B4
Lamb St BS2......... 143 C3
Lamington Cl BS13... 78 F6
Lamont Ho **7** BA1.... 85 C1
Lamord Gate BS34.... 36 E5
Lampard's Bldgs BA1 . 141 B4
Lampeter Rd BS9..... 49 A7
Lampley Rd BS21 .... 73 D2
Lampton Ave BS13... 79 E3
Lampton Gr BS13 .... 79 E3
Lampton Rd BS41.... 61 F1
Lanaway Rd BS16.... 51 B6
Lancashire Rd BS7... 49 E3
Lancaster Cl BS34.... 36 D4
Lancaster House Sch
  BS23................ 104 F8
Lancaster Rd
  Bristol BS2.......... 50 A2
  Yate BS37........... 27 E3
Lancaster St **10** BS5.. 64 C7
Lancelot Rd BS16 .... 50 E8
Landemann Cir BS23. 87 E1
Landemann Path **2**
  BS23................ 104 E8
Landmark Ct BS1 .... 142 C1
Landrail Wlk BS16 ... 50 F6
Landsdown View BA1. 84 B2
Landseer Ave BS7.... 50 B7
Landseer Cl BS22 .... 88 F3
Landseer Rd BA2 .... 101 B6
Land The BS36....... 38 C7
Lane End BS40....... 95 C5
Lane End Rd BS34.... 35 E6
Lanercost Rd BS10... 35 C2
Lanesborough Rise
  BS14................ 80 D7
Lanes Dairy BS34 .... 36 A3
Lanes End BS4....... 64 C1
Lane The BS35....... 22 F2
Laneys Dro BS24..... 105 E5
Langdale Ct BS34.... 36 A3
Langdon Rd BA2..... 101 D4
Langdown Ct BS14... 80 E5
Langfield Cl BS10 .... 34 E3

Langford Cl BS39 . . . . .132 D6
Langford Court Cotts
BS40. . . . . .109 E5
Langford La BS40 . . .109 E5
Langford Rd
Bristol BS13. . . . . .78 F8
Lower Langford BS40 . .109 C6
Weston-s-M BS23 . . .105 A6
Langfords La BS39 . . . .132 C8
Langford's La BS39. . .115 D1
Langford Way BS15 . . . .65 E7
Langham Pl BA11 . . . . .137 F1
Langham Rd BS4. . . . . . .64 B2
Langhill Ave BS4. . . . . . .79 D7
Langley Cres BS3 . . . . . .62 E1
Langley Mow BS16. . . . .52 B7
Langleys Cotts BA3. . . .138 B8
Langley's La BA3, BS39 132 C1
Langport Gdns BS48 . . .75 E8
Langport Rd BS23. . . . .104 E5
LANGRIDGE. 84 E7
Langridge La BA1. . . . . .84 D8
Langsdown Ho 7 BS2. .49 F1
Langthorn Cl BS36. . . . . .38 C7
Langton Court Rd BS4. .64 D5
Langton Ct 11 BS16 . . . .50 E3
Langton Ho 9 BS2. . . .143 C4
Langton Pk BS3. . . . . . .63 C4
Langton Rd BS4. . . . . . .64 D5
Langton Way BS4 . . . . . .64 F6
LANSDOWN
Bath 84 E1
Upper Langridge 84 B6
Lansdown BS37. . . . . . . .39 E8
Lansdown Cl BS15 . . . . .51 D2
Lansdown Cres
2 Bath BA1 . . . . .84 F1
Timsbury BA2. . . . . . . .116 C2
Lansdown Ct BS23 . . . .104 F8
Lansdowne BS16. . . . . . .37 C1
Lansdowne Ct 8 BS5. . .64 A8
Lansdown Gdns BS22 . . .89 B5
Lansdown Gr BA1 . . . . .141 B4
Lansdown Grove Ct
BA1 . . . . .141 B4
Lansdown Grove Lodge
BA1 . . . . .141 B4
Lansdown Ho
Bath 84 F1
Bristol BS15. . . . . .51 D2
Lansdown Hts BA1. . . . .84 F1
Lansdown La
Bath BA1 . . . . .84 B4
Upton Cheyney BS30 . . . .67 C1
Lansdown Mans BA1 . .141 B4
Lansdown Mews 9
BA1 . . . . .141 B3
Lansdown Pk BA1. . . . . .84 E3
Lansdown Pl
Bristol BS8. . . . . .142 A3
High Littleton BS39 . . . .115 D1
Lansdown Pl E BA1 . . .141 B4
Lansdown Pl W 1 BA1. .84 F1
Lansdown Rd
Bath BA1 . . . . .84 E2
Bristol BS8. . . . . .142 A3
Bristol, Kingswood BS15 51 D2
Bristol, Redland BS6 . . . .49 C1
6 Bristol, Upper Easton
BS5 . . . . .64 B8
Pucklechurch BS16 . . . . .53 C6
Saltford BS31. . . . . .82 E3
Lansdown Terr BS6. . . . .49 D5
Lansdown View
Bath BA2 . . . . .101 C5
Bristol BS15. . . . . .65 F8
Faulkland BA3 . . . . . . .135 D1
Timsbury BA2. . . . . . . .116 C2
Tunley BA2. . . . . .117 B4
Lanson Roberts Rd
BS35. . . . . .22 D5
Lanthony Cl BS24 . . . .106 A8
Lapdown La GL9 . . . . . . .41 D1
Laphams Ct 11 BS30. . .65 F4
Lapwing Cl BS32. . . . . . .24 D2
Lapwing Gdns
Bristol BS16. . . . . .50 F6
Weston-s-M BS22 . . . . .88 F1
Larch Cl
Churchill BS40. . . . . . . .109 A5
Lyde Green BS16. . . . . . .52 D8
Nailsea BS48. . . . . .60 A2
Larch Ct BA3 . . . . .139 D8
Larches The BS22 . . . . . .89 A3
Larchgrove Cres BS22. . .88 F1
Larchgrove Wlk BS22 . . .88 F1
Larch Rd
Bristol BS15. . . . . .51 E3
Colerne SN14. . . . . .70 F6
Larch Way BS34. . . . . . .35 E7
Larchwood Ct BA3 . . . .134 A3
Lark Cl BA3. . . . . .139 B8
Larkfield BS36. . . . . .38 D7
LARKHALL. 85 C2
Larkhall Pl BA1. . . . . . . .85 C2
Larkhall Terr BA1. . . . . .85 C2
Larkhill Rd BS24 . . . . .106 B6
Lark Pl BA1. . . . . .101 D7
Lark Rd BS22 . . . . .88 F1

Lark Rise BS37. . . . . . . .27 F4
Larks Field BS16. . . . . . .50 E5
Lark's La BS37. . . . . . . .26 B7
Larksleaze Rd BS30 . . . .65 F2
Larkspur Cl BS35. . . . . . . .8 D1
Lasbury Gr BS13 . . . . . . .79 C5
Lascelles Ave BA2. . . . .102 C8
Latchmoor Ho BS13. . . .79 A8
Late Broads BA15 . . . . .120 D7
Latimer Cl BS4. . . . . . . .64 E4
LATTERIDGE. 26 B6
Latteridge La
Latteridge BS37. . . . . . .26 A7
Tytherington BS35. . . . . .15 F1
Latteridge Rd
Iron Acton BS37. . . . . . .26 D4
Latteridge BS37. . . . . . .26 C6
Latton Rd BS7. . . . . .49 F8
Launceston Ave BS15 . . .65 B5
Launceston Rd BS15 . . . .51 B1
Laura Pl BA2. . . . . .141 C3
Laurel Cl
Colerne SN14. . . . . .70 F6
Lyde Green BS16. . . . . . .52 C8
Nailsea BS48. . . . . .59 F2
Paulton BS39. . . . . . . .132 E5
Weston-s-M BS23 . . . .104 E2
Laurel Gdns
Timsbury BA2. . . . . . . .116 B1
Yatton BS49. . . . . .74 B1
Laurel Ho BS25 . . . . . .125 A8
Laurel St BS15. . . . . . . .65 D8
Laurels The
Bristol, Catbrain BS10. . .35 A6
Bristol, Mangotsfield
BS16. . . . . .52 A6
Churchill BS25. . . . . . . .108 F4
Weston-s-M BS23 . . . .104 E2
Westwood BA15. . . . . . .120 F3
Laurel Terr BS49. . . . . . .74 B1
Laurie Cres BS9. . . . . . . .49 D6
Laurie Lee Ct 3 BS30. .66 A5
Lavender Cl
Thornbury BS35. . . . . .8 D1
Weston-s-M BS22 . . . . .89 A5
Lavender Ct BS5. . . . . . .50 F1
Lavender Way BS32 . . . .36 F7
Lavenham Rd BS37. . . . .27 B2
Lavers Cl BS15. . . . . . . .65 E6
Lavington Cl BS21. . . . . .57 D1
Lavington Rd BS5. . . . . . .65 B6
Lawford Ave BS34. . . . . .36 C6
Lawfords Gate BS2. . . .143 C3
Lawfords Gate Ho 17
BS2. . . . . .143 C3
Lawford St BS2 . . . . . .143 C3
Lawn Ave BS16. . . . . . . .51 B5
Lawn Cl 5 BS7. . . . . . .50 C8
Lawn Rd BS16. . . . . .51 B5
Lawnside BS48. . . . . . . .76 B5
Lawns Rd BS37. . . . . . . .27 F2
Lawns The
Bristol BS11. . . . . .47 E7
Weston-s-M BS22 . . . . .89 B3
Yatton BS49. . . . . .74 A1
Lawnwood Ind Units 14
BS5. . . . . .64 B8
Lawnwood Rd 15 BS5 . .64 B8
Lawrence Ave BS5 . . . . .50 B1
Lawrence Cl
Bristol BS15. . . . . .52 A2
Weston-s-M BS22 . . . . .88 E2
Lawrence Dr BS37. . . . . .27 B2
Lawrence Gr BS9. . . . . . .49 B5
Lawrence Hill BS5. . . . . .64 B7
Lawrence Hill Ind Pk
BS5. . . . . .64 B8
Lawrence Hill Rdbt
BS5. . . . . .64 A7
Lawrence Hill Sta BS5. . .64 B7
Lawrence Mews BS22 . . .88 E2
Lawrence Rd
Weston-s-M BS22 . . . . .88 E2
Wrington BS40. . . . . . . .92 E2
LAWRENCE WESTON. . . .34 A1
Lawrence Weston Rd
Avonmouth BS11. . . . . . .33 F4
Bristol BS11. . . . . .34 A2
Laws Dr BS24. . . . . . . .105 F7
Lawson Cl BS31. . . . . . . .82 C2
Laxey Rd BS7. . . . . .49 F7
Laxton Cl BS35. . . . . . . .14 A3
Laxton Dr GL12 . . . . . . .11 F4
Laxton Way BA2. . . . . .134 D7
Lays Dr BS31. . . . . .81 C5
Lays Farm Bsns Ctr
BS31. . . . . .81 C4
Lays Farm Trad Est
BS31. . . . . .81 C4
Lays La BS40. . . . . .110 D4
Leach Cl BS21. . . . . .57 F1
Lea Croft BS13. . . . . . . .79 A4
Leader St BS7. . . . . .64 C8
Leading Edge The
BS8. . . . . .142 B2
Leadmine La BS40 . . . .127 E4
Leafy Way BS24. . . . . . .106 B4
Lea Grove Rd BS21. . . . .57 E4
Leaholme Gdns BS14. . .80 A3

Leaman Cl BS37 . . . . . . .28 B1
Lea Pound St BS34. . . . .35 F6
Leap Vale BS16. . . . . . . .52 A8
Leap Valley Cres BS16 . .52 A8
Lear Cl BS30. . . . . .66 B5
Leawood Ct 3 BS23. . . .87 C1
Leaze La BS40 . . . . . . .127 E8
Leaze The
Radstock BA3. . . . . . . .139 D8
Yate BS37. . . . . .27 D2
Leda Ave BS14. . . . . . . .80 A7
Ledbury Rd BS16. . . . . . .51 C4
Leechpool Way BS37. . . .27 C5
Lee Cl BS34. . . . . .35 F8
Leedham Rd
Locking BS24. . . . . . . .106 C5
Locking BS24. . . . . . . .106 C5
Leeming Way BS11. . . . .47 C8
Lees Ct BS15. . . . . .51 E1
Lees Hill BS15. . . . . .51 E2
Leeside BS20. . . . . .45 C5
Lees La BS30. . . . . .66 D5
Leewood Rd BS23. . . . . .87 C1
Leg La BS40. . . . . .110 B3
Leicester Sq BS16. . . . . .51 D3
Leicester St 6 BS3 . . . .63 D4
Leicester Wlk BS4 . . . . .64 F5
Leigh Cl BA1. . . . . .85 A2
Leigh Court Bsns Ctr
BS8. . . . . .48 A2
Leigh Ct BS9. . . . . .48 D3
Leigh La
Cold Ashton BA1. . . . . . .69 B3
Westerleigh BS37. . . . . .39 B1
Leigh Rd BS8. . . . . .142 B4
Leigh St BS3. . . . . .63 A4
Leighton Cres BS24. . . .122 A8
Leighton Rd
Bath BA1 . . . . .84 A3
Bristol, Southville BS3. . .63 B4
Bristol, Upper Knowle
BS4. . . . . .64 B2
Leigh View Rd BS20 . . . .45 E7
Leighwood Dr BS48. . . . .59 B1
LEIGH WOODS. 62 D8
Leigh Woods Forest
Walks ★ BS8. . . . . .48 C1
Leinster Ave BS4. . . . . . .79 D8
Leisure Rd BS15 . . . . . . .65 E5
Lemon La BS2. . . . . . . .143 C4
Lena Ave 3 BS5 . . . . . .50 C1
Lena St BS5. . . . . .50 C1
Lennox Way BS11. . . . . .33 B1
Lenover Gdns BS13 . . . .79 B4
Leonard La BS1. . . . . . .143 A3
Leonard Rd BS5. . . . . . .64 D7
Leonards Ave BS5. . . . . .50 C1
Leonides Ave BS24. . . .105 B4
Leopold Bldgs BA1. . . .141 C4
Leopold Rd BS6. . . . . . . .49 E2
Les Brown Ct BS2. . . . .143 C2
Lescren Way BS11 . . . . .33 D1
Leslie Rise BA15. . . . . .120 F3
Lester Dr BS22. . . . . . . .89 A3
Lewington Rd BS16. . . . .51 C4
Lewins Mead BS1. . . . .143 A3
Lewin St 9 BS5. . . . . . .64 D7
Lewis Cl
Bristol, Emerson's Green
BS16. . . . . .52 C5
Bristol, North Common
BS30. . . . . .66 D5
Chilcompton BA3. . . . . .138 C4
Lewisham Gr BS23. . . . .105 A8
Lewis Rd BS13. . . . . . . .79 A8
Lewis St BS2. . . . . .64 B5
Lewton La BS36. . . . . . . .37 E7
LEYHILL. 10 B4
Ley La BS35. . . . . .13 F3
Leyland Wlk BS13. . . . . .78 F4
Leys The BS21. . . . . .57 D1
Leyton Villas BS6. . . . . .49 B2
Liberty Gdns BS1. . . . .142 C1
Liberty Ind Pk BS3. . . . .63 A1
Liberty La BS40 . . . . . .110 E2
Lichfield Rd BS4. . . . . . .64 E6
Lilac Cl BS10. . . . . .35 C1
Lilac Ct BS31. . . . . .81 C4
Lilac Dr BS16. . . . . .52 C8
Lilac Terr BA3. . . . . . . .133 C2
Lilac Way BS22. . . . . . . .89 A5
Lilian Terr BS39. . . . . . .132 E5
Lillian St 5 BS5 . . . . . .64 C8
Lillington Cl BA3. . . . . .134 B2
Lillington Rd BA3. . . . .134 B2
Lilliput Ave BS37. . . . . . .40 A8
Lilliput Ct BS37. . . . . . . .40 B8
Lillypool Cheese & Cider
Farm ★ BS25. . . . . . . .125 F6
Lilstock Ave BS7. . . . . . .49 F4
Lilton Wlk BS13. . . . . . . .63 A1
Lilymead Ave BS4. . . . . .64 A3
Lime Ave GL9. . . . . .42 B8
Limebreach Wood
BS48. . . . . .59 D3
Limeburn Hill BS40 . . . .95 E5
Lime Cl
Bristol BS10. . . . . .35 B3
Locking BS24. . . . . . . .106 B4

Lime Cl continued
Weston-s-M BS22 . . . . .89 A1
Lime Croft BS37 . . . . . . .27 F4
Lime Ct BS31. . . . . .81 C4
Lime Gr
Alveston BS35. . . . . .14 F4
Bath BA2 . . . . .102 B6
Lime Grove Gdns BA2. .102 B6
Lime Kiln Ct BS34. . . . . .36 D3
Lime Kiln Ct BS35. . . . . .15 F3
Lime Kiln Gdns BS32. . . .24 D2
Limekiln La BA2. . . . . . .102 F4
Lime Kiln La BS21. . . . . .57 F3
Limekiln Rd BS37, GL12 .17 C2
Lime Kiln Rd BS1. . . . . .142 B2
Limekilns Cl BS31. . . . . .81 F5
Lime Rd
Bristol, Hanham BS15. . .65 A5
Bristol, Southville BS3. . .63 B4
Limerick Rd BS6. . . . . . .49 C2
Lime St BS14. . . . . .79 E5
Limes The
Badminton GL9. . . . . . . .30 E2
Bristol BS16. . . . . .37 B1
Limestone La BS37. . . . .28 A2
Limestone Link BS40. . .128 D6
Lime Terr BA3 . . . . .133 D1
Lime Tree Gr BS20. . . . . .47 D3
Lime Trees Rd BS9. . . . . .49 D6
LIMPLEY STOKE. 120 A6
Limpley Stoke Rd
BA15. . . . . .120 D6
Lincoln Cl BS31. . . . . . . .81 C4
Lincoln Ct BS16. . . . . . . .50 D6
Lincoln St BS5. . . . . .64 B7
Lincombe Ave BS16. . . . .51 C6
Lincombe Rd
Bristol BS16. . . . . .51 C6
Radstock BA3. . . . . . . .139 D8
Lincott View BA2. . . . . .134 C8
Linden Ave BS23. . . . . .105 B8
Linden Cl
Bristol BS14. . . . . .80 E6
Bristol, Mayfield Park
BS16. . . . . .51 A2
Colerne SN14. . . . . .70 F6
Radstock BA3. . . . . . . .139 E8
Winterbourne BS36. . . . .37 E6
Linden Dr BS32. . . . . . . .36 E8
Linden Gdns BA1. . . . . .101 D8
Linden Grange BS6. . . . .49 C3
Linden Ho BS16. . . . . . . .50 C5
Linden Quarter 13 BS3 .63 C3
Linden Rd
Bristol BS6. . . . . .49 B4
Clevedon BS21. . . . . . . .57 F4
Lindens The BS22. . . . . .88 E4
Lindisfarne Cl BA15 . . .120 E6
Lindon Ct 4 BS15. . . . .51 B1
Lindon Ho BS4. . . . . .64 E3
Lindrea St 3 BS3. . . . . .63 B3
Lindsay Rd BS7. . . . . . . .50 A4
Lindsey Cl BS20. . . . . . . .44 F4
Linemere Cl BS48. . . . . .76 D6
Lines Way BS14. . . . . . . .80 C3
Lingfield Pk BS16. . . . . .37 F2
Link La
Burrington BS40 . . . . . .109 F8
Monkton Farleigh BA15 103 F8
Linkmead BA3. . . . . . . .138 F2
Link Rd
Bristol BS34. . . . . .36 B3
Nailsea BS48. . . . . .59 F2
Portishead BS20. . . . . . .45 C5
Yate BS37. . . . . .27 F1
Link Sch The BA2 . . . . .118 E8
Links Ct BS23 . . . . .104 D4
Linkside BS21. . . . . .57 G6
Links Rd BS23 . . . . .104 C2
Linley Cl BA2. . . . . .101 A5
Linleys The BA1. . . . . . .101 C7
Linne Ho BA2. . . . . .101 A5
Linnell Cl BS7. . . . . .50 B6
Linnet Cl
Bristol BS34. . . . . .35 E8
Weston-s-M BS22 . . . . .88 E1
Linnet Gdns BS20. . . . . .45 F6
Linnet Way
Keynsham BS31. . . . . . . .81 C3
Keynsham BS31. . . . . . . .81 C3
Midsomer Norton BA3. .139 B8
Lintern Cres BS30. . . . . .66 B6
Lintham Dr BS15. . . . . . .65 F6
Linton's Wlk BS14. . . . . .80 A7
Lion Cl BS48. . . . . .59 D2
Lipgate Pl BS20. . . . . . . .45 D3
Lippiat Hill BA3. . . . . . .135 C3
Lippiatt La
Shipham BS25. . . . . . . .125 FR
Timsbury BA2. . . . . . . .116 B3
LIPYEATE. 139 E1
Lipyeate La BA3. . . . . . .139 E2
Lisburn Rd BS4. . . . . . . .63 E1
Lisle Rd BS22. . . . . .89 B4
Lister Gr BA15 . . . . .120 F3
Litfield Pl BS8. . . . . .62 F7
Litfield Rd BS8. . . . . .62 F8
Litt Hill BA3. . . . . .130 F2

Little Ann St BS2, BS5. .143 C4
LITTLE BADMINTON. . . .30 E5
Little Birch Croft BS14 .80 A3
Little Bishop St BS2. . . .143 B4
LITTLE BRISTOL. 11 B3
Little Bristol Cl GL12 . . .11 B4
Little Bristol La GL12 . . .11 B4
Littlebrook BS39. . . . . .132 E6
Little Caroline Pl 4
BS8. . . . . .62 F5
Littlecross Ho BS3. . . . . .63 B4
Littledean BS37. . . . . . . .39 E7
Little Dowles BS30 . . . . .66 A4
Littlefields Ave BS29 . .107 B3
Littlefields Rd BS29 . . .107 B3
Littlefields Rise BS29. .107 B3
Little George St
Bristol BS2. . . . . .143 C4
Weston-s-M BS23 . . . .104 E2
Little Green La BS35 . . . .22 A7
Little Halt BS20. . . . . . . .44 E4
Little Ham BS21. . . . . . . .73 C8
Little Hayes BS16. . . . . . .51 B6
Little Headley Cl BS13. . .79 B7
Little King St BS1. . . . . .143 A2
Little La BA2. . . . . .116 A6
Little Mdw BS34. . . . . . . .37 A6
Little Mead BS11. . . . . . .34 B1
Little Mead Cl BS24 . . .105 E3
Little Meadow End
BS48. . . . . .75 E8
Little Mead Prim Sch
BS10. . . . . .35 C2
Little Orch BS23 . . . . . .104 D1
Little Paradise BS3. . . . . .63 D3
Little Parr Cl BS16. . . . . .50 C5
Little Paul St BS2. . . . . .142 C4
LITTLE SODBURY. 29 B3
LITTLE SODBURY END. . .28 B3
Little Solsbury La BA1. . .85 F4
Little Stanhope St
BA1 . . . . .141 A2
LITTLE STOKE. 36 D7
Little Stoke La BS34. . . .36 D6
Little Stoke Prim Sch
BS34. . . . . .36 D6
Little Stoke Rd BS9 . . . .48 E4
Little Stony Leas BS16. .50 D8
Little Thatch Cl BS14 . . .80 C6
LITTLETON. 95 C4
Littleton Ct BS34. . . . . . .23 F1
LITTLETON DREW. 43 E5
Littleton Drew La GL9 . .43 A6
Littleton La
Wellow BA2. . . . . .135 C7
Winford BS40. . . . . .95 D5
Littleton Mills BS40 . . . .95 D4
Littleton Rd BS3. . . . . . . .63 D2
Littleton St 4 BS5. . . . .50 C1
LITTLETON-UPON-
SEVERN 13 E8
Little Withey Mead
BS9. . . . . .48 F5
Littlewood Cl BS14. . . . .80 B3
Littlewood La BS49. . . . .75 C2
LITTON. 130 F2
Litton BS24. . . . . .105 A2
Litton Rd BA3. . . . . .131 A1
Livingstone Mews 11
BS3. . . . . .63 C3
Livingstone Rd BA2. . . .101 D5
Livingstone Terr BA2. . .141 A1
Llanarth Villas 3 BS6 . .49 D1
Llewellyn Ct BS9. . . . . . .49 A8
Llewellyn Way BS22. . . .89 B3
Lobelia Rd BS16. . . . . . .38 D1
Lockemor Rd BS13. . . . .79 F4
Lockes Paddock BS22. . .89 C3
Lock Gdns BS13. . . . . . .78 E7
LOCKING. 106 A4
Locking Farm Ind Est
BS24. . . . . .106 A5
Locking Head Dro
Locking BS24. . . . . . . .105 F5
Locking BS24. . . . . . . .106 A6
Weston-s-M BS24 . . . .106 A8
Locking Moor Rd
Locking BS24. . . . . . . .106 B5
Weston-s-M BS22 . . . .105 D8
Locking Parklands
BS24. . . . . .106 B5
Locking Prim Sch
BS24. . . . . .106 B4
Locking Rd BS22, BS23 105 B7
Locking Road Bsns Pk
BS23. . . . . .105 A7
Lockingwell Rd BS31. . . .81 D5
LOCKLEAZE. 50 C7
Lockleaze Prim Sch
BS7. . . . . .50 B6
Lockleaze Rd BS7. . . . . .50 A6
Lockleys Way BS16. . . . .50 D8
Lock's Acre BS35 . . . . . .15 B5
LOCKSBROOK. 101 B6
Locksbrook Ct 8 BA1 101 B6
Locksbrook Pl 6 BA1 101 C7

Locksbrook Rd
 Bath BA1........101 C6
 Weston-s-M BS22.....89 B5
Locksbrook Trad Est **7**
 BA1...........101 B6
Lockside BS20.......45 E7
Lockside Sq BS20....45 E7
Lock's La BS37.......25 E4
Locks Yd BS3........63 B1
Lodge Causeway Trad Ctr
 BS16...........50 F3
Lodge Cl BS49.......91 B8
Lodge Cswy BS16.....51 A3
Lodge Ct BS9........48 E4
Lodge Dr
 Bristol BS30........66 C2
 Long Ashton BS41....62 B2
 Weston-s-M BS23.....88 A1
Lodge Gdns BA2......101 D1
Lodge Hill BS15......51 C2
Lodge La BS48.......60 B2
Lodge Pl BS1........142 C3
Lodge Rd
 Bristol BS15........51 C1
 Wick BS30..........53 B1
 Yate BS37..........27 A3
Lodgeside Ave BS15...51 C1
Lodgeside Gdns BS15..51 C1
Lodge St BS1........142 C3
Lodges The BA3......138 D1
Lodge The BS40......92 E2
Lodge Wlk BS16......51 D6
Lodore Rd BS16......50 F3
LODWAY...........47 B5
Lodway BS20........47 C4
Lodway Cl BS20......47 C5
Lodway Gdns BS20....47 C4
Lodway Rd BS4.......64 C2
Logan Rd BS7.......49 D3
Logus Ct **14** BS30....65 F4
Lombard St BS3......63 D4
Lombardy Cl **5** BS22..105 E8
Lomond Rd BS7......35 F1
Londonderry Farm
 BS30............82 A8
London Rd
 Bath BA1..........141 C4
 Bristol, St Pauls BS2...49 F1
 Bristol, Warmley BS30..66 D7
 Wick BS30..........67 E6
London Rd E BA1.....86 A3
London Rd W BA1....85 E2
London Sq BS20......45 E7
London St
 Bath BA1..........141 C4
 Bristol BS16........65 D8
Longacre BS21.......73 B8
Long Acre BA1.......141 C4
Long Acre Ho BA1....141 C4
Long Acre Rd BS14...80 A3
Long Acres Cl BS9....48 D7
LONG ASHTON.......62 A1
Long Ashton Bsns Pk
 BS41............62 B1
Long Ashton By-Pass
 Barrow Gurney BS48...77 D7
 Bristol BS41........62 C1
 Bristol BS41........78 B8
Long Ashton Rd BS41..62 B2
Long Ave BS21.......57 D2
Long Barnaby BA3....133 A2
Long Beach Rd BS30...66 B3
Longbottom BS25.....126 A6
Longbrook Trad Est
 BS3.............62 E3
Long Cl
 Bristol, Fishponds BS16..51 C6
 Bristol, Little Stoke BS32.36 E6
Long Croft BS37......27 D4
Longcross GL12......10 B1
LONG CROSS........94 D7
Long Cross
 Bristol, Lawrence Weston
 BS11............34 B2
 Bristol, Shirehampton
 BS11............47 F8
 Felton BS40........94 D7
Longden Rd BS16.....51 F6
Longdown Dr BS22....89 B4
Long Eaton Dr BS14...80 B7
Longfellow Ave BA2...101 F4
Longfellow Rd BA3....139 C8
Longfield Rd BS7.....49 E3
Longford BS37.......39 C6
Longford Ave BS10...49 D8
Long Fox Manor BS4...65 A1
Long Ground BS34....36 A7
Long Handstones BS30.66 A4
Long Hay Cl BA2......101 B5
LONGHOUSE.........117 D5
Long La
 Backwell BS48.......76 C2
 Felton BS40........94 A3
 Wrington BS40......93 B2
Longlands Ho **13** BS5..64 C7

Long Lease SN14......43 C1
Longleat Cl BS9......49 C5
Longleaze Gdns BS24..105 F3
Long Leaze Rd BS34...35 F7
Long Mdw BS16......50 D6
Long Mead
 Lockleaze BS7......50 C8
 Yate BS37..........27 E5
Longmead Ave BS7....49 D5
Longmead Cl BA2.....136 F4
Longmead Croft BS13..78 F4
Longmeadow Rd BS31..81 C4
Longmead Rd BS16....38 B1
Longmoor Ct BS3.....63 A2
Longmoor Rd BS3.....63 A2
Longney Pl BS34......23 F1
Long Rd BS16........52 A5
Longreach BS31......82 C4
Longreach Gr BS14....80 D6
Longridge Way BS24...105 F7
Long Row BS1........143 B2
Longs Dr BS37........27 C2
Longs View GL12......11 A5
Long-Thorn BS48.....75 F6
Longthorne Pl BA2....101 F2
Long Thorn La BS40...111 E7
Longton Grove Rd **3**
 BS23............104 E8
Longton Ind Est BS23..104 F6
Long Valley Rd BA2...100 F5
Longvernal BA3......132 F1
Longvernal Prim Sch
 Midsomer Norton BA3..132 E1
 Midsomer Norton BA3..132 F1
Longway Ave BS13,
 BS14............79 F4
LONGWELL GREEN....65 E3
Longwell Green Prim Sch
 BS30............65 F3
Longwell Green Trad Pk
 BS30............65 E4
Longwell Ho BS30.....65 F3
Longwood BS4.......65 A2
Longwood Ho BS8.....61 D4
Longwood La BS8, BS41.61 F4
Long Wood Mead BS7..50 C8
Long Wood Rd BS7....50 C8
Lons Ct BS30........66 C1
Lonsdale Ave BS23....104 F4
Lonsdale Bsns Ctr BS15 51 C2
Loop Rd BS14........52 A3
Lorain Wlk BS10......34 F2
Lorne Rd BA2........101 D6
Lorton Cl BS10.......35 B1
Lorton Rd BS10.......35 B1
Lotts' Ave BS48.......76 B5
Lotus Ct BS22........88 C1
Loughman Cl **2** BS15..65 E8
Louisa St BS2........143 C2
Louise Ave BS16......52 A5
Love La
 Chipping Sodbury BS37..40 A8
 Yate BS37..........28 A4
Lovelinch Gdns BS41...61 F1
Lovell Ave BS30......66 D4
Lovell Dr BS39.......113 C4
Lovell's Hill BS15.....65 B5
Lovells Mill BS39.....113 D4
Lovells The BS20......47 B4
Loveridge Ct BS36....38 B7
Loveringe Cl BS10....34 F4
Lovers La BA3, BS39...133 A5
Lovers' Wlk BS23......104 D8
Loves Hill BA2........116 A1
Love's La BA2........115 F6
Lowbourne BS14......79 F6
LOWER
 ALMONDSBURY......24 A6
Lower Ashley Rd
 Bristol, Baptist Mills BS2,
 BS5............50 A1
 13 Bristol, St Pauls BS2..49 F1
Lower Batch BS40.....96 B3
Lower Borough Walls
 BA1............141 C2
Lower Bristol Rd
 Bath BA2..........101 B6
 Clutton BS39.......114 F4
Lower Burlington Rd
 BS20............45 E7
Lower Camden Pl
 BA1............141 C4
LOWER CANADA.....105 F2
Lower Castle St BS1...143 B3
Lower Chapel La BS36..38 C7
Lower Chapel Rd BS15..65 C5
Lower Cheltenham Pl
 BS6.............49 F1
Lower Church La BS2..143 A3
Lower Church Rd
 Carlingcott BA2.....117 C1
 Weston-s-M BS23....104 D8
LOWER CLAVERHAM...74 F2
Lower Claverham BS49..74 F3
Lower Clifton Hill BS8..142 B2
Lower Cock Rd BS15...65 E5
Lower College St BS1..142 C2
Lower Conham Vale
 BS15............65 A5

Lower Court Rd BS32..24 A5
Lower Down Rd BS20..45 B5
Lower East Hayes BA1..102 B8
LOWER EASTON......50 D2
Lower Failand La BS14..79 F3
LOWER FAILAND.....61 A8
Lower Farm La BA2....100 B7
Lower Gay St BS2.....143 A4
Lower Grove Rd BS16..50 F4
Lower Guinea St BS1...143 A1
LOWER HAMSWELL...68 C3
Lower Hanham Rd
 BS15............65 C6
LOWER HAZEL.......14 F3
Lower Hedgemead Rd
 BA1............141 C4
Lower High St BS11....47 D7
Lower Ho BS34.......36 A3
Lower House Cres
 BS34............36 B4
Lowerhouse La GL11...5 D5
Lower Kewstoke Rd
 Weston-s-M BS22....88 E3
 Weston-super-Mare
 BS22............88 E3
Lower Kingsdown Rd
 SN13............86 F3
Lower Knole La BS10...35 A3
LOWER KNOWLE.....63 E1
Lower Knowles Rd
 BS21............57 E2
Lower Lamb St BS1....142 C2
LOWER LANGFORD...109 C5
Lower La The BA2.....118 C4
Lower Leaze BS34.....35 E6
Lower Linden Rd BS21..57 F3
Lower Maudlin St BS1..143 A3
Lower Moor Rd BS37...27 C4
LOWER MORTON......8 C4
Lower Northend BA1...85 F5
Lower Norton La
 Weston-s-M BS22....88 E4
 Weston-s-M, Norton
 BS22............88 C4
Lower Oldfield Pk
 BA2............141 A1
Lower Parade Ground Rd
 BS24............106 C5
Lower Park Row BS1...143 A3
LOWER PEASEDOWN..134 B8
Lower Queen's Rd
 BS21............57 F3
Lower Rd BS39.......130 E6
Lower Redland Mews **2**
 BS6.............49 B2
Lower Redland Rd BS6..49 B2
Lower Shockerwick La
 BA1............86 D5
Lower Sidney St BS3...63 A4
LOWER SOUNDWELL...51 F2
Lower St SN14.......54 D4
Lower Station Rd
 6 Bristol, Ridgeway
 BS16............51 A4
 Bristol, Staple Hill BS16..51 C4
Lower Stoke BA2......120 A8
Lower Stone Cl BS36...38 C7
LOWER STONE.......3 C1
LOWER STRODE.....112 A8
Lower Strode BS40....112 A7
Lower Strode Rd BS21..73 A7
LOWER SWAINSWICK..85 C3
Lower Thirlmere Rd
 BS34............36 A8
Lower Tockington Rd
 BS32............14 B1
LOWER WESTON.....101 C7
Lower Whitelands
 BA3............134 B3
LOWER WICK........4 E3
LOWER
 WRITHLINGTON....134 C3
Lowlis Cl BS10.......34 F3
Lowry Grove BS7.....50 C8
Lowther Rd BS10.....35 C2
Low Veale La BS39....114 A4
Loxley Gdns BA2......101 C4
LOXTON...........123 C4
Loxton Dr BA2.......101 B6
Loxton Rd BS23......104 F2
Loxton Sq BS14......80 A6
Lucas Cl BS4........64 D1
Luccombe Hill BS6....49 B2
LUCKINGTON........31 F4
Luckington Com Sch
 SN14............31 E5
Luckington Court Gdns★
 SN14............31 F5
Luckington Cross
 BA11............140 B2
Luckington Rd
 Acton Turville GL9....43 A7
 Bristol BS7........49 E8
Lucklands Rd BA1.....84 C1
Luckley Ave BS13.....79 C5
Luckwell Prim Sch BS3..63 A3
Luckwell Rd BS3......63 B3
Lucky La BS3........63 D4

Ludlow Cl
 Bristol, St Pauls BS2...49 F1
 Bristol, Willsbridge BS30..66 B2
Ludlow Ct BS30......66 B1
Ludlow Rd BS7.......50 A7
Ludwell Cl BS36......37 D5
Ludwells Orch BS39...132 E5
Luggard's Cross BS21..57 C2
Luke's Cl BA3........133 F3
Lullington Rd BS4....64 B2
LULSGATE BOTTOM...94 A8
Lulsgate Rd BS13.....79 A8
Lulworth Cres BS16...51 F8
Lulworth Rd BS31.....81 E4
Lundy Gate BS20.....45 F6
Lunty Mead BS48.....75 F6
Lupin Cl BS16........52 C8
Lurgan Wlk BS4......63 D1
Lutyens Cl BS16......50 E8
Luvers La BS40.......110 D1
Lux Furlong BS9......48 B7
Luxton St BS5........64 B8
Lwr Station App Rd
 BS3............143 C1
Lychgate Pk BS24.....106 A4
Lydbrook Cl BS37.....39 D8
Lyddieth Ct BA15.....120 E7
Lyddington Rd BS7....49 F8
Lyddon Rd BS22......89 B3
Lyde Gn BA2........136 E5
LYDE GREEN.........52 E8
Lyde Green Prim Sch
 BS16............52 C8
Lyde Green Rdbt BS16..52 B8
Lydford Wlk BS3......63 C2
Lydia Ct BA15.......120 E7
Lydney Rd
 Bristol, Southmead
 BS10............35 D1
 Bristol, Staple Hill BS16..51 E4
Lydstep Terr BS3......63 C4
LYE CROSS.........93 C1
Lye Cross Rd BS40....93 C1
Lyefield Rd BS22......88 E4
LYE HOLE.........93 E2
Lye Hole La BS40.....93 D2
Lye Mead BS40......95 A6
Lyes The BS49.......91 D3
Lyme Gdns BA1......101 B7
Lyme Rd BA1........101 B7
Lymore Ave BA2......101 C5
Lymore Gdns BA2.....101 C5
Lymore Terr BA2......101 C4
LYMPSHAM.........122 B1
Lympsham CE Fst Sch
 BS24............122 B1
Lympsham Gn BA2....118 D8
Lympsham Rd BS24...122 B1
Lynbrook BS41.......61 F1
Lynbrook La BA2......101 F3
Lynch Cl BS22........88 F3
Lynch Cres BS25.....124 F7
Lynch Ct BS30.......65 F4
Lynch Hill BA3.......138 A3
Lynchmead BS25.....125 A7
Lynch The BS25......124 F7
Lyncombe Hall BA2...102 A4
LYNCOMBE HILL.....102 A4
Lyncombe Hill BA1....141 C1
LYNCOMBE VALE....102 A3
Lyncombe Vale BA2...102 B4
Lyncombe Vale Rd
 BA2............102 A4
Lyncombe Wlk BS16...51 B2
Lyndale Ave BS9......48 D5
Lyndale Rd
 Bristol BS5........64 D8
 Yate BS37..........27 D1
Lynde Cl BS13.......79 B4
Lyndhurst Rd
 Bath BA2..........101 C6
 Bristol BS9........48 F7
 Keynsham BS31......81 F3
 Midsomer Norton BA3..139 B8
 Weston-s-M BS23....104 E4
Lyndhurst Terr BA1...141 C4
Lynfield Pk BA1......84 C1
Lynmouth Cl BS22....89 A2
Lynmouth Rd **3** BS2..50 A2
Lynn Rd BS16........50 D5
Lynton **3** BS15......66 A8
Lynton Cl BS20......45 E4
Lynton Pl **9** BS5......64 C8
Lynton Rd
 Bristol BS3........63 D2
 Midsomer Norton BA3..139 B8
Lynton Way BS16.....37 B1
Lynwood Cl BA3......139 A8
Lynwood Ct BS13.....79 B6
Lynwood Rd BS3......63 B2
Lynx Cres BS24......105 B2
Lyons Court Rd BS14..80 D7
Lyons Ct BS23.......104 F7
Lyppiatt Rd BS5......64 D8
Lyppincott Rd BS10...35 A3
Lypstone Cl BS24.....106 A8
Lysander Rd BS10, BS34 35 C6
Lysander Wlk BS34....36 E5

Lytchet Dr BS16......51 F8
Lytes Cary Rd BS31...82 A3
Lytham Ho BS4.......64 D1
Lytton Gdns BA2.....101 B4
Lytton Gr
 Bristol BS7........50 A8
 Keynsham BS31......82 A5
Lyveden Gdns BS13...79 B5
Lyvedon Way BS41....62 B1

M

Mabberley Cl BS16....52 C5
Macaulay Bldgs BA2..102 C4
Macauley Rd BS7.....50 A8
Macdonald Wlk **3**
 BS15............65 D8
Macey's Rd BS13.....79 D3
Macfarlane Chase
 BS23............105 A5
Machin Cl BS10......34 F3
Machin Gdns BS10....35 A3
Machin Rd BS10......35 A3
Macies The BA1......84 B3
Mackie Ave BS34.....36 B2
Mackie Gdns BS34....36 B2
Mackie Rd BS34......36 B2
Mackley La BA2......136 E3
Macleod Cl BS21.....57 C2
Macquarie Farm Cl
 BS49............74 A1
Macrae Ct BS15......65 E8
Macrae Rd BS20......47 E4
Madam La
 Weston-s-M BS22....88 F2
 Weston-s-M BS22....89 A3
 Weston-s-M BS22....89 A3
Madam's Paddock BS40 96 B3
Madeira Ct BS23......104 C8
Madeira Rd
 Clevedon BS21......57 F3
 Weston-s-M BS23....87 C1
Madeline Rd BS16....50 F2
Madison Cl BS37.....27 D2
Madison Way BS35....22 D1
Maesbury BS15......65 E6
Maesbury Rd BS31....82 A2
Maesknoll La BS14,
 BS39............97 B8
Maesknoll Rd BS4....64 A2
Magdalena Ct BS1....143 B1
Magdalen Ave BA2...141 B1
Magdalene Pl BS2....49 F1
Magdalene Rd BA3....134 C2
Magdalen Rd BA2....141 B1
Magdalen Way BS22...89 A3
Magellan Cl BS22.....88 F4
Maggs Cl BS10.......35 C3
Maggs Folly BS39....115 D2
Maggs Hill BA2......116 B2
Maggs La
 Bristol BS5........50 E2
 Whitchurch BS14....80 C4
Magnolia Ave BS22...89 A1
Magnolia Cl BS22....105 E7
Magnolia Gdns BS32...24 E5
Magnolia Grange BS22 88 F1
Magnolia Rd BA3.....133 C1
Magpie Bottom La
 Bristol, Kingswood
 BS15............65 C6
 Bristol, St George BS5..65 B6
Magpie Cl BS22......105 E8
MAIDEN HEAD.......78 F1
Maidenhead Rd BS13..79 D3
Maiden Way BS11.....47 C8
Maidstone Gr BS24...105 A1
Maidstone St BS3.....63 F3
Main Dr BS10........34 E1
MAINES BATCH......92 E3
Main Rd
 Bristol BS16........52 D5
 Brockley BS49......75 D2
 Flax Bourton BS48....76 F7
 Hutton BS24.......105 E2
Main St BS39.......132 A6
Main View BS36......38 D7
Maisemore BS37.....39 E6
Maisemore Ave BS34..24 B1
Maize Cl BS35........8 B3
Makin Cl BS30.......66 C5
Malago Dr BS3.......63 C2
Malago Rd BS3.......63 D3
Malago Vale Trad Est
 BS3............63 D3
Malago Wlk BS13....78 E4
Malden Mead BS13...79 A4
Maldowers La **2** BS5..65 A8
Malin Par BS20......45 F6
Mallard Cl
 Bristol BS32.......24 D2
 Bristol, Crofts End BS5..50 F1
 Chipping Sodbury BS37..40 A8
Mallard Wlk **7** BS22..105 E8
Mallet Gr BA2.......102 A2
Mallow Cl
 Clevedon BS21......57 G2
 Thornbury BS35......8 D2

Mallow Rd G12 . . . . .11 B5
Mall The
  Bath BA1 . . . . .141 C2
  Bristol, Clifton BS8 . . . . . .62 F7
Mall The BS34 . . . . .35 D6
Malmains Dr BS16 . . . . . . .37 B1
Malmesbury Cl
  Bristol, Bishopston BS6 . .49 C4
  Bristol, Longwell Green
    BS30 . . . . .65 F5
Malpass Dr BS15 . . . . . . .65 D4
Maltings Ind Est The
  BA1 . . . . .101 B6
Maltings The
  Midford BA2 . . . . .119 C5
  Weston-s-M BS22 . . . . . .88 F2
Maitlands BS22 . . . . .105 D8
Malvern Bldgs BA1 . . . . . .85 A2
Malvern Ct BS5 . . . . .64 F7
Malvern Dr
  Bristol BS30 . . . . .66 C5
  Thornbury BS35 . . . . .15 D8
Malvern Rd
  Bristol, Crew's Hole
    BS5 . . . . .64 F7
  Bristol, Kensington Park
    BS4 . . . . .64 D3
  Weston-s-M BS23 . . . . . .104 E5
Malvern Terr **3** BA1 . . .85 A1
Malvern Villas **2** BA1 . .85 A1
Mamba Gr BS24 . . . . .105 B4
Manchester Cotts BS22. .88 E3
Mancroft Ave BS11 . . . . . .47 F7
Mandy Mdws BA3 . . . . . .132 F1
MANGOTSFIELD 51 F6
Mangotsfield CE Prim Sch
  BS16 . . . . .52 B6
Mangotsfield Rd BS16 . . .52 A5
Mangotsfield Sch BS16. .52 B4
MANIARDS GREEN 2 C2
Manilla Cres BS23 . . . . . . .87 C1
Manilla Pl BS23 . . . . .87 C1
Manilla Rd BS8 . . . . .142 A3
Manmoor La BS21 . . . . . . .58 A1
Manning Rd BS4 . . . . .79 F7
Manorbrook Prim Sch
  BS35 . . . . .8 C2
Manor Cl
  Easton-in-G BS20 . . . . . . .47 A4
  Farrington Gurney BS39 132 A3
  Frampton Cotterell BS36 .38 C6
  Portishead BS20 . . . . .45 A5
  Tockington BS32 . . . . .14 C1
  Wellow BA2 . . . . .118 D1
Manor Cl The BS8 . . . . . . .62 A8
Manor Coalpit Heath CE
  Prim Sch The BS36 . . . . .38 D6
Manor Copse Rd BA3. .134 C2
Manor Cotts GL11 . . . . . . .5 F5
Manor Court Dr BS7 . . .49 E7
Manor Ct
  Backwell BS48 . . . . .76 A5
  Bristol, Fishponds BS16. .50 E4
  9 Bristol, Upper Easton
    BS5 . . . . .50 B1
  Locking BS24 . . . . .106 B4
  Weston-s-M BS23 . . . . . .105 A8
Manor Dr BA1 . . . . .86 C2
Manor Farm
  Aust BS35 . . . . .13 B7
  Bristol BS32 . . . . .36 D8
Manor Farm BS22 . . . . . . .88 E5
Manor Farm Cl BS24 . . .105 B2
Manor Farm Cres
  Bristol BS32 . . . . .36 D8
  Weston-s-M BS24 . . . . . .105 B2
Manor Farm La
  Cowhill BS35 . . . . .7 A4
  Littleton-upon-Severn BS35 6 F4
Manor Farm Rd BS40. .127 D4
Manor Gardens Ho
  BS16 . . . . .50 F5
Manor Gdns
  Farmborough BA2 . . . . .115 F6
  Farrington Gurney BS39 132 A3
  Locking BS24 . . . . .106 A4
  Weston-s-M BS22 . . . . . .88 B4
Manor Gr
  Bristol BS34 . . . . .24 B2
  Bristol, Mangotsfield
    BS16 . . . . .52 A4
Manor Grange BS24. . .122 B7
Manor Ho
  6 Bristol, Lower Easton
    BS5 . . . . .50 B1
  Bristol, Tyndall's Park
    BS2 . . . . .142 C3
Manor House La BS14 . .80 C6
Manor La
  Abbots Leigh BS8 . . . . . . .61 F8
  Charfield GL12 . . . . .11 A4
  Winterbourne BS36 . . . . . .37 F7
Manor Park Cl BA3. . .134 C2
Manor Pk
  Bath BA1 . . . . .101 B8
  Bristol BS6 . . . . .49 B3
  Radstock BA3 . . . . .134 C2
  Tockington BS32 . . . . .14 C1
  Weston-s-M BS23 . . . . . .104 E1

Manor Pl
  Bristol, Frenchay BS16 . . .37 C1
  Bristol, Stoke Gifford
    BS34 . . . . .37 A4
Manor Rd
  Abbots Leigh BS8 . . . . . . .61 F7
  Bath BA1 . . . . .84 C1
  Bristol, Bishopston BS7. .49 E4
  Bristol, Bishopsworth
    BS13 . . . . .79 A6
  Bristol, Fishponds BS16. .51 A5
  Bristol, Mangotsfield
    BS16 . . . . .52 A4
  Radstock BA3 . . . . .134 C2
  Rangeworthy BS37 . . . . . .27 A7
  Saltford BS31 . . . . .82 C2
  Weston-s-M BS23 . . . . . .105 A8
  Wick BS30 . . . . .67 C5
Manor Terr BA3 . . . . . . .134 C2
Manor Valley BS23 . . . . . .88 A1
Manor Villas BA1 . . . . . . .84 C1
Manor Way
  Chipping Sodbury BS37 . .28 C2
  Failand BS8 . . . . .61 C4
Manor Wlk BS35 . . . . .4 B8
Mansbrook Ho **3** BA3 133 A1
Mansel Cl BS31 . . . . .82 C3
Mansell Rd BS34 . . . . .35 F6
Manser Rd BS24 . . . . . . .106 C5
Mansfield Ave BS23 . . . .105 B8
Mansfield Cl BS23 . . . . . .105 B8
Mansfield St BS3 . . . . .63 C2
Manston Cl BS14 . . . . .80 C7
Manvers St BA1 . . . . .141 C1
Manworthy Rd BS4 . . . . . .64 D3
Manx Rd BS7 . . . . .49 F8
Maple Ave
  Bristol BS16 . . . . .51 C3
  Thornbury BS35 . . . . .8 C1
Maple Cl
  Bristol BS14 . . . . .80 D5
  Bristol, Little Stoke BS34 36 C7
  Bristol, Oldland BS30. . . .66 B4
  Weston-s-M BS23 . . . . . .105 A8
Maple Ct
  5 Bristol BS15 . . . . . . .51 D1
  Bristol BS9 . . . . .48 F8
  9 Weston-s-M BS23 . . .87 C1
Maple Dr BA3 . . . . .133 E1
Maple Gdns BA2 . . . . . . .101 E4
Maple Gr BA2 . . . . .101 E4
Maple Ho BS2 . . . . .143 A4
Maple Leaf Ct BS8 . . . . .142 A3
Mapleleaze BS4 . . . . .64 D3
Maplemeade BS7 . . . . . . .49 C4
Maple Rd
  Bristol, Horfield BS7 . . . .49 E5
  Bristol, St Anne's BS4 . . .64 D5
Mapleridge La BS37 . . . . .28 D7
Maple Rise BA3 . . . . .134 B2
Maples The BS48 . . . . . . .59 C1
Maplestone Rd BS14 . . . .80 A3
Maple Wlk
  Keynsham BS31 . . . . .81 D4
  Pucklechurch BS16 . . . . . .53 C5
Mapstone Cl BS16 . . . . . . .37 B3
Marbeck Rd BS10 . . . . . . .35 B1
Marbled White Cl BS35. .8 C3
Marchant's La BA2 . . . .119 F4
Marchfields Way
  BS23 . . . . .105 A5
Marconi Cl BS23 . . . . . . .105 B7
Marconi Rd BS20 . . . . . . .44 F5
Mardale Cl BS10 . . . . .35 C2
Marden Rd BS31 . . . . .82 A4
Mardon Rd BS4 . . . . .64 D6
Mardons Cl **2** BA3. . . .139 B8
Mardyke Ferry Rd BS1 142 B1
Margaret Rd **4** BS13. .78 F7
Margaret's Bldgs BA1 141 B3
Margaret's Hill BA1 . . . .141 C4
Marguerite Rd BS13. . . .78 F7
Margate St BS3 . . . . .63 F3
Marigold Cl BS16 . . . . . . .52 D8
Marigold Wlk BS3. . . . . . .63 A2
Marina Gdns BS16 . . . . . .50 E3
Marindrin Dr BS22 . . . . . .89 B4
Marine Hill BS21 . . . . .57 E5
Marine Par
  Clevedon BS21 . . . . .57 E4
  Pill BS20 . . . . .47 C5
  Weston-s-M BS23 . . . . . .87 B1
  Weston-s-M BS23 . . . . . .104 D6
Mariners Cl BS48 . . . . . . .76 A6
Mariner's Cl BS22 . . . . . .88 D1
Mariners Dr
  Backwell BS48 . . . . .76 A6
  Bristol BS9 . . . . .48 D4
Mariner's Way BS20 . . . . .47 C5
Marion Rd BS15 . . . . .65 B3
Marion Wlk BS5 . . . . .65 A7
Marissal Cl BS10 . . . . .34 E3
Marissal Rd BS10 . . . . . . .34 E3
Maritime Way BS20 . . . . .66 C6
Maritime Heritage Ctr★
  BS1 . . . . .142 B1
Marjoram Pl BS32 . . . . . . .36 F7
Marjoram Way BS20. . . .45 F5
Market Ave BS22 . . . . . . .89 C3

Market Gate BS2 . . . . . .143 C3
Market Ind Est BS49. . . .74 B1
Market La BS23 . . . . .104 D8
Market Pl
  Marshfield SN14 . . . . . . .70 A8
  Radstock BA3 . . . . .133 F2
  Winford BS40 . . . . .94 F7
Marketside BS2 . . . . .64 B4
Market Sq BS16 . . . . .51 C3
Mark La BS1 . . . . .142 C2
Marklands BS9 . . . . .48 E3
MARKSBURY 99 B1
Marksbury Bottom BA2 99 B2
Marksbury CE Prim Sch
  BA2 . . . . .99 B2
Marksbury La
  Farmborough BA2 . . . . .116 E7
  Priston BA2 . . . . .117 A6
Marksbury Rd BS3 . . . . . .63 D2
Marlborough Ave **13**
  BS16 . . . . .50 E3
Marlborough Bldgs
  BA1 . . . . .141 A3
Marlborough Dr
  Bristol BS16 . . . . .37 B1
  Weston-s-M BS22 . . . . . .89 B2
Marlborough Flats **8**
  BS2 . . . . .143 A4
Marlborough Hill BS2 .143 A4
Marlborough Hill Pl
  BS2 . . . . .143 A4
Marlborough Ho **15**
  BS2 . . . . .143 A4
Marlborough La BA1 . .141 A3
Marlborough St
  Bath BA1 . . . . .141 A4
  Bristol BS2 . . . . .143 A4
  Bristol, Eastville BS5 . . . .50 E3
Marlepit Gr BS13 . . . . . . .78 F6
Marle Pits **1** BS48 . . . . .76 A6
Marlfield Wlk BS13. . . . . .78 E7
Marling Rd BS5 . . . . .64 F8
Marlowe Ho **3** BS23 . .104 F4
Marlwood Dr BS10 . . . . . .35 A3
Marlwood Sch BS32 . . . . .14 F5
Marmaduke St BS3 . . . . . .63 F3
Marmalade La BS4 . . . . . .64 D6
Marmion Cres BS10 . . . . .34 F3
Marne Cl BS14 . . . . .80 D5
Marron Cl BS26 . . . . .125 C2
Marsden Rd BA2 . . . . . . .101 B3
Marshacre La BS35 . . . . . .13 F6
Marshall Ho **1** BS16 . . .50 F4
Marshall Wlk BS4 . . . . . . .79 D7
Marsham Way BS30 . . . . .65 F4
Marsh Cl BS36 . . . . .37 E5
MARSH COMMON 22 E4
Marsh Common Rd
  BS35 . . . . .22 E3
MARSHFIELD 69 E8
Marshfield CE Prim Sch
  SN14 . . . . .70 B8
Marshfield La BS30 . . . . . .67 D1
Marshfield Path GL9 . . . .19 F1
Marshfield Pk BS16 . . . . .51 C8
Marshfield Rd
  Bristol, Frenchay BS16 . .51 C8
  Bristol, Hillfields BS16. . .51 C4
  Tormarton GL9 . . . . .41 E1
Marshfield Way BA1 . . . .85 A1
Marsh La
  Bristol, Ashton Vale
    BS3 . . . . .63 B2
  Bristol, Barton Hill BS5 . .64 C6
  Burton SN14, GL9 . . . . . .43 C4
  Easton-in-G BS20 . . . . . . .47 A4
  Farrington Gurney BS39 132 A3
  Portbury BS20 . . . . .46 F6
  Temple Cloud BS39 . . . .115 A1
Marsh Lane Ind Est
  BS20 . . . . .46 F7
Marsh Rd
  Bristol BS3 . . . . .62 F3
  Rode BA11 . . . . .137 F1
  Yatton BS49 . . . . .91 B8
Marsh St
  Avonmouth BS11 . . . . . . .47 C8
  Bristol BS1 . . . . .143 A2
Marshwall La BS32 . . . . . .23 E6
Marson Rd BS21 . . . . .57 F3
Marston Rd BS4 . . . . .64 B2
Martcombe Rd BS20 . . . .47 C2
Martha's Orch BS13 . . . .78 E7
Martin Cl BS34 . . . . .35 E8
Martin Ct **12** BS16 . . . . .50 E3
Martindale Ct BS22 . . . .105 D8
Martindale Rd BS22 . . . .105 D8
Martingale Rd BS4 . . . . . .64 D4
Martins Cl BS15 . . . . .65 C5
Martins Gr BS22 . . . . .88 E2
Martin's Rd BS15 . . . . . . .65 C5
Martin St **2** BS3 . . . . . .63 B3
Martins The BS20 . . . . . . .46 A6
Martock Cres BS3 . . . . . . .63 C1
Martock Rd
  Bristol BS3 . . . . .63 C2
  Keynsham BS31 . . . . .82 A3
Martor Ind Est SN14. . . .56 A2

Mart The **6** BS23 . . . . .104 E7
Marwood Rd BS4 . . . . . . .79 E8
Marybush La BS2 . . . . . .143 B3
Mary Carpenter Pl **15**
  BS2 . . . . .49 F1
Mary Ct BS5 . . . . .64 D8
Mary Elton Prim Sch
  BS21 . . . . .57 D1
Marygold Leaze BS30 . . .66 A4
Mary Seacole Ct **8**
  BS2 . . . . .50 A2
Mary St BS5 . . . . .64 D8
Mascot Rd BS3 . . . . .63 D3
Masefield Ho BS23 . . . . .105 A4
Masefield Way BS7. . . . . .50 A6
Maskelyne Ave BS10 . . . .49 D7
Masons View BS36 . . . . . .37 F7
Matchells Cl BS4 . . . . .64 E6
Materman Rd BS14. . . . . .80 E5
Matford Cl
  Bristol BS10 . . . . .35 D4
  Winterbourne BS36 . . . . .37 E5
Matford La GL13 . . . . .3 F4
Matthews Cl BS14 . . . . . . .80 F6
Matthew's Rd **17** BS5. .64 C7
Maules Gdns BS16 . . . . . .36 F2
Maules La BS16 . . . . .36 F2
Maunsell Rd
  Bristol BS11 . . . . .34 B2
  Weston-s-M BS24 . . . . . .105 E7
Maurice Rd BS6 . . . . .49 E2
Mautravers Cl BS32 . . . .36 D7
Mawdeley Ho **11** BS3. .63 C4
Maximus Gdns BS30. . . .81 F8
Max Mill La BS25. . . . . . .124 C8
Maxse Rd BS4 . . . . .64 B2
Maybank Rd BS37. . . . . . .27 D1
Maybec Gdns BS5. . . . . . .65 A6
Maybourne BS4 . . . . .65 A6
Maybrick Rd BA2 . . . . . .101 D5
Maycliffe Pk BS6 . . . . .49 F2
Mayfair Ave BS48 . . . . . . .59 F1
Mayfield Ave
  Bristol BS16 . . . . .51 A2
  Weston-s-M BS22 . . . . . .88 E1
Mayfield Cl BS16 . . . . .51 A3
MAYFIELD PARK 51 A2
Mayfield Pk BS16 . . . . . . .51 A2
Mayfield Pk N BS16 . . . . .51 A2
Mayfield Pk S BS16 . . . . .51 A2
Mayfield Rd BA2 . . . . . . .101 D5
Mayfields BS31 . . . . .81 E5
Mayflower Gdns BS48. . .60 A2
May Gr GL12 . . . . .11 B5
Maynard Cl
  Bristol BS13 . . . . .79 C5
  4 Clevedon BS21 . . . . .57 H3
Maynard Rd BS13 . . . . . . .79 C5
Maynard Terr BS39 . . . .114 F3
Mayors Bldgs BS16. . . . . .51 B5
May Park Prim Sch
  BS5 . . . . .50 C2
Maypole Cl
  Clutton BS39 . . . . .114 E3
  Hawkesbury Upton GL9 . .20 A2
Maypole Ct **1** BS15 . . . .65 B5
Mays Cl BS16 . . . . .38 D7
Maysfield Cl BS20 . . . . . . .45 D3
Maysgreen La BS24 . . . . .90 B3
MAYSHILL 26 E1
May's La BS24 . . . . .90 C3
Maysmead La BS40 . . . .109 C6
May St BS15 . . . . .51 C1
May Tree Ave BS13 . . . . . .79 B7
Maytree Cl BS13 . . . . .79 B7
May Tree Cl BS48 . . . . . . .59 C1
May Tree Rd BA3 . . . . . .133 E1
Maytrees BS5 . . . . .50 C2
Mayville Ave BS34. . . . . . .36 A3
Maywood Ave **3** BS16. .51 B4
Maywood Cres BS16 . . . .51 B4
Maywood Rd BS16 . . . . . .51 C4
Maze St BS5 . . . . .64 B6
McAdam Way BS1. . . . . . .62 F5
McCrae Rd BS24 . . . . . . .106 B5
McLaren Rd BS11 . . . . . . .33 B1
Mead Cl
  Bath BA2 . . . . .101 C3
  Bristol BS11 . . . . .47 E6
Mead Ct BS36 . . . . .37 E6
Mead Ct Bsns Pk BS35 . .15 B8
Meade Ho BA2 . . . . .101 A5
Meadgate BS16 . . . . .52 B7
MEADGATE EAST 116 E2
MEADGATE WEST 116 D2
Mead La
  Blagdon BS40 . . . . .110 E3
  Ingst BS35 . . . . .13 D2
  Saltford BS31 . . . . .82 F4
  Sandford BS25 . . . . .107 C4
Meadlands BA2 . . . . .100 B7
Meadowbank BS22 . . . . . .88 F3
Meadowbrook Prim Sch
  BS32 . . . . .36 A6
Meadow Brown Cl BS35 . 8 C4
Meadow Cl
  Backwell BS48 . . . . .76 B6
  Bristol BS16 . . . . .51 F7
  Farrington Gurney BS39 132 A3

Meadow Cl *continued*
  Nailsea BS48 . . . . .59 E3
Meadow Court Dr BS30 66 C3
Meadowcroft BS16 . . . . . .52 A8
Meadow Croft BS24 . . . .105 B2
Meadow Ct BA1 . . . . . . .101 A7
Meadow Dr
  Bath BA2 . . . . .118 D8
  Locking BS24 . . . . .106 B4
  Portishead BS20 . . . . .44 F1
Meadow Gdns BA1 . . . . . .84 A1
Meadow Gr BS11 . . . . .47 D7
Meadow La BA2 . . . . .85 D1
Meadowland BS49 . . . . . .74 A1
Meadowland Rd BS10 . . .34 E4
Meadowlands BS22 . . . . .89 C2
Meadow Mead
  Frampton Cotterell
    BS36 . . . . .38 B8
  Yate BS37 . . . . .27 C5
Meadow Pk BA1 . . . . .86 B3
Meadow Pl BS22 . . . . .89 D3
Meadow Rd
  Chipping Sodbury BS37 . .28 A1
  Clevedon BS21 . . . . .57 G3
  Leyhill GL12 . . . . .10 B4
  Paulton BS39 . . . . .132 F4
Meadows Cl BS20 . . . . . . .44 F5
Meadows End BS25 . . . .108 D4
Meadowside **2** BS35. . .15 D8
Meadowside BS14. . . . . . .80 A3
Meadows Prim Sch The
  BS30 . . . . .82 D8
Meadow St
  Avonmouth BS11 . . . . . . .33 A1
  Axbridge BS26 . . . . .125 C2
  Weston-s-M BS23 . . . . . .104 E7
Meadows The
  Bristol BS15 . . . . .65 D4
  Luckington SN14 . . . . . . .31 F4
Meadowsweet Ave
  BS34 . . . . .36 B3
Meadowsweet Rd **1**
  BS16 . . . . .52 C7
Meadow Vale BS5 . . . . . . .51 A1
Meadow View
  Frampton Cotterell
    BS36 . . . . .38 D7
  Radstock BA3 . . . . .134 A1
Meadow View Cl BA1. .101 A8
Meadow Villas **14**
  BS23 . . . . .104 E8
Meadow Way BS32. . . . . .36 E7
Mead Rd
  Bristol BS34 . . . . .36 F5
  Chipping Sodbury BS37 . .28 C1
  Portishead BS20 . . . . .45 C2
Mead Rise BS3 . . . . .63 F4
Mead St BS4 . . . . .143 C1
Meads The
  Bristol BS16 . . . . .51 F7
  Burton SN14 . . . . .43 B3
Mead Terr BS40 . . . . .110 E2
Mead The
  Alveston BS35 . . . . .15 A5
  Bristol BS34 . . . . .36 B4
  Clutton BS39 . . . . .114 E3
  Dundry BS41 . . . . .78 D2
  Farmborough BA2 . . . . .116 A6
  Keynsham BS31 . . . . .81 D3
  Paulton BS39 . . . . .132 D5
  Shipham BS25 . . . . .125 E8
  Stratton-on-t-F BA3 . . . .138 F2
  Timsbury BA2 . . . . .116 C3
  Winsley BA15 . . . . .120 E7
Mead Vale BS22 . . . . . . .105 E8
Mead Vale Prim Sch
  BS22 . . . . .88 E1
Meadway
  Bristol BS9 . . . . .48 C6
  Farmborough BA2 . . . . .116 A6
  Temple Cloud BS39 . . . .114 E1
Mead Way BS35 . . . . .15 B7
Meadway Ave BS48 . . . . .59 D2
Mearcombe La BS24 . . .122 F6
Meardon Rd BS14 . . . . . . .80 E6
Meare BS24 . . . . .104 F2
Meare Rd BA2 . . . . .102 A2
MEARNS 115 E2
Mede Cl BS1 . . . . .143 B1
Media Ho BS8 . . . . .142 B3
Medical Ave BS2, BS8. .142 C3
Medina Cl BS35 . . . . .15 C7
Medlar Cl BS10 . . . . .35 B6
Medway Cl BS31 . . . . .82 A3
Medway Ct BS35 . . . . .15 D8
Medway Dr
  Frampton Cotterell
    BS36 . . . . .38 B7
  Keynsham BS31 . . . . .82 A3
Meere Bank BS11 . . . . . . .34 B1
Meetinghouse La BS49 75 A1
Meg Thatcher's Gdns
  BS5 . . . . .65 B7
Meg Thatchers Gn BS5 . 65 B7
Melbourne Dr BS37 . . . . .28 C1

Melbourne Rd BS7.....49 D4
Melbourne Terr **2**
BS21............57 F2
Melbury Rd BS4......64 A2
Melcombe Ct BA2....101 D4
Melcombe Rd BA2....101 D4
Melita Rd BS6.......49 E3
Mellent Ave BS13....79 C3
Mells BS31..........82 A2
Mells La BA3........134 B1
Melrose Ave
Bristol BS8.........142 B4
Yate BS37...........28 A2
Melrose Cl BS37......28 A2
Melrose Gr BA2......101 B3
Melrose Pl BS8......142 B4
Melrose Terr BA1.....85 A2
Melton Cres BS7.....50 A7
Melville Rd BS6......49 B1
Melville Terr BS3......63 C3
Melvin Sq BS4........63 E1
Memorial Cl BS15....65 B4
Memorial Rd
Bristol BS15........65 B4
Wrington BS40......92 E2
Memorial Stadium (Bristol
Rovers FC)★ BS7...49 F6
Mendip Ave BS22....88 F2
Mendip Cl
Axbridge BS26......125 D2
Keynsham BS31......81 D5
3 Nailsea BS48......59 E1
Paulton BS39.......132 E4
Yatton BS49.........91 B7
Mendip Cres BS16...52 A8
Mendip Ct BS16......36 E1
Mendip Edge BS24...121 F8
Mendip Fields BA3...138 C2
Mendip Gdns
Bath BA2...........118 D8
Yatton BS49.........91 B7
Mendip Gn BA3......139 B6
Mendip Green Fst Sch
Weston-s-M BS22.....88 E1
Weston-s-M BS22.....88 F2
Mendip Lodge BS25..125 A8
Mendip Rd
Bristol BS3..........63 D3
Locking BS24........106 D4
Portishead BS20.....45 B5
Weston-s-M BS23....105 A7
Yatton BS49.........91 B7
Mendip Rise BS24....106 B4
Mendip View BS30....67 C2
Mendip View Ave BS16.51 A3
Mendip View Bsns Pk
BS24..............90 C5
Mendip Villas
Cheddar BS27.......126 A1
Compton Martin BS40..128 F4
Mendip Way BA3.....133 F3
Menhyr Gr BS10......35 B3
Menlea BS40........110 D3
Mercer Ct BS14......80 B8
Merchants Almshouses
BS1...............143 A2
Merchants Ct BS8....142 A1
Merchants Quay BS1.143 A1
Merchants Rd
Bristol BS8.........142 A1
Bristol, Hotwells BS8..142 A1
Merchants Row BS1...142 C1
Merchant St BS1.....143 B3
Merchants The SN14..31 E4
Merchants Trad Pk
BS2...............64 C6
Mercia Dr BS2.......50 A2
Mercier Cl BS37.....27 C2
Meredith Ct BS1.....142 A1
Merfield Rd BS4......64 B2
Meriden BA1........101 D8
Meridian Pl BS8......142 B3
Meridian Rd BS6.....49 C1
Meridian Vale BS8...142 B3
Meriet Ave BS13......79 B4
Merioneth St BS3.....63 F3
Meriton St BS2.......64 B5
Merlin Cl
Bristol BS9..........48 F8
1 Weston-s-M BS22..105 E8
Merlin Cres BS12.....11 A5
Merlin Ct BS10.......49 B7
Merlin Pk BS20.......45 A4
Merlin Rd BS10, BS34..35 C6
Merlin Ridge BS16....53 C4
Merlin Way
Chipping Sodbury BS37..39 F9
3 Radstock BA3......139 B8
Merrett Ct BS7.......50 B6
Merrick Ct BS1......143 A1
Merrick Fields BA3...138 C4
Merrimans Rd BS11...47 D8
Merritt Way BS16.....52 A3
Merryfield Rd BS24..106 B6
Merryholes La BS12...14 D3
Merryweather Cl BS32.36 D8

Merryweathers BS4.....64 E2
Merrywood Cl **5** BS3...63 C4
Merrywood Ct BS4.....64 B2
Merrywood Rd BS3.....63 C4
Merstham Rd **18** BS2....50 A2
Merton Dr BS24......106 A8
Merton Rd BS7......49 E5
Mervyn Rd BS7......49 E4
Meryl Ct BS6.........49 B1
Metford Gr BS6......49 B3
Metford Pl BS6......49 C3
Metford Rd BS6......49 C3
Methwyn Cl BS22....105 C7
Metropolitan The BS1.143 B1
Mews The BA1.......101 A8
Mewswell Dr BS27...126 B1
Mezellion Pl **14** BA1...85 B1
Michaels Mead BA1...84 B2
Middle Ave BS1......143 A2
Middledown Rd SN14..55 C1
Middleford Ho BS13...79 C4
Middle La
Bath BA1...........85 B1
Kingston Seymour BS21..72 F4
Middlemead BA3.....138 F3
Middlepiece La BA2,
BS31..............99 B7
Middle Rd BS15......51 F3
Middle St BS40......129 F4
Middle Stoke BA2....120 A6
Middleton Rd BS11....47 F8
Middlewood Cl BA2...101 C2
Middle Yeo Gn BS48...59 D3
MIDFORD............119 C6
Midford BS24........104 F2
Midford Hill BA2.....119 C5
Midford La BA2......119 E7
Midford Rd BA2......119 B7
Midhaven Rise BS22...88 E4
Midland Bridge Rd BA1,
BA2..............141 A2
Midland Mews BS2...143 C3
Midland Rd
Bath BA1...........101 D7
Bristol BS2.........143 C3
Bristol, Staple Hill BS16..51 D4
Midland Road Bsns Pk
BS16..............51 D4
Midland St BS2......143 C2
Midland Terr BS16....50 F3
Midland Way BS35....15 C7
Midland Way Bsns Pk
BS35..............15 B8
Midsomer Ent Pk BA3.133 C2
MIDSOMER NORTON..133 B3
Midsomer Norton Prim
Sch BA3...........133 B1
Midsomer Norton South★
BA3..............133 A8
Midsummer Bldgs BA1..85 B2
Milburn Rd BS23.....104 F7
Milbury Gdns BS22...88 C2
Mildred St BS5.......64 C7
Miles Cl BS20........47 E3
Miles Ct
Bristol, Cadbury Heath
BS30..............65 F4
Bristol, Clifton BS8...49 A1
Miles Rd BS8........49 A1
Miles's Bldgs BA1....141 B3
Miles St BA2........141 C1
Milestone Ct BS22....89 D2
Mile Wlk BS14.......80 A6
Milford Ave BS30.....67 B7
Milford St BS3.......63 C4
Milk St BA1.........141 B2
Millard Cl BS10......35 D2
Millards Ct BA3......133 B3
Millards Hill BA3.....133 B3
Millard's Hill BA3....133 C3
Millar Ho BS8.......142 A3
Millbank Cl BS4......64 E3
Millbook Ct **3** BS6....49 E1
Millbourn Cl BA15...120 D7
Millbrook Ave BS4....64 F3
Millbrook Cl BS30....66 C6
Millbrook Ct BA2....141 C1
Millbrook Pl BA2.....141 C1
Millbrook Rd BS37....27 B2
Mill Cl
Frampton Cotterell
BS36..............38 C7
Portbury BS20......46 D2
Mill Cotts BS31......82 F2
Mill Cres BS37.......39 B4
Millcross BS21.......73 C8
Mill Ct **1** BA3.......133 A1
Millennium Cl BS36...38 D7
Millennium Prom BS1.142 C1
Miller Cl BS23.......104 F8
Millers Cl BS20......47 C4
Millers Ct BS21......73 E8
Millers Rise BS22....89 A4
Miller Wlk BA2......85 F1
Millfield
Midsomer Norton BA3..138 F8
Thornbury BS35......8 C2

Millfield Dr BS30.....66 C6
Millground Rd BS13...78 F5
Millgrove St N BS2...143 A4
Mill Hill BA2........118 E1
Millhill La BS35......12 F5
Mill Ho
Bristol BS1.........143 A2
11 Bristol, Baptist Mills
BS5..............50 A1
Millier Rd BS49......92 B8
Milliman Cl BS13.....79 C5
Mill La
3 Bath BA2........101 B6
Bathampton BA2......85 F2
Bitton BS30.........82 E8
Bristol, Southville BS3..63 D4
Bristol, Warmley BS30...66 C5
Butcombe BS40......111 A8
Chew Stoke BS40.....112 D8
Chipping Sodbury BS37..40 E6
Compton Martin BS40..129 A6
Congresbury BS49....91 D4
Doynton BS30.......53 F1
Falfield GL12........9 F7
Frampton Cotterell BS36..26 B1
Hambrook BS16......37 D3
Monkton Combe BA2..119 E8
Portbury BS20.......46 E3
Priston BA2.........117 A7
Timsbury BA2.......116 B1
Tockington BS32......14 B1
Upton Cheyney BS30...66 F1
Wrington BS40......109 F8
Mill Leg BS49.......91 D4
Millmead Ho BS13....79 C4
Millmead Rd BA2.....101 C5
Millpill Cl BS9.......48 D5
Millpond Prim Sch BS5.50 A1
Millpond St **10** BS5....50 A1
Millpool Ct BS10.....49 B8
Mill Rd
Radstock BA3.......134 B2
Winterbourne BS36....37 D4
Mill Road Ind Est BA3.134 B3
Mill Steps BS36......37 E4
Mill Stream Cl BS26..125 C1
Millward Gr BS16.....51 C4
Millward Terr BS39...132 E6
Milner Gn BS30......66 A5
Milner Rd BS7.......49 F5
Milsom Pl BA1.......141 B3
Milsom St
Bath BA1...........141 B3
Bristol BS5.........64 A4
MILTON.............88 C2
Milton Ave
Bath BA2...........101 F4
Weston-s-M BS23....105 A8
Milton Brow BS22....88 B2
Milton C
Nailsea BS48........59 E3
Yate BS37...........27 D2
Milton Ct BS23......105 A8
Milton Gn BS22.....88 C1
Milton Hill BS22.....88 B2
Milton Park Prim Sch
BS22..............88 C1
Milton Park Rd BS22..88 C1
Milton Pk **1** BS5.....64 C7
Milton Rd
Bristol BS7..........49 E6
Radstock BA3.......133 C1
Weston-s-M BS22, BS23.105 B8
Yate BS37...........27 D2
Milton Rise BS22.....88 C1
Miltons Cl BS13......79 D4
Milverton BS24......104 F2
Milverton Gdns BS6...49 F2
Milward Rd BS31.....81 E6
Mina Rd BS2.........50 A2
Minehead Rd BS4.....63 F1
Miners Cl BS41......61 F2
Minerva Ct BA2......141 C3
Minerva Gdns BA2...101 C4
Minett Rd BS37......27 E5
Minor's La BS10......34 A8
Minsmere Rd BS31...82 A4
Minster Ct **1** BS37....39 D7
Minster Way BA2....102 C8
Minton Cl BS14......80 B5
Minto Rd BS2........50 A2
Minto Road Ind Ctr **9**
BS2..............50 A2
Mission Rd BS37.....27 B4
Mitchell La BS1......143 B2
Mitchell Wlk BS30....66 D7
Mitford-Slade Ct BS49..91 C7
Mivart St BS5.......64 C7
Mizzymead Cl **1** BS48..59 D1
Mizzymead Rd BS48..59 E1
Mizzymead Rise BS48..59 E1
Modecombe Gr BS10..34 F3
Mogg St BS2........50 A2
Moles Rd BS40......109 B6
Molesworth Cl BS13...79 A4
Molesworth Dr BS13..79 A4
Mollifriend La BA2...116 B8
Molly Cl BS39.......131 E8
Monarch Ct BS16.....38 A1

Monarch Ho **11** BS3...63 B3
Monger Cotts BS39...132 F4
Monger La
Greenhill BA3........133 A3
Midsomer Norton BA3..133 A3
Paulton BS39........133 A4
Monica Willis Ho **18**
BS3..............63 C3
Monk Rd BS7........49 D4
Monks Ave BS15.....65 B8
Monksdale Rd BA2...101 D4
Monks Hill BS22.....88 B3
Monks Ho **3** BS37....39 D7
Monk's Park Ave BS7..49 E8
Monks Park Way BS7..49 E8
Monkton Ave BS24...105 A2
MONKTON COMBE....102 F1
Monkton Combe Jun Sch
(Pre-Prep) BA2.....102 C1
Monkton Combe Sch
BA2..............102 E1
MONKTON FARLEIGH.103 F7
Monkton Prep Sch
BA2..............102 C1
Monkton Rd BS15....65 B5
Monmouth Cl BS20...44 F4
Monmouth Ct
Bath BA1...........141 A2
Pill BS20...........47 C5
Monmouth Hill BS23..23 E4
Monmouth Paddock
BA2..............136 E5
Monmouth Pl BA1...141 B2
Monmouth Rd
Bristol BS7..........49 D4
Keynsham BS31......81 D5
Pill BS20...........47 C5
Monmouth St
Bath BA1...........141 B2
Bristol BS3.........63 F3
Monsdale Cl BS10....35 A2
Monsdale Dr BS10....35 A2
Montacute Cir **4**
BS22..............105 F8
Montacute Ct BS22...105 F8
Montague Cl BS34....36 E5
Montague Ct **4** BS2..143 A4
Montague Flats **6**
BS2..............143 A4
Montague Hill BS2...143 A4
Montague Hill S **5**
BS2..............143 A4
Montague Ho **8** BA1..85 C1
Montague Pl BS6....143 A4
Montague Rd
Saltford BS31.......82 D2
Shoscombe BA2.....134 E5
Montague St BS1.....143 A4
Montepelier BS23....104 F8
Montgomery St BS3...63 F3
MONTPELIER.........49 E2
Montpelier Central **1**
BS6..............49 E1
Montpelier Ct BS6....49 E2
Montpelier E BS23.....87 F1
Montpelier High Sch
BS6..............49 E1
Montpelier Sta BS6...49 E2
Montreal Ave BS7.....50 A8
Montreaux Ct **9** BS16..51 D3
Montreaux Ho **2** BS5..65 A7
Montrose Ave BS6....49 C1
Montrose Cotts BA1...84 C1
Montrose Dr BS30....66 B6
Montrose Pk BS4.....64 D2
Montroy Cl BS9......49 C6
Montsurs Cl BA3.....138 D3
Mont The **2** BS6.....49 E1
Moon St BS2........143 B4
Moor Croft Dr BS30...65 F3
Moor Croft Rd BS24..105 E3
Moordell Cl BS37.....27 D1
MOOREND...........37 E2
Moorend Farm Ave
BS11..............33 E5
Moorend Gdns BS11..47 F7
Moorend Rd BS16.....37 D3
Moor End Spout BS48..59 D2
Moorfield Rd BS48....76 A6
MOORFIELDS........64 C8
Moorfields Cl BA2....101 D3
Moorfields Ct BS48...59 D2
Moorfields Dr BA2....101 D4
Moorfields Ho
Bristol BS5.........64 C7
Nailsea BS48........59 D2
Moorfields Rd
Bath BA2...........101 D4
Nailsea BS48........59 D2
Moor Gn BS26.......125 C2
Moor Gr BS11.......48 A8
Moorgrove Ho BS9....48 C7
Moorham Rd BS25...108 A1
Moorhen Ho
Kingston Seymour BS49..73 F2
Kingston Seymour BS49..73 F2
Moorhill St **17** BS5....50 B1
Moorhouse Cl BS10...34 B4
Moor House Cvn Pk
BS10..............34 A4

Moorhouse La BS10....34 B4
Moorings The
Bath BA2...........102 B6
Pill BS20...........47 C4
Pucklechurch BS16...53 C4
Moor La
Backwell BS48.......75 F6
Clapton in G BS20....45 E1
Clevedon BS21.......57 G2
Clevedon BS21.......58 A2
Hutton BS24........105 D3
Tickenham BS21......58 F4
Tockington BS32.....24 A8
Walton in G BS21....58 C6
Weston-s-M BS24....105 F7
Moorland Cotts BS26.124 F2
Moorland Pk BS24....90 E5
Moorland Rd
Bath BA2...........101 D5
Weston-s-M BS23....104 E4
Yate BS37...........27 D1
MOORLANDS........101 D3
Moorlands Cl BS48....59 D2
Moorlands Inf Sch
BA2..............101 D4
Moorlands Jun Sch
BA2..............101 D3
Moorlands Rd
Bristol, Mayfield Park
BS16..............51 A2
Bristol, Ridgeway BS16..50 F3
Moorland St BS26....125 C1
Moorlands The BA2...101 D3
Moorlay Cres BS40....94 F8
MOORLEDGE.........96 C6
Moorledge La BS39,
BS40..............113 F7
Moorledge Rd BS40....96 B1
Moorpark Ave BS37...27 D1
Moor Pk BS21.......57 G2
Moor Rd
Banwell BS29.......107 B5
Yatton BS49.........74 B2
Moorsfield BS39.....114 F3
Moorside BS49......74 B1
Moorside Ct BS21.....57 G2
Moorside Villas BS21..57 G2
MOORSLADE..........3 D1
Moorslade La GL12.....3 D1
Moravian Ct **4** BS15..65 D8
Moravian Rd BS15....65 D8
Moravian Rd Bsns Pk
BS15..............65 D8
Morden Wlk BS14....80 D7
Moreton Cl BS14.....80 A4
Moreton La BS40.....112 B2
Moreton Mans **5** BS23.87 C1
Morford St BA1......141 B4
Morgan Cl
Saltford BS31.......82 D2
Weston-s-M BS22....106 B4
Morgan Pl BS48......77 B8
Morgans Bldgs BS20..59 F8
Morgans Hill Cl BS48...75 D8
Morgan's La BS40....129 F2
Morgan St BS2.......49 F1
Morgan Sweet Pl
BS25..............108 A4
Morgan Way BA2....134 E7
Morley Ave BS16.....52 A4
Morley Cl
Bristol, Little Stoke
BS34..............36 C7
Bristol, Staple Hill BS16..51 D4
Morley Rd
Bristol, Southville BS3..63 C4
Bristol, Staple Hill BS16..51 D3
Morley Sq BS7.......49 E4
Morley St
Bristol, Baptist Mills
BS2..............49 F1
Bristol, Russell Town BS5.64 B7
Morley Terr
1 Bath BA2........101 D6
1 Bristol BS15......51 D1
Radstock BA3.......134 A3
Mornington Rd **14** BS8.49 A2
Morpeth Rd BS4......79 D8
Morris Cl BA1........86 B3
Morris La BA1.......86 B3
Morris Rd BS7.......50 A5
Morse Rd BS5........64 C7
Morston Ct BS22....105 C1
Mortimer Cl BA1.....84 B2
Mortimer Rd
Bristol BS8.........142 A3
Bristol, Filton BS34....36 B2
MORTON.............8 D3
Morton Mill BS35.....8 C3
Morton St
Bristol BS5.........64 B7
Thornbury BS35.....8 C4
Morton Way BS35.....8 D1
Moseley Gr BS23....104 E2
Mosquito End BS23..105 B4
Motorway Distribution Ctr
BS11..............33 C2
Mottershead Ave
BS24..............106 C5

Mountain Ash BA1 . . . . . 84 D1
MOUNTAIN BOWER 56 E3
Mountain Mews 5 BS5 65 A7
Mountain's La BA2. . . . 115 E6
Mountain Wood BA1 . . . 86 C2
Mountbatten Cl
Weston-s-M BS22 . . . . . . 88 E4
Yate BS37. . . . . 27 D3
Mount Beacon BA1 . . . . 85 A1
Mount Beacon Pl 3
BA1 . . . . 84 F1
Mount Cl BS36. . . . . 37 F8
Mount Cres BS36 . . . . . . 37 E5
Mounteney's La GL12 . . 18 D7
Mount Gdns BS15. . . . . . 65 D6
Mount Gr BA2 . . . . 101 B3
Mount Haviland BA1 . . . 84 B3
MOUNT HILL 65 E6
Mount Hill Rd BS15 . . . . 65 D6
Mount Pleasant
Bath BA2 . . . . 102 D1
Hallen BS10 . . . . 34 C4
Pill BS20. . . . . 47 D4
Radstock BA3. . . . . 134 B2
Mount Pleasant Terr
BS3. . . . . 63 C4
Mount Rd
Bath BA1 . . . . 141 B4
Bath, Southdown BA2 . . 101 B3
Mount The BS49 . . . . 91 C8
Mount View
Bath, Beacon Hill BA1 . . . 85 A1
Bath, Southdown BA2 . . 101 B3
Mow Barton
Bristol BS13. . . . . 78 F6
Yate BS37. . . . . 27 D2
Mowbray Rd BS14. . . . . . 80 C7
Mowcroft Rd BS13 . . . . . 79 D4
Moxham Dr BS13 . . . . . . 79 C4
Muddy La BS22 . . . . 89 A8
Mud La BS49 . . . . 74 D2
Muirfield
Bristol BS30. . . . . 66 A6
Yate BS37. . . . . 39 E8
Mulberry Ave BS20. . . . . 45 E5
Mulberry Cl
Backwell BS48 . . . . 76 A6
1 Bristol BS15 . . . . 65 E8
Portishead BS20 . . . . 45 F5
Weston-s-M BS22 . . . . . . 89 A1
Mulberry Ct BS4 . . . . 64 D4
Mulberry Dr BS15. . . . . . . 51 F1
Mulberry Gdns 10 BS16 51 D3
Mulberry La BS24 . . . . . 122 C6
Mulberry Mews BA1 . . . . 84 C1
Mulberry Rd BS49. . . . . . 91 E3
Mulberry Way BA2 . . . . 102 A2
Mulberry Wlk BS9 . . . . . 48 C8
Mule St GL13 . . . . 4 B3
Muller Ave BS7 . . . . 49 F4
Muller Rd BS5, BS7 . . . . . 50 B3
Mulready Cl BS7 . . . . 50 C6
Mumbleys Hill BS35. . . . 14 E7
Mumbleys La
Thornbury, Alveston Down
BS35 . . . . 14 E6
Thornbury, Kington BS35 14 E8
Mundy La BS35 . . . . 8 A1
Munscroft Ct BS23 . . . . 104 F8
Muntjac Rd BS40. . . . . . 109 B6
Murdoch Sq BS7. . . . . 49 F8
Murford Ave BS13. . . . . . 79 B4
Murford Wlk BS13 . . . . . 79 B4
Murhill BA2 . . . . 120 C6
Murray St 9 BS3 . . . . . . 63 C4
Musgrove Cl BS11. . . . . . 34 C2
Mus of Bath at Work★
BA1. . . . . 141 B4
Mus of Costume★
BA1. . . . . 141 B3
Mus of East Asian Art★
BA1. . . . . 141 B3
Myrtleberry Mead BS22 89 A5
Myrtle Ct BS3. . . . . 63 B4
Myrtle Dr BS11 . . . . 47 E5
Myrtle Farm Rd BS22. . . . 88 C4
Myrtle Gdns BS49 . . . . . . 91 C8
Myrtle Hill BS20 . . . . 47 C5
Myrtle Rd BS2 . . . . 142 C4
Myrtle St BS3. . . . . 63 B3
Myrtles The BS24 . . . . . 105 D2
Myrtle Tree Cres BS22 . . 88 A6

N

Nags Head Hill BS5 . . . . 65 A7
NAILSEA 59 E3
Nailsea and Backwell
Station BS48 . . . . 75 F7
Nailsea Cl BS13. . . . . 79 A7
Nailsea Moor La BS48 . . 74 F7
Nailsea Park Cl BS48. . . . 59 F2
Nailsea Pk BS48 . . . . 59 F2
Nailsea Sch BS48 . . . . . . 59 F1
Nailsea Wall BS21. . . . . . 74 C8
Nailsea Wall La BS48. . . . 74 E7
Nailsworth Ave BS37 . . . 27 E1
NAILWELL. 117 D6
Naishcombe Hill BS30. . 67 C7
Naishes Ave BA2 . . . . . . 134 D7
Naish Farm BA3 . . . . . . 138 D3
Naish Hill BS20 . . . . 45 F1
Naish Ho BA2. . . . . 101 A6
Naish La BS48 . . . . 77 D3
Naish's Cross BA3 . . . . 138 D3
Naite The BS35. . . . . 7 D6
Nanny Hurn's La BS39 114 A1
Napier Ct BS1 . . . . 142 B1
Napier Ho BS6. . . . . 49 B2
Napier Miles Rd BS11 . . 48 A8
Napier Rd
Avonmouth BS11 . . . . 33 B1
Bath BA1 . . . . 84 A3
Bristol, Baptist Mills BS5 50 B2
Bristol, Redland BS6 . . . . 49 B2
Napier Sq BS11 . . . . 33 A1
Napier St BS5 . . . . 64 B6
Narroways Rd BS2 . . . . . 50 A3
Narrow La BS16. . . . . 51 E4
Narrow Plain BS2. . . . . 143 B2
Narrow Quay BS1 . . . . . 143 A2
Naseby Wlk BS5 . . . . 50 F1
Nash Cl BS31 . . . . 82 A5
Nash Dr BS7. . . . . 50 C7
Nates La BS40 . . . . 92 F1
Naunton Way BS22. . . . . 88 B2
Neads Dr BS30. . . . . 66 C5
Neale Way BS11 . . . . 33 C1
Neate Ct BS34 . . . . 36 C8
Neath Rd BS5. . . . . 64 D8
Nelson Bldgs BA1. . . . . 141 C4
Nelson Ct BS22 . . . . 88 E4
Nelson Ho
Bath BA1 . . . . 141 A3
6 Bristol BS1 . . . . 143 A3
8 Bristol, Staple Hill
BS16 . . . . 51 D5
Nelson Par 10 BS3 . . . . . 63 D4
Nelson Pl BA1 . . . . 141 C4
Nelson Pl E BA1 . . . . . . 141 C4
Nelson Pl W BA1. . . . . . 141 A2
Nelson Rd
Bristol BS16. . . . . 51 D5
4 Bristol, Staple Hill
BS16 . . . . 51 D4
Nelson St
Bristol BS1. . . . . 143 A3
Bristol, Ashton Vale BS3 . 63 A2
Nelson Villas BA1 . . . . . 141 A2
Nelson Ward Dr BA3 . . 134 A1
Nempnett St BS40 . . . . 111 D5
NEMPNETT
THRUBWELL 111 D5
Neston Wlk BS4 . . . . 79 F8
NETHAM 64 D6
Netham Ct 22 BS5. . . . . . 64 D7
Netham Gdns 21 BS5. . . 64 D7
Netham Park Ind Est
BS5. . . . . 64 D6
Netham Rd BS5. . . . . 64 D6
Netham View Ind Pk 20
BS5. . . . . 64 D7
Netherdale Cvn Site
BS25. . . . . 125 B6
Netherton Wood La
BS48. . . . . 75 A6
Netherways BS21 . . . . . . 57 D1
Nettlefrith La TA8 . . . . . 121 B1
Nettlestone Cl BS10. . . . 34 E4
NETTLETON GREEN 43 B1
Nettleton Rd SN14 . . . . . 43 B2
Nevalan Dr BS5. . . . . 65 A6
Neva Rd BS23. . . . . 104 E6
Neville Rd BS15. . . . . 51 E2
Nevil Rd BS7. . . . . 49 E4
Newark St BA1 . . . . 141 C1
New Bldgs
Bristol BS16. . . . . 50 F4
Peasedown St John
BA2 . . . . 134 B8
New Bond St BA1 . . . . . 141 C2
New Bond Street Pl
BA1 . . . . 141 C2
Newbourne Rd BS22 . . 105 C8
Newbrick Rd BS34 . . . . . 37 A5
NEWBRIDGE 101 B8
Newbridge Cl BS4 . . . . . 64 D5
Newbridge Ct BA1 . . . . 101 B7
Newbridge Gdns BA1 . 101 A8
Newbridge Hill BA1. . . . 101 B7
Newbridge Ho BS9. . . . . 48 C4
Newbridge Prim Sch
BA1 . . . . 101 B7
Newbridge Rd
Bath BA1, BA2 . . . . 101 B7
Bristol BS4. . . . . 64 E6
Newbridge Trad Est
BS4. . . . . 64 D5
New Bristol Rd BS22 . . . 89 A2
New Brunswick Ave
BS5. . . . . 65 B7
NEWBURY 140 B1
Newbury Rd BS7. . . . . . . 50 A7
New Charlotte St BS3 . . 63 D4
New Charlton Way
BS10. . . . . 35 A6
NEW CHELTENHAM 51 F1
New Cheltenham Rd
BS15. . . . . 51 E1
New Church Rd BS23. . 104 D2
Newclose La BS40 . . . . 112 D1
Newcombe Dr BS9 . . . . . 48 C4
Newcombe La BS25 . . . 125 B7
Newcombe Rd BS9. . . . . 48 F7
New Cut Bow BS21. . . . . 73 A6
Newditch La BS40. . . . . . 77 C1
Newdown La BS41 . . . . . 79 B2
New Ear La BS22. . . . . . . 89 E5
NEW ENGLAND 52 B7
Newent Ave BS15 . . . . . . 65 B7
Newfields BS40 . . . . 127 C8
New Fosseway Rd BS14 80 B6
New Fosseway Sch
BS14. . . . . 80 B6
Newfoundland Rd
Bristol BS2. . . . . 143 C4
6 Bristol, Baptist Mills
BS2 . . . . 50 A1
Newfoundland St BS2 143 C4
Newfoundland Way
Bristol BS2. . . . . 143 C4
Portishead BS20 . . . . 45 E6
Newgate BS1 . . . . 143 B3
Newhaven Pl BS20 . . . . . 44 E4
Newhaven Rd BS20 . . . . 44 D4
New John St 17 BS3. . . . 63 C3
New Kings Ct BS7. . . . . . 49 C4
New Kingsley Rd BS2 . 143 C2
New King St BA1. . . . . . 141 B2
New La BS35. . . . . 15 C5
Newland Dr BS13 . . . . . . 79 A4
Newland Ho BA1. . . . . . . 84 F1
Newland Hts 12 BS2. . . . 49 F2
Newland Rd
Bristol BS13. . . . . 79 A3
Weston-s-M BS23 . . . . . 104 F6
Newlands Ave BS36 . . . . 38 C7
Newlands Cl BS20. . . . . . 45 C5
Newlands Gn BS21 . . . . . 57 G1
Newlands Hill BS20 . . . . 45 C4
Newlands La BS16 . . . . . 52 C8
Newlands Rd BS31 . . . . . 81 D4
Newlands The BS16 . . . . 51 B7
Newland Wlk BS13. . . . . 79 A3
NEWLEAZE. 36 B2
Newleaze BS34 . . . . 36 A2
New Leaze BS32 . . . . 24 C3
Newleaze Ho BS34 . . . . . 36 B2
Newlyn Ave BS9 . . . . 48 D5
Newlyn Way BS37. . . . . . 27 F2
Newlyn Wlk BS4 . . . . 64 B1
Newman Cl BS37. . . . . . . 39 B4
Newmans La BA2 . . . . . 116 B2
Newmarket Ave 11
BS1. . . . . 143 A3
New Mdws BS14 . . . . 80 A6
New Mills La GL12 . . . . . 19 E8
Newnham Cl BS14 . . . . . 80 D7
Newnham Pl BS34 . . . . . 23 F1
New Oak Prim Sch
BS14. . . . . 80 A7
New Orchard St BA1 . . 141 C2
New Park Ho BS21 . . . . . 57 F5
NEW PASSAGE 12 A1
New Passage Rd BS35. . 12 A1
New Pit Cotts BA2 . . . . 116 F1
Newpit La BS30. . . . . 66 F2
NEWPORT. 4 B8
Newport Cl
Clevedon BS21. . . . . 57 E2
Portishead BS20 . . . . 44 F4
Newport Rd BS20 . . . . . . 47 C5
Newport St BS3. . . . . 63 E3
Newquay Rd
Bristol BS4. . . . . 63 F1
Bristol BS4. . . . . 79 F8
New Queen St
Bristol, St George BS15. . 65 B8
Bristol, Windmill Hill BS3 63 E4
New Rd
Banwell BS29. . . . . 106 E4
Bathford BA1. . . . . 86 D2
Bristol, Filton BS34 . . . . . 35 F3
Bristol, Harry Stoke BS34 36 D3
Churchill BS25 . . . . 108 F4
Clevedon BS21. . . . . 57 F2
Freshford BA2 . . . . 120 B5
High Littleton BS39 . . . . 115 C3
Kilmersdon BA3. . . . . . . 140 E4
Kingswood GL12 . . . . 11 F6
North Nibley GL11 . . . . 5 E4
Olveston BS35 . . . . 14 A2
Pensford BS39. . . . . 97 D3
Pill BS20. . . . . 47 C4
Rangeworthy BS37 . . . . . 27 A8
Rangeworthy, Hall End
BS37 . . . . 17 C1
Redhill BS40. . . . . 94 A4
Shipham BS25 . . . . 108 E1
Tytherington GL12. . . . . . 16 C6
New Rock Ind Est BA3 138 D2
New Rock Rd BA3. . . . . 138 D1
Newry Wlk BS4 . . . . 63 E1
New Sandringham Ho 6
BS7. . . . . 49 D2
New Siblands Sch BS35 . 8 D1
Newsome Ave BS20 . . . . 47 C4
New St
Bath BA1 . . . . 141 B2
Bristol BS2. . . . . 143 C3
Charfield GL12. . . . . 11 A6
New Stadium Rd BS5. . . 50 B2
New Station Rd BS16. . . 51 A4
New Station Way BS16 . 51 A4
New Street Flats 4
BS2. . . . . 143 C3
New Thomas St BS2. . . 143 C2
NEWTON
Bristol 64 A7
Thornbury 8 D6
Newton Cl
Bristol BS15. . . . . 52 A1
West Harptree BS40 . . . 129 E6
Newton Dr BS30 . . . . 66 A5
Newton Gn BS48 . . . . 75 C8
Newton Rd
Bath BA2 . . . . 100 F6
Bristol BS30. . . . . 66 A5
Weston-s-M BS23 . . . . . 104 E6
NEWTON ST LOE. 100 D6
Newton's Rd
Weston-s-M BS22 . . . . . . 88 E3
Weston-s-M BS22 . . . . . . 88 E4
Newton St BS5. . . . . 64 A8
NEWTOWN. 124 D2
Newtown GL12. . . . . 11 A5
NEW TOWN
Bishop Sutton 113 D7
Hinton Charterhouse . . . 136 F8
Paulton. 132 D6
Newtown Chapel
BS39. . . . . 132 D5
New Tyning La BS37 . . . . 29 C4
New Walls BS2. . . . . 63 F4
New Wlk BS15 . . . . 65 B5
Niblett Cl BS15 . . . . 65 F6
Niblett's Hill BS5 . . . . . . 65 A6
NIBLEY 27 A1
Nibley Bsns Pk BS37 . . . 27 A1
NIBLEY GREEN 5 C5
Nibley La BS37. . . . . 26 F3
Nibley Rd BS11 . . . . 47 E5
Nicholas La BS5 . . . . 65 A6
Nicholas Rd BS5 . . . . 50 B1
Nicholas St BS3. . . . . 63 E4
Nicholettes BS30. . . . . . . 66 D5
Nicholls Ct BS36 . . . . 37 E7
Nicholls La BS36. . . . . . . 37 E6
Nichol's Rd BS20. . . . . . . 44 F5
Nigel Pk BS11 . . . . 47 E7
Nightingale Cl
Bristol BS4. . . . . 64 E6
Frampton Cotterell BS36 38 A6
Thornbury BS35. . . . . 8 D2
Weston-s-M BS22 . . . . . . 88 E1
Nightingale Ct
Bristol BS4. . . . . 64 D3
Weston-s-M BS22 . . . . . . 88 E1
Nightingale Gdns BS48 59 D2
Nightingale La BS36 . . . 38 A8
Nightingale Rise BS20. . 44 F3
Nightingale Way BA3. . 139 B8
Nile St BA1 . . . . 141 A2
Nimbus Rd BS24 . . . . . . 105 C5
Nine Tree Hill 16 BS1 . . . 49 E1
Ninth Ave BS7 . . . . 36 B1
Nippors Way BS25 . . . . 124 F8
Nithsdale Rd BS23 . . . . 104 E4
Nixon Trad Units
BS24. . . . . 105 A3
No 1 Royal Cres Mus★
BA1. . . . . 141 B3
Noah's Ark Zoo Farm★
BS48 . . . . 60 B6
Noble Ave BS30. . . . . 66 C4
Nomis Pk BS49 . . . . 91 E2
Nordrach La BS40. . . . . 128 D5
Nore Gdns BS20 . . . . 45 C6
Nore Park Dr BS20. . . . . 44 F5
Nore Rd BS20. . . . . 45 A6
Norfolk Ave
Bristol BS2. . . . . 143 B4
Bristol, Montpelier BS6 . . 49 E2
Norfolk Bldgs BA1 . . . . 141 A2
Norfolk Cres BA1 . . . . . 141 A2
Norfolk Gr BS31 . . . . 81 C4
Norfolk Hts 10 BS2. . . . 143 B4
Norfolk Pl BS3. . . . . 63 C3
Norfolk Rd
Portishead BS20 . . . . 45 E4
Weston-s-M BS23 . . . . . 104 F5
Norland Rd BS8. . . . . 62 F8
Norley La GL9 . . . . 41 D2
Norley Rd BS7 . . . . 49 F7
Normanby Rd 20 BS5. . . 50 B1
Normandy Dr
Yate BS37. . . . . 27 F1
Yate BS37. . . . . 39 F8
Norman Gr BS15 . . . . 51 D2
Norman Rd
Bristol, Baptist Mills
BS2 . . . . 50 A2
Bristol, Warmley BS30. . . 66 B8
Saltford BS31. . . . . 82 E3
Norman's Cotts BS36. . . 37 D7
Normans The BA2. . . . . . 85 F1
Normans Way BS20 . . . . 46 E7
Normanton Rd 16 BS8. . 49 A2
Norrisville Rd 8 BS6. . . 49 E1
Northampton Bldgs
BA1 . . . . 141 B4
Northampton Ho BS48 . 60 D3
Northampton St BA1 . . 141 B4
Northanger Ct 5 BA2 141 C3
Northavon Bsns Ctr
BS37. . . . . 27 C3
North Chew Terr BS40. . 96 B3
North Cnr 8 BS3 . . . . . . 63 B3
NORTH COMMON 66 D6
North Contemporis
BS8. . . . . 142 A3
NORTH CORNER 25 F1
Northcote Ho BS8. . . . . 142 A3
Northcote Rd
Bristol, Clifton BS8 . . . . . 48 F1
Bristol, Crew's Hole BS5 64 E7
Bristol, Mangotsfield
BS16 . . . . 51 F6
Northcote St 18 BS5. . . . 50 B1
North Croft BS30. . . . . . . 66 D4
North Ct BS32 . . . . 24 D3
North Devon Rd BS16 . . 51 A5
North Down Cl BS25 . . 125 F8
North Down La BS25 . . 125 F8
Northdown Rd BA3. . . . 133 E5
North Dro BS48 . . . . 59 A2
North East Rd BS35 . . . . . 8 C2
North Elm La BS40 . . . . . 96 B4
NORTHEND 85 F5
NORTH END
Clutton 114 E5
Yatton. 73 F3
North End
Luckington SN14 . . . . 31 E5
Midsomer Norton BA3 . . 133 B2
Northend Ave BS15 . . . . 51 D2
Northend Gdns BS15 . . . 51 D2
Northend Rd BS15 . . . . . 51 E1
North End Rd BS49. . . . . 73 F3
Northern Way BS21 . . . . 57 H3
NORTHFIELD 134 B1
Northfield
Radstock BA3. . . . . 134 A3
Timsbury BA2. . . . . 116 C3
Winsley BA15. . . . . 120 F7
Yate BS37. . . . . 39 D8
Northfield Ave BS15. . . . 65 D5
Northfield Ho
Bath BA1 . . . . 84 F1
10 Bristol BS3 . . . . 63 C4
Northfield La SN14. . . . . 55 F1
Northfield Rd
Bristol BS5. . . . . 65 B7
Portishead BS20 . . . . 44 E3
Northfields BA1. . . . . 84 F1
Northfields Cl BA1 . . . . . 84 F1
Northgate St BA1 . . . . . 141 C2
North Gr BS20 . . . . 47 C4
North Green St 12 BS8 . 62 F6
North Hills Cl BS24. . . . 105 B2
North La
Bath BA2 . . . . 102 D5
Nailsea BS48 . . . . 59 B1
2 Weston-s-M BS23. . . . 104 E7
Northleach Wlk BS11. . . 47 F5
North Leaze BS41 . . . . . . 62 B2
Northleaze CE Prim Sch
Long Ashton BS41 . . . . . . 62 B1
Long Ashton BS41 . . . . . . 62 B1
Northleigh Ave BS22 . . . 88 C1
North Mdws BA2. . . . . . 134 E8
Northmead Ave BA3. . . 132 F2
Northmead Cl BA3 . . . . 132 F2
Northmead La BS37. . . . 26 D6
Northmead Rd BA3 . . . 132 F2
NORTH NIBLEY 5 D4
North Nibley CE Prim Sch
GL11. . . . . 5 D5
Northover Ct BS35 . . . . . 22 E6
Northover Rd BS9. . . . . . 35 A1
North Par
Bath BA2 . . . . 141 C2
Yate BS37. . . . . 27 E2
North Parade Bldgs 8
BA1 . . . . 141 C2
North Parade Pas 7
BA1 . . . . 141 C2
North Parade Rd BA2 . 102 B6
North Pk BS15 . . . . 51 E1
North Rd
Banwell BS29. . . . . 107 A3
Bath, Bathwick BA2. . . . 102 C6
Bath, Combe Down BA2 102 B2
7 Bristol BS3 . . . . 63 A4
Bristol, Montpelier BS6 . . 49 E2
Bristol, Stoke Gifford
BS34 . . . . 36 F4
Leigh Woods BS8. . . . . . . 62 D7
Lympsham BS24. . . . . . . 122 D2
Midsomer Norton BA3. . 133 A1
Thornbury BS35. . . . . 8 C2

North Rd continued
Timsbury BA2 . . . . **116** C2
Winterbourne BS36 . . . **37** F7
Yate BS37 . . . . **27** B3
Yate, Engine Common
BS37 . . . . **27** B5
Northridge Bsns Ctr
BS37 . . . . **27** C2
North Road Com Prim Sch
BS37 . . . . **27** B4
North Side Rd BS48 . . . **93** F8
North Somerset Mus★
BS23 . . . . **104** E8
North St
Bristol BS1 . . . . **143** B4
Bristol, Downend BS16 . . **51** E5
Bristol, Oldland Common
BS30 . . . . **66** C4
Bristol, Southville BS3 . . . **63** B3
Nailsea BS48 . . . . **59** B1
Norton St Philip BA2 . **136** E4
Weston-s-M BS23 . . . . **104** E8
Wickwar GL12 . . . . **18** A6
NORTH STOKE **83** C6
North Stoke La BS30 . . **83** B8
Northumberland Bldgs [1]
BA1 . . . . **141** B2
Northumberland Pl [1]
BA1 . . . . **141** C2
Northumberland Rd
BS6 . . . . **49** D2
Northumbria Dr BS9 . . . **49** B4
North View
Bristol BS6 . . . . **49** A4
Bristol, Mangotsfield
BS16 . . . . **51** E5
Bristol, Upper Soundwell
BS16 . . . . **51** D4
Midsomer Norton BA3 . **133** B2
Radstock BA3 . . . . **134** B2
North View Cl BA2 . . . **101** B5
North View Dr BS29 . . **107** C2
NORTHVILLE **36** A1
Northville Rd BS7 . . . . **36** A1
North Way
Bath BA2 . . . . **101** A5
Bristol BS34 . . . . **36** B4
Midsomer Norton BA3 . **133** A1
NORTH WESTON **45** C2
NORTHWICK **12** E2
NORTH WICK **96** D8
Northwick Gdns BS39 . **113** D4
Northwick Rd
Bristol BS7 . . . . **49** F8
Chew Magna BS39, BS41 **96** D7
Northwick BS35 . . . . **12** E1
NORTH WIDCOMBE . . . **113** B1
North Wlk BS37 . . . . . . **27** E1
Northwoods BS10 . . **35** D3
North Worle Sh Ctr
BS22 . . . . **89** B2
NORTON **88** D4
Norton Cl
Bristol BS15 . . . . **65** F7
Chew Magna BS40 . . . . . **96** B3
Norton Farm Rd BS9 . . **34** D3
Norton Grange BA2 . **136** E5
NORTON HAWKFIELD . **96** F6
NORTON HILL **139** B7
Norton Hill Sch BA3 . . **139** B8
Norton Ho
[7] Bristol BS1 . . . . . . **143** B1
Bristol, Patchway BS34 . . **23** F1
Norton La
Chew Magna BS39,
BS40 . . . . **96** D5
Wellow BA2 . . . . **136** B7
Weston-s-M BS22 . . . . . **88** C4
Whitchurch BS14 . . . . . . **80** C2
NORTON MALREWARD . **97** B7
Norton Rd BS4 . . . . **64** A3
NORTON ST PHILIP . . . **136** F4
Norton St Philip CE Fst
Sch BA2 . . . . **136** E4
NORTON'S WOOD **58** C5
Nortons Wood La BS21 **58** A5
Norwich Dr BS4 . . . . . . **64** E6
Norwood Ave BA2 . . . . **102** E5
Norwood Farm★ BA2 . **136** F7
Norwood Gr BS20 . . . . **44** F5
Notgrove Cl BS22 . . . . . **88** B2
Nottingham Rd BS7 . . . **49** E3
Nottingham St BS3 . . . . **63** F3
Nova Scotia Pl BS1 . . **142** A1
Nova Way BS11 . . . . . . **33** B1
Novers Cres BS4 . . . . . . **79** C8
Novers Hill BS4 . . . . . . **79** C8
Novers Hill Trad Est
BS3 . . . . **63** C1
Novers La BS4 . . . . **79** D7
NOVERS PARK **79** D8
Novers Park Cl BS4 . . . **63** C1
Novers Park Dr BS4 . . . **79** C8
Novers Park Rd BS4 . . . **79** D8
Novers Rd BS4 . . . . **79** C8
Nowhere La BS48 . . . . . **60** A1

Nugent Hill BS6 . . . . . . **49** D1
Nunney Cl BS31 . . . . . . **82** A2
Nupdale La BS35 . . . . . **14** D8
NUPDOWN **2** A4
Nupdown Rd BS35 . . . . . **1** E5
Nurseries The GL12 . . . **16** B5
Nursery Gdns BS10 . . . **35** A3
Nursery Rise BA3 . . . . **138** E4
Nursery The BS3 . . . . . **63** B3
Nutfield Gr BS34 . . . . . **36** B2
Nutfield Ho BS34 . . . . . **36** B1
Nutgrove Ave BS3 . . . . **63** E3
Nutgrove La BS40 . . . . . **96** A4
Nuthatch Dr BS16 . . . . **50** F6
Nuthatch Gdns BS16 . . **51** A6
Nutwell Rd BS22 . . . . . **88** E2
Nutwell Sq BS22 . . . . . **88** E2
NYE **107** E8
Nye Dro BS24 . . . . **107** E8
Nye Rd BS25 . . . . **107** F5
Nympsfield BS15 . . . . . **51** D1

O

Oak Ave BA2 . . . . **101** C3
Oak Cl
Bristol BS34 . . . . **36** D7
Yate BS37 . . . . **27** D3
Oak Ct
Bristol BS14 . . . . **80** A5
Weston-s-M BS22 . . . . . . **89** C3
Oakdale Ave BS16 . . . . **51** D8
Oakdale Cl BS16 . . . . . **51** E8
Oakdale Ct BS16 . . . . . **51** D7
Oakdale Gdns BS22 . . . **88** F2
Oakdale Rd
Bristol BS14 . . . . **80** A8
Bristol, Downend BS16 . . **51** E8
Oakdene Ave BS5 . . . . . **50** D3
Oak Dr BS20 . . . . **45** B4
Oakenhill Rd BS4 . . . . . **64** E2
Oakenhill Wlk BS4 . . . . **64** E2
Oakes La GL9 . . . . **42** B5
Oakfield Bsns Pk BS15 . **65** D7
Oakfield Cl BA1 . . . . . **101** D8
Oakfield Gr BS8 . . . . . **142** B4
Oakfield Mans BS8 . . . **142** B4
Oakfield Pl BS8 . . . . . **142** B4
Oakfield Rd
Bristol BS8 . . . . **142** B4
Bristol, Kingswood BS15 . **65** D7
Keynsham BS31 . . . . **81** F2
Oakford Ave BS23 . . . **104** F8
Oakford La
Batheaston BA1 . . . . **86** A8
Marshfield SN14 . . . . **70** B2
Oak Gr BS20 . . . . **47** C5
Oakhanger Dr BS11 . . . **34** B1
Oakhill BS24 . . . . **105** A2
Oakhill Ave BS30 . . . . . **66** C2
Oakhill Cl BS48 . . . . . . **60** B1
Oakhill La BS10 . . . . . . **34** C4
Oakhill Rd BA2 . . . . . **101** F2
Oak Ho BS13 . . . . **79** D4
Oakhurst Rd BS9 . . . . . **48** F5
Oak La BS5 . . . . **50** F2
Oakland Bsns Pk BS37 . **27** A3
Oakland Dr BS24 . . . . **105** E3
Oakland Rd
Bristol, Crew's Hole
BS5 . . . . **64** E8
[6] Bristol, Redland BS6 . . **49** B1
Oaklands
Clevedon BS21 . . . . **57** E4
Paulton BS39 . . . . **132** E4
Temple Cloud BS39 . . . **114** E1
Oaklands Cl BS16 . . . . . **52** B5
Oaklands Dr
Almondsbury BS32 . . . . . **24** A4
Bristol, Frenchay BS16 . . . **51** A7
Bristol, Oldland Common
BS30 . . . . **66** C2
Oaklands Rd BS16 . . . . **52** A5
Oakleaze BS36 . . . . **38** D7
Oak Leaze BS34 . . . . . . **35** F6
Oakleaze Rd BS35 . . . . . **8** C1
Oakleigh Ave BS5 . . . . . **50** D1
Oakleigh Cl BS48 . . . . . **76** B5
Oakleigh Gdns BS30 . . . **66** C2
Oakley
Bath BA2 . . . . **102** E5
Clevedon BS21 . . . . **73** B8
Oakley Rd BS7 . . . . **49** F7
Oak Lodge BS37 . . . . . . **39** D8
Oakmeade Pk BS4 . . . . **64** B2
Oak Rd
Bristol BS7 . . . . **49** E5
Colerne SN14 . . . . **70** F5
Winscombe BS25 . . . . . **125** A8
Oakridge Cl
Bristol BS15 . . . . **66** A7
Winscombe BS25 . . . . . **125** A8
Oakridge La BS25 . . . . **125** C6
Oaksey Gr BS48 . . . . . . **60** A1
Oak St BA2 . . . . **141** B1
Oaks The
Bristol BS7 . . . . **49** E4

Oaks The continued
Nailsea BS48 . . . . **60** A2
Winford BS40 . . . . **94** F7
Oak Terr BA3 . . . . **133** D1
Oak The BS9 . . . . **48** D3
Oak Tree Ave BS16 . . . . **53** B4
Oak Tree Cl BS15 . . . . . **65** C3
Oaktree Cres BS32 . . . . **24** C2
Oaktree Ct BS11 . . . . . . **47** E7
Oaktree Gdns BS13 . . . **78** E5
Oaktree Pk BS24 . . . . **105** E5
Oaktree Pl BS22 . . . . . . **89** C3
Oak Tree Wlk BS31 . . . . **81** D3
Oakwood Ave BS9 . . . . . **49** C6
Oakwood Dr BS16 . . . . . **38** C1
Oakwood Gdns BS36 . . . **38** E7
Oakwood Pk BS16 . . . . . **51** A3
Oakwood Rd BS9 . . . . . **49** B6
Oasis Acad Brislington
BS4 . . . . **80** F8
Oasis Acad Long Cross
BS11 . . . . **47** F8
Oatfield BS48 . . . . **76** F1
Oatlands Ave BS14 . . . . **80** A5
Oatley Ho BS9 . . . . **49** A5
Oatley Trad Est [6]
BS15 . . . . **51** D1
Oberon Ave BS5 . . . . . . **50** E2
Observatory Field
BS25 . . . . **125** B8
Observatory The BS22 . . **88** D3
Octavius Rd BS31 . . . . . **81** F8
ODD DOWN **101** D2
Odeon Bldgs BS23 . . . **104** E7
Odins Rd BA2 . . . . **101** D1
Okebourne Cl BS10 . . . . **35** B4
Okebourne Rd BS10 . . . **35** B4
Okeford Ho BS9 . . . . . . **48** F7
Old Acre Rd BS14 . . . . . **80** A3
Old Ashley Hill BS6 . . . . **49** F2
Old Aust Rd BS32 . . . . . **24** C6
Old Banwell Rd BS24 . **106** B4
Old Barn La BS40 . . . . . **94** A5
Old Barrow Hill BS11 . . . **47** D7
Old Bond St [4] BA1 . . **141** B2
Old Bread St BS2 . . . . **143** C2
Old Brewery The BS20 . . **47** C4
Old Brewhouse The
BA1 . . . . **84** B2
Oldbridge Rd BS14 . . . . **80** C3
Old Bristol Rd
Ridge BS40 . . . . **129** A3
Weston-s-M BS22 . . . . . . **89** A2
Old Bromley Heath Road
BS16 . . . . **37** D2
Old Burnett La BS31 . . . **99** A7
Oldbury Chase BS30 . . . **66** A2
Oldbury Court Dr BS16 . **51** B6
Oldbury Court Prim Sch
BS16 . . . . **51** C7
Oldbury Court Rd BS16 . **51** A5
Oldbury La
Thornbury BS35 . . . . **8** B4
Wick BS30 . . . . **67** D5
OLDBURY NAITE **7** E7
OLDBURY-ON-SEVERN . . **7** C6
Oldbury-on-Severn Prim
Sch BS35 . . . . **7** B5
Old Butchers Yd BS26 . **125** C2
Old Chapel BA1 . . . . . **141** C4
Old Chapel La BS48 . . . **74** F7
Old Chelsea La BS8 . . . . **61** C4
Old Church Cl BS30 . . . . **66** D7
Old Church Rd
[1] Axbridge BS26 . . . . **125** C1
Clevedon BS21 . . . . **57** E3
Nailsea BS48 . . . . **75** D8
Weston-s-M BS23 . . . . **104** D2
Old Coach Rd BS26 . . . **124** C2
Old Dairy Ct BS21 . . . . . **57** G3
Old Dairy The BA2 . . . **101** D4
OLD DOWN **14** D6
Old Down Hill BS32 . . . **14** B2
Old Down Rd GL9 . . . . . **42** C8
Old Drill Hall The BS2 . **143** C3
Old England Way BA2 . **134** E8
Old Farm La BS5 . . . . . . **65** B6
Old Ferry Rd BA2 . . . . **101** C6
Oldfield BS21 . . . . **57** G1
Oldfield Girls Sch BA1 . **83** F1
Oldfield La BA2 . . . . . **101** E4
OLDFIELD PARK **101** E4
Oldfield Park Inf Sch
BA2 . . . . **101** D6
Oldfield Park Jun Sch
BA2 . . . . **101** C4
Oldfield Park Sta BA2 . **101** D6
Oldfield Pl BS8 . . . . **62** F5
Oldfield Rd
Bath BA2 . . . . **141** A1
Bristol BS8 . . . . **142** A1
Oldfields La BS35 . . . . . **25** D7
Old Forge Mews BS49 . . **91** D8
Old Forge The BA2 . . . **117** B4
Old Forge Way BA2 . . . **134** E8
Old Fosse Rd BA2 . . . . **101** C1
Old Frome Rd BA2 . . . **118** E8
Old Gloucester Rd
Alveston BS35 . . . . **15** B5

Old Gloucester Rd continued
Bristol, Stoke Gifford
BS16 . . . . **37** B4
Hambrook BS16 . . . . **37** B2
North Corner BS36 . . . . . **25** D3
Thornbury BS35 . . . . **9** B2
Old Hill
Winford BS40 . . . . **94** D6
Wrington BS40 . . . . **92** F3
Oldhill Farm La BS40 . . **94** D6
Old House The BA2 . . . **120** C5
Old Hundred La GL9 . . . **41** D2
Old Junction Rd BS23 . **105** B5
Old King St BA1 . . . . . **141** B3
Old King Street Ct
BS1 . . . . **143** B3
Old La
Bristol BS16 . . . . **52** C6
Farmborough BA2 . . . . **116** A6
Nailsea BS21 . . . . **59** C4
OLDLAND **66** A3
OLDLAND COMMON . . . **66** D3
Oldland Common Sta★
BS30 . . . . **66** C3
Oldlands Ave BS36 . . . . **38** C6
Old Malthouse The
BS2 . . . . **143** C4
Old Manor Cl GL12 . . . . **11** A5
Old Market Rdbt BS2 . . **143** C3
Old Market St BS2 . . . . **143** C3
Oldmead Wlk BS13 . . . . **78** E7
Old Midford Rd BA2 . . . **119** B7
Old Millard's Hill BA3 . **133** B3
Old Mill Cl BS37 . . . . . . **39** B4
Old Mill Rd BS20 . . . . . **45** D5
OLD MILLS **132** D3
Old Mills Ind Est BS39 . **132** E2
Old Mills La BS39 . . . . **132** D3
Old Mill Way BS24 . . . **106** A8
OLDMIXON **105** B1
Oldmixon Cres BS24 . . **105** A3
Oldmixon Prim Sch
BS24 . . . . **105** A2
Oldmixon Rd BS24 . . . **105** B1
Old Mixon Rd BS24 . . . **105** C2
Old Newbridge Hill
BA1 . . . . **101** A8
Old Orchard BA1 . . . . **141** C3
Old Orchard St BA1 . . **141** C2
Old Orchard The BS16 . **52** B5
Old Park Hill BS2 . . . . **142** C3
Old Park Rd
Bristol BS11 . . . . **47** D7
Clevedon BS21 . . . . **57** G4
OLD PASSAGE **12** F6
Old Pensford La BS31 . . **81** D1
Old Pit Rd
Radstock BA3 . . . . **139** C8
Yate Rocks BS37 . . . . . . **27** C5
Old Pit Terr BA3 . . . . . **133** E4
Old Pk BS2 . . . . **142** C3
Old Police Sta The BS4 . **64** A3
Old Pooles Yd BS4 . . . . **64** E2
Old Post Office La
BS23 . . . . **104** D8
Old Priory Rd BS20 . . . . **47** B4
Old Quarry BA2 . . . . . **101** D2
Old Quarry Gdns BS15 . **50** F4
Old Quarry Rd BS11 . . . **47** E7
Old Quarry Rise BS11 . . **47** E7
Old Rd
Pensford BS39 . . . . **97** E3
Radstock BA3 . . . . **134** C1
Old Rectory Rd GL12 . . . **11** F4
Old School Cl BS25 . . . **108** F4
Old School Ct SN14 . . . . **70** A8
Old School Hill BA2 . . . **118** F7
Old School Ho BS4 . . . . **64** B2
Old School Ho The
BA1 . . . . **141** B4
Old School House The
BS2 . . . . **143** C4
Old School La BS24 . . . **122** C6
Old Smiths Yd BS15 . . . **65** D5
Old Sneed Ave BS9 . . . . **48** D4
Old Sneed Cotts BS9 . . . **48** D4
Old Sneed Pk BS9 . . . . . **48** D4
Old Sneed Rd BS9 . . . . . **48** D4
OLD SODBURY **41** B8
Old Sodbury CE Prim Sch
BS37 . . . . **41** B8
Old St BS21 . . . . **57** G3
Old Station La BS40 . . . **92** D1
Old Tannery The [20]
BS2 . . . . **143** C3
Old Tarnwell BS39 . . . . . **97** B2
Old Tk BA2 . . . . **119** F7
Old Vicarage Ct BS14 . . **80** C4
Old Vicarage Gn BS31 . . **81** E6
Old Vicarage Pl BS8 . . . **49** A1
Old Vicarage The
Bristol BS13 . . . . **78** F6
Bristol, Montpelier BS6 . . **49** E1
Oldville Ave BS21 . . . . . **57** F2
Old Walcot Sch The
BA1 . . . . **141** C3
Old Wall BS24 . . . . **121** D5
Old Water Gdns The
BS40 . . . . **110** E2

Old Wells Rd BA2 . . . . . **101** F3
Old Wesleyan Chapel The
BS30 . . . . **66** B5
Old Weston Rd
Congresbury BS49 . . . . . **91** B5
Flax Bourton BS48 . . . . . **77** B8
Oldwood La BS37 . . . . . **27** B8
Old Work Ho The BS5 . . **64** E8
Olive Gdns BS35 . . . . . . **14** F2
Oliver Brooks Rd BA3 . **138** E7
OLVESTON **14** B3
Olveston CE Prim Sch
BS35 . . . . **14** A3
Olveston Rd BS7 . . . . . . **49** E5
Olympus Cl BS34 . . . . . **36** D6
Olympus Rd BS34 . . . . . **35** D7
Onega Ctr BA1 . . . . . . **141** A3
Onega Terr BA1 . . . . . **141** A3
Oolite Gr BA2 . . . . **101** D1
Oolite Rd BA2 . . . . **101** D1
Oram Ct BS30 . . . . **65** F4
ORANGE END **19** C4
Orange Gr BA1 . . . . . . **141** C2
Orange St BS2 . . . . . . **143** C4
Orchard Ave
Bristol BS1 . . . . **142** C2
Midsomer Norton BA3 . **132** F1
Portishead BS21 . . . . **58** E4
Thornbury BS35 . . . . **8** D1
Orchard Bvd BS30 . . . . . **66** B4
Orchard Cl
Banwell BS29 . . . . **107** B3
Bishop Sutton BS39 . . . . **113** C8
Bristol, Kingswood BS15 . **65** E8
Bristol, Westbury on T
BS9 . . . . **48** F5
Charfield GL12 . . . . **11** A5
Congresbury BS49 . . . . . **91** D4
Felton BS40 . . . . **94** C8
Flax Bourton BS48 . . . . . **77** A8
Keynsham BS31 . . . . **81** D6
Locking BS24 . . . . **105** F4
Portishead BS20 . . . . **45** D5
Weston-s-M, Kewstoke
BS22 . . . . **88** B3
Weston-s-M, Worle
BS22 . . . . **88** F2
Westwood BA15 . . . . . **120** F3
Winterbourne BS36 . . . . **37** E5
Wrington BS40 . . . . **92** E2
Yate BS37 . . . . **27** F2
Orchard Cotts
[11] Bristol BS16 . . . . . . **51** D5
Keynsham BS31 . . . . **81** B2
Timsbury BA2 . . . . **116** F1
Orchard Cres BS11 . . . . **47** D7
Orchard Ct
Bristol BS9 . . . . **48** C3
Bristol, Filton BS34 . . . . . **36** A2
[19] Bristol, Pile Marsh
BS5 . . . . **64** D7
Claverham BS49 . . . . **74** F1
Yate BS37 . . . . **27** B3
Orchard Dr
Aust BS35 . . . . **13** A7
Bristol BS13 . . . . **79** A6
Sandford BS25 . . . . **108** A4
Orchard End BS40 . . . . **129** F4
Orchard Gate BS32 . . . . **24** C2
Orchard Gdns
Bristol BS15 . . . . **65** F8
Paulton BS39 . . . . **132** E6
Orchard Grange BS35 . . **8** B2
Orchard Ho
[2] Bristol BS5 . . . . **64** F8
Weston-s-M BS22 . . . . . . **88** F2
Orchard La BS1 . . . . . . **142** C2
Orchard Lea
[6] Alveston BS35 . . . . . . **15** A5
Pill BS20 . . . . **47** D4
Orchard Lodge BA2 . . . **102** F3
Orchard Pk BS14 . . . . . . **80** D4
Orchard Pl [1] BS23 . . **104** E7
Orchard Rd
Axbridge BS26 . . . . **125** C1
Backwell BS48 . . . . **76** A5
Bristol, Ashley Down BS7 **49** E4
Bristol, Crew's Hole BS5 . **64** F8
Bristol, Kingswood BS15 . **65** E8
Clevedon BS21 . . . . **57** F2
Frampton Cotterell BS36 . **38** D7
Hutton BS24 . . . . **105** E2
Long Ashton BS41 . . . . . **61** F1
Nailsea BS48 . . . . **59** D1
Paulton BS39 . . . . **132** E6
Pucklechurch BS16 . . . . . **53** B5
Orchard Rise BS35 . . . . **14** A3
Orchard Sch Bristol
BS7 . . . . **49** F8
Orchard Sq BS5 . . . . . . **64** D7
Orchard St
Bristol BS1 . . . . **142** C2
Weston-s-M BS23 . . . . **104** E8
Orchards The
Bristol, Kingswood
BS15 . . . . **65** F7
Bristol, Shirehampton
BS11 . . . . **47** E6
Orchard Terr [5] BA2 . . **101** B6

Orchard The
Banwell BS29........**107** A3
Bath, Combe Down BA2 **102** B1
Bath, Newbridge BA1 ..**101** A7
Bristol BS34...........**36** F5
Corston BA2...........**100** B8
Frampton Cotterell BS36 **38** C8
Freshford BA2........**120** C5
Locking BS24.........**106** A5
Pensford BS39.........**97** E4
Pill BS20..............**47** C4
Tytherington GL12 .....**16** B5
Upper Stanton Drew
  BS39.................**97** A2
Orchard Vale
Bristol BS15...........**65** F7
Midsomer Norton BA3..**132** F1
Orchard Vw G12 ....**9** E7
Orchard Way BA2 .....**134** D7
Orchard Wlk
Churchill BS25........**108** E4
Kingswood GL12 ......**11** F4
Orchid Cl BS16........**52** C7
Orchid Dr BA2 ....**101** C1
Oriel Gdns BA1 ....**85** C2
Oriel Gr BA2..........**101** B4
Orion Dr BS34 ....**36** D6
Orland Way BS30 ......**66** A3
Orlebar Gdns BS11....**34** B2
Orme Dr BS21 ....**57** F5
Ormerod Rd BS9......**48** E5
Ormonds Cl BS32 .....**24** E1
Ormrod Gr BS24 .....**106** C5
Ormsley Cl BS34......**36** C8
Orpen Gdns BS7......**50** B5
Orpen Pk BS32........**24** B3
Orpheus Ave BS34 ....**36** D6
Orwell Dr BS31 ....**82** A4
Orwell St BS3.........**63** E3
Osborne Ave
Bristol BS7............**49** F3
Weston-s-M BS23 .....**104** F7
Osborne Cl BS34......**36** D4
Osborne Rd
Bath BA1 ....**101** B7
Bristol, Clifton BS8 .....**49** A1
Bristol, Southville BS3 ...**63** C4
Severn Beach BS35......**22** A7
Weston-s-M BS23 .....**104** F7
Osborne Terr [10] BS3 ..**63** B2
Osborne Villas BS2....**142** C4
Osborne Wallis Ho
BS8..................**142** A1
Osmond Rd [2] BS24...**105** F7
Osprey Ct BS14.......**79** D5
Osprey Gdns BS22.....**88** F1
Osprey Pk BS35........**8** D3
Osprey Rd [15] BS5 ....**64** C7
Ostlings La BA1.......**86** B2
Otago Terr [5] BA1.....**85** C2
Ottawa Rd BS23.......**104** F3
Otterford Cl BS14.....**80** B5
Otter Rd [1] BS21......**57** G1
Otter Way BS35........**8** D3
Ottery Cl BS11........**34** A1
Ottrells Mead BS32 ....**24** C3
Our Lady of Lourdes RC
  Prim Sch BS15......**65** E7
Our Lady of the Rosary RC
  Prim Sch BS11......**48** A8
OVAL THE **101** C4
Oval The BA2 ....**101** C4
OVER **23** D2
Overdale
Clandown BA3 ....**133** E5
Peasedown St John
  BA2.................**116** F3
Over Dr BS34 ....**35** F7
Overhill BS20...........**47** D4
Over La BS35...........**23** D2
Overndale Rd BS16....**51** C6
Overndale Sch BS37 ...**41** A7
Overnhill Ct BS16......**51** D5
Overnhill Rd BS16......**51** D5
Overnhurst Ct [2] BS16 .**51** D5
Overstables La BS21 ...**57** F3
Overton [5] BS4 ....**64** D1
Overton Rd BS6........**49** E2
Owen Dr BS8 ....**61** B4
Owen Gr BS9 ....**49** B5
Owen Henry Ho BS2...**50** A1
Owen St [18] BS5......**64** B8
Owls Head Rd BS15....**65** E6
Oxbarton BS34........**36** F5
Oxenham Ct BS5......**64** D8
Oxen Leaze BS32.......**24** E2
Oxford Pl
Bath BA2 ....**102** C2
[21] Bristol, Clifton BS8...**62** F6
[14] Bristol, Upper Easton
  BS5.................**50** B1
Weston-s-M BS23 .....**104** D7
Oxford Sq BS24........**106** B6
Oxford St
Bristol BS2...........**143** C2
[7] Bristol, Redfield BS5 .**64** C7
Bristol, The Dings BS2..**64** A6

Oxford St continued
Bristol, Tyndall's Park BS2,
  BS6.................**142** C4
Bristol, Windmill Hill BS3.**63** F4
Weston-s-M BS23 .....**104** D7
Oxhouse Gdns BS10....**34** E3
Oxhouse Ind Est BS22 ..**89** A5
Oxhouse La
Failand BS8 ....**61** B6
Winford BS40..........**94** D6
Oxleaze BS13..........**79** D4
Oxleaze La BS41.......**78** E3
Oxleaze Way BS39 ....**132** D6
Oxleigh Way BS16......**36** F3
Oxney Pl BA2.........**134** C7
Oxwick Farm La BS37 ..**28** A8
Ozenhay BS39 ....**130** E6
Ozleworth BS15........**66** A8

P

Packgate Rd BS11 .....**33** F4
Pack Horse La BA2...**118** F7
Pacquet Ho BS20 ......**47** D5
Paddock Cl
Bristol BS32...........**24** E2
Bristol, Emerson's Green
  BS16.................**52** C6
Paddock Gdn BS14.....**79** F4
Paddock Gdns BS35....**15** A5
Paddock Park BS22.....**89** B2
Paddock Rd BS35 ......**8** B3
Paddocks The
[5] Bath BA2 ....**102** B1
Bristol BS16...........**38** A1
Sandford BS25........**108** C4
Thornbury BS35........**8** D1
Weston-s-M BS23 ....**104** D2
Paddock The
Banwell BS29..........**107** A3
Clevedon BS21.........**57** F2
Corston BA2...........**100** B7
Portishead BS20.......**45** D4
Paddock Woods BA2 ..**102** D2
Padfield Cl BA2.......**101** B5
Padleigh Hill BA2.....**101** B2
Padmore Ct [7] BS5....**64** D7
Padstow Rd BS4 ....**79** F8
Pagans Hill BS40......**95** D2
Page Ct BS16..........**51** F4
Page Rd BS16.........**51** D4
Page's Ct BS49........**91** C8
Pages Mead BS11......**47** C8
Painswick Ave BS34....**36** B8
Painswick Dr BS37......**27** E1
Paintworks BS4........**64** B4
Palace Yard Mews
BA1 ....**141** B2
Palmdale Cl BS30......**66** A3
Palmer Ave BS35.......**22** C3
Palmer Row [7] BS23 ..**104** E8
Palmers BS30..........**66** A6
Palmer's Elm BS24.....**90** B4
Palmers La BA2.......**117** B3
Palmer St BS3.........**104** E8
Palmerston Rd BS6....**49** C4
Palmerston St BS3.....**63** C3
Palmer's Way BS24 ...**105** D2
Palmyra Rd BS3........**63** B2
Pamela Ho [9] BS16....**51** D5
Panoramic The BS1....**142** C3
Pantile The [16] BS3....**63** C3
Paper Mill Gdns BS20 ..**45** F6
Parade The BS5........**50** F2
Parade The
[1] Bath BA2 ....**101** B6
Bristol BS34...........**23** F1
Bristol, Bishopsworth
  BS13.................**79** A6
Bristol, Shirehampton
  BS11.................**47** E6
Chipping Sodbury BS37 ..**28** A1
Paradise Row BS39 .....**98** A6
Paragon Ct [13] BS23 ..**87** C1
Paragon Rd BS23......**87** C1
Paragon Sch The BA2 .**102** A3
Paragon The
Bath BA1 ....**141** C3
Bristol BS8............**62** F6
Parbrook Ct BS14......**80** B5
Parfitt's Hill [8] BS5 ....**64** F6
Parish Brook Rd BS48 ..**59** B2
Parish The BS3........**142** B1
Park Ave
Bath BA2 ....**141** B1
Bristol BS32...........**24** A2
Bristol, Eastville BS5....**50** D3
Bristol, Rose Green BS5 .**64** E8
Bristol, Windmill Hill BS3.**63** E3
Frampton Cotterell BS36 .**38** B6
Winterbourne BS36......**37** E7
Yatton BS49...........**74** B1
Park Batch BS40......**110** F3
Park Cl
Bristol, Cadbury Heath
  BS30 ....**66** B5
Bristol, Kingswood BS15 .**65** E7

Park Cl continued
Keynsham BS31.........**81** D5
Paulton BS39 ....**132** D5
Park Cnr
Paulton BS39 ....**132** D6
Sharpstone BA2.......**120** A4
PARK CORNER...........**120** A4
Park Cres
Bristol, Cadbury Heath
  BS30 ....**66** B5
Bristol, Frenchay BS16 ...**37** C1
Bristol, Rose Green BS5 .**64** E8
Park Ct [5] BS23.......**104** E5
Park Edge BS5.........**64** E8
Park End BS29.........**106** E4
Parkers Ave BS30......**67** C7
Parkers Barton BS5....**64** B6
Parkers Cl BS10........**35** E4
Parker St [5] BS3.......**63** B3
Parkes Rd BS24.......**106** C5
Park Farm Bsns Pk
BS36.................**94** B7
Park Farm Ct [13] BS30 .**65** F4
Park Farm Village Gn
BS36..................**38** B6
PARKFIELD..............**53** A7
Parkfield BS26........**125** D1
Parkfield Ave [3] BS5 ..**64** D7
Parkfield Gdns BS39 ..**113** D3
Parkfield Rank BS16....**53** A7
Parkfield Rd BS16......**53** A6
Park Gdns BA1.........**101** D8
Park Gr BS9...........**49** C5
Park Hill BS11.........**47** F6
Park Ho BA2..........**101** E4
Parkhouse La BS31.....**81** C2
Parkhurst Ave [4] BS16 .**51** B4
Parkhurst Rd BS23.....**105** A7
Park La
Bath BA1 ....**101** D7
Blagdon BS40.........**110** F3
Bristol BS2...........**142** C3
Faulkland BA2........**135** B1
Frampton Cotterell BS36 .**38** B6
North Nibley GL11 ......**5** E7
Parklands
Bristol BS8...........**142** C4
Bristol, Kingswood BS15 .**65** E8
High Littleton BS39 ....**115** D2
Parklands Ave BS22....**89** A4
Parklands Educate
  Together Prim Sch
BS24.................**106** B6
Parklands Rd BS3......**62** E4
Parkland Way BS35.....**8** C3
Park Leaze
Bristol BS34...........**23** E1
Kendleshire BS36......**38** A6
Park Pl
Bath BA1 ....**141** A4
Bristol, Kingsdown BS8 .**142** B3
Bristol, Upper Eastville
  BS5.................**50** E3
Bristol, Victoria Park
  BS2.................**142** C3
Weston-s-M BS23 .....**104** D8
Park Prim Sch The
Bristol BS15...........**65** E8
Bristol BS30...........**66** E8
Park Rd
Bath BA1 ....**101** B7
Bristol BS3...........**142** B1
Bristol, Cadbury Heath
  BS30 ....**66** B5
Bristol, Kingswood BS15 .**65** D8
Bristol, Northville BS7....**36** A1
Bristol, Shirehampton
  BS11.................**47** F6
Bristol, Staple Hill BS16 .**51** E5
Bristol, Stapleton BS16 ..**50** D5
Clevedon BS21........**57** F4
Congresbury BS49......**91** E3
Keynsham BS31........**81** E4
Leyhill GL12 ....**10** B4
Paulton BS39 ....**132** D5
Thornbury BS35........**8** B2
Park Row
Bristol BS1...........**142** C3
Frampton Cotterell BS36 **38** A8
Parkside Ave BS36......**37** E6
Parkside Gdns BS5.....**50** B4
Park St
Bath BA1 ....**141** A4
Bristol BS1...........**142** C3
Bristol BS4............**64** A4
Bristol, Crew's Hole BS5 .**64** F8
Bristol, Totterdown BS4..**64** A3
Hawkesbury Upton GL9..**20** A2
Iron Acton BS37 ....**26** D4
Parkstone Ave BS7.....**49** F6
Park Street Ave BS1...**142** C3
Park Street Mews
BA1 ....**141** A4
Park The
Bristol BS32...........**24** C3
Bristol, Frenchay BS16 ...**37** C1
Bristol, Kingswood BS15 .**65** E8
Bristol, Willsbridge BS30 **66** B1
Keynsham BS31.........**81** E6

Park The continued
Portishead BS20 ....**45** F5
Yatton BS49...........**74** B1
Park View
Bath BA2 ....**101** D6
Bristol, Kingswood BS15 .**65** E7
Bristol, Southville BS3...**63** C4
Yate BS37...............**39** E8
Park View Ave BS35 ....**8** C2
Park View Ct BS16......**51** E5
Park View Terr BS5.....**64** E8
Park Villas BS3........**104** D8
Parkwall Cres BS30.....**65** F4
Parkwall Prim Sch
BS30.................**66** A4
Parkwall Rd BS30.......**66** A4
Parkway
Bristol BS34...........**37** A4
Timsbury BA2.........**116** E2
Parkway La BA2.......**116** D3
Parkway N BS34........**37** A4
Parkway Trad Est [10]
BS2..................**49** F2
Park Wlk BS20.........**47** D4
Park Wood Cl BS14.....**79** F4
Parliament St BS4......**64** A4
Parnall Cres BS37......**27** C2
Parnall Rd BS16........**51** A3
Parnall Road Ind Est
BS16.................**51** A3
Parnell Rd
Bristol BS16...........**50** E7
Clevedon BS21.........**57** F3
Parry Cl BA2..........**101** B4
Parrys Cl BS9.........**48** E5
Parrys Gr BS9.........**48** E5
Parry's La BS9.........**48** F5
Parslow Barton [4] BS5 **65** A7
Parsonage Cl BS40.....**94** F6
Parsonage Ct BS20.....**45** D4
Parsonage La
Axbridge BS26.........**125** E2
Bath BA1 ....**141** B2
Chilcompton BA3 ....**138** C4
Pensford BS39.........**97** D6
Winford BS40..........**94** F6
Parsonage Rd BS41.....**62** C2
Parson St Prim Sch
BS3..................**63** C2
Parsons Ave BS34......**36** F5
Parsons Gn
Clevedon BS21.........**73** C8
Weston-s-M BS22 ......**89** A3
Parsons Mead BS48....**76** F7
Parsons Paddock BS14 **80** A7
Parson St BS3.........**63** B2
Parson Street Prim Sch
BS3..................**63** C2
Parson Street Sta BS3.**63** B2
Parsons Way BS25.....**124** E6
Parsons Wlk BS30......**66** D7
Partis College BA1....**101** A8
Partis Way BA1........**101** A8
Partition St BS1.......**142** C2
Partridge Cl
Weston-s-M BS22 ......**88** F1
[2] Yate BS37...........**27** F4
Partridge Dr BS16......**51** C6
Partridge Rd BS16......**53** C4
Passage Leaze BS11 ...**47** D6
Passage Rd
Aust BS35.............**12** F7
Bristol, Brentry BS10....**34** F3
Bristol, Westbury on Trym
  BS9.................**49** A8
Passage Road Brentry Hill
BS9, BS10.............**35** A2
Passage St BS2.......**143** B2
Pastoral Rd BS35 ......**8** B4
Pastures Ave BS22......**89** C3
Pastures The BA15....**120** E3
Patch Croft BS21......**73** C8
Patch Ct BS16.........**52** A8
Patch Elm La BS37.....**26** F7
Patch La BS37.........**27** A8
Patch St BA2..........**102** A2
PATCHWAY.............**24** B2
Patchway Brook BS32 ..**24** C2
Patchway CE Prim Sch
BS34.................**24** C1
Patchway Com Coll
BS32.................**24** B1
Patchway Sta BS34.....**36** C6
Patchway Trad Est
BS34.................**35** E7
Patchwood Rd BS48....**77** F7
Patterson Ho [8] BS1...**143** B1
Paul Alan Ho [21] BS5 ..**64** C7
Paulman Gdns BS41....**77** F8
Paulmont Rise BS39...**114** E1
Paul's Cswy BS49......**91** D4
Paul St BS2...........**142** C4
Paulto' Hill BA3, BS39.**133** B6
PAULTON **132** F5
Paulton Dr BS7........**49** C4

Paulton Jun & Inf Sch
BS39.................**132** E5
Paulton La BA2, BA3...**133** D7
Paulton Memorial Hospl
BS39.................**132** F4
Paulton Rd
Farrington Gurney
  BS39...............**132** B4
Hallatrow BS39........**132** B7
Midsomer Norton BA3...**132** F1
Paultow Ave BS3........**63** E3
Paultow Rd BS3........**63** E3
Paulwood Rd BS39....**114** E1
Pavey Cl BS13.........**79** C4
Pavey Rd BS13........**79** C4
Pavilions The BS4......**64** C1
Pawlett BS24..........**105** A2
Pawlett Rd BS13.......**79** C3
Pawlett Wlk BS13......**79** C3
Paxton BS16...........**50** E8
Paybridge Rd BS13.....**78** F4
Payne Dr BS5..........**64** B7
Payne Rd BS24........**105** D2
Paynes Ho [17] BS23...**104** E8
Paynes Orchard Pk
BS10.................**35** D5
Paywell La BS40......**127** E5
Peache Ct BS16........**51** E6
Peache Rd BS16........**51** F6
Peacock Rd BS25.......**8** C3
Peacocks La BS15......**65** C7
Pearces Hill BS16......**51** B7
Pearl St BS3...........**63** B3
Pearsall Rd BS30.......**65** E2
Pearse Cl BS22........**89** B5
Peart Cl BS13..........**78** E5
Peart Dr BS13.........**78** E4
Pear Tree Ave BS41....**77** E8
Peartree Cl BS13......**79** B4
Peartree Field BS20 ....**45** F5
Peartree Gdns BS24...**122** C6
Pear Tree Hey BS37 ...**27** E5
Pear Tree Ind Est
BS40.................**109** C4
Peartree La
Bristol, Lower Soundwell
  BS15...............**51** F2
Bristol, St George BS15..**65** B6
Pear Tree Leaze BS34 ..**35** F6
Pear Tree Rd BS32......**24** C2
Pear Tree Way BS16....**52** D8
PEASEDOWN ST
  JOHN **134** C8
Peasedown St John Prim
  Sch BA2............**134** C7
Peats Hill BS39.........**97** F5
Pedder Rd BS21........**57** F1
Peelers Ct [2] BS26....**125** C1
Peel St BS5...........**143** C4
Pegasus Lodge BS23 ..**104** D5
Pegasus Pk BS34......**36** C6
Pegasus Pl BS25......**107** C4
Pegasus Rd BS34......**35** D7
Peg Hill BS37..........**27** F4
Pegwell Close BS34.....**35** E6
Pelican Cl BS22.......**105** E8
Pemberton Ct BS16....**51** C5
Pembery Rd BS3........**63** B3
Pembroke Ave BS11....**47** E6
Pembroke Ct BS21......**57** E4
Pembroke Gate BS8....**49** A1
Pembroke Gr BS8.....**142** A3
Pembroke Ho [1] BS23..**87** C1
Pembroke Lodge BS8 .**142** A4
Pembroke Mans BS8 ..**142** A4
Pembroke Pl BS8......**142** A1
Pembroke Rd
Bristol BS8...........**142** A4
Bristol, Kingswood BS15 .**51** E2
Bristol, Shirehampton
  BS11.................**47** E6
Bristol, Southville BS3...**63** C4
Portishead BS20.......**44** E4
Weston-s-M BS23 .....**104** F4
Pembroke St BS2......**143** B4
Pembroke Vale BS8 ...**142** A4
Penard Way BS15.......**65** F7
Penarth Dr BS24......**105** A1
Pendennis Ave BS16 ...**51** D4
Pendennis Ho [5] BS16 .**51** D5
Pendennis Pk
Bristol, Brislington BS4..**64** D2
[1] Bristol, Staple Hill
  BS16...............**51** D4
Pendennis Rd BS16 ....**51** D5
Pendle Cl BS25........**125** A7
Pendlesham Gdns BS23 **88** A1
Pendock Cl BS30.......**66** C1
Pendock Ct BS16......**52** B7
Pendock Rd
Bristol BS16...........**51** C6
Winterbourne BS36......**37** E5
Penfield Cl BS2.........**50** A2
Penfield Rd BS2........**50** A2
Penlea Ct BS11........**47** D7
Pennard BS24 ....**105** A2

Pennard Ct
 Bath BA2 . . . . .101 A6
 Bristol BS14 . . . . .80 B5
Pennard Gn BA2 . . . . .101 A6
Penn Ct BS26 . . . . .125 C1
Penn Dr BS16 . . . . .37 C1
Penn Gdns BA1 . . . . . .101 A8
Penngrove BS30 . . . . . .66 A3
Penn Hill La BS31 . . . .81 A3
Penn Hill Rd BA1 . . . . .84 A1
Pennine Gdns BS23 . . . .88 A1
Pennine Rd BS30 . . . . .66 C4
Pennings The BS26 . . . .125 C2
Pennington Rd GL12 . . .18 B4
Pennlea BS13 . . . . .79 C7
Penn Lea Ct BA1 . . . . . .101 B8
Penn Lea Rd BA1 . . . . . .101 B8
Pennon Rise BS1 . . . . . .142 C1
Penn St BS1 . . . . .143 B3
Penns The BS21 . . . . . . .57 G2
PENNSYLVANIA 68 F7
Pennsylvania Vw BA1 . .84 E4
Penn Way BS26 . . . . . . .125 C1
Pennycress BS22 . . . . .105 D7
Pennycress Cl BS16 . . .52 D8
Pennyquick BA2 . . . . . . .100 D6
Pennyquick Hill BA2 . .100 F4
Pennyquick View BA2 . .100 F6
Pennyroyal Gr BS16 . . . .50 E4
Pennywell Ct 3 BS5 . . .64 A8
Pennywell Est 3 BS21 . .57 F2
Pennywell Rd BS2, BS5 . .64 A8
Pen Park Rd BS10 . . . . .35 D2
Penpole Ave BS11 . . . . . .47 E6
Penpole Cl BS11 . . . . . . .47 D7
Penpole La BS11 . . . . . .47 E7
Penpole Pk BS11 . . . . . .47 E7
Penpole Pl BS11 . . . . . . .47 E6
Penrice Cl BS22 . . . . . . .88 C2
Penrith Gdns BS10 . . . .49 D8
Penrose BS14 . . . . .79 F7
Penrose Dr BS32 . . . . . .36 D7
Pensfield Pk BS10 . . . . .35 D4
PENSFORD 97 E4
Pensford Ct BS14 . . . . .80 D5
Pensford Hill BS39 . . . .97 D5
Pensford La BS39 . . . . . .97 A3
Pensford Old Rd BS39 . .97 E3
Pensford Prim Sch
 BS39 . . . . .97 D4
Pentagon The BS9 . . . . .48 B5
Penthouse Hill BA1 . . . .85 F3
Pentire Ave BS13 . . . . . .79 A6
Pentland Ave BS35 . . . .15 E8
Peony Rd BS16 . . . . .38 C1
Peppershells La BS39 . .98 C6
Pepys Cl BS31 . . . . .82 D2
Pera Pl BA1 . . . . .141 C4
Pera Rd BA1 . . . . .141 C4
Percival Rd BS8 . . . . . . .62 F8
Percival Terr BS39 . . . .131 F4
Percy Pl 13 BA1 . . . . . . .85 B1
Percy St 8 BS3 . . . . .63 D4
Percy Walker Ct BS16 . .51 C6
Peregrine Cl BS22 . . . . .88 F1
Perfect View BA1 . . . . . .85 A1
Peritrack La BS23 . . . . .105 B4
Perrett Ho 22 BS2 . . . . .143 C3
Perretts Ct BS1 . . . . . . .142 C1
Perrett Way BS20 . . . . .47 E4
Perrin Cl BS39 . . . . .131 E8
Perrings The BS48 . . . . .75 E8
Perrinpit Rd BS36 . . . . .25 E2
Perrott Rd BS15 . . . . . . .52 A1
Perry Cl BS36 . . . . .37 D4
Perry Court E-Act Acad
 BS14 . . . . .80 A6
Perrycroft Ave BS13 . . .79 A6
Perrycroft Rd BS13 . . . .79 A6
Perrymans Cl
 Bristol BS16 . . . . .51 A6
 Doynton BS30 . . . . . . .68 A8
PERRYMEAD 102 B3
Perrymead
 Bath BA2 . . . . .102 B3
 Weston-s-M BS22 . . .89 B5
Perrymead Ct BA2 . . . . .102 B4
Perrymead Pl BA2 . . . . .102 B4
Perry Mead Rd BS40 . .130 C5
Perry Rd
 Bristol BS1 . . . . .143 A3
 Long Ashton BS41 . . . . . .61 F1
Perrys Lea BS32 . . . . . . .24 D2
Perry St BS5 . . . . .64 A8
Pesley Cl BS13 . . . . .79 A4
Petercole Dr BS13 . . . . .79 A6
Peterside BS39 . . . . . . .131 E8
Peterson Sq BS13 . . . . .79 C3
Peter's Terr BS5 . . . . . . .64 B7
Petersway Gdns BS5 . . .65 A6
Petherbridge Way BS7 . .50 A3
Petherton Cl BS15 . . . . .65 E5
Petherton Gdns BS14 . .80 B7
Petherton Rd BS14 . . . .80 B7
Pethick Ho BS4 . . . . .79 F8

Peto Garden at Iford
 Manor The★ BA15 . . .120 E3
Peto Gr BA15 . . . . .120 F3
Pettigrove Gdns BS15 . . 65 E7
Pettigrove Rd BS15 . . . .65 E6
PETTY FRANCE 30 A7
Pevensey Wlk BS4 . . . . .79 D7
Peverell Cl BS10 . . . . . .34 F3
Peverell Dr BS10 . . . . . .34 F3
Pheasant Row BS49 . . .73 F2
Philippa Cl BS14 . . . . . .80 A7
Philips Ho 2 BS2 . . . . .143 B4
Philip St
 Bristol, St Philip's Marsh
   BS2 . . . . .64 B5
 Bristol, Windmill Hill BS3 . 63 D4
Phillips Rd BS23 . . . . . .105 A6
Phillis Hill BS39 . . . . . . .132 F4
Phippen St 1 BS1 . . . . .143 B1
Phipps Barton BS15 . . .65 B8
Phipps St BS3 . . . . .63 B4
Phoenix Bsns Pk BS3 . .63 A2
Phoenix Gr BS6 . . . . . . .49 C5
Phoenix Ho
 Bath BA1 . . . . .141 B4
 Bristol BS5 . . . . .64 B6
Phoenix Way BS20 . . . .45 F6
Piccadilly Pl
 Bath BA1 . . . . .102 B8
 5 Bath BA1 . . . . .102 B8
Pickedmoor La BS35 . . .7 E5
Pickwick Rd BA1 . . . . . .85 A2
Picton La BS6 . . . . .49 E1
Picton Mews 6 BS6 . . .49 E1
Picton St BS6 . . . . .49 E1
Pier Cl BS20 . . . . .45 E7
Pier Rd BS20 . . . . .45 E7
Pierrepont Pl 9 BA1 . .141 C2
Pierrepont St BA1 . . . . .141 C2
Pigeon House Dr BS13 . 79 D4
Pigeon La BS40 . . . . . . .93 E1
Pigott Ave BS13 . . . . . . .79 A4
Pilemarsh BS5 . . . . .64 D7
PILE MARSH 64 D7
Pilgrims Way
 Avonmouth BS11 . . . .47 C7
 Bristol BS16 . . . . .51 D8
 Chew Stoke BS40 . . . .112 D8
 Weston-s-M BS22 . . .88 E3
Pilgrims Wharf BS4 . . .64 E7
Pilkington Cl BS34 . . . .36 C2
PILL 47 C4
Pillingers Gdns BS6 . . .49 B2
Pillingers Rd BS15 . . . .65 C7
Pill Rd
 Abbots Leigh BS8 . . . .47 F1
 Pill BS20 . . . . .47 E2
Pill St BS20 . . . . .47 D4
Pill Way BS21 . . . . .57 D2
PILNING 22 D7
Pilning Prim Sch BS35 . 22 E6
Pilning St BS35 . . . . . . .23 C8
Pilning Sta BS35 . . . . . .22 F5
Pimms La BS23 . . . . .88 B3
Pimm's La BS22 . . . . . . .88 B2
Pimpernel Mead BS32 . 36 E7
Pinchay La BS40 . . . . . .95 A5
Pinckney Gn BA15 . . . .103 E5
Pincots La GL12 . . . . . .18 B3
Pine Cl
 Thornbury BS35 . . . . . . .8 C1
 Weston-s-M BS22 . . .88 D2
Pinecroft
 Bristol BS14 . . . . .79 F7
 Portishead BS20 . . . . .44 F6
Pine Ct
 Chew Magna BS40 . . .96 B3
 Keynsham BS31 . . . . . .81 C4
Pinefield BS9 . . . . .49 B7
Pine Gr BS7 . . . . .36 A1
Pine Grove Pl BS7 . . . .49 D3
Pine Hill BS22 . . . . .88 D2
Pine Lea BS24 . . . . .122 B6
Pine Rd BS10 . . . . .35 B3
Pine Ridge Cl BS9 . . . .48 C4
Pines Cl BA3 . . . . .138 D3
Pines La BS35 . . . . .14 D3
Pines Rd BS30 . . . . .66 C1
Pines The
 Bristol, Lower Soundwell
   BS15 . . . . .52 A3
 Bristol, Sneyd Park BS9 . 48 D3
Pines Way
 Bath BA2 . . . . .141 A2
 Radstock BA3 . . . . . . .134 A2
Pines Way Ind Est
 BA2 . . . . .141 A2
Pinetree Rd BS24 . . . . .106 D4
Pine Wlk BA3 . . . . .133 E1
Pinewood BS15 . . . . . . .51 F1
Pinewood Ave BA3 . . . .132 F1
Pinewood Cl BS9 . . . . . .49 B7
Pinewood Gr BA3 . . . . .132 F1
Pinewood Rd BA3 . . . . .132 F1
Pinewood Way SN14 . . .70 F7
Pinhay Rd BS13 . . . . . . .79 B6
Pinkers Mead BS16 . . .52 C6
Pinkhams Twist BS14 . .80 A5

Pinnell Gr BS16 . . . . . . .52 C7
Pioneer Ave BA2 . . . . .101 F1
Pioneer Pk BS4 . . . . . . .64 C5
Pipehouse BA2 . . . . . . .119 E4
Pipehouse La BA2 . . . . .119 F4
Pipe La BS1 . . . . .142 C2
Piper Rd BS37 . . . . .27 E3
Pippin Cl BA2 . . . . .134 D7
Pippin Ct 3 BS30 . . . .65 F4
Pippins The BS20 . . . . .45 F5
Pitchcombe BS37 . . . . .39 C7
Pitchcombe Gdns BS9 . .48 D7
Pitching The BA3 . . . . .138 D5
Pitch La BS6 . . . . .49 D1
Pitch & Pay La BS9 . . .48 E3
Pitch & Pay Pk BS9 . . .48 E3
Pitfour Terr BA2 . . . . . .116 B2
Pithay Ct BS1 . . . . .143 A3
Pithay The
 Bristol BS1 . . . . .143 A3
 Paulton BS39 . . . . .132 E6
Pit La
 Backwell BS48 . . . . . . .76 A4
 Ubley BS40 . . . . .111 F5
Pitlochry Cl BS7 . . . . . .35 F1
Pitman Ct BA1 . . . . .85 C2
Pitman Ho BA2 . . . . . . .101 D4
Pitman Rd BS23 . . . . . .104 E6
Pit Rd BA3 . . . . .133 B1
PITT COURT 5 F5
Pitt Rd BS7 . . . . .49 E5
Pittville Cl BS35 . . . . . .8 C3
Pitville Pl 16 BS6 . . . . .49 B1
Pitway Cl BS39 . . . . . . .131 F4
Pitway La BS39 . . . . . . .131 E4
Pixash La BS31 . . . . . . .82 C5
Pixash Works BS31 . . .82 C5
Pixey Hole La BS40 . . .111 E3
Pizey Ave BS21 . . . . . . .57 D2
Pizey Ave Ind Est BS21 . 57 E2
Pizey Cl BS21 . . . . .57 D2
Plain The
 Norton St Philip BA2 . .136 E4
 Thornbury BS35 . . . . . . .8 B1
Platts Wood BS16 . . . . .50 D8
Players BS16 . . . . .37 B3
Playford Gdns BS11 . . .47 E8
Plaza The BS2 . . . . .143 C2
Pleasant Ho 4 BS16 . .51 D5
Pleasant Pl BA1 . . . . . .86 D2
Pleasant Rd BS16 . . . .51 D5
Pleshey Cl BS22 . . . . . .88 D2
Plimsoll Ho
 3 Bristol BS1 . . . . . .143 B1
 5 Bristol, Woolcott Park
   BS6 . . . . .49 B1
Ploughed Paddock
 BS48 . . . . .59 D1
Plover Cl
 Weston-s-M BS22 . . . . .88 F1
 Yate BS37 . . . . .27 C2
Plovers Rise BA3 . . . . .134 A3
Plowright Ho 8 BS15 . .65 B5
Plumers Cl 4 BS21 . . .57 G1
Plumley Cres BS24 . . .106 A4
Plumley Ct BS23 . . . . . .104 E8
PLUMMER'S HILL 132 E6
Plummer's Hill BS5 . . .64 E8
Plumpton Ct BS16 . . . .37 F1
Plumptre Cl BS39 . . . .132 E5
Plumptre Rd BS39 . . . .132 E5
Plumtree Cl BS25 . . . . .108 A1
Plum Tree Rd BS22 . . .105 E8
Plunder St BS49 . . . . . .92 B7
Podgers Dr BA1 . . . . . .84 B2
Podium The BA1 . . . . . .141 C2
Poets' Cl BS5 . . . . .64 D8
Poets Cnr BA3 . . . . .139 C8
Polar Gdns SN14 . . . . .31 E4
Polden Cl BS48 . . . . . . .59 E1
Polden Ho BS3 . . . . .63 D3
Polden Rd
 Portishead BS20 . . . . .45 B5
 Weston-s-M BS23 . . .104 F8
Polden Wk BA3 . . . . . . .139 B6
Polestar Way BS24 . . .106 A8
Pollard Rd BS22 . . . . . .105 F8
Polly Barnes Cl 6
 BS15 . . . . .65 B5
Polly Barnes Hill BS15 . .65 B5
Polygon Rd BS8 . . . . . .142 A2
Polygon The
 Avonmouth BS11 . . . .33 D1
 16 Bristol BS8 . . . . . .62 F6
Pomfrett Gdns BS14 . .80 E5
Pomphrey Hill BS16 . . .52 C4
Pond Cotts BA3 . . . . . .135 D2
Pond Head BS20 . . . . . .47 D4
Ponsford Rd BS4 . . . . .64 B1
Ponting Cl BS5 . . . . . . .51 A1
Pool Cnr BS32 . . . . .14 B2
Poole Court Dr BS37 . . .27 D2
Poole Ho BA2 . . . . .100 F5
Poolemead Rd BA2 . . .100 F5
Poole St BS11 . . . . .47 B8
Pooles Wharf BS8 . . . .142 A1
Pooles Wharf Ct BS8 . .142 A1
Pool Farm BS37 . . . . . .39 D5
Pool Ho BS34 . . . . .36 A8

Pool La BS40 . . . . .95 A2
Pool Paddock BS34 . . .35 F6
Pool Rd BS15 . . . . .51 E3
Poor Hill BA2 . . . . .115 F6
Pope's Wlk BA2 . . . . . .102 B3
Poplar Ave BS9 . . . . . . .48 D6
Poplar Cl
 Bath BA2 . . . . .101 D4
 Bristol BS30 . . . . .66 C6
Poplar Dr BS16 . . . . . . .53 B5
Poplar Fields BS30 . . .66 D6
Poplar Gardens Ho 3
 BS15 . . . . .65 E8
Poplar La GL12 . . . . . . .18 B4
Poplar Pl
 Bristol BS16 . . . . .51 A3
 16 Weston-s-M BS23 . .104 E8
Poplar Rd
 Bath BA2 . . . . .118 D3
 Bristol, Hanham BS15 . .65 A5
 Bristol, Highridge BS13 . .78 F7
 Bristol, North Common
   BS30 . . . . .66 D6
 Bristol, Speedwell BS5 . .50 F1
Poplar Rdbt BS11 . . . . .33 E5
Poplars The
 Easton-in-G BS20 . . . .47 B4
 Weston-s-M BS22 . . .89 A1
Poplar Terr BS15 . . . . . .65 F8
Poplar Way SN14 . . . . .70 F5
Poplar Way E BS11 . . .33 F4
Poplar Way W BS10,
 BS11 . . . . .33 D6
Poplar Wlk BS24 . . . . .105 E5
Pople's La BA11 . . . . . .140 F1
Pople Walk BS7 . . . . . .49 F3
Poppy Cl
 Harry Stoke BS34 . . . .36 F3
 Weston-s-M BS22 . . .89 A5
Poppy Mead BS32 . . . .36 E7
Porlock Cl
 3 Clevedon BS21 . . .57 G1
 Weston-s-M BS23 . . .104 F2
Porlock Gdns BS48 . . .59 E1
Porlock Rd
 Bath BA2 . . . . .102 A1
 Bristol BS3 . . . . .63 D3
Portal Rd BS24 . . . . . . .106 D4
PORTBURY 46 E3
Portbury Comm BS20 . .45 E4
Portbury Gr BS11 . . . . .47 D6
Portbury Hundreds The
 BS20 . . . . .46 C4
Portbury La BS20 . . . . .60 E7
Portbury Way BS20 . . .46 E5
Portbury Wlk BS11 . . .47 D6
Port Elizabeth Ho BS10 . 35 B1
PORTISHEAD 45 B4
Portishead Bsns Pk
 BS20 . . . . .45 E5
Portishead Lodge BS20 . 45 D6
Portishead Office Pk
 BS20 . . . . .45 E5
Portishead Prim sch
 BS20 . . . . .45 E6
Portishead Rd BS22 . . .89 B4
Portishead Way BS3 . . .62 E3
Portland Cl BS48 . . . . .59 D1
Portland Ct
 Bristol BS16 . . . . .51 D3
 Bristol, Upper Soundwell
   BS16 . . . . .51 D3
Portland Dr BS20 . . . . .45 E4
Portland Lofts 8 BS2 . .143 B4
Portland Mans 9 BA2 . 143 B4
Portland Pl
 Bath BA1 . . . . .141 B4
 Bristol BS16 . . . . .51 D3
Portland Rd BA1 . . . . . .141 B4
Portland Sq BS2 . . . . . .143 B4
Portland St
 Bristol, Clifton BS8 . . .62 F7
 Bristol, Staple Hill BS16 . .51 D3
Portland Terr BA1 . . . . .141 B4
Portmeade Dro BS25 . .125 C1
Portmeirion Cl BS14 . . .80 B5
Port Side Cl 5 BS5 . . .64 F6
Port View BS20 . . . . . . .47 C5
Portview Rd BS11 . . . . .47 B8
Portwall La BS1 . . . . . .143 B1
Portwall La E 10 BS1 . .143 B1
Portway
 Bristol BS8 . . . . .48 C3
 Bristol, Shirehampton
   BS11 . . . . .47 C6
Portway Com Sch BS11 . 47 E7
Portway La BS37 . . . . . .28 E2
Portway Rdbt BS11 . . .47 C8
Poskett Way G12 . . . . .11 A5
Post Office La
 Blagdon BS40 . . . . . . .110 D3
 Flax Bourton BS48 . . .76 C1
Post Office Rd BS24 . .106 C5
Poston Way BA15 . . . .120 D7
POTTERS HILL 77 B1
Potters Hill BS40 . . . . .94 A8
Potters View BS49 . . . .91 E2
Potterswood Cl BS15 . .65 D7
Pottery Cl BS23 . . . . . .105 A6

Potts Cl BA1 . . . . .85 F3
Pound Dr BS16 . . . . . . .50 F3
Pound La
 Bristol BS16 . . . . .50 F4
 Nailsea BS48 . . . . .59 D3
Pound Mead BS40 . . . .94 C8
Pound Mill Bsns Ctr
 BS35 . . . . .8 C5
Pound Rd BS15 . . . . . . .51 F2
Pound The
 Almondsbury BS32 . . . . . .24 A5
 Oldbury-on-S BS35 . . .7 B6
 Redhill BS40 . . . . .93 D3
Pountney Dr 2 BS5 . . .64 B8
Powel Ct BS30 . . . . .53 E1
Powells Acres BS21 . . .57 G3
Powis Cl BS22 . . . . .88 C2
Powlett Ct BA2 . . . . . . .102 B7
Powlett Rd BA2 . . . . . .102 B8
Pow's Hill BA3 . . . . . . .133 D5
Pow's Orch BA3 . . . . . .133 A1
Pow Rd BS15 . . . . .65 D7
Poyntz Ct BS30 . . . . . . .65 F3
Poyntz Rd BS4 . . . . . . .79 F8
Pratten's La 2 BS16 . .51 D4
Preacher Cl BS5 . . . . . .65 B6
Preachers Wlk BS15 . .65 D5
Preanes Gn BS22 . . . . .89 A2
Precinct BS49 . . . . .91 D3
Precinct The BS20 . . . .45 D5
Preddy's La BS5 . . . . . .65 A6
Prescot Cl BS22 . . . . . .88 B2
Prescott BS37 . . . . .39 D8
Press Moor Dr BS30 . .65 F4
Prestbury BS37 . . . . . . .39 D8
Preston Wlk BS4 . . . . .64 A1
Prestwick Cl BS4 . . . . .64 D1
Pretoria Rd BS34 . . . . .35 F8
Prewett St BS1 . . . . . . .143 B1
Priddy Cl BA2 . . . . .101 B5
Priddy Ct BS14 . . . . . . .80 B5
Priddy Dr BS14 . . . . . . .80 B5
Priests Way BS22 . . . . .88 D2
Priestwood Cl BS10 . . .35 A3
Primrose Alley BA2 . . .99 D2
Primrose Cl
 Bristol BS32 . . . . .24 D2
 Bristol, St George BS15 . .65 C8
Primrose Dr BS35 . . . . .8 D2
PRIMROSE HILL 84 D1
Primrose Hill BA1 . . . .84 D1
Primrose La
 Bristol BS15 . . . . .51 C1
 Midsomer Norton BA3 . .133 B1
Primrose Terr BS15 . . .51 C1
Princes Bldgs BA1 . . . .141 B3
Prince's Bldgs 19
 BS8 . . . . .62 F6
Princes Ct BS30 . . . . . .65 F4
Princes' La BS8 . . . . . . .62 F6
Princes' Pl BS7 . . . . . . .49 E3
Prince's Rd BS21 . . . . .57 F3
Princess Cl BS31 . . . . .81 E4
Princess Gdns BS16 . .50 D6
Princess Row BS2 . . . .143 A4
Princess St
 Bristol, Newton BS2 . . .64 A7
 Bristol, Windmill Hill BS3 . 63 E4
Princes St BA1 . . . . . . .141 B2
Prince's St
 Bristol BS2 . . . . .143 C4
 Clandown BA3 . . . . . . .133 C5
Princess Victoria St
 BS8 . . . . .62 F6
Prince St BS1 . . . . .143 A1
Prinknash Ct 6 BS37 . .39 C7
Prior La BS37 . . . . .27 E6
Prior Park Bldgs BA2 . .102 B5
Prior Park Coll BA2 . . .102 C2
Prior Park Cotts BA2 . .141 C1
Prior Park Gdns BA2 . .102 B5
Prior Park Landscape
 Gdn★ BA2 . . . . .102 C3
Prior Park Rd BA2 . . . .102 B4
Priors Hill BA2 . . . . . . .116 A2
Prior's Hill 12 BS6 . . . .49 D1
Priors Lea BS37 . . . . . .27 E1
Priory Ave BS9 . . . . . . .49 A7
Priory Cl
 Bath BA2 . . . . .102 B2
 Midsomer Norton BA3 . .133 A1
Priory Com Sch BS22 . .89 B3
Priory Court Rd BS9 . . .49 A7
Priory Ct
 Bristol, Hanham BS15 . . .65 C3
 Bristol, Upper Knowle
   BS4 . . . . .64 C2
Priory Dene BS9 . . . . . .49 A7
Priory Farm Trad Est
 BS20 . . . . .46 D3
Priory Gdns
 Bristol, Horfield BS7 . .49 F8
 Bristol, Shirehampton
   BS11 . . . . .47 D7
 Easton-in-G BS20 . . .47 B4
Priory Mews BS23 . . .105 B7
Priory Rd
 Bristol BS8 . . . . .142 D3

Priory Rd *continued*
Bristol, Shirehampton
 BS11 . . . . .47 D6
Bristol, Upper Knowle
 BS4 . . . . .64 B2
Easton-in-G BS20 . . . . . .47 B4
Keynsham BS31 . . . . . . .81 E7
Portbury BS20 . . . . .46 D3
Weston-s-M BS23 . . . . .105 A7
Priory Wlk BS20 . . . . . . .46 D3
PRISTON 117 B5
Priston Cl BS22 . . . . . . .89 B5
Priston Hill BA2 . . . . . . .117 C5
Priston La
Farmborough BA2 . . . . .116 C7
Farmborough BA2 . . . . .116 C8
Priston BA2, BA3 . . . . . .117 A5
Priston Rd BA2 . . . . . . .117 D6
Pritchard St BS2 . . . . . .143 B4
Pritchard Way BS37 . . .27 D6
Privet Dr BS13 . . . . .79 C5
Probyn Cl BS16 . . . . . . .51 A7
Pro-Cathedral BS8 . . . .142 B3
Proctor Cl BS4 . . . . .64 D1
Proctor Ho BS1 . . . . . . .143 B1
Promenade The BS7 . . .49 D2
Prospect Ave BS15 . . . . .51 B1
Prospect Cl
Easter Compton BS35 . . .23 A2
Frampton Cotterell BS36 . .37 F8
Winterbourne BS36 . . . . .37 E4
Prospect Cres BS15 . . . .51 F2
Prospect Gdns BA1 . . . .85 F5
Prospect Ho BS22 . . . . .88 E3
Prospect La BS36 . . . . . .37 F8
Prospect Pl
Bath, Beacon Hill BA1 . . .85 A1
Bathford BA1 . . . . .86 D2
Bath, Weston BA1 . . . . . .84 C2
1 Bristol, Montpelier
 BS6 . . . . .49 D2
Bristol, Moorfields BS5 . .64 C8
9 Weston-s-M BS23 . . . .104 E8
Prospect Rd
Bath BA2 . . . . .102 C4
Severn Beach BS35 . . . . .22 A5
Prospect Terr 5 BS3 . . .63 C3
Protheroes Ho BS1 . . . .142 C2
Proud Cross BS40 . . . . .129 E4
Providence La BS41 . . . .61 F2
Providence Pl BS2 . . . . .143 C2
PROVIDENCE PLACE . .132 F1
Providence Rise BS41 . .61 F2
Providence View BS41 . .62 A1
Prowse Cl BS35 . . . . .8 C1
Prowse's La BS26 . . . . .125 A1
Prudham St 7 BS5 . . . . .50 C1
PUBLOW 97 F5
Publow La BS39 . . . . . . .97 E5
PUCKLECHURCH 53 A5
Pucklechurch CE Prim Sch
 BS16 . . . . .53 C6
Pucklechurch Trad Est
 BS16 . . . . .53 B4
Pudding Pie Cl BS40 . . .109 A5
Pudding Pie La BS40 . .109 A6
Puffin Cl BS22 . . . . .105 F8
PULLENS GREEN 7 C5
Pullin Ct BS30 . . . . .66 D4
Pullins Gn 3 BS35 . . . . . .8 B1
Pulteney Ave BA2 . . . . .102 B6
Pulteney Bridge BA2 . . .141 C2
Pulteney Gdns BA2 . . . .102 B6
Pulteney Gr BA2 . . . . . .102 B6
Pulteney Mews BA2 . . . .102 B7
Pulteney Rd BA2 . . . . . .102 B6
Pulteney Terr BA2 . . . . .102 B6
Pump La
Bathford BA1 . . . . .86 B2
Bristol BS1 . . . . .143 B1
Redhill BS40 . . . . .93 D2
Tockington BS32 . . . . . . .14 D4
Pump Sq BS20 . . . . .47 D5
Purcell Wlk BS4 . . . . . . .79 D7
Purdown Rd BS7 . . . . . . .49 F5
Purdue Cl BS22 . . . . .89 B3
Purlewent Dr BA1 . . . . . .84 C1
PURN 122 A7
Purn La BS24 . . . . .122 A8
Purn Rd BS24 . . . . .121 F8
Purn Way BS24 . . . . . . .122 B7
Purple Emperor Rd
 BS35 . . . . .8 C3
Pursey Dr BS32 . . . . .36 F6
Purton Cl BS15 . . . . .65 E6
Purton Rd BS7 . . . . .49 D2
Purving Row BS24 . . . . .122 C1
Purving Row La BS24 . . .122 C1
Puttingthorpe Dr
 BS22 . . . . .105 C2
Puxley Cl BS14 . . . . .80 E6
PUXTON 90 D3
Puxton La BS24 . . . . .90 D3
Puxton Moor La BS24 . . .90 E2
Puxton Rd BS24 . . . . .90 D3
Pye Cnr BS25 . . . . .108 D4
PYE CORNER 37 D3
Pye Croft BS32 . . . . .24 E3

Pyecroft Ave BS9 . . . . . .49 C7
Pyghtell The SN14 . . . . .31 E5
Pylewell La BS25 . . . . . .108 D1
Pylle Hill Cres BS3 . . . . .63 F4
Pyne Point BS21 . . . . . . .57 E3
Pynes The BS31 . . . . . . .82 B4
Pynne Cl BS14 . . . . .80 F5
Pynne Rd BS14 . . . . .80 F5
Pyracantha Wlk BS14 . . .80 A6

Q

QEH Theatre ★ BS8 . . . .142 B3
Quadrangle The BS37 . . .39 C4
Quadrant BS32 . . . . .24 B3
Quadrant E BS16 . . . . . . .51 C3
Quadrant The BS32 . . . . .24 A3
Quadrant W BS16 . . . . . .51 C3
Quadrilles The BS35 . . . .22 A6
Quaker Ct 1 BS35 . . . . . .8 B1
Quaker La BS35 . . . . .8 B1
Quaker's Cl BS16 . . . . . . .51 D8
Quakers' Friars BS1 . . . .143 B3
Quaker's Rd BS16 . . . . . .51 E8
Quantock Cl
Bristol BS30 . . . . .66 C5
Midsomer Norton BA3 . .139 B4
Quantock Ct BS16 . . . . . .36 E1
Quantock Rd
Bristol BS3 . . . . .63 D3
Portishead BS20 . . . . . . .45 B5
Weston-s-M BS23 . . . . .104 E4
Quantocks BA2 . . . . .102 A1
Quarries The BS32 . . . . . .24 C6
Quarrington Rd BS7 . . . .49 E5
Quarry Bank BS37 . . . . . .28 B2
Quarry Barton BS16 . . . .37 C4
Quarry Cl
Bath BA2 . . . . .101 F1
Limpley Stoke BA2 . . . . .120 C1
Quarry Hay BS40 . . . . . .112 D8
Quarry La
Bristol BS11 . . . . .34 C1
Winterbourne BS36 . . . . .37 E4
Quarrymans Ct 1
 BA2 . . . . .102 B1
Quarry Mead BS35 . . . . .14 F5
Quarry Rd
Alveston BS35 . . . . .14 F5
Bath BA2 . . . . .102 D6
Bristol, Frenchay BS16 . . .51 C7
Bristol, Kingswood BS15 . .65 D6
Chipping Sodbury BS37 . . .28 A1
Portishead BS20 . . . . . . .45 C4
Sandford BS25 . . . . . . .108 A2
Quarry Rise BS24 . . . . . .121 F8
Quarry Rock Gdns
 BA2 . . . . .102 D4
Quarry Steps BS8 . . . . . .49 A2
Quarry The BS11 . . . . . . .34 C1
Quarry Vale Cotts 2
 BA2 . . . . .102 B1
Quarry Way
Bristol, Emerson's Green
 BS16 . . . . .38 A1
Bristol, Fishponds BS16 . .50 E5
Nailsea BS48 . . . . .59 D2
Quays Ave BS20 . . . . .45 E5
Quayside La 4 BS5 . . . . .64 F6
Quay St BS1 . . . . .143 A3
Quays The BS1 . . . . .142 C1
Quebec BA2 . . . . .101 A4
Quedgeley BS37 . . . . . . .39 C8
Queen Ann Rd BS5 . . . . .64 B6
Queen Charlotte St
 BS1 . . . . .143 A2
QUEEN CHARLTON 81 B3
Queen Charlton La
 BS14 . . . . .80 E2
Queen Elizabeth's Hospital
Sch BS8 . . . . .142 B3
Queen Quay BS1 . . . . . . .143 A2
Queens Apartments
 BS8 . . . . .142 C3
Queen's Ave
Bristol BS8 . . . . .142 B3
Portishead BS20 . . . . . . .45 C5
Queenscote BS20 . . . . . . .45 F5
Queens Ct BS31 . . . . .81 E5
Queen's Ct BS8 . . . . .142 B3
Queensdale Cres BS4 . . . .64 A1
Queens Down Ct BS4 . . . .64 C3
Queensdown Gdns BS4 . .64 C2
Queens Down Gdns
 BS4 . . . . .64 C3
Queens Dr BS15 . . . . . . .65 B4
Queen's Dr
Bath BA2 . . . . .102 A2
Bristol BS7 . . . . .49 C5
Queens Gate BS9 . . . . . . .48 D5
Queenshill Rd BS4 . . . . . .64 A1
Queensholm Ave BS16 . . .37 E1
Queensholm Cl BS16 . . . .37 E1
Queensholm Cres BS16 . .37 E1
Queensholm Dr BS16 . . . .37 E1
Queens Mans BS8 . . . . . .142 B3

Queens Par BS1 . . . . . . .142 C2
Queens Par BA1 . . . . . . .141 B3
Queen's Parade Pl
 BA1 . . . . .141 B3
Queens Pl BA2 . . . . .102 B5
Queen Sq
Bath BA1 . . . . .141 B2
Bristol BS1 . . . . .143 A2
Saltford BS31 . . . . .82 F3
Queen Square Ave 10
 BS1 . . . . .143 A2
Queen Square Ho BS1 . .143 A2
Queen Square Pl BA1 . . .141 B2
Queens Rd
Banwell BS29 . . . . .107 A3
Bristol RS4 . . . . .64 C2
Keynsham BS31 . . . . . . .81 D4
Nailsea BS48 . . . . .59 D1
Portishead BS20 . . . . . . .44 E4
Queen's Rd
Bristol BS8 . . . . .142 B3
Bristol, Ashley Down BS7 .49 F5
Bristol, Bishopsworth BS13,
 BS41 . . . . .78 F4
Bristol, Cadbury Heath
 BS30 . . . . .66 B4
Bristol, Crew's Hole BS5 . .64 F7
Clevedon BS21 . . . . .57 F3
Pucklechurch BS16 . . . . .53 B5
Radstock BA3 . . . . .134 B2
Weston-s-M BS23 . . . . . .87 D1
Queen St
Avonmouth BS11 . . . . . . .33 A1
Bath BA1 . . . . .141 B2
Bristol BS2 . . . . .143 B3
Bristol, Eastville BS5 . . . .50 D3
Bristol, St George BS15 . .65 B8
Queensway
Bristol BS34 . . . . .36 D6
Weston-s-M BS22 . . . . . .88 F4
Queens Way BS20 . . . . . .44 E4
Queensway Ctr BS22 . . . .89 B2
Queens Wlk BS35 . . . . . . .8 B3
Queen Victoria Rd BS6 . .49 A4
Queen Victoria St BS2 . . .64 A6
Queenwood Ave BA1 . . . .85 A1
Quickthorn Cl BS14 . . . . .80 A6
Quiet St BA1 . . . . .141 B2
Quilter Gr BS4 . . . . .79 D7

R

Raby Mews BA2 . . . . . . .102 B7
Raby Pl BA2 . . . . .102 B7
Raby Villas BA2 . . . . . . .102 B7
Rackfield Pl BA2 . . . . . . .101 B6
Rackham Cl BS7 . . . . .50 B6
Rackhay BS1 . . . . .143 A2
Rackley La BS26 . . . . . . .124 B2
Rackvernal Ct BA3 . . . . .133 B1
Rackvernal Rd BA3 . . . . .133 B1
RADFORD 133 C8
Radford Hill
Camerton BA2, BA3 . . . .133 C7
Timsbury BA2 . . . . .116 C1
Radley Rd BS16 . . . . .51 B4
Radnor Bsns Ctr BS7 . . . .49 E5
Radnor Rd
Bristol, Horfield BS7 . . . .49 E5
Bristol, Westbury on Trym
 BS9 . . . . .49 B5
RADSTOCK 133 E1
Radstock Mus ★ BA3 . . .133 F2
Radstock Rd BA3 . . . . . .133 C2
Raeburn Rd BS5 . . . . .65 B6
Rag Hill BA3 . . . . .134 D5
Rag La GL12 . . . . .17 D5
Raglan Cl BA3 . . . . .138 C4
Ragland La BA1 . . . . .85 A2
Ragland St BA1 . . . . .85 A2
Raglan La
Bristol BS5 . . . . .65 A7
Winford BS40 . . . . .94 E7
Raglan Pl
Bristol BS7 . . . . .49 D3
Thornbury BS35 . . . . . . .15 B8
20 Weston-s-M BS23 . . . .87 C1
Raglan Rd BS7 . . . . .49 D3
Raglan Terr BA1 . . . . .85 A2
Raglan Villas BA1 . . . . . .85 A1
Raglan Wlk BS31 . . . . . . .81 D4
Railton Jones Cl BS34 . . .36 E3
Railway Arches BS2 . . . .143 C2
Railway Cotts BS37 . . . . .40 E8
Railway La BA2 . . . . .118 D1
Railway Pl BA1 . . . . .141 C1
Railway St BA1 . . . . .141 C1
Railway Terr
Bristol BS16 . . . . .51 E4
Shoscombe BA2 . . . . . . .134 E4
Railway View Pl BA3 . . . .133 B2
Rainbow Ct BS37 . . . . . . .27 B3
Rainham Ct 2 BS23 . . . . .87 C1
Rains Batch BS40 . . . . . .127 E6
Raleigh Cl BS31 . . . . .82 D2
Raleigh Ct 3 BS23 . . . . .104 E6
Raleigh Rd BS3 . . . . .63 B4
Raleigh Rise BS20 . . . . . .45 B5

Ralph Allen Dr BA2 . . . .102 B3
Ralph Allen Sch BA2 . . . .102 E2
Ralph Rd BS7 . . . . .49 F4
RAM HILL 38 D4
Ram Hill BS36 . . . . .38 D4
Ram Hill Bsns Pk BS36 . .38 D5
Ramsay Cl BS22 . . . . .88 E4
Ramscombe La BA1 . . . . .85 F6
Ramsey Rd BS7 . . . . .49 F7
Rams Leaze BS34 . . . . . .36 A7
Ranchways BS20 . . . . . . .44 F4
Randall Cl BS15 . . . . .51 F2
Randall Rd BS8 . . . . .142 B2
Randolph Ave
Bristol BS13 . . . . .79 B5
Yate BS37 . . . . .27 D4
Randolph Cl BS13 . . . . . .79 B5
Rangers Wlk BS15 . . . . . .65 C4
RANGEWORTHY 27 B8
Rangeworthy CE Prim Sch
 BS37 . . . . .16 F1
Rankers La BS39 . . . . . . .98 C5
Rannoch Rd BS7 . . . . .35 F1
Ranscombe Ave BS22 . . . .88 D2
Ransford BS21 . . . . .57 D1
Raphael Ct BS1 . . . . .143 B1
Ratcliffe Dr BS34 . . . . . . .36 E5
Rathbone Cl BS36 . . . . . .38 C5
Raven Cl BS22 . . . . .88 E1
Raven Ct BS9 . . . . .48 F8
Ravendale Dr BS30 . . . . .66 B2
Ravenglass Cres BS10 . . .35 D2
Ravenhead Dr BS14 . . . . .80 B8
Ravenhill Ave BS3 . . . . . .63 F2
Ravenhill Rd BS3 . . . . . . .63 F3
Ravenscourt Rd BS34 . . . .36 B7
Ravenswood BS30 . . . . . .66 B3
Ravenswood Rd BS6 . . . .49 C1
Ravenswood Sch BS48 . . .59 D3
Rawlins Ave BS22 . . . . . .89 A5
Rawnsley Ho 13 BS5 . . . .50 A1
Rayens Cl BS41 . . . . .61 F1
Rayens Cross Rd BS41 . . .61 F1
Rayleigh Rd BS9 . . . . .48 E7
Raymend Rd BS3 . . . . . . .63 E3
Raymend Wlk BS3 . . . . . .63 E2
Raymill BS4 . . . . .65 A2
Raymond Ho BS16 . . . . . .51 F4
Raymore Rise BS41 . . . . .61 F1
Raynes Rd BS3 . . . . .63 A3
Rayneswood BS23 . . . . .104 F8
Raysfield Inf Sch BS37 . . .39 F8
Raysfield Jun Sch BS37 . .39 F8
Reade Cl BS15 . . . . .65 D4
Reading Ct BS15 . . . . . . .65 B8
Rearing Unit The BS35 . . .7 E7
Rector's Way BS23 . . . . .104 F6
Rectory Cl
Farmborough BA2 . . . . .116 A6
Wraxall BS48 . . . . .60 A2
Yate BS37 . . . . .27 F3
Rectory Dr BS49 . . . . .91 C7
Rectory Farm La BA2 . . .100 D2
Rectory Gdns BS10 . . . . .34 E2
Rectory La
Bleadon BS24 . . . . .122 C6
Bristol BS34 . . . . .36 A3
Compton Martin BS40 . .129 B6
Cromhall GL12 . . . . .17 A8
Timsbury BA2 . . . . .116 B2
Rectory Rd
Easton-in-G BS20 . . . . . .47 B3
Frampton Cotterell BS36 . .38 A8
Rectory Way
Lympsham BS24 . . . . . .121 F2
Yatton BS49 . . . . .91 C7
Recurium Lodge BS26 . .125 B2
Redacre BS40 . . . . .93 D3
Red Admiral Way BS35 . . .8 C3
Redcar Ct BS16 . . . . .37 F1
Redcatch Rd BS4 . . . . . . .63 F2
Redcliff Backs BS1 . . . . .143 B2
Redcliff Cres BS3 . . . . . . .63 E4
REDCLIFFE BAY 44 E4
Redcliffe Cl BS20 . . . . . . .44 E3
Redcliffe Par E BS1 . . . . .143 A1
Redcliffe Par W BS1 . . . .143 A1
Redcliffe Way BS1 . . . . . .143 B1
Redcliff Hill BS1 . . . . . . .143 B1
Redcliff Mead La BS1 . . .143 B1
Redcliff St BS1 . . . . .143 B2
Redcroft BS40 . . . . .93 D3
Redcross Mews 14
 BS2 . . . . .143 C3
Redcross St BS2 . . . . . . .143 C3
Redding Pit La BS40 . . . .94 E4
Reddings The
Bristol BS15 . . . . .51 F2
Compton Martin BS40 . .129 B6
REDFIELD 64 C7
Redfield Edge Prim Sch
 BS30 . . . . .66 D4
Redfield Gr BA3 . . . . . . .139 A8
Redfield Hill BS30 . . . . . .66 D4
Redfield Rd
Bristol BS34 . . . . .36 B7
Midsomer Norton BA3 . .139 A8
Redford Cres BS13 . . . . . .78 F3
Redford La BS16 . . . . . . .53 D4

Redford Wlk BS13 . . . . . .78 F3
Redham La BS35 . . . . . . .22 F8
REDHILL 93 D3
Red Hill
Peasedown St John
 BA2 . . . . .116 E1
Redhill BS40 . . . . .93 D2
Redhill Cl BS16 . . . . .50 E3
Redhill Dr BS16 . . . . .50 E3
Redhill Farm Bsns Pk
 BS35 . . . . .13 F6
Redhill La BS35 . . . . .13 E6
Red House La
Almondsbury BS32 . . . . .24 B4
Bristol BS9 . . . . .48 E6
REDLAND 49 C3
Redland Ave BS20 . . . . . .46 F6
Redland Court Rd BS6 . . .49 C3
Redland Gr BS6 . . . . .49 C3
Redland Green Rd BS6 . . .49 B3
Redland Green Sch
 BS6 . . . . .49 C2
Redland Hill BS6 . . . . . . .49 B2
Redland Pk
Bath BA2 . . . . .100 F8
Bristol BS6 . . . . .49 B2
Redland Rd BS6 . . . . .49 C2
Redland Sta BS6 . . . . . . .49 C2
Redland Terr BA3 . . . . . .138 F8
Redland Terr 8 BS6 . . . . .49 B2
Red Lodge Bsns Pk
 BS24 . . . . .89 D1
Red Lodge The ★ BS8 . . .142 C3
Redlynch La BS31 . . . . . . .81 D2
Red Maids Jun Sch The
 BS9 . . . . .49 A6
Red Maids Sch The
 BS9 . . . . .49 A6
Redpoll Dr BS20 . . . . .46 A6
RED POST 134 B7
Red Post Ct BA2 . . . . . . .134 B7
Red Rd TA8 . . . . .121 A2
Redshard La BS40 . . . . . .109 B7
Redshelf Wlk BS10 . . . . . .35 C3
REDWICK 22 B8
Redwick Cl BS11 . . . . . . .34 C2
Redwick Crossroads
 BS35 . . . . .22 C7
Redwick Gdns BS35 . . . . .22 C7
Redwick Rd
Pilning BS35 . . . . .22 C8
Redwick BS35 . . . . .22 B8
Redwing Dr BS22 . . . . . . .88 F1
Redwing Gdns BS16 . . . . .50 E6
Redwood Cl
Bristol BS30 . . . . .66 A3
Nailsea BS48 . . . . .60 A2
Radstock BA3 . . . . .139 E8
Redwood Dr BS8 . . . . . . .61 F4
Redwood Ho BS13 . . . . . .79 D3
Redwood La BS48 . . . . . . .77 C7
Redwoods The BS31 . . . . .81 D6
Reed Cl BS10 . . . . .49 D6
Reed Ct BS30 . . . . .65 F3
Reedley Rd BS9 . . . . .48 F5
Reedling Cl BS16 . . . . . . .50 E6
Reed Rd BS37 . . . . .27 E5
Reed's Row GL12 . . . . . . .19 D7
Reed Way BS22 . . . . .89 C3
Regency Dr BS4 . . . . .65 A2
Regent Apartments
 BS6 . . . . .49 C3
Regent Rd BS3 . . . . .63 D4
Regents Cl BS35 . . . . .8 B2
Regents St BS8 . . . . .142 A2
Regent St
Bristol, Kingswood
 BS15 . . . . .65 D8
Weston-s-M BS23 . . . . .104 E7
Regents The BS31 . . . . . .81 F6
REGIL 94 F2
Regil La BS40 . . . . .95 A6
Regil Rd BS40 . . . . .94 F3
Regina The BA1 . . . . .141 B3
Remenham Dr BS9 . . . . . .49 B5
Remenham Pk BS9 . . . . . .49 B5
Rendcomb Cl BS22 . . . . . .88 B2
Rendle Ho BS16 . . . . .51 F4
Rene Rd 12 BS5 . . . . .50 B1
Rennison Ct BS23 . . . . . .104 E4
Repton Hall BS10 . . . . . . .35 B2
Repton Rd BS4 . . . . .64 D3
Retford Ho BA2 . . . . .102 C5
Retort Rd BS11 . . . . .33 C3
Retreat The
Radstock BA3 . . . . .134 E3
Weston-s-M BS23 . . . . . .87 C1
Reubens Ct BS22 . . . . . . .88 F3
Reubins The BS5 . . . . . . .51 A2
Reynolds Cl BS31 . . . . . . .82 A5
Reynold's Wlk BS7 . . . . . .50 A7
Rhode Cl BS31 . . . . .82 A3
Rhodyate BS40 . . . . .110 D2
Rhodyate Hill BS49 . . . . .91 F6
Rhodyate La BS49 . . . . . .92 A7
Rhodyate The BS29 . . . .107 C1

Rhyne Terr BS23........104 D2
Rhyne View BS48......59 B1
Rialls Ground BS34.....35 F6
Ribblesdale BS35.....15 D8
Richards Cl BS22.......89 B4
Richard Stephens Rd
  BS16.................50 F8
Richeson Cl BS10....34 F2
Richeson Wlk BS10....34 F2
Richmond Apartments
  BS6..................49 C3
Richmond Ave
  Bristol, Montpelier BS6..49 C3
  Bristol, Stoke Gifford
  BS34................36 E5
Richmond Cl
  Bath BA1............84 F1
  Keynsham BS31......81 D4
  Portishead BS20.....45 E5
Richmond Ct
  Bristol BS34.........23 F1
  7 Bristol, Clifton BS8..49 A2
  2 Bristol, Windmill Hill
  BS3.................63 F4
Richmond Dale **6** BS8..49 A2
Richmond Gn BS48....59 F1
Richmond Hill
  Bath BA1............84 F1
  Bristol BS8.........142 B3
Richmond Hill Ave
  BS8................142 B3
Richmond Hts
  Bath BA1............84 F2
  Bristol BS8.........142 B3
Richmond La
  Bath BA1............84 F1
  Bristol BS8.........142 A3
Richmond Mews BS8..142 A3
Richmond Park Rd
  BS8................142 A3
Richmond Pl BA1......84 F1
Richmond Rd
  Bath BA1............84 F1
  Bristol, Mangotsfield
  BS16................52 A5
  Bristol, Montpelier BS6..49 E1
  Bristol, Pile Marsh BS5..64 E7
Richmond St
  Bristol BS3..........63 F4
  Weston-s-M BS23....104 D7
Richmond Terr
  Avonmouth BS11......33 B1
  Bristol BS8.........142 A3
Ricketts La BS22.......89 A2
RICKFORD.............110 B3
Rickford Cotts BS40....110 B4
Rickford La BS40.......110 A3
Rickford Rise BS40.....110 A3
Ricklands The BS40.....95 A6
Rickyard Rd BS40.......92 E2
Ride The BS15.........52 A2
RIDGE................129 C5
Ridge Cl BS20..........45 A4
Ridge Cres BS40.......129 E6
Ridge Green Cl BA2....118 D8
Ridgehill BS9..........49 C6
Ridge Jun Sch The
  BS37................27 F2
Ridge La BS40........129 D5
Ridgemeade BS14......80 D4
Ridgemount Gdns
  BS14................80 B5
Ridge The
  Bristol, Hengrove BS14..80 C5
  Bristol, Shirehampton
  BS11................47 E2
  Frampton Cotterell BS36 38 C7
  Yatton BS49.........91 B8
Ridgeview BS41........62 B2
Ridgeview Ho BS20.....45 E3
RIDGEWAY............50 F3
Ridgeway
  Frampton Cotterell
  BS36................38 D7
  Nailsea BS48........59 C1
  Yate BS37...........28 A2
Ridgeway Ave BS23..104 E6
Ridgeway Cl BS40....129 E6
Ridgeway La
  Bristol BS14.........80 C5
  Bristol, Henbury BS10..35 A1
Ridgeway Gdns BS14...80 C5
Ridgeway Ind Ctr BS5..50 E3
Ridgeway La BS14.....80 B5
Ridgeway Par BS5.....50 E3
Ridgeway Rd
  Bristol BS16.........50 F3
  Long Ashton BS41....62 A2
Ridgeway The
  Bristol BS10.........35 A1
  Weston-s-M BS22.....88 A3
Ridgewood BS9........48 D3
Riding Barn Hill BS30..67 A6
Ridingleaze BS11......34 A1
Ridings Cl BS37........28 D1

Ridings Federation Yate
  Int Acad The BS37....27 E1
Ridings' Federation Yate
  Int Acad The BS37....39 E8
Ridings Rd BS36.......38 C6
Ridings The
  Bristol BS13.........78 E4
  Frampton Cotterell BS36 38 C6
Ridley Ave BS15, BS16..52 B3
Ring Mead BS34.......36 A6
Ringspit La
  Blackrock BS39.......97 E8
  Bristol BS14, BS39...97 E8
Ringswell SN14.......70 A7
Ringswell Gdns BA1...85 B1
Ringwell BA2........136 E4
Ringwell La BA2......136 E4
Ringwood Cres BS10...35 D1
Ringwood Gr BS23.....88 A1
Ringwood Rd BA2....101 C6
Ripley Rd BS5.........51 A1
Ripon Ct BS16.........37 F2
Ripon Rd BS4.........64 E6
Rippleside BS20.......45 C5
Rippleside Rd BS21....57 G2
Ripple The BS21.......59 D4
Risdale Rd BS3........62 F1
Risedale Ho BS15.....65 D5
Risedale Rd BS25....125 A8
Rivendell BS22........89 A4
Rivergate BS1........143 C2
Riverland Dr BS13.....78 F5
Riverleaze
  Bristol BS9..........48 C5
  Portishead BS20.....44 F6
River Mead
  Clevedon BS21.......73 D8
  Yate BS37...........27 C3
River Pl BA2.........101 B6
River Rd
  Chipping Sodbury BS37..28 A1
  Portbury BS20.......46 F8
RIVERSIDE...........138 F7
Riverside BS24, BS29...107 B5
  Bath BA2...........141 B1
  Bristol BS4..........64 D6
Riverside Bsns Pk
  Bath BA2...........141 B1
  Bristol BS4..........64 D6
Riverside Cl
  Bristol BS11.........47 F5
  Clevedon BS21.......57 D1
  Midsomer Norton BA3..138 F7
  Weston-s-M BS22.....89 C3
Riverside Cotts
  Bristol BS15.........65 B1
  Radstock BA3.......134 C2
Riverside Ct
  Bath BA2...........141 B1
  2 Bristol BS4......64 F6
Riverside Dr BS16.....51 C7
Riverside Gdns
  Bath BA1...........141 B2
  Midsomer Norton BA3..138 F7
Riverside Mews BS4...64 F6
Riverside Pk BS35.....21 F6
Riverside Rd
  Bath BA2...........141 B2
  Midsomer Norton BA3..138 F7
Riverside Steps BS4....64 F7
Riverside Way BS15....65 C3
Riverside Wlk
  6 Bristol BS5.......64 F6
  Midsomer Norton BA3..138 F7
Rivers Rd BA1........141 C4
Rivers St BA1.........141 B3
Rivers Street Mews
  BA1................141 B3
River St BS2.........143 C3
River Street Pl **5**
  BA1................141 B3
River Terr BS31.......81 F5
River View BS16.......50 E5
Riverway BS48.........59 F3
River Wlk BS22........89 D2
Riverwood Ho BS16....37 C1
Riverwood Rd BS16....37 C1
Riviera Cres BS16.....51 E4
Riviera Way BS34.....37 A4
Roach's La GL9.......30 D2
Road Green GL11......5 A7
Road Hill
  Batheaston SN13.....86 E8
  Colerne SN14........70 D1
Road Two BS10........22 A3
Roath Rd BS20........45 D5
Robbins Cl
  Bristol BS32.........36 F6
  Marshfield SN14.....69 F8
Robbins Ct BS16.......52 B6
Robel Ave BS36........38 A8
Robert Ct
  Bristol BS16.........52 B7
  Leigh Woods BS8.....62 D7
Robertson Dr BS4.....64 F6
Robertson Rd BS5.....50 C2
Robert St
  Bristol, Baptist Mills
  BS5.................50 B2
  16 Bristol, Russell Town
  BS5.................64 B7

Robin Cl
  Bristol BS14.........80 D6
  Bristol, Brentry BS10...35 B2
  Midsomer Norton BA3..139 B8
  Weston-s-M BS22....105 E8
Robin Dr BS24.......105 E2
Robinia Wlk BS14.....80 A7
Robin La BS21.........57 F5
Robinson Cl BS48.....76 A5
Robinson Dr BS5......64 A8
Robinson Way BS48...76 A5
Robin Way BS37.......40 A7
Rob-Lynne Ct BS25...124 F8
Rochester Cl BS24...105 A1
Rochester Rd BS4.....64 F5
Rochfort Ct BA1......102 B8
Rock Ave BS48........59 C2
Rock Cl BS4..........64 E2
Rock Cotts BS20......47 E4
Rockeries Dr BS25....124 F8
Rockhall Cotts BA2...102 B1
Rock Hall Cotts BA2..102 B1
Rockhall Ho
  Bath BA2...........102 B1
  10 Weston-s-M BS23..87 C1
Rock Hall La **4** BA2..102 B1
ROCKHAMPTON.......8 E7
Rockhampton Rhine
  BS35.................8 B6
Rockhill Est BS31.....81 F4
Rock Ho BS10.........35 C3
Rockingham Gdns
  BS11................48 A8
Rockingham Gr BS23..88 A1
Rockingham Rdbt BS11 33 D6
Rock La
  Bath BA2...........102 B1
  Bristol BS34.........36 F4
Rockland Gr BS16.....50 D5
Rockland Rd BS16.....51 D7
Rockleaze
  Bristol BS9..........48 E2
  9 Thornbury BS35....8 B1
Rockleaze Ave BS9....48 E3
Rockleaze Ct BS9......48 E3
Rockleaze Mans **12**
  BS23................87 C1
Rockleaze Rd BS9......48 E3
Rockliffe Ave BA2....102 B8
Rockliffe Rd BA2.....102 B8
Rock Rd
  Chilcompton BA3....138 D2
  Keynsham BS31.......81 E5
  Midsomer Norton BA3..133 B2
  Wick BS30...........67 D8
  Yatton BS49.........91 C7
Rockside Ave BS16....51 F8
Rockside Dr BS9......49 C6
Rockside Gdns
  Bristol BS16.........51 F8
  Frampton Cotterell BS36 38 C8
Rocks La BS40.........77 E1
Rock St BS35..........15 B8
Rockstowes Way BS10..35 D3
Rock The BS4.........64 E3
Rockwell Ave BS11....34 B1
Rockwood Ho BS37....28 A4
Rodborough BS37......39 C7
Rodborough Way BS15..66 A7
Rodbourne Rd BS10...49 E6
RODE................137 F1
Rode Hill BA11.......137 E1
Rodfords Mead BS14...80 A7
Rodford Way BS37.....39 D7
Rodmead Wlk BS13....79 A4
Rodmoor Rd BS20.....45 D6
Rodney BS24.........105 A2
Rodney Ave BS15......65 A8
Rodney Cres BS34.....36 A4
Rodney Ho BA2......101 A6
Rodney Pl BS8........142 A3
Rodney Rd
  Backwell BS48........76 A6
  Bristol BS15.........65 A8
  Saltford BS31........82 E2
Rodney Wlk BS15......51 A1
Rodway Ct BS16.......52 A5
Rodway Hill BS16.....52 B3
Rodway Hill Rd BS16..52 A4
Rodway Rd
  Bristol BS34.........36 A8
  Bristol, Mangotsfield
  BS16................52 A5
  Bristol, Patchway BS34...35 F7
Rodway View BS15.....51 F3
Roebuck Cl BS22......89 B4
Roegate Dr BS4.......64 E6
Roegate Ho BS5.......51 A1
Rogers Cl
  Bristol BS30.........66 B5
  Clutton BS39........114 E3
  Yate Rocks BS37.....27 E6
Rogers Ct BS37.......28 C1
Rogers Wlk BS30......66 D7
Rokeby Ave BS6.......49 C1
ROLSTONE...........89 F2
**Roman Baths & Pump
  Room The**★ BA1....141 C2
Roman Farm Ct BS11...34 C2

Roman Farm Rd BS4...79 E7
Roman Ho BA1.......141 C4
Roman Rd
  Bath BA1...........141 C3
  Bleadon BS24.......122 C8
  Bristol BS5..........50 B1
  Sandford BS25......107 F4
Roman Way
  Bristol BS15.........65 D4
  Bristol BS9..........48 C4
  Paulton BS39.......132 C6
  Peasedown St John BA2 134 E7
Roman Wlk
  Bristol, Kensington Park
  BS4.................64 C3
  Bristol, Stoke Gifford
  BS34................36 E5
Romney Ave
  Bristol BS7..........50 B6
  Locklease BS7.......50 C7
Romo Ct BS16.........51 C4
Romulus Cl BS31......81 F7
Ronald Rd BS16.......50 F6
Ronaldson BS30......66 C2
Ronayne Wlk BS16....51 C6
Ron Jones Ho **3** BS1..143 B4
Ron Stone Rd BS5.....50 F1
Rookery Cl BS22......88 E3
Rookery La
  Pilning BS35.........23 A6
  Pucklechurch BS30, SN14 53 F4
Rookery Rd BS4.......64 A3
Rookery Way BS14....79 F4
Rooksbridge Wlk BA2 101 B5
Roper's La BS40.......92 E3
Rope Walk Ho **23** BS2..143 C3
Rope Wlk BS48........76 A5
Rosary Rdbt The BS16..52 D7
Rosary The
  Bristol BS16.........52 D7
  Harry Stoke BS16....36 F2
Ros Broomhead Cl
  BS16................50 F8
Rose Acre BS10.......35 A3
Rosebay Mead BS16...50 E5
Roseberry Pk BS5.....64 D8
Roseberry Pl BA2.....101 C6
Roseberry Rd
  Bath BA2...........101 C6
  Bristol BS5..........64 C7
Rosebery Ave BS2.....50 A1
Rosebery Ct **7** BS2...50 A1
Rosebery Terr BS8....142 B2
Rose Cl BS36..........37 E4
Rose Cotts BS22......89 C2
Rosedale Ave BS23...105 A7
Rosedale Rd BS16.....51 C3
Rose Gdns BS22.......89 B4
ROSE GREEN........50 E1
Rose Green Cl BS5....50 E2
Rose Green Rd BS5...50 D2
Rose Hill BA1.........85 C3
Rose La BS36.........38 D6
Roseland Cl BA1......85 C3
Roselarge Gdns BS10..35 A2
Rosemary Cl BS32.....36 F7
Rosemary Cres BS20...45 F5
Rosemary La
  Bristol BS5..........50 C2
  Freshford BA2......120 B4
Rose Mead BS7.......50 A7
Rose Meare Gdns BS13..78 E7
Rosemont Terr BS8...142 A2
Rosemount Ct BS15....65 B8
Rosemount La BA2....102 B4
Rosemount Rd BS48...77 B8
Rosenberg Ho **6** BA1 141 B2
Rose Oak Dr BS36.....38 D7
Rose Oak Gdns BS36..38 D7
Rose Oak La BS36.....38 D7
Rose Rd BS5..........64 E7
Rosery Cl BS9........49 A8
Rosery The BS16......51 C3
Rose Terr
  Bath BA2...........102 C2
  Bristol BS8.........142 B3
Rose Tree Ho BS16....51 F4
Rosevear BS2.........64 A7
Roseville Ave BS30....66 A2
Rosewarn Cl BA2....101 A4
Rosewell Ct BA1......141 B2
Rose Wlk BS16........51 C3
Rosewood Ave BS35...14 F5
Roshni Gar E **16** BS5..50 B1
Roshni Gar W **15** BS5..50 B1
Rosling Rd BS7.......49 E6
Roslyn Ave BS22......88 C1
Roslyn Hill BS6.......49 C1
Rossall Ave BS34......36 C6
Rossall Rd BS4........64 D3
Ross Cl BS37..........28 B1
Rossendale Cl BS22...88 F3
Rossiter Grange **5**
  BS13................78 F4
Rossiter Rd BA2......141 C1
Rossiter's La BS5.....65 A6
Rossiter Wood Ct BS11..34 B2
Rosslyn Cl **1** BA1....101 B7
Rosslyn Rd BA1......101 B7

Rosslyn Way BS35......8 C3
ROTCOMBE..........115 D2
Rotcombe La BS39....115 D2
Rotcombe Vale BS39..115 D2
Roughcroft La GL13....2 C6
Rounceval St BS37.....28 A1
Roundhill Gr BA2.....101 B3
Roundhill Pk BA2.....101 A4
Roundmoor Cl BS31...82 D3
Roundmoor Gdns BS14 80 D7
Round Oak Rd BS27..126 A1
Roundways BS36.......38 D6
Rousham Rd BS5......50 A3
Rowacres
  Bath BA2...........101 B3
  Bristol BS14.........79 F6
Rowan Cl
  Bristol BS16.........51 A2
  Nailsea BS48........60 A2
Rowan Ct
  10 Bristol BS5......64 B7
  Radstock BA3.......133 E1
  Yate BS37...........27 C3
Rowan Dr
  Catbrain BS10.......35 B5
  Lyde Green BS16.....52 C2
Rowan Ho BS13.......79 D4
Rowan Pl BS24........89 B1
Rowan St BS14........79 E5
Rowans The
  Bristol BS16.........37 B1
  Portishead BS20.....45 B4
Rowan Tree Ho BS16..51 F4
Rowan Way
  Bristol BS15.........65 B3
  Churchill BS40......109 A5
Rowan Wlk BS31......81 C4
ROWBERROW........109 A1
Rowberrow BS14......79 F7
Rowberrow La BS25..125 F8
Rowberrow Way BS48..59 E1
Rowdell Ave BS36.....38 A6
Rowland Ave BS16....50 D4
Rowlands Cl BA1......86 B2
Rowley Farm La BA2..118 D5
Rowley St BS3........63 C3
Rownham Cl BS3......62 E4
Rownham Ct BS8.....142 A1
Rownham Hill BS8....62 E6
Rownham Mead BS8..142 A1
Row Of Ashes La BS40..93 F4
Rows The BS22.........88 E2
Row The BS35.........13 A7
Roxburgh BS8.........62 F8
Royal Albert Rd BS6..49 A4
Royal Ave BA1.......141 B3
Royal Cl BS10.........34 D3
Royal Cres BS23......104 D4
Royal Ct BS23.......104 D4
Royal Fort Rd BS2,
  BS8................142 C3
Royal High Sch
  Bath BA1...........141 B4
  Bath, Lansdown BA1...84 F7
Royal National Hospl for
  Rheumatic Diseases
  BA1................141 B2
Royal Par
  Bristol BS8.........142 B3
  Weston-s-M BS23...104 D8
Royal Park Mews BS8.142 A3
Royal Pk BS8.........142 A3
Royal Portbury Dock Rd
  BS20................46 E5
Royal Prom BS8......142 B3
Royal Rd BS16........52 A6
Royal Sands BS23....104 D4
Royal United Hospl
  BA1................101 B3
Royal Victoria Pk BS10 35 B2
**Royal West of England
  Acad**★ BS8........142 B3
Royal York Cres BS8...62 F6
Royal York Ho **7** BS8..142 A2
Royal York Mews **6**
  BS8................142 A2
Royal York Villas BS8..142 A2
Royate Hill BS5.......50 D2
Roycroft Rd BS34.....36 B2
Roy King Gdns BS30..66 C6
Royston Lodge BS23..104 D6
Royston Wlk BS10.....35 D2
Rozel Ho **14** BS23....87 C1
Rozel Rd BS7.........49 E5
Rubens Cl BS31.......82 A5
Ruby St BS3..........63 B3
Ruckley Ford BA3....135 A2
Rudford Cl BS34......24 B1
Rudge Cl BS15.......51 F2
RUDGEWAY..........14 F1
Rudgeway Pk BS35....14 F1
Rudgeway Rd BS39...132 E4
Rudgewood Cl BS13...79 D4
Rudgleigh Ave BS20...47 C4
Rudgleigh Rd BS20...47 C4
Rudhall Gn BS22.....89 B3

Rudhall Gr BS10 . . . . **49** E7
Rudmore Pk BA1. . . . . .**101** A7
Rudthorpe Rd BS7 . . . . . **49** E5
Ruett La BS39. . . . .**132** B4
Ruffet Rd BS36 . . . . **38** B4
Rugby Rd BS4 . . . . **64** D3
Rugmoor La BS40. . . . .**111** D3
Rumney Penrose Rd
 BS16. . . . . **50** F8
Runnymead Ave BS4. . . **64** D2
Runnymede BS15 . . . . . **51** E1
Runswick Rd BS4 . . . . . **64** C3
Rupert Ho BS2. . . . . . .**142** C4
Rupert St
 Bristol BS1. . . . .**143** A3
 Bristol, Redfield BS5 . . **64** C7
Rusham BS13. . . . . **78** F4
Rush Cl BS32 . . . . **24** D2
Rushgrove Gdns BS39 **113** C4
RUSH HILL **101** B2
Rush Hill
 Bath BA2 . . . .**101** C2
 Farrington Gurney BS39 **131** F3
Rushmead La SN14. . . . . **55** F2
Rushmoor BS21. . . . . . . **57** C1
Rushmoor Gr BS48. . . . . **76** A5
Rushmoor La BS48. . . . . **76** A5
Rushton Dr BS36. . . . . . .**38** D7
Rushway BS40 . . . .**109** F4
Rushy BS30. . . . . **66** A4
Rushy Leaze BS34. . . . . **36** A7
Rushy Way BS16 . . . . . . **38** A1
Ruskin Gr BS7 . . . . **50** A8
Ruskin Ho BS34. . . . . . . **36** A8
Ruskin Rd BA3. . . . . . .**133** C1
Rusling La BS40. . . . .**94** A1
Russell Ave BS15. . . . . . **65** E7
Russell Cl BS40 . . . . **95** A6
Russell Gr BS6. . . . . **49** C5
Russell Rd
 Bristol, Chester Park
 BS16 . . . .**51** B2
 Bristol, Westbury Park
 BS6 . . . . **49** B4
 Clevedon BS21. . . . . . . **57** E3
 Locking BS24. . . . .**106** C6
Russell St BA1. . . . . . .**141** B4
RUSSELL TOWN **64** B7
Russell Town Ave BS5 . . **64** B8
Russell Town Ind Pk **18**
 BS5. . . . . **64** C7
Russet Cl BS35. . . . . **14** A3
Russet Ct GL12. . . . . **11** F4
Russets The BS20 . . . . . . **45** F4
Russett Cl BS48. . . . . . . **76** B6
Russett Gr BS48. . . . . . . **75** C8
Russet Way BA2 . . . . . .**134** D7
Russ St BS2 . . . .**143** C2
Rustic Pk BS35 . . . . **22** A6
Rustic Way BS35. . . . . **8** B4
Rust La BS21 . . . . **73** E4
Rutherford Cl BS30. . . . . **66** A3
Ruthven Rd BS4 . . . . **79** E8
Rutland Ave BS30. . . . . . **66** A2
Rutland Cl BS22. . . . . . .**105** C8
Rutland Rd BS7 . . . . **49** E3
Rydal Ave BS24 . . . .**106** A4
Rydal Ho BS34. . . . . **36** A8
Rydal Rd BS23 . . . .**104** F4
Ryde Rd BS4. . . . . **64** B2
Rye Cl BS13 . . . . **78** E6
Ryecroft Ave BS22 . . . . . **88** E2
Ryecroft Ct BS36. . . . . . . **38** C7
Ryecroft Rd BS36 . . . . . . **38** C8
Ryecroft Rise BS41. . . . . **62** B2
Ryedown La BS30. . . . . . **66** D2
Ryland Pl **1** BS2 . . . . . . **50** A2
Rylestone Cl BS36. . . . . . **37** F8
Rylestone Gr BS9 . . . . . . **48** F5
Rysdale Rd BS9 . . . . **48** F6

S

Sabin Cl BA2 . . . .**101** B3
Sabrina Way BS9. . . . . . . **48** C4
Saco Ho
 11 Bath BA1 . . . .**141** B2
 Bristol BS1. . . . .**143** B2
Sadbury Cl BS22 . . . . **89** B4
Saddlers Ct BS15 . . . . . . **51** D1
Sadlier Cl BS11 . . . . **48** A8
Saffron Ct BA1. . . . .**141** C1
Saffron Ho **10** BS23 . . . .**104** E8
Saffrons The **7** BS22. . . **89** B4
Sage Cl BS20 . . . . **44** E4
Sages Mead BS32. . . . . . **36** E8
St Agnes Ave BS4 . . . . . . **63** F2
St Agnes Cl BS48. . . . . . . **60** A1
St Agnes Gdns BS4. . . . . **63** F2
St Agnes Wlk BS4 . . . . . . **63** F2
St Aidan's Cl BS5 . . . . . . **65** B6
St Aidan's Rd BS5. . . . . . **65** B6
St Alban's Rd BS6. . . . . . **49** B4
St Aldams Dr BS16. . . . . **53** B5
St Aldwyn's Cl BS7 . . . . . **49** F8
St Andrews
 Bristol BS30. . . . . **66** B6
 Yate BS37. . . . . **27** F1

St Andrew's CE Prim Sch
 BA1 . . . .**141** B4
St Andrew's CE Prim Sch
 GL12. . . . . **10** A1
St Andrews Cl
 Nailsea BS48. . . . . **60** A1
 Weston-s-M BS22 . . . . . **88** F3
St Andrew's Cl BS49 . . . . **91** C4
St Andrew's Dr BS21 . . . . **57** C2
St Andrews Gate Rdbt
 BS11. . . . . **33** B2
Saint Andrews Mews
 BS6. . . . . **49** E3
St Andrew's Par **1**
 BS23. . . . .**104** F4
St Andrew's Prim Sch
 BS49. . . . . **91** C4
St Andrews Rd BS48. . . . **76** B5
St Andrew's Rd
 Avonmouth BS11 . . . . . . **33** B1
 Bristol BS6. . . . . **49** E2
St Andrews Road Sta
 BS11. . . . . **33** B4
St Andrew's Terr BA1. .**141** B3
St Andrews Trad Est
 BS11. . . . . **33** C2
ST ANNE'S **64** E5
St Anne's Ave BS31 . . . . **81** D6
St Anne's CE Prim Sch
 BS30. . . . . **66** C3
St Anne's CE Prim Sch
 BS24. . . . . **90** B5
St Annes Cl **7** BS5. . . . . **64** F6
St Anne's Cl BS30. . . . . . **66** B4
St Annes Ct BS4 . . . . **64** D5
St Annes Ct BS31. . . . . . . **81** D6
St Annes Dr BS30 . . . . . . **66** C2
St Anne's Dr
 Frampton Cotterell
 BS36. . . . .**38** C5
 Wick BS30. . . . . **67** B7
St Anne's Inf Sch BS4 . . **64** D5
St Anne's Jun Sch BS4 . **64** D5
ST ANNE'S PARK. **64** E6
St Anne's Park Prim Sch
 BS4. . . . . **64** E5
St Anne's Park Rd BS4 . **64** E5
St Anne's Rd
 Bristol, St Anne's Park
 BS4 . . . . **64** D6
 Bristol, St George BS5. . **65** B6
St Anne's Terr BS4 . . . . . **64** E5
St Ann's Pl BA1 . . . .**141** B2
St Ann's Way BA2 . . . . .**102** C6
St Anthony's Cl BA3. . . .**133** A2
St Anthony's Dr BS30. . . **67** B7
St Aubin's Ave BS4. . . . . **64** F3
St Aubyn's Ave BS23 . .**104** D2
St Augustines of
 Canterbury RC Sch
 BS16. . . . . **51** F7
St Augustine's Par
 BS1. . . . .**143** A2
St Augustine's Pl **1**
 BS1. . . . .**143** A2
St Austell Cl BS48. . . . . . **76** A8
St Austell Rd BS22 . . . . .**105** B8
St Barnabas CE Prim Sch
 Bristol, Montpelier BS6. . **49** F1
 Bristol, North Common
 BS30. . . . .**66** C6
 Portishead BS20 . . . . . . **45** B5
St Barnabas Cl
 Bristol, Lower Knowle
 BS4. . . . . **63** F1
 Bristol, Warmley BS30. .**66** C7
 Midsomer Norton BA3. .**133** B3
St Barnabas Ho BS30. . .**66** C7
St Bartholomew's Rd
 BS7. . . . . **49** F3
St Bede's RC Coll BS11. **34** B2
St Bede's Rd BS15 . . . . . **51** D2
St Benedict's RC Prim Sch
 BA3 . . . .**139** C7
St Bernadette RC Prim Sch
 BS14. . . . . **80** B6
St Bernadette RC Sch
 BS14. . . . . **80** B6
St Bernard's RC Prim Sch
 BS11. . . . . **47** E6
St Bernard's Rd BS11. . . **47** E6
St Bonaventure's RC Prim
 Sch BS7 . . . . **49** D4
St Brelades Gr BS4. . . . . **64** F5
St Brendans Rdbt BS11 **33** C1
St Brendan's Sixth Form
 Coll BS4 . . . . **65** A1
St Brendan's Way BS11. **33** B1
St Brenda's Ct BS8. . . . .**142** A3
St Briavels Dr BS37 . . . . **39** D8
St Bridges Cl BS22 . . . . . **88** A6
St Bridges Ct BS22 . . . . . **88** A6
St Cadoc Ho BS31. . . . . . **81** F5
ST CATHERINE. **69** F1
St Catherine La BA1. . . . **69** D2
St Catherine's Cl BA2 .**102** C6
St Catherines Ct BS4. . . **64** A2
St Catherine's Hosp **11**
 BA1 . . . .**141** C2

St Catherine's Ind Est
 BS3. . . . . **63** D3
St Catherine's Mead
 BS20. . . . . **47** D3
St Catherines Pl **7**
 BS3. . . . . **63** D4
St Catherine's Terr
 BS3. . . . . **63** D3
St Chad's Ave BA3 . . . .**133** A1
St Chad's Gn BA3 . . . . .**139** A8
St Charles Cl BA3 . . . . .**133** A2
St Christophers Cl
 BA2 . . . .**102** C8
St Christopher's Ct
 BS21. . . . . **57** E5
St Christopher's Sch
 BS6. . . . . **49** B4
St Clements Ct
 Bath BA1 . . . . **84** C1
 Bristol, St Pauls BS2 . .**143** C4
 5 Bristol, Upper Soundwell
 BS16 . . . .**51** D3
 Clevedon BS21. . . . . . . **57** E4
 Keynsham BS31. . . . . . . **81** E4
 2 Weston-s-M BS22 . . . **89** A2
St Clements Rd BS31. . . **81** F4
St Cuthberts Dr BS4. . . . **64** F3
St David's Ave BS30. . . . **66** B5
St David's Cl BS22 . . . . . **88** B2
St David's Cres BS4 . . . . **64** F6
St David's Ct BS21 . . . . . **73** E8
St Davids Mews BS1 . .**142** C2
St Dunstans Cl BS31. . . . **81** E6
St Dunstan's Rd BS3 . . . **63** C2
St Edward's Rd BS8 . . .**142** B2
St Edyth's Rd BS9 . . . . . **48** C6
SS Peter & Paul RC Cath★
 BS8 . . . .**142** A4
SS Peter & Paul RC Prim
 Sch BS8 . . . .**142** C4
St Fagans Ct BS30 . . . . . **66** B2
St Francis Dr
 Wick BS30. . . . . **67** B7
 Winterbourne BS36. . . . . **37** F6
St Francis RC Prim Sch
 BS31. . . . . **59** F1
St Francis Rd
 6 Bristol BS3 . . . . **63** A4
 Keynsham BS31. . . . . . . **81** D6
St Gabriel's Bsns Pk **24**
 BS5. . . . . **64** B8
St Gabriel's Rd BS5 . . . . **64** B8
ST GEORGE **65** A7
St George CE Prim Sch
 BS1. . . . .**142** B2
ST GEORGES **89** D3
St George's★ BS1. . . . .**142** C2
St Georges Ave **10** BS5 . **64** F6
St Georges Bldgs BA1 **141** A3
St George's Hill
 Bath BA2 . . . .**102** D8
 Easton-in-G BS20. . . . . . **47** A3
St Georges Ho BS5. . . . . **64** B8
St George's Ho BS8 . . . .**142** B2
St George's Hts **12** BS5 **64** D7
St Georges Ind Est
 BS11. . . . . **33** B3
St Georges Pl BA1 . . . . .**141** A3
St Georges Prim Sch
 BS22. . . . . **89** C3
St George's Rd BS1. . . .**142** C2
St George's Rd
 Keynsham BS31. . . . . . . **81** D6
 Portbury BS20 . . . . **46** E7
St Giles Barton GL12 . .**19** D8
St Gregory's RC Sch
 BA2 . . . .**118** D8
St Gregory's Rd BS7. . . . **49** F8
St Helena Rd BS6 . . . . . . **49** B4
St Helens CE Prim Sch
 BS35. . . . . **15** A4
St Helens Dr
 Bristol BS30. . . . . **66** C2
 Wick BS30. . . . . **67** C7
St Helen's Wlk BS5 . . . . **51** A1
St Helier Ave BS4 . . . . . . **64** F3
St Hilary Cl BS9. . . . . **48** D5
St Ivel Way BS30 . . . . . . **66** C6
St Ives Cl BS48. . . . . **60** A1
St Ives Rd BS23 . . . .**105** A5
St James BS24 . . . .**105** E7
St James Cl BS35 . . . . **8** C3
St James Ct BS32 . . . . . . **24** C3
St James Pl BS16 . . . . . . **52** A5
St James's Ct BS8 . . . . . **49** B1
St James's Par BA1. . . .**141** B2
St James's Pk BA1. . . . .**141** B4
St James's Sq BA1 . . . .**141** A4
St James's St
 Bath BA1 . . . .**141** B4
 Bristol BS16. . . . . **52** A5
St James St BS23 . . . . .**104** D7
St John's BA1 . . . .**101** B8
St John's Ave BS21. . . . . **57** F3
St John's Bridge **5**
 BS1. . . . .**143** A3
St John's CE Prim Sch
 BS8. . . . . **49** A2

St John's CE Prim Sch
 BS31. . . . . **81** E5
St John's CE Prim Sch
 BA3 . . . .**133** A1
St John's Cl
 Peasedown St John
 BA2 . . . .**134** B7
 Weston-s-M BS23 . . . . . **87** D1
St John's Cres
 Bristol BS3. . . . . **63** E2
 Midsomer Norton BA3. .**133** A2
St Johns Ct
 Axbridge BS26 . . . .**125** B2
 Bath BA1 . . . .**141** C3
 Bristol BS16. . . . . **51** A3
 Bristol, Bedminster BS3 .**63** D2
 Keynsham BS31. . . . . . . **81** E6
St John's Ho BS5 . . . . . . **64** D8
St John's La BS3 . . . . . . **63** E2
St John's Mead CE Prim
 Sch BS37. . . . . **28** B1
St John's Pl BA1 . . . . . .**141** B2
St John's RC Prim Sch
 BA2 . . . .**102** B6
St John's RC Prim Sch (Inf)
 BA2 . . . .**101** D4
St Johns Rd BA2. . . . . .**116** B1
St John's Rd
 Backwell BS48. . . . . **76** B5
 Bath BA2 . . . .**141** A4
 Bath, Lower Weston
 BA1 . . . .**101** C7
 Bristol, Bedminster BS3 .**63** D3
 Bristol, Clifton BS8 . . . . **49** A1
 Bristol, Southville BS3. . **63** D4
 Clevedon BS21. . . . . . . **57** F3
St Johns St
 Bristol BS3. . . . . **63** C3
St John's St BS3 . . . . . . **63** C2
St John St **2** BS35. . . . . . **8** B1
St Johns Way BS37. . . . . **28** C2
St John the Evangelist CE
 Prim Sch
 Clevedon BS21. . . . . . . **57** C1
 Clevedon BS21. . . . . . . **57** E1
St Joseph's RC Prim Sch
 Bristol BS16. . . . . **51** B3
 Portishead BS20 . . . . . . **45** D3
St Joseph's Rd
 Bristol BS10. . . . . **35** B3
 Weston-s-M BS23 . . . . . **87** E1
St Judes Ho **21** BS2 . . .**143** C3
St Jude's Terr BS22 . . . . **88** C1
St Julian's CE Prim Sch
 BA2 . . . .**118** E1
St Julian's Cl BS39 . . . .**132** E4
St Julian's Rd BA2 . . . .**134** F5
St Katharine's CE Prim Sch
 BS40. . . . . **94** A7
St Katherine's Sch
 BS20. . . . . **47** E3
St Kenya Ct BS31. . . . . . **81** F5
St Keyna Ct BS31. . . . . . **81** F5
St Keyna Rd BS31. . . . . . **81** F5
St Kilda's Rd BA2 . . . . .**101** D5
St Ladoc Rd BS31. . . . . . **81** D6
St Laud Cl BS9. . . . . **48** D5
St Leonard's Rd
 Bristol, Horfield BS7 . . . **49** E5
 Bristol, Lower Easton
 BS5 . . . . **50** C2
St Loe Cl BS14. . . . . **79** F3
St Lucia Cl BS7 . . . . **49** E7
St Lucia Cres BS7 . . . . . **49** E7
St Lukes Cl BS16. . . . . . . **52** C7
St Luke's Cres BS3 . . . . **63** F4
St Luke's Ct BS3 . . . . . . **63** E4
St Luke's Gdns BS4 . . . . **64** E2
St Luke's Mews BS4. . . . **64** E2
St Luke's Rd
 Bath BA2 . . . .**101** F3
 Bristol BS3. . . . . **63** E4
 Midsomer Norton BA3. .**132** F2
St Luke St **13** BS5 . . . . . **64** B7
St Margarets Cl BS48. . . **76** A5
St Margaret's Cl BS31. . **81** D6
St Margaret's Dr BS9. . . **49** C5
St Margaret's La BS48. . **76** A5
St Margaret's Terr
 BS23. . . . .**104** D8
St Mark's Ave **1** BS5 . . **50** B1
St Marks Church Ho **4**
 BS5. . . . . **50** B1
St Marks Cl BS31. . . . . . **81** E6
St Mark's Ecumenical CE/
 Methodist Prim Sch
 BS22. . . . . **88** F4
St Marks Gdns BA2. . . .**141** C1
St Mark's Gr **8** BS5. . . . **50** B1
St Mark's Ho **13** BS5 . . **50** B1
St Mark's Rd
 Bath BA2 . . . .**141** C1
 Bristol BS5. . . . . **50** B1
 Midsomer Norton BA3. .**133** A2
 Weston-s-M BS22 . . . . . **89** A3
St Mark's Sch BA1 . . . . **85** B2
St Mark's Terr **11** BS5 . . **50** B1
St Mark's VA Prim Sch
 BS22. . . . . **88** F4
St Martins BS21. . . . . . . **57** E5

St Martin's CE Jun Sch
 BS22. . . . . **88** D2
St Martins Cl BS4 . . . . . . **64** B1
St Martins Cl BS22. . . . . **88** E3
St Martins Ct BA2 . . . . .**101** E1
St Martin's Garden Prim
 Sch BA2 . . . .**101** D1
St Martins Gdns BS4. . . **64** B1
St Martins Hospl BA2 .**101** E1
St Martins Ind Pk BS11. **33** F5
St Martin's La SN14 . . . . **69** F8
St Martin's Pk SN14. . . . **69** F8
St Martin's Rd BS4. . . . . **64** B2
St Martin's Wlk BS4. . . . **64** B1
St Mary CE Prim Sch
 BA2 . . . .**102** C8
St Mary Redcliffe CE Prim
 Sch BS3 . . . . **63** E4
St Mary Redcliffe CE VC
 Prim Sch BS3 . . . . **63** E4
St Mary Redcliffe &
 Temple Sch BS1. . . . .**143** B1
St Mary's Bldgs BA2 . .**141** B1
St Mary's CE Prim Sch
 Radstock BA3. . . . .**134** C1
 Thornbury BS35. . . . . **8** A2
St Mary's CE Prim Sch
 Timsbury BA2. . . . .**116** C3
 Yate BS37. . . . . **27** E2
St Mary's CE VA Prim Sch
 BS20. . . . . **46** E3
St Marys Cl
 Bristol BS30. . . . . **66** B5
 Hutton BS24. . . . .**105** D2
St Mary's Cl
 Bath BA2 . . . .**102** B6
 Timsbury BA2. . . . .**116** B2
St Mary's Ct BS24 . . . . .**105** A1
St Mary's Gdns BS40 . .**109** B5
St Mary's Gr BS48 . . . . . **75** C8
St Mary's Hospl BS8 . .**142** B3
St Mary's Park Rd BS20 **45** C4
St Mary's Pk BS48. . . . . **75** C8
St Marys RC Prim Sch
 BS34. . . . . **37** A7
St Mary's RC Prim Sch
 BA1 . . . . **84** B1
St Mary's Rd
 Bristol BS11. . . . . **47** D7
 Hutton BS24. . . . .**105** D2
 Leigh Woods BS8 . . . . . **62** D6
 Portishead BS20 . . . . . . **45** C4
St Marys Rise BA3 . . . .**134** C2
St Mary's St BS26 . . . . .**125** C2
St Mary St BS35. . . . . . . **15** B8
St Marys Way **6** BS35. . . **8** B1
St Mary's Way BS37 . . . . **27** F2
St Mary's Wlk BS11 . . . . **47** D6
St Matthew's Ave **11**
 BS6. . . . . **49** D1
St Matthew's Cl BS23 . . **87** D1
St Matthews Hall **20**
 BS5. . . . . **64** C7
St Matthew's Pl BA2 . .**102** B5
St Matthew's Rd BS6. .**143** A4
St Matthias & Dr Bell's CE
 Prim Sch BS16 . . . . . . **51** A4
St Matthias Ho BS2 . . .**143** C3
St Matthias Pk BS2 . . .**143** C3
St Michael on the Mount
 CE Prim Sch BS2 . . . .**142** C3
St Michael's Ave
 Clevedon BS21. . . . . . . **57** F1
 Weston-s-M BS22 . . . . . **89** A3
St Michael's CE Jun Sch
 BA2 . . . .**101** A6
St Michaels CE Prim Sch
 BS36. . . . . **37** E6
St Michael's CE Prim Sch
 BS34. . . . . **36** E5
St Michaels Cl BS7. . . . . **49** E4
St Michael's Cl BS36 . . . **37** E7
St Michaels Cl BS15. . . . **65** B8
St Michael's Ct BA2 . . .**119** E8
St Michael's Hill BS2. .**142** C4
St Michael's Hospl
 BS2. . . . .**142** C4
St Michael's Pk BS2. . .**142** C4
St Michael's Pl BA1 . . .**141** B2
St Michaels Rd BA2 . . .**101** A5
St Michael's Rd BA1 . .**101** D7
St Monica Ct BS9 . . . . . . **49** A5
St Nicholas Almshouses **7**
 BS1. . . . .**143** A2
St Nicholas CE Prim Sch
 BA3 . . . .**133** D1
St Nicholas' CE Prim Sch
 BA3 . . . .**134** A2
St Nicholas Chantry CE
 Prim Sch BS21 . . . . . .**57** G3
St Nicholas Chantry CE VC
 Prim Sch BS21 . . . . . . **57** E3
St Nicholas Cl BA15. . . .**120** D7
St Nicholas Ct BA2. . . . . **85** F1
St Nicholas of Tolentine
 RC Prim Sch BS5 . . . . **64** A8

St Nicholas Pk 10 BS5 . . 50 B1
St Nicholas Rd
　Bristol BS2 . . . . .143 C4
　Weston-s-M BS23 . . . . .104 D2
　Whitchurch BS14 . . . . . . .80 C4
St Nicholas' Rd BS2 . . . 49 F1
St Nicholas St BS1 . . . . .143 A2
St Nicholas Way BS48 . .75 D2
St Oswald's Ct BS13 . . . .79 A8
St Oswald's Ct BS6 . . . . .49 B3
St Oswald's Rd BS6 . . . . 49 B3
St Patricks Ct BS31 . . . . 81 E5
St Patrick's Ct BA2 . . . .102 B6
St Patrick's RC Prim Sch
　BS5 . . . . .64 D7
ST PAULS 143 C4
St Pauls Ho 13 BS3 . . . .63 D4
St Pauls Pl
　Bath BA1 . . . . .141 B2
　Midsomer Norton BA3 . .133 C2
St Paul's RC Prim Sch
　BS37 . . . . 39 E8
St Paul's Rd
　Bristol BS8 . . . . .142 B4
　2 Bristol, Southville BS3 63 D4
　Weston-s-M BS23 . . . . .104 E5
St Paul St BS2 . . . . . . .143 B4
St Peter's Ave BS23 . . . .87 D1
St Peter's CE Prim Sch
　BS20 . . . . .45 D4
St Peter's Cres BS36 . . . 38 B8
St Peters Ct 12 BS3 . . . .63 D4
St Peter's Ho BS1 . . . . .142 B2
St Peters Lodge BS20 . . 45 D4
St Peter's Pl 5 BA2 . . .101 D6
St Peters Rd BS20 . . . . . 45 D4
St Peter's Rd BA3 . . . . .139 C8
St Peter's Rise BS13 . . . .79 B7
St Peter's Terr 6 BA2 .101 D6
St Peter's Wlk 3 BS9 . . 49 B6
St Philips Central BS2 . . 64 A5
St Philip's CE Prim Sch
　BA2 . . . . .101 D2
St Philips Cswy BS2 . . . .64 B5
ST PHILIP'S MARSH 64 B5
St Philips Rd BS2 . . . . .143 C3
St Philips Trad Pk BS2 . .64 B4
St Phillips Rd BS2 . . . . . 64 A7
St Pias X RC Prim Sch
　BS13 . . . . .79 A5
St Pierre Dr BS30 . . . . . 66 B6
St Ronan's Ave BS6 . . . . 49 C1
St Saviour's CE Inf Sch
　BA1 . . . . 85 B2
St Saviour's CE Jun Sch
　BA1 . . . . 85 B2
St Saviours Ho BS4 . . . . 63 F2
St Saviour's Rd BA1 . . . . 85 C2
St Saviour's Rise BS36 . 38 B6
St Saviour's Terr 10
　BA1 . . . . 85 B1
St Saviours Way 4
　BA1 . . . . 85 C1
St Stephen's Ave 3
　BS1 . . . . .143 A2
St Stephens Bsns Ctr
　BS30 . . . . .66 C5
St Stephen's CE Jun Sch
　BS15 . . . . 51 D2
St Stephen's CE Prim Sch
　BA1 . . . . 84 F1
St Stephens Cl
　Bristol, Brentry BS10 . . . .35 C2
　Bristol, Upper Soundwell
　BS16 . . . . 51 E3
St Stephen's Cl BA1 . . . . 84 F1
St Stephen's Ct BA1 . . .141 B4
St Stephen's Pl BA1 . . .141 B4
St Stephen's Rd
　Bath BA1 . . . . .141 B4
　Bristol BS16 . . . . 51 D2
St Stephen's St BS1 . . .143 A2
St Swithin's Pl BA1 . . . .141 C4
St Swithin's Yd BA2 . . .141 C3
St Teresa's RC Prim Sch
　BS7 . . . . 35 C1
St Thomas Pl BS1 . . . . .143 B2
St Thomas Rd BA3 . . . .133 C2
St Thomas St E BS1 . . .143 B2
St Thomas St BS1 . . . . .143 B2
St Ursula's E-ACT Acad
　BS9 . . . . 49 A6
St Vigor & St John CE
　Prim Sch BA3 . . . . . . .138 E3
St Vincent's Hill 11 BS6 . 49 A2
St Vincent's Rd BS8 . . .142 A2
St Vincents Trad Est
　BS2 . . . . .64 D6
Saint Way BS34 . . . . . . .37 A4
St Werburgh's Pk BS2 . . 50 A2
St Werburgh's Prim Sch
　BS2 . . . . .50 A2
St Werburgh's Rd BS2 . . 49 F2
St Whites Cl BS14 . . . . .80 D3
St Whytes Rd BS4 . . . . .79 D8
St Winifreds Dr BA2 . . .102 D2

Salcombe Gdns BS22 . . .89 A2
Salcombe Rd BS4 . . . . . .64 A1
Salem Rd BS36 . . . . 37 F7
Salisbury Ave BS15 . . . . 65 B8
Salisbury Dr BS16 . . . . . 51 E6
Salisbury Gdns BS16 . . . 51 E5
Salisbury Pk BS16 . . . . . 51 E6
Salisbury Rd
　Bath BA1 . . . . .85 B2
　Bristol, Mangotsfield
　BS16 . . . . 51 E6
　Bristol, Redland BS6 . . . .49 D2
　Bristol, St Anne's BS4 . . .64 D5
　Paulton BS39 . . . . .132 F4
　Weston-s-M BS22 . . . . . . 88 C1
Salisbury St
　Bristol, Pile Marsh BS5 . .64 E7
　Bristol, Russell Town BS5 64 B6
Salisbury Terr BS23 . . . .104 D7
Sallybarn Cl BS30 . . . . . 65 C2
Sally Hill BS20 . . . . 45 E7
Sally In The Wood BA1,
　BA15 . . . . .103 D6
Sally Lunn's Kitchen Mus *
　BA1 . . . . .141 C2
Sallysmead Cl BS13 . . . .79 B4
Sally's Way BS36 . . . . . .37 F7
Salmon Cl BS35 . . . . . . .22 A6
Salmon Mead BS14 . . . . 80 D3
Salmons Way BS16 . . . . .52 B8
SALTFORD 82 D2
Saltford CE Prim Sch
　BS31 . . . . 82 E2
Saltford Ct BS31 . . . . . . 82 E3
Salthouse Ct BS21 . . . . .57 D2
Salthouse Farm Pk
　BS35 . . . . .22 A7
Salthouse Rd BS21 . . . . .57 D2
Salthrop Rd BS7 . . . . . . 49 E4
Saltings Cl BS21 . . . . . . 57 D2
Saltmarsh Dr BS11 . . . . 34 A1
Salway Cl BS40 . . . . . . .95 E1
Sambourne La BS20 . . . .47 C4
Samian Way BS34 . . . . . 36 E5
Sampson House Bsns Pk
　BS10 . . . . 34 D7
Sampsons Rd BS13 . . . . .79 D4
Samuel St 3 BS5 . . . . . .64 C8
Samuel White Rd BS15 . 65 C4
Samuel White's Inf Sch
　BS15 . . . . 65 C4
Samuel Wright Cl BS30 66 D5
San Andreas BS34 . . . . . 35 E6
Sanctuary Gdns BS9 . . . 48 D3
Sanctuary The BS11 . . . . 47 E4
Sandbach Rd BS4 . . . . . .64 D4
Sandbed Rd BS2 . . . . . . 50 A2
Sandburrows Rd BS13 . . 78 F6
Sandburrows Wlk BS13 . 78 F6
Sandcroft BS14 . . . . 79 F6
Sandcroft Ave BS23 . . . .104 D2
Sand Farm La BS22 . . . . .88 A6
SANDFORD 108 A3
SANDFORD BATCH 107 F2
Sandford Cl 2 BS21 . . . .57 D1
Sandford Prim Sch
　BS25 . . . . .108 B4
Sandford Rd
　Bristol BS8 . . . . .142 A1
　Weston-s-M BS23 . . . . .105 A7
　Winscombe BS25 . . . . . .107 F2
Sandgate Rd BS4 . . . . . .64 D3
Sand Hill BS4 . . . . 64 C4
Sandholme Cl BS16 . . . . 51 E8
Sandholme Rd BS4 . . . . .64 D4
Sandhurst BS37 . . . . 39 D8
Sandhurst Cl BS34 . . . . .24 B1
Sandhurst Rd BS4 . . . . . 64 D4
Sandling Ave BS7 . . . . . .50 A7
Sandmead Rd BS25 . . . .108 A4
Sandown Cl BS16 . . . . . 37 F1
Sandown Rd
　Bristol, Filton BS34 . . . . .36 C3
　Bristol, Kensington Park
　BS4 . . . . .64 D4
Sandpiper Dr BS22 . . . . .88 F1
Sandpits La GL9 . . . . . . 20 A2
Sand Rd BS22 . . . . 88 B5
Sandringham Ave BS16 . 51 E8
Sandringham Ct 2
　BS23 . . . . .104 F5
Sandringham Pk BS16 . . 51 E8
Sandringham Rd
　Bristol, Kensington Park
　BS4 . . . . .64 D4
　Bristol, Longwell Green
　BS30 . . . . 65 F2
　Bristol, Stoke Gifford
　BS34 . . . . 36 D4
　1 Weston-s-M BS23 . . . .104 F5
Sands Hill SN14 . . . . . . .54 E3
Sands La BS36 . . . . 25 F1
Sandstone Rise BS36 . . . 37 E4
Sandwich Rd BS4 . . . . . .64 D4
Sandy Cl BS32 . . . . .36 E6
Sandy La
　Aust BS35 . . . . 13 A7

Sandy La continued
　Aust BS35 . . . . .13 A8
　Bristol BS5 . . . . .50 C3
　Easton-in-G BS8 . . . . . . .61 A8
　Failand BS8 . . . . 61 C7
　Stanton Drew BS39, BS40 96 E3
Sandyleaze BS9 . . . . 48 E7
Sandy Lodge BS37 . . . . . 39 E8
Sandy Park Rd BS4 . . . . .64 C3
Sarabeth Dr BA2 . . . . . .117 A4
Saracen St BA1 . . . . . . .141 C3
Saracens The BS7 . . . . . .49 E5
Sarah St BS5 . . . . 64 B7
Sargent St BS3 . . . . 63 E4
Sarum Cl BS16 . . . . .52 C6
Sarum Cres BS10 . . . . . .35 C1
Sassoon Ct BS30 . . . . . . 65 F5
Satchfield Cl BS10 . . . . .34 F2
Satchfield Cres BS10 . . . 34 F2
Satellite Bsns Pk BS5 . .64 D6
Sates Way BS9 . . . . .49 C6
Saunders Rd BS16 . . . . . 51 E4
Saunton Wlk BS4 . . . . . .79 E8
Savages Wood BS32 . . . .36 E8
Savages Wood Rd
　BS32 . . . . .36 D8
Savernake Rd BS22 . . . . 88 F3
Saville Cres BS22 . . . . .105 C8
Saville Gate Cl BS9 . . . .48 F4
Saville Mews BS6 . . . . .143 A4
Saville Pl BS8 . . . . .142 A2
Saville Rd
　Bristol BS9 . . . . .48 F3
　Weston-s-M BS22 . . . . .105 C8
Saville Row BA1 . . . . . .141 B3
Savoy Rd BS4 . . . . 64 D4
Savoy The BS11 . . . . 47 E6
Saw Cl BA1 . . . . .141 B2
Sawmill Gdns BA3 . . . . .138 D3
Saw Mill La 5 BS35 . . . . .8 B1
Sawyers Cl
　Chilcompton BA3 . . . . . .138 D3
　Wraxall BS48 . . . . .60 A2
Sawyers Ct BS21 . . . . . .57 G3
Saxby Cl
　Clevedon BS21 . . . . .57 D1
　Weston-s-M BS22 . . . . . .89 B4
Saxon Cl BS14 . . . . .80 D3
Saxon Ct
　Axbridge BS26 . . . . .125 C1
　Weston-s-M BS22 . . . . . .89 D3
Saxon Rd
　Bristol BS2 . . . . .50 A2
　Weston-s-M BS22 . . . . .105 C8
Saxon St BS40 . . . . .109 D6
Saxon Way
　Bristol BS32 . . . . .24 C1
　Bristol BS34 . . . . .24 C1
　Peasedown St John BA2 134 E8
　Winsley BA15 . . . . .120 F7
Sayer Pl BS10 . . . . 49 E7
Says La BS40 . . . . .109 B4
Say Wlk BS30 . . . . .66 D7
SBI Ctr BS15 . . . . 65 B5
Scafell Cl BS23 . . . . 88 A1
Scandrett Cl BS10 . . . . . 34 E2
Scantleberry Cl BS16 . . . 51 D8
Scarf Dr BS24 . . . . .106 C5
Scaurs The BS22 . . . . . . 88 F2
School Cl
　Banwell BS29 . . . . .107 B3
　Bristol BS14 . . . . .79 F4
　Bristol, Eastville BS5 . . . .50 D2
　Bristol, Patchway BS34 . .36 C8
　Hillesley GL12 . . . . 19 E8
School Ct BS34 . . . . 37 A5
School La
　Badminton GL9 . . . . .30 E2
　Barrow Gurney BS48 . . . .77 D5
　Batheaston BA1 . . . . .85 F4
　2 Bristol BS16 . . . . .50 E5
　Chew Stoke BS40 . . . . . .112 D8
　Farrington Gurney BS39 132 A4
　Felton BS48 . . . . .94 A8
　Kilmersdon BA3 . . . . . . .140 A6
　Rowberrow BS25 . . . . . .109 A1
　Wick St L BS22 . . . . .89 B7
School of Christ the King
　RC Prim Sch BS4 . . . . . 79 E8
School Pl BA2 . . . . .103 B5
School Rd
　Bristol BS15 . . . . .65 C8
　Bristol, Broom Hill BS4 . .64 E3
　Bristol, Cadbury Heath
　BS30 . . . . .66 A4
　Bristol, Oldland Common
　BS30 . . . . .66 C3
　Bristol, Totterdown BS4 . .64 A3
　Frampton Cotterell BS36 38 A8
　Wrington BS40 . . . . .92 E2
School View BS48 . . . . . 60 B1
School Way BS35 . . . . . . 22 A6
School Wlk
　Bristol BS5 . . . . .50 D1
　Yate BS37 . . . . 27 C2
Scobell Rise BS39 . . . . .115 C2
Scop The BS32 . . . . .24 B5
Score La BS40 . . . . .110 E2
Score The BS40 . . . . . . .110 E2

Scotch Horn Cl BS48 . . . 59 F2
Scotch Horn Way 5
　BS48 . . . . 59 F2
Scot Elm Dr BS24 . . . . . 89 D1
Scot La BS40 . . . . .95 D1
Scotland La BS4, BS14 . .81 A7
Scots Pine Ave 3 BS48 . 59 F2
Scott Ct BS30 . . . . 65 F5
Scott Lawrence Cl
　BS16 . . . . 51 A7
Scott Rd BS23 . . . . .105 A4
Scott Way BS37 . . . . 39 F8
Scott Wlk BS30 . . . . 66 D7
Scumbrum La BS39 . . . .115 C2
Scythe Way BS35 . . . . . . .8 B3
Sea Bank Rd BS20 . . . . . 32 E1
Seabrook Rd BS22 . . . . . 88 D1
Seagry Cl BS10 . . . . 35 E1
Sea King Way BS24 . . . .105 C5
SEA MILLS 48 B6
Sea Mills Inf Sch BS9 . . 48 C7
Sea Mills Jun Sch BS9 . 48 B5
Sea Mills La BS9 . . . . . . 48 C5
Sea Mills Sta BS9 . . . . . .48 B4
SeaQuarium * BS23 . . . .104 D6
Searle Court Ave BS4 . . .64 E4
Searle Cres BS23 . . . . . .105 A6
Searle Ct BS21 . . . . .57 G2
Seaton Ct BS3 . . . . 63 D1
Seaton Rd BS5 . . . . 50 C1
Seavale Mews BS21 . . . .57 E4
Seavale Rd BS21 . . . . . . 57 E4
Seaview Rd
　Portishead, Redcliffe Bay
　BS20 . . . . .44 F4
　Portishead, West Hill
　BS20 . . . . .44 F6
Seawalls BS9 . . . . 48 D2
Seawalls Rd BS9 . . . . . . 48 D2
Second Ave
　Bath BA2 . . . . .101 D5
　Bristol BS14 . . . . .80 B7
　Radstock BA3 . . . . .139 C7
Second Way BS11 . . . . . .33 D1
Seddon Rd 4 BS2 . . . . . 50 A2
Sedgefield Gdns BS16 . . 37 F1
Sedgemoor Cl BS48 . . . . 75 E8
Sedgemoor Rd
　Bath BA2 . . . . .101 F2
　Weston-s-M BS23 . . . . . .87 F1
Sedgewick Ho BS11 . . . . 34 A7
Sefton Park Jun & Inf Schs
　BS7 . . . . 49 F3
Sefton Park Rd BS7 . . . . 49 F3
Sefton Sq BS24 . . . . . . .106 A4
Selborne Rd BS7 . . . . . . 49 F5
Selbourne Cl BA1 . . . . .101 A8
Selbourne Rd BS23 . . . .104 E4
Selbrooke Cres BS16 . . . 51 C6
Selby Rd BS5 . . . . .50 F1
Selden Rd BS14 . . . . 80 E5
Selkirk Rd BS15 . . . . 51 C1
Selley Wlk BS13 . . . . . . .79 A5
Selway Ct BA2 . . . . .102 B2
Selwood Cl BS22 . . . . . .105 C7
Selworthy BS15 . . . . 65 E7
Selworthy Cl BS31 . . . . . 81 D5
Selworthy Gdns 4
　BS48 . . . . 59 E1
Selworthy Ho BA2 . . . . .101 F2
Selworthy Rd
　Bristol BS4 . . . . .64 B2
　Weston-s-M BS23 . . . . .105 A4
Selworthy Terr BA2 . . . .101 F2
Seneca Pl 11 BS5 . . . . . .64 D7
Seneca St BS5 . . . . 64 D7
Septimus Bldgs BS14 . . .79 D5
Serbert Cl BS20 . . . . 45 E5
Serbert Rd BS20 . . . . . . .45 E5
Serbert Way BS20 . . . . . 45 E5
Sercombe Pk BS21 . . . . .57 G1
Serlo Ct BS22 . . . . .89 A4
Serridge La BS36 . . . . . . 38 D4
Serse Cl BS31 . . . . 81 C2
Sevastopol Rd BS7 . . . . .49 E7
Seven Acres La BA1 . . . .85 F5
Seven Acres The 3
　BS24 . . . . .105 F7
Seven Dials BA1 . . . . . .141 B2
Seventh Ave
　Bristol BS14 . . . . .80 A7
　Bristol, Filton BS7 . . . . . .36 B1
Severn Acre Lea BS34 . . 35 E6
Severn Ave BS23 . . . . . .104 C5
SEVERN BEACH 22 B6
Severn Beach Prim Sch
　BS35 . . . . .22 A6
Severn Beach Sta BS35 22 A6
Severn Cl GL12 . . . . 11 A4
Severn Dr BS35 . . . . .8 B2
Severn Grange BS10 . . . 34 D3
Severn Ho BS10 . . . . . . .34 D3
Severn La GL13 . . . . .2 F8
Severnleigh Gdns BS9 . . 48 F3
Severnleigh Ho BS9 . . . .48 F3
Severnmeade BS20 . . . . .44 F5
Severn Rd
　Bristol BS11 . . . . .47 D6
　Hallen BS10 . . . . 34 A7

Severn Rd continued
　Pill BS20 . . . . .47 C5
　Portishead BS20 . . . . . . 45 C5
　Severn Beach BS35 . . . . 21 F3
　Weston-s-M BS23 . . . . .104 E5
Severnside Trad Est
　BS11 . . . . 33 C5
Severn View BS10 . . . . . 34 C1
Severn View Ind Pk
　BS10 . . . . 21 F3
Severn View Rd BS35 . . . .8 C2
Severn Way
　Bristol BS34 . . . . .23 F1
　Keynsham BS31 . . . . . . .82 A5
Severnwood Gdns
　BS35 . . . . .22 A5
Severus St BS31 . . . . 81 F8
Sevier Rd BS26 . . . . . . .123 C3
Sevier St BS2 . . . . .49 F2
Seville Ct BS20 . . . . 45 E7
Seville Rd BS20 . . . . 45 E7
Seward Terr BA3 . . . . . .134 C2
Sewell Ho BS25 . . . . . . .125 A8
Seymour Ave BS7 . . . . . . 49 E4
Seymour Cl
　Clevedon BS21 . . . . .57 G3
　Weston-s-M BS22 . . . . . .88 F4
Seymour Pl BS36 . . . . . . 38 B6
Seymour Rd
　4 Bath BA1 . . . . .85 A1
　Bristol, Ashley Down BS7 49 E4
　Bristol, Kingswood BS15 . 51 C1
　Bristol, Staple Hill BS16 . 51 E4
　Bristol, Upper Easton
　BS5 . . . . 50 A1
Seyton Wlk BS34 . . . . . . 36 E5
Shackel Hendy Mews
　BS16 . . . . 52 B5
Shackleton Ave BS37 . . . 39 F8
Shadow Wlk BS24 . . . . .106 C3
Shadwell Rd BS7 . . . . . . 49 D3
Shaftesbury Ave
　2 Bath BA1 . . . . .101 C7
　Bristol BS6 . . . . .49 E1
Shaftesbury Cl BS48 . . . 75 D8
Shaftesbury Crusade
　BS2 . . . . .64 A6
Shaftesbury Mews 7
　BA2 . . . . .101 D5
Shaftesbury Rd
　Bath BA2 . . . . .101 D5
　Weston-s-M BS23 . . . . .105 B8
Shaftesbury Terr
　8 Bristol BS5 . . . . .64 D7
　Radstock BA3 . . . . .134 A3
Shaft Rd
　Monkton Combe BA2 . . .102 E1
　Severn Beach BS35 . . . . .22 A8
Shakespeare Ave
　Bath BA2 . . . . .101 F4
　Bristol BS7 . . . . .50 A8
Shakespeare Ct BS23 . .104 F2
Shakespeare Rd BA3 . . .133 C1
Shaldon Rd BS7 . . . . . . .50 A4
Shallowbrooks La SN14 31 F8
Shallows The BS31 . . . . .82 F3
Sham Castle La BA2 . . .102 C7
Shamrock Rd BS5 . . . . . .50 D3
Shanklin Dr BS34 . . . . . .36 B3
Shannon Ct BS35 . . . . . . 15 D8
Shannon Wlk BS20 . . . . .45 F6
Shapcott Cl BS4 . . . . . . .64 B1
Shaplands BS9 . . . . 48 F4
Sharland Cl BS9 . . . . 48 E3
Sharland Gr BS13 . . . . . .79 C4
Sharples Dr BS7 . . . . 50 C8
SHARPSTONE 120 C8
Shaw Cl
　Bristol BS16 . . . . .52 B3
　3 Bristol, Upper Easton
　BS5 . . . . 64 B8
Shaw Gdns BS14 . . . . . . 80 A8
Shaws Way BA2 . . . . . . .100 F5
Shaymoor La BS35 . . . . .23 A4
Shearmore Cl BS7 . . . . . 50 A4
Shearwater Ct BS16 . . . . 50 F6
Sheene Ct Ind Est 12
　BS3 . . . . 63 C3
Sheene Rd BS3 . . . . .63 C3
Sheene Way BS3 . . . . . . .63 C3
Sheepfair La SN14 . . . . .69 F8
Sheephouse Cvn Pk
　BS20 . . . . .46 E7
Sheeps Croft BS13 . . . . .79 A5
Sheepwash The BS35 . . . .7 D5
SHEEPWAY 46 B5
Sheepway BS20 . . . . 46 B5
Sheepway La BS20 . . . . . 46 A5
Sheepwood Cl BS10 . . . . 35 A2
Sheepwood Rd BS10 . . . 35 A2
Sheiling Sch BS35 . . . . . . 8 B2
Sheldare Barton BS5 . . . 65 B7
Sheldon Cl BS21 . . . . . . 57 H2
Sheldrake Dr BS16 . . . . . 50 E6
Shellard Rd BS34 . . . . . . 36 A2
Shellards La BS35 . . . . . . 15 E2
Shellards Rd BS30 . . . . . 65 D3
Shelley Ave BS21 . . . . . . 57 C2
Shelley Cl BS5 . . . . 64 F8

Shelley Ho BS34 . . . . . . 24 A1
Shelley Rd
  Bath BA2 . . . . .101 F4
  Radstock BA3. . . . . . . .133 C1
  Weston-s-M BS23 . . . .105 A4
Shelley Way BS7 . . . . . .50 A8
Shellmor Ave BS34. . . . .24 B1
Shellmor Cl ■ BS32. . . .24 D1
Shepherds Cl
  Bristol BS16. . . . . .51 E5
  Chipping Sodbury BS37 . . 40 F3
Shepherds Way BS22. . .89 C2
Shepherds Wlk
  ■ Bristol BS32 . . . . .24 D1
  Bristol BS32. . . . . .36 D8
Sheppard Rd BS16 . . . . .51 C6
Sheppards Gdns BA1. . . .84 B1
Sheppards Wlk BA3. . . .138 D3
SHEPPERDINE 1 D3
Shepperdine Rd BS35 . . .1 D2
Sheppy's Mill BS49. . . . .91 D5
Shepton BS24 . . . . .105 A2
Shepton Wlk BS3 . . . . . .63 C2
SHERBORNE 130 D3
Sherbourne Ave BS32 . . 36 E7
Sherbourne Cl BS15. . . .51 E7
Sherbourne's Brake
  BS32. . . . . .36 E6
Sherbourne St BS5. . . . .64 E7
Sheridan Rd
  Bath BA2 . . . . .100 F5
  Bristol BS7 . . . . .50 A4
Sheridan Way BS30 . . . .66 A2
Sherrings The BS34 . . . .36 B8
Sherrin Way BS13. . . . . .78 E3
Sherston Cl
  Bristol BS16. . . . . .51 B5
  Nailsea BS48 . . . . .60 A1
Sherston Rd
  Bristol BS7 . . . . .49 E8
  Luckington SN14 . . . . . .31 F5
Sherwell Rd BS4. . . . . . .64 E3
Sherwood Cl BS31 . . . . .81 E5
Sherwood Cres BS22 . . . 88 F3
Sherwood Rd
  Bristol BS15. . . . . .51 B1
  Keynsham BS31. . . . . . .81 E5
Shetland Rd BS10. . . . . .35 D1
Shetland Way BS48 . . . .60 A1
Shickle Gr BA2 . . . . . . .101 D1
Shield Ct BS15. . . . . . . .65 D5
Shield Ret Ctr BS34. . . .36 A3
Shield Road Prim Sch
  BS7. . . . . .36 A1
Shields Ave BS7 . . . . . . .36 A1
Shiels Dr BS32. . . . . . . .36 D7
Shilton Cl BS15 . . . . . . .65 F7
Shimsey Cl ■ BS16 . . . .51 C6
Shiners Elms BS49 . . . . .91 B8
Shingle La BS10 . . . . . . .21 F4
SHIPHAM 125 F7
Shipham CE Fst Sch
  BS25. . . . . .125 E8
Shipham Cl
  Bristol BS14. . . . . .80 B5
  Nailsea BS48 . . . . .75 F8
Shipham Hill BS25 . . . .125 F5
Shipham La BS25 . . . . .108 B1
Shipham Rd BS27 . . . . .126 A3
Ship La BS1 . . . . .143 B1
SHIPLATE 122 F6
Shiplate Rd BS24 . . . . .122 E6
Shipley Mow BS16 . . . . .52 B6
Shipley Rd BS9 . . . . . . .49 A8
Shipman Ct BS16 . . . . . .51 E4
Shire Gdns BS11 . . . . . .47 D8
SHIREHAMPTON 47 E7
Shirehampton Prim Sch
  BS11. . . . . .47 D6
Shirehampton Rd BS9. . 48 C6
Shirehampton Sta
  BS11. . . . . .47 D5
Shire Hill SN14 . . . . . . .56 A7
Shire Way BS37 . . . . . . .39 D6
Shirreff Ct ■ BS6. . . . . .49 B1
SHOCKERWICK 86 E5
Shockerwick Farm La
  BA1. . . . . .86 E6
Shockerwick La BA1 . . .86 D4
Shophouse Rd BA2. . . .101 B5
Shop La GL9. . . . . .30 E2
Shopland Ho ■ BS21 . . 57 E2
Shoredtch BS40. . . . . . .112 C7
Shorland Ho BS8. . . . . . .49 A1
Shorthill Rd BS37 . . . . .39 C4
Short La
  Litton BA3 . . . . .130 F2
  Long Ashton BS41 . . . . .62 A2
Shortlands Rd BS11. . . .34 A1
Short St BS2. . . . . .64 A5
Short Way
  Failand BS8 . . . . .61 B4
  Thornbury BS35 . . . . . . .15 B7
SHORTWOOD. 52 D4
Shortwood Hill BS16 . . .52 E4
Shortwood La BA3 . . . .130 F2
Shortwood Rd
  Bristol BS13. . . . . .79 E3
  Pucklechurch BS16 . . . . .53 A4

Shortwood View BS15 . . 65 F8
Shortwood Wlk BS13. . .79 E3
SHOSCOMBE 134 E5
Shoscombe CE Prim Sch
  BA2. . . . . .134 F5
SHOSCOMBE VALE 134 E5
Showering Cl BS14. . . . .80 D5
Showering Rd BS14 . . . .80 D5
Shrew Gdns BS35 . . . . . .8 D2
Shrewsbury Bow
  BS24. . . . . .106 A8
Shrowle BS40. . . . . . . .130 A6
Shrubbery Ave BS23. . . .87 D1
Shrubbery Cotts ■
  BS6. . . . . .49 B2
Shrubbery Ct ■ BS16 . .51 D5
Shrubbery Rd
  Bristol BS16. . . . . .51 D5
  Weston-s-M BS23 . . . . . .87 D1
Shrubbery Terr ■
  BS23. . . . . .87 C1
Shrubbery Wlk BS23 . . .87 D1
Shrubbery Wlk W BS23 87 D1
Shubb Leaze BS7 . . . . . .50 C8
Shums Ct ■ BA1. . . . . .141 C2
Shuter Rd BS13. . . . . . . .78 E5
Sibland BS35 . . . . .15 D8
Sibland Cl ■ BS35. . . . .15 D8
Sibland Rd BS35 . . . . . .15 D8
Sibland Way BS35. . . . . .15 D8
SIDCOT. 125 C7
Sidcot BS4 . . . . .65 A2
Sidcot Dr BS25 . . . . . . .125 A7
Sidcot Jun Sch BS25 . .125 C8
Sidcot La BS25. . . . . . . .125 A7
Sidcot Sch BS25 . . . . . .125 B7
Siddeley Cl BS10. . . . . . .35 D4
Sideland Cl BS14. . . . . . .80 E6
Sidelands Rd BS16. . . . . .51 C6
Sidelings The BS40. . . .128 D8
Sidings The
  Bristol, Lower Soundwell
    BS16. . . . . .52 B2
  Bristol, Newleaze BS34 . . 36 C2
  Charfield GL12. . . . . .11 B5
  Haywood Village BS23 . .105 B4
Sidmouth Cl BS3. . . . . . .63 D1
Sidmouth Gdns BS3. . . .63 D2
Sidmouth Rd BS3 . . . . . .63 E2
Sidney Hill Cottage Homes
  BS25. . . . . .108 E4
Signal Rd BS16. . . . . . . .51 F4
Silas Rd BS37. . . . . .27 E5
Silbury Rd BS3. . . . . . . .62 E2
Silbury Rise BS31. . . . . .82 A2
Silcox Rd BS13. . . . . . . .79 C4
Silklands Gr BS9. . . . . . .48 C6
Silver Birch Cl BS34 . . . .36 D7
Silvercombe ■ BS23. . .104 E5
Silver Ct BS48 . . . . .59 C2
Silverhill Brake BS35. . . .14 E1
Silverhill Rd BS10. . . . . .34 E4
Silverhill Sch BS36. . . . .37 E7
Silverlow Rd BS48 . . . . .59 D2
Silver Mead BS49 . . . . . .91 D2
Silver Moor La BS29. . .106 F7
Silver St
  Bristol BS1. . . . . .143 A3
  Chew Magna BS40. . . . . .96 B3
  Congresbury BS49. . . . . .91 D2
  Holcombe BA3 . . . . . . .139 C1
  Kilmersdon BA3. . . . . . .140 B5
  Midsomer Norton BA3. .139 A4
  Nailsea BS48 . . . . .59 D2
  Portishead BS20 . . . . . . .44 F1
  ■ Thornbury BS35 . . . . . .8 B1
  Wrington BS40. . . . . . . .92 E2
Silverstone Way BS49 . .91 D3
Silverthorne La BS2. . . . .64 A6
Silverthorne Wharf
  BS2. . . . . .64 B6
Silverton Ct BS4 . . . . . . .63 F1
Silverweed Rd BS16. . . .52 D7
Simmons Bldgs BS16 . . . 37 C3
Simmons View BS34 . . . .36 F5
Simons Cl BS22. . . . . . . .89 A2
Simon's Cl BS39 . . . . . .132 F5
Simons Mews ■ BS23 104 F7
Sinclair Ho
  Bristol BS8. . . . . .142 A2
  Bristol, Filton BS34 . . . . .36 A2
Singapore Rd BS23. . . .104 E3
SINGLE HILL. 135 A5
Single Hill BA2 . . . . . . .134 F5
SION HILL. 84 E1
Sion Hill
  Bath BA1 . . . . .84 E1
  Bristol BS8. . . . . .62 F7
Sion Hill Pl BA1. . . . . . .84 E1
Sion La BS8. . . . . .62 F7
Sion Pl
  Bath BA2 . . . . .102 B6
  Bristol BS8. . . . . .62 F7
Sion Rd
  Bath BA1 . . . . .84 E1
  Bristol BS3. . . . . .63 C3
Sir Bernard Lovell Sch
  BS30. . . . . .66 C4

Sir Bernard Lovell Sch
  (annexe) BS30. . . . . . .66 D5
Sir Bevil Grenville's Mon★
  BA1. . . . . .68 A1
Sir John's La
  Bristol BS7. . . . . .50 B5
  Bristol, Eastville BS5. . . . .50 B4
Siskin Cl BS20 . . . . .45 F6
Siskin Wlk BS22 . . . . . .105 F8
SISTON. 52 F3
Siston Cl BS15. . . . . . . .52 A2
Siston Comm BS15. . . . .52 A2
Siston Common BS30 . . 52 B1
Siston Ctr The BS15 . . . .52 A2
Siston Hill BS30. . . . . . .52 B1
Siston Hill Rdbt BS15. . .52 B2
Siston La BS30 . . . . .52 F2
Siston Pk BS15 . . . . .52 A2
Sixpence BS39. . . . . . . .115 D2
Six Streams BA1. . . . . . .84 B2
Sixth Ave
  Bristol BS14. . . . . .80 A7
  Bristol, Filton BS7. . . . . . .36 B1
Sixty Acres Cl BS8 . . . . .61 B4
Six Ways BS21 . . . . .57 E4
Skinners Cft BS34. . . . . .36 A7
Skinner's Hill BA2 . . . . .133 F7
Skinners La BS25 . . . . .108 F4
Skippon Ct BS15 . . . . . .65 E5
Skylark Ave BS21 . . . . . .44 B1
Skylark Dr BS31. . . . . . .81 C3
Skylark Gr BS49. . . . . . .73 F2
Skypark Rd BS3. . . . . . . .63 C3
Sladacre La BS40 . . . . .110 E2
Slade Baker Wy BS16. . .50 F8
Sladebrook Ave BA2. . .101 C3
Sladebrook Ct BA2. . . .101 C3
Sladebrook Rd BA2. . . .101 B4
Slade La
  Barrow Gurney BS48. . . .77 C4
  Lympsham BS24. . . . . . .122 B1
Slade Rd BS20. . . . . . . .45 D5
Slades Ct ■ BS48. . . . . .76 A6
Slad The BS35. . . . . .15 F6
Slate La SN14. . . . . .98 B7
Slaughter La BS30 . . . . .67 D2
Sleep La BS14. . . . . .80 D3
Slimbridge Cl BS37 . . . .39 F7
Sloan St BS5. . . . . .64 D8
Sloe Cl BS22. . . . . .105 D8
Sloe Way BS34. . . . . . . .36 F3
Slough La SN14. . . . . . . .68 F5
Slymbridge Ave BS10. . .35 A3
Smallbrook La BS39. . . .98 B6
Smallcombe Cl BA3. . . .133 E5
Smallcombe Rd BA3 . . .133 E4
Small Down End BS25 107 F2
Small La BS16. . . . . .50 E5
Small St
  Bristol BS1. . . . . .143 A3
  Bristol, St Philip's Marsh
    BS2. . . . . .64 A5
Smallway BS49 . . . . . . .91 D5
Smallwood View BA3. . .138 E7
Smarts Gn BS37. . . . . . .40 D8
SMART'S GREEN. 40 D8
Smeaton Rd BS1 . . . . . .62 F5
SMITHAM HILL 129 D2
Smitham's Hill BS40 . . .129 D2
Smithcourt Dr BS34. . . .36 D6
Smithmead BS13. . . . . . .79 B5
Smiths Ct BS34 . . . . . . .36 A8
Smith's Forge Ind Est
  BS49. . . . . .73 F3
Smoke La BS11. . . . . . . .33 D6
Smythe Croft BS14. . . . .80 A3
Smyth Ho BS8 . . . . .62 E6
Smyth La BS3. . . . . .63 A3
Smyth Rd BS3 . . . . .63 A3
Smyths Cl BS11. . . . . . . .33 B1
Smyth Terr ■ BS3. . . . . .63 C4
Snapdragon Way BS16 . .52 D7
Snatch BS40. . . . . .111 E2
Snatch La BS40 . . . . . .111 E2
SNEYD PARK. 48 D3
Sneyd Park Ho BS9 . . . .48 D3
Snowberry Cl
  Bristol BS32. . . . . .36 E8
  Weston-s-M BS22 . . . . . .89 A1
Snowberry Wlk BS5. . . .50 E1
Snowdon Cl BS16 . . . . . .50 F4
Snowdon Ho BS16 . . . . .50 F5
Snowdon Rd BS16 . . . . .50 F4
Snowdon Vale BS23 . . . .88 A1
Snowdrop Cl BS22 . . . . .89 A5
Snowdrop Dr BS16 . . . .52 C7
Snow Hill BA1 . . . . .85 A1
Snow Hill Ho
  ■ Bath BA1 . . . . .141 C4
  ■ Bathwick BA2 . . . . . .102 B8
Soapers La BS35. . . . . . .15 B8
Soaphouse Ind Est BS5. 64 E8
Sodbury La BS37. . . . . . .40 A5
Sodbury Rd
  Acton Turville GL9. . . . . .42 F7
  Wickwar GL12. . . . . .18 A4
Sodbury Vale BS37. . . . .28 B2
Soldiers Rd ■ BS34. . . . .35 F7
Solent Way BS35. . . . . . .15 D7

Solon Ct BS13 . . . . .78 F5
Solsbury Ct BA1 . . . . . . .85 F3
Solsbury View ■ BA1 . . 85 A1
Solsbury Way ■ BA1 . . .85 A2
Somer Ave BA3 . . . . . . .132 F2
Somerby Cl BS32 . . . . . .36 D7
Somer Ct BA3 . . . . .133 B1
SOMERDALE 81 E7
Somerdale Ave
  Bath BA2 . . . . .101 D2
  Bristol BS4. . . . . .64 A1
  Weston-s-M BS22 . . . . .105 C8
Somerdale Cl BS22. . . .105 C8
Somerdale Rd BS31. . . .81 F7
Somerdale View BA2. . .101 C2
Somerford Cl BS10. . . . .34 F1
Somer Ho ■ BA3 . . . . .133 A1
Somer La BS3 . . . . .63 C1
Somer Lea BA3 . . . . . . .138 D5
Somermead BS3. . . . . . .63 C1
Somer Rd BA3 . . . . .132 F2
Somer Ridge BA3 . . . . .132 F3
Somerset Ave
  Weston-s-M BS22,
    BS24. . . . . .106 A8
  Yate BS37. . . . . .27 F3
Somerset Cl GL12. . . . . .11 B5
Somerset Cres BS34 . . . 36 F5
Somerset & Dorset Joint
  Rly★ BA3. . . . . .139 A8
Somerset Folly BA2. . . .116 B2
Somerset Ho
  Bath BA2 . . . . .101 D3
  ■ Bristol BS2 . . . . .143 C3
  Portishead BS20 . . . . . . .45 D4
Somerset La BA1 . . . . . .84 E1
Somerset Mews
  Portishead BS20 . . . . . . .45 D4
  Weston-s-M BS23 . . . . .104 F6
Somerset Pl BA1. . . . . . .84 E1
Somerset Rd
  Bristol BS4. . . . . .64 B3
  Clevedon BS21. . . . . . . .57 G3
  Portishead BS20 . . . . . . .44 F5
Somerset Sq
  Bristol BS1. . . . . .143 B1
  ■ Nailsea BS48 . . . . . . .59 E2
Somerset St
  Bath BA1 . . . . .141 C1
  Bristol BS1. . . . . .143 B1
  Bristol, Kingsdown BS2 143 A4
Somerset Terr BS3 . . . . .63 D3
Somerset Way BS39. . . .132 E6
Somerton BS24 . . . . . . .105 A2
Somerton Cl BS15. . . . . .65 E7
Somerton Rd
  Bristol BS7. . . . . .49 E6
  Clevedon BS21. . . . . . . .57 G1
Somervale Rd BA3 . . . .133 C2
Somervale Sch BA3. . . .133 A1
Somerville Cl BS31. . . . .82 E2
Somerville Ho BS10. . . . 49 A8
Somerville Rd BS25 . . .108 A4
Sommerville Rd BS7 . . . 49 E3
Sommerville Rd S ■
  BS6. . . . . .49 F2
Sommerville Way BS30. 82 E8
Soper Gdns BS4 . . . . . . .79 D7
Sophia Gdns BS22 . . . . .89 B4
Sopworth Rd SN14. . . . .31 F5
Sorbus Cl BS32 . . . . . . .24 E5
Sorrel Cl BS35 . . . . .8 D2
Sorrel Pl BS16 . . . . .36 F3
Soundwell Rd BS15,
  BS16. . . . . .51 D2
Sour Mead BS16. . . . . . .50 D8
Southampton Gdns BS7 49 F5
Southampton Mews
  BS7. . . . . .49 F5
South Ave
  Bath BA2 . . . . .101 D5
  Portishead BS20 . . . . . . .45 D6
  Yate BS37. . . . . .27 B1
Southbourne Gdns BA1 85 B1
Southbourne Mans
  BA2. . . . . .141 C2
Southbow Ho ■ BS3. . . .63 A3
South Bristol Bsns Pk
  BS4. . . . . .79 E7
South Bristol Ret Pk
  BS3. . . . . .63 A3
South Bristol Trad Pk
  BS3. . . . . .62 F3
South Combe BS24. . . .122 B6
Southcot Pl BA2 . . . . . .141 C1
South Croft
  Bristol BS9. . . . . .49 C7
  Winscombe BS25. . . . . .107 F2
South Ct BS32 . . . . .24 D3
South Dene BS9 . . . . . . .48 F6
SOUTHDOWN. 101 B4
Southdown BS22. . . . . . .88 F4
Southdown Ave BA2. . .101 B3
Southdown Com Inf Sch
  BA2. . . . . .101 B3
Southdown Jun Sch
  BA2. . . . . .101 B3
Southdown Rd
  Bath BA2 . . . . .101 B4

Southdown Rd continued
  Bristol BS9. . . . . .48 F8
SOUTHEND. 5 E3
Southend Ho GL12 . . . . .18 A5
Southend Rd BS23 . . . .104 E4
Southernhay
  Bristol BS8. . . . . .142 B2
  Bristol, Staple Hill BS16 . .51 D4
Southernhay Ave BS8 . .142 B2
Southernhay Cres BS8 142 B2
Southern Way BS21 . . . .57 E1
Southey Ave BS15. . . . . .51 E1
Southey Ct BS15 . . . . . . .51 D1
Southey Rd BS21. . . . . . .57 E2
Southey St BS2 . . . . .49 F2
SOUTHFIELD 134 A2
Southfield
  Norton St Philip BA2 . . .136 F4
  Radstock BA3. . . . . .134 A2
Southfield Ave BS15. . . . 51 E1
Southfield Cl
  Nailsea BS48 . . . . .59 E3
  Weston-s-M BS23 . . . . .104 D2
Southfield Ct BS9 . . . . . .49 A7
Southfield Rd
  Bristol, Cotham BS6. . . . .49 D1
  Bristol, Westbury on Trym
    BS9. . . . . .49 A7
  Nailsea BS48 . . . . .59 F3
Southfield Rd Trad Est
  BS48. . . . . .59 F3
Southfield Way BS37 . . .28 A4
Southgate BA1. . . . . . . .141 C2
Southgate Sh Ctr BA1 141 C2
South Gloucestershire
  Central Teaching Unit
  BS16. . . . . .52 A5
South Gr
  Bristol BS6. . . . . .49 C5
  Pill BS20. . . . . .47 C4
South Green St ■ BS8 . 62 F6
South Hayes BS5. . . . . . .50 B4
South Hill BS25 . . . . . .107 F2
Southlands
  Bath BA1 . . . . .84 B1
  Bristol, Clifton BS8 . . . . .49 A1
  Bristol, Knowle Park BS4 . 64 B1
  Tytherington GL12 . . . . .16 B4
Southlands Dr BA2. . . .116 B2
Southlands Way BS49 . . 91 E5
South Lawn BS24 . . . . .105 F4
South Lawn Cl BS24. . .105 F4
South Lea Rd BA1. . . . .101 A8
Southleaze BS25. . . . . .125 A6
Southleigh BS25 . . . . . .124 F8
Southleigh Mews BS8 142 B4
Southleigh Rd BS8. . . .142 B4
South Liberty La
  Bristol BS3. . . . . .63 A1
  ■ Bristol BS3. . . . . .63 B2
South Mdws BS40. . . . . .92 E2
SOUTHMEAD. 35 D1
Southmead BS25. . . . . .125 A8
Southmead Hospl BS10 49 E8
Southmead Rd
  Bristol BS10, BS34. . . . . .35 E1
  Weston-s-M BS22 . . . . .105 B7
Southmead Way BS10. . .49 E8
Southover Cl BS9 . . . . . .49 A8
Southover Rd BS39. . . .115 D1
South Par
  Bath BA2 . . . . .141 C2
  Chew Magna BS40. . . . . .96 B3
  Weston-s-M BS23 . . . . .104 D8
  Yate BS37. . . . . .27 E1
South Parade Cotts
  BA2. . . . . .102 C1
South Parade Mans
  BS8. . . . . .142 B4
South Rd
  ■ Bristol, Bedminster
    BS3. . . . . .63 C3
  Bristol, Kingswood BS15 65 D8
  Bristol, Redland BS6 . . . .49 C2
  Lympsham BS24. . . . . . .122 B1
  Midsomer Norton BA3. .133 B1
  Portishead BS20 . . . . . . .45 D7
  Timsbury BA2. . . . . . . .116 B2
  Weston-s-M BS23 . . . . . .87 C1
  Woodhouse Down BS32. .24 E6
South Rock Ind Est
  BA3. . . . . .138 D1
Southsea Rd BS34 . . . . .36 A8
Southside BS23. . . . . . .104 E8
South Side BS49 . . . . . .91 E5
Southside Cl BS9 . . . . . .40 D0
Southside Cres BS22 . . .88 A4
South St
  Bristol BS3. . . . . .63 B3
  Stratton-on-t-F BA3. . . .138 F2
SOUTHSTOKE 118 E7
Southstoke La BA2. . . .118 F8
Southstoke Rd BA2 . . .101 F1
South Street Prim Sch
  BS3. . . . . .63 B3

South Terr
　6 Bristol BS6 . . . . 49 B2
　Weston-s-M BS23 . . . . 104 D8
SOUTH TWERTON 101 C5
South View
　Bristol BS16 . . . . 51 E5
　Clandown BA3 . . . . 133 E5
　Frampton Cotterell BS36 38 B7
　Monkton Combe BA2 . . 102 E1
　Paulton BS39 . . . . 132 E6
　Portishead BS20 . . . . . . 45 D7
　Timsbury BA2 . . . . 116 B2
South View Bsns Pk
　BS16 . . . . 51 F5
Southview Cl BS24 . . . 105 E2
South View Cres BS36 . . 38 D6
South View Rd BA2 . . . . 101 D6
South View Pl BA3 . . . . 133 E4
South View Rise BS36 . . 38 D6
South View Terr BS49 . . 74 B1
SOUTHVILLE 63 C4
Southville Pl BS3 . . . . . 63 D4
Southville Prim Sch
　BS3 . . . . 63 C4
Southville Rd
　Bristol BS3 . . . . 63 C4
　Weston-s-M BS23 . . . . 104 E4
Southville Terr BA2 . . . 102 B4
Southway Ct BS21 . . . . . 57 F1
Southway Dr BS15 . . . . . 66 D5
Southwell St BS2 . . . . . 142 C4
SOUTH WIDCOMBE . . . 130 C6
South Wlk BS37 . . . . . . 27 E1
Southwood Ave BS9 . . . 48 C8
Southwood Dr BS9 . . . . 48 B8
Southwood Dr E BS9 . . . 48 C8
Sovereign Sh Ctr
　BS23 . . . . 104 D8
Spalding Cl BS7 . . . . . . 50 A3
Spaniorum View BS35 . . 22 F2
Spar Rd
　Avonmouth BS11 . . . . . . 33 D4
　Yate BS37 . . . . 27 D2
Sparrowbill Way BS34 . . 36 A7
Spartley Dr BS13 . . . . . . 78 F6
Spartley Wlk BS13 . . . . . 78 F6
Speckled Wood Rd BS35 . 8 C3
Specklemead BS39 . . . . 132 D5
SPEEDWELL 51 A2
Speedwell Ave **5** BS5 . . 64 D7
Speedwell Cl BS35 . . . . . 8 D2
Speedwell Ind Est **1**
　BS21 . . . . 57 E2
Speedwell Rd BS5, BS15 51 A1
Speedwell Tech Coll
　BS15 . . . . 51 A1
Spencer Dr
　Midsomer Norton BA3 . . 133 A2
　Weston-s-M BS22 . . . . . 89 B3
Spencer Ho **6** BS1 . . . 143 B1
Spencers Belle Vue
　BA1 . . . . 141 B4
Spencers Ct BS35 . . . . . 15 B5
Sperring Ct BA3 . . . . . . 138 F8
Spey Cl BS35 . . . . 15 C8
SPIKE ISLAND 142 B1
Spike Island Artspace★
　BS1 . . . . 142 B1
Spindleberry Gr BS48 . . 60 A2
Spinners End BS22 . . . . 89 B4
Spinney Croft BS13 . . . . 78 F5
Spinney Rd BS24 . . . . . 106 D4
Spinney The
　Bristol BS32 . . . . 36 E7
　Frampton Cotterell BS36 . 38 B7
　Portishead BS20 . . . . . . 45 C4
　Weston-s-M BS24 . . . . 104 F1
Spinnings Dro BS48 . . . . 76 D2
Spires View **4** BS16 . . . 50 E5
Spratts Bridge BS40 . . . 96 A3
Sprigg Dr BS20 . . . . . . 44 F1
Spring Cres BA2 . . . . . 141 C2
Springfield
　Norton St Philip BA2 . . 136 E4
　Peasedown St John
　　BA2 . . . . 134 C7
　1 Thornbury BS35 . . . 15 D8
Springfield Ave
　Bristol, Horfield BS7 . . . 49 F5
　Bristol, Mangotsfield
　　BS16 . . . . 52 A7
　Bristol, Shirehampton
　　BS11 . . . . 47 D6
　Weston-s-M BS22 . . . . . 88 D1
Springfield Bldgs
　Midsomer Norton
　　BS39 . . . . 132 D2
　Radstock BA3 . . . . 134 A3
Springfield Cl
　Bath BA2 . . . . 101 B5
　Bristol BS16 . . . . 52 A7
　Cross BS26 . . . . 124 F2
Springfield Cotts BS30 . 83 A8
Springfield Cres BA3 . . 134 A3
Springfield Gdns
　BS29 . . . . 107 A3

Springfield Gr BS6 . . . . 49 C5
Springfield Ho
　Bristol BS6 . . . . 142 C4
　Portishead BS20 . . . . . . 45 C4
Springfield Hts BA3 . . . 133 E4
Springfield Lawns
　BS11 . . . . 47 D6
Springfield Pl
　Bath BA1 . . . . 84 F1
　Clandown BA3 . . . . 133 E4
Springfield Rd
　Bristol, Cotham BS6 . . . . 49 D1
　Bristol, Mangotsfield
　　BS16 . . . . 52 A7
　Pill BS20 . . . . 47 C4
　Portishead BS20 . . . . . . 45 B5
Springfields BS34 . . . . . 36 A2
Springfort BS9 . . . . 48 F3
Spring Gardens Rd
　BA2 . . . . 141 C2
Spring Gdns
　Bath BA2 . . . . 141 C2
　Bristol BS4 . . . . 64 A1
Spring Ground Rd
　BS39 . . . . 132 E5
Spring Hill
　Bristol BS2 . . . . 143 A4
　Bristol, Upper Soundwell
　　BS15 . . . . 51 E2
　Weston-s-M BS22 . . . . . 88 D2
Springhill Cl BS39 . . . . 132 C6
Spring Hill Dr BS22 . . . . 88 E1
Spring Ho **2** BS35 . . . . 15 C8
Spring La
　Bath BA1 . . . . 85 B2
　Dundry BS41 . . . . 79 A1
Springleaze
　Bristol, Knowle Park
　　BS4 . . . . 64 A1
　Bristol, Mangotsfield
　　BS16 . . . . 52 A7
Springly Ct BS15 . . . . . . 66 A8
Spring Rise BS20 . . . . . . 45 C3
Spring St BS3 . . . . 63 E4
Spring Street Pl BS3 . . . 63 E4
Spring Terr BS22 . . . . . . 88 C2
Spring Vale BA1 . . . . . . 85 B2
Spring Valley BS22 . . . . 88 C2
Springville Cl BS30 . . . . 66 A3
Springwater Pk Trad Est
　BS5 . . . . 64 C2
Springwood Dr BS10 . . . 34 D3
Spring Wood Gdns
　BS24 . . . . 105 E3
Spruce Way
　Bath BA2 . . . . 118 E8
　Bristol BS34 . . . . 35 F7
　Weston-s-M BS22 . . . . 105 E8
Square Leaze BS34 . . . . 35 F6
Square The
　Alveston BS35 . . . . 15 A4
　Axbridge BS26 . . . . . . 125 C2
　Banwell BS29 . . . . 107 B3
　Bath BA2 . . . . 141 B1
　Bristol BS1 . . . . 143 C2
　Bristol, Knowle Park BS4 64 A1
　Bristol, Staple Hill BS16 . 51 E4
　Shipham BS25 . . . . . . 125 E7
　Temple Cloud BS39 . . . 114 E1
　Timsbury BA2 . . . . 116 B2
　Wellow BA2 . . . . 118 D1
　Winscombe BS25 . . . . 124 E6
Squire La BS40 . . . . . . 111 C1
Squires Ct BS30 . . . . . . 65 F4
Squires Leaze BS35 . . . . 8 D2
Squirrel Cres BS35 . . . . . 8 D2
Stabbins Cl BS22 . . . . . . 89 B5
Stables The BA3 . . . . . 140 B5
Stable Yd BA2 . . . . 101 D6
Stable Yd The GL9 . . . . . 30 B7
Stackpool Rd BS3 . . . . . 63 C4
Staddlestones BA3 . . . . 138 F7
Stadium Rd BS6 . . . . . . 49 C5
Stafford Cres BS35 . . . . . 8 B1
Stafford Pl BS23 . . . . . 104 E8
Stafford Rd
　Bristol BS2 . . . . 50 A2
　Portishead BS20 . . . . . . 45 E4
　Weston-s-M BS23 . . . . 104 F7
Staffords Ct BS30 . . . . . 66 A6
Stafford St BS3 . . . . 63 D4
Stainer Cl BS4 . . . . 79 D7
Stalcombe La BA2 . . . . . 99 B4
Stall St BA1 . . . . 141 C2
Stambrook Pk BA1 . . . . . 86 A5
Stanbridge Cl BS16 . . . . 51 F6
Stanbridge Prim Sch
　BS16 . . . . 51 F6
Stanbridge Rd BS16 . . . . 51 F6
Stanbury Ave BS16 . . . . 51 C5
Stanbury Rd BS3 . . . . . . 63 E3
Stancombe La BS48 . . . . 76 E7
Stancombe View GL11 . . . 5 D5
Standfast Rd BS10 . . . . . 34 F3
Standing Cross BA2 . . . 117 D7
Standish Ave BS34 . . . . . 24 C1
Standish Cl BS10 . . . . . . 34 F1
Standon Way BS10 . . . . . 35 C2
Stane Way BS11 . . . . . . 47 C7

Stanfield Cl BS7 . . . . . . 50 C6
Stanford Cl BS36 . . . . . . 37 F8
Stanford Pl BS4 . . . . 79 D7
Stanhope Pl BA1 . . . . . 141 A2
Stanhope Rd
　Bristol BS30 . . . . 65 F2
　Weston-s-M BS23 . . . . 104 E3
Stanhope St BS2 . . . . . . 64 A5
Stanier Rd
　Bath BA2 . . . . 141 A2
　Bristol BS15, BS16 . . . . . 52 B3
Stanley Ave
　Bristol, Bishopston BS7 . . 49 E3
　Bristol, Filton BS34 . . . . 36 B2
Stanley Chase BS5 . . . . . 50 E2
Stanley Cres BS34 . . . . . 36 B2
Stanley Ct BA3 . . . . 133 B2
Stanley Gdns BS30 . . . . 66 B4
Stanley Gr BS23 . . . . . . 104 F2
Stanley Hill BS4 . . . . 64 A4
Stanley Mead BS32 . . . . 24 E2
Stanley Park Rd BS16 . . . 51 E3
Stanley Pk BS5 . . . . 50 C1
Stanley Rd
　Bristol, Cotham BS6 . . . . 49 C1
　Bristol, Warmley BS15 . . . 66 B8
　2 Weston-s-M BS23 . . 104 F2
Stanley Rd W BA2 . . . . 101 D5
Stanley St N **9** BS3 . . . 63 C3
Stanley St S BS3 . . . . . . 63 C2
Stanley St **4** BS3 . . . . . 63 C3
Stanley Terr
　3 Bristol BS3 . . . . 63 C2
　Radstock BA3 . . . . 134 A3
Stanley Villas **11** BA1 . . 85 A1
Stanshalls Cl BS40 . . . . . 94 C8
Stanshalls Dr BS40 . . . . . 94 C8
Stanshalls La BS40 . . . . . 94 C8
Stanshaw Cl BS16 . . . . . 51 A7
Stanshawe Cres BS37 . . . 27 E1
Stanshawes Court Dr
　BS37 . . . . 39 E8
Stanshawes Dr BS37 . . . . 27 D1
Stanshaw Rd BS16 . . . . . 51 A7
Stanshaws Cl BS32 . . . . . 24 C2
Stanton Cl BS15 . . . . 51 F1
STANTON DREW 96 F2
Stanton Drew Prim Sch
　BS39 . . . . 97 A2
**Stanton Drew Stone
　Circles★** BS39 . . . . . . 97 A3
Stanton La BS39 . . . . . . 97 D4
STANTON PRIOR 99 E2
Stanton Rd
　Bristol BS10 . . . . 35 E2
　Chew Magna BS40 . . . . 96 B3
STANTON WICK 114 D8
Stanton Wick La BS39 . . 97 B1
Stanway BS30 . . . . 66 C1
Stanway Cl BA2 . . . . . . 101 D1
Staple Gr BS31 . . . . 81 D5
Staple Grove Cres BS5 . . 65 E4
STAPLE HILL 51 E4
Staple Hill Prim Sch
　BS16 . . . . 51 D4
Staple Hill Rd BS16 . . . . 51 B4
Staples Cl BS21 . . . . 57 G1
Staples Gn BS22 . . . . . . 89 B3
Staples Hill BA2 . . . . . . 120 C4
Staples Rd BS37 . . . . . . 27 D2
STAPLETON 50 D4
Stapleton Cl BS16 . . . . . 50 D5
Stapleton Rd
　Bristol, Baptist Mills
　　BS5 . . . . 50 B1
　Bristol, Eastville BS5 . . . 50 C3
Stapleton Road Sta
　BS5 . . . . 50 B1
STAR 108 D1
Star Ave BS34 . . . . 37 A4
Star Barn Rd BS36 . . . . . 37 E7
Starcross Rd BS22 . . . . . 89 A2
Star La
　Bristol BS16 . . . . 50 F3
　Pill BS20 . . . . 47 D4
Starling Cl BS22 . . . . . . 105 E8
Starrs Cl BS26 . . . . 125 B2
STARVEALL 20 D4
Starveall Cl BS5 . . . . 51 A1
Station App
　Pensford BS39 . . . . 97 D5
　Weston-s-M BS23 . . . . 104 E7
Station Ave **3** BS16 . . . . 51 A4
Station Ave S **5** BS16 . . 51 A4
Station Cl
　Backwell BS48 . . . . 75 F7
　Bristol BS15 . . . . 66 C8
　Chipping Sodbury BS37 . . 40 D8
　Congresbury BS49 . . . . 91 C4
Station Ct BS5 . . . . 64 E8
Station La BS7 . . . . 50 A4
Station Lodge **8**
　BS23 . . . . 104 E7
Station Mead BA3 . . . . 138 D3
Station Rd
　Acton Turville GL9 . . . . . 42 F8
　Axbridge BS26 . . . . . . 125 C2
　Backwell BS48 . . . . 76 A6
　Bath BA1 . . . . 101 C7

Station Rd continued
　Blagdon BS40 . . . . 110 E3
　Bristol, Ashley Down BS7 49 F4
　Bristol, Filton BS34 . . . . 36 A3
　Bristol, Fishponds BS16 . . 51 A4
　Bristol, Henbury BS10 . . . 34 F4
　Bristol, Montpelier BS6 . . 49 E2
　Bristol, Newleaze BS34 . . 36 C2
　Bristol, Patchway BS34 . . 36 C7
　Bristol, Shirehampton
　　BS11 . . . . 47 D5
　Bristol, Shirehampton
　　BS11 . . . . 47 E6
　Bristol, Staple Hill . BS16 . 51 F3
　Bristol, Upper Knowle
　　BS4 . . . . 64 D2
　Bristol, Warmley BS30 . . 66 C7
　Charfield GL12 . . . . 11 B5
　Clevedon BS21 . . . . 57 F3
　Clutton BS39 . . . . 114 F3
　Congresbury BS49 . . . . 91 C4
　Flax Bourton BS48 . . . . 77 A8
　Frampton Cotterell BS36 38 C5
　Freshford BA2 . . . . 120 C5
　Iron Acton BS37 . . . . . . 26 D3
　Keynsham BS31 . . . . . . 81 E6
　Midsomer Norton BA3 . . 133 B2
　Nailsea BS48 . . . . 59 F2
　Pill BS20 . . . . 47 C4
　Pilning BS35 . . . . 22 F4
　Portbury BS20 . . . . 46 D3
　Portishead BS20 . . . . . . 45 D6
　Sandford BS25 . . . . . . 107 F4
　Severn Beach BS35 . . . . 22 A6
　Wellow BA2 . . . . 118 D1
　Weston-s-M BS23 . . . . 104 E7
　Weston-s-M, St Georges
　　BS22 . . . . 89 D2
　Weston-s-M, Worle BS22 . 88 F2
　Wickwar GL12 . . . . 18 B7
　Winterbourne BS36 . . . . 37 B4
　Wrington BS40 . . . . 92 D2
　Yate BS37 . . . . 27 C2
　Yatton BS49 . . . . 74 B1
Station Road Bsns Ctr
　BS15 . . . . 52 A3
Station Road Link BS15 52 A2
Station Road Workshops
　BS15 . . . . 52 A3
Station Yd BS36 . . . . 37 E4
Staunton Fields BS14 . . . 80 C4
Staunton La BS14 . . . . . . 80 D3
Staunton Way BS14 . . . . 80 D4
Staveley Cres BS10 . . . . 35 C2
Staverton Cl BS32 . . . . . 24 C1
Staverton Way BS15 . . . . 66 A7
Stavordale Gr BS14 . . . . 80 B6
Staynes Cres BS15 . . . . . 65 E8
Steam Mills BA3 . . . . . 138 F8
Steanbridge BS32 . . . . . 36 D6
Stean Bridge Rd BS32 . . 36 E6
Steel Ct BS30 . . . . 65 F2
Steel Mills BS31 . . . . 81 F4
STEEP HOLM 104 B2
Steevens Ho (Almshouses)
　13 BS2 . . . . 143 C3
Stella Gr BS3 . . . . 63 A2
Stennard Gn BA2 . . . . . 102 B2
Stephens Dr BS30 . . . . . 65 F5
Stephen St BS5 . . . . 64 C8
Stepney Rd BS5 . . . . 50 C1
Stepney Wlk BS5 . . . . . . 50 C1
Stepping Stones The
　BS4 . . . . 64 E6
Sterncourt Rd BS16 . . . . 51 A7
Stevens Cres BS3 . . . . . . 63 F4
Stevens La BS24 . . . . . . 122 C3
Stevens Wlk BS32 . . . . . 36 D8
Steway La BA1 . . . . 86 B6
Stibbs Ct BS30 . . . . 65 F4
Stibbs Hill BS5 . . . . 65 A7
Stickland BS21 . . . . 57 E1
STIDCOT 16 E6
Stidcote La GL12 . . . . . . 16 E5
Stidcot La GL12 . . . . 16 D5
Stidham La BS31 . . . . . . 82 B6
Stile Acres BS11 . . . . 34 A1
Stilemead La BS40 . . . . 111 D1
Stileway Bsns Pk BS21 . . 73 B8
Stillhouse La BS3 . . . . . . 63 D4
Stillingfleet Rd BS13 . . . 79 C5
Stillman Cl BS13 . . . . . . 78 E4
Stinchcombe BS37 . . . . . 27 E1
Stirling Cl BS37 . . . . 27 D4
Stirling Rd BS4 . . . . 64 C3
Stirling Way BS31 . . . . . 81 E4
Stirtingale Ave BA2 . . . 101 C3
Stirtingale Rd BA2 . . . . 101 C3
Stitchings La BA2 . . . . . 117 D7
Stitchings Shord La
　BS39 . . . . 113 C4
STOCK 109 B8
Stock Hill BS35 . . . . 7 C1
Stockhill Cl BA3 . . . . . . 138 C3
Stockhill Rd BA3 . . . . . 138 C2
Stock La BS40 . . . . 109 A7
Stockmead BS40 . . . . . 109 B5
Stockton Cl
　Bristol BS14 . . . . 79 F4

Stockton Cl continued
　Bristol, Oldland BS30 . . . 66 B3
Stock Way N BS48 . . . . . 59 F2
Stock Way S BS48 . . . . . 59 E2
Stockwell Ave BS16 . . . . 52 A6
Stockwell Cl BS16 . . . . . 51 F7
Stockwell Dr BS16 . . . . . 52 A6
STOCKWOOD 80 E5
Stockwood Chambers
　BS5 . . . . 64 C7
Stockwood Cres BS4 . . . 63 F2
Stockwood Green Prim
　Sch BS14 . . . . 80 E4
Stockwood Hill BS31 . . . 81 C7
Stockwood La
　Bristol BS14 . . . . 80 E5
　Keynsham BS14, BS31 . . 81 B7
Stockwood Mews BS4 . . 64 F5
Stockwood Rd BS4 . . . . . 64 F1
STOCKWOOD VALE 81 C6
Stockwood Vale BS31 . . . 81 C6
Stodelegh Cl BS22 . . . . . 89 B3
STOKE BISHOP 48 E5
Stoke Bishop CE Prim Sch
　BS9 . . . . 48 E5
Stoke Bridge Ave BS34 . . 36 D6
Stoke Cotts BS9 . . . . 48 E4
Stokefield Cl BS35 . . . . . . 8 B1
STOKE GIFFORD 36 F4
Stoke Gr BS9 . . . . 48 E6
Stoke Hamlet BS9 . . . . . 48 F6
Stoke Hill
　Bristol BS9 . . . . 48 E3
　Chew Stoke BS40 . . . . . 112 D7
Stoke La
　Bristol, Broomhill BS16 . . 50 E7
　Bristol, Patchway BS34 . . 36 C8
　Bristol, Westbury on T
　　BS9 . . . . 48 F6
Stokeleigh Wlk BS9 . . . . 48 C5
Stoke Lodge Prim Sch
　BS34 . . . . 36 C8
Stoke Mdws BS32 . . . . . 24 D1
Stokemead BS34 . . . . . . 36 C8
Stoke Mead BA2 . . . . . 119 F7
Stoke Paddock Rd BS9 . 48 D6
Stoke Park Rd BS9 . . . . . 48 F4
Stoke Park Rd S BS9 . . . 48 E3
Stoke Rd
　Bristol BS8, BS9 . . . . . . 48 F3
　Portishead BS20 . . . . . . 45 D5
Stokes Croft BS1 . . . . . 143 B4
Stokes Ct **1** BS30 . . . . . 66 A4
Stoke View BS34 . . . . . . 36 A3
Stoke View Bsns Pk **6**
　BS16 . . . . 50 F4
Stoke View Rd BS16 . . . . 50 F3
STONE 3 F3
Stoneable Rd BA3 . . . . . 134 A3
STON EASTON 131 E1
Stoneberry Rd BS14 . . . . 80 B3
STONEBRIDGE 107 A4
Stonebridge BS21 . . . . . . 57 F1
Stonebridge Pk BS5 . . . . 50 E2
Stonebridge Rd BS23 . . 104 F4
Stonechat Gdns BS16 . . . 50 E6
Stonechat Gn BS20 . . . . 46 A6
Stone Cl BS36 . . . . 37 E4
STONE-EDGE BATCH . . . 59 D4
Stonehenge La BS48 . . . 59 D4
Stonehill BS15 . . . . 65 E4
STONE HILL 65 E4
Stonehill Ctr BS30 . . . . . 65 E4
Stonehill Farm BS15 . . . . 65 E4
Stone Hill View BS15 . . . 65 C3
Stonehouse Cl BA2 . . . . 102 B2
Stonehouse La BA2 . . . . 102 B2
Stone House Mews
　BS37 . . . . 28 B1
Stone La BS36 . . . . 37 F3
Stoneleigh BS40 . . . . 96 B3
Stoneleigh Cres BS4 . . . . 64 A2
Stoneleigh Ct BA1 . . . . . 84 E3
Stoneleigh Dr BS30 . . . . 65 F5
Stoneleigh Ho BS8 . . . . 142 B3
Stoneleigh Rd BS4 . . . . . 64 A2
Stoneleigh Wlk BS4 . . . . 64 A2
Stone Monolith BS34 . . . 35 E6
Stone's Cross BA3 . . . . 133 B2
Stones Ct BS6 . . . . 49 B2
Stonewell Dr BS49 . . . . . 91 D3
Stonewell Gr BS49 . . . . . 91 D3
Stonewell La BS49 . . . . . 91 D3
Stonewell Park Rd
　BS49 . . . . 91 D3
Stoneyard La
　Litton BA3 . . . . 130 D2
　Maniards Green BS35 . . . 2 A1
　Shepperdine BS35 . . . . . . 1 F1
Stoneyfield Cl BS20 . . . . 47 B5
Stoneyfields BS20 . . . . . 47 B4
**Stoney Littleton Long
　Barrow★** BA2 . . . . . . 135 C2
Stoney Steep BS48 . . . . . 60 C5
Stoney Stile Rd BS35 . . . 15 A5
Stony La GL9 . . . . 19 C5
STONY LITTLETON 135 B6
Stormont Cl BS23 . . . . . 104 F3

Stormont Ct BS24 . . . . . . **105** E7
Stothard Rd BS7 . . . . . . **50** B7
Stottbury Rd BS7 . . . . . . **50** A3
Stoulton Gr BS10 . . . . . . **35** A3
Stourden Cl BS16 . . . . . . **51** A7
Stourton Dr BS30 . . . . . . **65** F4
Stover Rd BS37 . . . . . . **27** B2
Stover Trad Est BS37 . . . . **27** B2
Stowborough Cotts
  BA2 . . . . **134** C7
Stowell Hill Rd GL12 . . **16** B6
STOWEY **113** F4
Stowey Bottom BS39 . . **113** E5
Stowey Crossroads
  BS39 . . . . **113** F5
Stowey Pk BS49 . . . . . . **91** D7
Stowey Rd BS49 . . . . . . **91** C8
Stowey Road BS39 . . . . . **113** F2
Stow Hill Rd GL12 . . . . **16** B6
Stow Ho BS11 . . . . **47** E5
Stowick Gdns BS11 . . . . **34** C2
Stradbrook Ave BS5 . . . . **65** B7
Stradling Ave BS23 . . . . **104** F5
Stradling Rd BS11 . . . . . **34** C2
Stradlings Yd BS2 . . . . . **142** C4
Straightmead BA3 . . . . . **130** F1
Straight St BS2 . . . . **143** C2
Straits Par BS16 . . . . **51** B5
Stratford Cl BS14 . . . . . . **79** F3
Stratford Ct BS9 . . . . . . **48** F8
Stratford La BS40 . . . . . **112** E1
Strathearn Dr BS10 . . . . **35** B2
Strathmore Rd BS7 . . . . **49** F5
Stratton Cl BS34 . . . . . . **36** C7
Stratton La BS22 . . . . . . **88** A4
STRATTON-ON-THE-
  FOSSE **138** F1
Stratton Pl BS30 . . . . . . **65** F2
Stratton Rd BS31 . . . . . . **82** E3
Strawberry Cl BS48 . . . . **59** D1
Strawberry Field
  BS26 . . . . **125** D2
Strawberry Gdns BS48 . . **75** D8
Strawberry Hill BS21 . . . **57** H4
Strawberry La
  Bristol BS5 . . . . **64** E7
  Dundry BS13, BS41 . . . **78** E3
Strawberry Line BS49 . **108** A8
Strawbridge Rd **11** BS5 . **64** B7
Stream Cl BS10 . . . . **35** D3
Streamcross BS49 . . . . . **74** D1
Streamleaze
  Chew Magna BS40 . . . . **96** B3
  Thornbury BS35 . . . . . . **15** C8
Streamleaze Ct BS35 . . . **15** B8
Streamside
  Chew Magna BS40 . . . . **96** B3
  1 Clevedon BS21 . . . **57** H3
Stream Side BS16 . . . . . **51** F6
Streamside Rd BS37 . . . . **28** A1
Streamside Wlk BS4 . . . . **64** E3
Stream The BS16 . . . . . . **37** B2
STREET END **110** E2
Street End BS40 . . . . . . **110** D2
Street End La BS40 . . . . **110** D2
Street The
  Acton Turville GL9 . . . . **42** F6
  Alveston BS35 . . . . **15** B5
  Bishop Sutton BS39 . . . **113** D4
  Burton SN14 . . . . **43** B4
  Chew Stoke BS40 . . . . . **112** D8
  Chilcompton BA3 . . . . . **138** D5
  Compton Martin BS40 . . **129** B7
  Farmborough BA2 . . . . **115** F6
  Luckington SN14 . . . . . **31** E4
  North Nibley GL11 . . . . **5** D4
  Olveston BS35 . . . . **14** A3
  Radstock BA3 . . . . **133** F2
  Stowey BS39 . . . . **113** F4
  Ubley BS40 . . . . **111** D1
  Winford BS40 . . . . **94** F1
Stretford Ave BS5 . . . . . **64** D8
Stretford Rd BS5 . . . . . . **64** D8
Stride Cl BS35 . . . . **22** A6
STRODE **111** E7
Strode Comm BS35 . . . . **14** F5
Strode Gdns BS35 . . . . . **14** F5
Strode Rd BS21 . . . . **57** E2
Strode Way BS21 . . . . . . **57** D1
Stroud Rd
  Bristol, Patchway BS34 . . **35** F8
  Bristol, Shirehampton
  BS11 . . . . **47** E5
  Petty France GL9 . . . . . **30** B7
Stroud Way BS24 . . . . . . **105** E2
Stuart Ho BS23 . . . . **87** D1
Stuart Pl BA2 . . . . **101** D6
Stuart Rd BS23 . . . . **105** A5
Stuart St BS5 . . . . **64** C7
Studland Ct BS9 . . . . . . **49** B6
Stumpwell La GL12 . . . . **5** E2
Sturden La BS16 . . . . . . **37** C3
Sturdon Rd BS3 . . . . . . **63** A3
Sturmer Cl BS37 . . . . . . **27** E4
Sturmey Way BS20 . . . . **47** E3
Sturminster Cl BS14 . . . . **80** D6
Sturminster Lodge
  BS14 . . . . **80** D5
Sturminster Rd BS14 . . . **80** D7

Suffolk Ho BA1 . . . . **101** C8
Sulis Manor Rd BA2 . . . . **118** D8
Sullivan Cl BS4 . . . . **79** D6
Sumerlin Dr BS21 . . . . . **57** H3
Summer Ct BS8 . . . . **142** B3
Summerfield Rd BA1 . . . **85** A1
Summerfield BS22 . . . . . **89** A3
Summerfield Terr BA1 . . **85** A1
Summer Ground Dr
  BS13 . . . . **79** A5
Summerhayes BS30 . . . . **66** D5
Summer Hill BS4 . . . . . . **64** A4
Summerhill Jun & Inf Schs
  BS5 . . . . **64** E8
Summerhill Rd
  Bath BA1 . . . . **84** D1
  Bristol BS5 . . . . **64** F7
Summerhill Terr BS5 . . . **64** F7
Summerhouse BS21 . . . . **59** D4
Summer House Way
  BS30 . . . . **66** B7
Summer La
  Banwell BS29 . . . . **106** E5
  Burton SN14 . . . . **43** F3
  Monkton Combe BA2 . . **119** D8
  Weston-s-M BS22, BS24 . **89** B1
  Weston-s-M BS22,
  BS24 . . . . **106** C8
  Weston-s-M BS29 . . . . **106** D7
Summer La N BS22 . . . . **89** B2
Summerlands BS48 . . . . **76** B5
Summerlands Rd
  BS23 . . . . **105** B8
Summer Lane Park Homes
  BS29 . . . . **106** E4
Summerlays Ct BA2 . . . . **102** B6
Summerlays Pl BA2 . . . . **102** B6
Summerlea BA2 . . . . . . **117** A5
Summerleaze
  Bristol BS16 . . . . **51** C3
  Keynsham BS31 . . . . . . **81** E7
Summer Leaze BS39 . . . **113** D4
Summers Dr BS30 . . . . . **54** E1
Summers Mead BS37 . . . **27** E4
Summers Rd **4** BS2 . . . . **50** A1
Summer St **4** BS3 . . . . **63** C4
Summers Terr **3** BS2 . . **50** A1
Summer View GL12 . . . . **18** B4
Summit Cl BS15 . . . . **65** E8
SUNDAYSHILL **9** C8
Sundays Hill BS32 . . . . . **24** A4
Sundayshill La GL12 . . . . **9** D7
Sunderland Pl BS8 . . . . . **142** B3
Sunderland St **2** BA2 . . **141** C3
Sundew Rd BS16 . . . . . . **52** D7
Sundridge Pk BS37 . . . . **39** E8
Sunfield Rd BS24 . . . . . **105** E3
Sunningdale
  Bristol BS8 . . . . **142** B4
  Yate BS37 . . . . **39** E8
Sunningdale Cl BS48 . . . **60** A1
Sunningdale Dr BS30 . . . **66** B6
Sunningdale Rd BS22 . . . **88** F3
Sunnybank
  Bath BA2 . . . . **102** B4
  Bristol BS16 . . . . **51** E6
  Westerleigh BS37 . . . . . **39** A3
Sunny Bank
  Bristol BS15 . . . . **51** B1
  Wick BS30 . . . . **67** B7
Sunnybank Ct BS24 . . . . **89** B1
Sunnybank Way BS24 . . **89** B1
Sunnydene BS4 . . . . **64** D4
Sunny Hill BS9 . . . . **48** C7
Sunnyhill Dr BS11 . . . . . **47** E6
Sunnyhill Ho E BS11 . . . **47** E6
Sunnyhill Ho W BS11 . . . **47** E6
Sunnymead
  Bristol BS30 . . . . **66** D6
  Keynsham BS31 . . . . . . **81** F3
  Midsomer Norton BA3 . . **132** F2
  Stratton-on-t-F BA3 . . . **138** F2
Sunnymead La BS39 . . . **113** D3
Sunnymede Rd BS48 . . . **59** D3
Sunny Mount BA3 . . . . . **133** B2
Sunnyside
  Bristol BS9 . . . . **48** E5
  Clutton BS39 . . . . **115** A4
  Farrington Gurney BS39 . **132** B3
  Frampton Cotterell BS36 . **38** B8
Sunnyside Cres BS21 . . . **57** F3
Sunnyside Farm Trad Est
  BS20 . . . . **47** C2
Sunnyside Gdns BA2 . . . **116** B2
Sunnyside La
  Hambrook BS16 . . . . . . **37** C2
  Yate BS37 . . . . **27** C1
Sunnyside Rd
  Clevedon BS21 . . . . **57** F3
  Weston-s-M BS23 . . . . . **104** E5
Sunnyside Rd N BS23 . . **104** E5
Sunnyside View BA2 . . . **134** C7
Sunnyvale
  Camerton BA2 . . . . **133** E8
  Clevedon BS21 . . . . **57** D1
Sunnyvale Dr BS30 . . . . **66** B3
Sunny Wlk BS15 . . . . . . **51** B1
Sunridge BS16 . . . . **51** D6
Sunridge Cl BA3 . . . . . . **138** F8

Sunridge Pk BA3 . . . . . . **138** F8
Sunrise Gr BS4 . . . . **64** D4
Sunset Cl BA2 . . . . **134** C7
Surrey Rd BS7 . . . . **49** E3
Surrey St BS2 . . . . **143** B4
Sussex Pl
  Bath BA2 . . . . **141** C1
  Bristol BS2 . . . . **49** F1
Sussex St BS2 . . . . **64** A6
Sutcliffe Ho BA1 . . . . . . **102** B8
Sutherland Ave
  Bristol BS16 . . . . **51** E7
  Yate BS37 . . . . **27** D4
Sutherland Dr BS24 . . . **105** D2
Sutherland Pl **9** BS8 . . . **49** A2
Sutton Ave BS4 . . . . **64** D4
Sutton Cl BS22 . . . . **105** E8
Sutton Court BS39 . . . . **113** F5
Sutton Hill Rd BS39 . . . **113** D4
Sutton La BS40 . . . . **93** F1
Sutton Pk BS39 . . . . . . **113** D4
Sutton St BA2 . . . . **102** B7
SUTTON WICK **113** B2
Swainswick BS14 . . . . . . **79** F6
Swainswick Gdns BS10 . . **35** C2
Swainswick La BA1 . . . . **85** D4
Swainswick CE Prim Sch
  BA1 . . . . **85** B5
Swaish Dr **2** BS30 . . . . **66** A4
Swallow Cl BA3 . . . . . . **139** B8
Swallow Ct BS14 . . . . . . **80** F6
Swallow Dr BS34 . . . . . . **35** E8
Swallow Gdns BS22 . . . **105** E8
Swallow Pk BS35 . . . . . . **8** D3
Swallows Ct BS34 . . . . . **36** E4
Swallows The BS22 . . . . **105** D7
Swallowtail Cl BS35 . . . . **8** D3
Swan Cl BS22 . . . . **105** E8
Swancombe
  Blagdon BS40 . . . . **110** E2
  Clapton in G BS20 . . . . **59** E8
Swane Rd BS14 . . . . **80** F6
Swan Field BS37 . . . . . . **27** F2
Swangrove La GL9 . . . . . **30** D8
Swan La BS36 . . . . **37** C8
Swanley La GL13 . . . . . . **4** B5
Swanmoor Cres BS10 . . **35** A4
Sweetgrass Rd BS24 . . . **106** A8
Sweets Cl BS15 . . . . **51** E2
Sweets Rd BS15 . . . . **51** E2
Sweetwater La BS35 . . . . **14** D7
Swift Cl BS22 . . . . **88** F1
SWINEFORD **83** A7
Swinhay La GL12 . . . . . . **11** B8
Swiss Ct **13** BS23 . . . . . **104** E7
Swiss Dr BS3 . . . . **62** F2
Swiss Rd
  Bristol BS3 . . . . **62** F1
  Weston-s-M BS23 . . . . . **104** F7
Swithins La BS34 . . . . . . **35** F7
Sycamore Cl
  Bristol, Hanham BS15 . . **65** B3
  Bristol, Whitehall BS5 . . **50** E1
  Locking BS24 . . . . **105** E5
  Nailsea BS48 . . . . **59** E2
  Shipham BS25 . . . . **125** E8
  Weston-s-M BS23 . . . . . **105** A8
Sycamore Ct BS7 . . . . . . **49** E3
Sycamore Dr
  Bristol BS34 . . . . **35** F7
  Thornbury BS35 . . . . . . **8** C1
Sycamore Ho **6** BS16 . . **51** C6
Sycamore Rd BA3 . . . . . **134** B2
Sycamores BS23 . . . . . . **87** E1
Sydenham Bldgs BA2 . . **141** A2
Sydenham Hill BS6 . . . . **49** D1
Sydenham La BS6 . . . . . **49** D1
Sydenham Pl **15** BS6 . . . **49** E1
Sydenham Rd
  Bath BA2 . . . . **141** A2
  Bristol, Cotham BS6 . . . **49** D1
  Bristol, Totterdown BS4 . **64** A3
Sydenham Terr BA2 . . . **102** C1
Sydenham Way BS15 . . . **65** C3
Sydney Bldgs BA2 . . . . **102** B6
Sydney Ho BA2 . . . . . . **102** B7
Sydney Mews BA2 . . . . **102** B7
Sydney Pl BA2 . . . . **102** B7
Sydney Row BS1 . . . . . . **142** B1
Sydney Wharf BA2 . . . . **102** B7
Sylvan Way BS9 . . . . . . **48** B7
Sylvia Ave BS3 . . . . **63** F3
Symes Ave BS13 . . . . . . **79** C4
Symes Pk BA1 . . . . **84** A2
Symington Rd BS16 . . . . **51** B5
Syston View BS15 . . . . . **66** A8
Syston Way BS15 . . . . . . **51** D1

T

Tabernacle Rd BS15 . . . . **65** C6
Tackley Rd BS5 . . . . **50** B3
TADWICK **68** E1
Tadwick La BA1 . . . . **85** A6
Tailor's Ct **9** BS1 . . . . . **143** A3
Talbot Ave BS15 . . . . . . **51** C1

Talbot Ct BS4 . . . . **64** B2
Talbot Rd BS4 . . . . **64** C2
TALBOT'S END **10** C1
Talgarth Rd BS7 . . . . . . **49** F4
Tall Elms Rd BS34 . . . . . **36** A7
Tallis Gr BS4 . . . . **79** D6
Tamar Cl BS35 . . . . **15** D7
Tamar Dr BS31 . . . . **82** A4
Tamar Rd
  Bristol BS2 . . . . **64** C6
  Weston-s-M BS22 . . . . . **89** A2
Tamblyn Cl BA3 . . . . . . **134** A3
Tamsin Ct BS31 . . . . **81** F5
Tamworth Rd BS31 . . . . **81** E4
Tanhouse La BS37 . . . . . **27** D7
Tankard's Cl BS8 . . . . . **142** C3
Tanner Cl BS30 . . . . **65** F5
Tanner Ct BS30 . . . . **65** F5
Tanner Rd BS29 . . . . . . **106** C7
Tanners Ct
  Bristol, Frenchay BS16 . . **37** B1
  4 Bristol, Two Mile Hill
  BS15 . . . . **51** C1
  Thornbury BS35 . . . . . . **15** B8
Tanners La SN14 . . . . . . **69** F8
Tanners Wlk
  Bath BA2 . . . . **100** F5
  Marshfield SN14 . . . . . . **69** F8
Tanorth Cl BS14 . . . . . . **80** A3
Tanorth Rd BS14 . . . . . . **79** F3
Tansy La BS20 . . . . **45** F5
Tanyard The BS30 . . . . . **66** B2
Tapsters BS30 . . . . **66** A4
Tara Cl BS36 . . . . **25** F1
Tarn Ho BS34 . . . . **36** A8
Tarnock Ave BS14 . . . . . **80** A7
Tarnwell BS39 . . . . **97** A2
Tarragon Pl BS32 . . . . . **36** F7
Taunton Rd BS22 . . . . . . **89** B4
Taunton Wlk BS7 . . . . . . **50** A7
Taurus Rd BS34 . . . . . . **36** B5
Tavistock Rd
  Bristol BS4 . . . . **63** F1
  Weston-s-M BS22 . . . . . **89** A2
Tavistock Wlk BS4 . . . . . **63** F1
Tawny Way BS22 . . . . . **105** F8
Taylor Cl BS15 . . . . **65** F8
Taylor Ct BS22 . . . . **89** B4
Taylor Gdns BS13 . . . . . **78** F4
Taylors Bank **10** BS1 . . **143** A3
Taylors Fields BS29 . . . **107** B3
Tayman Cl BS10 . . . . . . **49** E6
Tayman Ridge BS30 . . . . **82** D8
Taynton Cl BS30 . . . . . . **66** C2
Teal Cl
  Bristol BS32 . . . . **24** D2
  Weston-s-M BS22 . . . . . **88** F1
Teal Way BS20 . . . . **45** F6
Teasel Cl BS16 . . . . **52** D8
Teasel Mead BS32 . . . . . **36** E7
Teasel Wlk BS22 . . . . . **105** D7
Teddington Cl BA2 . . . . **101** C4
Teesdale Cl BS22 . . . . . **105** D8
Teewell Ave BS16 . . . . . **51** E4
Teewell Cl BS16 . . . . **51** E4
Teewell Ct BS16 . . . . **51** E4
Teewell Hill BS16 . . . . . . **51** E4
Teignmouth Rd
  Bristol BS4 . . . . **63** F1
  Clevedon BS21 . . . . **57** G3
Telephone Ave BS1 . . . . **143** A2
Telford Ho
  Bath BA2 . . . . **101** D3
  Leigh Woods BS8 . . . . . **62** E7
Telford Wlk BS5 . . . . **51** A1
TELLISFORD **137** E4
Tellisford La BA2 . . . . . **136** F4
Tellisford Rd BA2 . . . . . **137** E7
Templar Rd BS37 . . . . . . **27** D7
Templars Ct **1** BS22 . . . **105** D7
Templars Way BS25 . . . . **125** E7
Temple Back BS1 . . . . . **143** B2
Temple Back East
  BS1 . . . . **143** C2
Temple Bridge Bsns Pk
  BS39 . . . . **131** F7
Temple Church ★ BS1 . **143** B2
Temple Circus Giratory
  BS1 . . . . **143** B1
TEMPLE CLOUD **114** E1
Temple Ct BS31 . . . . **81** E5
Temple Gate BS1 . . . . . **143** B1
Temple Gate District Ctr
  BS3 . . . . **63** F4
Temple Inn La BS39 . . . **114** E1
Templeland Rd BS13 . . . **78** F5
Temple Rose St BS1 . . . **143** B2
Temple St
  Bristol BS1 . . . . **143** B2
  Bristol, Bedminster BS3 . **63** D4
  Keynsham BS31 . . . . . . **81** F5
Temple Trad Est BS2 . . . **64** C5
Temple Way BS2 . . . . . **143** C2
Temple Way Underpass
  BS2 . . . . **143** C3

Ten Acre La BA2 . . . . . . **117** F6
Ten Acre Ri BS34 . . . . . . **35** E6
Tenby Rd BS31 . . . . **81** D4
Tenby St BS5 . . . . **64** B7
Tennessee Gr BS6 . . . . . **49** C5
Tennis Court Ave
  BS39 . . . . **132** D5
Tenniscourt Rd BS15 . . . **52** A1
Tennis Court Rd BS39 . . **132** D5
Tennis Rd BS4 . . . . **64** A2
Tennyson Ave BS21 . . . . **57** D2
Tennyson Cl BS31 . . . . . **81** F6
Tennyson Rd
  Bath BA1 . . . . **101** D7
  Bristol BS7 . . . . **49** E5
  Weston-s-M BS23 . . . . . **105** A3
Tenterk Cl BS24 . . . . . . **122** B6
Tenth Ave BS7 . . . . **36** B1
Tereslake Gn BS10 . . . . **35** D4
Terrace The BS25 . . . . . **125** E7
Terrace Wlk BA1 . . . . . . **141** C2
Terrell Gdns **14** BS5 . . . **64** D7
Terrell St BS2 . . . . **143** A4
Terris Ct BS34 . . . . **36** E4
Terry Hill BA3 . . . . **140** D8
Terry Ho BS1 . . . . **142** C3
Tetbury Gdns BS48 . . . . **60** A1
Tetbury Rd BS15 . . . . . . **65** B8
Teviot Rd BS31 . . . . **82** A4
Tewkesbury Rd **12** BS2 . **50** A3
Tewther Rd BS13 . . . . . . **79** D3
Teyfant Com Sch BS13 . . **79** E4
Teyfant Rd BS13 . . . . . . **79** E4
Teyfant Wlk BS13 . . . . . **79** E4
Thackeray BS7 . . . . **50** A8
Thackeray Ave BS21 . . . **57** G4
Thackeray Ho BS23 . . . **105** A5
Thackeray Rd BS21 . . . . **57** G4
Thames Cl GL12 . . . . . . **11** A4
Thames Ho **9** BS35 . . . . **15** C8
Thanet Rd BS3 . . . . **63** B2
Thatcher Cl BS20 . . . . . . **45** D4
Thatchers Cl BS5 . . . . . . **65** B7
Theatre Royal ★
  Bath BA1 . . . . **141** B2
  Bristol BS1 . . . . **143** A2
There-and-Back-Again La
  BS1 . . . . **142** C3
Theresa Ave BS7 . . . . . . **49** E4
Thermae Bath Spa ★
  BA1 . . . . **141** B2
Theynes Croft BS41 . . . . **62** B1
Thicket Ave BS16 . . . . . . **51** C3
THICKET MEAD **132** F3
Thicket Mead BA3 . . . . . **133** A2
Thicket Rd BS16 . . . . **51** C4
Thicket Wlk BS35 . . . . . . **8** C1
Thickthorn La BA3 . . . . . **138** A4
Thiery Rd BS4 . . . . **64** C2
Thingwall Pk BS16 . . . . . **50** E3
Third Ave
  Bath BA2 . . . . **101** D5
  Bristol BS14 . . . . **80** B7
  Bristol, Filton BS7 . . . . . **36** A1
  Radstock BA3 . . . . **139** D7
Third Way BS11 . . . . **33** C2
Thirlmere Ct BS30 . . . . . **66** D6
Thirlmere Rd
  Bristol BS34 . . . . **36** A8
  Weston-s-M BS23 . . . . . **105** A4
Thistle Cl BS16 . . . . **52** D8
Thistle St **1** BS3 . . . . . . **63** B3
Thomas Ave BS16 . . . . . **52** B8
Thomas Cl BS29 . . . . . . **107** A3
Thomas Ct BS1 . . . . **143** B2
Thomas La BS1 . . . . **143** B2
Thomas Lane Apartments
  BS1 . . . . **143** B2
Thomas Pring Wlk **1**
  BS5 . . . . **51** A1
Thomas St N **13** BS2 . . . **49** D1
Thomas St
  Bath BA1 . . . . **141** C4
  Bristol BS2 . . . . **143** B4
  8 Bristol, Russell Town
  BS5 . . . . **64** B7
  Bristol, St Pauls BS2 . . . **49** F1
Thomas Way BS16 . . . . . **50** E7
Thompson Rd BS14 . . . . **80** E6
Thomson Rd **7** BS5 . . . . **64** B8
Thornbank Pl BA2 . . . . **141** A1
THORNBURY **8** E2
Thornbury Dr BS23 . . . . **104** D2
Thornbury Hospl BS35 . . **8** C1
Thornbury Ind Est BS35 **15** B7
Thornbury Mus ★ BS35 . **15** B8
Thornbury Office Pk
  BS35 . . . . **15** B8
Thornbury Rd
  Alveston BS35 . . . . **15** A5
  Weston-s-M BS23 . . . . **104** C2
Thorn Cl
  Weston-s-M BS22 . . . . . **89** B2
  Yate BS37 . . . . **27** D1
Thorndale BS8 . . . . **142** A4

Thorndale Cl BS22 . . . .105 D8
Thorndale Mews BS8. .142 A4
Thornfield Rd BS10 . . . .35 A2
Thornhayes Cl BS36. . . . .38 A8
Thornhills The BS16. . . .51 B6
Thornleigh Rd BS7. . . . .49 E5
Thornmarsh Cl BS34. . . .37 A3
Thornmead Gr BS10. . . .35 A2
Thorns Farm BS37. . . . .27 E1
Thornycroft Cl BS7. . . . .50 B7
Thorpe Lodge **10** BS6 . .49 D1
Three Brooks La BS32. .36 E8
Three Oaks Cl BS16 . . . .51 C4
Three Queens' La BS1 143 B2
Threeways Sch
   Summerfield Site
   BA1. . . . . .84 D1
Three Wells Rd BS13 . .78 F4
Thresher Cl BS35 . . . . . . .8 B3
Thrissell St BS5. . . . . . .64 A8
Throgmorton Rd BS4. . .79 F8
Thrubwell La BS40. . . . .94 B4
Thrush Cl **4** BS22. . . .105 E8
Thurlestone BS14. . . . . .80 A6
Thurlow Rd BS5. . . . . . .50 C2
Thurston's Barton BS5. .50 E1
Thyme Cl BS20. . . . . . . .45 F5
Tibberton BS15. . . . . . . .66 A8
Tibbott Rd BS14. . . . . . .80 D5
Tibbott Wlk BS14. . . . . .80 D5
Tiberius Rd BS31. . . . . .81 F7
Tichborne Rd
   Bristol BS5. . . . . .64 C7
   Weston-s-M BS23. . . . .87 C1
TICKENHAM. 58 F4
Tickenham CE Prim Sch
   BS21. . . . . .58 F4
Tickenham Hill BS48. . . .59 E4
Tickenham Rd BS21. . . .58 A4
Tide Gr BS11 . . . . .48 A8
Tidenham Way BS34. . . .23 F1
Tiffany Ct BS1 . . . . . . .143 B1
Tiger Moth Rd BS24. . .105 C5
Tiledown Cl
   Farmborough BA2. . . .116 A5
   Keynsham BS31. . . . . .82 A2
Tilley La BA2 . . . . .116 A5
Tilling Rd BS10 . . . . . . .49 E7
Tilling Wlk BS10. . . . . .49 E7
Tilting Rd BS35. . . . . . . .8 B2
Timber Dene BS16. . . . .50 D4
Timberscombe Wlk
   BS14. . . . . .80 C5
Timbers The BA3. . . . .139 B7
TIMSBURY 116 B1
TIMSBURY BOTTOM. . .116 A1
Timsbury Rd
   Bristol BS3. . . . . .63 E2
   Farmborough BA2. . . .116 B5
   High Littleton BS39 . . .115 D1
Timsbury Village
   Workshops BA2 . . . . .115 F3
Timsbury Wlk BS3 . . . . .63 E2
Timsbury Workshop Est
   BA2. . . . . .115 F3
Tindell Ct **12** BS30 . . . .65 F4
Tinding Dr BS16. . . . . . .50 D8
Tinkers La BS48. . . . . . .76 F2
Tinker's La
   Compton Martin BS40. .129 B7
   Kilmersdon BA11. . . . .140 B1
Tintagel Cl BS31. . . . . .81 D4
Tintern Ave BS5. . . . . . .64 D8
Tintern Cl BS30. . . . . . .65 F6
Tippetts Rd BS15. . . . . .65 D6
Tirley Ho BS34. . . . . . . .23 F1
Tirley Way BS22. . . . . . .88 B2
Titan Barrow BA1. . . . . .86 C2
Titan Rd BS34 . . . . .36 B5
Tiverton Gdns BS22. . . .89 A2
Tiverton Rd **2** BS21. . .57 G1
Tiverton Wlk BS16. . . . .51 A2
Tivoli Ho BS23. . . . . . .104 E8
Tivoli La BS23 . . . . . . .104 E8
Tobias Gdns BS37. . . . .27 D1
TOCKINGTON. 14 C1
Tockington Gn BS32. . . .14 B2
Tockington La BS32. . . .24 A7
Tockington Manor Sch
   BS32. . . . . .14 C2
Tockington Park La
   BS32. . . . . .24 E8
Toddington Cl BS37. . . .39 D8
Tog Hill BS30 . . . . .68 B6
Toghill La BS30 . . . . . . .68 A8
Tolland BS24 . . . . .105 A2
Toll Bridge Rd BA1. . . . .85 E3
Toll Down Way SN14 . . .43 A3
Toll House Ct **5** BS3. . .63 A4
Toll Rd BS23 . . . . .121 F8
Tone Rd BS21. . . . . .57 F1
Top Rd BS25. . . . . .125 F7
Tor Cl BS22. . . . . .89 A2
TORMARTON 41 E2

Tormarton Cres BS10. . .34 F4
Tormarton Intc BS37. . . .41 B1
Tormarton Rd
   Acton Turville GL9 . . . .42 E6
   Marshfield SN14 . . . . . .56 A4
   Marshfield, East End
   SN14. . . . . .70 A8
Tormynton Rd BS22. . . .88 E3
Toronto Rd BS7. . . . . . .50 A8
Torpoint Rd BS3. . . . . . .63 D2
Torrance Cl BS30. . . . . .66 D6
Torridge Rd BS31. . . . . .82 A4
Torrington Ave BS4. . . .79 F8
Torrington Cres BS22 . .89 A3
TORTWORTH. 10 C7
TORTWORTH GREEN. . .10 C5
Tortworth Prim Sch
   GL12. . . . . .10 C7
Tortworth Rd BS7. . . . . .49 E5
Torwood House Sch
   BS6. . . . . .49 A3
Totnes Cl BS22. . . . . . . .89 A2
Totshill Dr BS13. . . . . . .79 E4
Totshill Gr BS13. . . . . . .79 E4
Tottenham Pl BS8. . . . .142 B3
TOTTERDOWN. 64 A4
Totterdown Bridge Ind Est
   BS2. . . . . .64 A4
Totterdown La BS24. . .105 A1
Totterdown Rd BS23 . .104 F4
TOTTEROAK. 28 F5
Touching End La SN14. .69 F8
Tovey Cl BS22. . . . . . . .88 E4
TOWERHEAD. 107 D4
Towerhead Rd BS29. . .107 C5
Tower Hill
   Bristol BS2. . . . . .143 B3
   Locking BS24. . . . . . . .106 D4
Tower House La BS48 . .60 A4
Tower La
   Bristol BS1. . . . . .143 A3
   Bristol, Cadbury Heath
   BS30. . . . . .66 B6
Towerleaze BS9. . . . . . .48 D3
Tower Rd
   Bristol BS15. . . . . .51 C1
   Portishead BS20 . . . . . .45 A4
Tower Rd N BS30. . . . . .66 B7
Tower Rd S BS30. . . . . .66 B5
Tower St BS1 . . . . .143 B2
Tower The
   Bristol BS1. . . . . .143 B2
   Bristol, Redland BS6. . . .49 C3
Tower Wlk BS23. . . . . . .87 D1
Town Barton BA2. . . . .136 F4
Town End BA2. . . . . . .136 F4
Townsend
   Almondsbury BS32. . . . .23 F4
   East Harptree BS40. . . .130 A5
TOWNS END. 132 E4
Townsend Cl BS14. . . . .80 F5
Townsend La BS32. . . . .24 A5
Townsend Rd BS14. . . . .80 F5
Townshend Rd BS22. . . .89 B5
TOWNWELL. 10 B2
Townwell GL12. . . . . . .10 B2
Tozers Hill BS4. . . . . . . .64 C2
Tracy Cl BS14. . . . . .79 F7
Trafalgar Ct
   Weston-s-M BS23 . . . .104 E7
   12 Weston-super-Mare
   BS23. . . . . .104 E7
Trafalgar Rd BA1. . . . . .84 B1
Trafalgar Terr **3** BS3. . .63 B2
Trajectus Way BS31. . . .81 F7
Tralee Wlk BS4 . . . . . . .79 D6
Tramshed The BA1. . . .141 C3
Tramway Rd BS4. . . . . .64 C3
Tranmere Ave BS10. . . .35 A4
Tranmere Gr BS10. . . . .35 A3
Transom Ho BS1 . . . . .143 B2
Tranton La GL13 . . . . . . .2 C4
Tratman Wlk BS10. . . . .34 F3
Travers Cl BS4. . . . . . . .79 D6
Travers Wlk BS34. . . . . .36 F5
Trawden Cl BS32. . . . . .88 A1
Tredegar Rd BS16. . . . . .51 B3
Treefield Pl **5** BS2. . . . .50 A2
Treefield Rd BS21. . . . . .57 F2
Tree Leaze BS37. . . . . . .27 F2
Treetops Cvn Pk BS16 . .51 A8
Tregarth Rd BS3 . . . . . .62 F1
Trelawn Cl BS22. . . . . . .89 D2
Trelawney Ave BS5. . . . .64 D8
Trelawney Pk BS4. . . . . .64 D3
Trelawney Rd BS6. . . . . .49 C1
Trelissick Gdns **3**
   BS22. . . . . .105 F8
Trellick Wlk BS16. . . . . .50 E8
Tremes Cl SN14. . . . . . .69 F8
Tremlett Mews **3**
   BS22. . . . . .89 B4
Trenchard Rd
   Locking BS24. . . . . . . .106 D4
   Saltford BS31. . . . . . . .82 D3
Trenchard St BS1. . . . .142 C3
Trench La BS32. . . . . . . .24 E2
Trendlewood Pk BS16. .50 E5

Trendlewood Way
   BS48. . . . . .60 A1
Trenleigh Dr BS22. . . . .89 A2
Trent Dr BS35. . . . . .15 D7
Trent Gr BS31. . . . . .82 A4
Trentham Cl **7** BS2. . . .50 A2
Trescothick Cl BS31. . . .81 E6
Trescothick Dr BS30. . . .66 D4
Tresham Cl BS32. . . . . .24 D2
Trevanna Rd BS3. . . . . .62 F1
Trevelyan Rd BS23. . . .104 F7
Trevelyan Wlk
   Bristol, Henbury BS10 . . .34 F3
   Bristol, Stoke Gifford
   BS34. . . . . .37 A5
Treverdowe Wlk BS10 . .34 D3
Trevethin Cl BS15. . . . . .65 D7
Trevisa Gr BS10. . . . . . .35 C4
Trewartha Cl BS23. . . .104 F8
Trewartha Pk BS23. . . .104 F8
Trewint Gdns BS4. . . . . .79 F8
Triangle Ct **2** BA2. . . .101 D5
Triangle Ctr The BS21. . .57 F3
Triangle E BA2. . . . . . .101 D5
Triangle N BA2. . . . . . .101 D5
Triangle S BS8. . . . . . .142 B3
Triangle The
   Clevedon BS21. . . . . . . .57 F3
   Paulton BS39. . . . . . . .132 E6
   Portishead BS20 . . . . . .45 B5
   Wrington BS40. . . . . . . .92 D2
Triangle Villas **1** BA2 .101 D5
Triangle W
   Bath BA2. . . . . .101 D5
   Bristol BS8. . . . . .142 B3
Trident Cl BS16. . . . . . . .38 A1
Trim Bridge **3** BA1. . .141 B2
Trim St BA1. . . . . .141 B2
Trinder Rd BS20. . . . . . .47 B4
Trinity CE Prim Sch
   GL9. . . . . .43 A6
Trinity CE VC Prim Sch
   BA3. . . . . .134 A4
Trinity Cl BA1. . . . . . . .141 B2
Trinity Coll BS9. . . . . . .48 E4
Trinity Ct
   5 Bristol BS15. . . . . . .65 E8
   Bristol, Horfield BS7 . . . .49 E5
   Nailsea BS48. . . . . .59 C1
Trinity La BS37. . . . . . . .28 C2
Trinity Mdws BS37. . . . .28 C2
Trinity Mews **15** BS2. .143 C3
Trinity Pl
   3 Bristol BS8. . . . . . .142 A2
   4 Weston-s-M BS23. . .87 C1
Trinity Rd
   Bath BA2. . . . . .102 B2
   Bristol BS2. . . . . .64 A7
   Nailsea BS48. . . . . .59 D1
   Weston-s-M BS23 . . . . .87 C1
Trinity St
   Bath BA1. . . . . .141 B2
   Bristol BS2. . . . . .64 A7
Trinity Wlk
   Bristol BS2. . . . . .143 C3
   Bristol, Newton BS2. . . .64 A7
Trin Mills BS1. . . . . . . .143 A1
Tripps Cnr BS49. . . . . . .91 D7
Tripps Row BS41. . . . . . .62 A1
Trollope's Hill BA2. . . .103 A1
Troon BS37. . . . . .39 E8
Troon Dr BS30. . . . . . . .66 B6
Troopers' Hill Rd BS5. . .65 A7
Trossachs Dr BA2. . . . .102 D8
Trowbridge Rd BS10. . . .35 C1
Trowbridge Wlk BS10. . .35 C1
Trubodys Yd BS30. . . . .66 E7
Trubshaw Cl BS7. . . . . .49 F6
Trumpet La BS5. . . . . . .65 B7
Truro Rd
   Bristol BS3. . . . . .63 B3
   Nailsea BS48. . . . . .60 A1
Trym Bank BS9. . . . . . . .48 D7
Trym Cross Rd BS9. . . . .48 C5
Trymleaze BS9. . . . . . . .48 C5
Trym Rd BS9. . . . . .49 A7
Trym Side BS9. . . . . . . .48 C5
Trymwood Cl BS10. . . . .34 F2
Trymwood Par BS9. . . . .48 D6
T T Trad Est BS37. . . . . .28 C1
Tucker's La BS40. . . . . .128 E8
Tucker St BS2. . . . . . . .143 C3
Tuckett Ho BS16. . . . . . .51 C7
Tuckett La BS16. . . . . . .51 C7
Tucking Mill La BS39 . . .98 E5
Tucking Mill Cotts
   BA2. . . . . .119 D7
Tuckingmill La BS39 . . .98 E5
Tuckmill BS21. . . . . .57 D1
Tudor Cl BS30. . . . . . . .66 C3
Tudor Rd
   Bristol, Hanham BS15. . .65 C5
   Bristol, Lower Easton
   BS5. . . . . .50 C1
   Bristol, St Pauls BS2 . . . .49 F1
   2 Portishead BS20. . . .45 B5
   Weston-s-M BS22. . . . . .89 A4
Tuffley Rd BS10. . . . . . .49 C8
Tufton Ave BS11. . . . . . .48 A8

Tugela Rd BS13. . . . . . .78 F7
Tuggy's La BA2. . . . . . .119 E1
Tunbridge Cl BS40. . . . .96 B2
Tunbridge Rd BS40. . . . .96 B2
Tunbridge Way BS16. . . .52 A8
TUNLEY. 117 B3
Tunley Hill BA2. . . . . . .116 E2
Tunley Rd BA2, BA3. . . .117 D5
Tunnel La BA3 . . . . . . .138 F5
Tunstall Cl BS9. . . . . . . .48 E4
TURLEIGH. 120 F6
Turleigh Hill BA15. . . . .120 F6
Turley Rd BS5. . . . . .50 D1
Turmo Rd BS23. . . . . . .105 B4
Turnberry
   Bristol BS30. . . . . .66 B6
   Yate BS37. . . . . .39 E8
Turnberry Wlk **3** BS4. .64 D1
Turnbridge Cl BS10 . . . .35 D4
Turnbridge Rd BS10. . . .35 C3
Turnbury Ave BS48. . . . .60 A1
Turnbury Cl BS22. . . . . .88 F3
Turner Cl BS31. . . . . . . .82 A5
Turner Ct BS22. . . . . . . .88 F3
Turner Dr BS37. . . . . . . .27 B1
Turner Gdns BS7. . . . . . .50 B6
Turners Ct **8** BS30. . . .65 F4
Turner Way BS21. . . . . .57 D1
Turner Wlk BS30. . . . . . .66 D7
Turnpike Cl BS37. . . . . .27 E2
Turnpike Gate GL12. . . .18 B6
Turnpike Rd
   Cross BS26 . . . . .124 E1
   Shipham BS25 . . . . . .125 E8
Turtlegate Ave BS13. . . .78 E4
Turtlegate Wlk BS13. . . .78 E4
Turville Dr BS7 . . . . .50 A6
Tuscany Ho BS6. . . . . . .49 A3
Tutton Way BS21. . . . . .57 F1
Tuttors Hill BS27. . . . . .126 C1
Tweed Cl BS35. . . . . . . .15 C8
Tweed Rd BS21. . . . . . . .57 E1
Tweed Rd Ind Est **2**
   BS21. . . . . .57 E1
Tweeny La BS30. . . . . . .66 D6
Twelve O'clock La
   BA2 . . . . .100 B3
Twenty Acres Rd BS10. .35 B2
TWERTON. 101 A5
Twerton Farm Cl **2**
   BA2. . . . . .101 B6
Twerton Inf Sch BA2 . . .101 A5
Twickenham Rd BS6. . . .49 C5
Twinhoe La BA2. . . . . . .118 E2
Twinnell Ho **5** BS5. . . .64 A8
Two Acres Cvn Pk BS21. 44 B2
Two Acres Rd BS14. . . . .80 A7
Two Mile Ct BS15 . . . . . .65 C8
TWO MILE HILL. 51 C1
Two Mile Hill Jun & Inf
   Schs BS15. . . . . .65 C8
Twomile Hill Rd BS15 . . .65 B8
Two Stones La BS37. . . .40 C8
Two Trees BS40. . . . . . .127 E8
Twynings The BS15. . . . .51 E2
Tybalt Way BS34. . . . . . .36 E5
Tydeman Rd BS20. . . . . .45 F5
Tyler Cl BS15. . . . . .65 E5
Tyler Gn **2** BS22. . . . . .89 B4
Tylers Farm BS37. . . . . .27 F4
Tyler's La BS16. . . . . . . .51 D5
Tyler St BS2. . . . . .64 A6
Tylers Way BS37. . . . . . .27 F5
Tyndale Ave
   Bristol BS16. . . . . .51 A4
   Yate BS37. . . . . .27 D3
Tyndale Cl GL11. . . . . . . .5 E4
Tyndale Cl **7** BS6. . . . .49 B1
Tyndale Mon The★ GL11. 5 E4
Tyndale Rd BS15. . . . . . .51 E2
Tyndale View BS35. . . . .15 B8
Tyndall Ave BS8. . . . . .142 C4
Tyndall Ho **5** BS2. . . .143 C3
Tyndall Rd BS5. . . . . . . .64 B8
Tyndalls Ct BS8. . . . . . .142 C4
Tyndalls Ho BS8. . . . . .142 C4
TYNDALL'S PARK. 142 C4
Tyndalls Park Mews
   BS2. . . . . .142 C4
Tyndall's Park Rd BS8 142 C4
Tyndalls Way BS10. . . . .49 E8
Tyne Gr BS20 . . . . .45 F6
Tyne Ho **8** BS35. . . . . .15 C8
Tyne Rd BS7. . . . . .49 D3
Tyne St BS2. . . . . .50 A7
TYNING
   Radstock. 134 D3
   Timsbury. 116 A2
Tyning Cl
   Bristol BS14. . . . . .80 A7
   Yate BS37. . . . . .27 E2
Tyning End BA2. . . . . . .102 B5
Tyning Hill BA3. . . . . . .134 B3
Tyning La BA1. . . . . .85 B1
Tyning Pl BA2. . . . . . . .102 C2
Tyning Rd
   Bath BA2. . . . . .102 C2
   Bathampton BA2. . . . . .85 F2

Tyning Rd continued
   Bristol BS3. . . . . .63 F3
   Peasedown St John
   BA2. . . . . .134 D7
   Saltford BS31. . . . . . . .82 E2
   Winsley BA15. . . . . . . .120 E7
Tynings BS39. . . . . .114 D3
Tynings Mews BS23. . .104 E4
Tynings Sch The BS16. . .51 E4
Tynings The
   Clevedon BS21. . . . . . . .57 C1
   Portishead BS20 . . . . . .44 F1
Tynings Way
   Clutton BS39. . . . . . . .114 E3
   Westwood BA15. . . . . .120 F3
Tyning Terr
   14 Bath BA1. . . . . . . .85 A1
   18 Bath BA1. . . . . . . .85 B1
Tyning The
   Bath BA2. . . . . .102 B5
   Freshford BA2. . . . . . .120 B4
Tynte Ave BS13. . . . . . . .79 E3
Tyntesfield BS48. . . . . . .61 A2
Tyntesfield★ BS48 . . . . .60 F4
Tyntesfield Rd BS13. . . .79 A8
Tyrone Wlk BS4. . . . . . .79 E8
Tyrrel Way BS34. . . . . . .36 E5
Tythe Ct SN14. . . . . .70 A8
TYTHERINGTON 16 C5
Tytherington Rd BS35. . .16 A3

U

UBLEY. 111 E1
Ubley CE Prim Sch
   BS40. . . . . .111 D1
Ubley Dro BS40. . . . . . .128 B7
UBLEY SIDELING. 128 D8
UDLEY. 92 C4
Ullswater Cl
   Bristol BS30. . . . . .66 D6
   Weston-s-M BS23 . . . .105 A4
   Yate BS37. . . . . .27 E3
Ullswater Dr BA1. . . . . .85 E3
Ullswater Rd BS10. . . . .35 C1
Uncombe Cl BS48. . . . . .76 D3
Underbanks BS20. . . . . .47 D4
Underdown Ho BS1. . . .143 A1
Underhill Ave BA3. . . . .132 F2
Underhill Dr BS23. . . . .104 D1
Underhill La BA3. . . . . .132 F2
Underhill Rd GL12. . . . .11 A5
Under Knoll BA2. . . . . .134 E8
Underleaf Way BA2. . . .134 D7
Undertown BS40. . . . . .129 A7
Undertown La BS40. . . .129 A7
Under Tree Rd BA2. . . .134 A6
Underwood Ave BS22. . .88 B1
Underwood Cl BS35. . . . .15 A4
Underwood End BS25 .108 A4
Underwood Rd BS20 . . .45 A4
Unicorn Bsns Pk BS4. . .64 D5
Unicorn Pk BS4. . . . . . .64 D5
Union Pas BA1. . . . . . .141 C2
Union Pl BS23. . . . . . . .104 D7
Union Rd **2** BS2. . . . . .64 A6
Union St
   Bath BA1. . . . . .141 C2
   Bristol BS1. . . . . .143 B3
   Nailsea BS48. . . . . .59 C1
   Weston-s-M BS23 . . . .104 D7
Unite Ho BS1 . . . . .142 C2
Unity Ct BS31. . . . . .82 A5
Unity Rd BS31. . . . . . . .82 A6
Unity St
   Bristol BS2. . . . . .143 C3
   Bristol, Brandon Hill
   BS1. . . . . .142 C2
   Bristol, Kingswood BS15 65 C8
University Cl BS9. . . . . .48 F4
University of Bristol
   Dorothy Hodgkin Bldg
   BS1. . . . . .143 A4
University Rd BS8. . . . .142 C3
University Wlk BS8. . . .142 C3
Univ of Bath BA2. . . . .102 E5
Univ of Bristol BS8. . . .142 C3
Univ of Bristol Botanic
   Gdns★ BS9. . . . . .48 F4
Univ of Bristol Langford
   House Sch of Veterinary
   Science BS40 . . . . . . .109 B6
Univ of the West of
   England BS3 . . . . .62 E4
Univ of the West of
   England Faculty of
   Health & Social Care
   BS16. . . . . .50 E5
Univ of the West of
   England Frenchay
   Campus BS16 . . . . . . .36 E1
Univ of the West of
   England, St Matthias
   Campus BS16 . . . . . . .51 C4
UPHILL. 104 C2
Uphill Ct BS23. . . . . . .104 D2
Uphill Dr BA1. . . . . .85 B2

Uphill Farm Cvn Pk
  BS23. . . . . .104 E1
Uphill Prim Sch BS23 .104 D2
Uphill Rd BS7. . . . . 49 F5
Uphill Rd N BS23. . . . . .104 D4
Uphill Rd S BS23. . . . . .104 D2
Uphill Way BS23 . . . . . .104 D1
Upjohn Cres BS13. . . . . .79 D3
Uplands Cl BA2. . . . . . .119 F7
Uplands Dr BS31. . . . . . 82 F2
Uplands La BS31. . . . . . 81 F1
Uplands Rd
  Bristol BS16. . . . . .51 D3
  Saltford BS31. . . . . 82 F2
Uplands The BS48. . . . . 75 C8
Upper Bath Rd BS35. . . . 15 B8
Upper Belgrave Rd BS8 49 A2
Upper Belmont Rd BS7. 49 E3
Upper Berkeley Pl
  BS8. . . . . .142 B3
Upper Bloomfield Rd
  BA2 . . . . .101 D1
Upper Borough Walls
  BA1 . . . . .141 C2
Upper Bristol Rd
  Bath BA1 . . . . .101 D7
  Clutton BS39. . . . . . . .114 D3
  Weston-s-M BS22 . . . . .88 B1
Upper Byron Pl BS8. . .142 B3
Upper Camden Pl BA1 141 C4
UPPER CANADA. 106 A1
Upper Chapel La BS36. 38 C7
Upper Cheltenham Pl
  BS6. . . . . .49 E1
Upper Church La
  Bristol BS2 . . . . .142 C3
  Hutton BS24. . . . . . . .105 D2
Upper Church Rd BS23 .87 D1
Upper Church St BA1 .141 B1
Upper Conham Vale
  BS15. . . . . 65 A5
Upper Cranbrook Rd
  BS6. . . . . .49 B4
Upper East Hayes BA1. 85 B1
UPPER EASTON. 64 B8
UPPER EASTVILLE 50 E3
Upper Farm Cl BA2 . .136 F4
Upper Furlong BA2 . . .116 B3
Upper Green La BS40 .111 B7
Upper Hedgemead Rd
  BA1 . . . . .141 B4
UPPER HILL. 2 E5
Upper Horfield Prim Sch
  BS7. . . . . .50 A8
Upper Kewstoke Rd
  BS23. . . . . 87 B1
UPPER KILCOTT 20 C5
UPPER KNOWLE 64 B2
Upper Lambridge St
  BA1. . . . . .85 C2
UPPER LANGFORD. . . .109 C3
UPPER LANGRIDGE . . . 84 B7
Upper Lansdown Mews
  BA1 . . . . 84 F1
UPPER LITTLETON 95 C6
Upper Maudlin St BA3 143 A3
Upper Merryfield BA3 139 E1
UPPER MORTON 8 E4
Upper Mount Pleasant
  BA2. . . . . 120 A4
Upper Myrtle Hill BS20 47 C4
Upper New Rd BS27. . .126 A1
Upper Oldfield Pk
  BA2. . . . . 141 A4
Upper Perry Hill BS3. . 63 C4
Upper Pitching BA3. . .138 D5
UPPER RADFORD
  133 B8
  Withy Mills BS39 . . . . .133 B7
Upper Rd BS39. . . . . . .130 E6
Upper Sandhurst Rd
  BS4. . . . . .64 D4
UPPER SOUNDWELL . . 51 D3
Upper St
  Bristol BS4. . . . . .64 A4
  Dyrham SN14. . . . . 54 D4
Upper Stanton BS39. . . 97 A2
UPPER STANTON
  DREW 97 B2
Upper Station Rd BS16 51 D4
Upper Stone Cl BS36. . 38 C7
Upper Strode BS40. . . .111 F7
UPPER SWAINSWICK. . . 85 B5
Upper Sydney St BS3. . 63 B3
Upper Terr BS11 . . . . . . 34 B1
Upper Tockington Rd
  BS32. . . . . 14 A2
Upper Town La BS40 . . 94 C8
Upper Wells St BS1 . .142 C3
UPPER WESTON. 84 A3
UPPER WESTWOOD. . .120 E4
UPPER WICK. 5 A6
UPPER WRAXALL 56 C2
Upper York St BS2 . . .143 B4
Upton BS24. . . . . .105 A2
UPTON CHEYNEY 83 B8
Upton Cotts BS41. . . . . 95 F8
Upton La BS41. . . . . 96 A8
Upton Rd BS3. . . . . 63 B4

Urchinwood La BS49 . . . 91 F4
Urfords Dr ⬛ BS16. . . . .51 C6
Usk Ct ⬛ BS35. . . . . . . .15 C8

V

Valda Rd BS22 . . . . .88 C2
Vale Cres BS22. . . . . 89 C2
Vale Ct BS8. . . . . .142 A4
Vale End BS48. . . . . .59 D1
Vale Foundry La BS3 . . 62 F2
Vale La BS3. . . . . .79 C8
Vale Mill Way BS24. . . .105 F8
Valentine Cl BS14. . . . . 80 B5
Vale Orch GL13 . . . . 3 F3
Valerian Cl BS11 . . . . . . 47 F6
Valerian St BS16. . . . . . .38 D1
Vale St BS4. . . . . 64 A4
Vale The BS16. . . . . .52 F6
Valetta Cl BS23. . . . . . .104 F3
Vale View BA3 . . . . .134 A2
Vale View Pl ⬛ BA1 . . . . 85 B1
Vale View Terr BA1 . . . . 85 F3
Valley Cl ⬛ BS48. . . . . . 59 E2
Valley Ct BS20 . . . . 44 E3
Valley Gdns
  Bristol BS16. . . . . .51 F8
  Nailsea BS48. . . . . 59 E2
Valley Rd
  Bristol, Bedminster Down
    BS13. . . . . 79 A8
  Bristol, Mangotsfield
    BS16. . . . . .52 A5
  Bristol, Warmley BS30. . 66 D6
  Clevedon BS21. . . . . . . .57 H5
  Leigh Woods BS8. . . . . .62 C7
  Portishead BS20. . . . . . 45 A2
Valley View
  Chilcompton BA3 . . . . .138 D3
  Clutton BS39. . . . . . . .114 E3
Valley View Cl BA1 . . . . 85 B3
Valley View Rd
  Bath BA1 . . . . 85 C3
  Paulton BS39 . . . . .132 E6
Valley Way Rd BS48. . . .59 E3
Valley Wlk BA3 . . . . . . .133 B2
Valls The BS32 . . . . .36 F6
Valma Rocks BS5. . . . . . 65 A6
Vanbrugh La BS16 . . . . .50 E7
Van Diemen's La BA1 . . 84 F2
Vandyck Ave BS31. . . . . 81 F6
Vane St BA2 . . . . .102 B7
Vantage Office Pk
  BS34. . . . . 37 A6
Varsity Way BS24 . . . .106 B6
Vassall Ct BS16. . . . . . . 51 B5
Vassall Rd BS16. . . . . . . 51 B5
Vattingstone Ho BS35 . 14 F5
Vattingstone La BS35. . 14 F5
Vaughan Cl BS10. . . . . . 34 F3
Vauxhall Terr ⬛ BS3 . . 63 A4
Vayre Cl BS37. . . . . .28 C1
Veale The BS24 . . . . . . .122 C6
Vellore La BA2. . . . . . . .102 C7
Velvet Bottom BS40. . .127 E3
Venns Gate BS27. . . . . .126 A1
Ventnor Ave ⬛ BS5 . . . 64 F8
Ventnor Rd
  Bristol, Filton BS34 . . . .36 B3
  Bristol, St George BS5. . .50 D1
Venton Ct ⬛ BS15 . . . . 65 B5
Venture The BS4 . . . . . . 63 E1
Venue The BS10. . . . . . . 35 C6
Venus La BS39. . . . . . . .114 E3
Venus St BS49 . . . . 91 E2
Vera Rd BS16. . . . . 50 F2
Verbena Way BS22. . . . . 89 A1
Vereland Rd BS24. . . . .105 E3
Vernals La GL12. . . . . . .11 C8
Vernham Gr BA2. . . . . .101 C1
Vernhamwood Cl BA2 101 C1
Vernon Cl BS31. . . . . . . .82 D3
Vernon La BS26. . . . . . .124 B3
Vernon Pk BA2 . . . . . . .101 C6
Vernon St ⬛ BS2 . . . . . 63 F4
Vernon Terr BA2 . . . . . .101 C6
Verrier Rd BS5. . . . . 64 C7
Verwood Dr BS30 . . . . . 66 C2
Vian End BS37 . . . . 88 F4
Via Traversus BS31. . . . 81 F7
Viburnum Rd BS32. . . . . 24 D5
Vicarage Cl BS22. . . . . . 89 A3
Vicarage Cotts ⬛ BS16 51 D5
Vicarage Ct
  Bristol, Jefferies Hill
    BS15. . . . . 65 B5
  ⬛ Bristol, Russell Town
    BS5. . . . . .64 C7
Vicarage Gdns BA2. . . .134 B7
Vicarage La
  Barrow Gurney BS48. . . .77 C6
  Compton Bishop BS26 . .124 A3
  Compton Dando BS39. . . 98 D6
  Hillesley GL12 . . . . .19 D8
  Norton St Philip BA2 . . .136 E4

Vicarage La continued
  Olveston BS35 . . . . 14 B3
Vicarage Rd
  Bristol, Bishopsworth
    BS13. . . . . .79 A6
  Bristol, Hanham BS15 . . .65 B5
  Bristol, Moorfields BS5 . .64 C8
  Bristol, Southville BS3. . .63 B4
  Frampton Cotterell BS36 38 C6
  Leigh Woods BS8. . . . . .62 D6
  Pilning BS35. . . . . .22 C7
Vicars Cl BS16. . . . . 51 B4
Victor Ho BS34. . . . . 36 C7
Victoria Art Gall The★
  BA2. . . . . .141 C2
Victoria Ave BS5. . . . . . 64 C7
Victoria Bldgs BA2. . . .101 D6
Victoria Bridge Ct
  BA1 . . . . .141 A3
Victoria Bridge Rd BA1,
  BA2. . . . . .141 A2
Victoria Cl
  Bath BA2 . . . . .101 C5
  Portishead BS20 . . . . . .45 D5
  Thornbury BS35. . . . . . . 8 B3
Victoria Cotts BA2 . . . .118 F7
Victoria Cres BS35 . . . . 22 A6
Victoria Ct
  ⬛ Bristol, Cotham BS6. .49 D1
  Bristol, Redland BS6 . . . 49 A3
  Clevedon BS21. . . . . . . .57 E3
  Portishead BS20. . . . . . 45 D5
Victoria Gdns
  Batheaston BA1. . . . . . . 85 F3
  ⬛ Bristol BS6. . . . . . . .49 D1
Victoria Gr BS3 . . . . 63 E4
Victoria Ho
  Bath BA1 . . . . .101 D8
  Keynsham BS31. . . . . . . 81 F4
Victoria Jubilee Homes
  BS40. . . . . .109 C6
Victoria Lodge BS22. . . .88 E2
Victoria Par BS5 . . . . . . 64 C8
VICTORIA PARK. 142 B3
Victoria Park Bsns Ctr
  BA1. . . . . .101 D7
Victoria Park Com Inf Sch
  BS3. . . . . 63 E3
Victoria Park Com Jun Sch
  BS3. . . . . 63 E3
Victoria Park Ct BS3 . . 63 F3
Victoria Pk
  Bristol, Fishponds BS16. .51 A5
  Bristol, Kingswood BS15 51 D1
  Weston-s-M BS23 . . . . . 87 D1
Victoria Pl
  Bath, Combe Down
    BA2. . . . . 102 C1
  ⬛ Bath, Lambridge BA1 85 C1
  Bristol BS3. . . . . .63 C3
  Paulton BS39 . . . . .132 D5
  Weston-s-M BS23 . . . . .104 D8
Victoria Quadrant
  BS23. . . . . .104 E8
Victoria Rd
  Avonmouth BS11 . . . . . . 47 B7
  ⬛ Bath BA2 . . . . .101 D6
  Bristol, Hanham BS15 . . .65 C5
  Bristol, St Philip's Marsh
    BS2. . . . . .64 A5
  Bristol, Warmley BS30. . .66 D5
  Clevedon BS21. . . . . . . .57 E2
  Saltford BS31. . . . . 82 D3
Victoria Rooms★ BS8 .142 B3
Victoria Sq
  Bristol BS8. . . . . .142 A3
  Portishead BS20 . . . . . .45 D5
  Weston-s-M BS23 . . . . .104 D7
Victoria St
  Bristol BS1. . . . . .143 B2
  Bristol, Staple Hill BS16 .51 D5
Victoria Terr
  Bath BA2 . . . . .101 D6
  ⬛ Bristol, Clifton BS8. . .62 F6
  Bristol, St Philip's Marsh
    BS2. . . . . .64 B5
  Paulton BS39 . . . . .132 E6
Victoria Wlk BS6. . . . . . 49 D1
Victor Rd BS3. . . . . 63 C3
Victor St
  ⬛ Bristol, Russell Town
    BS5. . . . . .64 B6
  Bristol, St Philip's Marsh
    BS2. . . . . .64 A4
Vigor Rd BS13 . . . . 79 B5
Village Cl BS37 . . . . 27 D1
Village Farm BS35 . . . . 14 A6
Village Rd BA2. . . . . . . .100 C6
Village The BS16. . . . . . .52 C7
Villa Rosa ⬛ BS23 . . . . 87 C1
Villice La BS40. . . . . . . .129 A7
Villiers Rd BS5. . . . . 50 B1
Vilner La BS35. . . . . .15 B7
Vimpany Cl BS10. . . . . . 34 F3
Vimpennys La BS35 . . . 22 E1
Vincent Cl BS11. . . . . . . 34 C2
Vincent Ct ⬛ BS16. . . . .51 D3
Vine Gdns BS22 . . . . 89 A2
Viner's La GL9 . . . . 43 B5

Vinery The BS25. . . . . . .125 A7
Vineyard La GL12 . . . . . 11 F5
Vineyards BA1. . . . . . . .141 C3
Vining Wlk ⬛ BS5 . . . . 64 B8
VINNEY GREEN 52 A7
Vinney La BS37 . . . . 28 F8
Vinny Ave BS16 . . . . 52 A7
Vintery Leys BS9. . . . . . 49 B7
Viola Way BS16 . . . . 52 D7
Virginia Cl BS37. . . . . . . 28 A1
Vivian St BS3. . . . . 63 D3
Vivien Ave BA3. . . . . . . .133 A2
Vowell Cl BS13. . . . . 79 B4
Vowles Cl BS48. . . . . 60 A3
Voyager Cl BS34 . . . . . . 37 A4
Vulcan Ho BA2. . . . . . . .141 C2
Vynes Cl BS48 . . . . 60 A1
Vynes Ind Est BS48. . . . 60 A3
Vynes Way BS48. . . . . . . 60 A1
Vyvyan Rd BS8. . . . . . . .142 A3
Vyvyan Terr BS8. . . . . .142 A3

W

Wadehurst Ind Pk BS2 .64 A7
Wade Rd BS37. . . . . .27 A3
Wades Rd BS34. . . . . 36 B3
Wade St BS2. . . . . .143 C3
Wadham Dr BS16 . . . . . .37 B1
Wadham Gr BS16. . . . . . 52 B5
Wadham St BS23. . . . . .104 D8
Wagtail Gdns BS22. . . .105 E8
Wainblade Ct ⬛ BS37. . 27 F5
Wainbridge Cres BS35. .22 D7
Wainbrook Dr BS5 . . . . .50 D2
Wains Cl ⬛ BS21. . . . . . 57 E2
Wainwright Cl ⬛ BS22 .89 B4
Waits Cl BS29. . . . . .106 F3
Wakedean Gdns BS49 . .74 A1
Wakeford Rd ⬛ BS16. . .52 A7
Wakeford Way BS30. . . .66 D7
Wakehurst Gdns
  BS24. . . . . .105 E7
Walcot Bldgs
  Bath BA1 . . . . .102 B8
  Bath BA1 . . . . .141 C4
  ⬛ Bathwick BA2 . . . . .102 B8
Walcot Gate BA1. . . . . .141 C4
Walcot Ho BA1 . . . . . . .141 C4
Walcot Par BA1. . . . . . .141 C4
Walcot St BA1. . . . . . . .141 C3
Walcot Terr BA1 . . . . . .141 C4
Waldegrave Rd BA1. . . . 84 E1
Waldegrave Terr BA3. .134 A3
Walden Rd BS31. . . . . . . 82 A4
Walford Ave BS22. . . . . 89 C3
Waling La BA2 . . . . .100 D6
Walker Cl
  Bristol, Downend BS16 . .52 A7
  Bristol, Upper Easton
    BS5. . . . . .64 B8
Walker Ct BS16 . . . . 51 F5
Walkers Dr BS24. . . . . .105 F7
Walker St BS2. . . . . . . .142 C4
Walker Way BS35. . . . . . 15 B7
Walk Mill La GL12 . . . . . 11 F4
Walk The GL12 . . . . .11 F5
WALLACE 129 E3
Wallace La BS40 . . . . . .129 E3
Wallace Rd BA1. . . . . . . 85 B1
Wallcroft Ho BS6. . . . . . 49 A3
Wallenge Cl BS39 . . . . .132 F6
Wallenge Dr BS39. . . . .132 F6
Waller Gdns BA1. . . . . . . 84 E4
Walley La BS40 . . . . . . .113 B7
Wallflower Cl BS16. . . . .52 D7
Wall Gn BS26 . . . . .125 C1
Wallingford Rd BS4 . . . .79 D7
Walliscote Ave BS9 . . . . 49 C6
Walliscote Grove Rd ⬛
  BS23. . . . . .104 E7
Walliscote Prim Sch
  BS23. . . . . .104 E7
Walliscote Rd
  Bristol BS9. . . . . .49 C6
  Weston-s-M BS23 . . . . .104 D6
Walliscote Rd S BS23. .104 D4
Wallis Est BS2. . . . . 49 F3
WALL MEAD 116 C4
Wallscourt Rd BS34 . . . .36 B2
Wallscourt Rd S BS34 . .36 B1
Wallsend La SN14. . . . . 55 C5
Wallshut Wood BS7 . . . .50 C8
Wally Court Rd BS40. . .112 E8
Walmsley Terr ⬛ BA1 . . 85 B1
Walnut Ave BS37. . . . . . 28 D1
Walnut Bldgs BA3. . . . .134 A3
Walnut Cl
  Axbridge BS26 . . . . . . .125 B1
  Bristol BS15. . . . . .51 F1
  Easton-in-G BS20. . . . . .47 A3
  Frampton Cotterell BS36 38 C6
  Keynsham BS31. . . . . . . 81 C4
  Nailsea BS48. . . . . 75 E8
  Thornbury BS35. . . . . . . 8 D1
  Weston-s-M BS24 . . . . .105 B2
Walnut Cres BS15. . . . . 65 F8

Walnut Dr
  Bath BA2 . . . . .101 E4
  Colerne SN14. . . . . .70 F6
Walnut La BS15. . . . . . . .66 A8
Walnut Tree Cl
  Almondsbury BS32. . . . .24 A5
  Ubley BS40. . . . . .111 D1
Walnut Tree Ct BS49. . . 91 D4
Walnut Way ⬛ BS16 . . .52 C7
Walnut Wlk
  Bristol BS13. . . . . .79 A6
  Keynsham BS31. . . . . . . 81 C4
Walsh Ave BS14. . . . . . . 80 A7
Walsh Cl BS24. . . . . . . .105 B2
Walshe Ave BS37. . . . . . 28 C1
Walsingham Rd BS6. . . . 49 E2
Walter Rd BS36. . . . . . . .38 B6
Walter St BS3. . . . . 63 A4
Waltham End BS24. . . . .106 A8
Walton BS24. . . . . .105 A2
Walton Ave BS4. . . . . . . 64 D5
Walton Bay House Park
  Homes BS21. . . . . .44 B1
Walton Cl
  Bristol BS30. . . . . .66 C1
  Keynsham BS31. . . . . . . 81 D4
Walton Cres BS40. . . . . .94 F8
Walton Cross BS21. . . . . 58 B7
Walton Heath BS37 . . . . 27 F1
WALTON IN GORDANO. . 58 B7
Walton Rd
  Bristol BS11. . . . . .47 D6
  Clevedon BS21. . . . . . . .57 H4
Walton Rise BS9 . . . . . . 49 A7
WALTON ST MARY 57 G5
Walton St
  Bristol BS5. . . . . .50 B1
  Portishead BS21. . . . . . 44 A1
  Walton in G BS21. . . . . .58 A8
Walwyn Cl BA2 . . . . . . .101 A6
Walwyn Gdns BS13. . . . .79 C3
Wansbeck Rd BS31. . . . . 82 A4
Wansbrough Rd BS22 . . 89 B4
Wanscow Wlk BS9 . . . . . 49 B6
Wansdyke Bsns Ctr
  BA2. . . . . .101 D4
Wansdyke Ct BS14. . . . . 80 B5
Wansdyke Prim Sch
  BS14. . . . . 79 F4
Wansdyke Rd BA2. . . . .101 D1
Wansdyke Way BS14 . . .80 D3
Wansdyke Workshops
  Keynsham BS31. . . . . . . 82 A6
  Peasedown St John
    BA2. . . . . .134 D6
WAPLEY 39 E4
Wapley Hill BS37. . . . . . 39 E4
Wapley Rank BS37 . . . . .39 D5
Wapley Rd BS37. . . . . . . 40 B3
Wapping Rd BS1. . . . . .143 A1
Warbler Cl ⬛ BA3 . . . .139 B8
Warden Rd BS3. . . . . 63 C4
Wardour Rd BS4 . . . . . . .79 D8
Ware Ct BS36. . . . . 37 D5
Wareham Cl BS48. . . . . . 59 D1
Warend Hall GL11 . . . . . 5 F6
Waring Ho BS1. . . . . . . .143 A1
WARLEIGH 103 C6
Warleigh Dr BA1. . . . . . . 86 A3
Warleigh La BA1. . . . . . .103 C5
Warleigh Manor BA1. . .103 C6
Warleys La BS24. . . . . . . 89 C1
Warman Cl BS14. . . . . . . 80 F6
Warman Rd BS14 . . . . . . 80 F6
Warmington Rd BS14. . . 80 C8
Warminster Rd
  Bristol BS2. . . . . .50 A2
  Claverton BA2, BA3. . . .103 B5
WARMLEY 66 B7
WARMLEY HILL 65 E8
Warmley Park Sch
  BS30. . . . . 66 B7
WARMLEY TOWER 66 B6
Warne Pk BS23 . . . . . . .105 A6
Warner Cl
  Bristol BS15. . . . . .65 F6
  Cleeve BS49. . . . . .92 A7
Warne Rd BS23 . . . . . . .105 A6
Warns The BS30. . . . . . . 66 A4
Warren Cl
  Bristol BS32. . . . . .24 D3
  Hutton BS24. . . . . .105 D2
Warren Croft GL11. . . . . 5 E4
Warren Gdns BS14. . . . . 80 F5
Warren La BS41. . . . . . . .77 E8
Warren Rd BS34 . . . . . . .36 B3
Warren's Cl BS27 . . . . .126 B1
Warrens Hill BS27. . . . .126 B1
Warrens Hill Rd
  BS27. . . . . .126 D4
Warren Way BS37. . . . . .27 E3
Warrilow Cl BS22 . . . . . .89 B5
Warrington Rd BS4 . . . . 64 D2
Warry Cl BS48. . . . . 60 B2
Warth La BS22. . . . . .89 A8
Warwick Ave ⬛ BS5 . . . 50 B1

Warwick Cl
Bristol BS30 . . . . 66 B2
Weston-s-M BS22 . . . . . 105 C8
Warwick Gdns BS39 . . . . 114 D3
Warwick Pl BS35 . . . . 8 A1
Warwick Rd
[3] Bath BA1 . . . . 101 B7
Bristol, Baptist Mills BS5 50 B1
Bristol, Redland BS6 . . . 49 B1
Keynsham BS31 . . . . 81 D4
Washingpool Hill BS35 . 14 E1
Washingpool Hill Rd
BS32 . . . . 14 D2
Washingpool La BS11 . 33 F7
Washing Pound La
Bristol BS14 . . . . 80 B4
Nailsea BS48 . . . . 59 B4
Washington Ave BS5 . . 50 C1
Washpool La BA2 . . . . . . 100 F2
Watch Elm Cl BS32 . . . . . 36 E6
Watch House Pl BS20 . . 45 E7
Watch House Rd BS20 . . 47 D4
Watchill Ave BS13 . . . . . . 78 F6
Watchill Cl BS13 . . . . 78 F6
Watcombe Cl BS22 . . . . . 88 E1
Waterbridge Rd BS13 . . 78 F4
Watercress Cl BS48 . . . 60 B2
Watercress Rd BS2 . . . . . 49 F3
Waterdale Cl BS9 . . . . . . 49 C7
Waterdale Gdns BS9 . . . 49 C7
Waterford Cl BS35 . . . . . 15 D8
Waterford Pk BA3 . . . . . . 133 E1
Waterford Rd BS9 . . . . . . 49 B6
Waterfront Ho BA2 . . . . 141 B1
Waterhouse La BA2 . . . 119 F8
Water La
Bristol BS1 . . . . 143 B2
Bristol, Hanham Green
BS15 . . . . 65 B2
Bristol, Upper Knowle
BS4 . . . . 64 D2
Bristol, Windmill Hill BS3 . 63 F3
Paulton BA3, BS39 . . . . 133 A4
Pill BS20 . . . . 47 C4
Waterloo Bldgs [4] 101 B6
Waterloo Ho BS20 . . . . 47 D5
Waterloo Pl [19] BS2 . . 143 C3
Waterloo Rd
Bristol BS2 . . . . 143 C3
Radstock BA3 . . . . 134 A2
Waterloo St
Bristol BS2 . . . . 143 C3
[10] Bristol, Clifton BS8 . . 62 F7
Weston-s-M BS23 . . . . . 104 E8
Watermead Cl [13] BA1 . 141 B2
Watermill Cl GL12 . . . . . . 9 E7
Watermore Cl BS36 . . . . 38 C7
Watermore Gdns BS36 . 38 C8
Watermore Prim Sch
BS36 . . . . 38 C8
Waters Edge BS20 . . . . . 45 E7
Watershed Media Ctr★
BS1 . . . . 143 A3
WATERSIDE 133 E1
Waterside Cres BA3 . . . 133 D1
Waterside Dr BS32 . . . . 24 A1
Waterside La BS3 . . . . . . 140 A6
Waterside Pk BS20 . . . . 44 D4
Waterside Rd BA3 . . . . . 133 D1
Waterside Way BA3 . . . 139 D8
Water's La BS9 . . . . 49 A7
Waters Rd BS15 . . . . 65 C8
Water St BS40 . . . . 129 F4
Watery La
Bath BA2 . . . . 101 A6
Doynton BS30 . . . . 68 A8
Marshfield SN14 . . . . 69 F6
Nailsea BS48 . . . . 59 B2
Stratton-on-t-F BA3 . . . 139 A3
Winford BS40 . . . . 95 B4
Wathen Rd BS6 . . . . 49 F3
Watkins Yd BS9 . . . . 49 A8
WATLEY'S END 37 F7
Watley's End Rd BS36 . 37 F7
Watling Way BS11 . . . . . . 47 D7
Watson Ave BS4 . . . . 64 D4
Watson's Rd BS30 . . . . . 65 F3
Watters Cl BS36 . . . . 38 D6
Wavell Cl BS37 . . . . 27 D3
Waveney Rd BS31 . . . . . 82 A3
Wavering Down Rise
BS26 . . . . 125 A3
Waverley Ho BS1 . . . . . 142 C1
Waverley Rd
Backwell BS48 . . . . 76 A7
Bristol, Cotham BS6 . . . 49 C1
Bristol, Shirehampton
BS11 . . . . 47 E6
Weston-s-M BS23 . . . . 104 F4
Yate BS37 . . . . 27 B2
Waverley St [9] BS5 . . . 50 A1
Waverly Ct BS49 . . . . . . 91 C8
Wayacre Dro BS24 . . . 121 E6
Waycroft Prim Sch
BS14 . . . . 80 E5

Wayfarer Cl BS23 . . . . . 105 B4
Wayfarer Rd BS10 . . . . . 35 B6
Wayfield Gdns BA1 . . . . 85 F4
Wayford Cl BS31 . . . . . . 82 A3
Wayland Ct [7] BS16 . . . 51 A4
Wayland Rd BS22 . . . . . . 88 E3
Wayleaze
Frampton Cotterell
BS36 . . . . 38 D7
Wapley BS37 . . . . 39 F3
Wayside BS22 . . . . 88 D2
Wayside Cl BS36 . . . . . . 38 B7
Wayside Dr BS21 . . . . . . 57 G5
WAY WICK 89 E1
WCA Ho BS1 . . . . 143 A2
Weal Terr BA1 . . . . 84 B2
Weal The BA1 . . . . 84 C2
Weare Ct BS1 . . . . 142 A1
We are Curious★ BS1 142 C2
Weatherly Dr BS20 . . . . 44 F3
Weatherly Ave BA2 . . . 101 D2
Weavers Cl GL12 . . . . . . 11 F4
Weavers La BS37 . . . . . . 27 B6
Weavers Orch BA2 . . . . 118 D1
Weavers Way BS37 . . . . 28 B2
Webb Cres BS37 . . . . 27 E5
WEBBINGTON 123 E4
Webbington Rd BS26 . . 124 C3
Webbs Heath BS30 . . . . 66 E8
WEBB'S HEATH 66 E8
Webbs Mead BS40 . . . . 112 D8
Webb St BS5 . . . . 64 A8
Webbs Wood BS32 . . . . 36 F7
Webbs Wood Rd BS32 . . 36 F7
Wedgewood Rd BS16 . . 37 D1
Wedgwood Cl BS14 . . . 80 B5
Wedgwood Rd BA2 . . . 101 A5
Wedlock Way BS3 . . . . . . 62 F3
Wedmore Cl
Bath BA2 . . . . 101 A3
Bristol BS15 . . . . 65 F7
Weston-s-M BS23 . . . . . 104 F2
Wedmore Pk BA2 . . . . . 101 A3
Wedmore Rd
Clevedon BS21 . . . . 57 D1
Nailsea BS48 . . . . 75 E8
Saltford BS31 . . . . 82 D4
Wedmore Vale BS3 . . . . 63 E2
Weedon Cl [6] BS2 . . . . 50 A2
Weekesley La BA2 . . . . 116 D1
Weetwood Rd BS49 . . . 91 E5
Weight Rd [2] BS5 . . . . . 64 C7
Weind The BS22 . . . . 88 D2
Weir La
Abbots Leigh BS8 . . . . . 61 F5
Marshfield SN14 . . . . . . 69 F8
Weir Rd BS49 . . . . 91 E3
Welland Rd BS31 . . . . . . 81 F4
Wellard Cl [1] BS22 . . . 89 B4
Well Cl
Long Ashton BS41 . . . . . 62 B1
Weston-s-M BS24 . . . . . 105 B2
Winscombe BS25 . . . . . . 125 A8
Wellesley Prim Sch
BS37 . . . . 39 D6
Wellgarth Ct BS4 . . . . . . 64 A2
Wellgarth Rd BS4 . . . . . 64 A2
Wellgarth Wlk BS4 . . . . 64 A2
Well House Cl BS9 . . . . . 48 E3
Wellington Ave BS6 . . . 49 E1
Wellington Bldgs BA1 . . 84 B2
Wellington Cres BS7 . . 49 E6
Wellington Ct
[11] Bristol BS6 . . . . 49 E1
Clevedon BS21 . . . . 57 E5
Wellington Dr
Bristol BS9 . . . . 49 D6
Yate BS37 . . . . 27 B2
Wellington Hill BS7 . . . 49 E4
Wellington Hill W BS9 . . 49 D7
Wellington La BS6 . . . . . 49 E1
Wellington Mews BS11 47 D5
Wellington Pk BS8 . . . . 49 A2
Wellington Pl
Bristol BS16 . . . . 37 B1
Weston-s-M BS23 . . . . . 104 D7
Wellington Rd
Bristol BS2 . . . . 143 C4
Bristol, Kingswood BS15 51 D2
Yate BS37 . . . . 27 E3
Wellington Terr
[20] Bristol BS8 . . . . . . 62 F6
Clevedon BS21 . . . . 57 F5
Wellington Wlk BS10 . . 49 C7
Well La
Badminton GL9 . . . . 30 E5
Banwell BS29 . . . . 106 E3
Yatton BS49 . . . . 91 C8
WELLOW 118 D1
Wellow Brook Cl BA3 . 133 B3
Wellow Brook Mdw
BA3 . . . . 133 B2
Wellow La
Hinton Charterhouse
BA2 . . . . 119 D1
Norton St Philip BA2 . . 136 D5
Peasedown St John
BA2 . . . . 134 C6
Shoscombe BA2 . . . . . . 134 E6

Wellow Mead BA2 . . . . 134 B7
Wellow Rd BA2 . . . . 135 B8
Wellow Tyning BA2 . . . 134 D7
Well Pk BS49 . . . . 91 E4
Wells Cl
Bristol BS14 . . . . 80 C5
Nailsea BS48 . . . . 60 B1
Wellsea Gr BS23 . . . . . . 105 B7
Wells Rd
Bath BA2 . . . . 141 B1
Bristol, Hengrove BS14 . . 80 C7
Bristol, Upper Knowle
BS4 . . . . 64 B2
Chilcompton BA3 . . . . . 138 F4
Clevedon BS21 . . . . 57 F1
Corston BA2 . . . . 100 B7
Dundry BS40, BS41 . . . 95 F7
Hallatrow BS39 . . . . 132 B7
Norton St Philip BA2,
BA3 . . . . 136 C3
Radstock BA3 . . . . 133 E2
Wells Sq BA3 . . . . 133 D1
Wells St BS3 . . . . 63 A4
Wellstead Ave BS37 . . . 27 D1
Wellsway BA2 . . . . 101 F3
Wellsway Cl BA2 . . . . . 101 D1
Wellsway Pk BA2 . . . . . 118 D8
Wellsway Rd BS31 . . . . 81 F3
Wellsway Sch BS31 . . . 82 A5
Well The BS9 . . . . 48 E3
Welsford Ave BS16 . . . 50 D4
Welsford Rd BS16 . . . . . 50 C4
Welsh Back BS1 . . . . 143 A2
WELTON 133 B2
Welton Gr BA3 . . . . 133 B3
WELTON HOLLOW 133 D2
Welton Prim Sch BA3 . 133 C2
Welton Rd BA3 . . . . 133 E2
Welton Vale BA3 . . . . . . 133 B2
Welton Wlk BS15 . . . . . 51 C2
Wemberham Cres BS49 74 A1
Wemberham La BS49 . . 90 E8
Wenmore Cl BS16 . . . . . 37 D1
Wentforth Dr [2] BS15 . 51 C2
Wentwood Dr BS24 . . . 105 A1
Wentworth
Bristol BS30 . . . . 66 A6
Yate BS37 . . . . 27 E1
Wentworth Cl BS22 . . . 89 A3
Wentworth Rd BS7 . . . . 49 D3
Wescott Gr BS11 . . . . . . 34 C2
Wesley Ave
Bristol BS15 . . . . 65 D5
Radstock BA3 . . . . 133 C1
Wesley Cl
[6] Bristol, Upper Soundwell
BS16 . . . . 51 D3
Bristol, Whitehall BS5 . 50 D1
Wesley Ct BS23 . . . . 104 F8
Wesley Dr BS22 . . . . 89 A3
Wesley Hill BS15 . . . . . . 51 D1
Wesley La BS30 . . . . 66 B5
Wesley Pl BS8 . . . . 49 A2
Wesley Rd
Bristol BS7 . . . . 49 E4
Radstock BA3 . . . . 133 D1
Wesley St BS3 . . . . 63 C3
Wessex Ave BS7 . . . . . . 49 F7
Wessex Ct BS7 . . . . 49 F7
Wessex Ho [10] BS2 . . . 143 C3
Wessex Rd BS24 . . . . . . 105 B2
West Ave BA2 . . . . 101 C5
Westaway Cl BS49 . . . . 91 C7
Westaway Pk BS49 . . . 91 C7
Westbourne Ave
Clevedon BS21 . . . . 57 D2
Keynsham BS31 . . . . 81 E5
Westbourne Cl [2] BS5 . . 52 A7
Westbourne Cres BS21 . 57 D2
Westbourne Ct BS5 . . . 64 B8
Westbourne Gr [15] BS3 . . 63 C3
Westbourne Ho BA2 . . 141 C2
Westbourne Pl BS8 . . . 142 B3
Westbourne Rd
Bristol, Downend BS16 . . 51 F8
[8] Bristol, Upper Easton
BS5 . . . . 64 B8
Westbourne Terr BS16 . . 51 B7
West Broadway BS9 . . . 49 D6
Westbrooke Ct BS1 . . . 142 A1
Westbrook Pk BA1 . . . . 84 A2
Westbrook Rd
Bristol BS4 . . . . 80 D8
Weston-s-M BS22 . . . . . 88 D1
Westbury Court Rd BS9 49 A7
Westbury Cres BS23 . . 104 F2
Westbury Ct BS9 . . . . . . 49 A7
Westbury Hill BS9 . . . . . 49 A7
Westbury La BS9 . . . . . . 48 C7
Westbury Mews [6] BS9 49 A7
WESTBURY ON TRYM . . 48 F7
Westbury-on-Trym CE
Prim Sch BS9 . . . . 49 A8
WESTBURY PARK 49 A3
Westbury Park Prim Sch
BS6 . . . . 49 B3
Westbury Pk BS6 . . . . . . 49 A4
Westbury Rd BS6 . . . . . . 49 A4

Westbury Terr BA2 . . . 117 E5
Westbury View BA2 . . . 134 E8
West Cl BA2 . . . . 101 A5
West Coombe BS9 . . . . . 48 D6
West Country Water Pk★
BS36 . . . . 24 F2
Westcourt Dr BS30 . . . 66 B4
West Croft
Blagdon BS40 . . . . 110 E2
Bristol BS9 . . . . 49 C7
Clevedon BS21 . . . . 57 D2
West Ct BS20 . . . . 45 D4
West Dene BS9 . . . . 48 E6
West Dundry La BS41 . 78 E2
WESTEND 7 B6
WEST END
Blagdon 110 E3
Clevedon 57 D2
Nailsea 74 F7
Wickwar 17 E5
West End
Bristol BS3 . . . . 142 C1
Bristol, Kingsdown BS2 143 A4
Oldbury-on-S BS35 . . . . 7 C6
West End Farm Cvn Pk
BS24 . . . . 105 E4
Westend La BS37 . . . . . . 7 B6
West End La BS48 . . . . . 75 A8
Westend Rd GL12 . . . . . 17 E5
West End Trad Est
BS48 . . . . 59 B1
Westering BS16 . . . . 52 A5
WESTERLEIGH 39 B4
Westerleigh Bsns Pk
BS37 . . . . 27 B1
Westerleigh Cl BS16 . . 51 F7
WESTERLEIGH HILL . . . 39 D3
Westerleigh Rd
Bath BA2 . . . . 102 B1
Clevedon BS21 . . . . 57 D2
Henfield BS36 . . . . 38 D2
Pucklechurch BS16 . . . 53 C7
Westerleigh BS36, BS37 . 39 B5
Yate BS37 . . . . 39 C8
West App Distribution
Pk BS35 . . . . 22 B4
Western Approach
Distribution Pk BS35 . . 22 C4
Western Ave BS36 . . . . . 26 A1
Western Ct
Bristol BS34 . . . . 37 A4
Clevedon BS21 . . . . 57 F3
Western Dr BS14 . . . . . . 79 E6
Western Grange BS34 . 36 A3
Western La BS40 . . . . . 129 C3
Western Rd BS7 . . . . 49 E6
Western-S Ho BS23 . . . 105 B5
WESTFIELD 139 C8
Westfield BS21 . . . . 73 D8
West Field [2] BS34 . . . 35 F7
Westfield Cl
Backwell BS48 . . . . 76 A6
Bath BA2 . . . . 101 E3
Bristol BS15 . . . . 65 D5
Keynsham BS31 . . . . 81 C5
Weston-s-M BS23 . . . . . 104 D2
Westfield Cres BS29 . . 107 A3
Westfield Dr BS48 . . . . 76 A6
Westfield Ho
Bath BA2 . . . . 101 E3
Stoke Bishop BS9 . . . . . 48 F5
Westfield Ind & Trad Est
BA3 . . . . 139 C7
Westfield La BS34 . . . . 36 E3
Westfield Pk
Bath BA1 . . . . 101 A7
Bristol BS6 . . . . 49 B1
Westfield Pk S BA1 . . . 101 A7
Westfield Pl BS8 . . . . . . 62 F7
Westfield Prim Sch
BA3 . . . . 139 C8
Westfield Rd
Backwell BS48 . . . . 76 A6
Banwell BS29 . . . . 107 A3
Bristol BS9 . . . . 49 A8
Weston-s-M BS23 . . . . . 104 D2
Westfield Terr BA3 . . . 133 D1
Westfield Way BS32 . . 24 D2
West Garston BS29 . . . 107 A3
Westgate BS1 . . . . 142 B1
Westgate Bldgs BA1 . . 141 B2
Westgate St BA1 . . . . . 141 B2
West Gr BS6 . . . . 49 F1
Westhall Rd BA1 . . . . . 101 D7
WEST HARPTREE 129 E6
West Harptree Rd
BS40 . . . . 129 F5
Westhaven Cl BS48 . . . 76 A6
Westhaven Sch BS23 . 104 D2
West Hay Rd BS40 . . . . 92 C3
WEST HEWISH 90 A5
WEST HILL
Nailsea 60 A5
Portishead 45 A5
West Hill
Nailsea BS48 . . . . 60 A5
Portishead BS20 . . . . . . 45 B5
West Hill Ct BS20 . . . . . 45 C6

WEST HILL GARDENS . 133 E1
Westhill Gdns BS20 . . . 45 C5
West Hill Gdns
Radstock BA3 . . . . 133 D1
Radstock BA3 . . . . 133 E1
West Hill Rd BA3 . . . . . . 133 D1
WEST KINGTON 56 F7
West La BS40 . . . . 94 C8
Westland Ave BS30 . . . 66 C4
Westland Distribution Pk
BS24 . . . . 105 B3
West Lea Rd BA1 . . . . . 84 A1
West Leaze Pl BS32 . . . 36 E6
Westleigh Cl
Bristol BS10 . . . . 35 D1
Yate BS37 . . . . 27 C1
Westleigh Ct BS37 . . . . 27 C1
West Leigh Inf Sch
BS48 . . . . 76 A6
Westleigh Pk BS14 . . . 80 B8
Westleigh Rd BS10 . . . 35 D1
West Links BS23 . . . . . . 104 D2
West Links Cl BS22 . . . 88 B3
West Littleton Rd
Marshfield SN14 . . . . . . 69 F8
West Littleton SN14 . . . 55 E2
West Mall BS8 . . . . 62 F7
Westmarsh Way BS22 . 89 A4
Westmarsh La BS35 . . . 7 B5
Westmead BA3 . . . . 138 D3
Westmead Gdns BA1 . . 84 A2
Westmead Ho BS11 . . . 33 B1
Westmead Rd BS5 . . . . 65 B7
Westminster Cl [1] BS9 . 49 A7
Westminster Rd BS5 . . . 64 D8
Westmoreland Dr
BA2 . . . . 141 A2
Westmoreland Rd
Bath BA2 . . . . 141 A1
Bristol BS6 . . . . 49 B3
Westmoreland St BA2 141 A2
Westmoreland Station Rd
BA2 . . . . 141 A1
Westmorland Ho BS6 . 49 A3
Westmorland Terr
BS37 . . . . 41 A4
WESTON 84 A2
Weston All Saints CE Prim
Sch BA1 . . . . 84 A2
Weston Ave [4] BS5 . . . 64 D7
Weston Bsns Pk BS24 . 105 E5
Weston Cl BS9 . . . . 48 C7
Weston Coll BS48 . . . . . 59 E2
Weston College BS23 . 104 D8
Weston Coll Univ Campus
BS23 . . . . 104 F2
Weston Coll (Westcliff)
BS23 . . . . 87 B1
Weston Cres BS7 . . . . . 49 E6
Weston Ct BS24 . . . . . . 105 B3
Weston Dro BS20 . . . . . 58 F8
Weston Euro Pk BS24 . 105 B4
Weston Express Bsns Pk
BS22 . . . . 105 C6
Weston Farm La BA1 . . 84 C2
Weston Gateway Tourist
Pk BS24 . . . . 89 C1
Weston General Hospl
BS23 . . . . 104 E2
Westonia BS22 . . . . 88 D2
Westonian Ct BS9 . . . . . 48 C4
Weston Ind Est BS24 . 105 C6
WESTON IN GORDANO . 44 B4
Weston La
Bath BA1 . . . . 101 C8
Christon BS26 . . . . 123 C2
Weston Lock Ret BA2 . 101 C6
Weston Lodge
Bath BA1 . . . . 84 A2
Weston-s-M BS23 . . . . . 104 D8
Weston Milton Sta
BS22 . . . . 105 C7
Weston Miniature Rly★
BS23 . . . . 104 D5
WESTON PARK 84 C1
Weston Park Ct BA1 . . . 84 D1
Weston Pk BA1 . . . . 84 C1
Weston Pk E BA1 . . . . . 84 C1
Weston Pk W BA1 . . . . 84 C1
Weston Rd
Bath BA1 . . . . 101 D8
Brean TA8 . . . . 121 A5
Congresbury BS49 . . . 91 B5
Failand BS8 . . . . 61 C3
Long Ashton BS41 . . . . 77 D3
Weston Ret Pk BS23 . 105 C4
Westons Brake BS16 . 38 A1
Westons Hill Dr BS16 . . 38 A1
WESTON-SUPER-
MARE 104 B8
Weston-Super-Mare Sta
BS23 . . . . 104 F2
Westons Way BS15 . . . 65 F7
Weston Way BS24 . . . . 105 D2
Weston Wood Rd BS20 . 45 C3
Westover Cl BS9 . . . . . . 34 F1
Westover Dr BS9 . . . . . . 35 A1
Westover Gdns BS9 . . . 48 F8

Westover Rd
 Bristol BS9 . . . . .35 A1
 Bristol BS9 . . . . .48 F8
Westover Rise BS9 . . . . .35 A1
West Par BS9 . . . . .48 C7
West Park Rd BS16 . . . .51 E5
West Pk BS8 . . . . 142 B4
Westpoint Trad Est
 BS15 . . . . .65 D7
West Priory Cl BS9 . . .49 A7
West Rd
 Lympsham BS24 . . . . . .122 B1
 Midsomer Norton BA3 . .133 A3
 Yatton BS49 . . . . .91 B7
West Ridge BS36 . . . . . .38 C7
West Rocke Ave BS4 . . .48 D6
West Rolstone Rd BS24 90 A1
West Shrubbery 5 BS6. 49 B2
West St
 Axbridge BS26 . . . . . . .125 B2
 Banwell BS29 . . . . .107 B3
 Bristol BS2 . . . . .143 C4
 Bristol, Bedminster BS3 .63 C3
 2 Bristol, Kingswood
 BS15 . . . . .65 D8
 Bristol, Oldland Common
 BS30 . . . . .66 C4
 Tytherington GL12 . . . . . .16 B5
 Weston-s-M BS23 . . . . . .104 D8
West Terr BA2 . . . . .137 C1
WEST TOWN
 Backwell 75 F5
 Ubley 111 B6
West Town Ave BS4 . . . .64 D1
West Town Dr 2 BS4. . .64 D1
West Town Gr BS4 . . . . .80 D8
West Town La BS4,
 BS14 . . . . .64 D1
West Town Lane Prim Sch
 BS4 . . . . .64 D1
West Town Pk BS4 . . . . .64 D1
West Town Rd
 Backwell BS48 . . . . .76 A5
 Bristol BS11 . . . . .47 C7
West Tyning BA2 . . . . . .99 B1
Westview BS39 . . . . . . .132 C5
West View
 Alveston BS35 . . . . .14 F4
 Bristol BS16 . . . . .52 A6
Westview Orch BA2 . . .120 B5
West View Rd
 Batheaston BA1 . . . . .86 A3
 Bristol BS3 . . . . .63 B3
 Keynsham BS31 . . . . .81 E5
Westward BS41 . . . . . . .62 B2
Westward Cl BS40 . . . . .92 D2
Westward Dr BS20 . . . .47 C4
Westward Gdns BS41. . .62 B2
Westward Rd BS13 . . . .78 F7
Westway BS48 . . . . .59 E2
West Way
 Bristol BS10, BS34 . . . . . .35 E4
 Clevedon BS21 . . . . .57 E3
Westway Farm BS39 . .113 C6
WEST WICK 89 C1
West Wick BS24 . . . . . . .89 C1
West Wick Rdbt BS22,
 BS24 . . . . .106 B8
West Wlk BS37 . . . . .27 E1
WESTWOOD 120 E3
Westwood BA2 . . . . . . .102 C6
Westwood Ave BS39. . .115 C2
Westwood Cl 2 BS22 . .88 F2
Westwood Cres BS4 . . . .64 D5
Westwood Rd BS4 . . . .80 D8
Westwoods BA1 . . . . . . .86 B3
Westwood-with-Iford
 Prim Sch BA15 . . . . . . .120 F3
Wetherby Ct BS16 . . . . .37 F1
Wetherby Gr 1 BS16. . .37 F1
Wetherell Pl BS8 . . . . . .142 B3
Wetlands La BS20 . . . . .45 C3
Wexford Rd BS4 . . . . . . .79 D8
Weymouth Rd BS3 . . . .63 D2
Weymouth St BA1 . . . . .102 B8
Wharfedale BS35 . . . . . .15 D8
Wharf La BS20 . . . . .46 B5
Wharf Rd
 5 Bristol BS16 . . . . .50 F4
 Haywood Village BS24 . .105 B4
Wharfside BS24 . . . . . . .121 E3
Wharnecliffe Cl BS14 . .80 B5
Wharnecliffe Gdns
 BS14 . . . . .80 B5
Whartons 8 BS4 . . . . . .64 D1
Whatley Ct 9 BS8 . . . . .49 B1
Whatley Rd BS8 . . . . . . .49 B1
Wheatcar Rd BS49 . . . . .73 F2
Wheatfield Dr
 Bristol BS32 . . . . .24 D1
 Weston-s-M BS22 . . . . . .89 A5
Wheatfield Prim Sch
 BS32 . . . . .24 D1
Wheathill Cl BS31 . . . . .81 D5
Wheatsheaf La BA2 . . . .99 C6
Wheelers Cl BA3 . . . . . .133 D2
Wheelers Dr BA3 . . . . .133 C2

WHEELER'S HILL 133 C2
Wheelers Patch BS16 . . .52 B5
Wheelers Rd BA3 . . . . .133 D2
Whinchat Gdns BS16 . . .50 F6
Whippington Ct BS1 . .143 B3
Whistle BS16 . . . . .52 B2
Whistley La BS40 . . . . .129 F6
Whitaker Rd BA2 . . . . .102 A2
Whitby Rd BS4 . . . . .64 C4
WHITCHURCH 80 D4
Whitchurch District Ctr
 BS14 . . . . .80 A5
Whitchurch La
 Bristol BS14 . . . . .79 E5
 Bristol, Bishopsworth
 BS13 . . . . .79 B5
 Bristol, Hartcliffe BS13 . .79 C5
 Dundry BS41 . . . . .79 C1
Whitchurch Prim Sch
 BS14 . . . . .80 C4
Whitchurch Rd BS13 . . .79 A6
Whitebeam Ct BS5 . . . . .64 E8
Whitebeam Ho 7
 BS16 . . . . .51 C6
Whitebridge Gdns
 BS35 . . . . .15 C7
Whitebrook La BA2 . . .134 A8
Whitecroft Way BS15. . .66 A7
WHITE CROSS
 Bishop Sutton 113 E1
 Hallatrow 131 F6
White Cross BS39 . . . . .131 F6
Whitecross Ave BS14 . . .80 C6
White Cross Gate
 BS39 . . . . .131 F6
Whitecross La BS29 . . .107 A4
Whitecross Rd
 East Harptree BS40 . . . .129 F4
 Weston-s-M BS23 . . . . . .104 E6
Whitefield Ave
 Bristol, Hanham BS15 . .65 D5
 Bristol, Speedwell BS5 . .51 A1
Whitefield Cl
 Batheaston BA1 . . . . .86 B4
 7 Bristol BS16 . . . . .51 D3
Whitefield Fishponds
 Com Sch BS16 . . . . .50 F4
Whitefield Rd BS5 . . . . .51 A2
Whitefields BS37 . . . . . .28 C1
Whitegate Cl BS24 . . . .122 B6
Whitegates BS36 . . . . . .37 D6
WHITEHALL 50 D1
Whitehall Ave BS5 . . . . .50 E1
Whitehall Gdns BS5 . . . .50 D1
Whitehall Prim Sch
 BS5 . . . . .50 D1
Whitehall Rd BS5 . . . . . .64 C8
Whitehall Trad Est 4
 BS5 . . . . .64 C8
WHITE HILL 134 F6
White Hill BA2 . . . . .134 F6
Whitehorn Vale BS10. . .35 C3
White Horse Rd BA15 .120 E7
White House Bsns Ctr The
 BS15 . . . . .65 D7
Whitehouse Ctr (PRU)
 BS13 . . . . .79 C5
Whitehouse La
 Bristol BS3 . . . . .63 D4
 Litton BA3 . . . . .130 D3
 Pilning BS35 . . . . .22 C7
 Wraxall BS48 . . . . .60 A6
White House La BS26 .123 A3
Whitehouse Pl BS3 . . . . .63 E4
Whitehouse Rd BS49 . . .91 F8
Whitehouse St BS3 . . . . .63 E4
Whiteladies Rd BS8 . . .142 B4
Whitelands Hill BA3. . .134 B3
Whiteleaze BS10 . . . . . . .49 C8
White Lodge Pk BS20 . .45 D6
White Lodge Rd BS16 . .51 F4
Whitemead Ho 3 BS3. .63 A3
Whitemore Ct BA1 . . . . .86 A4
Whiteoak Way BS48 . . .75 D8
White Ox Mead La
 BA2 . . . . .117 F1
White Ox-mead La
 BA2 . . . . .134 E8
White Post BA3 . . . . . . .139 B6
Whitesfield Ct BS48 . . . .59 D2
Whitesfield Rd BS48 . . . .59 D1
WHITESHILL 37 D3
Whiteshill BS16 . . . . .37 D3
Whiteshill La SN14 . . . . .55 D3
White St BS5 . . . . .143 C4
Whitestown La BS40 . .128 E3
White Tree Rdbt BS9 . . .49 A4
White Tree Rd BS9 . . . . .49 B4
Whitewall La BS35 . . . . . .8 F1
WHITEWAY
 Bath 101 A4
 Bristol 51 A1
Whiteway Cl
 Bristol, St Anne's Park
 BS4 . . . . .64 E6
 Bristol, St George BS5. .65 A8
Whiteway Ct 1 BS5. . . .65 A8
Whiteway Mews BS5 . . .65 A8

Whiteway Rd
 Bath BA2 . . . . .101 A3
 Bristol BS5, BS15. . . . . . .51 A1
Whitewells Rd BA1. . . . .85 A2
Whitewood Rd BS5 . . . . .50 F1
WHITFIELD 9 C3
Whitfield Ho 7 BS15. . .65 D8
Whitfield Rd BS35. . . . . . .8 C2
Whiting Rd BS13 . . . . . . .79 A4
Whitland Ave BS13 . . . . .79 B5
Whitland Rd BS13. . . . . .79 B5
WHITLEY BATTS 97 F2
Whitley Cl BS37 . . . . . . .27 C3
Whitley Mead BS34 . . . .36 E3
Whitling St BS40 . . . . . . .95 A2
Whitmead Gdns BS13 . .79 C4
Whitmore Ave BS4 . . . . .65 A3
Whitson Ho 1 BS2. . . .143 C3
Whitson St BS1 . . . . . . .143 A4
Whitsun Leaze BS34 . . .35 F6
Whitting Rd BS23 . . . . .104 E4
Whittington Dr BS22 . . .88 D2
Whittington Rd BS16. . .51 C6
Whittock Rd BS14 . . . . .80 D6
Whittock Sq BS14 . . . . .80 D7
Whittucks Cl BS15 . . . . .65 D4
Whittucks Rd BS15. . . . .65 C4
Whitwell Rd BS14 . . . . .80 B8
Whytes Cl BS9 . . . . .49 A8
WICK 67 D6
Wick CE Prim Sch
 BS30 . . . . .67 B6
Wick Cres BS4 . . . . .64 D3
Wick Ct BS24 . . . . .89 B1
Wickets The
 Bristol, Filton BS7 . . . . . .35 F1
 Bristol, Upper Soundwell
 BS15 . . . . .51 D2
Wicketts The BS7 . . . . . .35 F2
Wickfield BS21 . . . . .57 E1
Wickham Cl BS37 . . . . . .40 D8
Wickham Ct
 Bristol BS16 . . . . .50 D5
 Clevedon BS21 . . . . .57 E3
Wickham Hill BS16. . . . .50 D5
Wickham Theatre ★
 BS8 . . . . .142 C3
Wickham View BS16. . . .50 D4
Wick House Cl BS31. . . .82 D3
Wick La
 Lympsham BS24 . . . . . .121 E1
 Peasedown St John BA2,
 BA3 . . . . .116 F1
 Pensford BS39 . . . . .97 D3
 Upton Cheyney BS30 . . . .67 A2
WICKLANE 117 A1
Wicklow Rd BS4 . . . . . . .79 E8
Wick Rd
 Bishop Sutton BS39 . . . .113 C3
 Bristol BS4 . . . . .64 D4
 Greenways GL13 . . . . .2 B8
 Lympsham BS24 . . . . . .121 D2
 Pilning BS35 . . . . .22 C7
 Wick St L BS22 . . . . .89 B7
Wick Rdbt BS16 . . . . . . .38 A2
WICK ST LAWRENCE . . .89 B7
WICKWAR 18 B5
Wickwar Rd
 Kingswood GL12 . . . . . . .11 E4
 Rangeworthy BS37 . . . . . .17 B1
 Yate BS37 . . . . .28 B5
Wick Wick Cl BS16,
 BS36 . . . . .38 A2
WIDCOMBE 102 C4
Widcombe BS14 . . . . . . .80 A6
Widcombe CE Jun Sch
 BA2 . . . . .102 B5
Widcombe Cl 3 BS5. . . .65 A7
Widcombe Cres BA2 . . .102 B5
Widcombe Hill BA2 . . . .102 C4
Widcombe Inf Sch
 BA2 . . . . .102 B5
Widcombe Par BA2 . . .141 C1
Widcombe Rise BA2 . . .102 B5
Widcombe Terr BA2 . . .102 B5
Wider Mead 2 BS7 . . . . .50 C8
Widmore Gr BS13 . . . . . .79 B5
Wight Row BS20 . . . . . . .45 F6
Wigmore Gdns BS22 . . .88 D2
Wigton Cres BS10. . . . . .35 C2
Wilbye Gr BS4 . . . . .79 D7
Wilcox Cl BS15. . . . . .65 C6
Wildcountry La BS48 . . .77 E6
Wildcroft Ho BS9 . . . . . .49 B4
Wildcroft Rd BS9 . . . . . .49 B4
Wilder Ct BS2 . . . . .143 B4
Wilder St BS2. . . . . .143 B4
Wild Flower Rd BS35. . . .8 B4
Willada Cl BS3. . . . . .63 B2
William Daw Cl BS29 .106 F3
William Herschel Mus ★
 BA1 . . . . .141 B2
William Mason Cl 19
 BS5 . . . . .64 B7
Williams Cl BS30. . . . . . .65 F3
Williamson Rd BS7. . . . .49 F3
William St
 Bath BA2 . . . . .141 C3
 Bristol, Fishponds BS16. .51 B3

William St continued
 8 Bristol, Moorfields
 BS5 . . . . .64 C8
 Bristol, Newton BS2 . . . . .64 A6
 Bristol, St Pauls BS2 . . . .49 F1
 Bristol, Windmill Hill BS3 .63 E4
Williamstowe BA2 . . . .102 C1
Willinton Rd BS4. . . . . . .79 F8
Willis Rd
 Bristol BS15 . . . . .51 F2
 Fox Hill BA2 . . . . .102 B2
Williton Cres BS23 . . . .104 F3
Willment Way BS11 . . . .33 D1
Willmott Cl BS14 . . . . . .79 F3
Willoughby Cl
 Alveston BS35 . . . . .15 A4
 Bristol BS13 . . . . .79 B7
Willoughby Rd BS7. . . . .49 E5
Willow Bank BS10. . . . . .49 C7
Willow Bed Cl BS16 . . . .51 B6
Willow Cl
 Bath BA2 . . . . .118 E8
 Bristol, Patchway BS34 . .35 E7
 Bristol, Warmley BS30 . .66 D6
 Charfield GL12 . . . . .11 A4
 Clevedon BS21 . . . . .57 G3
 Long Ashton BS41 . . . . . .61 F1
 Portishead BS20 . . . . . . .45 C4
 Radstock BA3 . . . . .133 E2
 Weston-s-M, St Georges
 BS22 . . . . .89 D2
 Weston-s-M, Uphill
 BS23 . . . . .104 E2
 Wick BS30 . . . . .67 B6
Willow Ct BS7 . . . . .50 A7
Willowdown BS22 . . . . . .88 E4
Willow Dr
 Bleadon BS24 . . . . .122 C6
 Hutton BS24 . . . . .105 E2
 Weston-s-M BS24 . . . . . .105 E5
Willowfalls BA1 . . . . . . .85 E3
Willow Gdns BS22. . . . . .89 D2
Willow Gn BA2 . . . . . . .101 D4
Willow Gr 1 BS16 . . . . .51 C2
Willowherb Rd
 Lyde Green BS16 . . . . . . .52 C8
 Lyde Green BS16 . . . . . . .52 C8
Willow Ho BS13 . . . . . . .79 D4
Willow Rd BS15 . . . . . . .65 C3
Willow Sh Ctr The
 BS16 . . . . .51 E6
Willows The
 Bristol BS16 . . . . .51 E4
 Bristol, Bradley Stoke
 BS32 . . . . .36 D8
 Bristol, Frenchay BS16 . .37 B1
 Frampton Cotterell BS36 .38 F7
 Keynsham BS31 . . . . .81 E6
 Nailsea BS48 . . . . .59 F3
 Yate BS37 . . . . .27 D2
Willow The BA3 . . . . . . .138 F2
Willow Way BS36 . . . . . .38 C6
Willow Wlk
 Bristol BS10 . . . . .35 B3
 Keynsham BS31 . . . . .81 D4
WILLSBRIDGE 66 B1
Willsbridge Hill BS30. . .66 A2
Willsbridge Mill ★ BS30 66 B2
Wills Dr BS5 . . . . .64 A8
Wills Way BS4 . . . . .79 D6
Willway St BS3 . . . . .63 D4
WILMINGTON 100 A1
Wilmington Hill
 Englishcombe BA2 . . . . .100 C2
 Marksbury BA2 . . . . .99 E1
Wilmot Ct BS30 . . . . . . .66 A6
Wilmots Way BS20 . . . . .47 D4
Wilshire Ave BS15. . . . . .65 D5
Wilson Pl BS2 . . . . .143 C4
Wilson St BS2 . . . . .143 C4
Wilton Cl BS10 . . . . .35 C1
Wilton Ct BS23 . . . . . . .104 D7
Wilton Gdns BS23 . . . . .104 D7
Wiltons BS40 . . . . .92 D2
Wiltshire Ave BS37 . . . . .28 A3
Wiltshire Pl BS15 . . . . . .51 E3
Wiltshire Way BA1 . . . . .85 A2
Wilverley Ind Est BS4 . .64 E1
Wimbledon Rd BS6 . . . . .49 C5
Wimblestone Rd BS25 .107 F2
Wimborne Rd BS3 . . . . .63 C1
Winash Cl BS14 . . . . . . .80 D7
Wincanton Cl
 Bristol BS16 . . . . .37 F1
 Nailsea BS48 . . . . .60 B1
Winchcombe Cl BS48 . . .76 A8
Winchcombe Gr BS11 . .47 F5
Winchcombe Rd BS36. . .38 C6
Winchester Ave BS4. . . .64 D3
Winchester Ct BS16 . . . .50 E6
Winchester Rd
 5 Bath BA2 . . . . .101 D5
 Bristol BS4 . . . . .64 D3
Wincombe Trad Est
 BS2 . . . . .64 A4
Wincroft BS30 . . . . .66 C4
Windcliff Cres BS11 . . . .47 E7

Windell St BA2 . . . . . . .102 A2
Windermere Ave BS23 .104 F4
Windermere Rd BS34 . . .36 A8
Windermere Way BS30 .66 D6
Windmill Bsns Pk BS21. .73 E8
Windmill Cl
 Bristol BS15 . . . . .65 D5
 Bristol BS3 . . . . .63 E4
Windmill Farm Bsns Ctr
 BS3 . . . . .63 D4
WINDMILL HILL 63 E3
Windmill Hill
 Bristol BS3 . . . . .63 D3
 Hutton BS24 . . . . .106 A2
Windmill La BS10 . . . . . .34 D3
Windmill Rd BS21 . . . . . .73 E8
Windrush Cl BA2 . . . . . .100 F4
Windrush Ct BS35 . . . . . .15 C8
Windrush Gn BS31 . . . . .82 A4
Windrush Rd BS31 . . . . .82 A4
Windscreens Ave BS2 . .64 A7
Windsor Ave
 Bristol BS5 . . . . .65 B6
 Keynsham BS31 . . . . .81 E4
Windsor Bridge Rd BA1,
 BA2 . . . . .101 D7
Windsor Castle BA1. . .101 D7
Windsor Cl
 Bristol BS34 . . . . .36 E4
 Clevedon BS21 . . . . .57 F2
Windsor Cres BS10. . . . .34 C4
Windsor Ct
 4 Bath BA1 . . . . .101 C7
 14 Bristol, Clifton BS8. . .62 F6
 Bristol, Downend BS16 . .51 E7
 Wick BS30 . . . . .67 C7
Windsor Dr
 Nailsea BS48 . . . . .59 E2
 Yate BS37 . . . . .27 D2
Windsor Gr 20 BS5 . . . .64 B8
Windsor Pl
 5 Bath BA1 . . . . .101 C7
 Bristol, Clifton BS8 . . . . .62 F6
 Bristol, Mangotsfield
 BS16 . . . . .52 A5
Windsor Rd
 Bristol, Longwell Green
 BS30 . . . . .65 F2
 Bristol, Montpelier BS6 . .49 E2
 Weston-s-M BS22 . . . . . .88 C2
Windsor Terr
 Bristol, Clifton BS8 . . . . .62 F6
 Bristol, Windmill Hill BS3 .63 F4
 Paulton BS39 . . . . .132 E5
Windsor Villas 3 BA1 .101 C7
Windwhistle Circ
 BS23 . . . . .104 F4
Windwhistle La BS23 . .104 E3
Windwhistle Prim Sch
 BS23 . . . . .104 F3
Windwhistle Rd BS23 .104 F3
Windyridge BS16 . . . . . .51 E4
Wineberry Cl BS5 . . . . . .50 D1
Wine St
 Bath BA1 . . . . .141 C2
 Bristol BS1 . . . . .143 A3
Winfield Rd BS30 . . . . . .66 C7
WINFORD 94 F7
Winford Bsns Pk BS40. .95 C4
Winford CE Prim Sch
 BS40 . . . . .94 F7
Winford Cl BS20 . . . . . . .45 E4
Winford Ct BS6 . . . . .49 A5
Winford Gr BS13 . . . . . . .79 A8
Winford La BS41 . . . . . . .78 C1
Winford Rd BS40 . . . . . .95 F3
Winford Terr BS41 . . . . .78 C5
Wingard Cl BS23 . . . . . .104 D2
Wingard Ct 6 BS23 . . .104 E5
Wingfield Rd BS3 . . . . . .63 E2
Winifred's La BA1 . . . . . .84 F1
Winkworth Pl 4 BS2. . .49 F1
Winnowing End BS25 .108 A3
Winsbury View BA2 . . . .99 B1
Winsbury Way BS32. . . .24 D1
WINSCOMBE 124 F7
Winscombe Cl BS31. . . .81 D6
Winscombe Dro
 Shipham BS25 . . . . .125 D6
 Winscombe BS25 . . . . . .125 A5
Winscombe Hill BS25 .124 F5
Winscombe Rd BS23 . .105 A7
Winscombe Woodborough
 Prim Sch BS25 . . . . . . .125 A8
Winsford St 2 BS5. . . . .64 A8
Winsham Cl BS14 . . . . . .80 B5
WINSLEY 120 D7
Winsley Bypass BA15. .120 E7
Winsley CE VA Prim Sch
 BA15 . . . . .120 E7
Winsley Hill BA2 . . . . . .120 B6
Winsley Rd
 Bristol BS6 . . . . .49 D1
 Winsley BA15 . . . . .120 F7
Winstanley Ho 4 BS5. .64 B6
Winstone Ct BS2 . . . . . .142 C3

Winstones Rd
Barrow Gurney BS48 .... **77** F6
Bristol BS48 .... **78** A6
WINTERBOURNE **37** F6
WINTERBOURNE DOWN **37** F4
Winterbourne Hill BS36 .... **37** D5
Winterbourne Int Acad BS36 .... **37** D6
Winterbourne Rd BS34 . **36** E6
Winterfield Cl BS39 . **132** E4
Winterfield Pk BS39 . **132** E4
Winterfield Rd BS39 . **132** E5
WINTERHEAD **125** D8
Winters La BS40 ...... **93** D6
Winterstoke Cl 5 BS3 . **63** B2
Winterstoke Commercial Ctr BS23 ...... **105** A6
Winterstoke Ctr 1 BS3 . **63** B2
Winterstoke Ho 1 BS3 . **63** B2
Winterstoke Hundred Acad BS24 .... **105** D6
Winterstoke Rd
Bristol BS3 .... **63** A2
Weston-s-M BS23, BS24 **105** B4
Winterstoke Underpass BS3 .... **62** F4
Wint Hill BS29 ..... **107** B2
Winton St BS2 ...... **63** F4
Wisemans Ho BS8 .. **142** A4
Wishford Mews BA3 . **133** C2
Wisley Wlk BS22 ... **105** F1
Wistaria Ave BS37 .... **28** A1
Wisteria Ave BS24 ... **105** D2
Witchell Rd BS5 ..... **64** C7
Witch Hazel Rd BS13 .. **79** E3
Witcombe BS37 ..... **39** C7
Witcombe Cl BS15 ... **51** F1
Witham Rd BS31 .... **82** A3
Witherlies Rd BS16 .. **50** F6
Withey Cl E
Bristol BS9 .... **48** F6
Stoke Bishop BS9 .... **48** F6
Withey Cl W BS9 .... **48** F5
Witheys The BS14 ... **80** C4
Withies La BA3 ..... **139** A4
Withies Pk BA3 .... **138** F8
Withington Cl BS30 . **66** C2
Withleigh Rd BS4 .... **64** B2
Withy Cl BS48 ...... **59** F3
WITHYDITCH **117** C3
Withyditch La BA2 ... **117** C4
Withy La BS34 ...... **36** A7
Withymead Rd SN14 .. **70** A8
WITHY MILLS **133** A7
Withypool Gdns BS14 . **80** B5
Withys The BS20 .... **47** D4
WITHYWOOD **79** A4
Withywood Com Sch BS13 .... **79** A5
Withywood Gdns 1 BS13 .... **78** F4
Withywood Rd BS13 .. **78** F4
Witney Cl BS31 ..... **82** D3
Witney Mead BS36 ... **38** B8
Woburn Cl BS30 .... **65** F5
Woburn Rd BS5 ..... **50** B3
Wolferton Rd BS7 ... **49** F2
Wolfridge Gdns BS10 . **35** A4
Wolfridge La BS35 .... **14** F4
Wolfridge Ride BS35 .. **14** F4
Wolseley Rd BS7 .... **49** D3
Wolvershill Ind Units BS29 .... **106** C6
Wolvershill Pk BS29 . **107** A3
Wolvershill Rd BS29 . **106** C6
WONDERSTONE **122** D6
Woodacre BS20 ..... **45** E7
Woodbine Rd BS5 .... **64** D8
WOODBOROUGH **125** B8
Woodborough Cres BS25 .... **125** A7
Woodborough Ct BS25 .... **125** A8
Woodborough Dr BS25 .... **125** A8
Woodborough Hill Cotts BA2 .... **134** C4
Woodborough La BA3 **134** A4
Woodborough Rd
Radstock BA3 .... **134** A3
Winscombe BS25 ..... **124** F8
Woodborough St BS5 . **50** B1
Woodbridge Rd BS4 .. **64** C2
Woodbury La BS8 .... **49** A2
Woodchester
Bristol BS15 .... **51** E3
Yate BS37 .... **39** E7
Woodchester Rd BS10 . **49** C7
Woodcliff Ave BS22 .. **88** C1
Woodcliff Rd BS22 ... **88** C1
Woodcote BS15 ..... **65** D6
Woodcote Rd BS16 .. **51** B3

Woodcote Wlk BS16 .... **51** B2
Woodcroft BS39 ..... **113** C3
Woodcroft Ave BS5 .. **50** D1
Woodcroft Cl BS4 .... **64** E4
Woodcroft Rd BS4 ... **64** E4
Wooddene BS25 .... **125** A8
Woodend BS15 ...... **65** D6
Woodend La BS35 ..... **2** E1
Woodend Rd BS36 ... **38** C7
Wood End Wlk BS9 ... **48** C6
Woodfield Rd BS6 .... **49** B2
WOODFORD **4** A4
Woodford Cl BS48 ... **60** A1
Woodford Ct 2 BS23 . **104** E5
Woodford Gn GL13 .... **3** A4
Woodgrove Rd BS10 .. **34** D2
Woodhall Cl BS16 .... **51** F6
WOODHILL **45** D7
Woodhill BS49 ...... **91** E6
Woodhill Ave BS20 ... **45** D6
Woodhill Cl BS20 .... **45** D6
Woodhill Pk BS20 .... **45** D7
Woodhill Rd BS20 .... **45** D6
Woodhill Views BS48 . **59** F3
Woodhouse Ave BS32 . **24** D7
Woodhouse Cl BS32 .. **24** D6
WOODHOUSE DOWN .. **24** D7
Woodhouse Gr BS7 ... **49** E6
Woodhouse Rd BA2 . **101** A6
Woodhurst Rd BS23 . **105** A7
Woodington Ct 1 BS30 **65** F4
Woodington Rd BS21 . **57** E1
Wood Kilns The BS49 . **74** A1
Wood La
Axbridge BS26 ...... **125** D2
Clapton in G BS20 .... **59** E8
Horton BS37 .... **19** A1
Weston-s-M BS23 ..... **87** F1
Woodland Ave BS15 .. **51** D2
Woodland Cl
Bristol BS15 .... **51** C2
Failand BS8 .... **61** B4
Woodland Cotts BA2 . **120** D6
Woodland Ct
Bristol BS9 .... **48** C3
Bristol, Tyndall's Park BS8 .... **142** C4
Woodland Glade BS21 . **57** G5
Woodland Gr
Bath, Bushey Norwood BA2 .... **102** E5
Bath, Weston Park BA1 . **84** C1
Bristol BS9 .... **48** D6
Woodland Pl BA2 ... **102** D5
Woodland Rd
Bristol BS8 .... **142** C4
Leyhill GL12 .... **10** B4
Nailsea BS48 .... **59** E3
Weston-s-M BS23 .... **104** D4
Woodlands
Axbridge BS26 ...... **125** D2
Bristol BS9 .... **48** E3
Bristol, Downend BS16 . **51** E6
Bristol, Patchway BS32 . **24** D3
Tytherington GL12 .... **16** B6
Weston-s-M BS23 .... **87** D1
Woodlands Ct
Bristol, Patchway BS32 . **24** B3
Bristol, Shirehampton BS11 .... **47** E5
Woodlands Dr BA2 .. **120** B6
Woodlands La
Bristol BS32 .... **24** C3
Woodhouse Down BS32 . **24** E5
Woodlands Pk
Bath BA1 .... **85** C2
Bristol BS32 .... **24** C3
Woodlands Rd
Charfield GL12 .... **11** A4
Clevedon BS21 .... **57** E4
Portishead BS20 ..... **45** D8
Tytherington GL12 .... **16** B6
Woodlands Rise BS16 . **51** D6
Woodlands The BA2 . **116** F3
Woodland Terr
Bristol, Kingswood BS15 .... **65** E7
Bristol, Redland BS6 .. **49** B2
Woodland Way
Bristol BS15 .... **51** C2
Failand BS8 .... **61** B4
Woodleaze BS9 ..... **48** B6
Wood Leaze BS34 ... **35** F6
Woodleigh BS35 ...... **8** C1
Woodleigh Gdns BS14 . **80** C6
Woodmancote BS37 .. **39** D8
Woodmancote Rd 7 BS6 .... **49** E1
Woodmans Cl BS37 .. **40** B8
Woodmans Rd BS37 .. **40** C8
Woodmans Vale BS37 . **40** C8
Woodmarsh Cl BS14 .. **80** A4
Wood Mead BS34 .... **50** B8
Woodmead Gdns BS13 **79** C4
Woodmill BS49 ...... **74** A1
Woodnook The BS10 .. **35** C2

Woodpecker Ave BA3 . **139** B8
Woodpecker Cl BS31 .. **81** C3
Woodpecker Cres BS16 **53** C4
Woodpecker Dr BS22 **105** E8
Wood Rd BS15 ...... **65** D8
Woodsage Cres BS16 . **52** D7
Woods Hill BA2 ..... **120** A6
Woodside
Bristol BS9 .... **48** D3
Midsomer Norton BA3 **132** E1
Woodside Ave BS24 . **105** B2
Woodside Ct BS23 .. **105** A8
Woodside Dr BS32 ... **24** A4
Woodside Gdns BS20 . **44** E5
Woodside Gr BS10 ... **34** D3
Woodside Rd
Bristol, Downend BS16 . **51** C7
Bristol, Kingswood BS15 **65** C7
Bristol, St Anne's Park BS4 .... **64** E6
Clevedon BS21 .... **57** G5
Frampton Cotterell BS36 **38** B8
Woodspring Ave BS22 . **71** C1
Woodspring Cres BS22 **88** A3
Woodspring Priory ✱
BS22 .... **71** C1
Wood St
Bath BA1 .... **141** B2
Bath, Beechen Cliff BA2 **141** B1
Bristol BS34 .... **35** F7
Bristol BS5 .... **50** B2
WOODSTOCK **65** F7
Woodstock Ave BS6 .. **49** C1
Woodstock Cl BS15 .. **65** F8
Woodstock Rd
Bristol, Kingswood BS15 .... **65** F7
Bristol, Redland BS6 .. **49** C2
Weston-s-M BS23 ... **105** B8
Woodstock Sch BS10 . **34** E2
Woodview
Chilcompton BA3 .... **138** E5
2 Clevedon BS21 .... **57** H3
High Littleton BS39 .. **115** D1
Paulton BS39 .... **132** C5
Woodview Cl BS11 ... **47** E7
Woodview Cotts BS39 **132** B7
Woodview Dr BS49 ... **92** B8
Woodview Terr
Bath BA2 .... **100** F6
Nailsea BS48 .... **59** F2
Weston-s-M BS23 ... **105** A6
Woodward Ave BS37 .. **27** B1
Woodward Dr BS30 .. **65** F4
Woodwell Rd BS11 ... **47** E5
Woodyleaze Dr BS15 .. **65** D6
Wookey Cl BS48 ..... **75** F8
Woolcot St BS6 ..... **49** B2
WOOLCOTT PARK ... **49** B1
Wooler Rd BS23 ... **104** E8
WOOLLARD **98** A6
Woollard La
Bristol BS14, BS39 ... **98** A7
Whitchurch BS14 .... **80** E1
WOOLLEY **84** F5
Woolley La BA1 ..... **85** A4
Woolley Rd BS14 .... **80** E5
Woolvers Way BS24 . **106** B6
WOOLVERTON **137** C1
Wootton Cres BS4 ... **64** E6
Wootton Pk BS14, BS4 . **64** E1
Wootton Rd BS4 .... **64** F6
Worcester Bldgs BA1 . **85** B2
Worcester Ct
Bristol BS16 .... **51** B2
Peasedown St John BA2 .... **134** D7
Worcester Cres BS8 . **142** A4
Worcester Gdns BS48 . **75** C8
Worcester Pk BA1 ... **85** B2
Worcester Pl BA1 ... **85** B2
Worcester Rd
Bristol BS8 .... **142** A4
Bristol, Kingswood BS15 **51** D1
Worcester Terr
Bath BA1 .... **85** B2
Bristol BS8 .... **142** A4
Wordsworth Ho BS34 . **36** A8
Wordsworth Rd
Bristol BS7 .... **50** B7
Clevedon BS21 .... **57** E2
Weston-s-M BS23 ... **105** A3
Workshop La BA2 ... **100** C6
Worldsend La GL13 .... **2** E7
World's End La BS31 . **82** C5
WORLE **88** F2
WORLEBURY **88** A2
Worlebury Cl BS22 ... **88** B3
Worlebury Hill Rd BS22, BS23 .... **88** B2
Worlebury Park Rd BS22 .... **88** A2
Worlebury St Pauls CE VA Fst Sch BS22 ..... **88** B3
Worle Com Sch BS22.. **88** E1
Worle Ct BS22 ...... **88** F3

Worle Ind Est BS22 ... **89** B2
Worle Moor Rd BS24 **105** E7
Worle Sta BS22 ..... **89** B1
Worle Village Prim Sch BS22 .... **88** E2
Wormcliff La SN13 ... **86** F3
Worrall Mews 10 BS8 . **49** A2
Worrall Pl 11 BS8 .... **49** A2
Worrall Rd BS8 ..... **49** A2
Worrel's La BS16, BS36 . **37** D3
Worsley St BS5 ...... **64** D7
Worthing Rd BS34 ... **35** F8
Worthings The BS24 . **122** B1
Worthy Cl BS15 ..... **65** F6
Worthy Cres BS24 .. **122** B1
Worthy La 5 BS23 .. **104** E8
Worthy Pl 4 BS23 .. **104** E8
Worthy Rd BS11 .... **33** D7
Worthys The BS34 ... **37** A6
Wotton Rd
Charfield GL12 .... **11** B5
Iron Acton BS37 ..... **26** F5
Kingswood GL12 ..... **11** F5
Wrangle Farm Gn BS21 **57** G2
WRANGLE THE **129** A5
Wrangle The 5 BS24 **105** E7
WRAXALL **60** C3
Wraxall CE VA Prim Sch BS48 .... **60** B4
Wraxall Gr BS13 ..... **79** A8
Wraxall Hill BS48 ... **60** C5
Wraxall Rd BS30 .... **66** A6
Wrenbert Rd BS16 ... **51** D5
Wren Cl
Bristol BS16 .... **50** E7
Weston-s-M BS22 ... **105** D8
Wren Dr BS16 ...... **51** A6
Wright Way BS16 ... **50** E8
WRINGTON **92** E1
Wrington CE Prim Sch BS40 .... **92** E2
Wrington Cl BS34 ... **36** C7
Wrington Cres BS13 .. **79** A7
Wrington Hill BS40 .. **92** F5
Wrington La BS49 ... **91** E5
Wrington Mead BS49 . **91** E5
Wrington Rd BS49 ... **91** F4
WRITHLINGTON **134** C2
Writhlington Ct BA3 . **134** C1
Writhlington Sch BA3 **134** C1
Wroughton Dr BS13 .. **79** D4
Wroughton Gdns BS13 **79** D4
Wroxham Dr BS34 ... **36** C8
Wyatt Ave BS13 ..... **78** F5
Wyatt Cl BS13 ...... **78** F5
Wyatt's Cl BS48 ..... **59** D2
Wyatts View BS4 .... **64** E6
Wychwood BS15 .... **65** E6
Wyck Beck Rd BS10 .. **35** A3
Wycliffe Rd BS9 .... **49** B7
Wycliffe Row 9 BS3 . **63** F4
Wycombe Gr BS4 .... **64** D2
Wycotte Hill BA2 ... **118** C6
Wye Croft Cl BS10 ... **35** D3
Wye Ct BS35 .... **15** C8
Wyedale Ave BS9 ... **48** C7
Wykis Ct BS15 ...... **65** E5
Wylington Rd BS36 .. **38** B6
Wyllie Ct BS22 ..... **89** A5
Wymbush Cres BS13 .. **79** C5
Wymbush Gdns BS13 . **79** C5
Wyndam Ct BS2 .... **143** B4
Wyndham Cres
Bristol BS4 .... **65** A3
Easton-in-G BS20 .... **47** B4
Wyndham Way BS20 . **45** E5
Wyndham Way Ret Pk BS20 .... **45** D5
Wynstones The BS15 . **65** C7
Wynter Cl BS22 ..... **89** A3
Wyvern Cl BS23 .... **104** F7
Wyvern Com Sch BS23 .... **104** F5
Wyvern Mews 5 BS23 **104** F7
Wyvern Villas BS9 ... **49** A8

Y

Yadley Cl BS25 ..... **125** A7
Yadley La BS25 ..... **125** A6
Yadley Way BS25 ... **125** A7
Yanel La BS25 ..... **108** B5
Yanleigh Cl BS13 ... **78** D6
YANLEY **78** C8
Yanley La BS41, BS13 . **78** D6
Yarbury Way BS24 ... **89** B1
Yard The BS2 .... **50** A3
Yarrow Cl 5 BS16 ... **52** C7
Yarrow Ct BS22 ..... **89** A5
Yarrow Wlk BS16 ... **52** D7
YATE **27** C1
Yate Court La BS37 ... **27** D8
Yate Her Ctr ✱ BS37 . **27** E2
Yate Rd BS37 .... **26** F3
YATE ROCKS **27** F6
Yate Rocks BS37 .... **27** F7

Yate Sta BS37 ...... **27** C2
YATTON **91** C1
Yatton CE VA Jun & Inf Schs BS49 .... **91** C8
Yatton Cl BS13 ..... **78** E3
Yatton Inf Sch BS49 .. **91** C8
Yatton Station BS49 .. **74** A1
Yeaman's Ho BS1 ... **143** B1
Yeates Ct BS21 ..... **57** G3
Yeatman Cl BS39 ... **113** D4
Yelverton Rd BS4 ... **64** E1
Yeo Bank La
Icelton BS22 .... **89** D7
Kingston Seymour BS21 . **72** F1
Yeo Cl BS23 .... **105** A5
Yeo Ct
Clevedon BS21 .... **57** E2
Congresbury BS49 ... **91** D4
Yeo La BS41 .... **61** F1
Yeolands Dr BS21 ... **57** D1
Yeomans Cl BS9 .... **48** D5
Yeomanside BS14 ... **80** C5
Yeomans Orch BS40 .. **92** E3
Yeomead BS48 ...... **59** F3
Yeomeads BS41 ..... **61** F1
Yeo Moor BS21 ..... **57** G2
Yeo Moor Inf Sch BS21 **57** G2
Yeo Moor Jun Sch BS21 .... **57** G2
Yeo Moor Prim Sch BS21 .... **57** E2
Yeo Valley Way BS48 . **60** B2
Yeoward Rd BS21 ... **57** G1
Yeo Way BS21 ...... **57** D2
Yewcroft Cl BS14 .... **80** A4
Yewtree Batch BS40 .. **94** A1
Yew Tree Cl
Bishop Sutton BS39 . **113** D4
Lower Langford BS40 . **109** E6
Nailsea BS48 .... **59** C1
Yew Tree Cotts BS40 **110** E3
Yew Tree Ct BS14 ... **80** B5
Yew Tree Dr
Bristol BS15 .... **51** F3
Weston-s-M BS22 ... **106** B8
Yew Tree Gdns
Nailsea BS48 .... **59** C1
Pill BS20 .... **47** C4
Sandford BS25 ..... **108** A4
Yew Tree La
Compton Martin BS40 **129** A7
Kingston Seymour BS21 . **73** B1
Yew Tree Pk BS49 ... **91** D3
Yomede Pk BA1 .... **101** A7
York Ave BS7 ...... **49** F4
York Bldgs
Bath BA1 .... **141** B3
Bristol BS3 .... **63** E4
York Cl
Bristol, Bromley Heath BS16 .... **37** F1
Bristol, Stoke Gifford BS34 .... **36** D4
Weston-s-M BS22 .... **89** A4
Yate BS37 .... **27** E4
York Ct BS2 .... **143** B4
York Gdns
Bristol BS8 .... **62** F6
Winterbourne BS36 ... **37** F8
York Ho BS8 ...... **142** A3
York Pl
Bath BA1 .... **102** B8
Bristol, Brandon Hill BS1 .... **142** C2
Bristol, Victoria Park BS8 .... **142** B3
York Rd
Bristol BS2 .... **143** C1
Bristol, Lower Easton BS5 .... **50** C1
Bristol, Montpelier BS6 . **49** E1
Bristol, Staple Hill BS16 . **51** E4
Bristol, Windmill Hill BS3 **63** E4
York St
Bath BA1 .... **141** C2
Bristol BS2 .... **143** B4
Bristol, Baptist Mills BS2 **50** A2
2 Bristol, Clifton BS8 .. **49** A2
9 Bristol, Redfield BS5 . **64** C7
Weston-s-M BS23 ... **104** D7
Youngs Ct BS16 .... **52** B8
Youngwood La BS48 . **75** D7
Yoxter Rd
Charterhouse BA5 ... **127** F1
Ubley Sideling BS40 . **128** B2

Z

Zetland Rd BS6 ..... **49** D2
Zig Zag BS21 .... **57** F4
Zinc Rd BS11 .... **33** C3
Zion Hill BA3 ..... **138** B7
Zone The 7 BS5 .... **65** A8